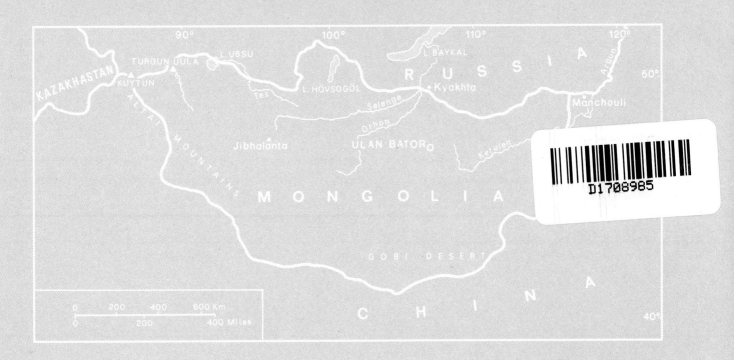

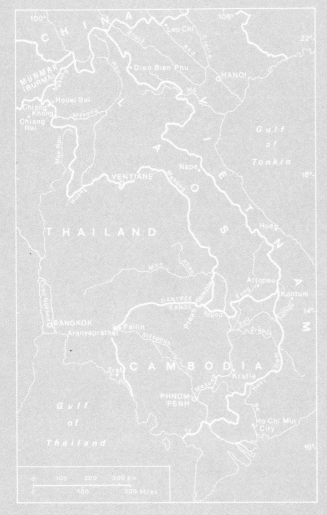

THE ENCYCLOPEDIA
OF INTERNATIONAL
BOUNDARIES

"THE ENCYCLOPEDIA OF INTERNATIONAL BOUNDARIES"

GIDEON BIGER

in collaboration with

THE INTERNATIONAL BOUNDARIES RESEARCH UNIT

University of Durham, England

Facts On File®

AN INFOBASE HOLDINGS COMPANY

Facts On File, Inc.
11 Penn Plaza
New York NY 10001

Library of Congress Cataloging-in-Publication Data

Encyclopedia of international boundaries / Gideon Biger, editor-in-chief
        p.   cm.
    Includes bibliographical references and index.
    ISBN 0-8160-3233-5 (acid-free paper)
    1. Boundaries.   I. Biger, Gideon.
    JX4111.E53 1995
    911' .03--dc20   95-18364
                                                                 CIP

Facts On File books are available at special discounts when purchased in bulk quantities for businesses, associations, institutions or sales promotions. Please call our Special Sales Department in New York at 212/967-8800 or 800/322-8755.

Jacket design by Hadass Bar Yosef
Printed in Israel

10 9 8 7 6 5 4 3 2 1

This book is printed on acid-free paper.

EDITOR-IN-CHIEF

GIDEON BIGER

MANAGING EDITOR

RACHEL GILON

ASSISTANT EDITOR-IN-CHIEF

RACHEL FELDMAN (FINE)

CONSULTING EDITOR

GERALD BLAKE

MAP EDITOR

JACOB DORFMAN

CONTENTS

CONTRIBUTORS

GIDEON BIGER, Ph.D.
Senior Lecturer, Department of Geography,
Tel Aviv University, Israel

GERALD BLAKE, Ph.D.
Professor of Geography, Director, International Boundaries Research Unit,
University of Durham, England

JACOB DORFMAN, Ph.D.
Cartographic Laboratory, Department of Geography,
Tel Aviv University, Israel

LOUIS DE VORSEY, Ph.D.
Professor Emeritus, Department of Geography, University of
Georgia, Athens, Georgia, United States of America

MARTIN GLASSNER, Ph.D.
Professor of Geography, Southern Connecticut State University,
New Haven, Connecticut, United States of America

JACCI HIGGITT, B.Sc.
Research Staff, International Boundaries Research Unit,
University of Durham, England

PETER HOCKNELL, B.A.
Research Officer, International Boundaries Research Unit,
University of Durham, England

VICKI INNES, B.A. (Hons.)
Research Staff, International Boundaries Research Unit,
University of Durham, England

MLADEN KLEMENCIC, M.Sc.
Miroslav Krleza, Lexicographic Institute,
Zagreb, Croatia

JULIAN MINGHI, Ph.D.
Professor of Geography, University of South Carolina,
Columbia, South Carolina, United States of America

ANNA OXBURY, B.A. (Hons.)
Research Staff, International Boundaries Research Unit,
University of Durham, England

MARTIN PRATT, M.A.
Research Officer, International Boundaries Research Unit,
University of Durham, England

CLIVE SCHOFIELD, B.A.
Executive Officer, International Boundaries Research Unit,
University of Durham, England

WILLIAM STANLEY, Ph.D.
Professor of Geography, University of South Carolina,
Columbia, South Carolina, United States of America

FOREWORD

With over 200 independent states and some 35 dependencies in the world today, the issue of international boundaries has become increasingly complex. Modern territorial and maritime boundaries often present an indication of the history, geography and political stability of each state and of its relations with its neighbors. Geographers and generals, international lawyers and surveyors, have all played important roles in the delineation of boundaries. International land boundaries, as lines that were formed on the basis of international agreements, are the subject of this Encyclopedia.

WHAT IS INCLUDED?

This Encyclopedia includes only contemporary international land boundaries. It does not include maritime boundaries or divisions between internal states, provinces and districts. Maritime boundaries are now under processes of definition all over the world; but as less than half of them are delimited by international agreement they are not included here. An international boundary is a boundary line defined by international agreement or accepted by adjacent countries as their common international boundary. In any case, where there are different attitudes toward the exact position of a boundary line, we have tried to present both sides of the issue and to provide the reader with the latest information available. There are many cases in which the international agreement has not been publicized or in which no international agreement even exists, as is the case with some African boundaries. This, however, is a scholarly work, not a legal document. As boundary issues are very sensitive by nature, one may find some incorrect information according to a certain view. We welcome any comment and accurate information concerning the contents of the Encyclopedia.

ORGANIZATION

Entries are presented alphabetically. Each state is introduced with a brief description including its area, population, political structure and a historical summary. The boundaries of the state follow, each described with its geographical setting, historical background and present situation. Maps and photographs provide the reader with invaluable tools for understanding the geographical context of the boundaries. Cross references are used to facilitate finding articles of interest. The French border with Germany, for example, is discussed under **FRANCE — GERMANY**, an entry that can be found after the item **FRANCE**. Under **GERMANY — FRANCE** a cross reference appears: **see** FRANCE– GERMANY. Dependencies, such as Guam, Gibraltar and American Samoa, are treated as countries. Island states, such as Japan and Iceland which have no land boundaries, are likewise discussed as separate entries. Geographical features (such as rivers, mountains and towns) that have more than one name are presented by their common English names (e.g., *Cairo*) and/or by their local names (e.g., *Oder (Odra) River*).

SELECT BIBLIOGRAPHY

A select bibliography is found at the end of this Encyclopedia. It mostly includes books that cover several boundaries or one particular boundary. A major source of information that is principally not open to the general public is a series of International Boundary Studies, published by the Office of the Geographer, Bureau of Intelligence and Research, Department of State, USA. The bibliography includes only one entry for this source, although more than 200 separate studies were published. This also stands true for publications that include formal documents published by different foreign offices (British, French, American, etc.) in multiple volumes.

The bibliography is organized by continents and, for the English reader, primarily includes books that are published in the English language. However, other foreign-language books were also included where needed. As there are hundreds of articles that have been written on many of the boundaries, they could not be included in the bibliography.

MAPS

All the maps were created especially for this Encyclopedia. Three different kinds of maps appear in the Encyclopedia. There are maps of particular boundaries, placed with the corresponding entry; there are maps of states, placed usually with the state's entry; and there are regional maps, which include a number of states in one map and are placed with one of the states' items. All of the maps face north. At the end of the Encyclopedia the reader will find a list of all the international boundaries with a reference to the maps in which they appear.

INTRODUCTION

A century ago Lord Curzon, Britain's leading imperialist, described international boundaries as being "the razor's edge on which hang suspended the modern issues of war or peace, or life or death to nations." And, with the memory of the recent Gulf War in mind, it might fairly be asked if those boundaries have lost any of their significance? Would such an unprecedented coalition of states from the West and Middle East, from the First World powers and their former Third World colonies, have arrayed themselves against Iraq had not Kuwait's boundary and territorial integrity been violated? Most informed observers would not hesitate in answering this query with a resounding negative. But why should boundaries and territory be such important considerations in the affairs of a world community now comprised of more than 200 states?

It is because the state is a territorial organization that violation of its frontiers is inseparable from the idea of aggression against the state itself. The word "territory" is derived from the Latin root, *terra*, meaning "land" or "earth." Traditionally the term conveyed the idea of an organized area around a place that was characterized by an element of centrality and control exercised over the people inhabiting it. In its modern and legal use "territory" has come to designate a portion of earth space under the jurisdiction of certain people that is separated and distinct from adjacent territories that are under different jurisdictions. Separateness thus becomes an essential in the establishment of that other sine qua non of statehood—sovereignty. The hallmark of national separateness on the world political stage is the boundary.

Most often it is along their boundaries that the contrasting human energies latent in the cultures of adjacent sovereign states can and often do come into competitive contact. It comes as no great surprise to find that mentions of boundaries and "boundary problems" continue to punctuate and enliven today's headlines as they have the pages of our history books and chronicles. International boundaries can be likened to world political fault lines along which competing national aspirations are most likely to surface and come into direct contact. They mark the zones in which social, political or economic shock waves, all too often, have triggered the military conflicts Lord Curzon had in mind when he spoke of the "life or death to nations."

International boundaries reflect the historical moments in the life of a state, when its limits were made according to its force and ability at that time. Thus, today's boundaries are relics from the past and might be changed in the future. States have acquired their boundaries in a variety of ways: in some cases they marked the territorial limit of a phase of political expansion and conquest; in other cases they have been imposed by external powers, either through acts of conquest or through negotiation. They function as barriers to social and economic processes, which would otherwise transgress the lines without interference, as well as holding economic significance through their association with tariff and quota restrictions. The latter converted an otherwise open world economic network into a series of partially closed economic systems.

Boundaries appear on maps as thin lines between adjacent state territories, marking the limits of state sovereignties. The lines can be effective with regard to underground resources, marking the limits of ore and oil deposits, as well as above the ground, guarding the individual states' air space. In the past they were drawn for defensive purposes, as cultural divisions, according to economic factors, for legal and administrative purposes or on ideological bases. Sometimes they were drawn through essentially unoccupied territories, although they were usually superimposed on existing cultural patterns, disturbing the lives of the people living in the border areas.

Of the many criteria for establishing a boundary line the ethnic criteria are the those applied most often in modern times. Accordingly boundaries were drawn to separate culturally uniformed peoples so that a minimum of stress would be placed upon them. The heterogeneous world population, however, could not define boundaries that completely and exactly separated peoples of different character and as a result there are ethnic minorities in almost every state. The definition of peoples, according to race, language or religion, was used in several cases to delimit a state boundary. Other political boundaries lie along prominent physical features in the landscape. Such physiographic political boundaries, following rivers, mountain ranges or escarpments, sometimes termed "natural boundaries," seem to be especially acceptable criteria as such pronounced physical features often also separate culturally distinct areas. In the early days of boundary establishment, physiographic features were useful as they were generally known and could be visually recognized. However, many of the boundary lines that were based on such physiographic features have created major difficulties between states. Rivers tend to shift their course and having breadth as well as length and depth have led to countless disputes over whether the boundary should be along one of the river banks, along the *thalweg* (main navigation channel), through the median line of the water's surface or somewhere else. Any mountain range has recognized crest lines; but they rarely coincide with the region's watershed. The placing of boundaries along crest lines in mountainous areas has therefore led to water disputes concerning the use of rivers near their source.

Most of today's political boundaries were created by European nations. In fact, it is difficult to identify any international boundary that has not directly involved a European state at some stage of its evolution. The allocation of territory was usually determined by straight lines connecting known points or by features of the physical landscape, generally solving immediate territorial conflicts. The need for the delimitation of the boundaries emerged if the allocated borderland proved to have economic value or if disputes arose in the area. The delimitation of a boundary, which has usually been decided by agreement between two states or at postwar conferences, was generally a full definition and served as a guideline for the demarcation team. Today, even as many states are energetically seeking to fix and demarcate their boundaries, which were not accurately defined in the past, there are still a great many (over 100) boundary and territorial disputes around the world.

A famous American boundary scholar once wrote that a boundary, "like human skin, may have diseases of its own or may reflect the illnesses of the body." Indeed, a variety of boundary conflicts have developed over the centuries. At times states disputed the precise position of their limits according to the boundary agreements while some states laid claims to another's state territory, primarily due to the fact that the boundary, most often determined by an external force, did not coincide with any significant physical, historical or cultural division. Other controversies have concerned the use of transboundary resources, such as water and mineral ore. A number of boundary lines stood dormant for many years, coming under dispute only later, some of which are alive at present, while other boundaries are of uncertain status. The international boundaries of the world continue to evolve in terms of their definition, their function and position.

Louis De Vorsey   *Gideon Biger*
University of Georgia   Tel Aviv University

A

AFGHANISTAN A mountainous landlocked state in southwest Asia (area: 251,761 sq. miles [652,061 sq. km.]; population: 17,400,000 [1994]), Afghanistan is bounded in the north by Tajikistan (750 miles; 1,206 km.), Uzbekistan (85 miles; 137 km.) and Turkmenistan (462 miles; 744 km.), in the east by China (47 miles; 75 km.), south and southeast by Pakistan (1,510 miles; 2,430 km.) and west by Iran (582 miles; 936 km.). The capital of Afghanistan is Kabul.

Afghanistan first found unity as a nation under the rule of Ahmad Shah Abdal in 1747. The area was eventually colonized by the British after the First Afghan War (1838–1842). Throughout this period,

Afghanistan and its boundaries, southwest Asia

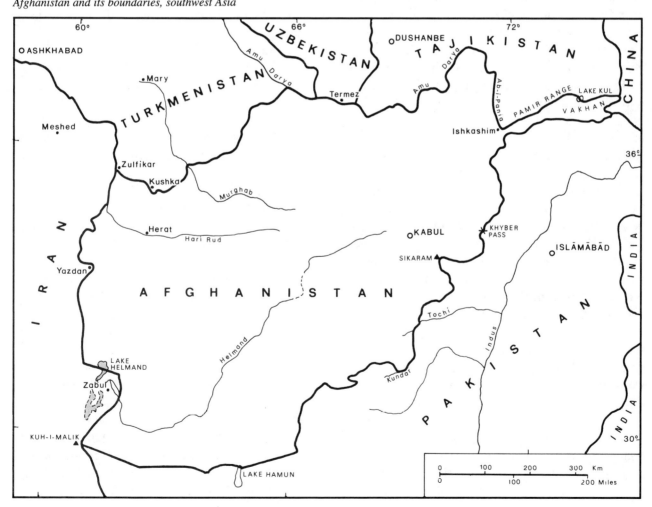

the Russians were also trying to gain control and in 1907 an Anglo-Russian agreement was signed which gave Afghans their own government (still influenced by the British). There was much turmoil throughout the twentieth century, resulting in many turnovers of power. The constitutional monarchy established in 1964 was ended by a coup in 1973. By 1978 the USSR was backing the People's Democratic Party of Afghanistan, who were in power. Beginning in the 1980s, a widespread rebellion against the Soviet-backed government grew into a civil war and by the end of the decade an estimated 1,000,000 Afghans had been killed. The Soviet-backed regime was ousted, but there is still much turmoil between the different factions over the balance of power.

AFGHANISTAN — CHINA

The boundary between these Asian countries runs 47 miles (75 km.) through the Pamirs of central Asia. At 18,000 feet (5,490 m.) above sea level, it is one of the highest boundary lines of the world, connecting two of the highest peaks in the region.

Geographical Setting. The boundary begins on the peak of Povalo Shveykovski, the tripoint boundary of Tajikistan, China and Afghanistan. From there it runs westward, connecting several mountain passes lying along the watershed between the Kara Chukur, located in China, and the Afghan rivers. From the Kara Jilga Pass it runs southwest, following the watershed between the Wakhjir (China) and the Darya (Afghanistan) rivers. It then turns southeast, between the watersheds of the Wakhjir and Ab-i Wakhan rivers, traversing the Wakhjir Pass (16,252 feet; 4,955 m.) to reach a mountain peak at an altitude of 18,471 feet (5,631 m.), at 74°34'E and 37°03'N, where it meets the Pakistan boundary junction.

Historical Background. Afghanistan acquired a common boundary with China by the terms of the 1895 Anglo-Russian agreement, by which the Wakhan strip and the Little Pamir mountain range became Afghan territory, thus separating the possessions of Russia in central Asia from British India. The Chinese government did not participate in the boundary negotiations; in fact, it only became aware of the line 68 years later, in 1963. A Sino–Afghan boundary was drawn, while China and Pakistan also reached a boundary agreement at that time, forming a junction with the Sino–Afghan boundary. A

Sino–Afghan boundary commission prepared a map of the area in 1964 and this map was attached to the demarcation protocol signed in Kabul, Afghanistan, in March 1965.

Present Situation. There is some disagreement over the location of the unnamed peak at the junction point with Pakistan. The Sino-Afghan agreement and the Sino-Pakistan agreement define the point 2 miles (3 km.) apart. This, however, does not cause any problems, the point in question being located in a mountainous, uninhabitable region. There are no known disputes concerning the Sino–Afghan boundary.

AFGHANISTAN— IRAN

The boundary between Afghanistan and Iran runs for 582 miles (936 km.), from the boundary junction with Turkmenistan in the Zulfikar pass on the Hari Rud River in the north to the boundary junction with Pakistan on Kuh-i-Malik Peak in the south. The boundary is demarcated along its entire length with boundary pillars.

Geographical Setting. Starting on the Zulfikar pass in the Hari Rud, the boundary follows the river southward to its confluence with the Kal-i-Kalla River, which it joins down to the Shorab pass. It continues southwestward to a point east of Karat (Iran), where the line swings southeast, reaching the southern edge of the Yal-i-Khar range at about 34°20'N and 60°55'E at the head of the Chah Surkh valley. The boundary line then runs eastward for about 30 miles (50 km.) until it turns southward to follow a straight line, crossing the large salt lake of Namakzar. To circumvent the Iranian town of Yazdan, the boundary line takes an easterly direction, circles the town and then runs southwest and south, where the boundaries of local farms are taken into consideration. It reaches the Kuh Peak (Siah Kuh), which stands at about 5,180 feet (1,579 m.) above sea level. From there it traverses eastward, crossing Lake Helmand, to the mouth of the Siskar River, where it enters the river. This river is followed southward to its confluence with the Pariun River, from which point they become the Helmand River. Along the Helmand River the boundary continues southward to a dam on the river in Band-i-Seistan where the Seistan River joins the Helmand River. The boundary line then leaves the river and takes a straight line southwestward for about 90 miles (145 km.) to reach Kuh-i-Malik Peak (5,425 feet;

1,654 m.), which constitutes the boundary tripoint with Pakistan.

Historical Background. The present boundary between Afghanistan and Iran was settled between 1872 and 1935. The southern section, between the peaks of Kuh-i-Malik and Kuh in the Seistan region, was long in dispute between Iran (formerly Persia) and Afghanistan. After 1860 there were increasing conflicts over water rights between Persian and Afghan groups. Britain offered to help settle the issue, whereupon a British officer was appointed as arbitrator. According to his decision of 1872, Seistan-proper was awarded to Persia while outer-Seistan was given to Afghanistan along the line extant today. In 1896 an exceptional flood burst the west bank of the Helmand River, forming a new outlet (the Pariun River) to the lake and driving the water from the Siskar channel, which put the irrigated areas of Afghanistan at risk. Although the Iranians allowed the Afghans to divert some water into their land, it was later deemed necessary to reconstruct the boundary and to regulate the general allocation of water in Seistan. Another British officer was appointed as arbitrator and in 1905 he delineated the boundary by placing 90 boundary pillars along the line.

The northern section of the boundary, from the Zulfikar pass to the Chah Surkh valley was established in 1891. The Afghan and Iranian governments requested further arbitration of the British authorities to settle their differences concerning water rights in the semidesert area. The British arbitrator took into consideration historical and agricultural claims and tried to utilize the geographical elements to settle the boundary location. He announced his award in December 1889 and the northern boundary line was marked with 39 boundary pillars in 1891, after both the Afghan and Iranian governments accepted the proposed line. The central part of the boundary, the 250 miles (402 km.) between Kuh Peak in the south and Chah Surkh in the north, is an area characterized by the absence of population settlement and low economic potential. Nevertheless, problems arose in connection with land and water rights along the line and in October 1934 a Turkish general was appointed as arbitrator for this section of the boundary. In May 1935, after solving some local boundary problems concerning winter pasture,

an acceptable line was designed and 51 boundary pillars were erected along it. The Turkish arbitrator also redefined the boundary along the Hari Rud in the north.

Present Situation. Since 1935 (when Persia formally became Iran) there have been no known disputes concerning the location of the boundary line. Although changes in the geographical features of the river area of Seistan might occur, the boundary is well demarcated and thus such permutations should not cause any further problems of definition.

AFGHANISTAN — PAKISTAN

The old boundary between British India and the Kingdom of Afghanistan has been kept to date as delineated in the 1893 Kabul Agreement. Extending 1,510 miles (2,430 km.), it was demarcated by joint British-Russian and British-Afghan commissions in 1894 and 1896 respectively.

Geographical Setting. The present boundary, known as the Durand Line, stretches across the mountainous region of Hindu Kush. It originates at Kuh-i-Malik-Siah, the tripoint boundary of Iran, Afghanistan and Pakistan, at approximately 29°N and 61°E and runs east and northeast to about 37°N and 75°E near Lake Zorkul at the China, Pakistan and Afghanistan tripoint. In its course it traverses watersheds, rivers, valleys, plains and mountain peaks. The desert region in the southwest gives way to the towering mountains of central Asia, with many peaks exceeding 24,000 feet (7,300 m.). It climbs the lofty Khanzah (17,500 feet; 5,330 m.) and Dorah (14,300 feet; 4,360 m.) passes before crossing the Khyber Pass—the main land route connecting India with central Asia. Only a small section of the boundary in the vicinity of the Khyber Pass has not been marked.

Historical Background. The establishment of the Durand Line in the nineteenth century was the climax of a lengthy process of negotiations to determine the extent of British influence in India and central Asia. Several armed conflicts, followed by intense negotiations between the Russian government and local Afghan rulers of West Indus, prompted Britain to dispatch Sir Mortimer Durand to the Afghan capital of Kabul to negotiate a permanent boundary line. A treaty signed on 12 November 1893 was reaffirmed in 1905; a Treaty of Peace was

Pashtun men near the Afghanistan–Pakistan boundary

concluded between the British government and Afghanistan on 8 August 1919 and a final treaty was signed on 22 November 1921.

In 1947 Pakistan inherited the Durand Line as its western boundary with Afghanistan. Successive Afghan governments questioned the line's legitimacy, claiming that its sanction had lapsed with the transfer of sovereignty from Britain to Pakistan. They demanded self-determination for the Pashtun tribes people living east of the line in Pakistan territory, claiming that all Pashtun peoples should be united under the Afghan flag. Such claims, raised in 1973, in 1975 and after the Russian intervention in Afghanistan in 1979, were backed by India. In 1950 and again in 1956 the United Kingdom declared that it regards the Durand Line as the international boundary, while Pakistan has repeatedly stated that it has no dispute with Afghanistan over the exact location of the line.

Activity in the border area increased during the Afghan civil war of the late 1980s as hundreds of thousands of Afghan refugees streamed into Pakistan. At the same time, the Western powers sent arms and supplies across the boundary line for the benefit of rebel Afghan forces.

Present Situation. At present the line is under quiet, unaggressive dispute.

AFGHANISTAN — TAJIKISTAN The boundary between Afghanistan and Tajikistan runs 750 miles (1,206 km.) between the border junction with China in the east and the border junction with Uzbekistan in the west. For the most part, the boundary follows the Amu Darya (Oxus) River and its tributaries. The present boundary is a segment of the boundary between Afghanistan and the former USSR.

Geographical Setting. The boundary line begins at the border junction with China on the peak of Povalo Schveykovski in the Little Pamir mountain range. It runs westward to Lake Zorkul crossing the Ak Su River, which is a tributary of the great Amu Darya River. The line runs along the southern shore of the lake, leaving it within Tajikistan, and joins the Pamir River, which runs from the lake westward. Following the river to its confluence with the Vakhjir River where they become the Ab-i-Pandj River, it continues to follow it westward. This section of the boundary line, together with the Pakistan–Afghanistan boundary to the south, creates the Wakhan, a narrow corridor of Afghan territory that gives it a common boundary alignment with China.

The boundary line continues to follow the Ab-i-Pandj River northward to its confluence with the Ak Su River near the Tajik town of Rushan, where they become the Amu Darya River. The boundary follows it northwestward, southwestward and then westward to the boundary junction with Uzbekistan.

Historical Background. The history of the boundary line between Afghanistan and Tajikistan dates back to the second half of the nineteenth century when Britain and Russia tried to established their sphere of influence in central Asia. The boundary along the Amu Darya River and its tributaries was agreed upon in 1872–1873 while the section from Lake Zorkul to the Chinese border was established in 1895. During this period Britain and Russia had a mutual interest in establishing a neutral zone between their respective territories in Asia: Britain wanted the Russians distanced as far as possible from Afghanistan while the Russians wanted to maintain a safe passage from the Caspian Sea into central Asia. Britain claimed the Amu Darya River as the northern boundary of Afghanistan, placing the Badakhshan and Wakhan territories under Afghan authority. Russia, on the other hand, called for the independence of these territories, but at last agreed to include them in Afghanistan. In January 1873 a British-Russian agreement was signed by which the Amu Darya River, from its tributary in Lake Zorkul to Kwaja Salar, would be the northern boundary of Afghanistan. No decisions were made concerning the ownership of islands in the Amu Darya and the issue was only resolved in 1945 with a settlement between Afghanistan and the Soviet Union.

The section of the Afghan–Russian boundary east of Lake Zorkul was established in 1895. The Russian officials made it clear to Britain that a clearly demarcated boundary between the lake and the Chinese border was necessary—unlike the border region of the Pamirs, which were so uninhabitable that there was no risk of collision between British and Russian forces. In March 1895 Britain agreed to extend the boundary eastward to the peak of Povalo Schveykovski, thus placing the entire Wakhan area within Afghanistan. The boundary line was demarcated in 1895 by 12 boundary pillars.

The creation of the USSR after World War I did not cause any changes to the boundary. In 1929

Tajikistan became a republic of the Soviet Union, its southern boundary adopting part of the former Afghanistan–Russia boundary. World War II also did not lead to any changes in the boundary and after 1945 agreements between Afghanistan and the Soviet Union reaffirmed the location of the boundary line. In 1991 Tajikistan became an independent country.

Present Situation. Since the establishment of Tajikistan as an independent country, no disputes concerning the boundary's position have been reported. The line along the course of the Amu Darya River is clear and it is well demarcated along the Pamirs.

AFGHANISTAN — TURKMENISTAN The boundary between Afghanistan and Turkmenistan runs for 462 miles (744 km.) between the boundary tripoint with Uzbekistan in the east and the boundary junction with Iran in the west. The present boundary is the outcome of the nineteenth-century British-Russian territorial power struggle in central Asia, and is the western section of the boundary between the former Soviet Union and Afghanistan.

Geographical Setting. The western terminus of the boundary is in the Zulfikar pass on the Hari Rud River, at the boundary junction with Iran. The boundary runs southeast for about 80 miles (130 km.), crossing some local rivers and reaching the town of Kushka (Turkmenistan) on the Kushka River. It turns northeastward to the Murghab River, which it follows downstream northward, leaving the city of Mari Chaq (Maruchak) within Turkmenistan. North of Mari Chaq, the boundary leaves the river and runs northeast for another 200 miles (320 km.), east of the Qaisar (Darya-ye-Qeysar) and Andkhoy rivers, both of which are left within Afghanistan. The boundary line reaches the town of Kwaja Salar (Afghanistan), which is located on the great Amu Darya (Oxus) River, enters the Amu Darya and follows it eastward to the boundary junction with Uzbekistan in the river and west of Tash Gozar (Afghanistan).

Historical Background. In the second half of the nineteenth century the British and Russian empires contended for control over central Asia and in 1869 a mutual desire for a neutral zone between their Asian territories became evident. Britain, which controlled Afghanistan, wanted Russia to remain distant from Afghanistan, while the Russians wished to secure a safe route from the Caspian Sea to central Asia along the Amu Darya River. The British proposed that the Amu Darya, south of Bukhara, serve as the boundary between the Russian Empire and Afghanistan. The proposal was accepted, but the western terminus of the line was not clear and Bukhara, which was under Russian control, owned territory south of the river. In 1872, after lengthy debate between the two countries, it was agreed that the boundary leave the river at the town of Kwaja Salar. This enabled Bukhara to maintain its control over its areas south of the river.

Between 1882 and 1884 there were further negotiations between Britain and Russia concerning the western section of the boundary—between Kwaja Salar and the Hari Rud River, which formed the eastern boundary of Iran. Russia proposed a line that would run up to Sarakhs on the Hari Rud, but Britain rejected it at first. Later, the Mary tribes, located south of the Aral Sea, submitted all their territory to Russia and thus Britain was forced to accept a boundary terminus in the Zulfikar pass, about 60 miles (100 km.) south of the original Russian recommendation. In September 1885 a protocol defining the boundary was signed. A demarcation team tried to place the boundary in the ground but found it difficult to establish the exact line, as it was agreed to leave some local tribes within Russia although their lands were irrigated by canals originating in Afghan territory. A line was then drawn and conditions were set to avoid conflicts over water rights. The boundary demarcation was completed in January 1888.

From then on the boundary line never changed. The establishment of the Soviet Union and the British withdrawal from the area did not affect it. Turkmenistan became a constituent republic of the Soviet Union in 1925 with the Afghan–Soviet Union border as its southern boundary.

In 1945, after World War II, Afghanistan and the Soviet Union signed additional treaties to establish their common boundary, which in the 1980s served as a military zone when some 120,000 Soviet soldiers were placed in Afghanistan. With the dissolution of the Soviet Union in 1991, Turkmenistan was established as an independent country. Turkmenistan then adopted the former Soviet–Afghanistan international boundary as its boundary with Afghanistan.

Present Situation. Since Turkmenistan gained independence, there have been no disputes concerning the boundary alignment.

AFGHANISTAN — UZBEKISTAN

The boundary between Afghanistan and Uzbekistan runs 85 miles (137 km.) along a river, between the boundary junction with Tajikistan in the east and the boundary junction with Turkmenistan in the west.

Geographical Setting. The eastern terminus of the boundary between Afghanistan and Uzbekistan is the border junction with Tajikistan, located in the Amu Darya River at 67°40'E. Following the median line of the river westward for 85 miles (137 km.), the boundary passes the town of Termez (Uzbekistan) and then reaches the tripoint border junction with Turkmenistan. The eastern point of the boundary is situated in the Amu Darya River, east of the Turkmen town of Kilif near 67°E.

Historical Background. The present boundary between Afghanistan and Uzbekistan is part of the boundary between Afghanistan and the former Soviet Union. In the British-Russian struggle for domination over central Asia, Uzbekistan was conquered by Russia in 1865. This rule lasted until 1869 when Britain and Russia decided to create a buffer zone between their Asian territories. It was agreed that Afghanistan take on the role of a neutral country between the empires and in January 1873 the Amu Darya River was established as the northern boundary of Afghanistan, south of the Russian provinces of Samarkand and Bukhara. The establishment of the USSR after World War I did not change the line's demarcation. Tashkent gradually extended its power between 1917 and 1924 and in 1925 Uzbekistan became a constituent republic of the USSR. After World War II Afghanistan and the Soviet Union confirmed their common boundary according to the nineteenth-century agreements, settling problems concerning the ownership of islands situated in the Amu Darya River. In 1991 Uzbekistan became an independent country and the former Afghan–Soviet Union boundary became the present boundary between Afghanistan and Uzbekistan.

Present Situation. There are no known disputes concerning the alignment of the boundary between the two countries.

ALBANIA (Shqipëri)   A country (area: 11,101 sq. miles [28,752 sq. km.]; estimated population: 3,400,000 [1994]) situated in the Balkan Peninsula of southeastern Europe, Albania is bounded in the north by Serbia (178 miles; 287 km.), in the east by Macedonia (94 miles; 151 km.), in the southeast by Greece (175 miles; 282 km.) and in the west by the Adriatic Sea. The capital of Albania is Tirana.

The Albanians never formed a state of their own until the twentieth century. During their long history, they were either under the rule of other powers— Byzantines, Serbs, Bulgars, Bosnians, Normans, Venetians and Ottomans—each of which promoted its own religion, or lived in their inaccessible mountains as independent tribes who shifted alliances among themselves and with the neighboring states whom they often supplied with mercenaries. Charles of Anjou was the first, and, until the twentieth century, the only monarch, to adopt the title "King of Albania," after he conquered the Albanian coast in 1272.

The Ottoman conquest of Albania, begun in 1385, was completed only in 1571. Apart form the country's rugged terrain and the resistance of Venice, they were thwarted by a series of local revolts. The most famous of these, between 1443 and 1470, was led by Skanderbeg, who was proclaimed a hero by the Albanian national movement in the nineteenth century.

Although they established their "*pax turcica*," the Ottomans never succeeded in extending their direct rule beyond the coastal plain and the lowlands. The mountain tribes, especially in the north, were left to their own devices as long as they kept the peace and supplied irregulars (one man per household) to the Ottoman army. Landlords in the lowlands, on the other hand, were fully absorbed into the Ottoman military administrative structure (the *timar*). Conversion to Islam was never a condition of this absorption and the islamization of the Albanians did not gain momentum until the eighteenth century.

Muslim Albanians were, and considered themselves, a part of the *stadtsvolk* of the Ottoman Empire, and as such contributed far beyond their share in the popularization to its expansion, maintenance and survival. An Albanian nationalism was first formulated in 1878, with the establishment of the "Albanian League for the Defense of the Rights of the Albanian People," which was actually instigated by the Ottoman authorities to influence the decisions of the Congress of Berlin. Yet, until the creation of an independent Albania in 1913, Albanian nationalism remained in an embryonic stage, striving for autonomy within the Ottoman Empire rather than for an independent state. The creation of Albania in 1913 was more the result of Italian and Austro-Hungarian efforts (both resisted any significant strengthening of Serbia and Greece) than of local nationalist activity.

After World War I Albania's independence was recognized, but the first years of the new state were marked by internal struggles. In 1924 Ahmed Zog seized power with Yugoslav help, proclaimed Albania a republic and declared himself president. In 1928 he proclaimed Albania a monarchy with himself as king. In the 1920s and 1930s a series of treaties with Italy placed Albania under Italian protection in all but name. Still, in 1939 Mussolini conquered the country.

Following World War II a Communist regime, headed by Enver Hoxha, was established in Albania. A staunch Stalinist, Hoxha broke with the Soviet Union in 1959 and with the People's Republic of China in 1975 for their "revisionism." Albania was declared, "the world's first atheist state," and was closed to the outside world, thus making it the poorest and most underdeveloped country in Europe. Following his death in 1985, his heirs, headed by Ramiz Alia, cautiously attempted to open the country to the world and started a slow process of liberalization, but the collapse of the Communist regimes in Eastern Europe soon brought down that of Albania as well.

In Yugoslavia, Tito recognized Kosovo's Albanian majority by declaring the region an Autonomous Province within Serbia. Following his death, however, and with the general rise of nationalism in Yugoslavia, tension and ethnic conflict developed in Kosovo. In 1989 Serbia dissolved the Autonomous Province of Kosovo and placed the territory under martial law.

ALBANIA — GREECE   The boundary between Albania and Greece is 175 miles (282 km.) long, stretching from the Corfu Channel in the Ionian Sea to the border junction with Macedonia, situated in Lake Prespa. About 17 miles (27 km.) of the line run across water (rivers and lakes), the majority of the line running through mountainous terrain.

Geographical Setting. The common boundary begins at the meeting point of Albania, Greece and Macedonia, southwest of Veliki Grad Island in Lake Prespa. From this point the boundary runs southward in a straight line, following the meridian toward Vissaronivie, a summit standing at a height of 4,006 feet (1,221 m.) on the southern shore of the lake. Thence it runs southwestward, following local watersheds and changing directions with the local topography. The line forms a connection between the high points of the area, the highest being Mount Tchioukapetsit, which towers 8,131 feet (2,479 m.) above sea level. At one point the boundary line enters the Sarandaporos River and follows its main channel to its confluence with the Vijose River. From there the boundary runs westward, climbing along a local crest and reaching a height of 7,249 feet (2,210 m.) in the Nemerchka mountain range. It then turns southward, changes its direction westward, then again runs southward, following the course of the highest local peaks and reaching Mount Chenndeli (3,465 feet; 1,056 m.). From this peak the boundary runs westward, reaching Phtelia Bay in the Corfu Channel, east of the Greek island of Corfu. The maritime boundary runs northward, binding the whole island with Greece, and then runs westward, leaving with Greece the two small islands of Erikousa and Fano. The boundary line is demarcated by 178 numbered and intervisible boundary pillars and many other unnumbered markers.

Historical Background. Sheltered by their mountains, the Albanians have preserved their identity and language to a remarkable degree, despite successive foreign invasions. Through the centuries they have changed their religion from Hellenism to Christianity and then to Islam but have always maintained their national character. From the fourteenth century to 1913 Albania was ruled by Ottoman Turkey but never as a separate province. Greece was established as an independent kingdom in May 1832 within a limited area that stretched up to central Greece of today. From then on it pressed for a larger territory, especially toward the north. In 1881 Greece acquired part of Epirus (northwest of today's Greece), thereby extending its boundary to the Arakhthos River. During the First Balkan War of 1912–1913, the joint armies of Greece, Montenegro and Serbia occupied the entire Adriatic coast, attempting to divide the Albanian territory between them. During the peace negotiations, however, the Austro-Hungarian Empire, which was the main European force in the Balkan area, induced the Great Powers of Europe to recognize Albania's autonomy. A German prince was chosen to act as Albania's ruler and an agreement on the Albanian boundaries was reached at the Conference of Ambassadors in London during the summer of 1913. The boundary between Albania and Greece was subsequently confirmed and delimited in December 1913 by the Greco-Albanian Protocol of Florence but a definitive settlement was not reached and the new regime failed to establish an organized administration. In October 1914 Greece occupied Northern Epirus (southern Albania) and from 1915 Austro-Hungarian forces occupied the north and center of the country while the Italians captured Vlonë. The survival of the Albanian state was subsequently threatened by the provisions of the secret Treaty of London signed in 1915. By this treaty, designed to bring Italy into World War I, the Allied Powers agreed to the partitioning of Albania. Greece was promised the south (Northern Epirus), Serbia the north and Italy, central Albania. The status of Albania and Northern Epirus in particular was confused still further as the war drew to a close. In 1917 the Italians declared that Albania was under their protection, while the French, then occupying the Korcë (Koritsa) region, backed the foundation of an independent republic there. Subsequently an Albanian Provisional Government was formed which coordinated successful guerrilla action against the occupying forces. Italy was forced to withdraw from Vlonë and in August 1920 recognized Albania's independence and territorial integrity. Thus, only after World War I, during the Paris Peace Conference, did the Conference of Ambassadors confirm in 1921, with some modification, the boundary determined in 1913. An International Boundary Commission then commenced demarcation between 1922 and 1925 and the final treaty was signed on 30 July 1926. The Commission International de Délimitation des Frontières de l'Albanie described the boundary line in detail, specifically mentioning the location of every village situated in the border region according to its nation. The entire length of the boundary was then demarcated with boundary pillars.

The result of the commission's work, however, was considered far from satisfactory by both parties. In November 1926 Albania and Italy signed a treaty of friendship and security. This agreement was followed by the occupation of Albania with Italian troops (1939). War ensued between Italy and Greece. The Italians pressed for the southward extension of Albanian territory as far as the Gulf of Arta to include the whole of Epirus within Albania. These proposals were never acted upon but after the war Greek sources accused the Albanian minority of southern Epirus of collaboration with the Axis forces with a view to bringing about a revision of the boundaries in the area in Albania's favor.

On 10 November 1945 the Greek government demanded "...the union of north Epirus with the Greek Motherland...." However, in August and September of the same year the Epirus issue was struck off the agenda of the Paris meeting of the Allied foreign ministers, by the US secretary of state, after protests from the Albanian leader Envar Hoxha. Thus the Allies gave de facto recognition of the 1921 boundary. On 2 July 1958 the Albanian government rejected a Greek statement that a state of war still existed between the two countries and asked for normal relations. Greece reiterated its claim and on 14 August it was rejected by Albania in a statement which affirmed that no state of war existed and that "...the question of north Epirus does not exist, as this is Albanian territory."

The Albano-Greek border was finally reopened for official traffic, trade and cultural exchanges in the mid-1980s and a protocol was signed by the two countries in July 1985 for the restoration of border markers and agreement on procedures for the settlement of border disputes. Official Greek hopes of a territorial realignment in their favor in the region were finally laid aside by virtue of a government statement on 23 August 1985 announcing the end to the state of war between the two countries (which, as far as the Greek government was concerned, had been uninterrupted since 25 October 1940).

Present Situation. Political changes in the Balkan area over the last 70 years never affected the boundary location. The existence of an Albanian population in Greece and of Greeks in Albania has created

some obstacles in the past; yet this does not seem to cast a problem at present. There are no known disputes concerning the delimitation of the boundary between Albania and Greece.

ALBANIA — MACEDONIA The boundary between Albania and Macedonia runs for 94 miles (151 km.), from the Albania–Macedonia–Serbia tripoint, mainly through mountainous terrain southward, to the Albania–Greece–Macedonia tripoint.

Geographical Setting. From the northern boundary tripoint the line follows the watershed on the Korab (9,065 feet; 2,764 m.) and Desat (7,790 feet; 2,375 m.) mountains and cuts through the valley of the Black Drin (Drim) River, then heading south along the crest of the Jablanica mountains to reach Lake Ohrid. The boundary runs across the lake, dividing it such that one-third is left within Albania and two-thirds in Macedonia. It climbs Galicica mountain, follows its crest and drops down the other side of the mountain to reach the Albania–Greece–Macedonia tripoint on Lake Prespa, which is divided between Albania and Macedonia such that two-fifths of the lake are left with Macedonia.

Historical Background. Albania and Macedonia have maintained as their common boundary the line that was established between Albania and the former Yugoslavia. The first delimitation in the area was carried out in 1913, after the First Balkan War between the newly independent Albania and the Kingdom of Serbia, which had expanded its territory to encompass today's Macedonia. In the course of 1913 the Great Powers of Europe fixed the boundaries of independent Albania. After World War I the 1913 boundary was confirmed as the boundary between Albania and the Kingdom of Serbs, Croats and Slovenes (later Yugoslavia) and was clarified with more precise detail by the Council of Ambassadors in the peace conference of November 1921. In 1925 an international commission completed the demarcation of the boundary, which was ratified in 1926. The same boundary line was confirmed again in 1947 by the Paris Treaty as the boundary between Albania and the reestablished Yugoslavia. In 1991 Macedonia gained independence from Yugoslavia and adopted the existing provincial boundary with Albania.

Present Situation. There are no disputes regarding

the boundary line itself. However within Macedonia, since it became an independent state in 1991, there has been ongoing agitation concerning the status of a significant Albanian ethnic minority (443,000 in number; 22.9% of the total population) concentrated in the boundary region, especially around the towns of Tetovo and Debar.

ALBANIA — SERBIA This boundary arches from the tripoint with Macedonia in the east to the Adriatic Sea at the mouth of the Buenë (Bojana) River in the west. Running for a total of 178 miles (287 km.), the western section is the Albania–Serbia (Montenegro) boundary (107 miles; 173 km.) while the eastern section is the Albania–Serbia boundary (71 miles; 114 km.).

Geographical Setting. Northward from the tripoint with Macedonia in the mountainous area of Korab, the boundary descends toward the valley of the White Drin (Drim) River and then climbs gradually into the Albanian Alps (Prokletije). East of the Montenegrin capital, Titograd, the boundary follows the Cijevna River until it reaches Lake Scutari. It runs across the lake—leaving roughly one-third within Albania and two-thirds in Serbia—and reaches the Buenë (Bojana) River southwest of Shkodër (Albania), which it follows to its mouth in the Adriatic Sea.

Historical Background. The only sections of the boundary that were delimited previous to the twentieth century are two short sectors that belonged to the former Kingdom of Montenegro and that were recognized by the 1878 Congress of Berlin. Until the Balkan Wars of 1912–1913, the present Albanian and most of the Yugoslav borderlands were under the rule of the Ottoman Empire. However, in the First Balkan War (1912) Montenegro and Serbia expanded their territories and Albania declared independence, which was recognized by the London Conference of May 1913. An international commission was then formed to determine the Albanian boundaries. After the Second Balkan War and by the end of 1913, an international commission settled the boundaries of Albania, leaving the Albanians of Kosovo outside the new state.

After World War I the 1913 boundary was largely confirmed as the boundary between Albania and the Kingdom of Serbs, Croats and Slovenes (later Yugoslavia). The Council of Ambassadors of the November 1921 Peace Conference fixed Albania's boundaries, somewhat increasing its area from that of 1913, but also benefiting Yugoslavia, the largest addition located near Prizren (Serbia). By 1925 the international commission had completed the demarcation of the boundary line, which was confirmed in 1926 and after World War II by the Paris Treaty of 1947.

Present Situation. Officially, there are no territorial claims along the border, but the situation in the region is highly sensitive. There is an Albanian ethnic minority in the border region of Kosovo, an autonomous region within Serbia since 1945 (inhabited by approximately 2,000,000 Albanians, or 90% of the total population). In 1989 this autonomy was abolished, following ethnic conflicts during the 1980s. Since then the Albanians of Kosovo have been repressed by the Serbs. Repeated incidents along the boundary have been reported, including the shooting of several people to death. A significant Albanian minority is also found in Montenegro, along the northern (Plav) and southern (Ulcinj) sections of the boundary.

ALGERIA (Algérie/Djazaïr) Algeria is a North African country (area: 919,355 sq. miles [2,381,129 sq. km.]; estimated population: 27,200,000 [1994]) situated in northwestern Africa. It is bounded in the northwest by Morocco (969 miles; 1,559 km.), in the west by Western Sahara (26 miles; 42 km.), southwest by Mauritania (288 miles; 463 km.) and Mali (855 miles; 1,376 km.), southeast by Niger (594 miles; 956 km.), east by Libya (610 miles; 982 km.) and Tunisia (600 miles; 965 km.) and north by the Mediterranean Sea. Algeria's capital is Algiers.

Since the departure of 1,000,000 French colonists, the population consists nearly exclusively of Muslims. The Algerians may descend from a mixture of indigenous Berbers and colonizing Phoenicians and Carthaginians. Later they were partially subdued and colonized by Rome. Irrigation and slave labor turned North Africa into the Western Empire's richest agricultural province, which was lost in the turmoil of tribal revolts and vandal invasions of the fourth–fifth centuries. Algerians received their strongest imprint in the seventh century from the conquering Arabs, who defeated the indigenous

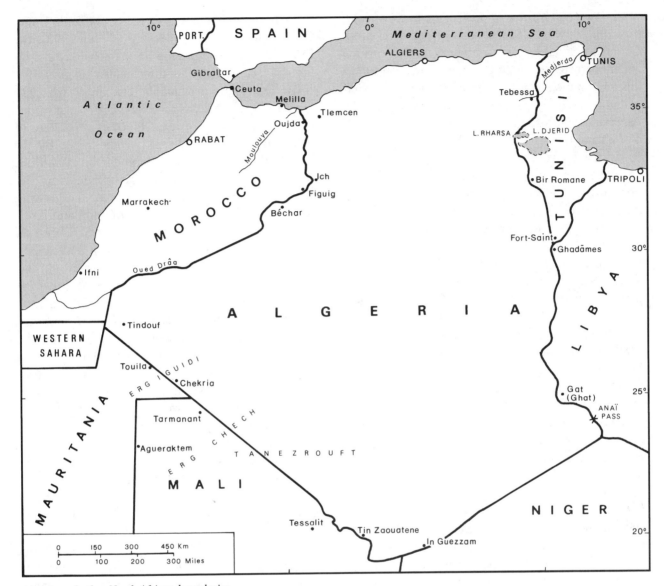

Algeria and other North African boundaries

Berbers and brought complete Islamization and incomplete arabization. Arabs became the ruling elite,
but Islam remained a minority religion until the
eleventh century, when competition between Sunni
and Shi'ite dynasties in North Africa led the Egyp-
tian-based Fatimids to send destructive Bani Hilal
nomad-settlers westward: they devastated the
Maghreb, and are blamed for a fateful decline in
agricultural and city life, and growth of pastoralism.
After having lived under Saharan Berber kingdoms
of the Almoravids and Almohads, Algerians were,
from the thirteenth to the sixteenth centuries, partitioned between Moroccan and Tunisian dynasties.
The "Barbary coast" was next contested between the

Spaniards and Turks, and won by the latter: Algeria
became an Ottoman province and a corsairs' den
whose lords grew rich from ransoming Christian
prisoners. After 1671 Algiers was a quasi-indepen-
dent backwater.

In 1830 military intervention by the French led to
the conquest of Algiers, provoking the fall of Ottoman overlordship throughout the whole of Algeria. But it took France time to decide what to do
with its colony. A revolt in the Oran region where
the Marabou leader Abd el-Kader created a strictly
Islamic state and initiated a holy war, ended in capit-
ulation, and lasting French occupation. Sporadic
tribal or Islamic revolts at the end of the nineteenth

century were powerless to prevent the massive colonization by which France consolidated its hold. Colonial policy toward assimilation, sedentarization and modernization on the one hand, and open subordination on the other. France systematically discriminated in favor of its *colons*, who transformed the Algerian countryside. By the 1930s they formed 2% of the rural population but owned one-quarter of all cultivated lands. However, most Europeans were city-dwellers: French, other Europeans (Italians, Spaniards, Maltese), and naturalized Jews ultimately totaled nearly 1,000,000.

Meanwhile the Muslim Algerians developed a national consciousness of their own, but the *colons* blocked even the slightest emancipation. After World War II, a restricted Muslim elite obtained a partial franchise, and complete equalization was broached for all. Hopes for peaceful improvement of the Muslims' position and the closure of a social-economic gap were gone. Decades of French rule had created an underdeveloped Algerian society. After a series of more limited (and cruelly suppressed) regional revolts, in 1954 the FLN (National Liberation Front) launched a full-scale war of independence. The armed insurrection was harshly repressed, but meanwhile the FLN gained wide international recognition.

Without hope of a military victory, the FLN combined international action with terrorism and strengthened its institutions. Meanwhile the European settlers rejected any compromise, armed themselves, and contemplated secession. After a particularly violent war (which may have cost up to 1,000,000 civilian lives), Algerians obtained full independence in 1962. As French *colons* departed, their estates became the booty for a new Arab bourgeoisie. The new rulers installed an authoritarian, one-party, socialized state, mixed from the onset with a dose of Islamic symbolism. Yet for all its proclaimed hegemony, the FLN failed to reform itself into a mass vanguard party. Houari Boumediene's rule (1965–1978) symbolized the concentration of power in the sovereign state, which from the late 1970s found it increasingly hard to fulfill the people's economic aspirations, or to lay a firm basis for a collective Algerian identity. The ideological vacuum has been filled by an increasingly vocal Islamic fundamentalist movement: the religious majority of the Algerians has never been secularized. Under Chadli Ben-Jedid's leadership (1978–1992), the FLN has attempted to prop up the economy and repossess Islamic elements from fundamentalists.

The expansion of education and industrialization (paid for by natural gas revenues) has not succeeded in keeping pace with the Algerians' high rate of population growth and rapid urbanization. By the mid-1980s economic development remained unspectacular and the party's image became tarnished. The absence of legal ways to express the growing discontent with the functioning of state and profiteering by new classes gave rise to social unrest. In 1988 massive riots, initiated by youth movements, forced the regime to permit political pluralism. This raised hopes for a democratic opening profiting three major tendencies: the intellectuals' and women's movement demanding secularization and modernization, Berbers demanding ethnic-linguistic pluralism, and anti-Western fundamentalists seeking a conservative religious-political program. Of these three, the fundamentalists are by far the strongest. In 1990 the Islamic Front won the municipal elections, defeating the FLN for the first time. In an atmosphere of religious intolerance and growing destabilization, the Islamic Front seemed on the verge of taking over the Algerian state. In 1991, after violent demonstrations, the army proclaimed a state of emergency, cracked down on the fundamentalist leadership, and delayed legislative elections. However, in Algeria's first-ever free elections the Islamic Front won by an overwhelming margin. Soon afterward, in 1992, the army took over, disbanded the Islamic front, and began to persecute the fundamentalists.

ALGERIA — LIBYA The boundary between Algeria and Libya runs for 610 miles (982 km.), from the boundary tripoint with Tunisia near Fort-Saint in the north to the boundary tripoint with Niger in the south. The boundary follows the former colonial boundary between the French and Italian possessions in northern Africa.

Geographical Setting. The northern terminus of the boundary line, boundary point no. 220, is located between Fort-Saint (Tunisia) and Ghadames (Libya). It forms a semicircular line westward to Garet Hamel, at boundary point no. 233, southwest of Ghadames. In a series of 20 straight lines the boundary runs 275 miles (442 km.) south, crossing the northern sector of the Sahara Desert to reach a point east of Tarat (Algeria) and from there heads southeastward to a point west of the Libyan town of Gat (Ghat), leaving the oil field of In Amenas within Algeria. From Gat southeastward to the tripoint with Niger, the line was detailed. It runs for about 190 miles (306 km.), passing through Takharkhouri Gap, the Anai Pass and a hill that stands some 3,030 feet (924 m.) above sea level. The boundary reaches the tripoint boundary junction with Niger just north of the Tropic of Cancer (23°N latitude).

Historical Background. Both Algeria and Libya were under Turkish Ottoman rule until the nineteenth century. The French established themselves on the Mediterranean coast of Algeria in 1830 and by 1847 controlled the whole northern territory of Algeria, which was divided into the three French districts in 1848 and integrated with France in 1881. The Sahara region of Algeria became a military zone, formally annexed by France on 24 December 1902. France and the Ottoman Turkish Empire signed a convention on 19 May 1910, defining the present boundary between Fort-Saint and Ghadames as a section of the entire boundary between the French and the Turkish possessions in northern Africa. This section was demarcated by boundary pillars in 1911.

The Italians occupied Libya from 1912 until 1942. After World War I, on 12 September 1919, France and Italy held an exchange of notes in which the sector from Ghadames down to Gat was established and the southern sector of the boundary, up to the boundary tripoint with Niger, was dealt with in general terms. Libya became independent on 24 December 1951 and on 10 August 1955 signed a treaty of friendship with France, in which the boundary line was confirmed and the southern sector was defined in sharper detail. Further clarifications and descriptions of the entire boundary was made with an exchange of letters on 26 December 1956. Algeria became independent on 3 July 1962, adopting the colonial boundary as its international boundary with Libya without any formal agreement.

Present Situation. Since achieving independence neither Algeria nor Libya has made claims on the other's territory and no disputes concerning the boundary alignment are known.

ALGERIA — MALI   This boundary is 855 miles (1,376 km.) long and courses along straight-line sectors, watersheds and wadis, from the boundary tripoint with Mauritania to the tripoint with Niger.

Geographical Setting. From the southeastern boundary tripoint with Niger, at about 19°08'30"N and 4°14'30"E, the boundary follows a straight line west-southwest for 63 miles (101 km.) to the In-Akantarer wadi at approximately 18°57'40"N and 3°20'E. From there it continues generally north along the In-Akantarer and Tin-Zaouâtene wadis and then west to the source of the latter, where it joins the watershed north of the Vallee du Tilemsi. It follows the watershed, passes westward between the N'Djouden and the In-Keouen rivers and turns northward to cross the N'Djouden. The line reaches the road that connects Bordj le Prieur (Algeria) and Tessalit (Mali), at about 21°06'15"N and 1°10'E. From this point the boundary forms a straight line for 452 miles (727 km.) to the boundary tripoint with Mauritania at 25°N and 4°50'W, north of Tarmant (Mali).

Historical Background. Mali developed out of the French occupation of Senegal, which began as early as 1558. The French sphere of influence spread inland in Haut-Senegal (which later became French Sudan, then the Republic of Mali) and the area became semi-independent in 1880. It was separated from Senegal by the Faléme River, but to the east its borders were to be as far as the French forces could carry them. Timbuktu was occupied by the French in 1893, in answer to an appeal from its people for protection, and war against the ruling Tuaregs in the north lasted until 1897. The Federation of Mali was made independent on 20 June 1960 and consisted of the former colonies of Senegal and French Sudan. However, the Federation was dissolved, the Republic of Sudan became independent on 20 August 1960 and on 22 September 1960 became the Republic of Mali.

The Saharan region of Algeria was formally annexed by France on 24 December 1902 and the area was administered as a regional unit called the Territory of South Algeria. The division between Algeria and French West Africa (which included French Sudan) was established by French administrators in 1905 and was defined with little detail in the Niamey Convention of June 1909. Under the Organic

Statute of Algeria of 20 September 1947 these territories were reorganized as departments. Algeria became independent on 3 July 1962. The tripoint with Mauritania was established in the Kayes Treaty of 16 February 1963 in which Mali and Mauritania delimited their boundary. Algeria was not a party to this agreement but a border demarcation agreement between Algeria and Mali was signed at Bamako on 26 April 1984.

Present Situation. This boundary is recognized by both countries.

ALGERIA — MAURITANIA

ALGERIA — MAURITANIA This boundary is delimited by a straight line, 288 miles (463 km.) long, that stretches from the boundary tripoint with Mali in the southeast to the northwestern tripoint with Western Sahara.

Geographical Setting. The Algeria–Mali–Mauritania boundary tripoint is located at 25°N and 4°50'W. From there the Algeria–Mauritania boundary runs in a straight line across an arid, sparsely populated tract—leaving Chekria within Algeria and Chegga and Touila in Mauritania—to the tripoint with Western Sahara, at approximately 27°17'40"N and 8°40'W. The northwestern terminus of the line is situated on the northern bank of a wadi that drains eastward to Tindouf (Algeria).

Historical Background. The French occupation of Algeria began in 1830 and arose largely from an attempt to protect French shipping by quelling a pirate stronghold at Algiers. At first France held only the coastal districts and, faced with difficult terrain and strong opposition, the interior was controlled indirectly through client chiefs. However, in 1840 France began complete occupation and colonization against the opposition of Emir Abd el-Kader, who was finally defeated in 1847. In 1848 the northern section of Algeria was proclaimed an integral part of France and was organized into three departments (Oran, Alger and Constantine). Colonel Lyautey, using tactics of "peaceful penetration" from 1903 to 1906, suppressed tribal revolts, extended the railways and established a network of military posts to the border with French West Africa (a federation of French dependencies that included today's Mauritania).

After the accession of Napoleon III France pursued a more vigorous policy of colonization. Between 1855 and 1858, under General Faidherbe, the French gained treaties with the Trarza and Brakna Arabs in the country north of the Senegal River that is now Mauritania. In 1880 and 1881 further treaties were made with the Arabs, concerning their caravan routes, and in 1892 the emir of Adrar agreed to deal with no foreign country other than France. Although Mauritania was generally recognized as being within the French sphere of influence, France undertook no properly organized penetration of the interior until it was made possible to build posts within the Trarza and Brakna Arab territory. Mauritania became a territoire civil in 1904. The colonial federation of French West Africa was reorganized by a decree of 18 October 1904. On 7 June 1905 a boundary agreement between the commander of the French region of southern Algeria and the commandant of Haut-Senegal et Niger outlined a border between Algeria and French West Africa. The principles of the boundary were completed by the Naimey Conventions of 20 June and 26 August 1909. On 4 December 1920 Mauritania acquired colonial status and in 1958 became a constituent member of the French Community. Mauritania gained total independence on 28 November 1960; Algeria on 3 July 1962. Neither challenged the existing border and on 9 April 1985, after three years of negotiations, a formal demarcation agreement was signed.

Present Situation. This boundary line is recognized by both countries.

ALGERIA — MOROCCO

ALGERIA — MOROCCO The boundary between Algeria and Morocco runs 969 miles (1,559 km.) between the Mediterranean coast in the northeast and the boundary tripoint with Western Sahara in the Ouarkziz range, on the 8°40'W meridian, in the southwest.

Geographical Setting. The northern terminus of the boundary line is located on the Mediterranean shore, west of the Algerian town of Nemours. It runs southward, leaves the town of Oujda with Morocco, and then follows a series of straight lines to Dougmount (Algeria) and turns southwestward to Ich (Algeria). Thence it runs generally southwestward for about 30 miles (50 km.) to reach the town of Figuig (Morocco) and turns westward to stretch some 90 miles (145 km.) in another straight line, reaching Grouz Mountain. Running southwestward again, the boundary line crosses the Guir River southeast of

Berbers visiting a sacred tomb near the Algeria–Morocco boundary

the town of Bouanane (Morocco) and travels westward in a straight line for about 50 miles (80 km.) to a point south of the town of Boudenib (Morocco). The boundary line changes its direction southward for about 120 miles (193 km.) and reaches a point east of the Algerian town of Abadla, north of the main road between the Mediterranean Sea and the west African shore of the Atlantic Ocean. Trending southwestward for about 200 miles (320 km.) the line reaches the Dra River south of Zagora (Morocco) and follows the river downstream to its intersection with the 8°40'W meridian. The boundary then follows the meridian southward to the boundary tripoint with Western Sahara at 27°17'40"N and 8°40'W.

Historical Background. Morocco was a north African independent empire from the seventeenth century that established a boundary with the Ottoman Empire (which ruled the rest of northern Africa) from the Mediterranean Sea to Figuig. From 1830 to 1870 France occupied most of the area that is now modern Algeria, and on 18 March 1845 Morocco and France adopted the Morocco–Ottoman Empire boundary that stretched from the Mediterranean Sea to Teniet-al-Sassi (Morocco) as their common international boundary in the Treaty of Lalla Marnia. This line was reconfirmed and extended to Figuig on 20 July 1901. France annexed the Sahara region of Algeria on 24 December 1902, extending the boundary line even further southwest.

On 30 March 1912 a French protectorate was established in Morocco under the Treaty of Fez, placing the French on both sides of the boundary, neither side anticipating a need to change or redefine it. However, the 44 years of French occupation saw conflict between the French rulers of Morocco and Algeria, as they abortively tried to established a boundary between the two regions.

The French controlled Morocco until 2 March 1956, when Morocco regained independence. Algeria became independent on 3 July 1962, adopting the French colonial boundary that was never defined west of Figuig. Morocco then began making territorial claims on the western sectors of southern Algeria—especially to the area of Tindouf, rich in iron ore. Armed conflicts with Algeria subsequently took place in 1962–1963. After peace was restored the two heads of state convened and, on 17 May 1970, provided for the constitution of a mixed demarcation commission. On 15 June 1972 both countries agreed to adopt a definitive line between them.

Present Situation. From 1972 onward, no disputes concerning the boundary alignment were reported. The boundary is not demarcated by pillars and only the river sections are defined on the ground.

ALGERIA — NIGER

ALGERIA — NIGER The boundary between Algeria and Niger runs across a sparsely populated tract of the Sahara for 594 miles (956 km.). It forms three straight-line sectors from the boundary tripoint with Mali in the southwest to the tripoint with Libya in the northeast.

Geographical Setting. From the tripoint with Mali, at about 19°08'30"N and 4°14'30"E, this boundary runs in a straight line east-northeast to In Guezzam (Algeria) on the Agadez (Niger)–Tamanrasset (Algeria) highway, at approximately 19°26'30"N and 5°48'45"E. There it bears northeast, follows the Tin Tarabine dry river for about 120 miles (200 km.) and continues to about 20°51'N and 7°27'E on the railway track 2 miles (3 km.) north of the In-Azaoua wadi. From there it continues up to the boundary tripoint with Libya at 23°30'54"N and 11°59'54.6"E, east of In Ezzane (Algeria).

Historical Background. French forces occupied Algiers in 1830, and by 1847 most of northern Algeria was under French administration. In 1848 Algeria was proclaimed an integral part of France and was organized into three departments: Oran, Alger and Constantine. With the establishment of a post at Zinder (southern Niger) in 1899, France achieved the creation of an African empire stretching from the Atlantic and the Mediterranean to the Congo; it was the largest tract of Africa controlled by any European power. Niger was part of French West Africa from 1904 and was made into a separate military territory with its headquarters at Zinder in 1912. It became a formal colony of French West Africa in 1922 and its capital was moved to Niamey in 1926. On 7 June 1905 an agreement between the comman-

dant of Upper Senegal and Niger and the military commander of the District of the Oasis (part of southern Algeria) determined a boundary between Algeria and French West Africa (which included present-day Mauritania, Mali and Niger). The 1905 agreement was completed by the Niamey Conventions of 20 June and 16 August 1909, which provided a more detailed description of the boundary between Niger and Algeria. In 1946, after World War II, Niger became an overseas territory of France, an autonomous member of the French Community in 1958 and an independent state on 3 August 1960. Algeria became independent on 3 July 1962 and on 5 January 1983 signed a demarcation agreement with Niger.

Present Situation. The Algeria–Niger boundary is recognized by both countries.

ALGERIA — TUNISIA

ALGERIA — TUNISIA The boundary between Algeria and Tunisia extends 600 miles (965 km.) from the Mediterranean Sea in the north to the boundary junction with Libya in the south. After crossing the Atlas Mountains it mainly runs in an uninhabited desert region.

Geographical Setting. The northern terminus of the boundary is situated on the Mediterranean shore, between the cities of Tabarka (Tunisia) and El Kala (Algeria). It runs southward, climbs the Medjerda Mountains and follows their crest southwestward, and then bears east to reach the Medjerda River, which flows eastward. The line crosses the river and runs in a southerly direction to cross some other local rivers. Forming a semicircle to the west, the boundary leaves the Rharsa and Djerid Lakes in Tunisia, and reaches the desert well of Bir Romane. From there it runs in a straight line southeast to Puits Mort and in another straight line south-southeast to the boundary junction with Libya, near Fort-Saint.

Historical Background. Until 1830 Algeria was under Turkish Ottoman rule. It was conquered by France between 1830 and 1870 and the Saharan area of Algeria was formally annexed by France on 24 December 1902. Tunisia was likewise a province of the Ottoman Empire in the nineteenth century, until French protection was imposed by force by a treaty signed on 12 May 1881. The boundaries between Algeria and Tunisia prior to the impositions of

French rule were uncertain. However, a definitive line between the French colony of Algeria and the protectorate of Tunisia was established during the period of French administration—from the Mediterranean as far south as Bir Romane. The precise location of the line was never published as the outcome of any formal agreement, but it does appear on maps published by the French between 1913 and 1935.

The section of the boundary from Bir Romane southward was not definitive. The boundary junction with Libya, on a local hill known as Garet Hamel, was demarcated in 1911 following a convention between France and Turkey (which then ruled Libya), which was signed on 19 May 1910. Some French maps, however, indicated another boundary junction, about 19 miles (30 km.) north of Garet Hamel.

Tunisia became an independent country on 20 March 1956, while Algeria gained independence on 3 July 1962, both assuming the status quo of the colonial period. The principle of the establishment of a common boundary between the two independent countries was agreed upon in a treaty of 6 April 1968, which was followed by an agreement signed on 6 January 1970. Neither Algeria nor Tunisia has challenged the northern sector of the line down to Bir Romane.

Present Situation. There are no known disputes concerning the boundary alignment between the two north African states.

ALGERIA — WESTERN SAHARA

The boundary between Algeria and Western Sahara is 26 miles (42 km.) long and follows a straight line between the tripoint with Mauritania in the north and the tripoint with Morocco in the south. It was demarcated by the Franco-Spanish commissions held between 1956 and 1958.

Geographical Setting. The boundary between Algeria and Western Sahara begins at the tripoint with Morocco, from where the boundary follows the line of the 8°40'W meridian for 26 miles (42 km.) along the rocky and sandy surfaces of the eastern tip of the small mountainous region of the Dra Desert (Dra Hamada). The boundary ends at the tripoint with Mauritania, the position of which is in dispute. The line has only two known pillars: no. 40 at 27°20'N and no. 41 at 27°40'N, which belong to the Maurita-

nia–Western Sahara series of boundary pillars that demarcate the entire southern boundary of Western Sahara.

Historical Background. The history of this boundary primarily dates back to the nineteenth century, when France and Spain were increasing their efforts to extend their spheres of influence in Africa. Spanish influences can be traced back to 1476 along the Moroccan coast, specifically Ifni, which Morocco ceded to Spain in 1860. French influence was increased in 1845 after French military forces occupied northern Algeria and by 1848 France had proclaimed the "Territoiries du Sud Algerien" an integral part of the country—although annexation into French sovereignty did not occur until December 1902. From 1934 to 1958 Río de Oro, Ifni and the Spanish southern zone of Morocco were administered under the auspices of Spanish West Africa. A decree of January 1958 created two provinces within this area and ceded the Spanish southern zone of Morocco to the Kingdom of Morocco. One of the two provinces created was Spanish Sahara, now known as Western Sahara. It was not until the early twentieth century that the two European countries began the delineation of their colonial boundaries. The Franco-Spanish Convention of June 1900 delimited southern and inland boundary sectors from 20°51'N to 26°N and 12°W. The 1904 convention established a line between French and Spanish spheres of influence along the 8°40'W meridian and northward from 26°N and 12°W to the Dra River (Oued Dra). December 1956 saw the signing of the Franco-Spanish Agreement, which delimited the Mauritania–Spanish Sahara boundary. In February 1976 Spain handed the territory of Spanish Sahara to Morocco and Mauritania; a partition was arranged whereby the Algeria–Western Sahara border was to be administered by Morocco. A number of governments, however, did not recognize this form of decolonization. The political situation within Western Sahara is unstable due to the above-mentioned territorial claims, the partition arranged between Morocco and Mauritania and the nationalist guerrillas fighting for self-determination.

Present Situation. The alignment of this boundary rests on the Franco-Spanish Convention of October 1904 and the line demarcated by the Franco-Spanish Commission between 1956 and 1958. No challenges

to the line have been reported. The tripoint with Mauritania, however, has no precise location due to French and Spanish territorial claims, although the French locate it at 8°40'W and 27°17'40"N.

AMERICA see UNITED STATES OF AMERICA.

AMERICAN SAMOA American Samoa lies in the South Pacific Ocean. It is constitutionally an unorganized and unincorporated territory of the United States, administered by the Department of Interior. The total area of the islands of American Samoa is 76 sq. miles (197 sq. km.) with an estimated population of 53,000 (1994). American Samoa has no land boundaries. Its capital is Pago Pago.

American Samoa has been administered by the United States since 1899.

ANDORRA Since 1278 Andorra has been a co-principality, ruled by the president (formerly the king) of France and the bishop of Urgel (Spain). It is a landlocked country (area: 175 sq. miles [453 sq. km.]; estimated population: 58,000 [1994]) situated in the eastern Pyrenees. It is bounded in the north by France (37.5 miles; 60 km.) and in the south by Spain (40 miles; 64 km.). The capital of Andorra is Andorra la Vella.

The 58,000 inhabitants of the small principality are Roman Catholics and speak Catalan, Spanish and French. Some 20% of the workforce is engaged in agriculture but tourism is also an important industry because of the country's status as a tax-free haven.

In recent years, there has been an increase in Andorran wishes to assert greater independence.

ANDORRA — FRANCE The boundary between Andorra and France runs for 37.5 miles (60 km.) along the Pyrenee Mountains, forming a break in the boundary terrain between Spain and France. The boundaries of Andorra are the oldest existing boundaries in the world, going back to the thirteenth century.

Geographical Setting. The boundary runs from the eastern border junction with Spain, located south of La Casa Pass, on the only access route between Andorra and France. The line travels northward for 3 miles (5 km.) to join the Ariège River. It follows the river, crossing the La Cassa Pass, and turns eastward for about 3.5 miles (6 km.) to reach the summit ring of the eastern Pyrenees. Then turning westward, the boundary follows the watershed between the eastern valley of Andorra (Valira del Orient) and the French Ariège valley for 19 miles (30 km.), along mountain peaks that range in altitude from 8,000 to 10,000 feet (2,400 to 3,000 m.). The line passes north of Andorra's El Serrat commune in the northern valley of Andorra and, turning southward, reaches the western boundary junction with Spain, situated at the highest source of a river that flows southeast to join the northern valley of Andorra. Apart from the eastern pass, the entire boundary line cannot be reached by vehicles; only a small number of footpaths cross it.

Historical Background. The existence of independent Andorra dates back to the Middle Ages. In a treaty contracted in 1278 to calm the French–Spanish border area, the country of the Valleys and Suzerainties was established as a joint principality

Andorra, forming a break in the France–Spain boundary

under the bishop of Urgel (Spain) and the count of Foix. The jurisdiction of the count was later transferred to the French crown and has now passed to the president of France.

Political changes and the long history of the French–Spanish border never affected the boundary

Andorra in the eastern Pyrenees

of Andorra, which has not been changed since 1278.
Present Situation. There are no disputes concerning
the alignment of the boundary between Andorra and
France.

ANDORRA — SPAIN   The boundary between
Andorra and Spain runs 40 miles (64 km.) from the
eastern boundary junction with France, situated
south of the La Cassa Pass on the Andorra–France
road, to the western boundary junction with France,
7 miles (11 km.) northwest of Andorra's capital, Andorra la Vella.
Geographical Setting. Running southwestward for
19 miles (30 km.) from the eastern border junction
with France, the boundary line runs along the watershed between the eastern valley of Andorra and the
Spanish Segre River until it reaches the Gran Valira
River, which flows south into Spain where it joins
the River Segre, a tributary of the Ebro River. The
line crosses the Gran Valira River and the road to
Spain and, turning north, it traverses 21 miles (34

km.) along the watershed between Andorra's eastern
valley and the Spanish Pallaresa valley until it
reaches the western boundary junction with France.
Historical Background. In 1278 Andorra, the
country of the Valleys and Suzerainties, was formed
as a shared principality between the bishop of Urgel
(Spain) and the count of Foix to settle disputes in
the France–Spain border region. French administration was later passed from the count to the French
crown, today under the authority of the French president. Since 1278, throughout the history of the
French–Spanish border region and despite political
changes and disputes, Andorra's boundary with
Spain has not been changed.
Present Situation. There are no boundary disputes
regarding the boundary between Andorra and Spain.

ANGOLA   Angola is an independent state (area:
481,231 sq. miles [1,246,388 sq. km.]; estimated
population: 10,900,000 [1994]) situated on the
southwestern coast of Africa. It is bounded by

Congo in the north along Angola's exclave of Cabinda (125 miles; 201 km.), by Zaire (1,560 miles; 2,511 km.)—including Cabinda's southern boundary—in the north and northeast, by Zambia (690 miles; 1,110 km.) in the east, by Namibia (855 miles; 1,376 km.) in the south and by the Atlantic Ocean in the west. Angola's capital is Luanda.

The Angolans achieved their independence from

Angola's boundaries in southwestern Africa

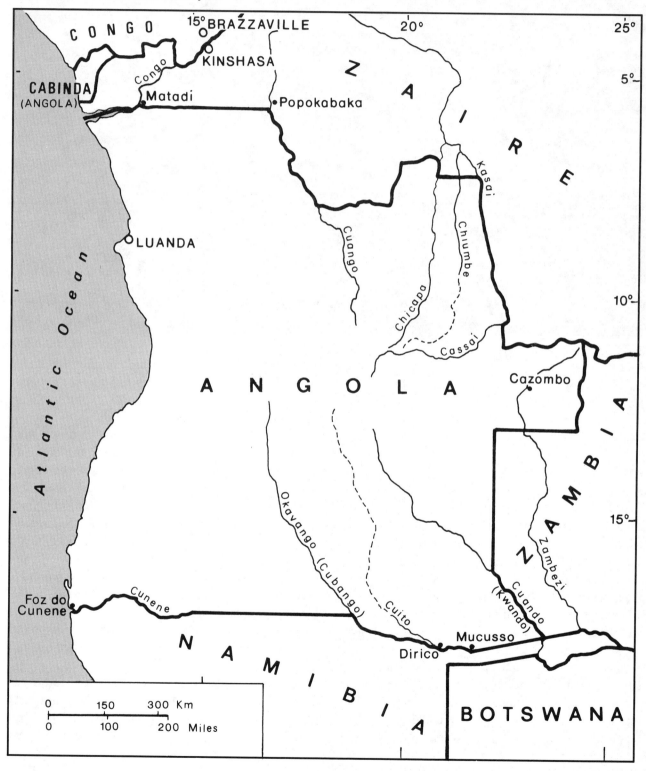

Portugal after a long and violent civil war which began in 1961 and was led by the National Front for the Liberation of Angola (FNLA) whose supporters were of the Kongo group; the Popular Movement for the Liberation of Angola (MPLA), supported by the Mbundu people; and the National Union for the total Independence of Angola (UNITA), dominated by the Ovimbundu. A characteristic of these organizations was their external basis of support. The MPLA was supported by the Soviet Union, UNITA received aid from China and South Africa, and the FNLA was backed by western and pro-western governments. Although all three groups were fighting a common adversary, they were never able to unite and, even after independence was achieved following the coup in Portugal in 1974, the conflict between the three movements continued.

The tensions between the movements exploded into a civil war, each side still receiving considerable aid from foreign governments.

The MPLA, led by Agostinho Neto, took over the government in 1976. Following the Marxist-Leninist model, it immediately sought to concentrate power in its own hands in the form of a one-party state and therefore did not allow any form of opposition to operate. As a result the other movements resorted to force. As the FNLA had been seriously weakened because of its defeat during the civil war, UNITA became the main source of opposition.

Supported by South Africa, the United States and other conservative African and Middle Eastern governments, UNITA launched attacks on a variety of targets. South Africa's 1984 proposal to withdraw troops from Angola precipitated a series of peace talks which lasted throughout the decade. In spite of a peace agreement between UNITA and the government, signed in March 1991, sustained peace has not been achieved.

ANGOLA — CONGO   The boundary between Angola and Congo is demarcated by nine pillars, along the northern border of Angola's exclave, Cabinda. It is 125 miles (201 km.) long and uses ridge lines and watersheds as its course for a considerable extent. Cabinda is separated from the Angolan mainland by some 25 miles (40 km.) of coastline, Zaire's corridor to the Atlantic.

Geographical Setting. Beginning at the Atlantic

seaboard the boundary heads inland in a northeasterly direction, along a ridge on the southern side of the River Loem valley. The boundary is then demarcated past the parallel of the Bilisi and Luali rivers' confluence and up to the Bamba mountain range. From the range the boundary changes direction to follow the line of the Niari ridge, bounding the Mayumbe forest in a southeasterly direction, until it reaches the Chiloango River at the boundary tripoint with Zaire.

Historical Background. Portuguese activity in this region can be traced back to the late fifteenth century, with the establishment of trading posts in the mouth of the Congo River. Portugal occupied the small enclave of Cabinda in 1783, although French interests in the area broke the occupation within 11 months. Through several treaties, Portugal attempted to reinstate its claim over the entire Atlantic coast of Africa between latitudes 5°12'S and 8°S. After several unsuccessful treaties, Portugal proposed the convention of an international conference to discuss these issues. The proposal led to the Berlin Conference (15 November 1884–26 February 1885), which recognized the Portuguese claims north of the Congo.

The boundary between the two countries was first aligned by a convention between Portugal and the International Association of the Congo on 12 May 1886, whereby the latter was guaranteed a narrow corridor to the Atlantic Ocean. The alignment was updated by the Franco-Portuguese Arrangement of January 1901. On 11 November 1975 Angola gained independence from Portugal—and with it Cabinda's stability was swayed: Angola's independence sparked Cabindan insurgency, which was subsequently quelled by Angolan sources. Albeit very small, Cabinda possesses strategic significance in the region, in that it restricts Zaire's access to the Atlantic Ocean and benefits Angola with offshore oil resources.

Present Situation. Since the independence of Congo (Brazzaville) on 15 August 1960, the principle of the alignment, set out in the Franco-Portuguese Arrangement of 1901, has not been challenged. Incidents and complaints to the UN Security Council in 1965–1966 indicated uncertainties regarding local alignments. The two governments involved refrained from challenging the alignment but stressed that detailed clarification and improved demarcation would be necessary to solve the local alignment disputes.

ANGOLA — NAMIBIA The boundary between Angola and Namibia (formerly South-West Africa) extends 855 miles (1,376 km.) from the Atlantic seaboard to the tripoint with Zambia. The length of the boundary is demarcated by rivers or pillars.

Geographical Setting. This boundary begins on the Atlantic coastal plain and follows the median line of the Cunene River for 213 miles (343 km.) from its mouth up to a point on the great Ruacana Falls and downstream from the Calueque Dam (Angola). From the falls the boundary heads in a straight line, due east, for 277 miles (446 km.) along 47 boundary pillars to the Okavango (Cubango) River, which it then follows for 230 miles (370 km.) up to a point between the towns of Mucusso (Angola) and Mukwe (Namibia). The line, again in a straight line, then heads east for 135 miles (217 km.) to the Kwando River, where it meets the boundary tripoint with Zambia. This part of the boundary is a section of a longer line that continues eastward to the Zambezi River and forms the western sector of the Namibia–Zambia boundary.

Historical Background. The delimitation of this border is based on conventions and agreements signed by the colonizing European countries in the nineteenth and twentieth centuries. The first Europeans to land on the shores of Angola and Namibia were Portuguese seafarers in the fifteenth century. German activity began in South-West Africa in the nineteenth century, acquiring land from local tribes through treaties of protection during the early 1880s. A mutually acceptable boundary line between the German and Portuguese possessions was concluded in the Declaration of December 1886, although a specific point on the Ruacana Falls, from which the line was to extend to the east along its parallel of latitude, was not specified. British protests to the agreement were lodged, claiming that it impinged on surrounding British territory. Hence, a treaty to define Anglo-Portuguese possessions was signed in June 1891. In the early twentieth century South-West Africa was consolidated as a German colony, but German administration ended during World War I, when the territory was occupied by Anglo-South

African forces. In 1915 the British and Portuguese administrations concluded a provisional agreement and in 1916 created a neutral zone, 6 miles (9.5 km.) wide, to be held under joint administration. A South African-Portuguese agreement in June 1926 finalized the undetermined point on the Cunene River at the Ruacana Falls (17°13'S) and stated that the boundary would follow the *thalweg* (main navigation channel) of the Cunene River, from its mouth to the parallel of latitude, passing a pillar erected on the left bank of the river adjacent to the Ruacana falls. On the basis of this agreement the boundary was demarcated, the neutral zone was abolished and the boundary as far as the Okavango River was fixed. However, the section east of the intersection with the Okavango River remained unclear, until it was surveyed and demarcated by a joint Portuguese–South African boundary commission in 1930–1931, which stated that the boundary should pass through the Zambian tripoint (at that time not fixed) to the Zambezi River. The Zambian tripoint was finalized with the Anglo-Portuguese agreements of November 1954 and October 1964.

Present Situation. The boundary is demarcated throughout by rivers or pillars and the principle of the alignment has never been challenged. Border tension was heightened as civil war raged in Angola during the 1970s and 1980s, although an internationally monitored cease-fire is now in enforced.

ANGOLA — ZAIRE The boundary between Angola and Zaire, including the Angolan exclave of Cabinda, is 1,560 miles (2,511 km.) long. The border is divided into several sections, which have been aligned by different conventions and treaties and demarcated with different instruments. Discussions regarding the boundary include the Cabinda boundary with Zaire, which runs for 140 miles (225 km.).

Geographical Setting. The Cabinda boundary sets out from the Atlantic seaboard and runs east and then north until it converges with the Chiloango River, which it follows to the boundary tripoint with Congo (Brazzaville), opposite a mountain ridge that forms the Angola–Congo boundary.

Some 25 miles (40 km.) south of the boundary with Cabinda on the Atlantic coast, the main Angola–Zaire boundary begins. It runs from the Atlantic Ocean along the Angolan side of the wide delta and channel of the Congo River up to a point near the town of Matadi. In a straight line eastward from the Congo River, the line enters a forested upland for 202 miles (325 km.) and then reaches a tributary that leads into the Kwango (Cuango) River, which is followed until the two rivers meet. The boundary then follows the *thalweg* of the Kwango River southeastward through forested areas for about 155 miles (250 km.), from its confluence with the Cuilo River to its confluence with the Utunguila River. From here eastward, the boundary skirts the edges of more forested areas and courses into an upland region, landscapes that emanate from Angola. Then turning north and again east, it meets the Chicapa River, a tributary of the Kasai River, and continues southward for about 12 miles (20 km.). Thence it runs eastward to reach the Kasai River, the course of which is followed southward to its source. The boundary then heads east to the tripoint with Zambia.

Historical Background. Portuguese interest in the region surrounding the former Congo (Zaire) is documented from early in the sixteenth century. In 1885 the Berlin-Africa Conference recognized the Portuguese claims to the territories north and south of the mouth of the Congo River. The boundaries between the Portuguese possessions and the Congo were mapped by treaties and conventions with France and Portugal in February 1885 and in May 1891. On 23 February 1885 the Belgian government recognized the International Association of the Congo within these limits. The International Association of the Congo was later renamed the Independent State of the Congo, with King Leopold II as its sovereign, and became a Belgian colony in November 1907. It became independent as the Republic of the Congo on 30 June 1960, changed its name to the Democratic Republic of the Congo on 1 August 1964, and finally became the Republic of Zaire on 21 October 1971. The Brussels Convention of 25 May 1891 set down the entire boundary, while later agreements and treaties verified this alignment. The Cabinda boundary was ratified by a protocol of 5 July 1913 and confirmed by a joint commission in 1925. Likewise, the westernmost line of the main boundary between Angola and Zaire was defined by a declaration of 24 March 1891 and later by the Procés-verbal of 30 June 1923. The segment from the junction of the Mepozo and Mia rivers to the intersection of the Duizi River and the line between pillars 11 and 12, is based on the convention of 22 July 1927 as was the central section of the boundary, between the Kwango River and the Kasai River. Finally, the easternmost section of the boundary was determined in an exchange of letters of 30 April–2 June 1910 and in a protocol of 18 September 1915, while the boundary tripoint with Zambia was settled by the Anglo-Portuguese agreements of November 1954 and October 1964.

Present Situation. The Republic of Zaire has not challenged the principle of the boundary. However, long-standing differences, concerning the ambiguity of several provisions in the Brussels Convention of May 1891 along the Congo River section, remain unresolved.

ANGOLA — ZAMBIA The Angola–Zambia boundary is 690 miles (1,110 km.) long. From the tripoint with Zaire in the north to the tripoint with Namibia in the south, it follows rivers and straight lines.

Geographical Setting. From the tripoint with Zaire, on the watershed between the Congo and Zambezi rivers, the boundary trends southward, roughly following the 24°E meridian, through high ground and dry, tropical forest, along various straight-line sections, between pillars, and along various river courses. The end of this northern section follows the Mininga River to its intersection with the 13th parallel. The boundary turns at a right angle westward and crosses the headwaters of the Zambezi River until it reaches the 22°E meridian. Forming another right angle, the boundary heads southward, crosses high ground, skirts the Nyengo swamp and reaches an intersection with the Kwando River, which it follows to the boundary tripoint with Namibia.

Historical Background. In 1888 the area that was later to be known as Northern Rhodesia or Zambia was proclaimed to be within the United Kingdom's sphere of influence, while Angola was a Portuguese possession. The boundary between the two territories was first established in a treaty of June 1891, which described the western dividing line as following the channel of the upper Zambezi River, from the Katima Rapids "up to the point where it reaches the territory of the Barotse Kingdom." The Barotse territory was to be within the British sphere of influence and its western limits were to "constitute the boundary between the British and Portuguese spheres of influence." An Anglo-Portuguese declaration of August 1903 passed the question of the Barotse boundary over to the arbitration of the king of Italy, who defined the "Barotse Kingdom" as the territory over which the king of Barotse had been paramount ruler on 11 June 1891. On 5 March 1915 an Anglo-Portuguese protocol demarcated the boundary from the boundary junction with Zaire to the "eastern side of the bed of the upper waters of the Kwando." This sector of the Angola–Zambia boundary remains demarcated as it was in the 1915 protocol.

On 18 November 1954 Portugal and the United Kingdom signed two agreements regarding the Kwando sector of the boundary: one concerning its alignment and demarcation and the other dealing with the movements and rights of peoples in the area of the boundary. The king of Italy's Award of 1905 contained the expression, "the eastern side of the bed of the upper waters of the River Kwando." As the Kwando River has an extensive flood zone, there were different interpretations of this statement. Thus, it was concluded in the Anglo-Portuguese Agreement that the 1905 Award should be replaced by the following criterion: "the normal limit of the waters of the River Kwando on its Eastern side when the river is in flood, a line which in general can be considered as following the edge of the woods or the so-called 'tree-line'." The agreement also provided for the demarcation of the boundary by a joint commission. The demarcation report was signed on 12 October 1964.

There is some incertitude as to the precise location of the tripoint with Zaire. The Anglo-Portuguese Protocol of 1915 demarcated the boundary southward from pillar no. 1 located at 10°53'18.3"S and 23°59'58.3"E—but there is no evidence that Belgium accepted this as the tripoint. The Anglo-Belgian Protocol of September 1934, concerning demarcation of this area of the Zaire–Zambia boundary, set the tripoint at pillar no. 46 in a series that runs from east to west; but this too was never ratified.

Present Situation. There have been no recorded disputes since Angola and Zambia achieved their independence; Angola in 1975 and Zambia in 1964.

ANGUILLA   A British dependency (area: 37 sq. miles [96 sq. km.]; population: 7,000 [1994]) in the Leeward Islands in the Caribbean Sea, Anguilla has no land boundaries. Its capital is The Valley.

ANTIGUA AND BARBUDA   A Caribbean state (area: 171 sq. miles [442 sq. km.]; estimated population: 77,000 [1994]), Antigua and Barbuda is comprised of three islands—Antigua, Barbuda, and Redonda—in the Lesser Antilles. It has no land boundaries. The capital of Antigua and Barbuda is Saint Johns on the island of Antigua.

ARGENTINA   A South American state (area: 1,068,298 sq. miles [2,766,890 sq. km.]; estimated population: 33,500,000 [1994]) situated in the southeastern region of the continent, Argentina is bounded in the north by Bolivia (517 miles; 832 km.), in the northeast by Paraguay (1,168 miles; 1,880 km.), in the east by Brazil (761 miles; 1,224 km.), Uruguay (360 miles; 579 km.) and the Atlantic Ocean and in the west by Chile (3,201 miles; 5,150 km.). The capital of Argentina is Buenos Aires.

About two-thirds of the 33,500,000 Argentines live in the pampa plains. Argentina gained independence in 1816 but civil unrest marked the years 1829–1862. A liberal oligarchical regime succeeded in developing the economy, and soon the country was known as one of the most modernized nationals in Latin America. By 1930 it led the continent in gross national product per capita, foreign trade, literacy, urbanization, area of farmland per person, and claimed the smallest proportion of the labor force employed in agriculture. The rapid economic growth prior to 1930 was aided by both the agro-export oriented economy and the political stability of almost 70 years of uninterrupted constitutional government.

However, since 1930 Argentina's economic growth has been sporadic and military intervention and dictatorship have been frequent. Peronist populism marked a new political and social era, characterized by a strong nationalist movement of workers and popular mass mobilization disputing the traditional oligarchical rule. After the fall of the first two Peronist governments, lack of political legitimacy and the consolidation of factional business and trades-union elites enabled authoritarian restorations that weakened the party representative system. With no legitimate source of authority, dictatorships took power in the 1960s and 1970s, the last of which, a regime based on military terror against civilian sectors, ruled from 1976 to 1983. The restoration of democracy in 1983 has paved the way for changes in civilian political organizations that may hold out prospects for political stability.

Argentina and its boundaries

ARGENTINA — BOLIVIA   The boundary between Argentina and Bolivia runs 517 miles (832 km.), beginning in the west at the boundary junction with Chile on Zapaleri Peak in the Andes. The boundary ends in the east at the boundary junction with Paraguay in the main navigation channel of the Pilcomayo River. It follows rivers and straight lines connecting high peaks and is demarcated along its entire length.

Geographical Setting. From its western terminus on Zapaleri Peak (18,641 feet; 5,683 m.) the boundary follows a direct line northeast to reach Brajma Peak, from there connecting seven peaks in the Andes Mountains in a series of straight lines, all of them above 15,150 feet (4,620 m.). The highest of these peaks are Negro and Tinte, standing at 18,745 feet (5,715 m.). From Panizos Peak the boundary follows the mountain ridge north-northeast along the chain of summits, until it reaches La Ramade Peak. In a straight line the boundary reaches the confluence of the San Antonio and San Juan rivers and continues downstream northward along the course of the San Juan River until it joins the Mojinete River. Running eastward in a straight line the boundary then reaches the summit of Branqui Peak, where it turns southeast and again follows mountain peaks until it reaches the valley of Huarja. Traversing over some local gorges and a line running eastward from a confluence of two local rivers, it reaches the Mecoya Peak (13,896 feet; 4,237 m.) and then descends toward the source of the Mecoyita Stream. Running along it downstream eastward to the Santa Rosa River, the boundary enters and follows the river until it joins the Santa Victoria River, forming the Condado River, in which the boundary line continues to reach the Bermejo River. It follows this river downstream in a southeasterly direction, finally joining the Tarija River, which it follows upstream northeastward until it meets the mouth of the Itau River. The boundary runs along the Itau River up to 22°S where it leaves it and follows the parallel eastward to the San Roque Stream. The line follows this and the Yacuiba and Pocitos streams, returning again to the 22°S parallel and following it eastward until it meets the Pilcomayo River. The boundary follows the main navigation channel of the river southeast, finally reaching the boundary junction with Paraguay situated in the river about 1,320 feet (400 m.) above sea level. From its starting point in the west to the boundary junction in the east, the line descends a total of some 17,325 feet (5,280 m.).

Historical Background. Like most of the South

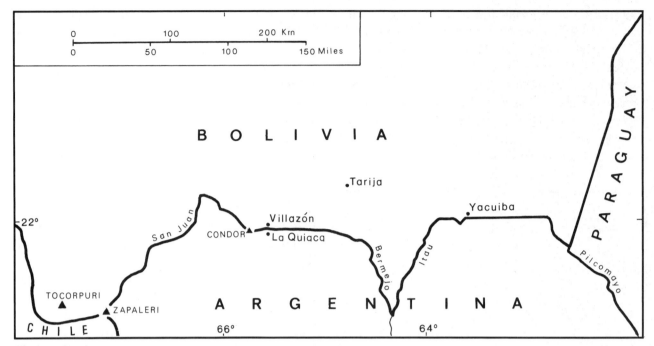

The boundary between Argentina and Bolivia

Argentina–Bolivia boundary

American boundaries, the boundary between Argentina and Bolivia dates back to the Spanish colonial rule. Until the early nineteenth century Bolivia was part of the Spanish viceroyalty of Peru while Argentina was under another Spanish viceroyalty. Argentina achieved full independence in 1816 and in 1825 Bolivia was liberated from the Spanish by Simon Bolivar. The boundary between the two countries, however, remained as it had been during the Spanish colonization.

The Bolivian wars with Chile (1879–1884) and Paraguay (1932–1935) affected the boundary location over the following decades. Previously, on 2 May 1865, a boundary treaty had been signed between Argentina and Bolivia. But Argentina then made claims on the Tarija region; a protocol signed in February 1869, after the Paraguayan War, canceled the Argentine claim and another protocol, signed on 11 June 1888, fixed the 22°S parallel as a provisional boundary in the Chaco plain. On 10 May 1889 a new boundary treaty was signed after some modifications were made on the former line. A treaty signed on 9 July 1925 determines the present boundary except for the section in the Pilcomayo River. The Bolivia-Paraguay agreement of 10 October 1938, which ended the Chaco War between them, placed their boundary terminus in the main navigation channel of the Pilcomayo River. This led to an agreement between Argentina and Bolivia concerning their common boundary in the river, which was reached in 1941 and finally ratified on 13 December 1956.

Present Situation. The boundary line is well demarcated. Similar river boundaries have been the cause of conflicts between other South American countries; Bolivia and Argentina, however, do not have this difficulty. The common boundary is a peaceful one with no known disputes concerning its alignment.

ARGENTINA — BRAZIL

The boundary between Argentina and Brazil is the longest river boundary that exists today. It follows four great rivers for 746 miles (1,200 km.) and about 15 miles (24 km.) of land boundary, from the boundary junction with Paraguay in the north to the boundary junction with Uruguay in the south.

Geographical Setting. The boundary line between Argentina and Brazil runs from the confluence of the Paraná River and the Iguaçu River, which forms the boundary junction point between Paraguay, Brazil and Argentina. The boundary follows the main navigation channel of the Iguaçu River eastward for 77 miles (124 km.), reaching its confluence with the San Antonio River. The boundary follows the San Antonio River southward for 81 miles (130 km.) to its source. From there it continues as a land boundary southward for 15 miles (24 km.) until it meets the principal source of the Pepiri-Guacu (Guazu) River. Following the main navigation channel of the river southward for 140 miles (225 km.) it reaches the confluence with the Uruguay River and follows it downstream, southwestward for 448 miles (721 km.) to its confluence with the Quaraí (Cuareim) River, which is the boundary junction with Uruguay. The islands of the Uruguay and Iguaçu rivers belong to the country indicated by the main navigation channels of the rivers.

Historical Background. The boundary between Argentina and Brazil follows the old boundary line between the Spanish and the Portuguese empires in

Argentina–Brazil boundary, mostly following rivers

South America, which was set along the great rivers. It was established in the late fifteenth century by two declarations made by the pope. Between the sixteenth and eighteenth centuries, however, the empires periodically changed the line between them and the last treaty was signed on 13 January 1750. When Argentina and Brazil gained independence (in 1816 and 1822 respectively), the boundary between them was reestablished according to the old colonial lines. The first boundary treaty was signed on 14 December 1857, in which both countries agreed to declare and acknowledge the Rivers Uruguay and Paraná as their common boundary. This treaty placed the area west of the River Uruguay, from its confluence with the Quaraí River to its confluence with the Pepiri-Guacu River, within Argentina while placing the area east of the river in Brazil. The boundary was confirmed along the Pepiri-Guacu River northward to its principal source, along the land area, the San Antonio River and the Iguaçu River up to its confluence with the Paraná River. In September 1885 a treaty for the survey of certain rivers and territories with a view to settling the boundary was signed. Differences regarding areas embraced by some rivers brought about an arbitration treaty that was placed before the president of the United States in 1889. On 5 February 1895, an award was made concerning the land boundary between the Pepiri-Guacu and the San Antonio rivers and boundary pillars were placed on the ground to mark the agreed line. A treaty settling the entire boundary between the two countries was signed on 6 October 1898, but it was another 12 years before a declaration confirming the demarcation of the boundaries between Argentina and Brazil was made. The final treaty, which dealt with the islands in the rivers and other minor points, was signed on 4 October 1910. There was one major problem concerning the southern terminus of the boundary, near Brazilera Island. A boundary convention signed by Argentina and Brazil on 27 December 1927, placed the boundary between the right bank of the Uruguay River and Brazilera Island. Uruguay, which is a partner to this boundary junction, never agreed to the location of the boundary terminus. In a treaty that was signed by Argentina and Uruguay on 7 April 1961 Uruguay declared that with the ownership of the island still unresolved, the location of this boundary junction would remain under dispute. **Present Situation.** The exact location of the boundary junction with Uruguay is still in dispute concerning the sovereignty of Brazilera Island; the controversy does not concern the Argentina–Brazil boundary. The boundary is very well defined and there are no problems concerning its alignment.

ARGENTINA — CHILE The boundary between Argentina and Chile runs for 3,201 miles (5,150 km.), between the northern tripoint with Bolivia in the Andes Mountains and the South Atlantic coast, east of Ushuaia in Tierra del Fuego (Argentina) in the south. It is the longest South American boundary. **Geographical Setting.** The highest regions of the Andes, through which the boundary threads, are scarcely populated. The mountains are dry in the north and grow gradually more humid toward the south. The southern Andes are cold, wet in the west and cool and relatively dry in Patagonia to the east.

The northern terminus of the boundary line is located on Zapaleri Peak (18,641 feet; 5,683 m.) in the Andes Mountains, north of Poquis Peak (18,832 feet; 5,741 m.). It runs southward along the highest peaks of the Andes Mountains, reaching Ojos del Salado Peak (22,575 feet; 6,883 m.) while leaving Aconcagua Peak, the highest peak in the American continent (22,829 feet; 6,960 m.), within Argentina. The boundary line crosses the main highways and railways running between Argentina and Chile, including the Mendoza (Argentina)–Valparaíso (Chile) and Salta (Argentina)–Antofagasta (Chile) routes, thence reaching the Maipo (17,457 feet; 5,322 m.) and Peteroa (13,497 feet; 4,115 m.) peaks. It runs close to the Pacific Ocean near the Gulf of Ancud and continues southward to cross the Buenos Aires and Cochrane lakes. Reaching Murallón Peak (11,880 feet; 3,622 m.), the boundary circles westward past Argentina Lake and down to the town of Río Turbio (Argentina). As the line leaves the cordilleran peaks it trends eastward to Vírgenes Cape in the northeastern entrance to the Strait of Magellan, which connects the Atlantic and Pacific Oceans. The boundary crosses the strait southward and reaches the island of Tierra del Fuego at Cape Espíritu Santo. Running in a straight line southward it divides the island between Argentina and Chile, crossing Fagnano Lake and reaching the northern shore of the Beagle Channel, west of Ushuaia (Argentina). The boundary turns eastward through the median line of the channel to its mouth in the South Atlantic Ocean.

Historical Background. In the inhospitable environment of the Andes Mountains, with no resources of commercial value, there was little need or desire to draw formal boundaries for more than three centuries. Pedro de Valdivia, a Spanish military leader,

the north was mostly uninhabited desert; to the south was Mapuche (Araucanian) Indian territory. To the east Chile nominally ruled the entire Patagonia region to the Atlantic Ocean—until the organization of the viceroyalty of the Río de la Plata in 1776, which later became Argentina. In fact, Chile seldom exercised any jurisdiction across the Andes.

The area now known as Argentina was explored along the Atlantic coast and along the Río de la

The Argentina–Chile boundary in Patagonia

arrived in Chile in 1540 and founded Santiago in 1541, the first permanent Spanish settlement in the country. He founded La Serena in the Coquimbo region in 1544 and Concepción on the northern edge of the mid-latitude rain forest in 1550. Throughout the Spanish colonial period the captaincy general of Chile, autonomous under the viceroyalty of Peru, nominally extended from the Bolivian littoral in the north to Cape Horn in the south; but in reality, La Serena and Concepción remained the northernmost and southernmost frontier towns, respectively. To

Plata by several Spanish expeditions between 1516 and 1580, when Buenos Aires was settled. Most Spanish settlements in the region consisted mainly of overflow from Chile, Peru and Paraguay and remained largely confined to the northern plains (Pampa and Chaco) and the Andean foothills (mostly on Tucumán, Córdoba, Salta and La Rioja) until well after independence. In the 1880s both the Argentine and the Chilean governments finally managed to subdue the Indians in their southern regions and to open them to European settlement.

By means of a treaty signed on 30 August 1855, Chile and Argentina established the boundary between them on the basis of the *uti possidetis* of 1810, the South American principle whereby the boundaries of the new states that emerged from the Spanish territories during the revolutionary period of 1810–1825 would continue to be the Spanish colonial boundaries. However, in Chile and Argentina no one knew exactly where that boundary lay in the Andes.

By a treaty of 23 July 1881, the two neighbors verified that their common boundary should lie along the highest line of the Andes, between Bolivia and the 52°S latitude, on the assumption that the line connecting the highest peaks was the same as the watershed, and that the Patagonia region was to be divided between them. An 1893 protocol further specified that the boundary was to be located in the main Andean cordillera along "the line of the highest peaks which divide the waters...." However, the line connecting the highest peaks does not coincide with the continental divide or watershed; numerous streams wind among the highest peaks, flowing into the Atlantic or the Pacific Oceans. Thus, the protocol that was intended to clarify the 1881 stipulation did not do so. A new treaty was negotiated on 17 April 1896 to supplement the 1881 treaty, providing for demarcation of the boundary down to 26°52'45"S. In 1898 the commission agreed to seek third-party help in delimiting the northernmost boundary sector, in the area known as Los Andes (part of the Puna de Atacama region). It was settled in 1899 with the aid of the United States and demarcation was completed in 1905.

Four major and a number of minor sections of the boundary remained undefined (20°52'45"S to 27°02'50"S; 40°06'01"S to 40°09'39"S; 41°12'18"S to 48°53'10"S; and 50°38'10"S to 52°S). Under the terms of the 1881 and 1896 treaties, these four segments were submitted to the British crown for arbitration. On 20 November 1902 the British arbitration commission compromised between the Argentine and Chilean claims. The first two awards were accepted; but the remaining two, the Palena-California sector and the Laguna del Desierto, were not. The Palena sector was once again submitted to a British commission in 1966 and this time both Argentina and Chile accepted the award, under which

Chile received about 30% of the disputed territory.

The final settlement of the Beagle Channel dispute in 1984 led to the Treaty of Peace and Friendship of 29 November 1984 between Argentina and Chile, under which the remaining boundary disputes were submitted to conciliation and arbitration. On 2 August 1991 the two presidents announced the settlement of 22 minor boundary problems, followed by one other settlement (of the Hielos Patagónicas between Monte Fitzroy and Cerro Daudet) shortly thereafter. The last outstanding boundary dispute, from Monte Fitzroy (Cerro Chaltel) northward in the Laguna del Desierto, was settled by an arbitral tribunal on 21 October 1994, awarding all but 12 of the roughly 205 sq. miles (530 sq. km.) to Argentina based on the location of the watershed and not the line of highest peaks.

Present Situation. There are no outstanding disputes between Chile and Argentina regarding their common boundary in South America.

ARGENTINA — PARAGUAY The boundary between Argentina and Paraguay runs 1,168 miles (1,880 km.) between the boundary junction with Bolivia in the west to the boundary junction with Brazil in the east. Apart for 102 miles (164 km.) of land boundary, it runs along river channels.

Geographical Setting. The western terminus of the boundary line is the boundary junction with Bolivia at a point called La Esmeralda in the Pilcomayo River. It follows the river for 475 miles (764 km.) in a southeasterly direction. As some sections of the river run through flooded areas between Punto Horqueta (at 23°52'22"S and 60°50'98"W, some 210 miles [338 km.] from the western boundary junction) and Salto Palmar (at approximately 24°19'45"S and 59°28'20"W) the boundary follows a series of straight lines for 102 miles (164 km.). From Salto Palmar the boundary line continues to follow the Pilcomayo River to its confluence with the Paraguay River south of Cerro Lambare. It follows the central channel of the Paraguay River downstream for 238 miles (383 km.) to its confluence with the Paraná River, leaving the island of Cerrito with Argentina. From the confluence of the two rivers the boundary line continues to follow the Paraná River 455 miles (732 km.) eastward and then northward, leaving Apipe Grande Island with Argentina and Yacyreta

Island with Paraguay, until its confluence with the Iguaçu River at the eastern junction with Brazil.

Historical Background. Paraguay, which gained independence from Spain on 14 May 1811, signed a treaty with Argentina on 12 October 1811 to maintain the colonial boundaries of Paraguay. On 31 July 1841 a provisional boundary treaty was signed by which some modifications were made to the established boundary. On 15 July 1852, following a war between Argentina and Paraguay, a new boundary treaty was signed by which the Paraná River was constituted as the boundary between the two rival states while the entire Paraguay River was to belong to Paraguay. Other sections of the boundary were not established then. Following the War of the Triple Alliance of Argentina, Brazil and Uruguay (1865 – 1870) a peace and boundary treaty was signed on 3 February 1876. This treaty established the present boundary between Argentina and Paraguay along the Paraná and the Paraguay rivers. The disagreements concerning the area west of the Paraguay River were presented before President Rutherford Hayes of the United States for arbitration. According to his decision of 12 November 1878, the boundary line was to be located such as to give Paraguay the entire area south of the main branch of the Pilcomayo River. On 11 September 1905 a convention was signed by Argentina and Paraguay concerning their common boundary in the Pilcomayo River and to establish the meaning of the main branch of the river mentioned in the 1878 arbitration. The attempted clarification was abortive, however, and the delimitation had to wait for another 34 years. Only on 5 July 1939 was a treaty formulated to confirm the common boundary line in the Pilcomayo River from its confluence with the Paraguay River to Salto Palmar and from Punto Horqueta to the boundary junction with Bolivia. The delimitation of the boundary line in the flooded areas along the Pilcomayo River was achieved only six years later, on 1 June 1945. Later that part of the boundary line was demarcated with pillars.

Present Situation. There are currently no known disputes between the two states concerning the alignment of their common boundary line.

ARGENTINA — URUGUAY

The boundary between Argentina and Uruguay is a water boundary, runs along the main navigation channel of the Uruguay River and is 360 miles (579 km.) long.

Geographical Setting. As a river boundary, the line follows the *thalweg* (main navigation channel) of the Uruguay River, starting at the border junction with Brazil near the southwestern corner of Brazilera Island at the confluence of the Uruguay and Quaraí (Cuareim) rivers. The northern part of the boundary, down to the town of Salto Grande (Uruguay), generally follows the median line of the present riverbed but is inflected at certain points where the river's islands were allocated to Argentina or Uruguay, although a dam built in the river near Salto Grande later changed the level of the water and the islands were submerged.

From Salto Grande the boundary continues to follow the main navigation channel, placing islands in Argentina or Uruguay. Downstream, the main navigation channel is divided: Filomena, the eastern channel, and El Medio, the western channel. Along this section of the boundary it was agreed to establish two different boundaries. Coinciding with the Filomena channel is the line dividing the waters; along the El Medio channel is the boundary dividing the islands between Argentina and Uruguay. Where the channels reconverge and the Paraná River joins the Uruguay River at a point (33°55'S and 58°25.3'W) parallel to Punta Gorda, the line follows the main navigation channel of the Uruguay River. The boundary then follows the joint river, Río de la Plata, along nine points, starting from the point parallel to Punta Gorda to a point immediately south of the island of Martin García (34°12'S and 58°15.1'W), which was placed under the jurisdiction of Argentina.

Historical Background. The peace convention between Argentina and Uruguay, signed on 27 August 1828, placed the boundary between the newly created independent countries in the Uruguay River and the Río de la Plata. No treaties concerning the boundary's delimitation were made for more than 100 years. Only on 6 April 1937 was a special commission created to study the problem of sovereignty over the islands in the Uruguay River and on 13 January 1938 an agreement that maintained the status quo was signed. It took another 23 years to conclude a final agreement. A treaty signed in Montevideo, Uruguay, on 7 April 1961, allocated the islands in the Uruguay River between Uruguay and Argentina, from Brazilera Island to the point in the river parallel to Punta Gorda. Some months earlier, on 20 January 1961, it was agreed that the boundary in Río de la Plata was to be determined by a straight line, but that section was remodified on 19 November 1973.

Present Situation. The agreement of 1973 was the final delimitation of the long-established boundary. There are no known disputes concerning the exact location of the line.

ARMENIA (Hayastan)   An independent state since December 1991, Armenia is a landlocked, mountainous country (area: 11,506 sq. miles [29,800 sq. km.]; population: 3,500,000 [1994]) situated in the Transcaucasian highlands that separate Europe and Asia. It is bounded in the north by Georgia (102 miles; 164 km.), east and south by Azerbaijan (489 miles; 787 km.), south and southwest by Iran (22 miles; 35 km.) and west by Turkey (167 miles; 267 km.). The capital of Armenia is Yerevan.

Armenia was the first country in the world to proclaim Christianity its state religion (297–301). Today most Armenians belong to the Armenian Apostolic church with its center in Echmiadzin (near Yerevan). There are also groups of Catholic and Protestant Armenians, as well as Armenian-speaking Muslims in northeast Turkey (in the region of Hemshin).

The Armenian people came into being at the beginning of the first millennium B.C.E. at the junction of the Upper Euphrates and Aratsani Rivers. They were conquered by Media, Achaemenid Iran and the Seleucids. In 189 B.C.E. two independent Armenian states were proclaimed; in the first century B.C.E., under Tigran II, the country became an empire extending from the Caucasus mountains to the Middle East, but lost its annexed territory at the end of that century during a war between Rome and Parthia. In 397 the Armenian kingdom was divided between Iran and Rome. From 438 to 481 the Armenians waged a religious war against the Sassanid states which tried to convert them by force to Zoroastrianism. Over the following centuries Armenia was invaded by Arabs, Seljuk Turks Mongols, Ottoman Turks, and others, with brief periods of independence, including the twelfth- to fourteenth-century kingdom of Cilicia.

Russia annexed a part of Persian Armenia in 1828–1829. Turkish Armenia became an arena of massacres; between 1894 and 1896, 500,000 Armenians were killed. During World War I there were 1,500,000 Armenian victims. Hundreds of thousands fled the country and swelled the Armenian diaspora, which had existed since the Middle Ages. In 1918 an independent republic was proclaimed in former Russian Armenia, but was abolished by the Communists, who established in its place the Armenian Soviet Socialist Republic (1920). After World War II about 200,000 Armenians from the diaspora settled in Armenia. The flow became much slower after 1949, and from the late 1960s it was reversed, many Armenians migrating to North America.

With the eclipse of the USSR tension erupted between Azerbaijan and Armenia over the Nagorno-Karabakh Autonomous *Oblast* (region) of Azerbaijan, inhabited predominantly by Armenians. The tension developed into a continuing military conflict. As a result, virtually all Armenians who lived in Azerbaijan (with the exception of those in Nagorno-Karabakh) left, mostly for Armenia, but also for Russia and other neighboring non-Muslim countries.

ARMENIA — AZERBAIJAN   The boundary between Armenia and Azerbaijan runs in two sections. The main boundary between Armenia and Azerbaijan runs for 352 miles (566 km.) from the boundary tripoint with Georgia in the north to the tripoint with Iran on the Aras (Araks) River in the south. The boundary between Armenia and the Azerbaijan province of Nakhichevan runs for 137 miles (221 km.) from the boundary tripoint with Turkey in the northwest to the boundary tripoint with Iran in the southeast, both of which are located on the Aras River.

Geographical Setting. The northern terminus of the main line is located on the 45°E meridian, south of the Georgian town of Rust'avi and near the Khrami River. It runs southeastward along the local watershed between Lake Sevana (Sevan) in the southwest and the Kura River and its tributaries, which run east to the Caspian Sea. On its way it leaves two Azerbaijani enclaves within Armenia, north of the small Armenian town of Ijevan, and the Armenian enclave of Artsvashan within Azerbaijan, northeast of Lake Sevana. East of the Armenian town of Sot'k the boundary turns south for 20 miles (32 km.), then runs west and again eastward, leaving the source of the Arp'a River in Armenia. The line then continues southeastward along the local watershed, reaching a point south of the small town of Laçin (Azerbaijan). There it bears southward, crossing the Vorotan (Bärgüsad) River and the railway that connects Kapan (Armenia) with the main railway. It then runs southward to the Aras River and reaches the tripoint with Iran, located in the main navigation channel of the river, southwest of the small Iranian town of Alajujeh.

The northwestern terminus of the boundary between Armenia and Nakhichevan is located on the main navigation channel of the Aras River, south of the Armenian town of Ararat. It runs northeastward for 20 miles (32 km.), crossing the main railway and road that run parallel to the Aras River, and then heads southeastward, crosses the Arp'a River and continues southeast to the road between Sahbuz (Nakhichevan) and Angeghakot' (Armenia). From there southward, the boundary traverses a local mountain range and reaches the Aras River, 22 miles (35 km.) east of the main tripoint with Iran. The southeastern terminus of the boundary line is located between the towns of Ordubad (Nakhichevan) and Meghri (Armenia), south of the railway and road junction between the two towns.

Historical Background. Armenia was one of the first kingdoms to be established in the Caucasia region, mainly based on its Armenian Christian religion. The Ottoman Empire occupied Armenia in 1473, Czarist Russia occupied northeastern Armenia from 1800 onward, and Muslim Azerbaijan was occupied by Russia in 1828. During World War I, however, the whole Transcaucasian region proclaimed its independence (20 September 1917) and it was partitioned into three republics on 26 May 1918: Georgia, Armenia and Azerbaijan. Azerbaijan was occupied by the Red Army in early 1920 while Armenia became an independent Communist Republic in December of that year. On 12 March 1922 the three republics formed the Transcaucasian Union, which subsequently entered the Soviet Union on 30 December 1922. With the reorganization of the Soviet Union in 1936, both Armenia and Azerbaijan became constituent republics of the So-

viet Union, their common boundary being established by the Central Authorities of Moscow, mainly based on national and religious divisions. However, this boundary never had the status of a state boundary. Frequent boundary modifications took place between the two national republics from 1936 to 1991, when the they both finally became independent states. At first both adopted the latest territorial division that had been established by the Soviet Union, but later they did not officially accept the internal line as an international boundary and the border area was left under civil dispute.

Present Situation. With the establishment of independent states out of the former Soviet Union arose the issue of the Nagorno-Karabakh Oblast's future. An Armenian Christian region, it is located within the boundaries of Muslim Azerbaijan that was still under the Soviet Union in January 1988. This district adopted a motion to secede from Azerbaijan and to become part of Armenia, marking the opening of the hardest, longest and bloodiest ethnic conflict in the former Soviet Union. To date, Azerbaijan still holds Nagorno-Karabakh but the dispute has yet to be resolved.

A second dispute concerns the future of southern Armenia and its border area with Iran—which Azerbaijan claims as its own territory. No other territorial claims are known, but the boundary lines between the two states are yet to be determined by a boundary treaty.

ARMENIA — GEORGIA   The boundary between Armenia and Georgia extends 102 miles (164 km.) from the boundary tripoint with Turkey in the west to the tripoint with Azerbaijan in the east. The undemarcated boundary follows the internal boundary between the republics of the former Soviet Union.

Geographical Setting. The western terminus of the boundary line is located on the ridge dividing Lake Çildir (Turkey) and the Arp'a Cayi (Akhuryan) River (Armenia), east of the Turkish town of Dogruyol. It runs eastward along a local watershed, crossing the Bolnisi (Georgia)–Step'anavan (Armenia) road to a point located about 1 mile (1.6 km.) west of the Debed River and the railway that links Alaverdi (Armenia) and T'bilisi (Georgia). From there the boundary line progresses northwestward for 10 miles (16 km.), turns eastward for about 15 miles (25 km.), crosses the Debed River and the main road and railway that connect Armenia and Georgia, and reaches the boundary tripoint with Azerbaijan on the 45°E median, south of the Georgian town of Rust'avi, near the Khrami River.

Historical Background. Armenia and Georgia, both ancient kingdoms, became Christian states in the fourth century: Armenia adopted Eastern Christianity while Georgia held by the Orthodox tradition. Both were occupied by the Turkish Ottoman Empire in the fifteenth century, until Russia entered the Caucasia region in the early nineteenth century and occupied Armenia and Georgia. During World War I both became independent, establishing the independent Transcaucasian Republic, with Azerbaijan, on 20 September 1917, only to be divided again on 26 May 1918 into three separate republics. Georgia was occupied by the Red Army early in 1921 while Armenia became an independent Communist Republic. However, on 12 March 1922 the three republics joined together to establish the Transcaucasian Union, which joined the Soviet Union on 30 December 1922. Until 5 December 1936 the area was in the Transcaucasian Soviet Republic, and was then divided again to form three separate constituent republics within the Soviet Union. In 1991, after the breakdown of the Soviet Union, Armenia and Georgia became independent states. Albeit with no formal agreement, they maintained the internal republic boundary line as their international boundary.

Present Situation. Armenia has claimed that the southern section of Georgia—the Dzhavaketia province—should be annexed to Armenia. Nevertheless, no official disputes have been recorded concerning the alignment of the boundary.

ARMENIA — IRAN The boundary between Armenia and Iran extends (22 miles; 35 km.) from the tripoint with Azerbaijan in the west to the tripoint with Iran in the east.

Geographical Setting. The entire length of the boundary between Armenia and Iran follows the main navigation channel of the Aras (Araks) River. The western terminus is located southwest of the Armenian town of Meghri, while the eastern terminus is located some 10 miles (16 km.) southwest of the Iranian town of Alajujeh.

Historical Background. The Transcaucasian region was a border zone between the Russian, Turkish and Persian empires for seven centuries. Armenia was captured by the Persians in 1405 but became a Turkish subject in 1473. The Persians recaptured it in 1605—only to be resettled by the Turks a few years later.

In the early nineteenth century Russia captured northwestern Persia and according to the Peace Treaty of Gulistan (1813) ruled part of Armenia. The Peace Treaty of Turkmanchai of 22 February 1828 established the boundary between Russia (Armenia) and Persia on the Aras River—where the present boundary stands. The establishment of Armenia as an independent republic in 1920, its transfer to the Soviet Union in 1922 and the establishment of the Armenian Soviet Socialist Republic (ASSR) in 1936 did not affect the boundary alignment. Armenia became independent in 1991, adopting, without any formal agreement, the Armenian section of the USSR–Iran boundary line as its international boundary with Iran.

Present Situation. Since the dissolution of the Soviet Union and the establishment of independent Armenia in 1991, there have been no reports of disputes concerning the alignment of the boundary line. Azerbaijan has made claims on the whole border area that separates its mainland from its province of Nakhichevan. Armenia has refused to cede the area to Azerbaijan, and for now, the established boundary between Iran and Armenia is maintained.

ARMENIA — TURKEY The boundary between Armenia and Turkey is the southern section of the former USSR–Turkey boundary. It extends 167 miles (267 km.) across mountainous terrain.

Geographical Setting. All but 40 miles (64 km.) of the boundary follow rivers. The line sets out from the Georgia, Armenia and Turkey boundary junction point, 18 miles (28.8 km.) southeast of Hazapin Lake. It runs southeastward, crosses the highway and rail line that link Leninakan (Armenia) with Kars (Turkey) and reaches the Arpa Cayi (Akhuryan) River. After following the main channel of the river southward for 67.5 miles (108 km.), it enters the main channel of the Araks River, along which it traverses eastward and then southeastward for 78.4 miles (125.5 km.) to the border junction with the Azerbaijan province of Nakhichevan on the west bank of the river.

Historical Background. The former USSR–Turkey boundary was established after World War I. From the fifteenth century, the region of Armenia, Azerbaijan and Georgia, known as Transcaucasia, was under Ottoman rule. The Russians advanced into the tract during the nineteenth century, gradually extending their boundaries southward at the expense of Turkey. In the Adrianople Treaty of 1829 the boundary between Russia and Turkey was established north of the cities of Batumi (now in Georgia) and Kars (now in Turkey). In 1878, by the Treaty of Berlin, Russia secured the provinces of Batumi, Ardahan and Kars from Turkey, establishing a line further south in the area. The Russian army occupied eastern Turkey during World War I, but by November 1920 the Turks had reoccupied the area and by the Treaty of Aleksandropol of December 1920 a new boundary was established. In exchange for the area surrounding Batumi, the Turks received a southern portion of the Russian province of Erivan (the capital of Armenia), shifting the boundary northward to the Aras River. This line was confirmed in the Soviet-Turkish Treaty of Moscow in March 1921. Since then, the boundary has remained unchanged. In 1936 the Soviet Republic of Armenia became a constituent republic of the Soviet Union, holding a section of the Turkish–Soviet Union boundary, which was further maintained with the establishment of the independent state of Armenia in 1992.

Present Situation. There are no known disputes between Armenia and Turkey concerning the location of the boundary between them.

ARUBA   The island of Aruba, a self-governing Dutch territory, lies in the southern Caribbean Sea, a few miles north of Venezuela. Its area is 75 sq. miles (194 sq. km.) with a population of 65,000 (1994). Aruba's capital is Oranjestad.

The inhabitants of the Caribbean island of Aruba, while still under a governor appointed by the Dutch, are scheduled for complete independence in 1996. The island's inhabitants, predominantly Roman Catholics, are most concentrated in and around the capital, Oranjestad. Their official language is Dutch, but Papiamento, a mixture of Spanish, Portuguese and Dutch, is most frequently spoken. Oil refining, the economic base of Aruba until its refinery closed in 1985, has been supplanted by tourism as the major income source for inhabitants of this semi-arid island.

AUSTRALIA   Australia is the largest island in the Pacific Ocean. Its area, including Tasmania but excluding external territories, covers a land area of 2,967,139 sq. miles (7,684,890 sq. km.) extending some 2,300 miles (3,680 km.) from Cape York (10°41'S) in the north to Tasmania (43°39'S) in the south, and some 2,500 miles (4,000 km.) from Cape Byron (153°39'E) in the east to Cape Cuvier in Western Australia (113°9'E). It has an estimated population of 17,800,000 (1994) and its capital is Canberra. Australia has no land boundaries.

In 1901 the former British colonies of New South Wales, Victoria, Queensland, South Australia, Western Australia and Tasmania were federated under the name of the Commonwealth of Australia. The designation "colonies" was at the same time changed to "states," except for the Northern Territory, which was transferred from South Australia to the Commonwealth as a "territory" in 1911. In the same year the Commonwealth acquired from the state of New South Wales the Canberra site for the Australian capital.

Traditionally Australian wealth was derived from agricultural production, especially pastoral development but also wheat. Pastoral industries, producing meat and wool, still play a major role in the Australian economy, although mining has developed substantially, particularly since the 1950s. Gold-mining encouraged a number of waves of immigration especially in the 1850s and between 1890 and 1910. However, iron ore, copper, lead, zinc and a wide range of other minerals are produced in large quantities in different locations around the continent. In the cities industrial production is prominent.

AUSTRIA (Österreich)   Austria is a landlocked country (area: 32,377 sq. miles [83,856 sq. km.]; estimated population: 7,900,000 [1994]) situated in Central Europe. It is bounded in the north by Germany (487 miles; 784 km.) and the Czech Republic (285 miles; 456 km.), in the east by Slovakia (56 miles; 90 km.) and Hungary (227 miles; 366 km.),

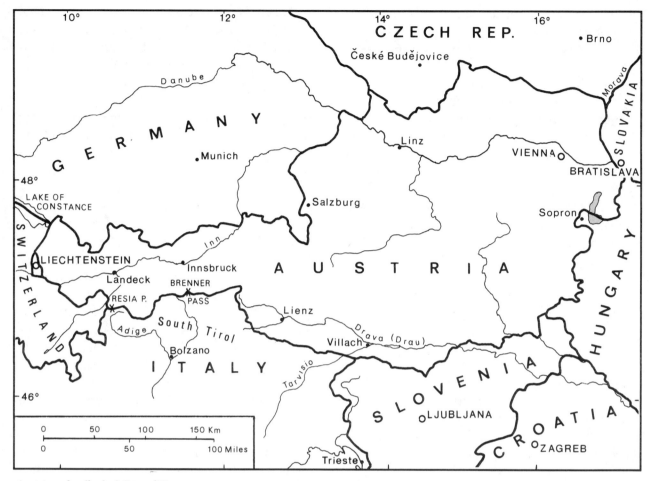

Austria, a landlocked Central European country

south by Slovenia (163 miles; 262 km.) and Italy (267 miles; 430 km.) and west by Switzerland (102 miles; 164 km.) and Liechtenstein (23 miles; 37 km.). The capital of Austria is Vienna.

From the thirteenth century Austria developed territorially from an ill-defined collection of original Habsburg regions; yet no Austrian nation as such existed before the twentieth century. The Austrian empire proper came into its own after the splitting of the Habsburg family estate among the Spanish and German branches in 1555. By the nineteenth century Austria had grown into the center of a sprawling multinational empire, eight times the size of its current territory, and ruling over Czechs, Slovaks, Hungarians, Croats, Serbs, Slovenes, Poles, Ruthenians, Jews, Bosnians, Romanians and many others. But "Austrians" as such did not yet exist.

Culturally, the Austrian (after 1866, Austro-Hungarian) Empire contributed to baroque art and classi-

cal music. In the nineteenth century, Vienna was the capital of central European civilization. However, the Austrians were ruling an empire which was an unintegrated collection of tongues, religions and enthnicities, kept together by monarchy and bureaucracy.

The empire's dismemberment in 1919 left modern Austria a more homogeneous Germanic and Catholic state. Consequently, Austrians gravitated toward Germany, and in the 1930s developed first a fascist-type dictatorship and then a strong Nazi movement of their own. The 1938 *Anschluss* led to denial of any Austrian particularism: paradoxically this stimulated a specifically Austrian nationalism. After 1945 the Austrians built their own neutral, democratic parliamentarian welfare state, with marked trade union and church influences.

AUSTRIA — CZECH REPUBLIC This border is some 285 miles (456 km.) long and extends from the tripoint with Slovakia in the east to the tripoint with Germany in the west. It follows river courses and parts of the old Habsburg Imperial provincial borders.

Geographical Setting. From the tripoint with Slovakia near the confluence of the Dyje (Thaya) and Morava (March) rivers in the east the boundary follows the Dyje River upstream north and west across Dlouhyvrch, Rosenbergen, Wolfsberg, Raistenberg and Kallerhaide. It then travels northwest to a point on the old administrative boundary between Lower Austria and Moravia, situated about 1,312 feet (400 m.) south of the point where the present boundary cuts the Mikulov (Nikolsburg)–Valtice railway. Thence westward, the line reaches a point about 2 miles (3 km.) east of the village of Franzenthal (Austria) and traverses along the old administrative border between Lower Austria and Bohemia. From there the line turns south to Gelsenberg, about 3 miles (5 km.) north-northwest of Gmünd (Austria), and passes east of the Rottenschachen (Austria)–Zuggers (Czech Republic) road and through Altnagelberg. It continues between Zuggers and Breitensee (Austria), then over the point furthest southeast of the railway bridge that crosses the Luznice (Lainsitz) River, leaving the town of Gmünd within Austria and the station and railway works of Gmünd (Wolshof) and the junction of the Gmünd–Ceske Budejovice and Gmünd–Trebon railways to the Czech Republic. The boundary line passes through Grundbuhol (1,719 feet; 524 m.) and north of Hohenberg (1,873 feet; 571 m.) and Lagerberg (2,247 feet; 685 m.) and then turns southward and west-northwestward to a point on the old administrative border between Lower Austria and Bohemia, some 656 feet (200 m.) north of the point where it cuts the main highway and railway between Linz (Austria) and Ceske Budejovice (Czech Republic). The boundary then travels southwest, along the old administrative border, and turns northwest to the old administrative border between Bohemia and Upper Austria, which it follows, crossing the road that links Aiger (Austria) and Krumlov (Czech Republic), to its boundary tripoint with Germany near Plockenstein (4,532 feet; 1,379 m.).

Historical Background. The borders of the Czech Republic originate from the Treaty of Versailles (1919), when the Habsburg Empire was abolished following World War I. The last emperor of the Austro-Hungarian Empire, Charles I, had tried to salvage his empire by transforming it into a federation of states. However, the conflict between the German nationalists and Slavs in Austria prevented this solution. Moreover, the Peace Commissioners at Versailles would not condone anything less than the destruction of the empire on which they blamed the origins of the Great War. Several nationalities nevertheless took advantage of the mechanism for federation, which had already been set up by Charles I, to declare their independence or unite themselves with fellow nationals on the empire's borders. From the provinces of Moravia, Slovakia, Ruthenia and the ancient kingdom of Bohemia the Czech and Slovak peoples formed Czechoslovakia. This, along with other territorial losses, left Austria so small and short of resources that its ability to survive was widely doubted and the new country made strenuous but fruitless efforts to retain the Sudeten area of Bohemia.

In the Lana Agreement of 16 December 1921, Austria finally renounced all claims on the Sudetenland to Czechoslovakia. On 1 January 1993 Czechoslovakia was divided, along its original provincial boundary, into the Republic of Slovakia and the Czech Republic, the latter adopting the northwestern section of the existing boundary with Austria.

Present Situation. The Austria–Czech Republic boundary is not in dispute.

AUSTRIA — GERMANY The Austria–Germany boundary extends for some 487 miles (784 km.) from Lake Constance (Bodensee), at the tripoint with Switzerland in the west, and follows mountainous terrain east to the valley of the Inn River at the tripoint with the Czech Republic.

Geographical Setting. From Lake Constance in the west to the Salzburg region this border follows the Allgäu, Bavarian and Salzburg Alps, mostly along the crests of the mountain range. It runs generally east, south of Weissensee, and crosses the Lech valley. It trends over the Sauling peaks (6,714 feet; 2,047 m.) and crosses the Ammer and Loisach valleys, southwest of Eibsee, to Zugspitze (9,715 feet; 2,962 m.). The line continues along the Wellerstein ridge, through Hochwaner (9,000 feet; 2,744 m.)

and Dreitorspitze (8,633 feet; 2,632 m.), crossing the Isar valley near Schanitz. Here the border turns north and east over west Karendelspitze (7,823 feet; 2,385 m.) and east Karendelspitze (8,321 feet; 2,537 m.), crosses the Vorderiss–Hinteriss road and trends over the Scharfreiter (6,895 feet; 2,102 m.) and Demeljoch (6,317 feet; 1,926 m.) peaks. After crossing the Achen valley and passing through the Achen Pass to Halserspitz (6,111 feet; 1,863 m.), the boundary follows the Mangfallgebirge ridge to the Ursprung Pass and crosses the Inn valley and the Rosenheim (Germany)–Innsbruck (Austria) highway before turning north along the Inn River to Windshausen. It then continues eastward along mountain crests, through Durrnbachhorn (5,825 feet; 1,776 m.) and Sonntagshorn (6,432 feet; 1,961 m.) to Stadelhorn (7,501 feet; 2,287 m.) and Gr. Hundstod (8,505 feet; 2,593 m.), forming a large loop around the Königsee Lake and Berchtesgaden basin to Kahlersberg (7,708 feet; 2,350 m.), Kehlstein (8,272 feet; 2,522 m.) and Untersberg (6,078 feet; 1,853 m.). It enters the Saalach valley and the Salzach River, which it follows to its confluence with the Inn. The boundary follows the Inn River past the Austrian town of Braunau to its confluence with the Danube (Donau) River near Passau (Germany), which it then follows to the south of Kasten. Turning north and east about 2 miles (3 km.) north of Engelhartszell (Austria), the line crosses the Passau–Freistadt road and continues north to the boundary tripoint with the Czech Republic at Plockenstein (4,532 feet; 1,379 m.).

Historical Background. The Austria–Germany boundary, including the German province of Bavaria, resulted from the defeat of Austria at Hradec Kralové (Königgrätz) in 1866, ending the six-week Austro-Prussian War over the control of Germany. The subsequent formation of the North German Confederation of German states under Prussian leadership excluded Austria and allowed the southern German states to define their own relationships with the confederation. In 1867 the Habsburg Empire became the dual monarchy of Austria-Hungary, although it did not unite the Slav and German components strongly enough to prevent the growth of nationalist movements. Austrians considered themselves part of the German nation and after World War I wanted to be attached to Germany.

However, in the Treaty of Versailles (1919), the boundaries of 1866 were restored and Austria was declared an independent republic and compelled to renounce all hopes of annexation with Germany. Furthermore, Germany was required to recognize Austria's independence.

However, in March 1938 Austria was united with Germany through the Anschluss. At a conference in Moscow in 1943, a public declaration was made by the Allies regarding their determination to liberate Austria and reconstitute it as an independent state. At the end of World War II Austria was partitioned between the East and West until a representative and democratic government could be established. The boundary of 1866 was then reaffirmed and was never changed.

Present Situation. The present boundary line is not disputed.

AUSTRIA — HUNGARY This boundary is 227 miles (366 km.) long and runs from the tripoint with Slovenia in the south to the tripoint with Slovakia in the north.

Geographical Setting. From the tripoint with Slovenia, about 2 miles (3 km.) east of Tauka, the boundary line runs northeast to a point 3.5 miles (6 km.) north-northeast of Szentgotthárd, and up to the customs post on the Rabafuzes–Dobersdorf road. It travels northward through three spot heights, runs east of Nagynarda and Rohoncz and west of Dozmat and Butsching, and reaches Geschreibenstein (2,900 feet; 884 m.), 5.5 miles (9 km.) southwest of Köszeg (Hungary). From here the line heads northeastward, passing southeast of Liebing, Olmond and Locsmand and northwest of the Köszeg–Salamonfa road, to reach Kamenje (869 feet; 265 m.), about 1 mile (1.5 km.) southeast of Nikiksch. It passes between Frankenau (Austria) and Peresznye (Hungary) to join the administrative border between the Hungarian provinces of Vas and Gyor-Sopron and continues north to skirt the surrounding area of the city of Sopron. It trends along the crest of the Ödenburg range and runs south of Schattendorf to the customs post at Klingenbach. From the customs post on the Sopron–Morbisch highway the boundary runs east to the shore of Neusiedler Lake and crosses the lake, passing south of its islands and turning south and then east to the opposite shore. The boundary line turns toward the Apetion–Pamhgaen road and heads south before meeting it. The boundary then turns eastward and runs north of the Einser canal and parallel to it for some 8.5 miles (14 km.). Turning north, the line then passes between Albertkazmerpuszta in the east and Halbturn (Austria) in the west to meet the Gattendorf–Budapest road at the customs post south of Nickelsdorf. The boundary then proceeds to the tripoint with Slovakia, about 2 miles (4 km.) east of Deutsch Zurndorf.

Historical Background. Under the Habsburg Empire Hungary's territory covered a large area, from Croatia in the west to Transylvania in the east, and from Russia to Romania. After World War I Hungary resisted attempts to turn the dual monarchy of Hungary-Austria into a federation and, following a revolution that began on 13 October 1918, its king abdicated and Hungary was proclaimed an independent republic on 16 November 1918. A Communist regime, under Béla Kun, lasted for 100 days in 1919, before being ousted by an opposition government with the support of the Romanian army. Hungary then became a constitutional monarchy under the Regency of Admiral Horthy in 1920.

Subsequently, the restoration of a Habsburg monarchy was vetoed by the Allies, and by the Treaty of Trianon (4 June 1920) Hungary lost the predominantly German-speaking Burgenland to Austria. This award was Austria's only territorial gain in the post-World War I negotiations.

Present Situation. The boundary line between Austria and Hungary has been maintained as it was defined in 1920 and is not disputed.

AUSTRIA — ITALY

The boundary between Austria and Italy runs for 267 miles (430 km.) from the boundary junction with Switzerland, at Piz Lad in the west, to the boundary tripoint with Slovenia at Patzen (Pec) peak on Mount Forno, in the east. Most of the boundary follows the main Alpine watershed.

Geographical Setting. From its eastern terminus, on Mount Forno (Ofen) (4,948 feet; 1,509 m.), the boundary runs westward for 4 miles (6.5 km.) to the Tarvisio Valley, through which the railway and the main road from Vienna to Venice pass. The line crosses the Tarvisio River and turns eastward for 6 miles (10 km.) to reach Mount Osternig (6,731 feet; 2,052 m.). From there it continues westward for 33 miles (53 km.) along the mountain crests to Plöken (Monte Croce) Pass and along the crest of the Carnic Alps for 23 miles (37 km.). Turning northwest, the boundary runs for 10 miles (16 km.) to reach the Dobbiaco Pass, which is situated in the Drava (Drau) Valley and constitutes the main passage for the Lienz (Austria)–Bolzano (Italy) road and railway. Here the headstream of the Drava River cuts across the boundary to flow from Italy into Austria. From the pass, the boundary line bears northward for 39 miles (63 km.) along the watershed to reach Dreiherrnspitze Peak (11,482 feet; 3,500 m.), on the western extremity of the Hohe Tauern mountain range. Continuing along the crest westward for another 42 miles (68 km.), the line reaches the Brenner Pass, through which the principal road and railway cross into Italy from Innsbruck (Austria).

For the next 73 miles (117 km.) the boundary line follows the Alpine watershed, running west and then southwest, climbing to a height of 12,257 feet (3,737 m.) in the Ötztaler Alps. It then travels northwest and west to Reschen Pass (Passo di Resia) and another 3 miles (5 km.) westward to the boundary junction with Switzerland, at Gruben Joch, near the northern slope of Piz Lad (7,155 feet; 2,181 m.).

Historical Background. The boundary between Austria and Italy is primarily a cultural boundary that divides the German-speaking and the Italian peoples. For a significant period northern Italy was part of the Austrian (later Austro-Hungarian) Empire and no international boundary existed in that area. Italy was unified and became an independent country in 1861 and the boundary with Austria was established five years later, at the Vienna Peace Treaty between Austria and Italy, signed on 3 October 1866. This treaty established the eastern sector of the boundary along the historic border of the Lombardo-Venetian kingdom.

The western section of the boundary runs south of the principal Alpine crest, along the southern border of the German-speaking Tirol region and was demarcated in 1911 and 1912. Italy had raised claims for the "natural boundary" along the main Alpine watershed but Austria refused to cede South Tirol (Alto Adige) to Italy. During World War I, Italy joined the Allied Powers with the anticipation of facilitating a northward shift of the boundary into the Brenner Pass. Austria's defeat led the way to the

Treaty of Saint-Germain (10 September 1919), in which Austria ceded the Tirol region, south of the Brenner Pass, to Italy. Some 5,400 sq. miles (14,000 sq. km.) of land, along with a population of about 240,000 (most of them German-speaking), were annexed to Italy. The task of demarcation was undertaken by an international commission including Britain, France, Japan and Austria, which was asked to delimit the boundary along existing administrative, cadastral and natural borders and limits. This work was completed, after much difficulty, in 1924 and in 1930 the detailed maps and pillar descriptions were published.

Following World War II the Treaty of Paris, signed by Italy and the Allied and Associated Powers on 10 February 1947, confirmed the Austria–Italy boundary as it had stood on 1 January 1938. This was reconfirmed in the Austrian State Treaty, which was signed at Vienna on 15 May 1955 between Austria and the Allied and Associated Powers.

Present Situation. Political changes that took place before and during World War II did not affect the boundary alignment, which has been maintained along the 1919 line. While there is no dispute between Austria and Italy concerning the location of the boundary line, the outstanding issue in the boundary area concerns the minority rights of about 250,000 German-speaking people who inhabit the former Austrian territory south of the Brenner Pass.

AUSTRIA — LIECHTENSTEIN The Austria–Liechtenstein boundary is 23 miles (37 km.) long and runs from north to south between two tripoints with Switzerland.

Geographical Setting. The area of Liechtenstein is roughly triangular, its Alpine boundary with Austria forming a hypotenuse. The boundary separates the Schellenberg, Planken and Triesenberg communes in Liechtenstein from the Vorarlberg state of Austria. From the Swiss tripoint on the Rhine River in the north, northwest of the town of Bangs, the line runs south and east, across the valley floor, to the crest of the Schellen Berg. It then follows the mountain tops, crosses the pass for the Feldkirch–Vaduz highway and railway and returns to the mountains. It trends over Rojasattel and Garsellinkopf (6,906 feet; 2,105 m.) to Galinakopf (6,700 feet; 2,043 m.) and turns generally south toward the peak of

Naafkopf (8,430 feet; 2,570 m.) and to the boundary tripoint with Switzerland in the south.

Historical Background. The Principality of Liechtenstein developed from the Roman province of Rhaetia. Under Charlemagne the province became an earldom of the Holy Roman Empire in the ninth century. It was divided in the course of time and by the fourteenth century the County of Vaduz was a separate territory, although awarded directly from the emperor. In 1608 Charles of Liechtenstein was created a Prince of the Holy Roman Empire and in order to qualify for a vote in the Diet of Princes he was required to hold territory directly allotted from the emperor. Vaduz and Schellenberg to the north were ideal for this purpose and the prince purchased both. The two territories were formally united in 1719 and named the Imperial Principality of Liechtenstein. Political independence was established after the Coalition War (1806), when Liechtenstein was included in Napoleon's Confederation of the Rhine. An Austrian general, the Prince of Liechtenstein fought against France at Aspern in 1809 and as the power of France began to wane, joined the Little Alliance against Napoleon. In 1815 Liechtenstein joined the German Confederation, until the latter dissolved in 1866.

The Austro-Hungarian Empire bordered Liechtenstein until the Treaty of Versailles of 1919 when today's Austria was formed.

Present Situation. Since 1719 the boundary has remained unaltered and there are no disputes over its alignment.

AUSTRIA — SLOVAKIA The boundary between Austria and Slovakia is 56 miles (90 km.) long and runs from the tripoint with Hungary in the south to the tripoint with the Czech Republic in the north. For most of its route it follows river courses and old Imperial Habsburg administrative borders.

Geographical Setting. From the tripoint with Hungary, some 610 feet (200 m.) north of the road between Rajka (Slovakia) and Zurndorf (Austria), the boundary heads generally northwestward in a series of short straight lines. It reaches the bend of the 1867 frontier between Austria and Hungary, 1.5 miles (2.5 km.) northeast of Berg, and crosses the road between Kittsee and Bratislava (Pressburg), about 1 mile (2 km.) north of Kittsee. It travels

The Austria–Liechtenstein boundary follows valleys and mountain tops

northward to a point on the *thalweg* of the Danube (Donau) River, 3 miles (4.5 km.) upstream from Bratislava Bridge, for the most part following the old frontier of 1867 along the Danube. Turning westward the boundary reaches the confluence of the Morava (March) and Danube rivers. It follows the Morava and Dyje (Thaya) rivers upstream to a point 1 mile (2 km.) southeast of the intersection of the Rabensburg–Postorna road with the Rabensburg–Breclav (Lundenburg) railway, about 1 mile (2 km.) north of Bernhardsthal, and arrives at the boundary tripoint with the Czech Republic.

Historical Background. The origins of Slovakia's boundaries are in the Treaty of Versailles (1919) and the Treaty of Trianon (4 June 1920). Slovakia was previously a part of the Hungarian section of the Habsburg Empire. In an effort to save the empire from disintegration, the last Habsburg emperor, Charles I, had proposed the formation of a federation, but his plans were foiled by the irreconcilable opposition of Austria's German nationalists and Slavs and by Hungary's refusal to grant autonomy to the nations in its part of the empire. Taking advantage of the national parliaments already set up under the emperor's federalist plan, the separate nations of the old empire either declared their independence or united with their fellow nationals beyond Austria-Hungary's borders. The Czechs and Slovaks formed Czechoslovakia from Moravia, Slovakia, Ruthenia and the ancient kingdom of Bohemia.

On 31 October 1918 a revolutionary war broke out in Hungary, aimed at establishing Hungary as a republic separate from Austria. On 13 November 1918 Charles I abdicated and a republic was declared. A Communist regime followed, under Béla Kun, which was swiftly swept aside by an opposition government backed by the Romanian army. Hungary then became a constitutional monarchy under the regency of Admiral Nicholas Horthy. By the Treaty of Trianon Hungary lost Burgenland to Austria and its boundaries with Czechoslovakia, Yugoslavia and Romania were established by a mixed commission. Certain sections of southern Slovakia were returned to Hungary by the Vienna Treaty of

2 October 1938 between Germany and Italy, although after World War II its 1920 boundaries were restored (excepting Ruthenia, which was retained by Russia). In 1991 the Czech and Slovakian parts of Czechoslovakia separated into two independent countries, Slovakia becoming the Republic of Slovakia and adopting the existing boundary with Austria.

Present Situation. There are no disputes regarding this boundary.

AUSTRIA — SLOVENIA Extending 163 miles (262 km.) the Austria–Slovenia boundary runs from the tripoint junction with Italy in the west to the tripoint with Hungary in the east. Most of its course follows the crest of the Karawanken Alps while the rest utilizes river courses and old administrative boundaries.

Geographical Setting. From the tripoint with Italy on the peak of Petzen (Pec) (4,599 feet; 1,509 m.) the boundary runs generally eastward across the Wurzen Pass and along the Karawanken Alps. It crosses Mittagskogel (6,532 feet; 2,143 m.), Kahikogel (5,593 feet; 1,835 m.) and Hochstuhl (6,821 feet; 2,238 m.) to the customs post on the Klagenfurt–Kranj highway. From there it continues to the customs post on the Völkermarkt–Kranj road. Further along the mountain range the line forms a large loop, south and then north, and travels northeast to Kordeschkogel (6,480 feet; 2,126 m.), passing south of Lavamünd before meeting the Drava (Drau) River. It follows the course of the river southeastward for approximately 4 miles (6 km.) and leaves it to cross the Lavamünd–Dravograd road and continue along the Karawanken range. The boundary passes through a spot height of 4,639 feet (1,522 m.) and trends eastward to cross the Krum River and the Eibiswald–Maribor (Marberg) road along the watershed between the Drava (Slovenia) and Saggau (Austria) rivers. It crosses the rail and road links between Graz and Maribor and joins the Mur (Mura) River. It then follows the Mur River downstream southeastward to its confluence with a stream from the north, which it then follows northward, turning east at Kalch (east of Saint Ama, Austria), and trends along the 1867 border between Austria and Hungary. The line runs between Bonisdorf and Kuzma, south past Tauka and on to the tripoint

with Hungary, about 1 mile (2 km.) east of Tauka.

Historical Background. Before World War I Slovenia belonged to the Hungarian section of the Austro-Hungarian Empire and formed the empire's border with Serbia (which, until 1878, was part of the Ottoman Empire). In the Pact of Corfu of 20 July 1917, Serbia and the Yugoslavian Committee in Exile decided to unite all Serbs, Croats and Slovenes as a single nation under a constitutional monarchy. This was to become Yugoslavia and included Dalmatia, Bosnia, Montenegro, Serbia, Slovenia and Croatia. Some of this territory had been promised to Italy by the Entente in a secret treaty (London, 1915), in return for joining the Allied cause in the war; under pressure from Italy, the Western powers withheld recognition of the new state.

Thus, the territories on the eastern side of the Adriatic Sea that were promised to Italy were now allying themselves with Yugoslavia. Nevertheless, despite opposition and much difficulty, the Kingdom of the Serbs, Croats and Slovenes was proclaimed by Prince Regent Alexander in Belgrade on 4 December 1918. Sensitivity was increased in the two Austrian provinces of Carinthia and Styria, across which the German–Slovene linguistic frontier ran, and in a plebiscite of 10 October 1920 Carinthia voted to remain wholly in Austria and the Karawanken Alps remained Austria's southern border. Meanwhile, in Styria to the east, the frontier drawn by the 1919 Peace Conference ran roughly along the linguistic divide. After a referendum on 23 December 1990, the Parliament of the Republic of Slovenia declared its independence from Yugoslavia on 25 June 1991 and accepted the existing boundary with Austria in the north.

Present Situation. This boundary is not disputed.

AUSTRIA — SWITZERLAND This boundary is 102 miles (164 km.) long and runs in two sections from the tripoint with Germany in Lake Constance (Bodensee) in the north to the northern tripoint with Liechtenstein and from the southern tripoint with Liechtenstein to the tripoint with Italy below Piz Lad.

Geographical Setting. From Lake Constance the boundary heads south, following the *thalweg* of the Rhine River upstream to the boundary tripoint of Saint Gall (Switzerland), Liechtenstein and Austria. From the southern tripoint with Liechtenstein and

Graubünden (Grisons), near the Naafkopf peak, the boundary line runs east and south, following the mountain crests of the Rhaetian Alps to Schesapland (9,037 feet; 2,965 m.) and Drusenfluh (8,617 feet; 2,827 m.). It continues past Sultzfluh and, after running briefly northeast, turns southward to the Madrisahorn (8,614 feet; 2,826 m.) and then southeastward along the peaks of the Silvreta mountains, over Piz Buin (10,095 feet; 3,312 m.) and Fluchthorn (11,162 feet; 3,662 m.). The line runs along the crest of Fimberthal to a point opposite Piz Rotz (9,440 feet; 3,097 m.), passes it northeastward along the crest of the Stamnaungruppe, and then drops down to the customs post at Spiss. It continues to the customs post on the Inn river and follows the river to the customs post on the road joining the Landeck (Austria)–Saint Moritz (Switzerland) and Landeck–Bolzano (Italy) highways. Running south it reaches the tripoint with Italy near Piz Lad.

Historical Background. Switzerland's boundaries were established in 1815 at the Congress of Vienna, following the Paris Peace Conference of 1814. Furthermore, in the Federal Pact of Zurich (1815) the country's perpetual neutrality and the inviolability of its borders were guaranteed for the first time.

At the end of World War I the Austro-Hungarian Empire was partitioned into independent countries. In 1919 the people of Vorarlberg, an Austrian state, voted to join Switzerland, but the Swiss were reluctant to gain territory at the expense of such a powerful neighbor and declined to alter their boundaries. Thus, the present boundary separates the Austrian district of Vorarlberg from the Swiss cantons of Saint Gall and Graubünden, both of which joined the Swiss Confederation in 1803 after a period of unrest and after the collapse of the French Helvetic Republic.

Present Situation. This boundary is not in dispute and has remained unchanged since 1815.

AZERBAIJAN The former Soviet Republic of Azerbaijan gained independence in August 1991. Azerbaijan (area: 33,436 sq. miles [86,600 sq. km.], including the Nakhichevan Autonomous Republic, which is surrounded by Armenia; estimated population: 7,200,000 [1994]) is situated in the eastern region of Transcaucasia and is partly a landlocked country open to the western shore of the Caspian Sea. Azerbaijan is bounded in the west by Armenia (489 miles; 787 km.), northwest by Georgia (200 miles; 322 km.), north by Russia (176.5 miles; 284 km.), east by the Caspian Sea, south by Iran (380 miles; 611 km.) and southwest by Turkey (5.5 miles; 9 km.). It also governs the largely Armenian inhabited Nagorno-Karabakh Autonomous Region. Azerbaijan's capital is Baku.

For centuries Azerbaijan was ruled by the Arabs and the Mongols. In 1918 Russian Azerbaijan was proclaimed an independent republic. However, in 1920 it was conquered by Soviet troops and became the Azerbaijan Soviet Socialist Republic. During World War II Iranian Azerbaijan was occupied by Soviet troops, who encouraged an autonomist movement there, and by the end of 1945 the Soviet-backed autonomy of Azerbaijan within the framework of Iran was proclaimed, which survived only for about a year.

For centuries the majority of Azerbaijani were occupied in agriculture and cattle-breeding, crafts and trading. Many areas of Azerbaijan are arid semi-deserts and plains. Agriculture and especially the growing of cotton were based on irrigation and animal husbandry on seasonal migrations from the plains to mountain pasturelands. The nomads among the Azerbaijani (including ethnic groups of Airum, Padar, Shahseven), settled on the land in the first quarter of the twentieth century.

In the second half of the nineteenth century there emerged an intelligentsia which acquired a European (i.e. Russian) education and advocated a Muslim nationalist reform. The development of an oil industry, particularly the Baku oil fields, created national classes of bourgeoisie and workers. Under the impact of the Russian, Persian and Turkish revolutions of 1905–1907 Azerbaijani nationalists developed political ideas, which for the first time focused on their own political-cultural identity.

During the seven decades of Soviet rule in Azerbaijan a tremendous social change produced new industries, towns, a reconstituted way of life and new institutions. However, Azerbaijani grievances against this imposed modernization gradually grew and became the basis for a mass public protest movement in the 1980s.

Since 1988 an armed Armenian-Azerbaijani conflict had been waged for Nagorno-Karabakh, which is an autonomous *Oblast* (region) within the framework of Azerbaijan, inhabited mainly by Armenians, in which hundreds of people from both sides were killed. Since then about 200,000 Azerbaijani previously living in Armenia have left for Azerbaijan. At the end of 1992 Azerbaijan announced its decision to withdraw from the Commonwealth of Independent States.

AZERBAIJAN — ARMENIA see ARMENIA–AZERBAIJAN.

AZERBAIJAN — GEORGIA The boundary between Azerbaijan and Georgia extends 200 miles (322 km.) between the tripoint with Russia in the northeast and the boundary tripoint with Armenia in the southwest. The undemarcated boundary follows the internal boundary between the republics of the former Soviet Union.

Geographical Setting. The boundary tripoint with Russia is located on the range that separates the Kura River and its tributaries in the south from the rivers that run in Russian territory. The boundary line runs southwestward, crosses the road between Lagodekhi (Georgia) and Zaqatala (Azerbaijan) and reaches the Alazani River. It follows the river downstream southeastward to its confluence with the Ayri River (Ayriçay), where they become the Qanix River. This river is followed southward to a point located 3 miles (5 km.) north of the man-made Mingäçevir Lake. The line turns westward and then southward to the northern shore of the lake, which it follows to the mouth of the Qabirri River. The boundary follows the river upstream westward for 22 miles (35 km.) and leaves it to head northwestward toward the Georgian city of Rust'avi. Some 15 miles (25 km.) east of Rust'avi the boundary line changes direction, running southwestward, and crosses the main Caucasian railway line that travels from the Black Sea via T'bilsi (the capital of Georgia) to Baku (the capital of Azerbaijan) on the Caspian Sea. The boundary then crosses the Kura River and reaches the boundary tripoint with Armenia, south of the Khrami River, on the 45°E meridian.

Historical Background. Both Azerbaijan and Georgia were occupied by Russia in the nineteenth century. Georgia was inhabited by Christians, while Azerbaijan was a Muslim region. During World War I both became independent and, together with Armenia, established the Transcaucasian Republic on 20 September 1917. On 26 May 1918 the Republic was partitioned into three separate republics. Azerbaijan was occupied by the Red Army in early 1920 and a Soviet republic was established on 28 April 1920. Georgia was occupied by the Red Army in February 1921. On 12 March the three republics were rejoined, under Soviet Union influence, establishing an independent republic that joined the Soviet Union on 30 December 1922 as the Transcaucasian Soviet Republic. On 5 December 1936 the Republic was again divided, establishing the constituent republics of Azerbaijan, Georgia and Armenia within the Soviet Union. Frequent changes took place between 1936 and 1990 along the Azerbaijan–Georgia border, establishing new internal boundaries that were primarily based on national and religious divisions. These lines never had the status of state boundaries, until 1991, when both republics became independent states, adopting the latest internal line, but without a formal agreement as to their international boundary.

Present Situation. There is an ethnic territorial conflict between Azerbaijan and Georgia, the former calling for the transfer of a southern section of Georgia to Azerbaijan. Others have made demands for the transfer of a northwestern section of Azerbaijan to Georgia. However, since the independence of the former Soviet republics there have been no official disputes concerning the boundary alignment.

AZERBAIJAN — IRAN Azerbaijan's boundary with Iran runs in two sections for a total of 380 miles (611 km.). The main boundary extends 269 miles (432 km.) from the shore of the Caspian Sea in the east to the boundary tripoint with Armenia in the west. The second boundary section, between Azerbaijan's province of Nakhichevan (dislocated from Azerbaijan by Armenian territory) and Iran, runs for 111 miles (179 km.) between the boundary tripoint with Turkey in the west and a second boundary tripoint with Armenia. All three boundary tripoints are located on the Aras (Araks) River. The line is a section of the boundary between the former Soviet Union and Iran.

Geographical Setting. The Nakhichevan boundary

with Iran follows the main navigation channel of the Aras River. Its northwestern terminus, the boundary tripoint with Turkey, is located about 4 miles (6.5 km.) south of the town of Sädäräk (Azerbaijan). It follows the Aras River downstream southeastward, to the boundary tripoint with Armenia, located southwest of the Armenian town of Meghri.

The western terminus of the Iranian boundary with mainland Azerbaijan, at the boundary tripoint with Armenia, is located in the main navigation channel of the Aras River, southwest of the small Iranian town of Alajujeh. The line follows the river downstream northeastward, to a point north of Parsabad (Iran). It leaves the river to head southeast in a straight line for about 30 miles (50 km.), until it reaches the Bolqar River (Bolqarçay), which it follows southwestward, southeastward and again southwestward to a point located on the 48°E meridian. From there the boundary trends southeastward to the Caspian Sea, at the southern terminus of the Transcaucasian railway, south of the small town of Astara (Azerbaijan).

Historical Background. The area settled by the Azerbaijani was a border region between Russia and Iran (Persia) for three centuries. The Persians captured the area in 1795, but in 1813 Czarist Russia secured the area that is mainly inhabited by the Shiah Muslim Tartars of Azerbaijan, by the Peace Treaty of Gulistan. They left the region and again occupied it in 1828, after a three-year war with Persia. In the Peace Treaty of Turkmanchai (22 February 1828) a boundary was established between the Russian and Persian empires—which is the present boundary between Azerbaijan and Iran. This line left about one half of the Azerbaijani with Russia and the other half with Persia, which established the Persian Azerbaijan province. Despite political developments which marked the history of the Transcaucasian territories from 1828 onward, the boundary alignment was never affected. After World War II, Persian Azerbaijan declared its independence as the Democratic Republic of Azerbaijan, but Iran reoccupied the area in December 1946, and reestablished the 1828 boundary line with the Soviet Union. When Azerbaijan became independent in August 1991, it adopted the Azerbaijani segment of the USSR–Iran boundary line as its international boundary with Iran without any formal agreement.

Present Situation. Since the independence of Azerbaijan in 1991, no disputes concerning the boundary alignment have been reported. Azerbaijan adopted its section of the former Soviet Union boundary with Iran, and Iran has not made claims on any areas north of the line. South of the present boundary is the region inhabited by Azerbaijani who are associated with their independent people in the north. This may cause some border problems in the future.

AZERBAIJAN — RUSSIA   The boundary between Azerbaijan and Russia (the province of Dagestan) runs for 176.5 miles (284 km.), between the boundary tripoint with Georgia in the west and the Caspian Sea in the east.

Geographical Setting. The western terminus of the boundary line, northwest of Zaqatala (Azerbaijan), is located on the main crest of the Caucasus Mountains, the watershed that stands between the Kura River and its tributaries in the south and the rivers running north and northeast. The line bears southeast along the crest and between the Ayriçay (Azerbaijan) and Samur (Russia) rivers, which run westward and eastward respectively. It reaches Mount Bazardyuze, the highest peak in the eastern Caucasus Mountains (14,698 feet; 4,481 m.), where it turns northeastward toward the Samur River, east of the small Russian town of Usukh-Chay. The boundary follows the river downstream northeastward for 22 miles (35 km.), departs from the river, continues northeast to cross the railway between Baku (Azerbaijan) and Makhachkala (Dagestan, Russia) and reaches the Caspian Sea, southeast of the mouth of the Samur River.

Historical Background. Azerbaijan, a Shiah Muslim Tartar region, was occupied by Czarist Russia from 1828 until World War I. The boundary between Russia and Persia (the former name of today's Iran) divided the Azerbaijani people and established a long disputed boundary line. In 1917 Azerbaijan joined Armenia and Georgia to form the Transcaucasian Federation within the traditional boundary of the Azerbaijani people, but the "Mussavat" (Nationalist) party, which dominated the National Council of the Tartars, declared Azerbaijan's independence on 28 May 1918. Two years later, in January 1920, Azerbaijan was captured by the Red Army and on 28 April 1920 was proclaimed a Soviet Republic and a section of the Transcaucasian Soviet Federal Socialist Republic. In 1936 it assumed the status of a constituent republic of the USSR. The boundary between Russia and Azerbaijan was established by internal decrees that, from time to time, modified the boundary alignment. The line never had the status of a state boundary—until Azerbaijan declared its independence on 30 August 1991, adopting (with no formal agreement) its last internal boundary with the Soviet Russian Republic as its international boundary with Russia.

Present Situation. Since independence, there have been no conflicting views between Azerbaijan and Russia concerning the alignment of the boundary line. Along their common boundary live the Lezgi people, who have been demanding the creation of a republic of Lezgistan as part of the Russian Federation or as an independent state. This claim, although currently inconsequential, may lead to future disputes in the borderland of Dagestan and Azerbaijan.

AZERBAIJAN — TURKEY The boundary between Azerbaijan and Turkey is part of the former Soviet Union–Turkey boundary. The establishment of Azerbaijan as an independent state in 1991 left it with a geographically dislocated province, Nakhichevan, which is surrounded by Armenia. The province has a common boundary with Turkey, a very small section (5.5 miles; 9 km.) of the former line that had measured 335 miles (539 km.).

Geographical Setting. The full length of the present boundary between Azerbaijan and Turkey follows the main channel of the Aras (Araks) River.

Historical Background. The boundary between Turkey and the former USSR was established after World War I. During the war the Russians occupied northeastern Turkey but after Russia's withdrawal from the war the Turks occupied the area. Armenia's independence was established in 1918, but by November 1920 the Turks and the Soviet forces had demolished Armenia's independence and established a new boundary between them by the Soviet-Turkish Treaty of Moscow, signed on 16 March 1921. This was further confirmed by the Treaty of Kars between Armenia and Turkey, signed on 13 October 1921. The international boundary has remained unchanged, but in 1936 the Nakhichevan province, a border area inhabited mainly by Muslim Tatars, was separated from the Soviet Socialist Republic of Armenia, which is mainly populated by

Road in Turkey near the Azerbaijan–Turkey boundary

Christian Armenians. Armenia surrounds the province on three sides, while Turkey lies along its southern border. The establishment of independent Armenia and Azerbaijan in 1991 left Nakhichevan to Azerbaijan, establishing a common boundary with Turkey.

Present Situation. There are no recorded disputes concerning the delimitation of the boundary line be- tween Azerbaijan and Turkey. During 1991–1993, however, Azerbaijan and Armenia struggled over the status of Nakhichevan, which is claimed by both countries. The status of the Muslim enclave, sur- rounded by Christian Armenian militants and with no geographical connection to the main area of Azerbaijan, is complex and Muslim Turkey stands in the background of the conflict.

B

BAHAMAS An independent state (area: 5,382 sq. miles [13,939 sq. km.]; estimated population: 270,000 [1994]) off the Florida coast, the Bahamas consist of some 700 islands, 30 of which are inhabited, and over 1,000 cays. It has no land boundaries. The capital of the Bahamas is Nassau.

The Bahamas, site of the first landing of Columbus, were originally inhabited by native Arawak. The first British settlements were established in the 1600s. During the American Revolution, loyalists fled there together with their slaves, establishing both the basis for what is now a substantial part of the Bahamian population and a plantation economy later ended by British abolition of slavery in 1834. Since independence, Bahamians have been ruled by a white minority; opposition of the black majority to this system, however, is increasing.

Tourism, which occupies two-thirds of the work force, and financial services currently contribute to a rapidly expanding Bahamian economy. Less important contributors to the economy include agriculture, including bananas, citrus fruit, vegetables and oil.

BAHRAIN (Al-Bahrayn) An independent archipelago, Bahrain consists of some 30 islands in the Persian Gulf, between Qatar and Saudi Arabia. Bahrain has no land boundaries, its area is 267 sq. miles (692 sq. km.), it has an estimated population (1994) of 570,000 and its capital is Manama.

Bahrain is noteworthy for its Shi'ite majority of nearly 60%, many of them of Iranian descent. Bahrain has functioned as an island station since Sumerian times. The region was Islamized in the eighth century: maritime trade in the Gulf was disrupted in 1514 by the arrival of the Portuguese. Bahrain was ruled by Iran from 1602 until 1783, when the presently ruling (Sunni) al-Khalifah family took control. Iranian influence still accounts for the tiny achipelago's preponderant Shi'ism.

In 1861 Bahrain became a British protectorate, and after Britain's retreat from Aden, its main pillar in the region. However, its small but well educated (and militant) labor class also made it harder to control. The ruling al-Khalifas suppressed attempts at installing a parliament. Upon reaching independence in 1971, Bahrain chose to remain outside the United Arab Emirates. Iran lays claim to Bahrain, and in 1978 Khomeini's Iran called on Bahraini Shi'ites to destabilize Bahrain's solute monarchy.

From 1934 oil has been Bahrain's main export. The traditional pearl industry has nearly disappeared. By 1980 Bahrain had taken over ownership of the Bahrain Petroleum Company and now features one of the Middle East's largest refineries. Bahrain is developing into a service center for Gulf trade and shipping as well as the main banking center of the Gulf. It has, however, suffered from the 1991 Gulf War, which caused not only pollution but also a massive draining of foreign capital.

BANGLADESH Situated in southern Asia, Bangladesh (area: 55,598 sq. miles [143,999 sq. km.]; estimated population: 122,280,000 [1994]) is bounded in the west, north and east by India (2,519 miles; 4,053 km.), southeast by Myanmar (120 miles; 193 km.) and south by the Bay of Bengal in the Indian Ocean. Its capital is Dacca.

The area now known as Bangladesh was once the eastern part of Bang, where the Hindus flourished for nearly 700 years, beginning in the fourth century. The Muslims took control of the area in the thirteenth century and held it for 500 years, withstanding attacks by Turkic peoples and Afghans. In the early part of the eighteenth century, the British gained control of the area. Tension was created between the Muslims, who did not accept British rule, and the Hindus, who did. In 1905 the British sectioned off the area now known as Bangladesh as a Muslim state, a decision they later rescinded as a result of a mainly Hindu public outcry.

Muslim became increasingly adamant about securing a separate state, and this led to the partition of British India into Pakistan and India at the time of independence in 1947. Pakistan was divided into two parts that were separated by India; West Pakistan, the dominant half, and East Pakistan, which is the area now known as Bangladesh. After 30 years of West Pakistani control, Bangladesh (with Indian Army help) won independence from West Pakistan in 1971.

BANGLADESH — INDIA   This boundary is 2,519 miles (4,053 km.) long and was created during the partition of India in 1947, when India became independent and its province of Bengal was divided into West Bengal and East Pakistan (later Bangladesh). It was subsequently modified, both by peaceful negotiation and during periods of hostility, and was inherited by Bangladesh in 1971. Except for 160 miles (257 km.) across the Chittagong Hill Tracts to the tripoint with Myanmar (Burma), the border covers alluvial plains laid down by the Ganges and Brahmaputra rivers. The line separates the plains from the hilly regions—largely coinciding with the ethnic divisions along the border.

Geographical Setting. Starting on the western side of Bangladesh in the Bay of Bengal, the boundary follows the previously existing boundaries between districts (*thanas*) of the State of Bengal northward. Where the boundary between Daulatpur and Karimpur meets the central channel of the Mathabhanga River it joins the river to its confluence with the Ganges River. It then continues along the Ganges River, which also forms a district boundary. The boundary leaves the river to separate Shibganj from Kaliachak and English Bazaar and continues to do so northward. From the boundary between Panchibi and Balurghat the border follows the western edge of the Bengal–Assam railway northward to its junction with the border between Phulbari and Balurghat. It continues north, again dividing *thanas* and districts, to the border between Haripur and the Indian province of Bihar, and from the point where

the dividing line between Phansidewa and Tetulia meets the province of Bihar the boundary runs generally eastward, along the northern corner of the *thana* of Debiganj to the boundary with the town of Cooch Behar. It then traverses the old border with Cooch Behar to the ancient Bengal–Assam (India) boundary, which it follows to Sylhet (Bangladesh). From here the boundary follows the main channel of the Kusiyara River, still dividing districts, to the boundary between Karimganj and Beani Bazaar. The line leaves the river and follows further divisions to the border with Tripura, which it follows to leave all of Tripura (except a small parcel that was ceded to East Pakistan [Bangladesh] to avoid cutting the railway line from Comilla to Sylhet) within India. The boundary separates the Chittagong Hill Tracts from India, and reaches the boundary tripoint with Myanmar to the east of Bangladesh.

Historical Background. In August 1947 a boundary commission was convened to delimit the line between East Pakistan and West Bengal. The commission consisted of two Hindu and two Muslim members from the Indian subcontinent and a chairman, Sir Cyril Radcliffe. The members' opposing interests were so disparate that Radcliffe himself was finally forced to set the line. He made concessions to both points of view, trying to avoid, wherever possible, dividing road and rail links and economically integral regions. A further Indo-Pakistan tribunal, led by Algot Bagge of Sweden, considered four disputed sections of the line in February 1950, which led to territorial exchanges in 1959. The province of Sylhet decided, by referendum, to join East Bengal, which allowed those adjacent Muslim areas in Assam be included in East Bengal. Nevertheless, problems continued to arise, especially regarding enclaves that each country had on either side of the boundary, between Cooch Behar and East Pakistan. These enclaves dated from the war between Cooch Behar and the Mogul Empire in 1661–1712, after which they were confirmed by a peace treaty. Although an agreement was made later to exchange these enclaves, no exchange took place either before or after Bangladesh was created.

The boundary continued to be a source of friction between Pakistan and India, primarily because the previous administrative divisions, upon which it was based, were themselves disputed. Seasonal claims also arose when falling flood levels exposed new char lands—fertile deposits of the annual river floods. These problems were finally overcome by a conference and agreements, which were signed in 1959. Only the disputed channel of the Fenni River, south of Tripura, remained unsettled when Bangladesh was created in 1971.

Present Situation. The boundary is not disputed, although India's increased utilization of the Ganges River, especially the Farakka barrage, 11 miles (18 km.) from the boundary line, has resulted in a lapse of the water-sharing agreements. India has refused to negotiate a new agreement and Bangladesh is now suffering the social, economic and ecological results of increased salinity in the Bay of Bengal as well as the loss of previously navigable rivers.

BANGLADESH — MYANMAR This boundary is 120 miles (193 km) long and runs from the tripoint with India in the north. It trends along hill ridges from the mountainous area of western Myanmar and then joins the course of the Naf River into the Bay of Bengal in the south.

Geographical Setting. From the northern tripoint, the Myanmar–Bangladesh boundary runs south along the watershed of the mountain ridge between the Sangu and Kaladan rivers. It turns west and northwest, crossing the watershed of the Sangu and Mayu rivers, before heading south again to follow the *thalweg* of the Naf river into its estuary in the Bay of Bengal.

Historical Background. The boundary between India and Burma was delineated and demarcated in the nineteenth century by the British, whose intentions were to form a convenient administrative line between the territorial responsibilities of British India and British Burma. Britain acquired all of Burma by 1886, and subsequently the Lushai area (India), south of Manipur, was pacified in 1895 and divided between Assam and Bengal. The southeastern boundary of the Lushai land today forms the border between Bangladesh and Myanmar. The intercolonial border became an international boundary when India became independent in 1947, followed by Burma in 1948. In 1959 a boundary commission was created, which has since chiefly dealt with the problems of delimitation in the Naf Estuary region. This tidal reach and its main channel frequently change

shape; the *thalweg* boundary that the countries had inherited was thus fixed by the terms of an agreement in 1966, which guaranteed navigation rights to both countries—regardless of the movements of the main channel. East Pakistan became Bangladesh in 1971 and maintained the prior boundary settlement. Burma changed its name to Myanmar in 1989.

Present Situation. The border agreements reached prior to 1971 are respected and unquestioned by both Bangladesh and Myanmar.

BARBADOS An island state (area: 166 sq. miles [430 sq. km.]; population: 265,000 [1994]) lying east of the Windward Islands in the Caribbean Sea, Barbados has no land boundaries. Its capital is Bridgetown.

Evidence indicates that the Spaniards landed on this island in 1518, and had exterminated the peaceful Arawak population by 1536. With the British takeover and the establishment of plantations, slaves were introduced in the early 1600s, and continued to produce substantial income for their British masters until 1838, four years after slavery was abolished. Barbados joined the West Indies Federation in 1958 and achieved independence in 1966.

BELARUS Independent since September 1991, Belarus is a landlocked country (area: 80,155 sq. miles [207,600 sq. km.]; estimated population: 10,400,000 [1994]) in east Central Europe. It is bounded in the west by Poland (376 miles; 605 km.), northwest by Lithuania (312 miles; 502 km.), north by Latvia (88 miles; 141 km.), east by Russia (596 miles; 959 km.) and south by Ukraine (554 miles; 891 km.). The capital of Belarus is Minsk.

The Belarussians are descendents of Slavic tribes, who settled on the western shores of the Dvina, the Upper Dnieper, the Neman, and the Pripet Rivers and assimilated the Baltic tribes who had inhabited the area from at least Iron Age times. Three large tribal groups subsequently developed: the Dregovichi, the Radimichi and the Krivichi. In the ninth century these were incorporated into the ancient Russian state of Kiev, from which emerged the three East Slavic nations of Russians, Ukranians and Belarussians.

In the second half of the thirteenth century the area was conquered by the Mongols and attacked by the Teutonic Order. It was subsequently under foreign rule for several centuries, first by Lithuanians and then by Poles. As a result, the ancestors of the Belarussians were separated from those of the other East Slavic peoples, and began to develop distinctive customs, culture, and language.

The Catholic Lithuanian-Polish rulers tried to enforce papal authority on their Eastern Orthodox, East Slavic subjects. The majority of landowners converted to the Catholic faith and were subsequently Polonized. The majority of the peasantry, however, retained their Eastern Orthodox identity.

In the wars that swept the region in the seventeenth century the area suffered devastation, famine and epidemics, which caused the population to decrease by almost half. The Northern War of 1700–1721 caused a further decline in population.

The partition of Poland brought all Belarussians under Russian rule after 1772. In their centralizing efforts the Russian authorities attempted to assimilate the Belarussians as they had assimilated the Ukrainians. In 1840 it was even forbidden to use the term "Belarussian."

Industrialization and urbanization in the nineteenth century created the socioeconomic base for national revival, which began, as in many other countries, with the creation of literature in the Belarussian language; the publication of Viccenti Rovinski's novel *Anaide* is considered to mark this point. By the time of the 1917 revolution, however, the Byelorussian national movement was still in an embryonic stage, and the creation of the Soviet Socialist Republic of Byelorussia was carried out by the Bolshevik government in Moscow. This republic included the eastern parts of Belarussia. The western parts were annexed from Poland in 1939, following the Molotov-Ribbentrop agreement.

Although Byelorussian self-identity was reinforced during the Soviet period, no separatist nationalist movement such as that of the Ukraine developed in Byelorussia. Its independence as Belarus following the disintegration of the USSR in 1991 was, therefore, as the creation of the republic had been, an external act rather than a response to internal demands and developments.

BELARUS — LATVIA

The boundary between Belarus and Latvia runs for 88 miles (141 km.) between the boundary tripoint with Russia in the northeast and the boundary tripoint with Lithuania in the southwest. It follows the internal boundary line between republics of the former Soviet Union.

Geographical Setting. The northeastern terminus of the boundary line is located north of the small Lake Osbi, about 12 miles (20 km.) southwest of the Russian town of Sebej. The line runs southwest for about 40 miles (65 km.) reaching the Dvina River north of the small town of Druya (Belarus). Thence it follows the Western Dvina (Daugava) River downstream westward for 6 miles (10 km.) and leaves it to form a semicircle southwestward, leaving the lakes and the small town of Braslav within Belarus. From a point northwest of Braslav the boundary trends westward for about 10 miles (15 km.), reaching the boundary junction with Lithuania south of Daugavpils (Latvia) and east of the Vilnius (Lithuania)–Daugavpils railway.

Historical Background. Belarus was never an independent state, until 28 March 1918, when it became the independent Republic of Byelorussia. This independence was short lived: Belarus was occupied by the Red Army on 1 January 1919 and by the Riga Treaty (1921) it was divided between Poland and the Soviet Union, which established Belarus as a Soviet republic.

After 200 years of Russian rule Latvia achieved independence in 1920, its southeastern sector bordering the Soviet Republic of Belarus. Latvia was occupied by the Soviet Union on 16 June 1940 and became a constituent Soviet republic of the Soviet Union on 3 August 1940. The boundary between the Latvian and Belarussian republics remained as it was instituted in 1920. During World War II the Germans occupied Latvia and Belarus, but after the war the two were reestablished with no changes in their common boundary line. Latvia declared its independence in May 1990, subject to a transitional period for negotiation. It achieved full independence in August 1991. Belarus became independent that month and the newly independent states adopted the internal line as their common international boundary without any formal agreement.

Present Situation. Unlike most of the internal boundaries of the former Soviet Union, the Belarus–Latvia boundary served as a state boundary and was even delimited in the 1920s, but its significance diminished during the Soviet rule. Originally the delimitation was geographically, historically and ethnographically based. However, disputes that were not raised during the Soviet era, between 1940 and 1991, came to the forefront. Currently, the principal issue is the future of the town and region of Daugavpils (Dvinsk) in southern Latvia, which has an individual ethnic identity. Some call for the provision of a special national status for the city, while others press for the transfer of the Daugavpils district, or even the entire southeastern Latvia region, to Belarus. No official claims have been raised concerning this issue, but the disputed future of the area is yet to be resolved.

BELARUS — LITHUANIA The Belarus–Lithuania boundary is 312 miles (502 km.) long, running between the boundary tripoint with Poland in the southwest and the tripoint with Latvia in the northeast. The line follows an internal boundary that formerly divided two Soviet republics.

Geographical Setting. The boundary tripoint with Poland is located west of a curve in the Neman River and northwest of Grodno (Belarus). It runs eastward for a short length, reaching and crossing the Neman River, and thence continues eastward, crossing the Vilnius (Lithuania)–Grodno and Vilnius–Lida (Belarus) railways. The line forms a semicircle south, east and northward, then continuing northward to cross the Vilnius–Minsk (Belarus) highway and railway. In the same direction the boundary crosses the Neris (Viliya) River and then heads northeastward for about 60 miles (95 km.) when it reaches the Disna River. It follows that river upstream westward, leaving the small town of Vidzy within Belarus, departs from the river and travels northward for 20 miles (32 km.) to the tripoint with Latvia, southwest of the Dvina River and west of the town and lakes of Braslav (Belarus).

Historical Background. At the beginning of the twentieth century Lithuania was a peripheral area of the Russian Czarist empire. In 1919, following World War I and the collapse of the Russian Empire, it was formed as an independent state by the League of Nations. The Soviet-Lithuanian Peace Treaty of 1920 established a common boundary line, but soon after Poland and the Soviet Union became embroiled in a war over the boundaries of western

Ukraine. Lithuania found itself caught in the middle as a battleground. Although both sides formally recognized Lithuania's claims to its historical capital, Vilnius, Poland captured the city and its surrounding areas in 1920, an act that was later recognized by the League of Nations. In October 1939, following the Molotov (Soviet Union)-Ribbentrop (Nazi Germany) agreement and the division of Poland between Germany and the Soviet Union after the outbreak of World War II, Lithuania was forced to allow the entry of the Red Army and the mobilization of military bases on its territory. To soften this blow the city of Vilnius and its district, amounting to 3,500 sq. miles (9,000 sq. km.), was transferred from Poland to Lithuania, thus establishing a boundary between Lithuania and the Soviet Republic of Byelorussia.

The occupation of Lithuania by German forces in 1941, its recapture by the Soviet Union in 1944 and the establishment of Lithuania as a Soviet socialist republic never affected the line. Both Lithuania and Belarus became independent in 1991 and, without a formal agreement concerning its precise alignment, adopted the 1939 line as their common international boundary.

Present Situation. The historical and national basis of the Belarus–Lithuania boundary has not eliminated the development of territorial claims in its region. While Lithuania has raised claims for the Russian exclave of Kaliningrad, Russia may "reconsider" the 1939 cessions of Vilnius and its vicinity. Moreover, there are some claims for the transfer of a southeast Lithuanian parcel to Belarus, as well as a counterclaim to cede parts of the Belarusian districts of Vitebsk, Grodno and Minsk to Lithuania. The boundary, which was never delimited in detail or demarcated, has yet to be agreed upon by the two states.

BELARUS — POLAND From the boundary junction with Lithuania in the north to the boundary junction with Ukraine in the south, the Belarus–Poland boundary follows a segment of the boundary between Poland and the former Soviet Union, which was established after World War II. The boundary is 376 miles (605 km.) long.

Geographical Setting. Some 20 miles (32 km.) northwest of the city of Grodno (Belarus), west of a curve in the Neman River, the northernmost point of the boundary between Belarus and Poland is located. From there it runs south for approximately 50 miles (80 km.) to a point east of the Polish town of Biatowieza. It turns southwestward and reaches the Bug River south of the town of Miclnic (Poland). The line follows the river southeast, leaving the city of Brest in Belarus, and upstream southward to the boundary tripoint with Ukraine at the river's intersection with the Brest (Belarus)–Chelm (Poland) railway, east of the Polish town of Wlodawa.

Historical Background. The boundary between Poland and Russia and later the Soviet Union has been one of the most variable boundary lines in Europe, its history marking the history of Eastern Europe for over 700 years. After 125 years of Russian occupation, Poland was revived as an independent republic in 1918. Its eastern boundary was established along a line proposed after World War I by the territorial commission of the Versailles Conference of 1919, based on the easternmost limits of areas predominantly inhabited by a Polish population. This boundary, known as the Curzon Line, acquired its name after Lord Curzon, the British foreign secretary who proposed it on 8 December 1919. The Poles invaded Russia in 1920 and the Polish army and the Red Army moved back and forth in Ukraine and Byelorussia, until the Riga Peace Treaty of 18 March 1921 settled the line 125 miles (200 km.) east of the Curzon Line, west of the Belarussian cities of Minsk and Polotsk. During World War II eastern Poland was occupied by the Soviet Union (1940–1941) and by Nazi Germany until 1945. After the war Poland and the Soviet Union contracted a new boundary treaty (September 1945), which returned Poland's eastern boundary to the Curzon Line, albeit with some minor modifications for Poland's benefit. Poland lost 70,050 sq. miles (181,350 sq. km.) in the east to the Soviet Union (but gained 39,000 sq. miles [101,000 sq. km.] in the west from Germany). The central section of the Poland–Soviet Union boundary constituted the eastern boundary of the Soviet Republic of Byelorussia, which became an independent state in 1991. Upon gaining independence Belarus adopted the Soviet Union–Poland boundary line as its international boundary with Poland, although no formal agreements regarding its alignment were made.

Present Situation. Since 1991 no disputes concerning the boundary alignment have been reported. Both Belarus and Poland then accepted the 1945 line and neither has made claims on the other's territory.

BELARUS — RUSSIA Running 596 miles (959 km.) between the boundary tripoint with Latvia in the northwest and the tripoint with Ukraine in the southeast, the boundary between Belarus and Russia follows the administrative division between two republics of the former Soviet Union.

Geographical Setting. The boundary tripoint with Latvia is located some 12 miles (20 km.) southwest of Sebej (Russia) and north of the small Lake Osbi (Belarus). From there it heads eastward for about 40 miles (65 km.), along a flat plain region, between small lakes and across the northern tributaries of the Dvina River. It turns southward, crosses the main road and railway that link Nevel (Russia) and Poltusk (Belarus) and continues eastward and again southward to reach the Dvina River about 30 miles (50 km.) northeast of Vitebsk (Belarus). It crosses the Dvina River and the Smolensk (Russia)–Orsha (Belarus) railway and bears southeast to reach the Sozh River east of Mstislavl (Belarus), which it follows downstream southward for 20 miles (32 km.) to its confluence with an eastern tributary. The boundary follows the tributary eastward, leaves it at a point north of the Roslavl (Russia)–Krichev (Belarus) railway, and runs south to a northern tributary of the Iput River. The line then follows the Iput River southwestward for 5 miles (8 km.) and runs southeastward for about 40 miles (65 miles). Thence westward, the line crosses the Suraze (Russia)–Orsha railway and the Beshed River. Once again the boundary line heads south and extends 140 miles (225 km.) between small rivers and flat plains, across the Gomel (Belarus)–Bryansk (Russia) railway and down to the boundary tripoint with Ukraine at the confluence of the two northern tributaries of the Desna River, about 40 miles (65 km.) southeast of Gomel.

Historical Background. The boundary between Belarus and Russia is an artificial administrative line created for internal regulation. The Byelorussians are descendents of Slavic tribes who settled between the second and the fifth centuries on the western shores of the Dvina, Upper Dnieper, Nemen and

Pripet rivers. The area then came under foreign rule (the Mongols, Lithuanians and Poles) for several centuries, separating these tribes from the other East Slavic peoples. They began to develop distinctive customs, culture and language.

Belarus declared its independence on 28 March 1918, but was occupied by the Red Army on 1 January 1919. The Polish-Soviet Union war over Belarussian territory (1919–1920) was ended with the Riga Peace Treaty (18 March 1921), by which Belarus was divided between Soviet Union and Poland. Soviet White Russia (Byelorussia) was established as a Soviet republic within the Soviet Union, its eastern boundary with the Soviet Republic of Russia undergoing various formations and changes in accordance with the needs of the central authorities in Moscow before and after World War II. Belarus declared its independence in August 1991, adopting its last internal dividing line as its international boundary with independent Russia without any formal agreement.

Present Situation. The boundary between Belarus and Russia was never demarcated, no boundary signs or boundary post were ever erected and the line never served as a state boundary. However, there are no serious disputes concerning its alignment and neither of the states has made any territorial claims on the other.

BELARUS — UKRAINE

This boundary is 554 miles (891 km.) long and runs from the boundary tripoint with Poland on the Bug River in the west to the boundary junction with Russia in the east. The line follows an undemarcated border that separated two Soviet republics of the former Soviet Union.

Geographical Setting. The boundary tripoint with Poland is located on the Bug River, where the Berst (Belarus)–Chelm (Poland) railway crosses the river, east of the small Polish town of Wlodawa. From there the boundary line runs eastward along the flat, plain region of the Pripet Marshes, north of the Pripet River. It crosses this river south of Pinsk (Belarus) and continues eastward to cross some of its southern tributaries (Sgyr, Golyn, Ubort). After crossing the main road and railway between Zhitomir (Ukraine) and Mozyr (Belarus) the line heads south for about 20 miles (30 km.) and then again eastward to the Pripet River. It crosses the river and

runs eastward to reach the Dnieper River, about 25 miles (40 km.) north of its confluence with the Pripet River. The line follows the Dnieper River northward upstream for about 50 miles (80 km.), leaves the river and runs eastward to the boundary tripoint with Russia, located in the confluence of two northern tributaries of the Desna River.

Historical Background. Ukraine was annexed by Czarist Russia in 1654 and over the following centuries the Ukrainians were regarded by the Russian authorities as part of the Russian people. Following the Russian Revolution of 1917 a national Ukrainian congress proclaimed in Kiev a "free sovereign" Ukrainian People's Republic. A civil war was fought between the Ukrainian republic and the Ukrainian Soviet government, which led to the annexation of most of Ukraine to the Soviet Union (formed after World War I) and Ukraine became one of the founding republics of the Soviet Union.

The Soviet Republic of Ukraine's boundary with the Soviet Republic of Byelorussia was established in 1921, following the Riga Peace Treaty which ended the war between the Soviet Union and Poland. This internal boundary was changed several times during the 1920s and 1930s. After World War II western Ukraine, which had been annexed by Poland since 1921, was returned to the Ukrainian republic and new dividing lines were delineated between the western republics of the Soviet Union. With the dissolution of the Soviet Union in 1991 both Ukraine and Byelorussia (under the name of Belarus) became independent states, adopting the last internal dividing line as their common international boundary without any formal agreement regarding its alignment.

Present Situation. The border line between the former Soviet republics of Ukraine and Byelorussia never served as a state boundary. It was purely an administrative line, settled with no intention of demarcation or concern for the geographical need for a boundary delimitation. As with other internal boundaries of the former Soviet Union that were created and modified with the state's recurring political-territorial reorganizations, the Belarus–Ukraine boundary holds a high potential to cause national conflict. In this vein are Ukrainian claims for the transfer of the Gomel district from Belarus, Belarussian calls for the transfer of the northern areas of the

Zhitomir district from Ukraine, and the creation of a Western Polesye (Pripet) autonomous territory in the borderland of Belarus and Ukraine. These and other national conflicts that can arise with the transformation of administrative borders into international boundaries still lie ahead of the two newly independent states.

BELGIUM (Belgique/België) Situated in Western Europe, Belgium (area: 11,783 sq. miles [30,518 sq. km.]; estimated population: 10,050,000 [1994]) is bounded in the north by Netherlands (280 miles;

450 km.), northwest by the North Sea, east by Germany (104 miles; 167 km.) and Luxembourg (92 miles; 148 km.) and west and south by France (386 miles; 620 km.). Its capital is Brussels.

The population of Belgium, divided between two distinct ethno-linguistical communities, the Germanic Flemings and the Romanic Walloons. Most Belgians are Catholic.

The Flemish-Walloon divide goes back to Roman times. After a period of romanization in Gaul Frankish invasions in the fifth century advanced to a line from Maastricht to Dunkirk. By the year 1000,

Belgium and its boundaries

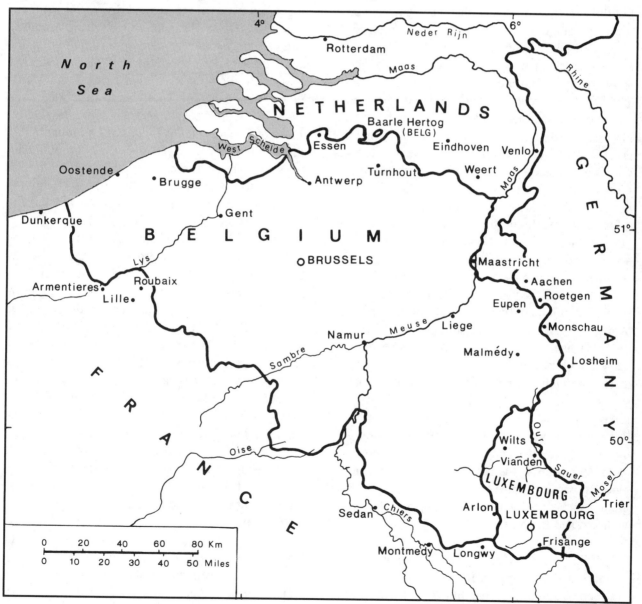

this boundary had frozen into a permanent language frontier. By the eleventh century seven feudal states had emerged in the area known today as Belgium, each nominally subject to the German emperor or French kings, but in practice independent. In the fourteenth century the Burgundian dukes coalesced the Seventeen Provinces into the Low Countries (or "nether lands"), a rich and highly urbanized region with a mixed Dutch-French population.

The revolt of the Low Countries in the sixteenth century, which led to the independence of Netherlands, left Belgium under Spanish rule until the Treaty of Utrecht transferred it to Austria in 1713. In 1797 Belgium was annexed by revolutionary France but the Congress of Vienna that was convened after the Napoleonic Wars (1800–1814), reunited Belgium and Netherlands under one kingdom on 24 August 1815. Spain reimposed Catholicism in its southern zone, and the cultural elite moved north. The French Revolution brought judicial and administrative modernization and stimulated industry, but also cemented French as the elite language. In 1830 an anti-Dutch revolt led by a coalition of conservative Flemish clergy and liberal Walloon bourgeoisie brought about the united Belgian kingdom, bilingual in theory but French-dominated in fact.

From the beginning the Belgians were beset by chronic ethnic disunity. Unilinguism was adopted in administration, education, etc., according to the dominant language in each region. However, only in the 1930s were the two languages treated equally. A completely Flemish-educated elite came of age after World War II. The language struggle exacerbated in 1960s: it has led to Belgium's progressive federalization, with cultural-educational autonomy and separate institutions for both communities and a special status for Brussels. Recently, each linguistic community has established its own legislature and executive, independent from the national center. Although community problems remain unresolved, no party is demanding the breakup of Belgium, and regionalist parties declined in the 1980s. In 1993 Belgium became a federal state, composed of Flanders, Wallonia and Brussels.

BELGIUM — FRANCE   The boundary between Belgium and France runs for 386 miles (620 km.) between the boundary tripoint with Luxembourg north of Longwy (France), and the North Sea coast, northeast of Dunkerque (Dunkirk).

Geographical Setting. The southeastern terminus of the boundary line is located on the northeastern tributary of the Chiers River, 2 miles (3 km.) south of the small Belgian town of Athus. It runs westward for 20 miles (32 km.) north of the Luxembourg–Longuyon (France) and Lunguyon–Montmédy (France) railways, reaching the aforementioned tributary east of Montmédy. The line runs parallel to the tributary to its confluence with the Torme River, another tributary of the Chiers River, west of Lamortedu (Belgium). There the boundary heads northwest for 35 miles (56 km.), following the watershed between the Semois River (Belgium) and the Chiers River (France) and reaching a point 2 miles (3 km.) southeast of Sugny (Belgium). Turning northward for about 30 miles (48 km.) the line crosses the Semois River and reaches the Meuse River west of the small Belgian town of Heer Agimant. It crosses the river and runs south, leaving the towns of Fumay and Givet and their surrounding areas within France. West of Fumay the boundary turns southwest and runs in that direction for 8 miles (13 km.) to a point south of Cul des Sarts (Belgium), where it bears westward for 15 miles (24 km.) to reach an eastern tributary of the Oise River. Thence it turns northward and extends 20 miles (32 km.) up to the Sambre River. It crosses the river and the Charleroi (Belgium)–Maubeuge (France) railway and runs westward, crosses the Mons (Belgium)–Maubeuge railway and continues in that direction for 12 miles (20 km.). It then runs northwestward, meandering between small towns and villages, crossing local streams and the main Brussels (Belgium)–Lille (France) railway and finally reaching the outskirts of the French town of Roubaix. There the boundary arches north, west and southwest along the Lys River for about 25 miles (40 km.) to a point north of Armentières (France) where it heads northwest for approximately 35 miles (55 km.) up to the coast of the North Sea, some 10 miles (16 km.) northeast of Dunkerque (France).

Historical Background. The Congress of Vienna established Belgium's southern boundary with France along the line that had been agreed upon in a treaty between Austria and the king of Netherlands, which had been signed on 31 May 1815 in Vienna.

This line had, in fact, been defined earlier by Article III of the Treaty of Paris of 30 May 1814. Belgium became independent on 4 October 1830, adopting the existing southern boundary with France as an international boundary.

Present Situation. Since 1815 no changes were made in the boundary's alignment and there are no disputes along this settled line. With the present steps toward uniting Europe there are very few restrictions and minimal control on boundary crossings.

BELGIUM — GERMANY

The boundary between Belgium and Germany runs for 104 miles (167 km.) from the tripoint with the Netherlands in the north to the boundary junction with Luxembourg in the south.

Geographical Setting. The boundary begins some 2 miles (3.2 km.) west of the German city of Aachen, running southeast in a series of broken lines through the hills of Ardennes, regardless of the physical landscape. Near the German town of Loshheim the boundary changes course, turning southwest to follow the Our Valley, leaving the Our River entirely in Belgium. The boundary ends at the tripoint with Luxembourg, located on the Our River near the German city of Hemmeres.

Historical Background. The history of the Belgium–Germany boundary dates back to 1815, when the European countries established a boundary between the Low Countries and Prussia. Belgium was established as an independent state 24 years later, in 1839, adopting the boundary line with Prussia, which became Germany in 1871 after the unification of the various small German states. However, the Treaty of Versailles, signed at Paris on 28 June 1919 after World War I, created an entirely new boundary by detaching Eupen, Malmédy and Moresnet from Germany and placing them in Belgium. The precise demarcation and delineation of the new boundary was concluded three years later, and the report of a Belgian–German boundary demarcation commission was subsequently signed at Aachen on 6 November 1922.

Since then, minor adjustments have been made to the boundary. Such modifications were deemed necessary because the area, though predominantly rural, is densely settled and contains many major transportation routes. Thus, in May 1935 two small parcels of land, totaling approximately 0.8 sq. miles (2 sq. km.), were ceded by Belgium to enable the orderly expansion of the Aachen freight yard. Likewise, in September 1949, seven parcels of German territory, covering about 8 sq. miles (20 sq. km.) and with a population of about 500, were transferred to Belgian administration.

Various problems concerning border administration, customs control, communications and river pollution caused some dissatisfaction in specific areas along the border. After lengthy discussions, a "Treaty Between the Federal Republic of Germany and the Kingdom of Belgium Concerning Rectification of the Germany–Belgium Boundary and other Questions" was signed in Brussels on 24 September 1956. According to this agreement Belgium ceded to Germany one parcel of land; Germany, in turn, ceded three to Belgium. Furthermore, the seven sections of territory administered by Belgium since 1949 were returned to German jurisdiction, with some minor rectifications. All these changes were made "in order to establish a suitable boundary line between the two countries, eliminating irregularities and conforming to local conditions and the requirements of transportation." The agreement was ratified by both countries in 1958.

Present Situation. Since the careful study of the boundary was made in 1956, there have not been any reports of disputes or problems concerning the boundary alignment.

BELGIUM — LUXEMBOURG

Belgium and Luxembourg share a boundary that runs for 92 miles (148 km.) between the boundary junction with Germany on the Our River in the north and the boundary junction with France in the south. It follows a dividing line that was established in the mid-nineteenth century between the Belgian province of Luxembourg and the independent Grand Duchy of Luxembourg.

Geographical Setting. Some 5 miles (8 km.) northeast of the small town of Heinescheid (Luxembourg) stands the northeastern terminus of the boundary line, on the Our River. The line runs westward for 10 miles (16 km.), reaching the main railway that travels between Liège (Belgium) and Luxembourg. It crosses the railway and turns southwestward, running parallel and southeast of the local railway to

Bastogne (Belgium). After crossing the Wiltz (Luxembourg)–Bastogne railway the boundary reaches the Sauer River, the main river of Luxembourg that crosses it from west to east. The boundary follows that river upstream southwestward to the town of Martelange (Belgium) and then heads southeast for about 15 miles (25 km.) to reach and cross the Luxembourg (Luxembourg)–Arlon (Belgium) railway. Finally, it runs southwestward for 10 miles (16 km.) to the boundary tripoint with France, 2 miles (3 km.) south of the small Belgian town of Athus.

Historical Background. By the eleventh century seven feudal states had emerged in the area known today as Belgium—one of them was Luxembourg. Luxembourg became a duchy in 1354, was included in the Habsburg domination of the feudal states from 1482 and later came under Spanish rule with all the Low Countries. The Treaty of Utrecht of 1713 transferred Belgium and Luxembourg to Austria and in 1797 both came under French Rule. In 1815, after the Napoleon era, the Congress of Vienna declared Luxembourg a grand duchy, ruled by the king of Netherlands, who also ruled Belgium. However, in 1830 both revolted against the Dutch rule. Belgium achieved independence on 20 January 1831—including in it the entire territory of Luxembourg. Netherlands never accepted this act and its army entered the newly established state. Only after French and British intervention did the London Treaty of 15 November 1831 establish the Belgian boundaries, leaving Luxembourg within Netherlands. Netherlands finally recognized Belgium's independence in 1838. The limits of Eastern Luxembourg (998 sq. miles [2,584 sq. km.] out of 2,700 sq. miles [7,000 sq. km.]) were established by the treaties of 19 April 1839 and the area was recognized as the independent Duchy of Luxembourg in 1848. The dividing line established in 1831 between Belgian and Dutch Luxembourg is the present boundary between the two independent states. The political changes that have taken place in Europe since 1838 have never affected the boundary line.

Present Situation. Since 1838 there have been no disputes concerning the alignment of the Belgium–Luxembourg boundary; neither state has ever raised any claims on the other's territory. Although it has not been demarcated, it is one of the most peaceful boundary lines in the world.

BELGIUM — NETHERLANDS The boundary between Belgium and Netherlands runs for 280 miles (450 km.) between the North Sea shore and the boundary tripoint with Germany, west of Aachen (Germany). There are some Belgian exclaves (Baarle-Hertog) in and around the Dutch city of Baarle-Nassau.

Geographical Setting. The southeastern terminus of the boundary line is located between the small towns of Vaals (Netherlands) and Gemmenich (Belgium), west of the German city of Aachen. The line trends westward for about 25 miles (40 km.) to reach the Meuse (Maas) River. It follows the main navigation channel of the river downstream northward for 3 miles (5 km.) and leaves it to form an arch northwestward and northeastward so as to leave the city of Maastricht within Netherlands. North of the city, the boundary line rejoins the Meuse River and follows it generally northward for 20 miles (32 km.) separating the Belgian and Dutch provinces of Limburg. North of Ophoven (Belgium) the boundary leaves the river and heads westward. Southwest of Weert (Netherlands) it crosses the Noord (North) Canal and continues westward, north of the Meuse-Escaut Canal. It reaches and crosses the main road and railway between Eindhoven (Netherlands) and Turnhout (Belgium) and then turns northward, leaving the small town of Poppel in Belgium. The boundary then bears southwestward for about 10 miles (16 km.) until it reaches the Tilburg (Netherlands)–Turnhout railway, leaving the Belgian town of Baarle-Hertog as an exclave in Dutch territory. It continues westward, reaches the Mark River and follows it north for 2 miles (3 km.) to its confluence with an eastern tributary. It follows the tributary east for 3 miles (5 km.), leaves the water line and runs north, west and south to leave the small towns of Meerle and Meer within Belgium. The boundary then runs westward again, crosses the Breda (Netherlands)–Antwerp (Belgium) highway and railway and again runs north, west and south, this time leaving the town of Essen in Belgium. East of Putte (Netherlands) the boundary trends westward to reach the eastern shore of the West Schelde estuary. The line crosses the mouth of the Schelde River southwestward, continues in that direction for 20 miles (32 km.) and thence, north of Selzaete (Belgium), heads north and west for 30 miles (50 km.) to the shore of the North Sea, 12 miles (19 km.) northeast of the city of Brugge (Belgium), between the small towns of Cadzand (Netherlands) and Knokke-Heist (Belgium).

Historical Background. Belgium and Netherlands, the Low Countries, were ruled by the duke of Burgundy and in 1504 were passed to the Spanish Habsburgs. The Dutch aspired to political freedom and Protestantism and from 1568 rebelled against the regime of the Catholic Philip II of Spain. The united provinces of the north ousted the Spanish in 1581, but the south (now Belgium and Luxembourg) was reconquered by Spain. The north maintained its freedom and in 1648 its independence as the Dutch Republic was finally recognized by the Treaty of Westphalia. Belgium was transferred to Austria in 1713 by the Treaty of Utrecht and was conquered by revolutionary France in 1797. The Congress of Vienna united Belgium and Netherlands in 1815 under a Dutch king, but historical differences made for a strained union. A Belgian rising in 1830 led it to a proclamation of independence on 4 October 1830, which was internationally recognized on 20 January 1831. Only Netherlands did not accept Belgium's independence and a Dutch army crossed the newly established boundary. French and British intervention saved Belgium, which was forced to accept territorial losses in its southeastern region, and the Treaty of London of 15 November 1831 defined all of Belgium's boundaries. Seven years later, in 1838, Netherlands finally recognized the independence of Belgium and accepted its northern boundary as their common boundary, which remains the same to the present day.

Present Situation. Since 1831 the boundary between the Low Countries has not changed. The boundary line has created a unique situation whereby the Belgian town of Baarle-Hertog lies within Netherlands. Moreover, some Dutch territories lie within this town and are enclaves within an enclave. This led to some unusual circumstances during World War I, when Netherlands was neutral while Belgium was occupied by German troops that could not enter the exclave town. Today the inhabitants of Belgian Baarle-Hertog living within Dutch territories have some different laws (drinking, gambling), but the establishment of the European Common Market and the open borders of Western Europe have made this unusual situation only an historic phenomenon.

BELIZE The only former British colony in Central America, Belize (area: 8,866 sq. miles [22,963 sq. km.]; estimated population: 202,000 [1994]) became independent in 1981. It is bounded in the north by Mexico (155.5 miles; 250 km.), in the west and south by Guatemala (165 miles; 266 km.) and in the east by the Caribbean Sea. The capital of Belize is Belmopan.

In 1862, the colony of British Honduras came into existence. Its status was disputed between Britain and Spain until the mid-nineteenth century. British Honduras experienced brief prosperity before World War I, but remained undeveloped. Mexico eventually recognized British dominion over the small territory, but Guatemala continued to claim British Honduras: until independence, Guatamalan maps labeled Belize "territory illegally held by great Britain." British Hondurans (as they were then called) drafted their first constitution in 1964, but did not achieve full independence until 1981, when a second constitutions was ratified. Today, although actual confrontations are rare, the old territorial dispute with Guatemala continues.

BELIZE — GUATEMALA From the Gulf of Honduras in the south, the Belize–Guatemala boundary runs generally north for 165 miles (266 km.) up to the boundary tripoint with Mexico.

Geographical Setting. The boundary begins at the mouth of the Sarstoon River in the Gulf of Honduras and proceeds westward along the *thalweg* of the river to Gracias a Dios Falls. There the line turns north and follows a straight line, drawn directly from Gracias a Dios Falls to Garbutt's Falls on the Belize River. The line continues northward up to the boundary junction with Mexico on the 17°49'N parallel.

Historical Background. Guatemala became independent from Spain on 15 September 1821 and considered Belize to be part of its territory inherited from the viceroyalty of New Spain. Britain had maintained a logwood settlement in the Gulf of Honduras since the latter half of the seventeenth century, with Spanish permission and under certain restrictions. Its rights were extended by the Treaty of Paris in 1763, after the Seven Years' War (1756–1763), but it was still not permitted to establish permanent agricultural settlements—and the treaty clearly dealt with Belize as part of Spanish territory. During the American War of Independence (1775–1781) Spain and France declared war on Britain, and Belize was saved from destruction by the chance arrival of British warships. Under the Convention of London in 1786, the logwood cutters gained a southern extension to their usufruct as well as permission to cut and export mahogany and to engage in farming. In return Britain agreed not to establish a colonial government in Belize. During the following years Belize was governed by superintendents appointed by the British monarchy.

In 1789 further hostilities between Britain and a Franco-Spanish alliance resulted in the expulsion of the Spanish from Belize. Although the Treaty of Amiens in 1802 required Britain to return territories conquered during this war, Belize was not mentioned at all. Furthermore, in 1814 the Treaty of Madrid confirmed the status of all treaties between Spain and Britain prior to 1797, specifically those concerning the woodcutters' rights in Belize.

It was only when the Federal Republic of Central America was established that Britain began making territorial and sovereignty demands for Belize and declined to recognize the new Federation when these were refused. In 1840 English law was proclaimed in the settlement and by the middle of the century Belize was well established as a separate administration with its own governance, justice system and trade relations.

In 1847 the United States sent a consul to Belize; however, in 1850 Britain and America signed the Clayton-Bulwer Treaty, agreeing that neither nation would exercise dominion or control over any part of Central America. Belize's status was clarified by the Dallas-Clarendon Agreement of 1856. This confirmed its exclusion from the terms of the 1850 treaty and required that its borders be fixed by a treaty with Guatemala. A treaty concluded on 30 April 1859 between Britain and Guatemala duly settled the boundary, but this was interpreted by Guatemala as a treaty of cessation under the guise of a border treaty in order not to infringe the terms of the 1850 Clayton-Bulwer Treaty. The 1859 treaty required the construction of a trade route between the

coast of Belize and the capital of Guatemala. Guatemala believed that the fact that this clause was not fulfilled made the entire treaty null and void. Britain, on the other hand, held that the 1859 treaty was indeed a boundary agreement that recognized the British occupation of Belize, and in 1862 Belize was declared the Crown Colony of British Honduras.

The northern boundary tripoint with Mexico was fixed by the Mexican-Guatemalan Treaty of 27 September 1882.

In 1880 and 1884 Guatemala repeated its demand that Britain build the road required by the 1859 treaty or forfeit sovereignty over Belize. The British refused and also rejected the suggestion of arbitration by the United States. In 1946, however, Britain offered to accept a ruling by the International Court of Justice (ICJ) in the Hague; this time Guatemala refused, on the grounds that the ICJ could not consider the wider aspects of the problem. The issue continued through the 1950s and 1960s, and when Britain proposed constitutional changes to give the colony internal self-government Guatemala demanded participation in decisions about the future of Belize and threatened war. In June 1978 a Memorandum of Understanding between Belize and Britain was issued, giving Belize rights of representation at negotiations with Guatemala and of referendum on any decisions reached. In September 1991 Guatemala recognized the sovereignty of Belize in return for access to its ports, but maintained its territorial claim.

Present Situation. This border remains insecure due to the Guatemalan territorial claims. In 1993 the British garrison was withdrawn from Belize.

BELIZE — MEXICO This boundary is 155.5 miles (250 km.) long, running from the mouth of the Hondo River on the Caribbean coast to the tripoint with Guatemala at 17°49'N.

Geographical Setting. From the mouth of the Hondo River in Chetumal Bay, the boundary follows the river's *thalweg* (deepest navigable channel) upstream westward and then southwestward, passing west of Albion island, to its confluence with the Blue Creek (Rio Azul) near Dos Bocest (Belize). It then follows the Blue Creek upstream westward, until it crosses the meridian of Garbutt's Falls, far south on the Belize River and north of the Mexico–Guatemala–Belize boundary intersection. From there it runs southward to latitude 17°49'N at the tripoint with Guatemala, leaving the Snosha (Xnohha) River within Mexico.

Historical Background. The British Bay Settlement, commonly called Belize in the early history of its occupation, was established in 1638. Although the Treaty of Madrid of 1670 recognized some de facto British possessions in the Caribbean, it did not accept that the Bay Settlement was one of them and in the Treaty of Paris in 1763 Spain maintained its claim to sovereignty over Belize, conceding to the British the right to continue its logging industry there. This was further confirmed in the Treaty of Versailles of 3 September 1783 regarding the area of northeast Belize, between the Hondo and Belize rivers. The Convention of London (14 July 1786) reiterated the logging rights and extended the concession beyond the Belize River to the Sibun River. In return, Britain renounced its claims to the Mosquito Coast.

Mexico gained independence from Spain on 16 September 1810 and in a treaty between Britain and Mexico, signed on 26 December 1826, recognized the limits of Belize as those of the Anglo-Spanish Treaty of 1786. On 30 August 1859 a treaty between Britain and Guatemala delimited their mutual boundary, extending the line from the Guatemala tripoint northward to the intersection of the Garbutt's Falls meridian with the Blue Creek river.

In 1862 the British Bay Settlement became the Colony of British Honduras. A treaty between Britain and Mexico, signed on 8 July 1893, delimited the present Belize–Mexico boundary by reference to the 1859 agreement between Belize and Guatemala and the Guatemala-Mexico agreement of 1882. British Honduras was renamed Belize on 1 June 1973.

Present Situation. The treaty of 1893 is mutually recognized and the boundary is not in dispute. This treaty also provided for the delimitation of a sea boundary.

BENIN Formerly known as Dahomey, Benin (area: 43,473 sq. miles [112,595 sq. km.]; estimated population: 5,160,000 [1994]) is situated in west Africa. It is bounded in the west by Togo (400

miles; 644 km.), in the north by Niger (165 miles; 266 km.) and Burkina Faso (190 miles; 306 km.), in the east by Nigeria (480 miles; 773 km.) and in the south by the Gulf of Guinea in the Atlantic Ocean. The capital of Benin is Porto-Novo.

The Beninians were ruled by the French from the beginning of the twentieth century, at which time the country was called Dahomey after the great kingdom that controlled the area in precolonial times. During the colonial period Dahomey was largely neglected by the French. However, it served as a source of African administrators for large parts of French-ruled West Africa and a relatively large number of Beninians studied abroad.

The Fon and Yoruba of the south enjoyed educational advantages while the northern peoples such as the Bariba and the Somba were less westernized. After independence, the existence of a large educated elite in a country with a slow and underdeveloped economy caused great instability in Benin's political life, which was dominated by a continuing struggle between regional elites. Three main forces in the country have been struggling for power since the colonial period: the southern peoples who formed their own party after World War II, led by Migan Apithy; the northern peoples led by Robert Maga; and the peoples living in the central region around the city of Abomey.

Until 1972 there was a series of military coups, followed by a long period of Mathiew Kerekou's military rule. In 1989, following severe popular unrest, Kerekou reluctantly agreed to begin a process of democratization. In 1991 the first multiparty elections since independence took place, and Nicepore Soglo was elected president.

BENIN — BURKINA FASO The boundary between Benin and Burkina Faso begins at the tripoint with Niger, at about 11°54'15"N and 2°25'10"E. It runs generally southwest, and primarily along the Mékrou and Pendjari rivers. In total, the line extends 190 miles (306 km.) to the tripoint with Togo.

Geographical Setting. The boundary follows the course of the Mékrou River over low, undulating plains southwestward, to approximately 11°25'30"N and 2°18'45"E. It then continues southwestward along the Atakora Mountains drainage divide to about 11°25'30"N and 2°00'15"E, where it turns west and, through a small tributary, reaches the Pendjari River, which it follows for 106 miles (170 km.) southwest to 11°01'25"N and 0°56'50"E. Finally, the boundary heads west along a straight line to the tripoint with Togo at 11°N and 0°55'E.

Historical Background. As Benin and Burkina Faso were both formerly French colonies in western Africa, the boundary between them is, in principle, the intercolonial boundary that was delimited by the French colonial administration. On 10 March 1893 the colony of Benin was created from the Establissements due Golfe de Guinee (the name given to the French protectorates along the Bight of Benin in 1883), and was renamed Dahomey one year later. A French decree of March 1901 specified a boundary between Dahomey and the military territories to its north—Haut Senegal and Niger (later Upper Volta, now Burkina Faso). In 1911, however, these territories were demilitarized and the French administration subsequently proceeded to respecify these sections of the boundary according to decrees passed between 1909 and 1938, which had presented descriptions of the then constituted regions of Kandi and Natitingou, both of which are adjacent to the boundary. In 1919 a decree was passed establishing the colony of Upper Volta by detaching a number of regions from Haut Senegal and Niger. On 5 September 1932 Upper Volta was dissolved and divided among the surrounding colonies. However, on 4 September 1947 it was reconstituted and became a French territory of the French Union, its boundaries positioned in accordance with the limits of Dahomey's northern territories as defined in the 1938 statute. Dahomey gained independence on 1 August 1960, followed by Upper Volta four days later, on 5 August 1960.

Present Situation. Although 85% of the boundary follows the Mékrou and Pendjari rivers, its entire length has remained undemarcated. Thus, there are a number of unresolved matters concerning the two sectors. It has never been determined whether the boundary follows the *thalwegs* or median lines of the rivers, and along the Pendjari River flooding areas are the cause of further delineation problems.

BENIN — NIGER From the tripoint with Burkina Faso the boundary between Benin and Niger runs northeast and then southeast to the tripoint with Nigeria. The line is 165 miles (266 km.) long.

Geographical Setting. The boundary between Benin and Niger begins at the tripoint with Burkina Faso at 11°54'15"N and 2°25'10"E on the Mékrou River. It follows the river's course in a northeasterly direction, through its low-lying valley, to its confluence with the Niger River. At the confluence the boundary turns southeast and continues along the course of the Niger River to the tripoint with Nigeria. The boundary runs at an almost equal distance from both the Mékrou and Niger rivers.

Historical Background. Niger and Benin were formerly French colonies in western Africa, divided by an intercolonial boundary that was delimited by the French colonial administration. The colony of Benin was created from the Establissements due Golfe de Guinee (the French protectorates along the Bight of Benin) on 10 March 1893 and in March 1894 the colony's name was changed to Dahomey. In March 1901 a French decree delimited a boundary between Dahomey and the three military territories to its north. In 1902 these military territories became the responsibility of the French colony of Senegambie et Niger, which in 1904 became the colony of Haut Senegal et Niger. The Niger military zone was detached from the colony in 1912, and in 1922 Niger became a colony of French West Africa in its own right. The French administration then determined and authorized the boundary between Dahomey and Niger on 27 October 1938, describing the then constituted region of Kandi, which is adjacent to the present area of Niger. At that time a large area of today's Burkina Faso was still part of Niger, following the abolition and partitioning of the colony of Upper Volta in 1932. However, on 4 September 1947 Upper Volta was reconstituted along the former colony boundaries in accordance with the limits set in the 1938 statute, thus establishing the present tripoint with Burkina Faso. There is some uncertainty regarding the accurate location of this tripoint. The American International Boundary Study locates it at 11°54'15"N and 2°25'10"E, but there is no official French instrument that describes it precisely. Dahomey and Niger were made overseas territories of the French Union in 1946; Niger became an autonomous member of the French Community in 1958; Dahomey gained independence on 1 August 1960 and two days later, on 3 August 1960, the

Republic of Niger became independent. Immediately after independence, negotiations were held regarding the attribution of the island of Lete in the Niger River, but a mixed commission failed to reach a solution and in 1963 the dispute flared up. Only on 19 January 1965 did representatives of the two states agree that the island was to be a common possession ("leur appartiendrait en commun"). For lack of available information, the questionable position of the boundary in the Niger and Mékrou rivers—along their *thalwegs* or median lines—has caused disputes over the sovereignty of various islands located in the rivers.

Present Situation. The French colonial administration's insufficient descriptions, regarding the division of the rivers and the allocation of islands along the boundary line, led to disputes that have yet to be solved. A joint border demarcation commission was being convened in 1994 to prevent and settle any border disputes.

BENIN — NIGERIA The Benin–Nigeria boundary is 480 miles (773 km.) long. From the Gulf of Guinea it runs north to the tripoint with Niger. Inland from the Gulf of Guinea the boundary is demarcated by pillars, up to the Okpara River.

Geographical Setting. From the coast of the Gulf of Guinea to the Okpara River, the boundary bears northward through coastal plains up to slightly higher ground. This section is demarcated by 142 beacons. The boundary joins the Okpara River at a point described as "800 metres north of Jabata (the point of permanent water supply)" and follows the *thalweg* of the Okpara River for approximately 100 miles (160 km.) until it turns north-northeast. From this point the boundary is demarcated in straight-lines and arcs and along sectors parallel to roads, up to its intersection with the median line of the Niger River, where the tripoint with Niger is located.

Historical Background. The present boundary was established by those European countries that had colonized the area during the nineteenth century. Along the coast of Nigeria and Benin (then known as Dahomey) both the United Kingdom and France were settling areas. By 1889 both were expanding inland, producing the need for a boundary between the two spheres of interest. Thus, it was fixed from the Gulf of Guinea north to the 9°N parallel. This

boundary was initially delimited by an Anglo-French convention in 1889. In 1898 another Anglo-French convention confirmed the 1889 delimitation and extended the boundary between the territories northward to the Niger River.

On 19 October 1906 an Anglo-French agreement detailed the northern section of today's boundary. The British interest, in the form of the Royal Niger Company, later surrendered its charter, annexing its southern territorial acquisitions to the Niger Coast Protectorate, which became the Protectorate of Southern Nigeria, while the Company's territories in the north became the Protectorate of Northern Nigeria. The two protectorates amalgamated in 1914 as the Colony and Protectorate of Nigeria. The positions of the 142 boundary markers and the point where the boundary enters the Okpara River were defined in the Anglo-French Exchange of Notes on 18 February of that year. In 1960 Dahomey gained independence from French Rule, becoming Benin in 1975, and on 1 October 1960 the independent Federation of Nigeria was established. On 24 May 1966 the Federal Republic of Nigeria became the Republic of Nigeria. Both countries adopted the colonial boundary as their common international boundary, without any official agreement.

Present Situation. With the passing of time roads and pillars used to demarcate the boundary have been lost. Although the boundary requires survey and updated location along its non-river sectors, there are no current areas of dispute, since the boundary does not impede movement of trade or people. 1994 saw calls for the improvement of conditions in Nigeria's border zones to curb economic emigration.

BENIN — TOGO From the Bight of Benin in the Gulf of Guinea, this boundary runs north for 400 miles (644 km.) to the boundary tripoint with Burkina Faso. It follows a coastal lagoon, several rivers and many straight-line segments. Numbered boundary posts were set up during 1908–1909 and 1911–1912.

Geographical Setting. From the intersection of the coast with the meridian at the western tip of Bayol Island, the boundary follows the meridian as far as the south bank of the lagoon, which it then follows to a distance of some 300 feet (100 m.) beyond the eastern tip of Bayol Island. Thence it runs directly north to a point midway between the south and north banks of the lagoon and follows it, meandering, always equidistant from the two banks, to the *thalweg* of the Mono River. It follows the Mono River to its intersection with 7°N and extends to the Bayol Island meridian, which it follows up to a point between Bassila (Benin) and Penesoulou. From there it extends to the Kara River, passing between Daboni and Alejo and between Sudu and Aledjo (Benin). It then runs through the *thalweg* of the Kara River for 3 miles (5 km.) and heads northward in a straight line to 10°N, leaving Semere in Benin. From there the boundary runs northwest to a point between Dje (Benin) and Gandou (Togo), continues northward, crosses the Uti River and reaches the boundary tripoint with Burkina Faso at 11°N and approximately 0°55'E.

Historical Background. In 1851 France concluded an agreement with the king of Dahomey for the site of a trading post, Porto-Novo, near Cotonou. After a suspension of control, France reestablished its rights in 1883 and extended its protection along the Bight of Benin. From 1893 France administered its territories from the Benin colony. The area was renamed Dahomey and in 1899 was included in French West Africa.

On 5 July 1884 Germany signed a treaty with the chief of Togo, by which German protection extended from east of Agbodrafo to west of Lome and by subsequent treaties Germany moved inland. A Franco-German Protocol of 24 December 1885 stated that the boundary between Dahomey and Togo would begin on the coast between Petit Popo and Agoue. A procès-verbal of 1 February 1887 delimited the boundary from the coast to 9°N. A Franco-German protocol of 9 July 1897 delimited the whole boundary between German Togo and the French area of French Dahomey and Upper Volta (today Burkina Faso) and a convention between France and Germany confirmed this protocol on 23 July 1897. A detailed delimitation of 28 September 1912 is the basis of the present alignment.

After World War I Togo was divided between the British and French who held mandates from the League of Nations, which were later converted into United Nations trusts. French Togo, in the east, had its own governmental structure while western Togo was administered by the British as an integral part of the Gold Coast (today Ghana). After a plebiscite in 1956 French Togo became an autonomous republic within the French Union. On 27 April 1960 it severed its ties with France and became an independent republic. Dahomey became an overseas territory and member of the French Union in 1946; on 4 December 1958 it became an autonomous republic of the French community and was proclaimed independent on 1 August 1960. Benin and Togo signed a Convention on Common Frontier Posts on 28 August 1962. A meeting that dealt with the frontier problems experienced by villagers at Agone and Agounegan, on either side of the lagoon, solved their controversies in 1975, but the actual position of the boundary was never at issue.

Present Situation. There are no disputes concerning the alignment of the Benin–Togo boundary.

BERMUDA   A British colony in the western Atlantic Ocean, Bermuda is situated 690 miles (1,110 km.) southwest of New York. It consists of a group of some 150 small islands. Its land area is 21 sq. miles (54 sq. km.) with a population of 61,000 [1994]. Bermuda has no land boundaries and its capital is Hamilton.

Over 60% of the inhabitants of Bermuda are of black African origin, the remainder being of European (mainly British or Portuguese) descent; religious affiliation is to a variety of Christian denominations. English is universally spoken. Tourism and an offshore financial sector stimulated by the absence of income and corporate taxes are the major foreign income earners.

BHUTAN (Druk-Yul)   A landlocked kingdom (area: 17,954 sq. miles [46,500 sq. km.]; estimated population: 1,700,000 [1994]) situated in the eastern Himalayas, on the border between China and India, Bhutan is bounded in the north by China (292 miles; 470 km.) and on all other sides by India (376 miles; 605 km.). The capital of Bhutan is Thimbu.

The term "Bhot" means Tibet and it is thought that this people originated in that country, as evidenced by the Tibeto-Burman dialect they speak. In contemporary India, however, other non-Tibetans occupying the same region are also referred to as Bhotia.

Most Bhutanese are Tibetan Buddhists although

Bon, a shamanist religion predating Buddhism, is also common, particularly in the remote regions of the Himalayas.

The Bhutanese are semi-nomadic and live in small, remote villages often separated by rugged mountain terrain which makes communications virtually impossible. There they engage in terrace agriculture, growing rice and other grains and herding yak. Traditionally they traded their produce in Tibet for salt, wool and livestock but this has become increasingly difficult since the Chinese occupation of that country.

Modernization has brought about other changes in the established Bhutanese lifestyle. Until the early 1960s they lived in a feudal society governed by a hereditary aristocracy and the enslavement of other peoples taken in battle was common. In 1960 the government of Bhutan abolished slavery and emancipated women, steps that were immediately adopted in the Bhutanese-settled regions of India as well.

BHUTAN — CHINA

The boundary between Bhutan and China runs for 292 miles (470 km.) between two boundary tripoints with India. It is one of few international boundaries that were never defined by any international agreement and its alignment is indistinct.

Geographical Setting. The eastern terminus of the boundary line is Che Dong in the eastern Himalayas, west of the Dangme River, a tributary of the Manas River, which is the main river of eastern Bhutan. The line runs westward, crosses the upper Manas River, and generally follows the watershed that separates the rivers running northward to the Chinese section of the Brahmaputra River from those that run southward toward its Indian section. The boundary passes between the Chinese peak of Monlakachung-la (24,852 feet; 7,575 m.) and the Bhutanese peak of Kulhakangri (23,858 feet; 7,272 m.) and near the 90°E meridian changes its direction southwestward, leaving the source of the Wong River within Bhutan and the Chomo Lhari (Chomolhari) peak (23,789 feet; 7,805 m.) in China. It also leaves the main road that connects India and Tibet via Sikkim in Chinese territory. It crosses the Aino River and reaches the boundary junction with India south of the Chinese town of Yatung (Yadong).

Historical Background. Bhutan, which was under Tibetan rule from the sixteenth century, was occupied by China in 1720. Britain became involved in Bhutan in 1773 and by 1864 recognized and guaranteed its independence in exchange for a trade agreement. By the Anglo-Bhutanese Treaty of 1910 Bhutan's foreign relations were placed under the control of the British Government of India. The boundary between Bhutan and China was never agreed upon by any known international agreement, but the British and Chinese "knew" where the boundary lay and never questioned it. In 1959 the Chinese annexation of Tibet placed it in direct contact with Bhutan—but still no boundary treaty was contracted or is known to exist.

Present Situation. Bhutan and China enjoy good relations and there have been no reports of boundary problems between them—despite the fact that the line has never been demarcated or officially and publicly agreed upon.

BHUTAN — INDIA

The boundary between Bhutan and India extends 376 miles (605 km.) between two boundary tripoints with China. The southern section of the boundary is demarcated.

Geographical Setting. The eastern terminus of the boundary is located in Che Dong in the Himalayas, northwest of the Indian town of Towang. The line runs southward for about 25 miles (40 km.) to reach and cross the Dangme River. It then runs eastward for 20 miles (32 km.) to a point southeast of Towang, where it turns southward for about 50 miles (80 km.) to reach the southern edge of the high mountainous area that stands on the northern edge of a forested tract known as the Duars, which is some 20 miles (32 km.) wide and is situated between the forested foothill of the Himalayas and the marshy grassland of the Brahmaputra River. From there the boundary line bears westward for about 300 miles (480 km.) along the Duars, crossing the Borolia River south of the town of Dewangiri (Bhutan). Continuing westward, the boundary line crosses the Manas and other rivers that run from the Himalayas southward to the great Brahmaputra River. North of the small Indian town of Metteli, the boundary changes its direction and runs northward for about 30 miles (50 km.) to the boundary tripoint with China, east of the Indian city of Gangtok and southeast of Jelep-la Pass, the main passageway between India and eastern Tibet.

Historical Background. Bhutan was under Chinese rule from 1720 and began official relations with the British in 1773, when the latter were establishing themselves in eastern India. The British drove the Bhutanese from the lower plains, leaving with Bhutan the entire Duars region—the long valley south of the eastern Himalayas. The British annexed Assam (northeast India) in 1826, placing itself in direct contact with Bhutan. In 1841 the area east of the Manas River was also annexed by the British and in 1864 the entire area south of Bhutan became a British possession. In 1865 Britain and Bhutan agreed on the alignment of the boundary along the Duars, but never defined the eastern and the western section of the border. In 1910 an Anglo-Bhutanese treaty placed Bhutan's foreign relations in British hands while, in exchange, Bhutan received an annual subsidy. India became independent in 1947, inheriting the British role in Bhutan. In 1950 a friendship treaty was signed between Bhutan and India, by which India retroceded 32 sq. miles (83 sq. km.) in the mouth of a principal mountain pass that is situated near Dewangiri.

Present Situation. Although the southern section of the boundary, which runs parallel to the Duars, is in consensus and is clearly demarcated, the eastern and the western sections, between the mountains and plains, were never settled by international agreement. However, since the 1950 agreement no disputes have been reported concerning the boundary alignment, including the eastern and western sections of the line.

BOLIVIA A landlocked country in central South America (area: 424,165 sq. miles [1,098,587 sq. km.]; estimated population: 8,010,000 [1994]), Bolivia is bounded in the north and east by Brazil (2,113 miles; 3,400 km.), in the south by Paraguay (466 miles; 746 km.) and Argentina (517 miles; 827 km.) and in the west by Chile (535 miles; 861 km.) and Peru (560 miles; 900 km.). The capital of Bolivia is La Paz.

The Bolivian white population is predominantly urban, while most of the Indians are part of the rural mining sector. Bolivia's troubled political history did not provide much ground for social, economic and national integration between the population groups until the 1950s. The revolution of April 1952 brought the Movement of National Revolution (MNR) and Victor Paz Estenssoro to power. As president, he nationalized the tin mines, reduced the army in favor of the popular militia, proclaimed universal suffrage, and, in the wake of land claims by the Indians, launched an agrarian reform.

The MNR governments lasted, through reelection, from 1952 to 1964 and its policies modernized and integrated Bolivian society. In 1964 a military coup took over and military governments were in power in Bolivia until 1982. Since then the redemocratization process is being built on the basis of strong neoliberal economic stabilization policies.

BOLIVIA — ARGENTINA see ARGENTINA–BOLIVIA.

BOLIVIA — BRAZIL Established in the late eighteenth century, this boundary mainly follows the line between the former Portuguese and Spanish possessions in South America. It runs for 2,113 miles (3,400 km.) from the boundary tripoint with Paraguay on the Paraguay River in the southeast to the boundary tripoint with Peru on the Acre River in the northwest.

Geographical Setting. The boundary tripoint with Paraguay is located at the confluence of the Negro (Otuquis) and Paraguay rivers (20°10'00.21"S and 58°10'11.14"W), north of Bahía Negra (Paraguay). The line follows the Paraguay River upstream northeastward for about 25 miles (40 km.), to a point west of Forte Coimbra (Brazil). There it leaves the river and runs in a straight line northwestward for another 25 miles (40 km.), reaching a small lake which is the source of the Negro River. Leaving the lake in Bolivia, the boundary runs in a straight line northeastward for 110 miles (177 km.) but forms a diversion eastward so as to leave the Caceres Lake in Bolivia. The boundary reaches the southern shore of Lake Mardiorè, runs in a straight line eastward to the Paraguay River and runs back to the lake in a northwesterly direction. The boundary follows the northeastern shore of the lake, leaving it in Bolivia and then, in a straight line, runs northwestward to the Guaiba (Gaiba) Lake. It crosses this lake and the nearby Uberaba Lake, reaching the mouth of the Candelaria River in that lake. The boundary follows the river northwestward to its confluence with the Las Petas River and follows the latter upstream northward to its confluence with one of its northern tributaries, which it follows to its source northeast of San Matías (Bolivia). Thence the boundary runs in a straight line westward for about 125 miles (200 km.) and north-northwest for about 90 miles (145 km.) to the Tarvo River. It follows the Tarvo River upstream eastward for 15 miles (24 km.) and in a straight line northward it reaches the source of the

Bolivia, a landlocked country in South America

Verde River, which it follows downstream northward to its confluence with the Iténez River. Along that river westward, the line reaches its confluence with the Paraguá River, where the two rivers become the Guaporé River. It follows the main navigation channel of the Guaporé River downstream westward for about 260 miles (420 km.) to its confluence with the Mamoré River. Thence it follows the Mamoré River downstream northward for some 180 miles (290 km.) to its confluence with the Abuná River, a tributary of the Madeira River and the Abuná River upstream westward to its confluence with the Rapirra River. This river is followed upstream to its source and then in a short straight line the boundary meets the Xipamanu River, follows it upstream westward to its source and in another straight line arrives at a southern tributary of the Acre River. It follows that tributary downstream to its confluence with the Acre River, north of Cobija (Bolivia), and follows the Acre River upstream westward until it reaches the tripoint with Peru between the small towns of Bolpebra (Bolivia) and Iñapari (Peru).

Historical Background. The Treaty of San Ildefonso (1 October 1777) placed the boundary between the Portuguese and Spanish possessions in central South America along a line that ran from Lake Caceres along the Paraguay River, the Jauru River and a straight line to the Guaporé River, the Guaporé River to its confluence with the Mamoré River, down the Mamoré and Madeira rivers to a point equidistant from the Marañón River and the mouth of the Mamoré and along an east–west line to the east bank of the Javari River.

Brazil became an independent kingdom in 1822, while Bolivia gained independence in 1825, and both initially adopted the colonial line as their common boundary. From 1837 onward a series of negotiations took place in order to establish the exact boundary line. Brazil wanted to place it west of the Mardiorè, Uberaba and Guaiba lakes, while Bolivia wanted to draw the line from the Paraguay River to the mouth of the Jauru, leaving the lakes within Bolivia. A treaty signed at La Paz on 27 March 1867 defined a line that divided the lakes between the two states and then followed the principles of the 1777 colonial line. Bolivia thus acknowledged Brazil's entitlement to an area of some 540,000 sq. miles

(1,398,060 sq. km.) of land along the Paraguay and Madeira rivers. Peru's boundaries with Brazil and Bolivia were not yet settled, leading Peru to protest the 1867 treaty, claiming that some of its territory was included in it, but these claims were ignored. The demarcation commission could not agree on the precise location of the line until 1896 and in 1874 a new dispute arose concerning the location of the source of the Javari River.

In the early years of the twentieth century the Acre area in northwestern Bolivia was disputed between the two states, as Bolivia tried to developed the rubber-plant area, which was a target for fortune seekers from Brazil and other regions. By a treaty signed at Petrópolis on 17 November 1903 the Acre area became Brazilian territory in exchange for a smaller parcel given to Bolivia (and the sum of £2 million)—and a new boundary line was delimited. A protocol of instructions for the demarcation commission was signed on 6 February 1907. The construction of new railways in the Acre area led to further demarcation in 1911 and another commission worked on the central section of the line in 1925. The final treaty, which settled minor problems and established the present line, was signed at Rio de Janeiro on 25 December 1928.

Present Situation. Since 1928 there have been no major disputes concerning the boundary's alignment. The Chaco Boreal War of 1932–1935 between Paraguay and Bolivia caused major changes in their common boundaries, but this never affected the boundary between Bolivia and Brazil, which has remained stable to date.

BOLIVIA — CHILE The boundary between Bolivia and Chile runs for 535 miles (861 km.) in the Andes Mountains, from the tripoint boundary junction with Peru in the north to the boundary junction with Argentina in the south. Most of the boundary consists of straight lines connecting mountain peaks.

Geographical Setting. Starting in the north at the boundary junction with Peru, located at 17°29'55.0"S and 69°28'28.8"W, the boundary runs southeastward in a straight line to boundary marker no. 94, east of the Chilean town of Visviri. In a straight line to the outlet of the Caquena (Cosapilla) River, the boundary follows its course downstream to Mount Carbiri. It trends along the local watershed southeastward, through 11 local peaks, up to Mount Toldo, west of Pisiga Socre (Bolivia), and in another straight line continues toward Panantala and southward along the mountain's ridge to Cerro Puguintica. Continuing in a series of straight lines southwestward to the summit of Torony and along the ridge southeastward to Mount Patalani, it then forms a series of straight lines connecting named peaks in a southerly direction. In some places the boundary follows local ridges instead of straight lines. It reaches the high point of Volcán Ollagüe (Oyahue), a volcanic peak at an altitude of 18,258 feet (5,990 m.) above sea level, just south of the Chilean city of Ollagüe, where the Antofagasta (Chilean coast)–Uyuni (Bolivia) railway crosses the boundary line. Further southward the line passes through Cerro de Tocorpuri (20,467 feet; 6,715 m.), the highest point of the boundary line, and reaches Mount Licancábur, another volcanic peak. Changing its direction, it runs east for about 50 miles (80 km.) to reach the boundary junction with Argentina, located on the highest peak of Cerro Zapaleri (Sapaleri) at an altitude of 18,641 feet (5,681 m.).

Historical Background. The original boundary between Bolivia and Chile dates back to the Spanish colonial period. When Bolivia became independent from Spain in 1825 it claimed the entire maritime territory westward, from the Andes to the Pacific Ocean, between the Salado River in the south and the Loa River in the north. Following the discovery of nitrate deposits in the Atacama Desert, Chile included that area in its claims. In the Treaty of Territorial Limits between Chile and Bolivia, signed in Santiago on 10 August 1866, it was agreed that their common boundary would follow the 24°S parallel. However, in February 1879, after a year of disputes concerning taxation on the production of the desert nitrate deposits, Chile occupied part of the Bolivian coastal area, thus beginning the Pacific War—in which Peru joined forces with Bolivia. The Chilean forces won the war and according to the terms of the truce signed in Valparaíso (Chile) by Bolivia and

Volcanic peak near the Bolivia–Chile boundary

Chile on 4 April 1884 Bolivia lost its Pacific littoral area south of the 23°S parallel, including the district of the port city of Antofagasta. The area north of the 23°S parallel, up to the Peruvian boundary on the Loa River, was to be administrated by Chile. A new boundary between this Chilean administrative region and Bolivia was established between the boundary tripoint with Argentina (Zapaleri Peak) and the Olca Peak on the 21°S parallel. A railway between the port city of Antofagasta and the Bolivian city of Uyuni gave Bolivia access to the Pacific

The Bolivia–Chile boundary

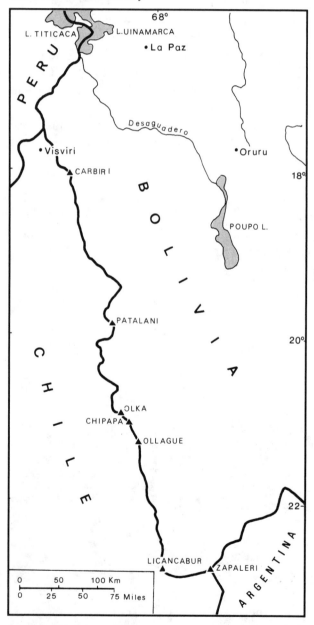

Ocean, thus easing its claim toward the Pacific coast. On 20 October 1904 a peace treaty between the two countries delimited the boundary through 96 detailed points, and boundary pillars were erected shortly after. Modifications were made in 1907 as Chile received an area that would enable the administration of a local railway, while Bolivia gained a parcel of land in the mountainous region. Another railway was constructed in 1913 between the Bolivian capital of La Paz and the Pacific port city of Arica (Chile), affording Bolivia a second route to the sea. The 1929 treaty between Chile and Peru gave the entire Pacific littoral area to Chile, up to Arica, thus extending the boundary between Bolivia and Chile northward along the former Peru–Bolivia boundary, up to the present tripoint with Peru, north of Charaña (Bolivia).

Present Situation. In 1962 Chile constructed a dam to divert the waters of the Lauca River, which flow into Bolivia, for irrigation. Bolivia was disquieted and the dispute was forwarded to be settled by the Organization of American States. Bolivia continues its aspirations for a territorial outlet to the Pacific Ocean. Despite these tensions there are no known disputes concerning the alignment of the present boundary.

BOLIVIA — PARAGUAY   The boundary between these two landlocked countries extends 466 miles (746 km.) between the boundary tripoint with Brazil on the Pilcomayo River and the boundary junction with Argentina on the Paraguay River, in the Chaco Boreal region of central South America.

Geographical Setting. The Bolivia–Paraguay boundary line runs in a series of straight lines connecting 11 boundary pillars. It begins in the *thalweg* (the deepest navigable channel) of the Pilcomayo river at the tripoint of Argentina, Paraguay and Bolivia near a point called La Esmeralda. From there it travels northeast for 85 miles (138 km.) to a point situated about 6 miles (10 km.) east of Puesto Estralla (Paraguay), and then directly northward to a point west of Villazon (Paraguay) on the Pan American Highway. Northeastward to boundary pillar no. 4 near Fortín Gabino Mendoza (Paraguay), the line continues up to boundary pillar no. 5 at Cerro Guarani (Cerro Capitan Ustares). From there the boundary line turns eastward for about 75 miles

Bolivia–Paraguay boundary

(120 km.) to the intersection of the Fortín Ravelo (Bolivia)–Fortín Ingavi (Paraguay) road with the southern limit of the Fortín Palmar de las Islas ravine and continues in a straight line to pillar no. 7 south of Fortín Paredes. It then stretches eastward to the highest point of Cerro Chovoreca, where it changes direction southeastward to Cerrito Jara in the Bambarral River. Without changing direction, the boundary line crosses the river to boundary pillar no. 10 in Rio Negro, following the *thalweg* of that river for 26 miles (42 km.) to its confluence with the Paraguay River, the boundary tripoint with Brazil. Each of the boundary pillars is strongly lodged in the ground.

Historical Background. Bolivia and Paraguay became independent in the first quarter of the nineteenth century. From then on the two countries disagreed on the ownership of the territory located between the Pilcomayo and Paraguay rivers, both claiming that the disputed area belonged to the Spanish provinces that became their respective independent states. For many years the two countries attempted to settle the dispute, but the endeavors proved futile until 1938. The first Bolivian-Paraguayan boundary treaty was signed on 15 October 1879 after the War of the Triple Alliance, in which Paraguay was defeated by Brazil, Argentina and Uruguay, but this was not approved by the Paraguayan Congress. Another treaty was signed on 17 February 1887 to replace the former treaty—but

again it was not ratified by Paraguay. A third treaty was signed in 1894, only to be rejected once again by the Paraguayan Congress, as it was considered unsatisfactory for the fulfillment of Paraguayan historical and national claims. On 12 January 1907 an agreement providing for the submission of the boundary dispute to the arbitration of the president of Argentina was signed. This time it was Bolivia that opposed the proposal and in 1913 declared the 1907 agreement void. Paraguayan settlers meanwhile established themselves in the disputed areas and Paraguay demanded possession of the region. In the Washington Conference of December 1928 an inquiry commission was established to investigate the boundary problem but never reached any agreement. In 1932 the Chaco War between Paraguay and Bolivia broke out and only after three years of fighting and the loss of some 60,000 Bolivian lives, Paraguay gained most of the disputed area. On 21 July 1938 a Treaty of Peace, Friendship and Boundaries was signed between Bolivia and Paraguay, by which a mixed commission, including representatives of Argentina, Brazil, Chile, Peru, Uruguay and the United States, was to settle the boundary problem. An agreement on the delineation of the line was finally reached in October 1938; in February 1939 a commission was appointed to demarcate the boundary. The agreement encompassed the entire length of the boundary, except for pillar no. 8, which was resolved in 1969, in Paraguay's favor.

Present Situation. As of 1969 the boundary between the two states has not been the cause of any contention.

BOLIVIA — PERU The Bolivia–Peru boundary generally follows the Spanish colonial division between its provinces in colonial South America. It is 560 miles (900 km.) long, extending northward from the boundary tripoint with Chile to the boundary tripoint with Brazil.

Geographical Setting. The southern terminus of the boundary between Bolivia and Peru is located at 17°29'57"S and 69°28'28.8"W, about 12,980 feet (4,000 m.) above sea level. It runs northward in a straight line, crosses the Mauri River, and then bears northwest for about 30 miles (50 km.). It trends northeast along a local watershed to the Desaguadero River, which is followed downstream northward. The boundary crosses the main highway between Puno (Peru) and La Paz (the Bolivian capital) and reaches the southern shore of Lake Uinamarca at an altitude of 12,506 feet (3,813 m.) above sea level, at the mouth of Desaguadero River. The boundary crosses the southern section of the lake to reach and cross the peninsula between Lake Uinamarca and Lake Titicaca, leaving the Bolivian town of Copacabana in a unique position, whereby it can be entered by land only through Peruvian territory. The boundary reaches Lake Titicaca west of Copacabana, crosses it in a northwesterly direction and arrives at its northern shore west of the Bolivian town of Puerto Acosta. Thence, in a semicircle westward, the boundary reaches the Suchi River and follows it upstream northwestward to its source. From there it runs north along the watershed between the basins of the Madre de Dios and Beni rivers, reaching the source of Heath River. The line follows that river downstream northward to its confluence with the Madre de Dios River at the town of Puerto Heath (Bolivia). It crosses the river and runs in a straight line northwest for about 130 miles (210 km.) to the Brazilian tripoint in the Acre River, situated between the towns of Iñapari (Peru) and Bolpebra (Bolivia).

Historical Background. Both Bolivia and Peru were constituents of the Spanish viceroy of colonial Lima. Peru gained its independence in 1824 and Bolivia in 1825 and during the first years of independence the states fought each other for improved boundaries. A boundary treaty that was procured to be signed on 15 November 1826 was not ratified by Peru and the ensuing two years of war brought about a peace treaty on 6 July 1828, but only a treaty that was signed at Arequipa on 8 November 1831 called for a boundary commission to delimit their common boundary line. Peru and Bolivia were

Lake Titicaca on the Bolivia–Peru boundary

united between 1835 and 14 August 1839 and then a new boundary was established between the separated states. Another war (1841–1842) brought about another treaty of friendship, signed on 3 November 1847, reiterating the 1831 boundary. No further progress was made and 16 years later, on 5 November 1863 it was agreed once again to define the common boundary.

The disputes concerning the boundary's alignment and the changes that took place during the War of the Pacific (1879–1884) between Bolivia and Peru on one side and Chile on the other, were ended by the treaty of peace signed at Ancón in October 1883 and promoted another boundary treaty that was signed by Bolivia and Peru at La Paz on 20 April 1886. This treaty again provided for a boundary commission to fix their common boundary line.

On 23 September 1902 a treaty concerning the demarcation of the new boundary was signed at La Paz. However, the boundary disputes were still not solved as Bolivia transferred the Acre region to Brazil on 17 November 1903, thus changing the position of its boundary with Peru. Bolivia and Peru agreed to submit their dispute for arbitration to the president of Argentina on 15 May 1906 and the award, accorded in Buenos Aires on 9 July 1909, gave Bolivia 22,000 sq. miles (57,000 sq. km.) of the disputed area and Peru 33,000 sq. miles (85,500 sq. km.), thereby establishing a new boundary line between the two states. Bolivia initially refused to accept the award but later both states signed a protocol effecting changes on 17 September 1909. A demarcation team was appointed on 15 April 1911 but only on 2 June 1925 was a demarcation agreement signed.

Present Situation. In 1925, after 100 years of boundary disputes, the line was established and for the next 70 years no disputes concerning its alignment were raised by Bolivia or Peru. Thus, the boundary is a peaceful demarcated line accepted by both states.

BOSNIA (AND HERZEGOVINA)   A southeastern European country situated in the Balkan Peninsula, Bosnia (area: 19,741 sq. miles [51,109 sq. km.]; estimated population: 4,400,000 [1994]) was part of the former Yugoslavia until 1991. Bosnia is bounded in the northwest and south by Croatia (523.5 miles; 842 km.) and in the east by Serbia (328 miles; 527 km.). It has an outlet to the Adriatic Sea in the south, cutting through Croatian territory. Bosnia's capital is Sarajevo.

Bosnia-Herzegovina, like its neighbors, Serbia and Croatia, was settled by Slavic tribes during the sixth and seventh centuries. However, the Slavs of Bosnia-Herzegovina were late in consolidating a unified political and cultural entity because they were subject to political and religio-cultural pressures from the two neighboring kingdoms. Only in the thirteenth century was a strong state created in Bosnia-Herzegovina, which reached its zenith during the rule of Tvrtko I (1353–1391), who assumed the title of king.

To withstand these pressures from east and west and to emphasize their independence, the Bosnian rulers adopted the Bogomil church (which originated in Bulgaria) and encouraged its spread. Yet the growing Ottoman threat made them turn for help to the west and yield to the pope's demands to suppress the "heresy." This in turn facilitated the final Ottoman conquest of the country (1461–1483) and its incorporation into the empire. It is believed that following the Ottoman conquest the bulk of the Bogomil following, as well as most of the nobility, converted to Islam, thus creating a massive Muslim population in Bosnia-Herzegovina.

During the Ottoman period the Bosnian Muslims were members of the *stadtsvolk* and as such contributed their share to the empire's administration and military. In Bosnia-Herzegovina itself they formed the majority in the cities, and former *bojars* (nobles) continued to rule the country as Ottoman officials, and since the seventeenth century as almost completely autonomous rulers. In the nineteenth century these Muslim *beks* and *agas* led a series of revolts against the attempts at modernization and centralization of the central authorities. The last of these revolts sparked off the great Balkan crisis of 1875–1878, following which Bosnia-Herzegovina was put under Austro-Hungarian administration.

During the period of Austro-Hungarian rule (1878–1918) and that of the new kingdom of Yugoslavia (1918–1941), the Muslims lost first their political and then—due to agrarian reforms promulgated by Yugoslavia—their economic superiority and tended to abstain from the new national politics.

Under Austro-Hungarian encouragement they developed their own communal institutions, which were kept apart from those of the rest of the Muslims in Yugoslavia, during the monarchy. The strong efforts by both Serbs and Croats to woo the Muslims to their fold failed, as was clearly demonstrated in the 1953 census when only 3.9% of the Muslims declared themselves Serbs and less than 1.7% Croats. The fact that almost 94.5% of the Muslims did not declare their nationality served as a justification for Tito to establish a separate People's Republic of Bosnia and Herzegovina.

Paradoxically, the communist regime in Yugoslavia seems to have promulgated a modern national identity and nationalism among the Bosnian Muslims. Until World War II the Muslims were the most conservative and least modernized community. The reforms promulgated by Tito, the forced opening-up of the community to outside contact, the rapid development of education, and the secularization process, taught Bosnian Muslims to express their identity in secular, nationalist terms, and showed them that only they were really interested in a separate Bosnian entity. The disintegration of Yugoslavia and the civil war in 1992 seem to have brought this process to its fruition.

BOSNIA — CROATIA

This boundary arches west and south, from the tripoint with Serbia on the Sava River to the tripoint with Serbia (Montenegro) southeast of Dubrovnik. The length of the boundary is 523.5 miles (842 km.).

Geographical Setting. From the tripoint junction with Serbia the boundary heads northward, following the Sava River upstream to the mouth of the Una River. It then runs along the Una upstream to Bosanski Novi (Bosnia), travelling through the hills on the river's right bank. Turning southwestward the boundary then follows the Pljesevica mountain, meeting the Una again south of the town of Bihac. The upper course of the Una River is then followed along the crest of the Dinaric Alps (Dinara), which run through the karstic areas of Dalmatian Zagora and Herzegovina. The boundary then enters the valley of the Neretva River, heads southwest and, northwest of Dubrovnik, cuts through Croatian territory, providing a narrow Bosnian exit to the Adriatic Sea at Neum. The final section of the boundary runs parallel to the coast a few miles inland to the boundary tripoint with Montenegro on Orjen Mountain.

Historical Background. The current boundary between Croatia and Bosnia-Herzegovina is the legacy of seventeenth- and eighteenth-century delimitations between Austrian Croatia, Ottoman Bosnia, Venetian Dalmatia and the former independent Republic of Dubrovnik. The northern section, along the Sava and Una rivers, was established by the Treaty of Karlowitz in 1699. Two minor parts of this section were later defined by the 1718 Treaty of Passarowitz. From Bihac to Dinara Mountain the line was determined by the Treaty of Sistova in 1791. Most of the boundary dividing the Croatian province of Dalmatia from Bosnia is based on the 'Linea Mocenigo' of Venetian Dalmatia in 1718. The Bosnian outlet to the Adriatic Sea at Neum was delimited in 1700 and the southeastern section of the boundary follows the frontier of the former Republic of Dubrovnik, which was established in the late fourteenth and early fifteenth centuries.

Throughout the nineteenth century and until 1918, the same line constituted the boundary between the Austrian (later Austro-Hungarian) provinces of Croatia-Slovenia and Dalmatia, which were unified under the Ottoman Empire, then becoming (since 1878) Austro-Hungarian Bosnia-Herzegovina. In 1945 the line was accepted as the boundary between the Yugoslav republics of Croatia and Bosnia-Herzegovina. The only changes that were made in the boundary line were carried out near Bihac in 1945 where a group of former Croatian villages was allotted to Bosnia, moving the line onto Pljesevica mountain. In the 1950s a few minor changes were made. In 1991 Bosnia and Croatia became independent from Yugoslavia and adopted the existing provincial boundaries.

Present Situation. Although the boundary line has been internationally recognized since 1992, its status is seriously disputed in practise. There are small self-proclaimed Serbian states on both sides of the border (the Serbian Republic of Krajina in Croatia and the Serbian Republic in Bosnia-Herzegovina), that share and control most of the boundary line. These units have openly sought to merge into one. The Serb-held Croatian borderland has been under international control as a United Nations Protected Area (UNPA Sectors West, North and South) since

March 1992. The future status of the boundary depends upon the resolution of the national dispute in Bosnia.

BOSNIA — SERBIA The boundary between Bosnia and Serbia runs for 328 miles (527 km.), from the tripoint with Croatia on the Sava River southward to a second boundary tripoint with Croatia near the Adriatic coast. Most of the boundary (203 miles; 326 km.) runs along rivers. Its northern section is the boundary between Bosnia and Serbia (194 miles; 312 km.), while the southern section is the boundary between Bosnia and Serbia (Montenegro) (134 miles; 215 km.).

Geographical Setting. From the northern boundary junction the line follows the Sava River and then turns generally southward to follow the Drina River. North of Visegrad it leaves the river and runs along the mountains on its right bank southeastward. Heading southwest it reaches the Tara River and follows it northwest to its confluence with the Piva River, which it follows south for a short distance. It then runs southwest through the high Maglic, Volujak and Golija mountains and meets the Croatian tripoint on the slopes of Orjen Mountain.

Historical Background. The present boundary between Bosnia and Serbia was established in the nineteenth century, during the Turkish Ottoman rule in the area. The boundary divided Bosnia and the Principality of Serbia, gradually developing between 1815 and 1833. It remained unchanged after the Congress of Berlin (1878), when Bosnia came under the influence of Austria-Hungary and Serbia was recognized as an independent state. Only the section south of the Lim River (toward the Tara River and southward) was delimited after the Balkan Wars of 1912–1913 and Serbia's expansion into the former Turkish sanjak of Novi Pazar. Both Ottoman and Austro-Hungarian Bosnia-Herzegovina had a narrow exit to the sea (Sutorina Strip) at the Bay of Kotor. In 1945 this area was assigned to Montenegro. Besides these modifications, the nineteenth-century boundary was accepted as a republican boundary between Bosnia-Herzegovina and Serbia and Montenegro after World War II.

Present Situation. Due to the war in Bosnia-Herzegovina, its boundary with Serbia is beyond the power of the Bosnian government. The entire borderland is under the control of rebelling Bosnian Serbs and their self-proclaimed Serbian Republic, which aims to unite with Serbia. Thus, the future status of the boundary is uncertain.

BOTSWANA Situated in southern Africa, Botswana is an arid country (area: 224,606 sq. miles [581,730 sq. km.]; estimated population: 1,400,000 [1994]), desert covering more then three quarters of its area. Botswana is a landlocked state, bounded in the west and north by Namibia (845 miles; 1,360 km.), northeast by Zambia at a junction point and Zimbabwe (505 miles; 813 km.) and east and south by South Africa (1,144 miles; 1,840 km.). The capital of Botswana is Gaborone.

In Botswana, the British ruled the Tswana indirectly through rural committees. When Botswana gained its independence in 1966, the government recommended major changes in the administration of rural committees in order to weaken the position of the traditional chiefs. Botswana became a multiparty democracy after independence.

BOTSWANA — NAMIBIA The boundary between these two countries mostly follows the rigid lines of longitude and latitude. From the tripoint with South Africa it heads north, then east and north again. It then follows a river to the boundary junction with Zambia and Zimbabwe. The total length of this boundary is 845 miles (1,360 km.).

Geographical Setting. Starting at the tripoint with South Africa, where the Nossob River intersects the 20°E meridian, the boundary heads directly northward, along the meridian and across the Kalahari Desert for approximately 180 miles (290 km.). As it meets 22°S, close to the settlement of Rietfontein, the line forms a right angle eastward to 21°E. Although physical marking of this section of boundary was difficult, as the terrain consists of permanent sand dunes, the demarcation was carried out. Another straight line is followed northward along this meridian for about 250 miles (400 km.), and then the boundary heads eastward, along the Caprivi Strip toward Chobe River. The boundary enters the *thalweg* of the river and reaches its confluence with the Zambezi River.

Historical Background. In 1833 a German merchant obtained land concessions from a local chief

Botswana and its boundaries

on the coast of southwestern Africa at Angra Pequena (Lüderitz), which extended from the northern bank of the Orange River to the 26th parallel and 20 miles (30 km.) inland. Germany claimed a protectorate over this area on 16 August 1884 and on 8 September of that year also declared the coast north of the 26th parallel up to Cape Fria to be under German protection, with the exception of the Walvis Bay area, which was claimed by United Kingdom. Further expansion inland soon increased German

South-West Africa to the present size of Namibia. Germany ceded its colonies to the Allies by the Treaty of Versailles (1919) after World War I and on 17 December 1920 the administration of South-West Africa was mandated by the League of Nations to South Africa. After World War II and the dissolution of the League of Nations the United Nations (UN) refused South Africa permission to annex South-West Africa and in turn South Africa refused to place the territory under a UN trusteeship agreement, claiming that the UN did not automatically replace the League of Nations. On 27 October 1966 the UN terminated South Africa's mandate, South-West Africa becoming a direct responsibility of the UN. By a UN resolution of 12 June 1968 South-West Africa became Namibia and in 1971 South Africa's presence there was declared illegal.

Botswana emerged as the British government concluded treaties with the chief of the Batlaping tribe on 3 May 1884 and with the chief of the Barolong tribe on 22 May 1884, conferring power and jurisdiction of the chiefs' territories to Britain. On 27 January 1885 the High Commissioner for South Africa issued a proclamation declaring a British protectorate over the areas of Bechuanaland, south of 22°S. The limits of the protectorate, as far north as the Zambezi River, were defined by the orders in council of 30 June 1890 and 9 May 1891. By an order in council of 3 October 1895 the Cape of Good Hope colony was given authority to annex British Bechuanaland. Botswana gained independence on 30 September 1966.

The alignment of the boundary between the two spheres of influence was first determined by the 1890 Anglo-German Agreement. This essentially constituted the present boundary between Botswana and Namibia. It was defined from the Nossob River up to 18°S and 21°E. The northern sector of the boundary (the Caprivi Strip), however, was not demarcated in the 1890 agreement, although references were made to the 18°S parallel. It seems that the northern sector was settled by an informal arrangement initiated by the British government, which was concerned with policing the strip at the time. The Colonial Office commented upon German maps that placed the northern boundary parallel to 18°S, hence making the width of the strip greater than 20 miles (30 km.) and incompatible with the 1890 agreement. Accordingly the British Government produced a map that illustrated the boundary line along the 21st meridian and then in a straight line eastward to Chobe River. Since around 1914 this view of the boundary has been accepted.

Present Situation. Since Botswana and Namibia have become independent there have been no major disputes regarding the boundary, despite uncertainty early in the twentieth century concerning the northern boundary line along the Caprivi Strip. However,

there is an ongoing dispute over the sovereignty of an island in the Chobe River.

BOTSWANA — SOUTH AFRICA   The boundary between Botswana and South Africa is 1,144 miles (1,840 km.) long and follows rivers for 90% of its length. It runs from the tripoint junction with Zimbabwe in the east to the tripoint with Namibia in the west. It is almost entirely demarcated, the small sectors that do not follow rivers being marked by physical features as hills, ridges and beacons. The principal rivers that form the boundary are the Limpopo, Molopo and Nossob.

Geographical Setting. From the boundary tripoint with Namibia, at the intersection of the Nossob River with 20°E, the course of the river is followed southeast, through Kalahari Gemsbok National Park to the confluence with the Molopo River. The boundary follows the course of the Molopo River northeast for 404 miles (650 km.) to the Ramatlhabama pool. From this point beacons are used to demarcate the boundary for a short distance, across the Dwarsberg mountain range to the Notwani River. The line then proceeds along the course of the Notwani River for a short distance and then beacons are again used northeastward to a point north of the town of Derdepoort, where the boundary intersects the Marico River. Along this river the line traverses through a low range of hills into the Limpopo River, which it follows to the tripoint with Zimbabwe.

Historical Background. In May 1884 the British government gained power and jurisdiction over tribal territories in southern Africa and in 1885 a British protectorate was proclaimed over Bechuanaland, south of 22°S. The total area of the British protectorate, up to the Zambezi River in the north, was defined by orders in council on 30 June 1890 and on 9 May 1891. British Bechuanaland was annexed to the Cape of Good Hope in 1895. The remaining area—Botswana—gained independence on 30 September 1966.

The Cape of Good Hope was ceded to Britain by the Dutch in 1814. To escape British rule Afrikaner farmers began to move northward (the Great Trek) and settled in the Orange Free State, Transvaal and Western Natal. Natal was annexed to the Colony of the Cape of Good Hope by Britain in 1843 and became a separate colony in 1856. Transvaal became

Botswana–South Africa crossing point

independent in 1852 and later became the South African Republic. In 1848 the governor of the Cape of Good Hope issued a proclamation declaring British sovereignty as far north as the Vaal River and eastward to the Drakensberg Mountains. In 1851 the Orange River territory, covering the regions north of the Orange River, established an independent government and on 23 February 1854 became the independent Boer Republic of the Orange Free State. Britain annexed the Orange Free State as the Orange River Colony, and the South African Republic as Transvaal during the Boer War (1899–1902). The Union of South Africa, a British dominion, was created on 31 May 1910, consisting of the Cape of Good Hope, the Orange River Colony, Natal and Transvaal. It became a sovereign state in 1931 and the Republic of South Africa on 31 May 1961.

The boundary between Botswana and independent Transvaal was established in the Pretoria Convention of 3 August 1881 and the sector from the tripoint with Zimbabwe to the Ramatlhabama pool was confirmed in the London Convention of February 1884. The western sector of the boundary, from the Namibian tripoint adjacent to the Cape of Good Hope province as far as the Ramatlhabama pool, was established as the northern boundary of British Bechuanaland in the proclamation of September 1885. It was restated by the British Order in Council of October 1895.

In 1961 South Africa gained complete independence and in 1968 representatives of the South African and Botswana governments signed a joint report on the boundary, in general adopting the line settled by the London Convention of 1884 and agreeing that unmarked sectors should be fenced.

Present Situation. There are no reported disputes regarding the boundary. However, the Sotho territories of the Tswana people were partitioned by the creation of British Bechuanaland and its annexation to the Cape of Good Hope at the end of the nineteenth century. Tswana groups remain dispersed between Botswana and the South African Tswana homeland of Bophuthatswana.

BOTSWANA — ZIMBABWE The boundary that runs between Botswana and Zimbabwe is 505 miles

(813 km.) long and runs generally southeastward. It begins at the quadripoint with Namibia and Zambia and extends to the confluence of the Shashi and Limpopo rivers. The boundary is almost entirely demarcated by rivers and pillars.

Geographical Setting. From the disputed quadripoint with Namibia and Zambia at the intersection of the Chobe and Zambezi rivers, the boundary travels southeast down the Pandamatenga (Hunter's) Road for 220 miles (354 km.). It takes an upland route, passing through several national parks and skirting a number of salt pans. Continuing southeast past an intersection with the Manzamnyama River and entering another upland region, the line reaches the watershed between the Ramaquabane and Shashi rivers and the headwaters of the Ramaquabane. The boundary then follows the river out of the mountainous region to its confluence with the Shashi River. It courses along the Shashi River, leaving it to form a 10-mile (16-km.) radius west of the town of Tuli (Zimbabwe) and returning to the Shashi River down to its confluence with the Limpopo River at the tripoint with South Africa.

Historical Background. In May 1884 the British government concluded treaties with the chief of the Batlaping tribe and with the chief of the Barolong tribe, thus assuming power and jurisdiction over their territories. Almost a year later, on 27 January 1885, the High Commissioner for South Africa declared a British protectorate over Bechuanaland areas, south of latitude 22°S. The limits of the protectorate, including the tribal and Bechuanaland areas, as far north as the Zambezi River, were set by orders in council in 1890 and 1891. However, this area was reduced in size as an order in council (3 October 1891) allocated British Bechuanaland to the colony of the Cape of Good Hope. The annexation took place on 16 November 1895. The remaining area became Botswana, which gained independence on 30 September 1966.

The area east and north of Bechuanaland, later to become Southern and Northern Rhodesia, was proclaimed a British sphere of influence in 1888. In 1889 Cecil Rhodes's British South Africa Company was granted a charter to operate in an imprecisely defined area between the Zambezi River and Bechuanaland. By an order in council of 18 July 1894 the Company became responsible for the administration of Matabeleland. Some areas of Bechuanaland were transferred to the Company in 1895, between the Shashi and Macloutsie rivers, but these transfers were rescinded after objections from some Tswana chiefdoms.

In the Administrator's Proclamation of 1 May 1895, defining the boundaries of provinces and districts under the administration of the British South Africa Company, a substantial part of the northern sector of the boundary was established along the Pandamatenga Road. The charter of the British South Africa Company was abrogated in 1923 and Southern Rhodesia was annexed by Britain as a self-governing colony. From 1 August 1953 to 31 December 1963 it belonged to the Federation of Rhodesia and Nyasaland. On 11 November 1965 it made a unilateral declaration of independence which was not recognized by Britain and in 1970 declared itself a republic. In 1980 Britain finally acknowledged Southern Rhodesia's independence, which then became Zimbabwe.

Present Situation. No disputes are known to exist over the alignment of the Botswana–Zimbabwe boundary, although its terminus point on the Zambezi River in the northwest is unspecified, leading to some controversy over whether it shares a boundary junction with Namibia and Zambia.

BRAZIL (Brasil) The largest country of South America (area: 3,285,650 sq. miles [8,509,833 sq. km.]; estimated population: 159,100,000 [1994]), Brazil is situated in the northeastern corner of the continent. It is bounded in the east, northeast and southeast by the Atlantic Ocean and on its northern, western and southern borders by all the South American countries except Ecuador and Chile. It is bounded in the north by French Guiana (418 miles; 673 km.), Suriname (371 miles; 597 km.), Guyana (695 miles; 1,119 km.) and Venezuela (1,367 miles; 2,200 km.), northwest by Colombia (1,022 miles; 1,644 km.), west by Peru (970 miles; 1,560 km.), southwest by Bolivia (2,113 miles; 3,400 km.), Paraguay (802 miles; 1,290 km.) and Argentina (761 miles; 1,224 km.) and south by Uruguay (612 miles; 985 km.). The capital of Brazil is Brasília.

The history of Brazil has had a direct impact on the development of the country's social and cultural patterns. After having been a Portuguese colony for nearly 300 years, Brazilians saw the arrival of Portugal's king João VI in 1807, when he fled the imminent invasion of his country by enemy forces. He brought with him some of the aristocratic customs of the royal court. Thirteen years later he was called back to Lisbon, and left the crown in his son's hands. In 1822 Pedro I declared Brazil a sovereign empire, cutting it loose from the mother-country without bloodshed. He and his son Pedro II ruled the empire until 1889, when the country was proclaimed a federated republic.

Brazil—near the Brazil–French Guiana border

BRAZIL — ARGENTINA see ARGENTINA–BRAZIL.

BRAZIL — BOLIVIA see BOLIVIA–BRAZIL.

BRAZIL — COLOMBIA The boundary between Brazil and Colombia is approximately 1,022 miles (1,644 km.) long, running between the boundary junction with Venezuela in the Rio Negro in the north and the boundary junction with Peru in the Amazon River in the south. About 502 miles (808 km.) of the boundary follow rivers, while 381 miles (613 km.) are straight lines and 139 miles (223 km.) are watershed lines.

Geographical Setting. The northeastern terminus of the boundary is marked by a stone located on the San Jose island in the Rio Negro at 1°13'27.2"N and 66°50'54.2"W. The island itself is split horizontally between Brazil and Colombia. The boundary runs westward to the right (western) bank of the Rio Negro and from there in a straight line to the head of the Macacuní Stream, a tributary of the Rio Negro. The boundary line then follows the watershed between the Xie' and Tomo rivers west, south and north as far as Cerro Caparro and finally reaching the main source of the Memachí River. Turning southward, the boundary line crosses elevated regions to a stream that is the main tributary of the Cuiarí River. The boundary traverses the course of the stream until it converges with the Cuiarí River, which it follows southeastward as far as its confluence with the Pegua River. The boundary line leaves the river at that point and travels in a straight line westward, along the parallel of the confluence to reach the Içana River. It follows that river westward to a point marked 1°42'57.3"N and 69°50'41.7"W. Southward along that meridian, the boundary line runs in a straight line to reach the Uaupés (Vaupés) River at its confluence with the Kerary (Querarí) River. The boundary courses along the Uaupés River eastward and then southward to its confluence with the Papurí River. Thence it follows the Papurí River westward to a point located at 0°33'47.6"N and 70°02'37.3"W and continues along the meridian southward to reach the Taraíra (Tracra) River, which is followed southeastward to its confluence with the Apaporis River. The boundary extends along the Apaporis southward to its confluence with the Japurá (Caquetá) River. Again in a straight line, the boundary stretches south-southwest to the Brazilian town of Tabatinga on the left (northern) bank of the Amazon River, and from there continues for a short distance to the tripoint boundary junction with Peru, at 4°13'30.5"S and 69°56'33.7"W.

Historical Background. The boundary between Brazil and Colombia originated in the late fifteenth century, when, in 1494, Pope Alexander VI bisected the world into Spanish and Portuguese domains by the Treaty of Tordesillas. A line was drawn from the North to the South Pole, running west of the Cape Verde Islands, opinions on its exact location varying between 42°30'W and 49°45'W. This line provided Portugal with a foothold in the central Amazon basin. For 250 years Spain and Portugal tried to delimit their common boundary in South America as their colonial empires expanded. In the treaties of Madrid (1750) and San Ildefonso (1777) a new line was established, placing the boundary on a straight line running from north to south through the confluence of the Marañón (Amazon) and Javari rivers (the present tripoint boundary between Peru, Colombia and Brazil), thousands of miles inland from the 1494 line. The empire of Brazil (independent from 1822) and the Republic of Gran Colombia (independent from 1819) made several attempts to define an acceptable boundary but these were abortive due to conflicting territorial claims among other Spanish successor states and the lack of reliable information concerning the geography of the disputed area. Gran Colombia's border disputes with Venezuela and Peru affected its border negotiations with Brazil. Venezuela and Brazil agreed on a common boundary between the Memachí and Negro rivers in 1859, which also involved an area claimed by Gran Colombia, which subsequently protested the agreement. Colombia, which became an independent republic in 1886, gained hold of the disputed territory in 1891, the delimited section of the Brazil–Venezuela boundary thus becoming part of the Brazil–Colombia boundary, although it took another 16 years to reach an agreement concerning the boundary's northern section. In 1907 a treaty signed in Bogotá, Colombia, established the boundary between the "Island of San Jose, opposite the Stone of Cocuy" on the Rio Negro and the confluence of the Apaporis and Caquetá rivers.

The southern section of the boundary results from the Brazil-Peru and Colombia-Peru boundary disputes. In 1851 Peru gained the disputed area between the Apaporis-Caquetá confluence and the Brazilian town of Tabatinga on the Amazon River. Colombia protested, claiming previous possession of the region. For over 70 years the area remained in dispute between Peru and Colombia—until 1922, when Peru relinquished all claims to the disputed

territory. It took another 12 years and the involvement of the League of Nations to reach a final agreement in 1934, which confirmed the 1922 settlement. The boundary between Peru and Brazil in the debated area became the Brazil–Colombia boundary. After some protest, Peru also signed the Rio de Janeiro agreement of 1928, accepting the old boundary with Peru as the southern section of its boundary with Colombia. From 1930 to 1936 a demarcation team established the exact line on the ground, making a few adjustments in the agreed line as the original descriptions had relied on faulty, inaccurate maps. The final authorization of the demarcation was made with an exchange of notes in 1937, which settled all the boundary disputes.

Present Situation. The settlement of 1937 ended over 440 years of boundary disputes. Since then no conflicts concerning the alignment of the boundary have been reported as neither of the countries has made further territory claims in the area.

BRAZIL — FRENCH GUIANA This is one of the rare land boundaries that still exists between a European colony and an independent state and reflects the prevalent relations between the French and Portuguese in South America. It runs from the mouth of the Oyapock (Oiapoque) River in the Atlantic Ocean in the northeast to the boundary tripoint with Suriname on the Itany (Litani) River in the southwest. The line is 418 miles (673 km.) long.

Geographical Setting. The northeastern terminus of the Brazil–French Guiana boundary is located in the middle of the estuary of the Oyapock River (where it enters the Atlantic Ocean), between the towns of Ponta dos Indios (Brazil) and Ouanary (French Guiana). The boundary follows the river inland southwestward for about 200 miles (320 km.) and reaches its source in the Tumuc-Humac Mountains (Serra Tumucumaque). It follows the watershed between the Jari River (Brazil) and the rivers that run north toward the Atlantic Ocean. The line extends through the Tumuc-Humac range for about 210 miles (340 km.), through its eastern and western peaks (1,476 feet [450 m.] and 2,274 feet [693 m.] respectively), and arrives at the boundary junction with Suriname, at the source of the Itany River, which then forms the southwestern section of the boundary between French Guiana and Suriname.

Historical Background. French traders established the town of Cayenne in 1635 on the northern coast of South America and the area of French Guiana became the property of the French crown in 1674. The area was occupied by the Portuguese from Brazil in 1809 but the French regained the area in 1817, after the Napoleonic era. The Franco-Portuguese treaty of 1815 and the convention of 28 August 1817 state that the eastern boundary of French Guiana is the Oyapock River, from its mouth in the Atlantic Ocean to its source, and that the southern section is the watershed between the Amazon basin and the rivers that run north toward the Atlantic Ocean, along the Tumuc-Humac range to Dutch Guiana. Brazil, which was under Portuguese rule from 1500, became an independent kingdom in 1822 and adopted the colonial line—which has never been changed since.

Present Situation. The boundary is located in an uninhabited jungle region and has not caused any known disputes concerning its alignment.

BRAZIL — GUYANA
The boundary between Brazil and Guyana runs for 695 miles (1,119 km.) between the boundary tripoint with Suriname at the source of the Kutari River in the east and the boundary tripoint with Venezuela on Mount Roraima in the northwest. It follows a colonial boundary between former British and Portuguese possessions in South America.

Geographical Setting. The eastern terminus of the boundary line is located in the source of the Kutari River, northwest of the Brazilian town of Aseonangka. It trends along Serra Acaraí on a watershed between some northern tributaries of the Amazon River (Cafuini, Tauini, Jauaperi, Caroaebe, Anauá) in the south and rivers that run north toward the Atlantic Ocean (Rupununi, New, Essequibo, Kwiparo). The line passes across the higher peaks of the range (2,972 feet [906 m.], 2,408 feet [734 m.] and 3,310 feet [1,009 m.]) and reaches the source of the Takutu (Tacutu) River. It follows the river downstream northward to its confluence with the Ireng River, north of the town of Lethem (Guyana) and follows the Ireng River upstream to its source in the Pakaraima Mountains. From Mount Caburai (4,777 feet; 1,456 m.) it heads westward, follows the watershed along the range and gains the boundary tripoint

with Venezuela on Mount Roraima (9,094 feet; 2,773 m.), the highest peak in northeast South America.

Historical Background. Guyana was a Dutch territory from the mid-seventeenth century and was acquired by Britain in 1799. The Dutch regained control of the area in 1802 but the British secured it again the following year and established the colony of British Guiana in 1831.

Brazil, which was ruled by the Portuguese from 1500, became an independent kingdom in 1822. Its boundary with British Guiana was never defined in the nineteenth century and it was assumed that the uninhabited range north of the Amazon basin was the boundary between Brazil and the European (British, French and Dutch) colonies of northern South America. In 1901, after long negotiations, Brazil and Britain agreed to accept arbitration, which was concluded in the arbitral decision given at Rome on 6 June 1904. It settled the disputed border between Brazil and British Guiana, although only on 22 April 1926 was it agreed to demarcate their boundary "along the watershed between the Amazon basin and the basins of the Essequibo and Courantyne rivers as far as the point of junction with Dutch Guiana." Ten years later, in 1936, Brazil, Britain and Netherlands (Dutch Guiana, later Suriname) agreed upon a boundary tripoint at the source of the Kutari River. British Guiana became independent in 1966, adopting the name Guyana and the 1926–1936 boundary with Brazil.

Present Situation. The Brazil–Guyana boundary line is demarcated and no disputes are known concerning its alignment.

BRAZIL — PARAGUAY
This boundary is 802 miles (1,290 km.) long and reaches northwestward from the boundary tripoint with Argentina at the confluence of the Paraná and Iguaçu (Iguazu) rivers to the boundary junction with Bolivia in the Paraguay River.

Geographical Setting. Setting out from the boundary junction with Argentina, at the confluence of the Paraná and Iguaçu rivers, the Brazil–Paraguay boundary follows the Paraná River upstream northward for approximately 120 miles (190 km.) to reach the Brazilian town of Guaria. There the boundary leaves the river and runs northwest and west along the watershed of the Maracaju Range to the town of Ypé Jhú (Paraguay). It then runs northward, following the watershed between the Paraná and Paraguay rivers, along Serra de Amambaí (Amambay Range). North of the town of Pedro Juan Caballero (Paraguay), the line reaches the source of the Apa River, which it follows downstream westward for about 130 miles (210 km.) to its confluence with the Paraguay River, west of San Lázaro (Paraguay). It heads north along the main navigation channel of the Paraguay River until it meets the Bolivian tripoint, which is located north of the town of Puerto Bahía Negra (Paraguay).

obtain a settlement that would allow free navigation of the rivers. In 1852 the Paraná River was declared free for navigation to vessels of all nations and subsequently, on 6 April 1856, Brazil and Paraguay signed a convention at Rio de Janeiro in which they agreed to settle their common boundary within six years, until then adopting the existing colonial line according to the *uti possidetis* principle. However, instead of a settlement, a war between the two states broke out in February 1865, in which Argentina and Uruguay joined Brazil against Paraguay in what became the Five Years' War. The three allies agreed to place the future boundary between Brazil and

Waterfalls on the Brazil–Paraguay boundary

Historical Background. The Spanish–Portuguese boundary northeast of Asunción (today a department of Paraguay) was fixed in the Treaty of San Ildefonso of 1 October 1777 along the Curitiba, Paraná, Iguary and Paraguay rivers with straight lines connecting them. Brazil became an independent kingdom in 1822 while Paraguay had gained independence in 1811. The boundary between the two independent states remained unsettled as both strove to

Paraguay according to Brazilian demands, which were forced on Paraguay in the treaty signed on 20 June 1870.

A boundary treaty between Brazil and Paraguay was signed at Asunción on 9 January 1872 and demarcation of the line was completed on 14 November 1874. The eastern section of the boundary line was established over 50 years later, when a complementary boundary treaty was signed on 21 May

1927 at Rio de Janeiro. The demarcation team worked between 1930 and 15 May 1932. Both states signed the South America Antiwar Pact of 10 October 1933, which declared that territorial questions ought not be settled by violence.

Present Situation. There are no known disputes concerning the alignment of this demarcated boundary line. Since 1932 the boundary has been peaceful and accepted by both states.

BRAZIL — PERU The Brazil–Peru boundary runs for 970 miles (1,560 km.) between the boundary junction with Bolivia on the Acre River in the south and boundary tripoint with Colombia at the confluence of the Amazon and Javari (Yavari) rivers in the north. It follows the eastern limit of the former Portuguese–Spanish colonial boundary in South America.

Geographical Setting. The boundary junction with Bolivia is located on the Acre River, between the

Brazil–Peru boundary

towns of Bolpebra (Bolivia) and Iñapari (Peru). It follows the Acre River upstream westward to its source and there continues westward for 12 miles (20 km.) to the 70°40'W meridian. It follows the meridian north for about 90 miles (145 km.) and reaches a southern tributary of the Purus River, which is followed east and north to its confluence with the Purus River. The line follows the Purus River downstream northeastward to its confluence with the Santa Rosa River, east of the town of Santa Rosa (Brazil). It follows the Santa Rosa River upstream southwestward to its source and along the local watershed, reaching the 10°S parallel. The boundary forms a straight line along the parallel for about 50 miles (80 km.) and then heads north and northwest along the watershed between the Brazilian Embira, Muru and Tarauacá rivers in the north and the Upper Juruá (Yuruá) River in the southwest. The boundary reaches the source of the Breu River and follows it downstream northwestward to its confluence with the Upper Juruá River, which it crosses west of Foz do Breu (Brazil). The line runs westward in another straight line to the watershed on Serra de Divisor, between the Juruá (Brazil) and Tamaya (Peru) rivers. It trends northward along the watershed and reaches the source of the Javari River west of the Brazilian town of Nossa Senhora da Gloria. Thence it follows the main navigation channel of the Javari River northeast and east for about 370 miles (595 km.) to its confluence with the great Amazon River at the boundary tripoint with Colombia.

Historical Background. The Treaty of San Ildefonso (1 October 1777) separated the Spanish and Portuguese possessions in South America, placing this boundary on the Javari and Amazon rivers to the confluence of the latter with the Yapurá River. Peru became an independent state in 1824 while Brazil had achieved independence in 1822. Since independence Peru has asserted claims to the land east of the Javari River and resisted application of the San Ildefonso line to determine its rights along the frontier. A treaty of friendship between Brazil and Peru, signed at Lima on 8 July 1841, affirmed the necessity of a precise boundary demarcation in accordance with the *uti possidetis* of 1810. However, the Bolivia-Peru War intervened and Brazil never ratified this treaty. Nevertheless, in a convention signed at Lima (23 October 1851), both Brazil and

above: Frito Moreno glacier near the Argentina–Chile boundary

below: The Argentina–Bolivia boundary in the Andes Mountains

98

above: A mountain peak along the Chile–Bolivia boundary

below: Argentina–Brazil boundary in the Iguacu Falls

above: Austria–Liechtenstein boundary crossing

below: Austria–Czech Republic boundary crossing

Bolivia–Paraguay boundary region, east of the Andes

above: Bolivia–Peru Lake Titicaca boundary

below: Bolivia–Argentina boundary crossing point

102

above: Niagara Falls—Canada–United States boundary

below: The Great Wall of China—the most impressive wall boundary in the world

The Pamir Mountains—China–Pakistan boundary region

China–Nepal boundary area

Tibet—near the China–India boundary

106

China–India boundary from the Indian side

China–East India boundary area

above: The India–China boundary in the Ladak region runs in a high mountainous area

below: China–Hong Kong boundary area

above: Israel–Jordan boundary crossing

below: China–Macao boundary

above: France–Spain boundary crossing

below: The Slovakian side of the Hungary–Slovakia boundary on the Danube River

above: The Indian side of the India–Nepal boundary

below: The Napo River, which crosses the Ecuador–Peru boundary

Germany–Switzerland boundary in the Rhine Falls

Peru accepted the principle of *uti possidetis* and recognized the town of Tabatinga as a frontier point, from where the boundary would run in a straight line north to the Japurá (Yapurá) River and south to the Javari River. In accordance with the agreement, a demarcation team worked between 1861 and 1874 along the proposed line. By a convention signed in Lima on 11 February 1874, the boundary line was established, but a year later Colombia protested a section of the boundary from Tabatinga to the Japurá River. No changes were made at that time, but in 1928 the area between the Japurá and Amazon rivers was transferred from Peru to Colombia and the boundary tripoint was established at the confluence of the Javari and Amazon rivers.

After Bolivia's interest in the Acre region, near the southern tripoint with Peru, had been transferred to Brazil by the Treaty of Petrópolis of 17 November 1903, the relations between Brazil and Peru became strained and conflicts developed between their respective inhabitants in the region of the upper Juruá River. The long controversy was settled by a treaty signed at Rio de Janeiro on 8 September 1909, modifying the 1851 boundary line to settle the disputes in the Acre region. By this treaty, of the 170,600 sq. miles (65,868 sq. km.) of disputed territory 155,600 sq. miles (403,000 sq. km.) became Brazilian and 15,000 sq. miles (38,850 sq. km.) remained with Peru. A protocol signed at Rio de Janeiro on 19 April 1913 called for the institution of a mixed demarcation commission. The final treaty was signed on 11 July 1918 and was ratified in 1927 by both Brazil and Peru.

Present Situation. Since 1927 the demarcated boundary has not been under dispute, both states maintaining the line peacefully.

BRAZIL — SURINAME   Following the earlier colonial boundary between Dutch and Brazilian possessions in South America, the Brazil–Suriname boundary is 371 miles (597 km.) long. It extends westward from the boundary tripoint with French Guiana on the Litani River to the tripoint with Guyana at the source of the Kutari (Cutari) River.

Geographical Setting. The entire boundary between Brazil and Suriname follows the western section of the Tumuc-Humac Mountains (Serra Tumucumaque), which is the watershed between the northern tributaries of the great Amazon River (Paru, Citare, Paru de Oeste, Marapi and Anamu) in the south and the rivers that run north toward the Atlantic Ocean. Its eastern terminus is located at the source of the Litani River and from there it runs west, reaching a peak at an altitude of 2,723 feet (830 m.). The line continues westward for about 80 miles (130 km.) to a point north of Maloca Veha (Brazil), where it turns south and trends in that direction for about 50 miles (80 km.). Heading westward again, it runs 60 miles (97 km.) to the boundary junction with Guyana in the source of the Kutari River.

Historical Background. Suriname was founded by British settlers, who established the town of Paramaribo in 1610. From the mid-seventeenth century it became a Dutch territory, between 1799 and 1815 it was again ruled by the British and in 1815 the Congress of Vienna returned it to the Dutch. While its eastern and western boundaries were negotiated in the nineteenth century, its southern boundary with Brazil, which became independent in 1822, was not defined at that time. An assumption was held that the Amazon basin belongs to Brazil while the mountainous range of northern South America constitutes the boundary between Brazil and the European colonies, which included Dutch Guiana. The line along the Tumuc-Humac Mountains, between the Litani and Courantyne rivers, was established on 5 May 1906 and only in 1936 did Brazil, Britain and Netherlands agree on a tripoint boundary junction at the source of the Kutari River, which is the western tributary of the Courantyne River.

Present Situation. The eastern and western boundaries of Suriname are sources of dispute. However, there are no disputes concerning the alignment of its southern boundary with Brazil.

BRAZIL — URUGUAY   The boundary between Brazil and Uruguay runs 612 miles (985 km.) between the boundary junction with Argentina at the confluence of the Uruguay and Quaraí (Cuareim) rivers in the west and the mouth of Arroyo Chuy in the Atlantic Ocean in the east. Most of the boundary line runs through rivers and lakes; other sections follow watersheds.

Geographical Setting. The western terminus of the boundary line has been under dispute. It was agreed in 1851 that the boundary reaches the confluence of the Uruguay and Quaraí rivers. At the confluence, however, lies Brazilera Island, over which both Brazil and Uruguay claim sovereignty. To date the dispute has not been resolved. The boundary line follows the Quaraí River eastward until it reaches a branch of the Invernada River. It follows the branch to its source on the Haedo ridge, then traversing across the height of that ridge and the ridge of Santa Ana up to the source of the San Luis River. Thence it follows the San Luis River downstream, to its confluence with Río Negro. In a straight line the boundary runs eastward to reach the headwaters of the Mina River, then, following the median line of that river and the Rivers Guaviyu and Chico, the boundary reaches the Jaguarão River. Coursing along that river downstream it reaches Lake Mirim, enters the lake in a southeasterly direction, dividing the lake's islands between Brazil and Uruguay, and reaches the median line of the lake. The line then traverses south through the lake to the mouth of San Miguel River. Along the river the boundary reaches its main defile and runs in a straight line to the main source of the Chuy River. It follows the median line of that river up to its mouth in the Atlantic Ocean at the eastern terminus of the boundary between Uruguay and Brazil.

Historical Background. The boundary between Brazil and Uruguay marks part of the boundary between the former Spanish and the Portuguese regions in South America. The history of the line dates back to the early days of European activities in the area in the late fifteenth century, but the present boundary goes back to the early nineteenth century.

In July 1821 the Province of Montevideo (which is Uruguay of today) was annexed by Brazil (then part of the Portuguese state), based on the colonial boundaries (according to the principle of *uti possidetis*), placing the boundary between Spain and Portugal in the region along Río de la Plata. On 28 August 1828, after the defeat of the Brazilian forces, the independent Oriental Republic of Uruguay was established to create a dividing area between Argentina and Brazil. Brazil and Uruguay signed a boundary treaty on 12 October 1851, forming the basis of today's boundary. From then on some modifications and improved demarcations were made: On 15 May 1852 the segment between the Chuy and Jaguarão rivers was modified; in 1909 and 1913 further modifications were made; and the land sections of the boundary were demarcated between 1920 and 1935. As late as 21 July 1972 the eastern terminus in the mouth of the River Chuy, which is subject to various fluctuations, was reestablished.

All these treaties, however, never solved two main boundary problems. One major dispute involves the sovereignty of Brazilera Island located at the confluence of the Quaraí and Uruguay rivers. Secondly, the definition of the boundary in the Invernada River, which forms a segment of the boundary line according to the treaty of 1851, became an issue as Brazil and Uruguay identified it as different streams. Although commissioners of both sides decided to actually delimit the boundary along the separate rivers, their respective governments never approved their demarcations, and the area between the two rivers remained in dispute.

Present Situation. Other than the two disputed areas, there are no known contentions concerning the boundary alignment. The disputes never elevated into major confrontations or local clashes between the two countries, but there are also no negotiations in progress at the present time to resolve them.

BRAZIL — VENEZUELA The boundary between Brazil and Venezuela runs for 1,367 miles (2,200 km.) between the boundary junction with Guyana in the east and the boundary junction with Colombia in the west. The main part of the line follows the watershed between the two South American Rivers—the Amazon River, which runs through Brazil and the Venezuelan Orinoco River. The entire length of the boundary is demarcated.

Geographical Setting. The eastern terminus of the boundary is located on Mount Roraima (9,094 feet; 2,773 m.), at 5°12'8.90"N and 60°44'7.50"W, which is the Brazil–Guyana–Venezuela boundary intersection. The boundary line runs westward, trending across the crest of the Pakaraima Mountains (Serra Pacaraima), the watershed between the northern tributaries of the Rio Negro, which is a branch of the great Amazon River, and the southern tributaries of the Orinoco River, until it reaches Masiati Peak (4,900 feet; 1,493 m.). The boundary line then turns southeastward and follows Sierra Parima for about 190 miles (305 km.) to meet 2°23'19.30"N and

63°21'23.50"W. From that point the boundary traverses along the crest of Sierra Tapirapecó southwestward, dividing the rivers running north to the Orinoco River and south to the Rio Negro. From the boundary point that is located at 0°37'53.10"N and 65°32'26.80"W, the line turns north and then west, following Sierra Imeri and reaching Sierra Cupy near the Húa Falls. From the falls it continues northwestward in a straight line to the boundary junction with Colombia on the San Jose island located in the Río Negro.

Historical Background. When the New World was divided by the Treaty of Tordesillas (1494) between Spain and Portugal, Spain received the main part of the American continent, while Portugal secured what later became the northeastern section of South America. Portugal then extended its hold westward, along the Amazon River, and Spain attempted to increase its territory east of the Andes. Indeed, by the end of the seventeenth century the majority of the Amazon basin came under Portuguese control. An attempt to settle the dividing line between the two empires was made by the Treaty of San Ildefonso of 1777, which placed the Amazon River and its tributaries up to the 70°W meridian under Portuguese domination. The watershed between the Orinoco and Amazon rivers formed a natural barrier between the Spanish and the Portuguese and helped to restore their common boundary—but the boundary descriptions were inaccurate and in some cases led to more confusion.

In 1819 the Spanish colony of New Granada became the independent Republic of Gran Colombia (which included today's Colombia, Ecuador, Panama and Venezuela) while Brazil became an independent empire in 1822. However, the two never reached an agreement concerning their common boundary. Venezuela declared its independence in 1830 and in 1852 concluded a treaty of limits with Brazil, defining a boundary similar to that which exists today, whereby the principle of *uti possidetis* was applied. This served as the basis for all South American boundaries, holding that rightful sovereignty should be based on occupation, utilization and effective control of territory—rather than written or verbal claims.

There were, however, some difficulties concerning the western section of the boundary, near the boundary junction with Colombia, as early maps mistakenly expanded the local ridges. To settle their differences, Brazil and Venezuela signed a boundary treaty in 1859 and 20 years later, in 1879, a demarcation commission began setting the boundary on the ground. In 1905 Brazil and Venezuela signed a protocol recognizing the demarcation work of the 1880s east of Sierra Cupy, while another round of talks in 1912–1915 established the boundary up to the Colombian boundary. The final demarcation protocol was signed in 1928, when a mixed commission was instituted to demarcate the entire boundary. By 1934 the boundary team had set marks along 100 miles (160 km.) of the line west of the boundary junction with Guyana; only after the introduction of aerial photography and aerial navigation in 1939 was the boundary team able to mark the boundary in the remote and isolated watershed area. In the 1970s the demarcation was completed satisfactorily.

Present Situation. There are no known disputes concerning the boundary line. Mixed boundary teams still continue peaceful allocations of boundary marks along the border. To date some doubts remain regarding the precise locations of various river sources that are to be separated by the line. Nevertheless, such uncertainties do not cause conflicts over the line's location.

BRUNEI An independent country since 31 December 1983, Brunei (area: 2,226 sq. miles [5,765 sq. km.]; estimated population: 280,000 [1994]) is an Asian state situated in the northwestern region of Borneo, an island between the Indian and the Pacific oceans. Brunei's geography is unusual in that the Malaysian province of Sarawak cuts into the country, splitting it into two discontinuous parts. Brunei is bounded in the northwest by the South China Sea and on all other sides by Malaysia (237 miles; 381 km.). Its capital is Bandar Seri Begawan.

Despite its small size, Brunei once dominated the entire island of Borneo (Kalimantan) and neighboring islands, including parts of the Philippines. In 1888, a treaty was signed making Brueni a protectorate of Great Britain. Independence was granted in 1984. Britain still has considerable control over the local economy and foreign affairs as does the Dutch-owned Shell oil company, which has developed the extensive Seria field since 1929. In recent

Brunei's boundaries with Malaysia

years, Japan's Mitsubishi corporation has begun developing natural gas resources.

BRUNEI — MALAYSIA The 237-mile (381-km.) boundary between Brunei and Malaysia is in two separate sections on the coast of the island of Borneo, divided by the Limbang River Valley. The western section of the boundary curves from the South China Sea to Brunei Bay and follows principal watersheds. The eastern section begins and ends in Brunei Bay, following the Pandaruan River and major water divides.

Geographical Setting. The western boundary begins on the coast of the South China Sea, east of the mouth of Sungai Belait, at roughly 114°0'47"E. It proceeds in a series of straight lines south across the coastal road then southeast, northeast and southeast again to run almost equidistantly between Batang Baram (Sarawak, Malaysia) and Sungai Belait (Brunei). It crosses the Pagalayan Canal between these rivers and runs south for about 1 mile (1.5 km.) before turning southeast to cross a marsh plain between Batang Baram and Sungai Mendaram. Turning southwest, it follows the watershed between the tributaries that run into Batang Baram and Sungai Mendaram and continues along the watershed until it trends south to cross the Marudi Forest Reserve. It then descends the eastern side of the hill ranges, keeping to the watershed and skirting the steep northern side of the valley of the Sungai Tutoh, turning northeast and dividing the waters that feed the Sungai Melinau and Sungai Medalam systems (Sarawak) from those feeding the Sungai Belait system (Brunei). Still following the watershed, the boundary swings northeastward to Bukit Ulu Tutong. It passes Bukit Bedawan and continues north along the watershed between the streams running east into the Limbang district of Sarawak and those running west into Brunei. At about 114°47'E and 4°44'N the line leaves the watershed and continues northeast across the plain to the headwaters of Sungai Manunggul and along its *thalweg* into Brunei Bay. The islands of Berbunot, Buruburu and Pepatan belong to Brunei.

The second, eastern area of Brunei which has no land connection with the western section, begins and ends its boundary with Malaysia in Brunei Bay. In the west, between the Limbang district (Sarawak) and the Temburong district (Brunei), the line sets out from a point between the Island (Pulau) of Siarau and Limbang and follows the *thalweg* of Sungai Pandaruan south to its headwaters at about 4°22'N. It then follows the watershed dividing the tributaries that run north into Brunei from those feeding the Sungai Medamit system in Limbang. It follows the watershed to form a wide loop north and west and then continues along it northward. It passes the peaks of Bukit Suang and Sagan 'A' Bukit, leaves the hills and takes a straight-line route to the headwaters of the Aru River. It follows the *thalweg* of the river to its confluence with other tributaries (forming Sungai Bangau) and along Sungai Bangau to its mouth in Brunei Bay.

Historical Background. By the nineteenth century

Brunei was bounded in the south by the Sultanate of Sambas and in the north by the Sultanate of Sulu, but its precise boundaries were yet undefined. The European partitioning of Brunei began in 1841 when James Brooke became governor in the Malaysian district of Sarawak. He enlarged his territory by piecemeal additions and in 1884 and 1890 took the Trusan and Limbang districts respectively. Sarawak's independence from Brunei was recognized by the British government in 1863 and in 1888 it was placed under British protection. Meanwhile the North Borneo Company had taken over Sabah and by constant concessions to the company and to Sarawak, Brunei was reduced to two enclaves completely surrounded by Sarawak territory. Although the British government did not approve of Brooke's having secured Limbang, it was decided that it should remain in Sarawak in return for "adequate pecuniary compensation." The sultan, in spite of acute poverty, refused to accept this offer and eventually the money deposited by Brooke was returned to him unclaimed. The sultan lost no opportunity to press the British government for the return of Limbang—but without success. Throughout the 1890s unrest in the area led the British government to contract a new treaty, by which a British resident could be appointed at the event of the sultan's death. Furthermore, the island of Labuan in Brunei Bay would be removed from the possession of the North Borneo Company and £20,000 would be "borrowed" from the Federated Malay States to redeem the mortgaged revenues of Brunei and to set up an administration. The sultan agreed and on 5 December 1905 the treaty was signed. This pledged the British to uphold the dynasty in Brunei and protected the state when the death of Sultan Hashim in 1906 gave rise to renewed demands by the rajah of Sarawak to annex Brunei. A British resident was appointed advisor to the sultan (Sir Omar, who ruled Brunei for 70 years, between 1916 and 1986) and the boundaries of Brunei were subsequently fixed under the first residents. Malaysia became an independent federation in 1963, including the British crown colonies of North Borneo, but Brunei refused to be included in the federation. Brunei gained independence in 1984 and both countries adopted the colonial boundary as their common international boundary without any formal agreement.

Present Situation. This border is mutually recognized by Brunei and Malaysia.

BULGARIA (Bâlgarija) An independent country since 1908 (area: 42,823 sq. miles [110,911 sq. km.]; population: 9,020,000 [1994]), Bulgaria is located in the Balkan Peninsula of southeastern Europe. It is bounded in the north by Romania (378 miles; 608 km.), in the east by the Black Sea, in the south by Turkey (149 miles; 238 km.) and Greece (307 miles; 494 km.) and in the west by Macedonia (92 miles; 148 km.) and Serbia (198 miles; 318 km.). The capital of Bulgaria is Sofia.

Slavic tribes settled the area between the Danube River and the Adriatic Sea in the sixth and seventh centuries. They seem to have forced out or annihilated many of the original Thraco-Illyarian, Latin and Greek inhabitants of the area and assimilated the rest. In 679 the Bulgars conquered present-day northeast Bulgaria and founded their state. The Bul-

gars (or Bulghars) were originally Turkic nomads who roamed the steppes north of the Black and Caspian seas and were gradually assimilated by the more numerous Slavs. They killed the Byzantine emperor and even besieged Constantinople. Their king Boris I (852–889) was baptized in 856, and in 870 converted his people to Orthodox Christianity, taking the title of czar. Under Simon (893–927) the first Bulgarian state reached its zenith, ruling over the areas between the Danube and the Adriatic and Aegean Seas. After Simon's death, however, his state declined rapidly and returned to Byzantine rule.

The second Bulgarian state was established in 1185, following a successful general revolt by the Bulgars and the Vlachs. Under Ivan Assen II (1318–1341) it reached its zenith but soon declined again. In 1330 the Serbs conquered Macedonia. In 1340 the Ottomans began their campaign against Bulgaria and by 1396 all Bulgaria and Macedonia

Bulgaria's boundaries in the Balkan Peninsula

was under their direct rule. It remained so for 482 years.

Under Ottoman rule the Bulgarians were part of the "Greek Orthodox nation" (*Rum milleti*), which was under the authority of the (Greek) Patriarchate of Constantinople. This gave rise to a slow hellenization of the Bulgarians, especially of the educated social strata. Thus, when Bulgarian nationalism made its appearance, it was directed against the Greek influence more than against the Turks. With Russian encouragement, Bulgarian nationalists revived the literary language and the Cyrillic alphabet (for a while Bulgarian was written in Greek letters) and established schools in which it was the language of instruction. A 40-year struggle ended in 1870 when the sultan reestablished the autonomy of the Bulgarian Church from Constantinople. From here to demands of political independence the distance was short.

In 1876 a rising was cruelly crushed by the Ottomans, which led to Russian military intervention. The treaty of San Stefano which concluded the Russo-Ottoman War of 1877 provided for the establishment of an independent Bulgaria in its widest borders, including eastern Thrace and Macedonia. The Congress of Berlin, however, introduced cardinal changes. A principality of Bulgaria under Ottoman suzerainty was established north of the Balkan mountains and an autonomous province of Rumelia to their south, within the Ottoman empire. Thrace and Macedonia remained under direct Ottoman rule. In 1885, however, the province of Rumelia was de facto united with Bulgaria. In 1908, following the Young Turk revolution, Ferdinand, the prince of Bulgaria, proclaimed the country's independence and took the title of czar.

In 1912 the Bulgarians, in coalition with the Serbs and the Greeks, attacked the Ottomans and conquered Thrace and Macedonia. However, as the three could not agree on the division of the spoils, the Bulgarians attacked their former allies in 1913, and Romania then attacked Bulgaria. Defeated, Bulgaria had to give up most of Macedonia to Serbia. In World War I Bulgaria fought on the side of the Central powers against Serbia, and lost some of its territory. It fought on the Axis side in World war II, and Germany fulfilled all its territorial demands, although Bulgaria never declared war on the Soviet Union, due to the overwhelming pro-Russian sentiments in the country.

In 1944 Soviet forces invaded Bulgaria, and by 1947 a communist regime was in power in Sofia. Since then, until its collapse in 1990, Bulgaria's communist regime was one of the strictest and most loyal to Moscow in Eastern Europe.

BULGARIA — GREECE The boundary between Bulgaria and Greece in the Balkan Peninsula runs in an east–west direction between the border junction with Turkey and the border junction with Macedonia. It is 307 miles (494 km.) long and is demarcated.
Geographical Setting. The boundary line begins on the Tumba Mountain peak on the ridge of Belasica Planina, at the border junction with Macedonia. It follows the ridge toward the confluence of the Struma and Bistrica rivers, runs along the Bistrica and then takes an easterly direction to the crest of Ali Butus (5,445 feet; 1,660 m.). The boundary follows the watershed, running eastward and then northeastward between the local peaks, and crossing in its course the Mesta and Despat rivers. Continuing its easterly direction, the boundary climbs Debikli Mountain (5,273 feet; 1,608 m.), which is marked by boundary pillar no. 233. In this direction the boundary traverses 153 miles (246 km.), following the watershed between the basin of the Maritsa River on the north and the basins of the Mesta and other rivers which flow directly into the Aegean Sea on the south and finally reaching the Daoul River, 2.5 miles (4 km.) north of the small town of Mikron Dherion (Greece). The boundary changes its direction northward to follow the main channel of the Daoul River and running to its source in the Kizil-Deli River. It then follows the local watershed, leaves it and runs to the Arda River, following the right bank of the river for a few miles, until turning northward in an almost straight line up to a height of 1,201 feet (366 m.). Thence, following the watershed between the Maritsa and Arda rivers, the boundary runs northeastward up to Mount Tazi-Tepesi (2,023 feet; 613 m.). From there it runs to the Ceremen-Dere stream, follows its course and then, in a straight line, courses northeastward into the Maritsa River. The boundary follows the Maritsa River for 9.5 miles (15.3 km.) southeastward until it reaches the border junction with Turkey.

Historical Background. Bulgaria and Greece gained independence from the Turkish Ottoman Empire in the nineteenth century; Greece received its independence in 1829, while Bulgaria was created a state in 1878, although the latter was still a subject of the Ottoman sultan.

When created, the two countries shared no common boundary, since a large area of Ottoman territory separated them. The years preceding World War I, however, brought great changes to the southern Balkan area. Bulgaria proclaimed itself an independent state in 1908 and by 1912 all the independent Balkan countries—Greece, Bulgaria, Montenegro and Serbia—joined together to drive Turkey out of the Balkans.

The First Balkan War of 1912–1913 succeeded in pushing the Turks up to 25 miles (40 km.) east of Istanbul, then forming a common boundary between Bulgaria and Greece. The conflicting ambitions of the victorious countries, especially concerning the border areas, brought about the Second Balkan War of summer 1913, during which Bulgaria lost most of its former gains. A Treaty of Peace was signed in Bucharest on 10 August 1913, in which the boundary between Bulgaria and Greece was delimited. That boundary ran eastward from the Struma River area in the west and then in a southerly direction to the Aegean Sea, converging with the Mesta River, thus giving Bulgaria a 70-mile (113-km.) strip of the Aegean coast.

Bulgaria joined the Central Powers (Germany, Austria and Turkey) during World War I and was defeated with them in October 1918. As a result, a new boundary between Bulgaria and Greece (which fought with the triumphant Allied Powers) was delimited in the Treaty of Neuilly on 27 November 1919, dislocating Bulgaria from the Aegean Sea. A commission demarcated the entire boundary in 1922 and the Treaty of Lausanne between Turkey and various Allied Powers, signed on 24 July 1923, defined the border junction with Turkey at a point on the Maritsa River.

Present Situation. The political changes of the last 70 years have not changed the boundary line. In 1947, after World War II, a treaty confirmed all Bulgarian boundaries that had existed before the war and since then there have been no known disputes concerning the boundary's location.

BULGARIA — MACEDONIA The boundary between Bulgaria and Macedonia runs 92 miles (148 km.) along mountain crests, between the boundary junction with Serbia in the north and the boundary junction with Greece on Mount Tumba in the south. It is the southern section of the former Bulgaria–Yugoslavia boundary established in 1919.

Geographical Setting. The southern point of the boundary is located on the summit of Mount Tumba (4,764 feet; 1,452 m.) in the Belasica range, at the boundary junction with Greece. The boundary line runs northward, reaching and crossing the Strumica River and the road between the towns of Petrich (Bulgaria) and Strumica (Macedonia). Turning northeastward it climbs the Males mountain range up to 4,740 feet (1,445 m.). Continuing northeastward and then northwestward, the line follows the watershed between the Struma River on the east and the northeastern tributaries of the Vardar River on the west, passing over the peak of Rujen (7,432 feet; 2,265 m.). The boundary line reaches the Kriva Palanka (Macedonia)–Kyustendil (Bulgaria) road, crosses it and runs northward for some 6 miles (10 km.) to reach the boundary junction with Serbia, located at a point that stands at a height of 4,372 feet (1,333 m.).

Historical Background. The area in which the present boundary line runs was under dispute for centuries between the Bulgars, the Greeks, the Turks and the local Macedonian people. In 1331 Stephen Dushan was crowned at his capital Skopje (which is today the capital of Macedonia), as emperor of the Serbs and Greeks. In 1389, the Serbs, aided by Bulgarian and Romanian allies, were defeated by the Turkish Ottoman Empire in the Battle of Kosovo, which led to over five centuries of Ottoman rule over Macedonia and Bulgaria.

In 1876 Bulgarian nationalists made an abortive attempt to free Bulgaria, leading to the Russo-Turkish War of 1877–1878. Under the terms of the Treaty of San Stefano (3 March 1878) that was concluded after the war, Bulgaria was established as an independent state including the large area of today's Macedonia. In July 1878, following the Congress of Berlin, Bulgaria lost the territories that had been gained in the west and became an autonomous province under the Ottoman sultan until 1908.

During the summer of 1912 a secret treaty between

Bulgaria and Serbia led to agreements with Greece and Montenegro to form an alliance to drive Turkey out of the Balkan region. According to these agreements, Bulgaria advocated the creation of an autonomous Macedonia, unless this goal would prove impractical, whereby Macedonia would be divided between Bulgaria and Serbia along a line from Kriva Palanka to Lake Ohrid. These arrangements led to the First Balkan War of 1912–1913. The Balkan allies succeeded in driving Turkey out of the Balkan area, but soon their different territorial claims led to further disputes between themselves: Serbia demanded a greater part of the Macedonian area as it occupied the Vardar Valley, Greece took southern Macedonia, while Bulgaria tried to clinch the areas for itself in accordance with the prewar agreement. Bulgaria attacked Serbia and Greece in Macedonia in June 1913, a move that began the short but intense Second Balkan War. Bulgaria was defeated, however, and according to the Treaty of Peace signed in Bucharest on 10 August 1913, most of Macedonia was left in Serbia. Only a small section of Macedonia, the Strumica valley, between the Struma and Vardar Rivers, was left to Bulgaria. The thwarting of Bulgaria's ambitions in the Balkan area led it to side readily with the Central Powers (the German, Austro-Hungarian and Ottoman empires) that were then defeated in World War I. Bulgaria subsequently lost that portion of Macedonia in the Strumica valley, excluding it entirely from the Vardar valley. The boundary between Bulgaria and the newly established Kingdom of the Serbs, Croats and Slovenes (later Yugoslavia) was defined by the Treaty of Peace between the Allied and Associated powers and Bulgaria, signed at Neuilly-sur-Seine on 27 November 1919. An international boundary commission demarcated the boundary in 1920–1922. Bulgaria joined forces with Germany again during World War II in order to gain a large area of Macedonia, but the Paris Peace Treaty of 1947 confirmed Bulgaria's boundary with Yugoslavia as it was established in 1919. Macedonia, which never had an independent status, became a federal republic in the Democratic Federal Yugoslavia at the end of World War II. Its eastern boundary was then the international border with Bulgaria. Following the breakdown of Yugoslavia in 1990, Macedonia became an independent state in 1992 and the southern section of the former Bulgaria–Yugoslavia boundary became the international boundary between Bulgaria and Macedonia.

Present Situation. There are no known disputes between the two countries concerning the boundary's alignment, as both countries have accepted the 1919 delimitation as their common boundary.

BULGARIA — ROMANIA

The boundary between Bulgaria and Romania runs for 378 miles (608 km.) from the boundary junction with Serbia in the west to the Black Sea in the east. Most of the boundary follows the Danube River (294 miles; 473 km.).

Geographical Setting. The boundary line begins at the confluence of the Timok and Danube rivers. It follows the principal navigation channel of the Danube River eastward for 294 miles (473 km.) up to the Bulgarian city of Silistra. The channel, for the most part, tends to flow within the Romanian rather than the Bulgarian boundary. At Silistra the boundary departs from the Danube and runs southeastward in a series of straight lines, separating Bulgarian and Romanian villages in the Dobruja region, to a point on the Black Sea situated 5 miles (8 km.) south of the center of the Romanian city of Mangalia.

Historical Background. From the fourteenth century on, following the Battle of Kosovo of 1389, the Ottoman Turkish Empire ruled the Balkan area. During the late nineteenth century nationalist agitation for liberation increased, aided by the growth of Czarist Russian influence in the Balkan region. In May 1876 revolutionaries in Bulgaria attempted to throw off the Turkish yoke, but were suppressed with great cruelty. This and other political events led to the Russo-Turkish war of 1877–1878, which positioned the Russian army near Istanbul. Britain and Austria-Hungary forced the Russians to stop their advance and the Treaty of San Stefano was signed on 3 March 1878. It created a greatly enlarged Bulgaria, extending from the Danube to the Aegean Sea, and proclaimed the total independence of Romania. The Great Powers, however, forced Russia to change the San Stefano Treaty and the Congress of Berlin modified it further on 13 July 1878, limiting the expansive proportions that Russia had ceded to Bulgaria, which then became a compact state that extended eastward from the Timok river between the Balkan Mountains and the Danube River. The boundary between Bulgaria and Romania in Dobruja was defined as "a line starting from the east of Silistra and terminating on the Black Sea, south of Mangalia." This line was demarcated in December 1878 and was modified in 1880 in Bulgaria's favor to maintain the Silistra–Karaorman road within Bulgaria's boundaries.

In 1913, following the Second Balkan War, the southern sector of Dobruja was transferred to Romania and the Treaty of Neuilly, signed on 27 November 1919 between Bulgaria and the Allied Powers and ending World War I, fixed the boundary with Romania along the same line as the 1913 boundary, "from the Black Sea to the Danube, thence to the confluence of the Timok and the Danube, along the principal channel of navigation upstream." No changes of the boundary location were made after World War II and the Treaty of Peace with Bulgaria, signed in Paris on 10 February 1947, confirmed all Bulgarian boundaries that had existed on 1 January 1914.

Present Situation. There are no known disputes concerning the delimitation of the Bulgaria–Romania boundary. The 1878 line still holds and is one of the oldest boundary lines extant in Europe today.

BULGARIA — SERBIA

The boundary between Bulgaria and Serbia, which is the northern section of the boundary between Bulgaria and the former Yugoslavia, runs for 198 miles (318 km.) between the boundary junction with Romania in the north and the boundary junction with Macedonia in the south. Primarily coursing along mountain crests, about 15 miles (24 km.) of the boundary line coincide with rivers.

Geographical Setting. The northernmost point of the boundary is located at the confluence of the Danube and the Timok rivers and serves as the boundary junction with Romania. It follows the course of the Timok River southwestward until it meets the road connecting Vidin (Bulgaria) and Negotin (Serbia). The boundary line leaves the river and continues southwestward, generally following the watershed between the basin of the Timok River on the northwest and the Delenja and Topolovitsa rivers on the southeast. Near the small Serbian town of Suka the boundary line changes its direction, run-

ning southeastward along the crest of Kom Balkan. It passes through the mountain pass of St. Nikola and the Midzor Peak (7,172 feet; 2,186 m.). Turning southwestward from Kom Balkan, the boundary crosses the Komstica River and the Dimitrovgrad (Serbia)–Sofia (Bulgaria) road along the watershed until it reaches the Lukavica River, a tributary of the Nishava River. It follows the river upstream to its confluence with the Jablanica River after crossing the Trun (Bulgaria)–Dimitrovgrad (Serbia) road. The boundary follows the Jablanica River westward, leaves the river and follows the crest of the Ruj Planina (its highest peak reaches 5,630 feet [1,716 m.] above sea level). About 10.5 miles (17 km.) west of Trun the boundary reaches the Golma Rudina Peak (5,003 feet; 1,525 m.) and from there runs southward, crossing the small Jerma and Dragovishtitsa rivers. It then follows the local watershed, traversing over peaks that reach a height of 5,679 feet (1,731 m.), and finally reaching the boundary junction with Macedonia at an altitude of 4,372 feet (1,333 m.) located 6 miles (10 km.) northwest of the road that connects Kriva Palanka (Macedonia) and Kyustendil (Bulgaria).

Historical Background. While the histories of Bulgaria and Serbia reach beyond the Middle Ages, both were born as modern states only as a result of the Congress of Berlin in 1878. Serbia then gained complete independence while Bulgaria became an autonomous region under the Ottoman sultan; the boundary between the two newly established states was placed along the Timok River. This line was maintained for over 30 years until the Balkan Wars of 1912–1913.

In 1912 both Bulgaria and Serbia joined forces with Greece and Montenegro to drive the Ottoman Turkish Empire from the Balkan region. Serbia and Bulgaria had set an agreement that their future boundary would divide the Macedonian region between them, running from Kriva Palanka to Lake Ohrid (now located between Macedonia and Albania), leaving the northern area to Serbia and the area south of that line to Bulgaria. The Balkan states succeeded in pushing Turkey eastward, but their alliance was short-lived. Bulgaria, Serbia and Greece were not able to solve their different territorial claims and another war, now between Bulgaria and its former allies, broke out in June 1913. Bulgaria attacked the Serb and Greek armies in the boundary area of Macedonia but was forced to accept an armistice and sign the Peace Treaty of Bucharest on 10 August 1913. According to the terms of this treaty only a small section of Macedonia—in the Strumica valley, between the Vardar and Struma rivers—was ceded to Bulgaria. This never satisfied Bulgaria, which subsequently joined Germany, Austria and the Ottoman Empire in World War I with the anticipation of gaining its territorial claims in the Balkan area. The defeat of these countries resulted in Bulgaria's loss of the areas along the former Serbia–Bulgaria line. In the Treaty of Neuilly, signed between the Allied and Associated powers and Bulgaria on 27 November 1919, some alterations were made in the locality of the Timok River and near the towns of Dimitrovgrad and Bosilegrad as the boundary line was moved eastward. Serbia united the various Slavic elements and led to the formation of the Kingdom of the Serbs, Croats and Slovenes in December 1918, later adopting the name Yugoslavia (1929). The demarcation of the common boundary was performed by an international boundary commission in 1920–1922. During World War II Bulgaria again joined forces with Germany to reclaim territories in the Balkan region. Bulgaria succeeded in occupying a large area of Yugoslavia, but the Paris Peace Treaty of 1947 restored Bulgaria's boundary with Yugoslavia to the 1919 line. From then on the boundary line never changed.

The collapse of the Federal Republic of Yugoslavia in 1990 led to the establishment of Serbia as a separate state, its boundary with Bulgaria constituting the northern section of the 1919 line.

Present Situation. Since 1990 the region of former Yugoslavia has been agitated with territorial claims by its former internal republics. During the 1950s and 1960s minor conflicts between Bulgarian and Serb boundary guards occurred and a Bulgarian minority (about 25,000 in number) is settled in Serbia in the vicinities of Dimitrovgrad and Bosilegrad. Nevertheless, at present there are no territorial disputes concerning the boundary between Bulgaria and Serbia.

BULGARIA — TURKEY The boundary between Bulgaria and Turkey runs 149 miles (238 km.) from the Black Sea to the border junction with Greece on the Maritsa River, situated in the southeastern extremity of Europe, in the Balkan Peninsula. About 85 miles (136 km.) constitute a land boundary while the other 64 miles (102 km.) course through rivers. The entire boundary is demarcated by 320 intervisible boundary pillars.

Geographical Setting. The boundary begins at the mouth of the Rezova River in the Black Sea, south of the monastery of St. Ivan. It follows the course of this river as far as the confluence of the Pirogu and Deliva rivers, then tracing the course of the Deliva northwestward for a distance of 9.5 miles (15.3 km.). The boundary line leaves the river and follows a mountain ridge in the same direction, reaching the Golema River. It follows the course of the river for 1.25 miles (2 km.) and reaches a confluence with another branch of that river. The boundary line then leaves the river and passes along ridges in a generally southwestward direction for some 59 miles (95 km.) to the Tunca River. The line turns southward, following the Tunca for a distance of 7.5 miles (12 km.), departing from the river's course to run southwestward on land for 11.5 miles (18.5 km.) to a tributary of the Kalamitsa River. The boundary follows the Kalamitsa for about 5.5 miles (8.8 km.) and, leaving the river, it runs in a straight line southeastward to the border junction with Greece on the Maritsa River.

Historical Background. Bulgaria was under Ottoman rule from 1389 until the Russo-Turkish War of 1877–1878. On 13 June 1878 the Conference of Berlin established the small state of Bulgaria, still under the Ottoman sultan, extending from the Danube River to the Balkan Mountains. In 1908 Bulgaria became an independent state with a czar of its own and in October 1912, with its allies in the Balkan area, Bulgaria started the First Balkan War, in which the Bulgarian army reached Edirne (the historic Adrianople) in western Turkey. In the Treaty of London, which ended the war on 30 May 1913, a line was drawn from Enez, on the Aegean Sea, to Midye, on the Black Sea, to mark the new boundary of the Bulgaria-Ottoman Empire. Shortly after, in June 1913, the Second Balkan War between Bulgaria and all the Balkan states, including Turkey, was started. Turkey recaptured Edirne; an armistice took place in July and a peace treaty between Turkey and Bulgaria was signed on 29 September

1913 in Istanbul. The boundary moved westward to the Maritsa River and Edirne was left in Turkish hands.

Turkey and Bulgaria became allies of the German Empire during World War I and in September 1915 signed the Treaty of Sofia in which Turkey agreed to give Bulgaria a certain area near Üsküdar (Shtit in Bulgaria of today) east of the Kalamitsa River, and to move the rest of the 1913 boundary to about one mile (1.6 km.) east of the Maritsa River. The defeat of both countries at the end of the war did not change their common boundary and in the Treaty of Peace between the Allied and Associated Powers and Bulgaria, signed at Neuilly-sur-Seine on 27 November 1919, the boundary was defined according to the 1913 and 1915 agreements. The entire boundary was demarcated by the Commission de délimitation de la frontière Greco-Bulgare in 1921 while the border junction with Greece was fixed on the Maritsa River by a demarcation commission in 1926.

Present Situation. Although there are some problems between Bulgaria and Turkey over the presence of a Muslim Turkish minority in Bulgaria, no disputes are known to exist over the location of the boundary between the two states.

BURKINA FASO Formerly known as Upper Volta, Burkina Faso is situated in West Africa. It is a landlocked state (area: 105,811 sq. miles [274,122 sq. km.]; estimated population: 9,810,000 [1994]), bounded in the north and west by Mali (622 miles; 1,000 km.), in the east by Niger (390 miles; 628 km.) and in the south by Benin (190 miles; 306 km.), Togo (78 miles; 126 km.), Ghana (341 miles; 549 km.) and Ivory Coast (363 miles; 584 km.). The capital of Burkina Faso is Ouagadougou.

The French occupied the territory of present day Burkina Faso, then called Upper Volta, in the late nineteenth century. Until 1947 it was ruled together with the Ivory Coast as a single territory, but with the postwar establishment of African political parties, Mossi chiefs demanded the separation of Upper Volta from the Ivory Coast to increase their political power. In this way the Mossi party gained considerable political power and dominated all political institutions created by the colonial administration. During the 1950s a group of young Mossi, who

were resentful of the chiefs' power, created their own party.

The main division in Upper Volta was between the east and the west, but within each region there was a further division between traditionalists and their opponents. Around the capital of Ouagadougou in the east live about 2,000,000 Mossi, largely adherents of traditional religions and mostly obedient to their chiefs. In the west there was a similar number of Bobo and other peoples: Muslims around the town of Bobo-Dioulasso and adherents of traditional religions in the rural areas. Cultural, geographic and economic ties between the peoples of the two regions were weak.

At independence the strongest party was the Union Democratique Voltaique led by Maurice Yameogo, himself a Mossi, who attempted to curb ethnic and regional separatism by forbidding all ethnic associations. After independence Yameogo banned all opposition parties and Burkina Faso became a one-party state. Although in the 30 years since independence Burkina Faso has been politically unstable, with power moving from civilian to military hands, the ethnic factor played a minor role in the country. In 1991 a process of democratization began with the emergence of new political groups.

BURKINA FASO — BENIN see BENIN–BURKINA FASO.

BURKINA FASO — GHANA The boundary between Burkina Faso and Ghana runs from south to north and then from west to east between the boundary junction with Ivory Coast on the Black Volta River in the west and the boundary junction with Togo in the east. Running 341 miles (549 km.), it follows the colonial boundary between the British Gold Coast and the French West Africa.

Geographical Setting. The boundary line runs from the Ivory Coast tripoint at the intersection of the Black Volta River with 9°N, south of the town of Batie (Burkina Faso). It follows the main channel of the Black Volta northward for 137 miles (220 km.) to the intersection of the river with 11°N, turning eastward to follow that parallel of latitude to the Red Volta River, leaving the parallel at certain points to place some villages within Burkina Faso to the north or within Ghana to the south. These departures are made in straight lines, running along meridians, right angles and even along some local streams. The boundary line courses some 6 miles (10 km.) along the main channel of the Red Volta River. Leaving the river, it runs northeastward for 30 miles (48 km.) to join the White Volta River, runs along it for 3 miles (5 km.), leaves it and traverses northeastward for some 12 miles (19 km.) to the boundary junction with Togo, east of the town of Bawku (Ghana). The boundary is very well demarcated.

Historical Background. The first arrangement concerning the boundary was concluded by Great Britain and France on 14 June 1898. The designation of the Gold Coast (now Ghana) as a separate British colony had been confirmed between 1886 and 1897 and the Ashanti region was formally annexed in 1901. The French, on the other hand, established themselves in western Africa during the second half of the nineteenth century. On 18 March 1904, in an exchange of notes between the British and the French foreign offices, sharper definitions were made of the 1898 demarcation and later, in the agreement between Great Britain and France regarding the boundary between the Gold Coast and French Sudan (now Mali), signed on 24 May 1906, a list of boundary pillars and maps illustrating their positions was presented. Thus, the agreements of 1904 and 1906 certified the original agreed delimitation and demarcation by setting boundary pillars along the line.

On 1 March 1919 the colony of Upper Volta was constituted and in 1925, following some misunderstandings concerning the exact delimitation, an Anglo-French commission redemarcated the sector near the Red Volta. Upper Volta became independent on 5 August 1960 (changing its name to Burkina Faso in 1984). The Gold Coast became independent three years earlier, on 6 March 1957, then changing its name to Ghana. The two countries deemed it necessary to redemarcate the boundary line as some of the old pillars had been dislocated and it did not serve the needs of the new independent countries. Arrangements for redemarcation were initiated in 1967 and it was partially completed in 1970. Work continued in 1974 but in 1977 the redemarcation was not finalized. Since then the entire boundary has been fully integrated.

Present Situation. Apart from the disrupted completion of the joint demarcation, there have been no known complications concerning the delimitation of the boundary line.

BURKINA FASO — IVORY COAST The boundary between Burkina Faso and Ivory Coast runs for 363 miles (584 km.) between the boundary tripoint with Ghana on the Black Volta River in the east and the tripoint with Mali, at the intersection of the Bani and Leraba rivers, in the west. The boundary follows the colonial border between former French administrative areas in western Africa.

Geographical Setting. The eastern terminus of the boundary line is located on the main navigation channel of the Black Volta River, at approximately 9°29'30"N. It runs along a local tributary southwest for 6 miles (10 km.) and then northwest, leaving the small town of Batié within Burkina Faso. The line runs for some 100 miles (160 km.) northwest and then west, along local rivers and straight lines to the Keleworo River, leaving the towns of Bouna and Tehini within Ivory Coast and the town of Gaoua in Burkina Faso. The boundary line follows the Keleworo River downstream southwestward for 20 miles (32 km.), leaves it and runs west to reach a tributary of the Comoé River. It follows the tributary southward to its confluence with the Comoé River, which it then follows upstream northwestward to its confluence with the Leraba River. It continues northwestward along the Leraba upstream for 105 miles (170 km.) to its confluence with the Bani River at the boundary tripoint with Mali.

Historical Background. Burkina Faso, which was ruled by the Mossi kingdom from the twelfth century, became part of the French colony of Haut-Senegal et Niger. By a decree of 1 March 1919 the colony was divided and the new colony of Upper Volta was constituted. Ivory Coast (Côte d'Ivoire) became a French colony as part of French West Africa in 1895. The boundary between the two colonies was never declared and was based on French administrative practice. Thus, the best evidence of the alignment is in the form of French colonial maps. Nevertheless, the alignment is sufficiently definitive in principle, substantially consisting of river segments. Both colonies became independent in August 1960, adopting the colonial boundary line without contracting an international agreement. Upper Volta changed its name to Burkina Faso in 1984.

Present Situation. Much of the boundary consists of segments that follow rivers and there is no evidence of demarcation along the line. The rivers tend to change their course seasonally and with no agreement concerning the boundary line, an element of doubt concerning the exact positioning of the river sectors inevitably exists. However, since the countries' independence no dispute concerning their common boundary has been reported.

BURKINA FASO — MALI From the boundary tripoint with Ivory Coast in the southwest to the Niger tripoint in the northeast, the Burkina Faso–Mali boundary runs for 622 miles (1,000 km.). It follows an administrative line that was determined during the French colonial period. A 20-year boundary dispute between the two states was solved by the International Court of Justice in 1986.

Geographical Setting. As there is no formal agreement concerning the boundary's alignment, this description is based on maps rather than written documents. The boundary tripoint with Ivory Coast is at the intersection of the Bani (a small tributary of the Leraba River) and Leraba rivers. It follows the Bani River upstream northward for about 20 miles (30 km.) and then northeastward to the source of the Bani River (a larger river than the tributary), which it follows northward to its confluence with an eastern tributary near the small town of Tiere (Mali). Proceeding mainly along the watershed between the Niger and Black Volta rivers, the line reaches a northern tributary of the Black Volta River, east of Kunda (Mali). In a series of straight lines northeastward it arrives at the Beni River region, runs eastward, crossing the river several times, and meets the boundary tripoint with Niger at about 14°59'30"N and 0°13'30"E, northeast of the small town of Oursi (Burkina Faso).

Historical Background. Both Burkina Faso and Mali were part of the French colonial area of French West Africa. By a decree of 1 May 1919 the French colony of Upper Senegal-Niger was divided and the new colony of Upper Volta was constituted. It was officially made up of seven districts and was created because of the "particularly homogeneous ethnic and linguistic character of the region." On 5

September 1932 the colony was dissolved but was reorganized on 4 September 1947, when it was decided that its boundaries should be maintained as they had stood on 5 September 1932. Mali, as French Sudan, was part of French West Africa from 1893 and became a member of the French Community in 1958. French Sudan and Senegal, which had also belonged to French West Africa, became independent as the Federation of Mali on 20 June 1960. Upper Volta became independent on 5 August 1960 while Mali achieved independence as the Republic of Sudan on 20 August 1960, becoming the Republic of Mali on 22 September 1960. The boundaries between the two as created by France were accepted in principle by both Mali and Upper Volta (which was named Burkina Faso in 1984) in their declarations of independence. The border problem concerning the exact alignment of the line in the Beli River region was first discussed at a bilateral meeting at San (Mali) on 18 and 19 November 1961, when it was agreed to have the frontier demarcated by a mixed commission. Extending along the northeastern border between the two states for about 90 miles (145 km.) at a width of between 9 and 12 miles (15–20 km.), this area had been in dispute since 1960. It contains a chain of pools, through which the Beli River flows, and is the only source of fresh water in the region. Both states made claims to the area; Mali's claim was based on ethnic arguments, as the inhabitants of the disputed area are mainly Malians, while Burkina Faso's claim was based on the French maps. The mixed commission determined that the boundary was to be as shown on a 1925 colonial map, in which the Beli region was in Burkina Faso. A boundary commission was appointed to solve the boundary problem in 1968, but in 1974 Mali declared that the commission had failed to carry out its instructions fully and that all negotiations were thereupon broken off. Armed clashes broke out in November 1974 and following mediation efforts a joint communiqué was signed on 26 December 1974 calling upon the parties to seek a solution to the dispute. Nevertheless, more border incidents were reported in early June 1975 and another round of peace talks took place in Lomé (Togo). On 9 March 1976 another joint commission was established, but no progress was made concerning the boundary dispute for another 10 years. After long negotiations both states agreed to place the disputes before the International Court of Justice (ICJ), which gave its final verdict on 22 December 1986. The boundary was placed as to divide the disputed area almost equally between the two. Burkina Faso received a larger share of territory in the east and Mali in the west. Both states then confirmed and accepted the ruling.

Present Situation. Burkina Faso and Mali accepted the ICJ ruling in 1986 and at present there are no known disputes concerning the boundary's alignment.

BURKINA FASO — NIGER Running 390 miles (628 km.), the boundary between Burkina Faso and Niger is the outcome of an internal organization of the former colonial French West Africa. From the boundary tripoint with Mali in the northwest it extends southeastward to the boundary tripoint with Benin on the Mékrou River.

Geographical Setting. From its northwestern terminus the boundary runs southward, crossing the Youmbam and Gorouol rivers, and then southeast for about 100 miles (160 km.) along astronomical points and local hills, crossing the road between Dori (Burkina Faso) and Téra (Niger) to reach the Sirba River near the village of Bosso Bangou (Niger). The boundary then follows the left bank of the river, which remains in Niger, upstream westward. It leaves the river, continues westward and then heads south to rejoin the river, including some villages, such as Alfassi, within Niger. The boundary crosses the river at a point parallel to the latitude of the town of Say (Niger) and thence runs east-southeast in a straight line for approximately 50 miles (80 km.). Then northeastward it reaches the confluence of the Dyamongou River (a tributary of the Niger River) with a local stream. The boundary crosses this river and trends southeast to reach the Tapoa River, which it follows upstream southwest for about 15 miles (25 km.) to a point that was the ancient frontier of the Say province (Niger). Leaving the river it runs 45 miles (72 km.) in a straight line southeastward to intersect the Mékrou River at the boundary tripoint with Benin.

Historical Background. Both countries were occupied by France in the second half of the nineteenth century as parts of French West Africa. In 1904 the French established the colony of Haut-Senegal et Niger (Upper Senegal-Niger) and in 1912 Niger was constituted as a separate entity within French West Africa. The border between Niger and what was then Haut-Senegal followed the Niger River. By a decree of 1 March 1919 the colony of Haut-Senegal et Niger was divided and consequently the new colony of Upper Volta was created. By a decree of 28 December 1926 sections of the provinces of Say (today in Niger) and Dori (today in Burkina Faso) were transferred from Upper Volta to Niger, establishing a new boundary line. This transfer was later modified and in the erratum to the decree of 31 August 1927 the present boundary was defined along local hills, villages, district boundaries, local streams and astronomical points. Niger gained independence on 3 August 1960 and Upper Volta became independent two days later, on 5 August 1960. The two newly established countries adopted the colonial administrative line as their common international boundary in an agreement signed on 23 June 1964. On 9 January 1968 the two governments negotiated various aspects concerning the application of the 1964 agreement.

Present Situation. The boundary line is not demarcated but the precise alignment is clear and there are no disputes concerning its location.

BURKINA FASO — TOGO The boundary between Burkina Faso and Togo extends 78 miles (126 km.) from the boundary tripoint with Benin in the east to the tripoint with Ghana in the west. It is based on the boundaries between the former German and French colonies in central and western Africa.

Geographical Setting. The western boundary point is located at about 11°08'33"N and 0°08'09"W, on the Kulutamsi River. In a straight line it heads east-southeast for some 55 miles (90 km.) to the Sansargou River at its intersection with the 11°N parallel. The boundary follows the river downstream southward for 6 miles (9 km.) and departs to run in a straight line east-northeast for 15 miles (25 km.) until it regains the 11°N parallel, which it follows for 22 miles (35 km.) to the tripoint with Benin at the convergence of the 11°N parallel with 0°55'30"E, west of the eastern source of the Oti River.

Historical Background. The imperial struggle between France and Germany in the late nineteenth century over western and central Africa led to the establishment of the present boundary. Germany created a protectorate over the coastal area of Togo in July 1884 and later expanded its territory inland. In 1897 the German protectorate reached the French sphere of influence that had been established over central Africa. On 23 July 1897 a Franco-German convention settled a boundary along the 11°N parallel between Togoland, ruled by Germany, and French Sudan. In 1904 the French established the colony of Haut-Senegal et Niger, which included a region called Upper Volta (from which the Black, Red and White Volta rivers originate).

On 28 September 1912 France and Germany modified and reestablished the boundary. Togoland was captured by Anglo-French forces during World War I and the area was divided between them in 1922 under a League of Nations mandate. The British section of Togoland (West Togo) voted in 1956 for integration with Ghana while French Togo became independent on 27 April 1960 as the Republic of Togo. In 1919 the colony of Upper Volta was established after the division of the French colony of Haut-Senegal et Niger. It became independent on 5 August 1960, changing its name to Burkina Faso in 1984. Both countries adopted the colonial boundary of 1912 as their common international boundary.

Present Situation. Although there are no demarcation pillars along the boundary line, no disputes exist concerning its alignment and it is one of the quietest boundaries in Africa.

BURMA see MYANMAR.

BURUNDI
A landlocked country (area: 10,746 sq. miles [27,832 sq. km.]; estimated population: 5,970,000 [1994]), Burundi is located in central Africa. It is bounded in the north by Rwanda (180 miles; 290 km.), in the east and south by Tanzania (280 miles; 451 km.) and in the west by Zaire (145 miles; 233 km.). The capital of Burundi is Bujumbura.

In the late nineteenth century the Germans occupied Burundi. After World War I the Belgians received the colony as a League of Nations mandated territory including neighboring Rwanda. Like the Germans before them, the Belgians ruled the Burundians indirectly through an intermediate princely class of the Tutsi. Before independence in 1962 the

Belgians held elections in Burundi. The head of the winning party was murdered immediately after the elections and his party proved unable to contain the ethnic tensions. The monarchy emerged as the only source of legitimacy of both the Tutsi and the Hutu.

In 1965 tensions reached a climax as a result of a coup attempt made by the Hutu-dominated gendarmerie and the ensuing massacre of the Hutu political elite and thousands of their rural supporters. These events ended any significant political participation of the Hutu for many years. A year later the monarchy was abolished in a coup carried out by Tutsi, who became increasingly dominant in the government.

In 1972, after an attempted Hutu-rebellion in which a few thousand Tutsi were killed, the government responded with a large-scale massacre of Hutu, especially the educated class. Estimates of the number of dead vary from 80,000 to 250,000. About 200,000 Hutu fled the country and all Hutu were eliminated from the armed forces.

Ethnic tensions continued to exist after 1972 and in 1988 erupted again in the north of the country when groups of Hutu, claiming Tutsi provocations, slaughtered hundreds of Tutsi. The Tutsi-dominated army was sent to restore order and in the following days more large-scale massacres took place.

The political situation remained tense until in mid-1989 the president, a member of the Tutsi, announced plans to combat all forms of discrimination against the Hutu. A commission for national unity was established and as a result 12 of the 23 portfolios in the government were given to Hutu ministers. However, the army was still reluctant to allow Hutu to enter its ranks.

BURUNDI — RWANDA
Most of the 180-mile (290-km.) boundary between Burundi and Rwanda follows rivers. It extends from the tripoint boundary junction with Tanzania in the east to the boundary junction with Zaire in the west. No boundary pillars demarcate the land boundary.

Geographical Setting. The boundary's eastern terminus lies in the confluence of the Kagera and Mwibu rivers. It follows the Kagera River downstream westward to Lake Rweru (Regwero) and crosses the lake to the mouth of the Bikare River, which it follows to its confluence with the Agatete

River. The line trends along the Agatete River to its source and then heads southwest in a straight line to the source of the Uruanda River. Following the Uruanda to its source, the boundary then forms another straight line to the source of the Kigeri River, which it follows to its mouth in the northeastern edge of Lake Coboba (Tshoboba). The line continues to the northwestern edge of the lake along the median line of its northern section, to reach the mouth of the Kamahozi River. Thence it progresses along the river westward to its confluence with the Kanyaru (Akanyaru) River and through the main navigation channel of the latter upstream southward and then westward to its sources. In a short straight line to the Sumu (Kakunamba) River, the boundary line then tracks it to its intersection with the Kabulantwa River and follows that river upstream northward for 6 miles (9 km.). It leaves the river, proceeds to Colline Umufu point and in a straight line reaches the source of the Ruwa (Luhwa) River near Twinyoni boundary point. Following the *thalweg* (main navigation channel) of the Ruwa River downstream westward and then southward the boundary reaches the Ruzizi River at the boundary tripoint with Zaire.

Historical Background. Burundi and Rwanda were both local monarchies settled mainly by Hutu people and ruled by Tutsi kings from the fifteenth century. The boundary between the monarchies was established primarily along local rivers, mainly the Ruwa, Kanyaru and Kagera rivers. In 1890 both countries were occupied by imperial Germany and became part of the German East African empire. The local rulers maintained their positions and there was no movement to change their common boundary. There were no legal documents that established the boundary between Urundi (the former name of Burundi) and Ruanda (today's Rwanda).

Both countries, which were bounded in the west by Belgian Congo (today's Zaire), were occupied by Belgian forces during World War I and became a mandate territory of Belgium in 1923, under the name of Ruanda-Urundi. The border between the two provinces was described in an ordinance published on 14 August 1949 and modified in 1958. On 1 July 1962 both gained independence and assumed their former tribal names—Rwanda and Burundi. They reestablished their old common boundary along the rivers, through the Coboba and Rweru lakes and along a number of straight lines linking stream sources.

Present Situation. There are no known boundary disputes between Burundi and Rwanda. The line is clearly demarcated by the rivers and lakes and is unequivocally recognized by the local inhabitants as their old, traditional boundary.

BURUNDI — TANZANIA The boundary between Burundi and Tanzania runs for 280 miles (451 km.) from the boundary tripoint with Rwanda in the north to the tripoint with Zaire in the south. For its most part the line follows rivers, connected by short straight lines.

Geographical Setting. The boundary junction with Rwanda in the north is located at the intersection of the main navigation channels of the Mwibu and Kagera rivers. It follows the Mwibu River upstream southward to the head of its southwestern branch. In a series of 17 short straight lines the boundary runs south for 10 miles (16 km.) to the head of the Mukana River. From there the line progresses along the main navigation channels of a series of rivers (about 40 in number), their confluences and short straight lines that connect them southeastward for about 75 miles (120 km.) and then southwestward for approximately 130 miles (210 km.). Thus it reaches Lake Tanganyika at the outlet of the Ndyakalika (Nyakolika) ravine, south of the small town of Nyanza (Burundi). A boundary pillar was erected about 13 feet (4 m.) from the water's edge and from there the line runs into the lake in a straight line westward. It reaches the median line of the lake, at approximately 4°27'S, which is the boundary tripoint with Zaire.

Historical Background. The Kingdom of Urundi and Tanganyika were parts of German East Africa, which was established in 1890. The limits of the Kingdom of Urundi were known and recognized by the local inhabitants long before the German occupation, but its boundary with Tanganyika was never declared during the German period.

Both areas became mandate territories under the League of Nations' system; Urundi (with Ruanda— later Rwanda) was placed under Belgian trust and Tanganyika was ruled as a mandate territory by Britain. The boundary between the Belgian and

British territories was described in very general terms in the British Mandate for East Africa on 20 July 1922 and the present boundary stems from the protocol of talks between Britain and Belgium that was signed on 5 August 1924, confirmed by an exchange of notes signed in Brussels on 17 May 1926 and approved by the Council of the League of Nations. A demarcation team erected 58 boundary pillars along the land segments while the river lines were well established. Tanganyika became an independent country on 9 December 1961, renaming itself Tanzania on 29 October 1964. Urundi became an independent country on 1 July 1962, then becoming Burundi. Both countries adopted the colonial mandate boundary.

Present Situation. Since Burundi and Tanzania gained independence, no disputes or issues concerning the boundary alignment have been reported.

BURUNDI — ZAIRE Extending 145 miles (233 km.), the boundary between Burundi and Zaire reaches from the boundary junction with Rwanda in the north to the boundary junction with Tanzania in the south. It is entirely a water boundary, following rivers and Lake Tanganyika—the only one of this kind in the world.

Geographical Setting. From the north, at the confluence of the Ruzizi and Ruwa (Luhwa) rivers, north of the small town of Kamanyola (Zaire), the boundary line follows the *thalweg* (main navigation channel) of the Ruzizi River downstream southward for 58 miles (93 km.). At the confluence of the Ruzizi with the Petite Ruzizi (Rusizi Rutoya) River it enters the *thalweg* of the latter and traverses southward for 8 miles (13 km.) to its mouth in Lake Tan-

ganyika. The line follows the median line of the lake southward for 79 miles (127 km.), down to the boundary junction with Tanzania in the middle of the lake. As the length of the whole boundary follows a water line, there are no land pillars and the entire demarcation lies in invisible lines.

Historical Background. The line between Zaire and Burundi follows the boundary between German East Africa (which included Rwanda, Burundi and Tanganyika), which was established in 1890 and the Belgian colony of Congo. It was established in a convention signed by Belgium and Germany on 11 August 1910, which defined it through Lake Tanganyika and northward along rivers up to Lake Kivu. After World War I Burundi and Rwanda (then Ruanda-Urundi) were placed under Belgian mandate while German Tanganyika became a British mandate area. The boundary junction between the Belgian and the British regions, which later became the Tanzania–Burundi–Zaire tripoint, was established by the Anglo-Belgian protocol of 1924. It was described as the point on the median line of Lake Tanganyika, west of boundary pillar no.1 situated on the eastern shore of Lake Tanganyika, 13 feet (4 m.) from the water's edge at the outlet of the Ndyakalika (Nyakolika) ravine. This line served the mandate area until 1962, when Urundi separated itself from Rwanda and established itself as independent Burundi, adopting the existing colonial boundaries with Belgian Congo, which became independent Zaire in 1960.

Present Situation. There are no official boundary disputes between Burundi and Zaire. Zaire's claims to the delta of the Petite Ruzizi area near Lake Tanganyika were never brought openly.

C

CAMBODIA (Kâmpuchéa)   A country in Southeast Asia (area: 69,879 sq. miles [180,986 sq. km.]; estimated population: 9,240,000 [1994]), Cambodia is bounded in the north by Laos (336.5 miles; 541 km.), in the north and west by Thailand (499 miles; 803 km.), in the east by Vietnam (763 miles; 1,228 km.) and in the south by the Gulf of Thailand. The capital of Cambodia is Phnom Penh.

The Khmer people of Cambodia probably migrated to their present location from the north in the early centuries C.E. They were the dominant ethnic group of the Chenla kingdom, which gained ascendancy over neighboring states during the sixth century. From the ninth to thirteenth centuries a Khmer kingdom known as Kambujadesa (the name Cambodia stems from the Hindi variant of the name, Kambuja) dominated southern Vietnam and significant portions of Laos and Thailand. Culturally, Kambujadesa was influenced by India, from which it adopted a writing system as well as Hinduism and Buddhism. Today the Khmer are predominantly Buddhist, although relics of traditional ancestor and spirit worship are also important. One of the most significant feats of the Kambuja state was the construction of the Angkor Wat complex of temples and public buildings, which can still be seen today. Also developed was a complex irrigation system which utilized waters from the Mekong River and Tonle Sap Lake to irrigate the flat interior Savannah. Upon the kingdom's downfall in 1432, the Khmer underwent a series of invasions by their neighbors, the Thais and Vietnamese, which culminated in the Khmer seeking the protection of the French in 1864.

Independence from France was granted in 1954, and the Khmer, under King Norodom Sihanouk, pursued a neutral stance to avoid entering the Vietnamese conflict. In 1965, a South Vietnamese air raid on Viet Cong bases in eastern Cambodia forced Cambodia into the war and provided impetus for its own Communist Khmer Rouge insurgency. The government collapsed in 1975 and the Khmer Rouge entered the capital, Phnom Penh.

The Khmer Rouge regime (1975–1979) nearly destroyed Cambodia. A radical variation of communism was pursued, cities were depopulated, and the entire

Boundaries of Cambodia and Laos

population was forced into the countryside as slave labor. Between one and three million people died of deprivation or were executed for crimes ranging from failing to produce rice efficiently, to having an education, or even wearing spectacles. Border skirmishes with the Vietnamese led to a full scale war and the conquest of the country in 1979. A pro-Vietnamese regime was established in Phnom Penh, but the country remains ravaged by warring factions.

Despite Khmer Rouge excesses, certain elements of Khmer culture survive. Ninety percent of the Khmer still live in small villages and grow rice in irrigated paddies. They still use the red and white checkered cloth, practically a national symbol, for everything from a headdress to a means of carrying young children. The influence of Buddhism is felt everywhere.

CAMBODIA — LAOS Mostly following watersheds and streams, the Cambodia–Laos boundary extends 336.5 miles (541 km.) from the tripoint with Vietnam in the east at approximately 107°32'E and 14°41'N to the boundary tripoint with Thailand in the west.

Geographical Setting. From the eastern boundary junction in the Annam Mountains the line bears southwest for 98 miles (157 km.) along the winding watershed between Se (Xe) Khong in Laos and Se San in Cambodia. Turning north for 30 miles (48 km.) it follows a minor water divide between the two tributaries of the Se Khong, reaching the main river 31 miles (49 km.) southwest of Attopeu (Laos). For the next 15 miles (24 km.) the line follows the river to a point about 0.3 miles (0.5 km.) below the confluence of Se Khong and Se Khampho, leaves the river to briefly follow a minor tributary and ascends the local watershed. Then following watersheds and crossing four streams (Houei Tin Hiang, Houei Loung, Houei Lane and Houei Khampha) southward, the boundary reaches Houei Khalieng, which forms the boundary for the next 15 miles (24 km.). The line runs north of Route Nationale 13 westward for about 10 miles (15 km.) and cuts across it, then reaching the Mekong River at a point immediately west of the Cambodian village of Voun Kham, which becomes accessible only through Laotian territory. From Voun Kham the boundary crosses the Mekong River westward to attain its west bank, where the river enters a narrower

channel and the boundary heads northwest for 8 miles (13 km.) and follows the Cambodian bank of the Mekong. From here the median line of the main channel that flows in close proximity to the Cambodian bank is followed to its confluence with the Tonle Ropou River, which it then follows to the border with Thailand at Preah Chambot pass.

Historical Background. The present boundary was established by the unilateral act of French administrators as separate segments, east and west of the Mekong River, early in the twentieth century. When the French acquired Thai territory on the east bank of the Mekong River by the French-Thai peace treaty of 1893, their new territories were divided into three sections. This division proved inconvenient, however, as some Laotian villages could only be reached by traversing through Cambodian territory, and led to the creation of a unified territory of Laos on 19 April 1899 as a French protectorate. Part of the southern division, the districts of Soeng Treng and Siempang, which had been under the administration of Cochin China, were transferred to Cambodia in 1904 and the boundary east of the Mekong River was then drawn along the existing line

The boundary west of the Mekong River was defined after Thailand ceded the area from the Dangrek mountains to the Mekong River to France in 1904. This region consisted of two separate areas: two ancient Cambodian provinces and the Kingdom of Bassac. The latter, situated in the east, had much in common with Laos, politically and ethnically, and a boundary was created to separate it from Phumi mbu Prey and Tonle Ropou. A decree of 28 March 1905 described the western section of the boundary along the main branch of the Tonle Ropou River to a col known as Preah Chambot at the eastern edge of the southern Dangrek range, at 105°10'E. With the collapse of Indochina Laos became partly independent on 19 July 1949, followed by Cambodia on 8 November 1949, both adopting the boundary defined at the beginning of the century. Full independence was acheived in 1954.

Present Situation. The Cambodia–Laos boundary is fully recognized by both parties.

CAMBODIA — THAILAND The boundary between Cambodia and Thailand was established as part of the old boundary between French Indochina and Thailand in the early twentieth century. It stretches 499 miles (803 km.) from the Gulf of Thailand to the tripoint boundary with Laos in the Preah Chambot pass, west of the Mekong River. Apart from a short section that crosses a valley, the boundary coincides with watersheds and rivers.

Geographical Setting. Beginning in the south, from the Gulf of Siam in the Indian Ocean, the boundary runs northward, following the watershed of the coastal range of the Cardamoms for a distance of 103 miles (166 km.). These isolated mountains, their peaks rising to 5,000 feet (1,520 m.), are subject to heavy annual rainfalls of about 200 inches (5,080 mm.), which generate dense tropical forest. The boundary joins some local rivers (Pailin, O Taker, Mongkol Boery) for about 25 miles (40 km.) and runs 10 miles (16 km.) in a series of straight lines to the O Dar River. Following the river for 18 miles (29 km.) and then traversing another two rivers, it reaches the city of Poipet. In a straight line northeastward, the boundary runs for 15 miles (24 km.), crossing the valley west of the Tonle Sap Lake, reaching a series of rivers and streams and following them to their source in the Dangrek Mountains. Turning eastward the boundary then follows the watershed along the Dangrek escarpment to the Preah Chambot pass, which is the source of the Ropou River, a tributary of the Mekong River, and the boundary junction with Laos.

Historical Background. Until the mid-nineteenth century the Southeast Asian states of Thailand, Laos, Annam and Tonkin were independent. Upon securing a foothold at the mouth of the Mekong River in 1862, France began making claims on Cambodia, a weak state also subject to Thai claims. The situation was resolved in July 1867: Thailand recognized Cambodia as a French protectorate in return for two of Cambodia's western provinces. France later expanded its Asian territories westward and on 3 October 1893 forced Thailand to accept the Mekong River as its eastern boundary. Further French claims on the area west of the Mekong River were realized on 13 February 1904, and France also obtained some 6,000 sq. miles (15,540 sq. km.) south of the Dangrek range. Another agreement made later that year (29 June 1904) granted France some 2,500 sq. miles (6,475 sq. km.) of the coastal plain in the Cardamoms peninsula, thereby extend-

ing French territory to the Gulf of Siam. On 23 March 1907 the Franco-Thai boundary was again rectified: France ceded the Cardamoms region and a small parcel of land in northern Thailand (total area: 950 sq. miles; 2,460 sq. km.) in exchange for the two provinces (12,400 sq. miles; 32,116 sq. km.) given to Thailand in 1867. The new treaty also made provisions for the demarcation of the boundary, which was completed by the end of 1908 with no serious difficulties arising. During World War II Thailand demanded that France return all the territories it had occupied during 1893–1907. France agreed, upon Japanese mediation, to return the two provinces taken in 1907, but after Japan's defeat demanded to reclaim them. This was provided for in an accord of 17 November 1946.

After Cambodia regained its full independence in 1954, a border problem arose involving the Preah Vihear temple, situated on the edge of the Dangrek range. According to the survey maps the temple was left south of the boundary, within Cambodia, even though the boundary had to follow the watershed and by doing so situated the temple in Thailand. The area was occupied by Thailand and the case was set before the International Court of Justice (ICJ). Thailand claimed that the boundary should follow the watershed according to the agreements, while Cambodia presented the maps that were made at the time and signed by Thai representatives, placing the temple within the French territory. The Thais accept the 1904 and 1907 treaties as having established the boundary, but reject the French maps as inaccurate and invalid. The verdict was in Cambodia's favor and the court ruled that the temple was Cambodian. Thailand maintains its reservation on the ICJ decision concerning the temple.

Present Situation. The border area between Thailand and Cambodia is not a settled area and there are occasional border incidents. Although no official questions have arisen as to the precise alignment of the boundary since the ICJ settlement of 1962 and the establishment of about 75 permanent boundary pillars in the area, the exact location of the entire boundary is yet to be settled.

CAMBODIA — VIETNAM   From the boundary tripoint with Laos to the Gulf of Thailand this boundary extends 763 miles (1,228 km.). Between

1869 and 1942 it was demarcated in four sections. Originally there were 124 pillars marking the route, which have since been supplemented to clarify difficult sections. Where the border consists of a waterway, the Cambodian bank of the stream usually constitutes the border.

Geographical Setting. Starting at the tripoint with Laos in the north the first 50 miles (80 km.) of the boundary follow the watershed between the Diak and Sathay rivers and the *thalweg* of the Sathay until the river turns west and north. Then the border continues south in a series of straight lines, arbitrarily traversing over the local topography, irrespective of notable features, for 55 miles (88 km.) to the confluence of the Srepok and Dam rivers. It follows the Dam River for a further 55 miles (88 km.) to its source at 12°40'N. Most of this route passes through forested and poorly inhabited country. From the headwaters of the Dam River the boundary crosses to the headwaters of the Hoyt River in a straight line and follows it to its confluence with the Kle River, where it joins the Djerman River at its headwaters and follows it until it crosses in a straight line to the Prek Chrieu, which it follows west to its intersection with the road to Kratie (Cambodia). In a straight line the boundary reaches the Can-le-Cham River at the point where it begins to turn south after its wide arc from its eastern headwaters. The line follows the river south to its confluence with the Saigon River and crosses rolling forested hills for about 50 miles (80 km.), along the borders of the Bang Chrum, Chon Ba Den and Hoa Ninh provinces. It reaches Cai Bach, follows it to Kompong Mean Chey and further south to its confluence with Cai Chey. From this point 3 miles (5 km.) of the border run in two straight lines and along the course of the Ta-So stream. The boundary then joins a line that was designed by its French surveyors to divide the areas between the branches of the Vaico rivers (Vam Co Tay and Vam Co Dong) and that is known as the "parrot's beak." This section of the border now shows a distinct demarcation between the rice paddies of Cambodia and the more densely forested areas of Vietnam. From its junction with the Vam Co Tay River the boundary continues to join the Cai Co River at Hung Nguyen and proceeds west for 21 miles (34 km.) along the bank of the Cai Co to its confluence with Tra Bec River and further along the

Song So Ha and Rach So Thuong rivers to the Mekong River. It then crosses the Mekong–Bassac interfluve in a series of straight lines westward to Bac Nam and then follows the Bassac upstream to Khanh Binh where the line follows the Rach Binh Ghi River to its confluence with Song Chan Doc. It travels south in a series of straight lines from a point less than 1 mile (1.5 km.) northwest of Chau Phu (Chau Doc) to the Kihn Vinh Te canal, which it follows on its northern bank westward, at a distance of about 0.5 miles (1 km.). Leaving the line of the canal at Giang Thanh the border reaches the harbor and follows the line of the outer ramparts, which are marked by old fortifications, 1.4 miles (2.3 km.) from the town of Ha Tien (Vietnam) and the limits of the village of Saky, to the edge of the extended lands of Saky. The boundary line then continues in a straight line to the coast of the Gulf of Thailand.

Historical Background. This boundary was established in four major sections between 1869 and 1942, when the French in Cochin China sought to define the extent of their influence in the decayed Annamite empire. Cambodia at the time was under pressure of resisting French incursions from the south and east and Thai expansionism from the north. The French seem to have taken advantage of the inexperience of the Cambodian commissioners in the first joint boundary commission that was convened to define their common frontiers in 1869, awarding the greatest advantages to themselves. The first section to be delimited, between 1869 and 1872, was the central area between the Cham and Cai Co rivers. After protests from the Cambodian king the original line, due south of Kompong Tasang to Hung Nguyen, was redrawn to include in Cambodia the tracts of land later known as the "parrot's beak." This modification left a small enclave along the Cai Chay in French hands, which was later returned to Cambodia under an agreement of 1914 when other French claims to coastal territories were answered.

The second section, east of the first, was unilaterally established by the French in 1871 and carried the border line to the headwaters of the Hoyt River. However, this was also modified by the agreement of 1914.

The third section, toward the tripoint with Laos was delimited during 1893–1929, when the French delineated the boundary between their Laotian and Annamite territories and established the size and status of the Darlac region.

The last section, from the coast to the Mekong and Bassac rivers, was mostly settled by 1873, but it was also modified in the 1914 agreement and later confirmed in 1935 when a dispute broke out over the Mekong–Bassac interfluve. It was altered again in 1942, when the island of Koki was transferred to Cochin China and a small area of land beside the Binh Ghi was returned to Cambodia. Cambodia achieved independence in 1954 while Vietnam became independent in 1954 as two states (North and South Vietnam) and was united in 1975.

Present Situation. Since independence, no boundary treaty or agreement has been negotiated between Cambodia and Vietnam, although there are several points of possible dispute. Both countries have accepted the French maps but both—from time to time—make claims to areas of the other's territory.

CAMEROON   Cameroon (area: 183,568 sq. miles [475,441 sq. km.]; estimated population: 12,800,000 [1994]) is situated on the west coast of central Africa. It is bounded in the west by the Gulf of Guinea, northwest by Nigeria (1,050 miles; 1,690 km.), east by Chad (680 miles; 1,094 km.) and the Central African Republic (495 miles; 797 km.) and south by Congo (325 miles; 523 km.), Gabon (185 miles; 298 km.) and Equatorial Guinea (118 miles; 189 km.). Its capital is Yaoundé.

Cameroon was a German colony until World War I. Following Germany's defeat it was divided as a mandate between France and Britain. After World War II, the French allowed party politics to develop. The first political party to emerge in French Cameroon was the UPC (Union des Populations du Cameroun), which demanded independence and supported unification with British Cameroon. It was supported mainly by the Bamileke and Duala, who were related to ethnic groups in the British part of Cameroon. Violent incidents in the 1950s led the French to ban the UPC, but the movement simply went underground to continue the struggle for independence. At independence the strongest, and later sole party, was the Union Camerounais of Ahmadou Ahidjo, a Muslim from the north who became the country's first president in 1960. Meanwhile vio-

lence broke out again, mainly in the Bamileke areas, over dissatisfaction of urban Bamileke at unemployment and overcrowded living conditions. Later known as the Bamileke revolt, it was joined by the Bassa-Bakoko, and only suppressed in the mid-1960s with the help of French troops. Ethnic incidents involving the Bamileke continued to occur sporadically, culminating in the Tombel Massacre of 1967, in which 230 Bamileke were killed.

The two parts of Cameroon became federated in 1961 and were unified in 1972. Ahidjo handed over his responsibilities to Paul Biya in 1982. Since 1991 there has been violent civil unrest and demand for political reform and democratization.

CAMEROON — CENTRAL AFRICAN REPUBLIC   Cameroon and the Central African Republic share a boundary that runs for 495 miles (797 km.) between the boundary tripoint with Chad, on the Mbéré River, in the north and the tripoint with Congo, on the Sangha River, in the south. It follows the colonial boundary between the former French and German possessions in central Africa.

Geographical Setting. Beginning at approximately 7°31'40"N and 15°29'40"E, in the median line of the Mbéré River, the boundary courses along the river upstream southwestward to its confluence with the Ngou River, which it follows upstream for about 15 miles (25 km.). It leaves the river, runs southwestward along a watershed that divides the rivers running to Lake Chad and those flowing to the Atlantic Ocean and reaches the source of the Kadei River. It trends along this river downstream southward to its confluence with one of its lesser tributaries. The line follows the tributary to its source and in a short straight line reaches the Boumbe River. The boundary line joins the river downstream southeastward for approximately 80 miles (130 km.) to its confluence with the Kadei River, which it follows again to its confluence with the Batouri River. Coursing along this river for 10 miles (16 km.) it reaches a point west of the town of Molai (Central African Republic), leaves the river and continues southeast in a straight line for 85 miles (137 km.) to the Nyoue River. Coursing along the river downstream to its confluence with the Sangha River, the boundary then follows the median line of the Sangha River downstream southward to the boundary tripoint with

Congo, located at approximately 2°13'20"N and 16°11'30"E.

Historical Background. Today's Cameroon was originally the German protectorate Kamerun, which was proclaimed on 12 July 1884. The Central African Republic was formerly part of the French colony of Oubangui-Chari-Tchad, which was occupied by the French in the late nineteenth century, became a unit of French Congo and from 1910 was a part of French Equatorial Africa. Dividing these French and German possessions in central Africa was a boundary that was defined in a convention that was concluded on 15 March 1894. A convention of 18 April 1908 restated the line, and it is along this latter delimitation that the present boundary stands.

The German colony of Kamerun was occupied by British and French forces during World War I, who later divided the area between them and held separate mandates in the region: Britain to the northwest and France to the southeast. French Cameroon became independent on 1 January 1960 while Oubangui-Chari became independent as the Central African Republic on 13 August 1960. With no formal agreement, both adopted the colonial boundary as their international boundary.

Present Situation. The ground sections of the boundary line are demarcated by pillars, but the river line is problematic. Like most African river boundaries, when large areas wind in many directions and become flood zones, delineation of the line is complicated. Since independence, however, no major doubts concerning the boundary alignment have transpired and neither country has raised boundary disputes.

CAMEROON — CHAD The boundary between Cameroon and Chad runs for 680 miles (1,094 km.) between the boundary junction with Nigeria, in Lake Chad, in the north and the boundary junction with the Central African Republic, in the principal navigation channel of the Mbéré River, in the south.

Geographical Setting. The northern terminus of the boundary line is located in the southeastern section of Lake Chad, at about 13°05'N and 14°05'E. The line runs eastward along the parallel to reach its intersection with 14°28'E. In a straight line it runs to the point where the principal navigable branch of

the Chari River empties into Lake Chad, north of Maski (Cameroon). It follows the main navigation channel of the Chari River upstream southeastward to its confluence with the Logone River near N'Djamena, the capital of Chad, and following the main navigation channel of the Logone River upstream southward it reaches a point on its right bank, 1.24 miles (2 km.) northwest of Ham (Chad). The boundary line then leaves the river, runs westward for 140 miles (225 km.) and arrives at the intersection of the Mayo Kebbi River and 14°E. In its course the boundary line crosses Lake Fianga and some local roads, between villages and small towns located on both sides of the boundary. In a straight line southeastward for 75 miles (121 km.) the line runs to the Sinabou River, follows it eastward for 12 miles (20 km.) and leaves it to continue southeast. Reaching the intersection of the Vina (Western Logone) and Mbéré rivers, west of Baibokoum (Chad), it courses along the Mbéré River upstream, through the center of its navigation channel, to the boundary junction with the Central African Republic, at approximately 7°31'40"N and 15°29'40"E.

Historical Background. During the late nineteenth century France extended its sphere of influence into central Africa and in the early years of the twentieth century Chad was a part of French Congo. In 1910 it became a unit within French Equatorial Africa. Cameroon became a German protectorate on 12 July 1884 as Kamerun. The border between the French and German spheres of influence was the origin of the present boundary between Chad and Cameroon and it resulted from the definitions of the Franco-German protocols of 24 December 1885 and 4 February 1894. Further delimitations took place following a convention of 15 March 1894, when the boundary between Cameroon and French Congo in the area of Lake Chad, along the Chari River and 15°E, was established. The present boundary closely follows the delimitations of the Franco-German Convention of 18 April 1908, which again established the boundary between the French and German possessions in central Africa and provided the demarcation of the line. Three years later, on 4 November 1911, the Logone River, from its confluence with the Chari River to the town of Ham (Chad), was established as a part of the boundary between Cameroon and Chad, thus awarding France the area south of Port-Lamy (today Chad's capital city, N'Djamena).

After World War I the German territories in Africa became mandate territories under the League of Nations. France and Britain divided Cameroon, France governing approximately 80% of the area while Britain administrated the remainder. The Treaty of Versailles of 1919 confirmed the 1911 Convention, restoring the boundary between Cameroon and Chad.

Cameroon became an independent state on 1 January 1960; Chad on 11 August 1960. The colonial boundary of 1911 was adopted as their common international boundary and redemarcation of the boundary by pillars was carried out by a mixed commission, completed on 9 December 1970.

Present Situation. The river sectors of the boundary were never determined and a number of complications are caused by flooding and the appearance or covering of islands. Thus it becomes difficult to determine the median lines or main navigation channels of these rivers, along which the boundary is defined. Nevertheless, no boundary disputes are known.

CAMEROON — CONGO   Following the colonial boundary between the former German and French possessions in central Africa, the Cameroon–Congo boundary runs 325 miles (523 km.) between the boundary tripoint with the Central African Republic on the Sangha River in the east and the boundary tripoint with Gabon in the west.

Geographical Setting. From the boundary tripoint with Gabon, at the intersection of the Ivindo (Ayina) River with the 2°10'20"N parallel, the line courses along the parallel eastward for 72 miles (115 km.). Reaching a point that stands south of the town of Eta (Cameroon) it trends across the watershed between the Masimbo (Cameroon) and Dja (Congo) rivers to their confluence, following the combined channel to its confluence with the Ngoko River. Constituting the main river boundary, the next section follows the Ngoko River downstream generally eastward for about 190 miles (310 km.) to its confluence with the Sangha River, north of the town of Ouesso (Congo). The boundary line then enters the main navigation channel of the Sangha River and courses through it northward for about 45 miles (75 km.) to the boundary tripoint with the Central

African Republic, which is located in the river at approximately 2°13'20"N and 16°11'30"E.

Historical Background. The French established themselves on the coast of central Africa in the late nineteenth century and Cameroon was established as a German protectorate (Kamerun) on 12 July 1884. France and Germany first established a boundary between their spheres of influence in central Africa on 24 December 1885, modifying it on 15 March 1894. The French established a colony in Congo in 1889, which became the colony of Moyen Congo in 1903 and the boundary was further altered and demarcated by the convention of 18 April 1908.

In 1910 the French established French Equatorial Africa, which included today's Chad, Gabon, the Central African Republic and French Congo. In 1911 some changes in the boundary alignment were made in favor of German Kamerun, but the earlier demarcation was restored in 1919. The power deficit of the German empire during World War I led to the division of Kamerun under the League of Nations as a French mandate in the southeast and a British mandate in the northwest. The southern boundary of French Kamerun with French Equatorial Africa was not changed.

French Cameroon became independent on 1 January 1960 and Congo gained its independence on 15 August of that year. The newly established independent states adopted the existing colonial line as their common international boundary without any formal agreement.

Present Situation. Since achieving independence neither Cameroon nor Congo have challenged the boundary's principle. No significant disputes concerning the boundary's alignment are known to exist.

CAMEROON — EQUATORIAL GUINEA   The boundary between Cameroon and Equatorial Guinea stretches for 118 miles (189 km.) from the Gulf of Guinea eastward. The western part of the boundary is formed by a river, while the eastern part follows a fixed latitude.

Geographical Setting. The western part of the boundary begins at the mouth of the Campo River, which enters the Gulf of Guinea south of the city of Tondfom. It follows the river to its intersection with 11°20'E and continues eastward to reach the tripoint boundary with Gabon, which is situated at

2°10'20"N and 11°20'E. The boundary cuts through a tropical rain forest situated along the southern bank of the Campo River.

Historical Background. The current boundary between Cameroon and Equatorial Guinea approximates the colonial boundary that had separated the German protectorate of Kamerun and Spanish Guinea. The boundary was formulated in the Franco-German agreements of 1885 and 1894 that outlined the European powers' spheres of influence in Africa. Both countries recognized Spanish interests along the coast and the extent of these interests was confirmed by the Franco-Spanish Convention of 27 June 1900. German Kamerun became the French mandate of Cameroon following World War I. It achieved independence on 1 January 1960. Spanish Guinea became the independent republic of Equatorial Guinea on 12 October 1968. Since obtaining independence neither state has challenged the principle of the boundary.

Present Situation. The straight segment of the boundary is marked by six pillars. The Campo River section is marked along the median line rather than the *thalweg* (deepest navigable channel) on maps. There are no known disputes concerning the location of the boundary.

CAMEROON — GABON   Extending 185 miles (298 km.), from the boundary tripoint with Congo on the Ayina River in the east to the boundary tripoint with Equatorial Guinea in the west, the Cameroon–Gabon boundary follows a dividing line between the former French and German colonial possessions in central Africa.

Geographical Setting. From the boundary tripoint with Congo in the east, at the intersection of the Ivindo (Ayina) River and the 2°10'20"N parallel, the boundary runs westward, following the river upstream to reach a flooded area south of Djoum (Cameroon). The boundary follows the main channel that crosses the flooded area westward and continues along the Kom River to its confluence with the Ntem River. It then proceeds in line with the Ntem River westward to its confluence with the Kyè River, which it follows southward to the point where it intersects the Mvèzeu River. From there the line courses in a straight line westward for 1 mile (1.6 km.) and reaches the tripoint with Equatorial

Guinea, which is located at 2°10'20"N and 11°20'E.

Historical Background. A German protectorate was proclaimed over Cameroon on 12 July 1884. Gabon was a French colony established in 1889 as part of French Congo and became a unit within French Equatorial Africa in 1910. The boundary between these French and German possessions was first established in 1885, although the present line results from the Franco-German Convention of 18 April 1908. After World War I southern Cameroon became a mandate area of France and gained independence on 1 January 1960. Later that month Gabon achieved independence from France and both countries adopted the colonial line as their international boundary.

Present Situation. The ground sector of the boundary is demarcated and no disputes concerning its alignment are known.

CAMEROON — NIGERIA   The Cameroon–Nigeria boundary is one of the few African boundaries that were determined by the local inhabitants and not by foreign powers as a colonial division. It is 1,050 miles (1,690 km.) long, reaching from the boundary tripoint with Chad in Lake Chad in the northeast to the Bight of Benin in the Gulf of Guinea in the southwest.

Geographical Setting. The northeastern terminus of this boundary is located in Lake Chad, at 13°05'N and approximately 14°05'E. It forms a straight line southward for about 40 miles (65 km.) and enters the El Beid River at its mouth on the southern shore of the lake. It follows the river upstream southeastward for about 50 miles (80 km.) to a point west of the small town of Djilbe Gana (Cameroon). There it leaves the river and runs southwest toward the foothills of the Mabuara Mountains, trends across the watershed of the range and reaches a northern tributary of the Benue (Bénoué) River, which it follows to reach the main river. The boundary follows the Benue River upstream eastward for about 5 miles (8 km.) to its confluence with a southern tributary and follows that tributary upstream southward to a point west of Touroua (Cameroon). Continuing southward the line meets the Alantika Mountains, follows the range southwestward, reaches the town of Kontcha (Cameroon) and continues in the same direction to Mount Kombon (7,378 feet; 2,249 m.). It turns westward, reaches the Donga River and follows it downstream northwestward for about 40 miles (65 km.). In a series of straight lines the boundary reaches the Katsina River, follows it for about 50 miles (80 km.), and heads southwestward in another series of straight lines to cross the Cross River. Bearing southward again, the boundary reaches the Bight of Benin in the Gulf of Guinea, west of the Bakassi peninsula and southeast of the Nigerian port city of Calabar.

Historical Background. The European powers occupied the northeastern corner of the Gulf of Guinea in the late nineteenth century. A German protectorate was proclaimed over the Cameroon region on 12 July 1884 while a British protectorate was established over the area between the protectorate of Lagos (Nigeria) and the western bank of the Rio del Rey (including the Bakassi peninsula) on 5 June 1885. The division between the British and German protectorates was first established during April–June 1885 and was followed by agreements in 1890, 1893, 1906 and 1909. The final Anglo-German delimitation was achieved by the agreements of 11 March and 12 April 1913. At the conclusion of World War I France and the United Kingdom agreed upon an administrative partition of the former German colony of Kamerun (10 July 1919). The zones were established respectively as British and French mandates in 1922. The boundary between the mandate areas was placed east of the former Anglo–German boundary in the areas south of Lake Chad and north of the Gulf of Guinea, while the central section of the boundary line was not changed.

French Cameroon was ruled as a separate region while British Cameroon was administrated as part of the colony of Nigeria. French Cameroon became independent on 1 January 1960 and Nigeria nine months later, on 1 October 1960. In 1959 and 1961 plebiscites were held in the British-ruled North and South Cameroon, which were divided by the Donga River. The final plebiscite indicated that the majority of North Cameroon's population was in favor of joining the independent Federation of Nigeria and that the majority of South Cameroon's population was in favor of joining the independent Republic of Cameroon. Both states adopted the plebiscite decision; North Cameroon joined Nigeria on 1 June 1961 and South Cameroon joined the Republic of Cameroon on 1 October 1961. Although both states accepted the new boundary line, the transfers were not peaceful. About 30% of the vote in South Cameroon was against its incorporation with Cameroon, claiming that the Bakassi peninsula, situated on Cameroon's side of the border and to the west of Rio del Rey River, was largely populated by Nigerians. In a border incident on 15 May 1981 five Nigerian soldiers were killed by Cameroonian forces. Nigeria claims that the incident took place on Nigerian soil while Cameroon holds that it was on territory that was not open to Nigerian forces. After long negotiations a peaceful solution was achieved to the boundary dispute, maintaining the 1961 line as it had been determined at the time of the transfers of North and South Cameroon to Nigeria and Cameroon respectively.

Present Situation. Since 1982 there have been some local incidents along the border and Nigeria even considered erecting a fence along its boundary, but neither state has challenged the boundary's 1961 alignment.

CANADA The largest country on the American continent and situated in its northern extremity, Canada (area: 3,851,791.5 sq. miles [9,976,140 sq. km.]; estimated population: of 28,100,000 [1994]) shares a boundary with the United States, which runs for 3,987 miles (6,416 km.) in the south, while its northwestern boundary with the state of Alaska runs for 1,538 miles (2,477 km.). Canada is also bounded by the Pacific Ocean in the west, by the Arctic Ocean in the north and by the Atlantic Ocean in the east. The capital of Canada is Ottawa.

The French established permanent settlements in Canada between 1632 and 1634. Over the next century, the territory repeatedly changed hands between Britain and France. Ultimate British control, achieved in 1755, resulted in the mass deportation of the local population to French colonies in Louisiana and the West Indies. Fewer than 3,000 Acadians remained in Canada, either as refugees in neighboring Quebec or in British prison camps. They were eventually released, and it is their descendants who constitute today's Acadians.

In the mid-1800s, Canada was granted internal self rule. Independence was achieved through a lengthy process in 1867. A century later, in the

1970s, Quebecois secessionist sentiment sparked a series of violent acts aimed at furthering the cause of independence. Since that time, tensions between the English and French communities have smoldered under the surface, sometimes threatening to erupt. Notable threats to the unity of the country occurred during both world wars (the French opposed conscription) and from the late 1960s to the present when a separatist party became an important factor in the provincial politics of French dominated Quebec. Recently, regionalism and even separatism have been felt in other parts of the country as well, sparked both by the sudden upturn in the local economy (as in western Canada since the discovery of oil) and a reluctance to allow concessions to Quebec in order to preserve the country. At the same time, indigenous groups have demanded that their rights be recognized and that they be granted autonomy. Until now, attempts to rewrite the constitution to the satisfaction of all Canadians have ended in failure.

CANADA — UNITED STATES The boundary between Canada and the United States of America consists of two sections. South of Canada the boundary runs 3,987 miles (6,416 km.) from the Atlantic Ocean in the east to the Pacific Ocean in the west. Northwest of Canada, marking the boundary between Canada and the state of Alaska, it runs 1,538 miles (2,477 km.) from the Pacific to the Arctic Ocean. The total length of the boundary is 5,525

miles (8,893 km.). The longest land boundary between any two countries in the world, it consists mainly of astronomical lines (latitudes and longitudes) connected by rivers, lakes and channels.

Geographical Setting. The vast length of the east–west boundary between Canada and the United States cuts across the north–south "grain" of the North American continent. Starting in the northeast, the boundary runs through Passamaquoddy Bay for 25.2 miles (40.5 km.) to the middle of the Saint Croix River and upstream for 129.4 miles (208.2 km.) to that river's source. From there the boundary runs overland for 670.3 miles (1,078.5 km.) between the Canadian provinces of New Brunswick and Quebec and the American states of Maine, New Hampshire, Vermont and New York, to the Saint Lawrence River. Most of the boundary from Passamaquoddy Bay to the Saint Lawrence River is located in the Northeastern Highlands ecoregion. Low mountains supporting forests of northern hardwoods dominate this thinly inhabited agricultural forestry area. North of Burlington, Vermont, the boundary cuts through the northern Appalachian plateau and uplands region where the mountains give way to hills and tablelands that present a landscape mosaic of croplands, pastures and forests.

The boundary line follows the Saint Lawrence River to its source in Lake Ontario and then runs west through the Great Lakes (Ontario, Erie, Huron and Superior) for a distance of 1,288.9 miles

Southern Canada–United States boundary

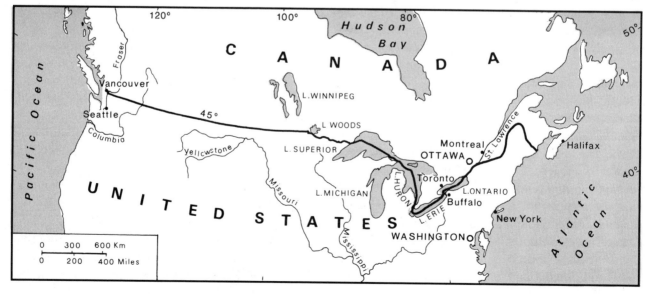

(2,073.8 km.). This portion of the boundary runs through the irregular plains that are dominated by croplands with pastures and woodlands as well as numerous small cities and manufacturing centers. After crossing the Great Lakes and their connecting waterways, the boundary follows a circuitous westerly course for 425.6 miles (684.8 km.), from the mouth of Pigeon River at Lake Superior, through the northern lakes and forests between the Canadian province of Ontario and the American state of Minnesota. Largely covered by forests and glacial lakes, this outlier of the Laurentian Highlands (Canadian Shield) remains a thinly inhabited recreation area. It reaches the Lake of the Woods, forms a northwestern angle through it and runs south from that point for 26.6 miles (42.8 km.) to the 49th parallel. In the area of Rainy Lake and Lake of the Woods the boundary crosses the ecoregion known as the Northern Minnesota Wetlands. As the name suggests, it is a poorly drained region of flat plains covered largely by unproductive swamp and marshland. The boundary follows the 49th parallel for 1,279.1 miles (2,058 km.) to the Gulf of Georgia and, after an additional 142 miles (228.5 km.) through the gulf, meets the Pacific Ocean opposite Cape Flattery on the Strait of Juan De Fuca. This section of the border crosses the towns of Emerson (Manitoba, Canada) and Pembina (North Dakota, United States) in the Red River Valley. Lakes are lacking in this broad north-south corridor flanking the Red River, where cropland dominates the landscape. For most of the boundary between North Dakota and Manitoba the northern glaciated plains present a landscape dominated by highly mechanized wheat cultivation. In western North Dakota the boundary begins to run through the slightly less favorable grain-growing and grazing areas that occupy the broad vistas of the Great Plains that extend across Montana and Saskatchewan to the foot of the eastern ranges of the Rocky Mountains. Except for relatively short stretches, where the line crosses the basin of the Columbia River and the Puget Lowland between British Columbia and Washington, the boundary transits mountainous terrain from the Great Plains to the Pacific Ocean.

Alaska's boundary with Canada begins in the south at Cape Muzon in the Dixon Entrance and runs directly eastward to the southern end of Tongass Passage. It runs up the Pearse and Portland canals to the 56th parallel. From this point the line roughly parallels the coast, running from one mountain summit to another above the heads of the region's fjords. At the head of the Lynn Canal it traverses through the White and Chilkoot passes and then takes a tortuous southwesterly course until it reaches Mount Fairweather (15,300 feet; 4,663 m.). From there the line follows the higher mountains around Yakutat Bay to Mount Saint Elias and the 141st meridian to the Arctic Ocean.

Historical Background. The original limits of the United States were first described, albeit imprecisely, in the provisional treaty of peace concluded in 1782 with Great Britain after the Revolutionary War (1775–1781). The terms used in the definitive treaty concluded the following year, on 3 September 1783, were very similar to those of the provisional treaty and were likewise imprecise. Almost from the time of its first description, the US–Canada boundary has been a source of dissension and controversy and its location the subject of numerous treaties, commissions and surveys. The first of these was the Treaty of London, signed on 19 November 1794, wherein provisions were made for the president of the United States and king of England to appoint commissioners who would decide which stream was the true Saint Croix River. On 25 October 1798 the commissioners agreed that a river sometimes called the Schoodiac was the true Saint Croix River and settled a dispute that had troubled relations between Massachusetts and Nova Scotia as early as 1764. The Treaty of Ghent (24 December 1814) included provisions for a final adjustment of the boundaries described in the treaty of 1783 that had not yet been ascertained and determined. Included were certain islands in the Bay of Fundy as well as the section that runs from the source of the Saint Croix River, through the Saint Lawrence River and the Great Lakes and reaches the northwesternmost point of the Lake of the Woods. Once again, commissioners were appointed. The first board of commissioners was responsible for settling the title to several islands in the Bay of Passamaquoddy and Grand Manan Island in the Bay of Fundy, while a second board took up the boundary from the Saint Croix River to the Saint Lawrence River. A third board of commissioners was to settle the boundary from the

Saint Lawrence River to the Lake of the Woods. The first and third boards reached an agreement but the second was unable to agree on any of the matters under its consideration. Nor could agreement be reached on a general map of the country exhibiting the boundaries claimed by each party.

In 1818 a convention concluded with Great Britain extended the boundary line due west along the 49°N parallel to the "Stony" (Rocky) Mountains and provided that the territory beyond the mountains should remain open to both parties for the next 10 years. In 1824 negotiations were resumed for the settlement of certain matters, including the boundary west of the Rockies. The British government argued that the boundary should follow the 49th parallel to the great northwestern branch of the Columbia River and thence down the middle of the Columbia to the Pacific Ocean, but no agreement was reached. Another round of negotiations was held in 1826, at which both parties tabled a number of compromising proposals, again without results.

The issue of the US–Canada boundary then remained in abeyance until 1842. During this period questions concerning the eastern part of the boundary persisted and it became necessary to refer the disputed matters to a friendly sovereign. When the parties outlined their respective positions, it was determined that an area of about 12,000 sq. miles (31,070 sq. km.) was in dispute. The king of Netherlands was selected in 1829 to serve as the arbiter, and each party laid before him all the evidence supporting its claims. After finding earlier treaty provisions "inexplicable and impractical," the king drew a line that fell between those argued for by the parties. The US government, however, rejected this solution on the grounds that the arbitration did not have the authority to change the boundary of the state of Maine without the state's consent. Maine entered a formal protest and the US Senate refused to ratify the arbiter's award.

Following the failed arbitration of the king of Netherlands, further unsuccessful negotiations on

Peace Arch State Park on the Canadian–USA border

the disputed boundary ensued. The subject soon became a matter of heightened irritation and collisions occurred in the disputed territory. For a time it seemed certain to many observers that the controversy would officially erupt into war between the US and Britain in the Aroostook River region of northern Maine. Both the Maine legislature and US Congress passed bills providing funds for military use should warfare break out. In 1839 Maine sent a party to expel New Brunswick lumbermen from the Aroostook valley. The party was surprised, however, and 50 members of the force were arrested and placed in a New Brunswick jail. Moderation displayed by local authorities on both sides of the conflict defused what became known as the "Aroostook War" before any fatalities were suffered. In an effort to remove causes for chronic friction the government of Great Britain dispatched Lord Ashburton to the United States in 1842 to reach an amicable settlement of the questions concerning both the northeastern boundary and the boundary west of the Rocky Mountains. Although negotiations on the western boundary produced no satisfactory result, the boundary between Maine and New Brunswick was settled to the satisfaction of all parties. Under the terms of the treaty concluded by Lord Ashburton and Secretary of State Noah Webster in 1842, the United States obtained more than one-half of the disputed area. Interestingly this was approximately 1,000 sq. miles (2,590 sq. km.) less than the king of Netherlands had originally recommended. Commissioners working under the terms of the Webster-Ashburton Treaty surveyed the northeastern boundary from the head of the Saint Croix River to the Saint Lawrence River during the period of 1843–1847. This period was also occupied by serious discussions regarding the western boundary. This resulted in a treaty in 1846, defining the line as far west as the Strait of Juan de Fuca. The treaty boundary followed the 49°N parallel from the Rocky Mountains to the Pacific Ocean but did not settle questions concerning the islands and passages in the Straits of Georgia and Juan de Fuca. This matter was finally settled by reference to the emperor of Germany as an arbiter in 1872.

Alaska was purchased from Russia in 1867 and was made a territory of the United States by a congressional act on 24 August 1912. The presidential proclamation admitting Alaska as the 49th state of the United States was issued on 3 January 1959. The territorial limits of Alaska had been defined in the convention of 1825 between Russia and Great Britain. The portion of the boundary following the 141st meridian was never questioned but, when the great mineral and other wealth of the area was realized, the location of the boundary from Mount Saint Elias southeastward came under the scrutiny of Canadian authorities. The coastline in the region is exceptionally irregular and deeply indented by fjords with no continuous mountain range paralleling the coast, so that the 1825 boundary description, which called for the boundary to "follow the summit of the mountains situated parallel to the coast" was

Canada–Alaska (USA) boundary

impossible to follow. For many years both sides tacitly agreed that the boundary should follow a winding line 10 marine leagues from the coast.

The discovery of gold in the Yukon River basin in Canada, coupled with the fact that the only feasible routes into the region lay through US territory, emphasized Canada's need for a port or ports on this coast. A claim was made by the British government on behalf of Canada before a joint commission on the boundary in August 1898, but was refused by the US commissioners. In 1903 an Alaskan Boundary Tribunal consisting of "six impartial jurists of repute," three selected by each side, was created to settle the boundary question. A majority, consisting of the British commissioner and the three Americans, agreed on a boundary that was eventually surveyed and demarcated. The irate Canadian commissioners were joined by the Canadian press and Parliament in expressing indignation for what was perceived as Britain's betrayal of Canada's interest. Control of this coastline by the US is still a point of resentment in many Canadian circles.

In the 1890s questions began to arise regarding the adequacy of the boundary's demarcation along the 49th parallel, west of the Rockies, in the east between New York and Quebec and in some other areas. A treaty concluded between the US and Great Britain in 1908 addressed these problems by describing the boundary in eight sections and providing for the appointment of a joint commission to recover or restore previously established boundary markers and to place new markers where they were lacking. In 1910 another treaty removed lingering uncertainties in the Passamaquoddy Bay area. Finally, in 1925, an agreement between the United States and Great Britain provided for the continued maintenance of the boundary under the supervision of the commissioners appointed in 1908 and their successors.

Present Situation. Since 1905 the boundaries between Canada and the United States have been well maintained. Problems have centered mainly on trans-boundary rivers, the Great Lakes and the anomalies in the boundary line. The small American town of Angel Inlet on the Lake of the Woods can be reached by land only through Canadian territory, as can Point Roberts in the Strait of Georgia. The exact location of the boundary in the Saint Lawrence River and the ownership of its islands in the Gulf of Saint Lawrence are still under deliberation, while an agreement on the maritime boundary in the Gulf of Maine was signed on 29 March 1979.

Today the International Boundary Commission consists of two commissioners, one of whom is appointed by the government of Canada and the other by the government of the United States. In the US the commissioner is appointed by the president and reports to the secretary of state, while Canada's is considered a career public servant and reports to the secretary of state for foreign affairs. Their mission includes periodic inspection of the boundary, repairing and replacing damaged boundary markers, maintaining a cleared vista through the vegetation along the line and helping in the resolution of disputes that involve the boundary as they arise. In recent years the chief regulatory problems along what is often described as the world's longest undefended border have involved such matters as fence and building encroachments in populated areas, fiber optic and telephone cable installations and the construction of pipelines. Drug and firearm violations are frequently detected at border crossings and turned over to local police authorities for investigation.

CAPE VERDE ISLANDS (Cabo Verde) A republic in the Atlantic Ocean, the Cape Verde Islands is located 386 miles (621 km.) west of the coast of Africa. It consists of 10 islands and 5 islets and has no land boundaries. Its area is 1,557 sq. miles (4,033 sq. km.) and it has an estimated population (1994) of 390,000. The capital of Cape Verde is Praia, located on the island of São Tiago.

The Portuguese arrived in the uninhabited archipelago in the fifteenth century and the islands later became a station in the Atlantic slave-trade. During the twentieth century many Cape Verdeans were still used as laborers by the Portuguese under slave-like conditions. Some were sent to another Portuguese colony, Guinea-Bissau, and became a leading force in its decolonization struggle. Following independence in 1975 the PAICV (Partido Africano da Independencia de Cabo Verde), the party that emerged from the Cape Verde liberation movement, dominated the country and converted it into a single-party state. Negotiations were begun with Guinea-Bissau, dominated after independence by Cape Verdeans, over unification of the two countries, but a 1980 coup in Guinea-Bissau put an end to Cape Verdean domination and unification plans were halted.

In 1990 Cape Verde became a multi-party state. Elections held in 1991 brought a new president to office.

CAYMAN ISLANDS A British colony consisting of three islands (area: 100 sq. miles [259 sq. km.]; estimated population: 30,000 [1994]), the Cayman Islands are located in the Caribbean Sea, northwest of Jamaica. The colony has no land boundaries and its capital is Georgetown.

CENTRAL AFRICAN REPUBLIC (République centrafricaine) A landlocked country (area: 240,324 sq. miles [622,439 sq. km.]; estimated population: 3,200,000 [1994]) situated in central Africa,

the Central African Republic is bounded in the north by Chad (744 miles; 1,197 km.), in the east by Sudan (724 miles; 1,165 km.), in the south by Zaire (980 miles; 1,577 km.) and Congo (290.5 miles; 467 km.) and in the west by Cameroon (495 miles; 797 km.). The capital of the Central African Republic is Bangui.

Of the country's ethnic groups, the riverine groups have played and still play a dominant social, economic and political role. Although they constitute only about 5% of the total population, during the French colonial period they held more than 60% of the administrative and civil positions in the colony and they continued to dominate the country after independence.

Upon achieving independence (1960), a Baya-dominated political party took control and banned all opposition parties. In 1965, a Mbaka, Jean-Bedel Bokassa, took power in a military coup. Initial Baya

Central African Republic and its boundaries

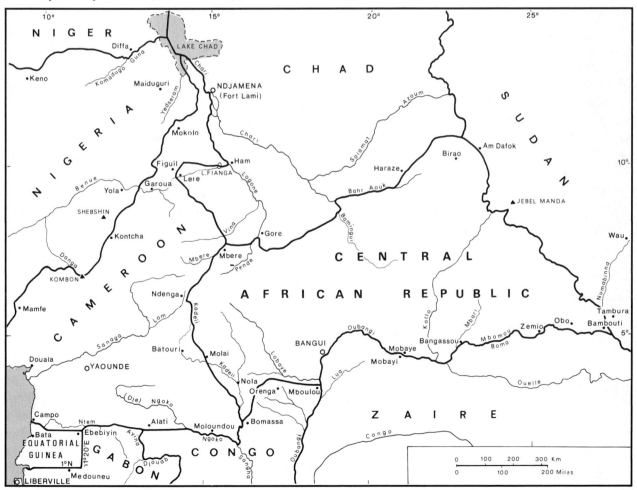

support, received for appointing a Baya as his head of the army, was lost following the appointee's execution. Bokassa's despotic rule was ended by a bloodless coup in 1979 and the first president regained power. Although the Central African Republic is still a one-party state, there has been popular pressure for political reform.

CENTRAL AFRICAN REPUBLIC — CAMEROON
see CAMEROON–CENTRAL AFRICAN REPUBLIC.

CENTRAL AFRICAN REPUBLIC — CHAD
The boundary between the Central African Republic and Chad runs for 744 miles (1,197 km.) between the boundary tripoint with Sudan in the east and the boundary tripoint with Cameroon on the Mbéré River in the west. The boundary is the outcome of a French administrative boundary that was established during the colonial era in central Africa.

Geographical Setting. There is no official agreement that describes the alignment of the Central African Republic–Chad boundary and the present line is mostly based on maps rather than written descriptions. The eastern terminus of the line was defined as located "one kilometer (0.6 miles) east of Mere de Tizi (Lake Tizi) at the point where a small westward-flowing stream crosses the former Anglo-Egyptian Sudan–French Equatorial Africa boundary." This description places the northwestern boundary terminus at approximately 10°57'N and 22°52.5'E. From there the line runs westward, following the small stream to its confluence with the Aouk River, which is followed downstream westward, southwestward and again westward for 385 miles (620 km.) to its confluence with the Chari River. The boundary courses along the Chari River upstream to its confluence with one of its sources, the Bamingui River. At this point the boundary line leaves the river and bears southward and westward in a series of straight lines to reach the Ouham River at its intersection with the Nana Bayara River. The latter is followed upstream westward to its confluence with the Bokola River and continuing westward the line follows local rivers (Pendé, Eréké, Lebe etc.), connecting them with short straight lines. The boundary reaches the boundary tripoint with Cameroon in the center of the Mbéré River, at 7°31'40"N and 15°29'40"E.

Historical Background. The Central African Republic and Chad constituted a French colony known as Oubangui-Chari-Tchad (Ubangi-Shari-Chad) when they were united in 1906 and became a section of French Equatorial Africa on 15 January 1910. On 30 July 1912 the boundaries of Oubangui-Chari were established in general terms when it was defined as an area located between German Kamerun in the west, the French military territory of Chad in the north, Egyptian Sudan in the east and Belgian Congo in the south. In 1920 Chad and the Central African Republic were separated; French Equatorial Africa was reorganized in 1934 and again in 1941, when the present boundary was set in general terms. Both territories became self-governing units within French Equatorial Africa, achieving full independence in August 1960. They both adopted the French administrative division at the time of independence, although no international agreements regarding the boundary alignment were ever signed.

Present Situation. The boundary line is not demarcated by pillars and the winding areas and flood zones of the river sections are not well marked, potentially contributing to the onset of boundary disputes. However, since independence there have been no disputes concerning the boundary's alignment or precise location.

CENTRAL AFRICAN REPUBLIC — CONGO
The Central African Republic–Congo boundary extends for 290.5 miles (467 km.), from the boundary tripoint with Zaire on the Ubangi River in the east to the boundary tripoint with Cameroon, located in the Sangha River, in the west. No formal agreement regarding the boundary was made.

Geographical Setting. The western terminus of the boundary line, at the boundary tripoint with Cameroon, is located in the *thalweg* (main navigation channel) of the Sangha River, at about 2°13'20"N. From there the line runs northeastward in a straight line for 48 miles (77 km.) to the source of the Makale River. Running northward it trends along the watershed that stands between the Sangha River in the west and the tributaries of the Ubangi River in the east, reaching the headwaters of the Ibenga River. Then turning eastward and following the watershed between the Ibenga (Congo) and Lobaye (Central African Republic) rivers and their tributaries for 175 miles (282 km.), the line reaches the Gouga River, which it follows to its confluence with the Ubangi River. As the line reaches the main navigation channel of the Ubangi River it arrives at the boundary tripoint with Zaire.

Historical Background. The Central African Republic (formerly known as Oubangui-Chari) and Moyen Congo were French colonies that became sections of French Equatorial Africa in January 1910. On 30 July 1912 the boundaries of landlocked Oubangui-Chari were established in general terms and the administrative boundary with Congo was later established (in 1921, 1936 and 1937). During World War II the district of Upper Sangha was transferred to Oubangui-Chari. Both countries became independent in August 1960 adopting, with no formal agreement, the last colonial administrative line as their common international boundary.

Present Situation. Although the boundary is one of the few African boundaries that does not run through rivers, its line follows watersheds that are not well defined. Nevertheless, since independence no disputes regarding the undemarcated boundary line have been reported.

CENTRAL AFRICAN REPUBLIC — SUDAN

Former British and French possessions in central Africa created administrative colonial boundaries that resulted in the present boundary between the Central African Republic and Sudan. It runs for 724 miles (1,165 km.) between the boundary tripoint with Chad in the northwest and the tripoint with Zaire in the southeast. It generally follows the watershed between the Congo River and the Nile drainage area.

Geographical Setting. The boundary tripoint with Zaire is located on a 15-foot (5-m.) boundary marker, at 5°01'10"N and 27°26'37"E, southeast of Obo (Central African Republic) and south of Tambura (Sudan). Heading northwest the boundary follows the principal central African watershed—between the Congo River basin in the southwest and the Nile River basin in the northeast—along a series of astronomically fixed boundary pillars. The rivers of the Central African Republic flow southwest toward the Ubangi River (which joins the Congo River in western Zaire) while most of the Sudanese rivers flow toward Bahr el Ghazal and the Sudd

swamp area. The line reaches Mount Tinga, which marks the northern point on the watershed between the Congo and Nile basins. Thence it runs northward to Mount Mishmira, following the watershed between the basins of the Nile and Lake Chad. Departing from the watershed, the boundary continues in a straight line northward for 17 miles (27 km.) to Mount Yarra and in another straight line northwest for 50 miles (80 km.) to the Kamar River (Wadi Towal). It then follows a road for 50 miles (80 km.) up to a point on the Auok River, 0.6 miles (1 km.) east of Lake Tizi (Tisi), which is the boundary tripoint with Chad—at approximately 10°57'N and 22°52.5'E.

Historical Background. Sudan was under British rule from 1896 and from 1899 was administrated as an Anglo-Egyptian condominium. The Central African Republic (then Oubangui-Chari) was a French protectorate. The boundary between the two was established in the Anglo-French Convention of 14 June 1898, in which the boundary alignment was described. The precise boundary line was further determined by an exchange of notes between the United Kingdom and France signed in London on 21 January 1924, ratifying the 1898 convention. Sudan became an independent state on 1 January 1956 and the Central African Republic gained independence on 13 August 1960. The newly established states mutually adopted the colonial boundary as their international boundary, although no formal agreement was reached.

Present Situation. Since 1960 no disputes have been raised concerning the alignment of the undemarcated boundary line. The absence of a formal demarcation and the dense forest area—through which the boundary runs—raised some local problems of definition, but no significant complications have arisen along this peaceful line.

CENTRAL AFRICAN REPUBLIC — ZAIRE

The boundary between the Central African Republic and Zaire runs in an east–west direction for 980 miles (1,577 km.). Except for a segment of about 0.5 miles (1 km.) in the easternmost part of the boundary, it is delineated along the *thalwegs* (deepest navigable channels) of rivers.

Geographical Setting. The boundary begins at the tripoint with Congo on the Ubangi River. From there it runs eastward to the confluence of the Mbomou and Ubangi rivers. It then follows the *thalweg* of the Mbomou River to its source, from where it travels in a straight line up to the crest that forms the watershed between the Nile and Congo rivers, reaching the tripoint boundary with Sudan. Being demarcated primarily by rivers, the boundary is particularly easy to follow.

Historical Background. The present boundary between the Central African Republic and Zaire is the former colonial boundary between Ubangi-Shari, a division of French Equatorial Africa, and the Belgian Congo. The line was established in a convention attended by both France and the International Association of the Congo on 5 February 1885 and was described in an agreement signed in Paris on 14 August 1894.

Present Situation. The Belgian Congo gained independence on 30 June 1960; the Central African Republic followed suit soon after, on 13 August 1960. Since that time, neither state has challenged the principle of the boundary.

CHAD (Tchad) A landlocked country situated in central Africa, Chad (area: 495,753 sq. miles [1,284,000 sq. km.]; estimated population: 6,100,000 [1994]) is bounded in the north by Libya (656 miles; 1,055 km.), east by Sudan (845 miles; 1,360 km.), south by the Central African Republic (744 miles; 1,197 km.) and west by Cameroon (680 miles; 1,094 km.), Nigeria (54 miles; 87 km.) and Niger (730 miles; 1,175 km.). The capital of Chad is N'Djamena.

Chad is one of the poorest and least developed countries in Africa. Its history since independence from the French in 1960 has been dominated by a lack of common interests and understanding between the peoples of the south and those of the north. The north is predominately Islamic and the peoples living there are mainly nomadic or semi-nomadic pastoralists of Arab origin; Arabic is the language of trade and is superimposed on local languages. There are two main ethnic groups divided into numerous clans—the Hassauna of the northwest and the Djoheina of the northeast—and ethnic rivalries in the north are strong.

The south of Chad is a smaller, better watered and more heavily populated area. Most of its inhabitants belong to the Sara people, a population of sedentary cultivators. The Sara are subdivided into several linguistically and culturally related groups. The other inhabitants of the south belong to numerous fragmented ethnic groups, the main ones of which are the Moundang, Toubouri, Masa, Musgum, Masalit and the Maba and the Lisi, both of which are also each subdivided into several subgroups.

Since the end of World War II, the people of the south have became modernized and westernized. Literacy advanced rapidly and Christianity attracted many adherents. By contrast, the northern peoples had shown reluctance toward modern education and clung to Islam. As a result, after independence most of the administrators and civil servants came from the south. The northern people, who were willing to accept French colonial rule, were not ready to be dominated by the southerners. This conflict between north and south made Chadian politics extremely unstable. Since independence there have been three civil wars in Chad which resulted in the intervention of the French.

CHAD — CAMEROON see CAMEROON–CHAD.

CHAD — CENTRAL AFRICAN REPUBLIC see CENTRAL AFRICAN REPUBLIC–CHAD.

CHAD — LIBYA The entire length of the Chad–Libya boundary stretches through the Sahara Desert. It is 656 miles (1,055 km.) long and runs in two straight lines from the boundary tripoint with Niger to the tripoint with Sudan. Although the line bears little relation to the tribal distribution in the region, since the International Court of Justice decision of March 1994 the debate over control of the area has been largely settled.

Geographical Setting. The Chad–Libya boundary is delimited by two geodetic lines that cross rocky, pebbly and sandy surfaces. The first line extends from the tripoint with Niger, which is located at 23°N and 15°E, to the intersection of the 16°E meridian with the Tropic of Cancer. It is part of a longer geodetic line that extends from an escarpment south of Tummo (Libya) to the intersection of 16°E with the Tropic of Cancer. The second geodetic line extends 586 miles (943 km.) between the intersection of the 16°E meridian and the Tropic of

Cancer and the Sudanese tripoint at 19°30'N and 24°E.

Historical Background. On 14 June 1899 the first ratified agreement concerning the Chad–Libya boundary was reached under an Anglo-French declaration that aimed at delimiting the British and French spheres of influence east of the Niger River. This was accepted by Italy in an exchange of notes on 1 November 1902—a significant agreement as Italy occupied Libya in 1911. In 1919 an Anglo-French convention determined the line's intersection with the 24°E meridian at 19°13'N. However, the declaration of 1899 did not appear to include a map and consequently the drafting did not provide a basis for the exact location of the boundary. In 1927 Fascist authorities in Libya laid claims to areas south of the 1899 line, based on the principle of *uti possidetis* (the legal principle that previously colonial states are entitled to maintain the colonial borders as international boundaries). An agreement of 7 January 1935 between France and Italy was to have ceded the disputed area, now designated the Aozou Strip, to Italy. However, this agreement was never ratified. Consequently, while the Libyan claims for this strip depended upon the validity of the 1935 agreement, Chad rejected them on the grounds that the agreement was never ratified or brought into force. Libya achieved independence in 1951 and on 10 August 1955 signed with France a Treaty of Friendship and Good Neighborliness, which Chad then cited as the continuing basis for the boundary in its present position.

Chad gained independence in 1960 and, taking advantage of factional fighting there, Libya occupied the strip in 1972 and officially annexed it in June 1975. This was widely interpreted as indicating a discovery of uranium deposits and it was thought that ownership of the strip would furnish Libya with nuclear independence. Relations between Libya and Chad later improved and it was even intimated that the strip was sold back to Chad—a charge denied by Chad. However, in 1976 Chad denounced the Libyan occupation.

In July 1977 the Organization of African Unity (OAU) set up a commission to handle the dispute, a government of national unity was established in Chad in 1979 and on 15 June 1980 a treaty of friendship was signed with Libya. President Oued-

dei of Chad accepted the Libyan annexation of the Aozou Strip as an accomplished fact on 26 December 1980. Libya's Mu'ammar Qadhafi then proposed a move toward full unity between the two countries, which was opposed by Chad and led to a series of wars in the 1980s. In 1987 Chad drove the Libyans beyond the Aozou Strip before the OAU mediated a cease-fire.

After five rounds of talks between senior Libyan and Chadian ministers had failed to settle the dispute, they both agreed to submit the case to the International Court of Justice (ICJ). The case appeared to rest on the interpretation of the 1935 treaty, the existence of minerals in the area and the strategic importance of the region. On 3 March 1994 the ICJ finally ruled that the Aozou Strip was Chad's territory. Libya formally agreed to hand over the disputed strip on 1 May 1994 in accordance with the ICJ decision.

Present Situation. Chad and Libya signed a cooperation agreement in June 1994, following the Libyan withdrawal from the Aozou Strip, and at present the boundary area is not under dispute.

CHAD — NIGER Extending 730 miles (1,175 km.), the boundary between Chad and Niger runs generally southward from the boundary junction with Libya to the boundary junction with Nigeria in the south. Most of the line runs through an uninhabited desert area and there are no known boundary pillars demarcating it.

Geographical Setting. At 23°N and 15°E the northern terminus of the boundary line is located, on the northwestern edge of the Tibesti Mountains, east of the Libyan town of Tummo. From there the boundary runs southeast in a series of straight lines, leaving the Tibesti Mountains within Chad, to a point situated on the 16°E longitude—on the northeastern edge of the Bilma desert (Grand Erge Bilma), west of Zouar (Chad). In straight lines the boundary heads southwest for 34 miles (55 km.) and south to a point west of the well of Siltou (Chad). Again southwestward in a series of straight lines, the boundary passes by the wells of Firkachi (Chad) and Fayenga (Niger) to the well of Molo (Niger). Southward in another set of straight lines, the line then reaches the northern edge of Lake Chad, enters the lake and stretches southeastward to the boundary junction with Nigeria,at approximately 13°42'58"N and 13°38'20"E, east of the town of Bosso (Niger).

Historical Background. The boundary line between these two independent countries corresponds with the former intercolonial boundary as it stood at the time of Chad's and Niger's independence. European explorers reached Niger in the late eighteenth century while Tuareg people entered the region from the north. France seized it from the Tuaregs in 1901 and Niger became an administrative unit of French West Africa from 1904. It remained in association with France until 1958.

Earlier known as Bornu, Chad was conquered by Sudan in the nineteenth century. In 1897 French expeditions began crossing the central Sahara and the Lake Chad region, establishing a military territory in Chad in 1900 and, in 1910, created French Equatorial Africa as a federation that included the territories of Tchad, Gabon, Middle Congo (today's Congo) and Ubangi-Shari (today's Central African Republic).

In 1912 the first alignment between these two French colonial territories was established, separating Niger from Chad along a line that reached from Molo to Lake Chad. In 1931 the section between the boundary junction with Libya (which was then an Italian colony) and Siltou was determined in general terms by a French memorandum. Niger and Chad achieved independence in August 1960, both countries accepting the colonial boundary as their common international boundary.

Present Situation. There are no official, written documents describing the alignment of the boundary line in detail, which has hindered the exact location of the available boundary data on the ground. However, the scope of uncertainty is minimal and there are no known disputes concerning the boundary's alignment.

CHAD — NIGERIA The Chad–Nigeria boundary runs for 54 miles (87 km.) from the boundary junction with Niger in the northwest to the boundary junction with Cameroon in the southeast. The entire boundary is located in Lake Chad.

Geographical Setting. The northwestern terminus of the boundary line, which is the boundary junction with Niger, is located in the northwestern section of Lake Chad, at 13°42'58"N and 13°38'20"E. From there the line runs in a straight line southeastward, passes through the salt encrusted islands of the archipelago of Bogomerom, and reaches its southeastern terminus, the boundary junction with Cameroon, at 13°05'N and approximately 14°05'E. The lake changes its area dramatically over the rainy and dry seasons and this line was established in order to secure for France, which ruled Chad and Niger, communication through the open waters the year round.

Historical Background. The boundary between Chad and Nigeria is a section of the former colonial boundary between the British (Nigeria) and French (Chad and Niger) possessions in central Africa. Chad was occupied by the French in 1900 and from 1910 was part of French Equatorial Africa. Northern Nigeria became a British protectorate in 1900 and was united with the protectorate of South Nigeria in 1914, establishing Britain's largest African colony. In 1898 Britain and France determined their spheres of influence in central Africa and the Anglo-French Convention of 8 April 1904 detailed the principles of their common boundary in Lake Chad. A convention of 28 May 1906 defined the boundary in Lake Chad as a straight line that reached from the mouth of the Yobe (Komadugu) River to its intersection with the meridian running 35' east of the center of Kukawa (Nigeria). The Anglo-French Agreement of 19 February 1910 established the precise parallel of the boundary in Lake Chad as 13°42'29"N. In 1906–1907 the boundary between the German possessions in Kamerun (today Cameroon) and Nigeria in Lake Chad was established and a Franco-German convention of 9 April 1908 established the boundary between Chad and Cameroon in the lake, thus creating the southeastern terminus of the boundary between Chad and Nigeria. After 1910 no changes were made in the boundaries that run through the lake. Chad and Nigeria both became independent countries in 1960, adopting the colonial frontier as their common international boundary.

Present Situation. Lake Chad varies in extent between rainy and dry seasons—from 20,000 to 7,000 sq. miles (50,000 to 20,000 sq. km.). For this reason a precise division in the lake had to be made to establish a firm line that could not be influenced by the changes. Today the Lake Chad basin is being jointly developed for oil exploitation by Cameroon, Chad,

Niger and Nigeria, an operation that accentuates the necessity for a precise alignment of the boundaries in the lake. There are no known disputes between Chad and Nigeria concerning their common boundary's location.

CHAD — SUDAN The northern section of the Chad–Sudan boundary runs in a straight line through a desert region, while the southern sector follows topographical features in savanna territory. The line follows a colonial boundary between former British and French spheres of influence in northern Africa. It is 845 miles (1,360 km.) long and reaches from the boundary tripoint with Libya in the north to the tripoint with the Central African Republic in the south.

Geographical Setting. The tripoint boundary junction with Libya is located in the Libyan Desert, at the intersection of 19°30'N and 24°E. From there the boundary runs directly southward for 261 miles (420 km.) along the 24°E meridian, until it reaches Wadi Howar at about 15°43'N. It follows the Howar valley west and then southwest for about 150 miles (240 km.) to its intersection with the dry Greigi River (Wadi Greigui). The valley is shared by the tribes living on its opposite banks, each tribe retaining rights to dig wells, cultivate and graze within its limits as they did prior to the delimitation of the boundary. The line courses along the Greigi River to its intersection with Wadi Tini, which it follows to Lake Undur. Heading southwestward the boundary reaches the Kaja River north of Adré (Chad). It follows that river downstream southward, for about 90 miles (145 km.), and leaves it east of Iffene (Chad), at the intersection of 12°02'17"N and 22°28'18"E. There the boundary line turns east and trends along a dry tributary of the Kaja River to its confluence with another dry river. It runs southward and then follows a straight line back to the Kaja River, which it follows again it to its confluence with the Azoum River. The boundary crosses that river and runs southeast in a series of straight lines and through dry riverbeds to reach the Central African Republic–Chad–Sudan tripoint, 0.6 miles (1 km.) east of the eastern shore of Lake Tizi (Tisi), at approximately 10°57'N and 22°52.5'E.

Historical Background. The Chad–Sudan boundary is a part of the dividing line between the British and French spheres of influence in northeastern Africa, which was settled in Paris on 14 June 1898 and completed by an Anglo-French declaration on 21 March 1899. The British established themselves in Sudan in 1895–1896 and it was ruled by an Anglo-Egyptian condominium. From 1897 France ruled Chad, which became part of French Equatorial Africa in 1910. The precise alignment of the boundary between the two resulted from a protocol of 10 January 1924, which was approved by an exchange of notes between the United Kingdom and France on 21 January 1924. Sudan gained independence on 1 January 1956; Chad on 11 August 1960. Both newly established independent states adopted the existing colonial boundary as an international border without a formal agreement.

Present Situation. The boundary line is precisely delimited along its entire length and since gaining independence neither state has raised any disputes concerning its alignment.

CHILE Situated on the southwestern coast of South America, Chile (area: 292,135 sq. miles [756,630 sq. km.]; estimated population: 13,800,000 [1994]) is bounded in the north by Peru (100 miles; 160 km.), in the east by Bolivia (535 miles; 861 km.) and Argentina (3,201 miles; 5,150 km.) and in the south and west by the Pacific Ocean. Its capital is Santiago.

Isolation and distance contributed to the development of a particular Chilean identity in South America during the period of Spanish colonization (sixteenth to nineteenth centuries). The war of independence (1810–1818), the establishment of an autocratic republic (1833), the wars against the Peruvian-Bolivian confederation (1836–1839) and the Pacific War between Bolivia, Chile and Peru (1879–1884), as a result of which Chile conquered the nitrate-rich areas of Atacama and Tarapaca, strengthened Chilean nationalism. The middle class developed rapidly after the 1930s and took an active part in the country's socioeconomic and political life. The predominance of the socioeconomic cleavage—reflected in the political crisis of the 1970s during which the Chileans polarized in terms of Left and Right, destroying the economy and democracy—brought about military dictatorship and economic stabilization policies that affected the middle

At the boundary crossing between Bolivia and Chile

and lower classes. Redemocratization in the 1990s is being carried out on the basis of national reconciliation and social development.

CHILE — ARGENTINA see ARGENTINA–CHILE.

CHILE — BOLIVIA see BOLIVIA–CHILE.

CHILE — PERU The boundary between Chile and Peru runs generally northeast for 100 miles (160 km.), from the Pacific Ocean to the boundary junction with Bolivia in the Andes Mountains. It is demarcated throughout by boundary pillars.

Geographical Setting. The Chile–Peru boundary line was formed as a series of straight lines connecting 80 established markers on the ground. It sets out from a point called Concordia (18°21'03"S and 70°22'56"W) on the coast of the Pacific Ocean and 6 miles (10 km.) north of a bridge over the Lluta River. The line runs east, northeast and north, parallel to the Chilean section of the Arica (Chile)–La Paz (Argentina) railway, at a distance of 6 miles (10 km.) from it. At some points deflections were made in accordance with local geographical features. After crossing the Azufre River, the boundary line runs north, leaving the mountain of Volcán Tacora, sul-

phur mines and the local railway branch within Chile. From the northwestern slope of the mountain, the line runs eastward to reach the southwestern point of the White Lake (Laguna Blanca), which it crosses northeastward, placing one half of the lake within each country. The boundary continues northeast, up to the boundary junction with Bolivia, located at 17°29'55"S and 69°28'28.8"W.

Historical Background. The original boundaries in the area, as in most regions in South America, date back to the Spanish colonial period. As the colonies gained independence they accepted the principles of *uti possidetis*, whereby the colonial boundaries would be maintained as state boundaries. Chile became independent in 1818, Peru in 1824 and Bolivia in 1825. Bolivia took possession of the area west of the Andes to the Pacific Ocean, including a section of the Atacama Desert, thus dividing Chile and Peru. The discovery of nitrate deposits in the desert led Chile to claim the Bolivian desert territory in 1842. A settlement was reached in 1866, setting the boundary between Chile and Bolivia along the 24°S parallel. In 1873 Bolivia and Peru signed a defensive agreement, joining forces in the Pacific War against Chile, which began in 1879. Chile won the war and in accordance with the terms of the Treaty of Ancón (20 October 1883), Peru ceded unconditionally to Chile the littoral province of Tarapaca, which lay north of Bolivian territory, and Bolivia ceded its Pacific coastal region. Thus, Chile expanded its territory northward to Camarones River. The provinces of Tacna and Arica, north of the Camarones River, which were part of Peru before the war, were to be administrated by Chile for a 10-year period, followed by a plebiscite to determine their future. Efforts to reach an agreement on the terms of the plebiscite failed and Chile remained in possession of Tacna and Arica, including the area surrounding the city of Tarata, which Peru insisted was located north of the agreed line. The dispute concerning these provinces was not settled until both countries presented their claims for the arbitration of the president of the United States. Between 1921 and 1929 three presidents (Warren G. Harding, Calvin Coolidge and Herbert Hoover) and two secretaries of state (Charles E. Hughes and Frank B.

Chile–Peru boundary

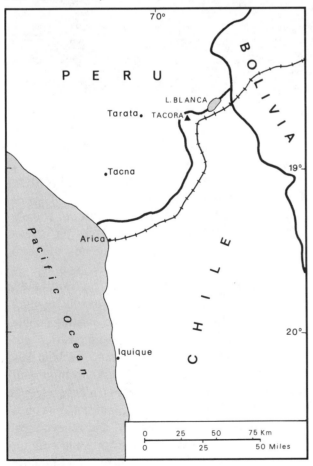

Kellogg) deliberated an agreement. In 1925 Chile delivered Tarata over to Peru, although efforts to organize a plebiscite came to nil. A treaty signed on 3 June 1929 delimited the international boundary between Chile and Peru, dividing the disputed area of Tacna and Arica between them. Peru held the province of Tacna but continued to use the port of Arica (Chile) as a terminus for the railway that traveled from Tacna to the Pacific Ocean. The placing of pillars to mark the boundary was completed in 1930 and a demarcation protocol was signed at Lima on 5 August 1930.

Present Situation. After the Arica-Tacna dispute was settled and the full demarcation of the line by 80 boundary pillars was completed, there were no more controversies concerning the alignment of the boundary between the two countries.

CHINA (Zhongguo)   A country in eastern and central Asia, China (area: 3,689,631 sq. miles [9,556,144 sq. km.]; estimated population: 1,185,000,000 [1994]) is located between the China Sea in the east and central Asia in the west. It is bounded by more countries than any other country in the world and the total length of its land boundaries (13,772 miles; 22,159 km.) is the longest in the world.

China is bounded in the north by Russia (2,265 miles; 3,645 km.) and Mongolia (2,904 miles; 4,673 km.), in the northwest by Kazakhstan (953 miles; 1,533 km.) and Kyrgyzstan (533 miles; 858 km.), in the west by Tajikistan (257 miles; 414 km.), Afghanistan (47 miles; 76 km.) and Pakistan (325 miles; 523 km.), in the south and southeast by India (2,101 miles; 3,380 km.), in the south by Nepal (768 miles; 1,236 km.), Bhutan (292 miles; 470 km.), Myanmar (1,358 miles; 2,185 km.), Laos (263 miles; 423 km.) and Vietnam (796 miles; 1,281 km.), in the southeast by the South China Sea, Macao (0.21 miles; 0.34 km.) and Hong Kong (19 miles; 30 km.) and in the east by the East China Sea, the Yellow Sea and North Korea (880 miles; 1,416 km.). The capital of China is Beijing.

China was first unified under the Qin dynasty (221–207 B.C.E.), while the formative years of the Han nationality were during the Han dynasty (206 B.C.E.–220 C.E.), which provided the group's self-designation. Early settlement in the Yellow and Wei

The Great Wall of China

rivers regions, which are often known as "the cradle of Chinese civilization," soon expanded eastward, and then to the south and southwest. Such expansion was generally accompanied by the forced assimilation of other ethnic groups. It was under the Tang dynasty (618–907) that China became the cultural and economic center of Asia, with commerce and trade flourishing and a series of successful wars in central Asia and Korea.

Although the Han have dominated China during most of the country's history, two foreign dynasties, the Mongolian Yuan (1271–1368) and the Manchurian Qing (1644–1911), also ruled. The Manchu in particular adopted Chinese culture, laws and bureaucratic procedures.

The Communists—who came to power under the leadership of Mao Zhedong in 1949, after nearly four turbulent decades of internecine conflict in China subsequent to the overthrow of the Manuchus

—launched a program of rapid industrialization and socialization until the economic crisis of the early 1960s forced a period of retrenchment and recovery lasting until 1965.

In that year Mao launched the Cultural Revolution, a movement that oversaw attacks on bureaucrats, intellectuals, scientists and individuals or groups with any foreign connections, and also encompassed a massive rustication movement whereby some 60,000,000 people (mostly aged between 16 and 30) were moved from existing population centers in an effort to relocate industries, provide human resources for agriculture, reclaim land in remote areas, settle borderlands, promote sinicization (the settlement of the Han Chinese in ethnic minority areas where they do not traditionally constitute a majority of the population) and relieve urban food and housing shortages. Despite the communists' sinicization policy, the Han remain a minority in the relatively sparsely-populated north and west of the country.

Having made significant steps toward normalizing relations with the capitalist West (a process fueled by the parties' mutual distrust of Soviet intentions) during the 1970s, China has expanded its attempts to modernize its industry, agriculture, national defense and science and technology.

However, liberalization has remained strictly confined to the economic sphere; China remains a gerentocratic Communist dictatorship as evidenced by the violent suppression by the military of peaceful pro-democracy student demonstrators in Tianenman Square in Beijing, the Chinese capital, in 1989. His action was condemned by China's Western trading partners and many countries imposed sanctions on Chinese trade as a result, but the perceived economic benefits of access to the huge Chinese market led to almost all sanctions being rescinded.

CHINA — AFGHANISTAN   see AFGHANISTAN–CHINA.

CHINA — BHUTAN   see BHUTAN–CHINA.

CHINA — HONG KONG   This boundary is 19 miles (30 km.) long and crosses the peninsula between Mirs Bay and Deep Bay, following two streams for the greater part of its length.

Geographical Setting. The eastern end of the China–Hong Kong boundary runs from the high watermark in the Starling Inlet (Sha Tau Kok Hui) of Mirs Bay where the 114°13'30"E meridian meets the eastern edge of the pier at Sha Tau Kok village (Hong Kong). It takes the road into the village and its main street northward to the Sha Tau Kok Hui stream, following its median line such that the land on the left bank of the river is in China and on the right bank is in British territory. The boundary leaves the river to join the road to Kang Hau village—the entire road being left in British territory but used by the inhabitants of both countries—and passes through an area about 500 feet (150 m.) above sea level to form the ridge that divides the Sha Tau Kok and Sham Chun valleys. This road takes the boundary down the northern side of the ravine and at the foot of the ravine the road crosses a stream (which is accessible to cultivators in both

countries) that flows from Ng Hung Shan and crosses it again within a distance of 300 feet (90 m.). The road then passes Kang To village on its right and reaches the Sham Chun River about 0.25 miles (0.4 km.) below Kang To. The boundary then follows the northern bank of the Sham Chun river down to Deep Bay, the river and the land south of it remaining in British territory. Pegs were located at various points along the boundary in 1899 but the line is now clearly marked by a high wire fence.

Historical Background. Before 1834 all British trade with China was conducted by the East India Company at Canton and Macao while diplomatic and commercial ties with the Chinese were generally through the merchant guild, the Co-hong. By such means China sought to limit the scope and extent of foreign influence. The European demand for tea and the difficulty in selling western products in China created an imbalance of trade which the British overcame by marketing opium. After 20 years of unrestrained importation of opium the economic and moral results for China were devastating and in an effort to impose a prohibition, which was enacted in 1800, Chinese officials seized huge stocks of the drug and war broke out. The British realized the advantages to be enjoyed at the deep sea harbor of Hong Kong after their retreat from Macao, and colonization was a fait accompli long before the First Opium War ended in 1842, when it was granted under the Treaty of Nanking. Claiming that Kowloon provided a haven for pirates, the British began to colonize it and after the second Opium War obtained a lease of the lower Kowloon Peninsula (1860), which they annexed that year under the Convention of Peking. The Franco-Russian Alliance of 1893 spurred the British to press for even more territory on the peninsula. When China was defeated by Japan in 1895, Britain took the opportunity to obtain further concessions and on 1 July 1898 it settled a 99-year lease that described the line, excluding the old walled city of Kowloon—until Britain unilaterally cancelled that part of the agreement. The New Territories, as the area was then known, comprised the peninsula between Mirs Bay and Deep Bay.

Present Situation. This boundary is not disputed, although some Chinese maps depict the boundary along the middle of the Sham Chun River, rather than its northern bank. The lease expires in 1997,

The crossing between Hong Kong and China

when the international boundary will cease to exist.

CHINA — INDIA The boundary between China and India runs for 2,101 miles (3,380 km.), according to India, or 1,337 miles (2,152 km.) according to the Chinese, in three separate sections. The easternmost section begins at the boundary tripoint with Myanmar (Burma) and ends at the eastern tripoint with Bhutan. The central section reaches from the western tripoint with Bhutan in the east to the eastern boundary junction with Nepal in the west. The westernmost section runs between the western boundary tripoint with Nepal and the tripoint with Pakistan in the west. The line is currently unsettled, as China and India have never agreed upon its alignment and large areas are disputed along the eastern and western sectors of the line.

Geographical Setting. The boundary, according to the Indian claim (the McMahon Line), lies on the high peaks of the Himalayas. Its eastern terminus, at the boundary junction with Myanmar, is located on the watershed between the Tsayul River and the tributaries of the Irrawaddy River in the Gamland L'ka region, at 28°30'N, east of Kahao (India). The boundary runs westward for about 70 miles (110 km.), crossing the Luhit River north of Kahlo (India) and leaving the Kadusam Peak (16,754 feet; 5,108 m.) within China. There it turns northward and then westward to leave the entire Dibang River basin in India. Continuing westward, the line crosses the Dihang River (which, from its confluence with the Dibang River, becomes the great Brahmaputra River), and thence runs for about 250 miles (400 km.) southwestward to reach the boundary tripoint with Bhutan, west of the Dangme Chu River, at a point called Che Dong. According to the Chinese claims, the eastern terminus of the boundary line is located about 60 miles (100 km.) south of

The China–India border runs through the Himalayas

the Indian point, and the boundary follows the foothills of the Himalayas, bordering the Brahmaputra River. While this section of the Indian line is 420 miles (676 km.) long the Chinese line is shorter, running for about 340 miles (550 km.) to the tripoint with Bhutan at the southeastern corner of Bhutan, still some 60 miles (100 km.) south of the Indian boundary tripoint.

The central section of the boundary line, which is less disputed than the other two sections, begins in the east at the boundary tripoint of Sikkim (India), Bhutan and China, south of Yatung (China). The line runs northward along a local watershed, crosses the India–Tibet road and reaches the Commo Yummo Peak (22,396 feet; 6,828 m.). It turns westward and meets the eastern tripoint with Nepal north of the Kanchenjunga Peak (28,201 feet; 8,598 m.), the third highest mountain in the world. This section is about 110 miles (177 km.) long.

The western section of the China–India boundary lies in the Ladakh region. Its eastern terminus, according to both sides, is located southeast of Pu-lan (China) on 81°E. It runs northwestward for about 50 miles (80 km.) toward the area of the town of Laptal, which both sides claim for themselves. It then continues northwestward, leaving the Kamet Peak (25,440 feet; 7,756 m.) in India and reaching the disputed region of Sang, which is also claimed by both sides as their own. It heads northward, running through six passes (Shipki Pass and five others) according to the Indian claim, while China holds that the passes are on Chinese soil. South of the Indus River the boundary runs eastward to a point southwest of Demchok (Pa-li-chia-ssu). Each state also claims that region for itself and again there are two views on the location of the boundary line in the area. The boundary crosses the Spanggur and Pangong lakes at an altitude of 13,930 feet, (4,247 m.)

in the southern part of the Aksai Chin region, which is the largest area of dispute between the two states. The Indian line runs northeastward from Khurnak Fort on the eastern shore of Pangong Lake, through Lanak Pass to the foothills of Kerian Mountains and westward across the Karakashin River to reach the boundary tripoint with Pakistan. The Chinese line on the other hand, runs from a point south of Lake Spanggur, crosses both that lake and the Pangong lake to the center of the northern shore of Lake Pangong, passes through the Kongka Pass and runs northwestward to place the entire region and the important Sinkiang–Tibet road in Chinese hands. The total area of this disputed sector is approximately 10,000 sq. miles (25,900 sq. km.). The westernmost terminus of the boundary line, at the boundary tripoint with Pakistan, is located about 15 miles (25 km.) east of the Karakoram Pass, which stands at an altitude of 18,290 feet (5,576 m.).

Historical Background. The cause of the boundary dispute between China and India is the result of China's claim that the line has never been formally delimited whereas India insists that it has been settled in a number of treaties. Regarding the northwestern section of the line, lying north of Shipki Pass, India refers to two treaties dated 1684, between the independent states of Tibet (now in China) and Ladach (now in India), and between Tibet and Kashmir (now in India). China repudiates the Indian view, holding that neither of the treaties actually describe the location of the boundary. Britain, controlling the area of India, attempted to draw a boundary through the region in 1899, suggesting a line that would extend between the Karakoram Pass and Nepal. China then received and considered the proposal but did not accept or reject it. India became independent in 1947 and China occupied Tibet in 1950. This brought about a Sino-Indian agreement concerning the area south of Shipki Pass, which was signed in 1954. China again claimed that the agreement made no mention of the location of the boundary, only specifying six passes where travelers may cross, while India claimed possession of the passes. In 1956–1957 China built a road connecting Sinkiang and Tibet, which runs through the disputed area of Aksai Chin. Clashes between Chinese and Indian troops led to a full-scale war between the two states in July 1962. Chi-

nese troops occupied the entire area east of the line claimed by China. In a cease-fire agreement of November 1962 China withdrew to a line 15 miles (20 km.) behind the line of control that had existed in 1959.

The boundary issue in the eastern section arises from the area's mountainous terrain and the limited control formerly exercised by the British over the tribal peoples living in the foothills of the Himalayas and the Chinese over Tibet. British annexation of Assam (East India) in 1838 brought it into direct contact with the tribal areas and an "Inner Line" was defined in 1873 regulating the entry of lowlanders into the area—but no agreement concerning an international boundary was signed. Following violations of the border in the early years of the twentieth century, a conference was held in Simla (India) in 1913–1914, at which Britain, China and Tibet were represented. The head of the British delegation, Sir Henry McMahon, proposed a boundary between India and Tibet that would follow the watershed of the Himalayas north of the tribal territories. The Tibetan delegation accepted what became known as the McMahon Line but the Tibetan government never ratified it. After 1938, however, the British authorities adopted a policy controlling the tribal area up to the McMahon Line, which from 1939 appeared on Indian maps as the boundary with China. When India became independent in 1947, the tribal area became part of India as Arunachal Pradesh.

China never recognized the McMahon Line as its boundary with India. Border incidents led to a Sino-Indian war in October 1962, when Chinese troops occupied areas as far as 100 miles (160 km.) south of the McMahon Line. A cease-fire agreement was reached in November 1962 and Chinese troops were placed about 12 miles (20 km.) north of the McMahon Line. No boundary agreement was signed and no settlement of the problem was reached.

Present Situation. Since the 1962 war between China and India little progress has been made toward a solution of the boundary dispute. Occasional border incidents occur, resulting in a number of fatalities. During 1981–1982 some preliminary negotiations took place on the border question but no agreement was reached. However, although China never recognized the McMahon Line officially, it does not cross it. The boundary will only be settled when both sides are prepared to negotiate without prior condition.

CHINA — KAZAKHSTAN

The boundary between China and Kazakhstan runs for 953 miles (1,533 km.), between the tripoint boundary junction with Russia in the Altai Mountains in the northeast and the boundary tripoint with Kyrgyzstan in the southwest. The line follows a segment of the Russian–Chinese boundary that was established in the nineteenth century and later became the boundary between China and the Soviet Union.

Geographical Setting. The northeastern terminus of the boundary line is located in the Altai Mountains, on Kuytun Mountain (Hüyten Orgil). From there it runs generally southwestward for about 150 miles (240 km.) to the upper Irtysh River, east of Lake Zaysan. The line crosses the river and heads southward to Saur Mountain. There it turns west and travels along the Tarbagatay Mountains (9,810 feet; 2,991 m.) until it reaches the 83°E meridian, where the boundary faces south and continues in that direction for approximately 160 miles (260 km.). It leaves the towns of T'a-ch'eng, Ma-ni-tu and Modu Barluk within China and the towns of Bakhty and Zharbulak in Kazakhstan. North of Ebi Nor (China) the boundary again changes its direction, running westward along the Dzungarian Ala Tau mountain range (15,380 feet; 4,690 m.), through Kara Pass and toward the source of the Khorgos (Ho-erh-kou-ssu) River. The boundary follows the river southward to its confluence with the Ili River. Continuing southward it crosses the Ili River and the main road—"The Silk Way"—between Alma-Ata (the capital of Kazakhstan) and Urumchi (China), reaching the Ketmen range. The boundary line crosses the range, follows the Tekes River for 6 miles (10 km.) and then climbs the Tien Shan mountains down to the boundary tripoint with Kyrgyzstan, north of the peak of Khan-Tengri and west of the principal mountain pass of Muzart.

Historical Background. The Czarist Empire of Russia entered Kazakhstan in 1718 and by 1740 the entire area of Kazakhstan was under Russian rule. For 100 years the boundary between Russia and China in that region was not defined (although the eastern Chinese–Russian boundary was delineated

from 1689). Finally, between 1860 and 1883, the western sector of the boundary between the empires of Russia and China was established. The 1860 treaty of Peking between Russia and China defined it in general terms and in 1864 a commission clarified it in a treaty concluded at Chuguchak (T'ach'eng), China. Muslim rebellions between 1864 and 1878 halted the boundary settlement and negotiations were resumed only in 1879 and concluded in the Treaty of Saint Petersburg in February 1881. The precise definition of the boundary was ratified by four protocols signed between 18 October 1882 and 21 September 1884. From that date on no changes were ever made in the boundary's alignment. Between 1917 and 1920 the local Kazakh people established an independent republic, which was occupied by the Red Army in 1920. In 1936 Kazakhstan became a recognized republic within the Soviet Union and gained independence in 1991. Kazakhstan adopted its section of the existing Soviet Union–China boundary as its international boundary with China without any formal agreement.

Present Situation. Since Kazakhstan's independence, no disputes concerning the boundary alignment have been reported. The line is clearly demarcated and the local inhabitants are familiar with its alignment.

CHINA — KOREA, NORTH

The boundary between China and North Korea runs for 880 miles (1,416 km.) between the Sea of Japan and Korea Bay in the Yellow Sea. Apart from 20 miles (32 km.) it coincides with the Tumen and Yalu rivers.

Geographical Setting. The eastern part of the boundary begins at the tripoint junction with Russia in the Tumen River, about 12 miles (19 km.) from its mouth, following the river to its source, near Pait'ou Shan. Then it runs southward, for about 20 miles (32 km.) and follows the watershed to An-Ping River, which is one of the tributaries of the Yalu River. The boundary follows this tributary to join the Yalu River, coursing along it to its opening in the Yellow Sea near the North Korean city of Sinuiju. This line forms a clear division between mainland China and the Korean peninsula and has functioned as some of the earliest political boundaries in that area.

Historical Background. The present boundary

dates back in history to a series of boundary treaties between China and Japan, signed between 1895 and 1911. After the war of 1894–1895 between Japan and China (won by Japan), China agreed to grant Korea its independence. A boundary treaty was signed in April 1895, in which the Yalu River was defined as the boundary between China and Korea, occupied then by the Japanese army. In September 1909 the eastern section of the boundary line, along the Tumen River, was established and in November 1911 it was confirmed that the center of the Yalu River would form the main part of the boundary between the two countries. This boundary line was never changed, despite the political changes that occurred in the area during the twentieth century. When the Korean peninsula was divided between North and South Korea after World War II, North Korea inherited the old boundary between China and Korea.

Present Situation. The main problem that is likely to be the cause of contention between the two countries concerning the boundary line, is the unclear definition of the boundary in the source of the Tumen River. The original agreement of 1909 gives contradictory definitions of the source of the Tumen River and an area of about 450 sq. miles (1,165 sq. km.) lies between the two possible lines. There is no known dispute between China and North Korea, however, and China accepts the Korean version for the time being, although future political changes could lead this unclear definition to an open dispute.

CHINA — KYRGYZSTAN Extending 533 miles (858 km.) between the boundary tripoint with Kazakhstan in the northeast and the tripoint with Tajikistan in the southwest, the China–Kyrgyzstan boundary is a section of the boundary between the former Soviet Union and China.

Geographical Setting. The boundary tripoint with Kazakhstan stands north of Khan-Tengri Peak (22,000 feet; 7,218 m.), in the Tien Shan mountains, and west of Muzart Pass. The line bears south, reaching Khan-Tengri Peak, turns southwest and trends through the Tien Shan mountain range, but not along the watershed. It meets the Pobeda Peak (22,674 feet; 7,439 m.) and about 50 miles (80 km.) west of the peak crosses the Kum Arik (A-ko-su) River. The line continues southwest for about 60

miles (100 km.), trends through Bedel Pass and, some 100 miles (160 km.) further, crosses the Ak Say (To-shin-kah) River. The boundary line then reaches its tripoint with Tajikistan, about 30 miles (50 km.) southwest of Irkeshtam (Kyrgyzstan).

Historical Background. The western boundary between the Russian and Chinese empires, along the region between Mongolia and Afghanistan, was established between 1860 and 1884. The Treaty of Peking in 1860 defined the boundary west of Kantegir River (a tributary of the Yenisei River) in general terms and a Russo-Chinese commission convened in 1864, concluding a treaty at Chuguchak (T'ach'eng), China.

This treaty defined the boundary in the Altai Mountains in the northeast and the Pamirs in the southwest. Kyrgyzstan was taken over by Russia that year (1864)—a move that influenced the boundary line by pressing the Chinese to define the boundary in that area. A Muslim revolt had begun in the southern region near the Pamir range, which halted the demarcation of the line and only in 1878, when order was enforced in the region, was a Chinese delegate sent to the Russian capital to negotiate the establishment of the boundary at Kyrgyzstan. After three years of negotiations the Treaty of Saint Petersburg established the line. The boundary between Kyrgyzstan (then part of Russia) and China was demarcated and defined in two protocols (25 November 1882 and 22 May 1884) and from then on it was never changed. After the collapse of the Russian Empire in 1917, Kyrgyzstan became part of an independent Turkistan republic and was incorporated in the Soviet Union in 1924. Kyrgyzstan became a constituent Soviet republic in 1936, its boundary with China following the 1882–1884 line. It became independent in December 1991, adopting, without a formal agreement, its section of the Soviet Union–China border as its international boundary with China.

Present Situation. Although Kyrgyzstan has many boundary disputes with other newly established states of the former Soviet Union, there are no reports of boundary conflicts with China. Both countries recognize the nineteenth-century agreement and accept the boundary's alignment.

CHINA — LAOS This demarcated boundary line

is 263 miles (423 km.) long and runs from the boundary tripoint with Vietnam in the east to the boundary tripoint with Myanmar (Burma) in the west.

Geographical Setting. In the west the boundary begins at the tripoint with Myanmar and runs eastward for 5 miles (8 km.), along the minor watershed between the Nan-la River and an unnamed tributary of the Mekong River to the south. The line then turns south to follow the minor watershed for 13 miles (21 km.) before crossing the Nan-jein River near the village of Meng-Jun (China). The sinuous line of the border continues for another 20 miles (33 km.) along the ridges of the water divide and then heads east for just over 50 miles (80 km.) and north for 81 miles (130 km.), leaving the drainage basin of the upper Nan-la River within China. Continuing generally north for 57 miles (92 km.) the boundary follows the main watershed between the Nam and Mekong rivers, and turns east along the water divide between the Mekong and Black rivers for 36 miles (58 km.) to the boundary junction with Vietnam, at about 22°24'N and 102°08'E. There are some 15 pillars marking this boundary.

Historical Background. The boundary between China and Laos was delimited as part of the line between China and Vietnam, when both Laos and Vietnam were under French administration. The boundary was established between France and China by the Treaty of Peace and Commerce (Treaty of Tientsin) of 1885, which included a provision for a boundary commission, which was appointed and concluded its work by 26 June 1887, when its results were summarized in a convention of that date. The boundary description seems to have depended upon rather imprecise geographical information and was amended in 1895, when a supplementary convention was signed, defining the section that is now the border with Laos. The Laotian section was negotiated with respect to China's commercial interests in the area, the inclusion of the upper Nan-la river valley within China protecting China's most commercial tea crop from I-Bang. It is one of the few boundaries between China and its various colonial European neighbors that the Chinese did not regard at the time as unfair. In 1954 Cambodia, Laos and Vietnam were created as independent states and the French colonial boundary was adopted as the north-

ern boundary between Laos and China. A bilateral agreement of October 1991 provided for a further demarcation of this boundary with boundary posts along its entire length.

Present Situation. The present government of China has never questioned the legality of the treaties regarding this boundary and it is shown in an identical location on both Chinese and French maps.

CHINA — MACAO The land boundary between China and Macao is 0.21 miles (0.34 km.) long and crosses the narrow isthmus between the Macao peninsula and the Chinese mainland. Including the maritime boundary, the total length of this boundary is 3 miles (5 km.).

Geographical Setting. The China–Macao boundary is marked by a wall 300 yards (274 m.) long, which was first built by the Chinese in 1573 across the narrow, sandy isthmus from east to west that joins Macao to mainland China.

Historical Background. The Portuguese arrived in southern China in 1514, setting up several trading stations from which they were subsequently expelled. In Macao, however, they were permitted to establish a colony from 1557. In order to control the import of supplies to the colony and to benefit from customs duty, the Chinese built a barrier across the isthmus, known to the Portuguese as "Porta Do Cerco." In 1662 an arrangement was reached by which the Portuguese paid 500 taels annually, in rent or tribute, to occupy Macao. China regarded the settlement as a trading post that remained Chinese territory, but Portugal considered it Portuguese and established a municipal government. In the nineteenth century governors were appointed to the colony and it was removed from the control of the governor of Portuguese India at Goa. It was declared a free port in 1845 to take advantage of the growing trade between China and Europe, and the following year the islands of Taipa and Colôane were also occupied. In 1848 the governor of Macao suppressed the Chinese Custom House and refused to pay the annual rent, acts that precipitated armed action by the Chinese, who had long been dissatisfied with Portugal's expansion in the Canton delta and its claims to Chinese territory.

By the Lisbon Treaty of Amity and Commerce of 1887, China recognized Portuguese sovereignty in

Macao in return for cooperation in the collection of an opium tax and a promise that the territory would not be alienated without China's consent. Negotiations that took place from 1901 to 1910 regarding the precise delimitation of the boundary were hampered by the dispute over control of the adjacent islands and no agreement was reached. Portugal adhered to the Nine-Power Treaty of 1922 and also concluded a further Treaty of Amity and Commerce with China at Nanking in 1928. Since then Portugal has offered to return Macao to the Chinese on two occasions: once in 1967, during China's Cultural Revolution, and again in 1974 after its own revolution. China felt it inappropriate to accept the offer on these occasions, but Macao will revert to China on 20 December 1999, under the terms of the Joint Declaration of 1987.

Present Situation. The alignment of this boundary is not in dispute.

CHINA — MONGOLIA The alignment of the China–Mongolia boundary was first delimited by the 26 December 1962 China–Mongolia Border Treaty. The full demarcation was later approved by the Sino–Mongolia Border Protocol of 30 June 1964. It runs for 2,904 miles (4,673 km.), from the western boundary tripoint with Russia in the Altai Mountains to the eastern tripoint with Russia.

Geographical Setting. The boundary begins at the western boundary junction with Russia on the Kuitun spur of the Altai Mountains. It heads southeastward following the main crests of the Altai chain to the Baytag (Pei-Ta) range at the southwestern foot of the Mongolian Altai chain. The boundary then crosses the Gobi desert eastward for over 930 miles (1,500 km.) only broken occasionally by rocky hills or shallow salt depressions. From the eastern fringes of the desert the boundary heads east toward China's Great Kingan mountains, first crossing steppe country and then the Dariganga flatlands. Upon reaching the Kingan range it bends first to the north then to the west, meeting the Herlen-Halhin peneplain. The boundary then bears northeastward until it meets its eastern tripoint with Russia.

Historical Background. The delimitation of the China–Mongolia boundary in December 1962 constituted a statement to the rest of the world that Mongolia had revoked all vestige of Chinese

suzerainty, although it still remained politically attached to the suzerainty of Russia.

Outer Mongolia tribes had acknowledged and paid tribute to the suzerainty of China since the seventeenth century. The Russians began to increase their interest in the area in the early eighteenth century as the reigning czar turned eastward instead of westward to increase Russia's sphere of influence. Settlements sprang up along the margins of the Xinjiang–Outer Mongolia–Manchuria frontier and the Sino-Russian Treaty of Kyakhta (12 October 1727) initiated the first demarcation of the Outer Mongolia–Russia boundary, with a series of guard and trade posts being set up along the border. Chinese interest in the area at this time was limited, but by 1900 Chinese interest grew and the China–Mongolia frontier no longer deflected Han Chinese penetrating the area from the southeast. The settlement of Mongolia was deemed a violation of historic agreements that justified Chinese suzerainty.

In December 1911 autonomous Mongolia ruled itself independent of China. However, with the birth of the Chinese Republic in 1912, its new leaders were quick to initiate procedures to reassimilate Outer Mongolia into China. During the internal struggle associated with the birth of the Republic, Russia was easily able to assume the role of Mongolia's suzerain, although a 1913 Sino-Russian convention seemed to have reestablished Chinese suzerainty. In the 1915 tripartite agreement it was agreed that neither China nor Russia would interfere in the internal administration of Outer Mongolia, although under Article II of the treaty China agreed to consult with Russia and Outer Mongolia on regional questions of a political or territorial nature, thus, in effect acknowledging Chinese suzerainty. The Bolshevik Revolution of 1917 saw the relations between Russia and Outer Mongolia weakening, which allowed Chinese forces to reoccupy it in 1919. This occupation only lasted until 1921, when the Chinese were defeated by combined Mongolian and Russian military forces. This led to the institution of a provisional government that was controlled by the communists and assumed all state power. The Mongolian People's Republic was established in 1924. From 1921 to 1962 the only portion of the China–Mongolia boundary subject to a delimitation agreement was in the east, in the region of Pei-erh

(Lake Buyr), due to the Japanese invasion of Manchuria in 1931. The Chinese hold over the area was not given up lightly, as it was felt that such a move would also threaten China's hold over Tibet and Xinjiang. Mongolia's vote for independence led to China's recognition of the Mongolian People's Republic in 1946, although delimiting a boundary between the two countries was near impossible due to the civil war raging in China. The situation was further complicated after China protested to the United Nations Security Council that Mongolian troops had intruded at least 60 miles (100 km.) into China through the Baytag mountains. (This protest was made at the time when Mongolia was seeking UN candidacy.) The territorial dispute over this region was mainly based on China's belief that the area was rich in precious metals while the Russians argued that the Baytag peoples had voted to belong to Mongolia, making a UN resolution difficult. The dispute led China to denounce recognition of the Mongolian People's Republic. Sino-Mongolian relations warmed, however, in 1960, after China's premier, Chou En-lai, paid a visit to the region. This period of good will led to the delimitation agreement of December 1962 and the completion of full demarcation by 1964. The boundary inspection, which was also provided for in the 1962 protocol, took place during February–April 1982.

Present Situation. There is currently no dispute over this border.

CHINA — MYANMAR   The boundary that separates China and Myanmar is 1,358 miles (2,185 km.) long, was established by a joint Sino-Burmese boundary commission in 1961 and is demarcated by 300 pillars and by flowering trees. It falls into two distinct sections lying north and south of the High conical peak. The line reaches from the boundary junction with India in the north down to the tripoint with Laos in the south.

Geographical Setting. From the High conical peak, situated at about 25°35'N and 98°14'E, the northern section of the China–Myanmar boundary follows the watershed between the Ta-ying and Nmai rivers in a northerly direction. It then travels through several passes to the source of Chu-Ita Ho. This river is followed to its junction with a tributary from the north, which it then pursues until it reaches the watershed

between the Hpimaw and Chu-Ita rivers. It then travels along the ridge through Luksang Bum and crosses the Gan River. The line reaches the Wu Chung River and follows it to its intersection with the Hsiao Chiang River, which is then followed. North of Kangfang village the border joins the watershed between the Hsao Hpawte and Ta Hpawte rivers to a point between the Salween and Nmai rivers. Then the watershed between the Salween, Tulung and Nmai rivers is followed through several passes. The border then heads through Aland L'Ka to Tusehpong Razi, then along the local ridge, reaching altitudes of 9,486 feet (2,892 m.) and 7,020.2 feet (2,140.3 m.), to the south bank of the Tulung River. The boundary then follows the watershed between the Tulung River and the upper tributaries of the Irrawaddy River, through several more passes. Thence it follows the watershed between the Tsayul River and the tributaries of the Irrawaddy River. Passing through Gamland L'ka it reaches the boundary tripoint with India.

The second section of the border runs in a southwesterly direction from the High conical peak, along the watershed between the Ta-ying and Nmai rivers. It then follows the Ta Pa Chiang to the Hkatong River and then to its source. The boundary tends along the watershed between the Mong Lai and Pajao rivers to the source of the Laisa stream. From there it heads to an intersection with the Ta-ying River, which it follows to a small ridge. The border then traverses across the watershed between the Kuli Hka stream and Ta-ying River. Following river sections to the Nam Che River, which it follows through Ching Shu Pass, and combining with several other rivers the line reaches a junction with the Shweli River. It stretches south in line with the Shweli River to the watershed between the Meng Peng Ho and the tributaries of the Salween River. It crosses to the confluence of the Nam Hpa and Nam Ting rivers and runs along the latter for about 3 miles (5 km.). The line trends along the northwestern slope of Kummuta Shan to its summit, follows a tributary of the Kung Meng Ho to its confluence with another and follows this second tributary to a point northwest of Maklawt Village. It then forms a straight line to reach a point southeast of the village and again in a straight line crosses a small stream to Shien Jen Shan. Along the watershed between these two tributaries and along the Mong Ling Shan ridge to its summit, the border reaches and follows the Nam Pan River to the source of the Nam It River, which it follows along with the Nam Mu River. The line then runs along the Nam Kunglong and Chawk Hkrak rivers to the source of the latter. From this point the border follows another watershed and then heads east to the source of a small river, a tributary of the Mongtum River, which it follows. Several more tributaries are then followed in a north-north-east direction to the watershed between the Mong-tum and Nam Ma rivers. Several tributaries are followed to the Angland Shan ridge and the boundary then heads toward the summit of Pang Shun Shan. It runs along several rivers to the source of the Nan Wo Kai Nan Shan and runs northeast to the west bank of the Nam Lam River. It then reaches the foot of the Chiu Na Shan, runs southwest, traveling through several passes, and heads northeast to the intersection with the Nam Lam River. From this point seven more river courses are followed and the boundary trends along the watershed between the Nam Nga and Nam Loi rivers to the top of Kwang Pien Nei Shan. Northeastward along the Hue Le River the boundary line arrives at an intersection with the Mekong River and follows it to its confluence with the Nan-la Ho at the boundary tripoint with Laos.

Historical Background. The Sino-Burmese Boundary Treaty of 1 October 1960 removed all formal territorial disputes between China and Burma (which changed its name to Myanmar on 19 June 1989) and, with only two exceptions, confirmed the boundary as it had been established in three earlier Sino-British treaties (1894, 1897 and 1941). It transferred 132 sq. miles (342 sq. km.) of Burma's territory south of the High conical peak to China (Hpi-maw and Panglao-Panghung) and 85 sq. miles (220 sq. km.) of the Namwan territory near the Shweli River to Burma. A Sino-Burmese protocol of 13 October 1961 then provided a detailed definition of the border, from its tripoint with Laos in the south to the tripoint with India in the north.

Present Situation. The 1961 definition of the boundary line is recognized by both parties.

CHINA — NEPAL

Between two tripoints with India the China–Nepal boundary runs for 768 miles (1,236 km.). The western tripoint is located east of the Urai Pass, the eastern point on Jongsong Peak on the border of the Indian Sikkim region.

Geographical Setting. At about 30°12'45"N and 81°E the watershed between the Kali and Tinkar rivers meets the watershed between the Tinkar River and the tributaries of the Mapchu (Karni) River. Here the China–Nepal boundary begins, heading southeast along the Himalayan watershed up to the Urai (Pai-Lin) Pass. Turning northward it reaches the Karnali (Ghaghara) River, follows it downstream for about 2 miles (3.5 km.) and returns to the watershed. The boundary follows the watershed east-southeast, passing through several mountain passes (Lapche, Manja, Thau, Marima and Pindu) and reaching the Mustang valley. There it leaves the water divide and encompasses the valley, leaving it within Nepal. After leaving the valley the boundary line follows the watershed from the Lugula peak, continuing generally east-southeast through other mountain passes and northeast to reach Khojang Peak. Thence it runs south for about 25 miles (40 km.) and turns east toward Gosainthan Peak (26,305 feet; 8,630 m.). From there the boundary runs southeastward to the lowest pass in the mountains and crosses the highway between Katmandu (the capital of Nepal) and Lhasa (Tibet, China) and a tributary of the Sun Kosi River before it regains the main watershed of the Himalaya mountains. It trends eastward, reaching Nangpa Pass and then the world's highest peak, Mount Everest (29,141 feet; 9,561 m.), and Makalu Mountain (27,790 feet; 9,117 m.). The line continues east toward Popti Pass, crossing the Arun River, and then runs through Rakha Pass for 50 miles (80 km.) to the boundary junction with India on Jongsong Peak (24,500 feet; 8,038 m.).

Historical Background. The history of Nepal, up to the nineteenth century, is predominated with the rise and fall of local kingdoms. A Sino-Nepalese treaty was signed in 1792, ceding the area south of the Himalayas to Tibet. By the beginning of the nineteenth century the Gurkha Kingdom became a powerful force in Nepal, expanding its territory northward to Tibet. During 1854–1856 a war between Nepal and Tibet led to a peace treaty that was signed on 24 March 1856, by which Tibet was to give certain territories to Nepal. After the establishment of the People's Republic of China in 1949, China signed an agreement that abrogated all previous treaties, to maintain the friendly relations between "the Tibet region of China" and Nepal. On 21 March 1960 a boundary treaty was signed, based on the existing traditionally recognized line. The complete delimitation of the boundary, created by a joint commission, was agreed upon in a boundary treaty between the People's Republic of China and the Kingdom of Nepal, signed on 5 October 1961. A total of 99 boundary pillars were erected and the final boundary treaty was signed on 23 January 1963.

Present Situation. The treaties of 1960–1963 established a demarcated boundary between China and Nepal for the first time. This eliminated the potential causes of friction regarding the alignment of the boundary and since then no disputes concerning the boundary area have been recorded.

CHINA — PAKISTAN

The China–Pakistan boundary is one of the highest boundary lines in the world, running through the world's second highest peak, K2 (26,246 feet; 8,611 m.). The line is 325 miles (523 km.) long and extends from the boundary tripoint with Afghanistan in the northwest to the tripoint with India in the southeast.

Geographical Setting. The northwestern terminus of the boundary is located on an unnamed peak on the watershed between the Wakhjir (China), Wakhan (Afghanistan) and Hunza (Pakistan) rivers, at 74°36'E and 37°03'N. This point is 2' (2 miles; 3 km.) east of the point mentioned in the 1963 Sino–Afghan boundary treaty. From there, the boundary runs eastward for about 50 miles (80 km.), trends through Kilik Pass, follows the watershed between the Kara Chukur River (China), the Khunjerab River and the upper tributary of the Hunza River (Pakistan), and traverses along the Taghdumbash Pamir range. Thence it runs southeast, reaching the Khunjerab Pass and the source of the Uprang Jilga River. It follows the river downstream southeastward for some 40 miles (65 km.) to its confluence with the Shaksgam (Muztagh) River, leaves the river and runs south for about 50 miles (80 km.) to the Muztagh Pass. It runs eastward along the main watershed of the Karakoram Range, reaching the Gasherbrum Saddle Pass, and then continues southeastward for about 80 miles (130 km.). It passes along the peak of K2 (Godwin Austen) and reaches

the main Karakoram Pass (18,290 feet; 5,576 m.), along which the main China–Pakistan road runs. From there it heads east for 20 miles (32 km.) and reaches the boundary tripoint with India.

Historical Background. During the last years of the nineteenth century Britain ruled India, while Russia and China struggled to control the Pamir range in the northwestern Himalayas. In 1895 an Anglo-Russian commission established the Afghanistan–Russia boundary in the Little Pamir range, but the boundary along the Karakoram Range was not settled. This led Britain to fear that the Russians would establish themselves in the important passes in the area. China controlled the Kunlun Shan range, northeast of the Karakoram Range, and in 1899 Britain (which ruled the Kashmir and Hunza regions) proposed to China a boundary line that would follow the Karakoram Range and would halt Russian progression into the Kashmir region. China did not accept the boundary line but did not reject it. This remained unsettled and the area between British Kashmir and Chinese Sinkiang and Kunlun Shan was left as no-man's-land.

When Britain left the area in 1947, giving independence to India and Pakistan, the Kashmir area was a cause of conflict between the two newly established states.

On 27 July 1947 a cease-fire line was established between them, placing the Karakoram Range and northwestern Kashmir (the Jammu district) in Pakistan. This brought about the need to establish a boundary line between China and Pakistan. A treaty was agreed upon in November 1963 in which a boundary was delimited for the first time between Chinese Sinkiang and the area of Kashmir occupied by Pakistan. A demarcation commission was appointed and its work was completed by 25 March 1965, when the final protocol was signed.

Present Situation. Since 1965 no territorial claims have been made between China and Pakistan. The present boundary seems to be fair to both sides and about 40 pillars are located in the main passes and in the lower valley areas. As the dispute over Kashmir has yet to be finally settled, the future of the boundary line is unknown: on the one hand China could negotiate with the future sovereign power of that area; on the other hand, if Pakistan remains in control, the boundary would not be altered.

CHINA — RUSSIA This boundary is divided into two sectors by the Mongolian People's Republic. The western section is 25 miles (40 km.) long and runs from the boundary tripoint with Kazakhstan to the western tripoint with Mongolia. The eastern section leads from the eastern tripoint with Mongolia to the boundary tripoint with North Korea and is 2,240 miles (3,605 km.) long. In total, the China–Russia boundary is 2,265 miles (3,645 km.) long.

Geographical Setting. The western sector of the boundary begins at the tripoint with Kazakhstan and trends generally eastward across the Altai Mountains to meet the western Mongolian tripoint. The eastern section of the China–Russia boundary begins at the eastern tripoint with Mongolia and follows the Argun River to its confluence with the Shilka and Amur rivers. The Chinese hold that the main channel of the Amur River is followed northeast to a point opposite the city of Khabarovsk. The Russians, on the other hand, claim that the line follows the Kazakevicheva channel southeastward to the Ussuri River. However, from a point on the Ussuri River the alignment is more precise. It proceeds along the Ussuri River upstream southward to the Songacha River and then on to Lake Khanka (Hanka). It crosses the lake westward, and southwestward from the lake a minor watershed is followed. From there the boundary forms straight-line sectors across the Sui-fen lowland. After crossing the Sui-fen stream the boundary trends along the southern bank of the Ta-wu-she River to the coastal drainage divide. Then the boundary heads for the North Korean tripoint in the Tumen River, about 10 miles (16 km.) above the estuary and west of the Sea of Japan.

Historical Background. The boundary between these two countries was developed as imperial Russia began to build its empire. Blocked by European powers in the West, Russia looked to the East to extend its territory and began by colonizing Siberia. By 1638 Russia had expanded across Asia from the Urals to the Pacific Ocean. As they pushed across Asia the Russians clashed with Manchurian tribes, who were then near the height of their power. The Treaty of Nerchinsk (27 August 1689) created the first boundary between the Russian and Manchu empires, followed by the Bur (Bura) Treaty of 20 August 1727 and its protocols (12 and 27 October

China–Russia boundary

1727) and the Kiachta Treaty of 27 October 1727. These agreements defined the limits of the two states from the Argun River westward, through the Abagetuy (Tarbagatay) region north of Mongolia to the valley of the upper Irtysh river, giving Russia roughly 40,000 sq. miles (103,560 sq. km.) of territory south of the previous line.

This delimitation was valid for over one and a quarter centuries—until 16 May 1858, when the Treaty of Aigun was signed. This treaty delimited the boundary eastward along the Amur River, from the Shilka River to the sea, leaving some 130,000 sq. miles (336,570 sq. km.) of territory between the Amur and Ussuri rivers and the sea in doubt. On 2 November 1860 the Peking Additional Treaty solved the doubtful sovereignty of this territory by ceding it to Russia. This treaty also completed delimitation of the entire Manchurian boundary, including a Manchu–Russian boundary in Turkistan, described as the existing line of Chinese pickets.

The last section of the western sector is along the Pamirs. The Chinese occupied this region but abandoned it under Afghan pressure in 1892. No subsequent Chinese government has accepted the Pamir boundary although the extent of their claims has varied. The delimitation of the modern boundary was established by the 12 February 1881 Treaty of Saint Petersburg. Since 1991 most of that line became the international boundary line between China on the one hand and Kazakhstan, Kyrgyzstan and Tajikistan on the other, leaving only a small portion (25 miles; 40 km.) as part of the China–Russia boundary.

The eastern sector of the boundary is more disputed that its western counterpart. The Tsitsihar Agreement of 20 December 1911 redefined the boundary between Mongolia and the Argun River, ceding approximately 375 sq. miles (970 sq. km.) to Russia, although China has since claimed that this agreement was void due to a lack of ratification. The 4 January 1915 Russo-Mongolian-Chinese agreement delimited an autonomous Outer Mongolia, but under republican Chinese suzerainty the 1911 Mongolian declaration of independence was negated. The de facto detachment from China of Tannu Tuva and Mongolia completed the establishment of the present boundary between China and Russia and by 14 August 1945 the two countries recognized the independence and territorial integrity of Outer Mongolia with an exchange of notes. This independence was again repudiated by the Republic of China, although envoys for the communist Chinese government and Mongolia signed a border delimitation agreement that confirmed the common tripoints of the Mongolian, Chinese and Russian boundaries on 26 December 1962.

Present Situation. The Russo–Chinese Border Agreement was ratified on 13 February 1991, supposedly settling the long-running disputes over the border east of Mongolia. However, in practise the two sides are arguing over the right to control islands in the Amur and Ussuri rivers—even though it was established in the agreement that the line was to run through the median lines of the main navigable and unnavigable channels. Attempts to rectify this situation were helped by the beginning of demarcation work along the Argun and Amur rivers on 25 May 1993. Dialogue has continued, although the border is considered stable at present.

CHINA — TAJIKISTAN

The China–Tajikistan boundary is 257 miles (414 km.) long and runs from a northern boundary tripoint with Kyrgyzstan to a southern boundary tripoint with Afghanistan. It follows the westernmost section of the boundary between China and the former Soviet Union.

Geographical Setting. The northern terminus of this boundary is the point that marks the western extremity of China. It is located on the Ka-shin-ka-erh River, east of the town of Irkeshtam (Kyrgyzstan), at 39°41'N and 73°55'E. The line runs southward for some 75 miles (120 km.), across high mountainous terrain (13,000 feet; 4,300 m.), to the Uch-bel Pass. From there it proceeds eastward for about 60 miles (100 km.) and turns south to trend along the watershed between the east-flowing tributaries of the Yarkand River (China) and the west-flowing tributaries of the Amu Darya. The southwestern terminus of the boundary line, which is the tripoint with Afghanistan, is located on Povalo Shveykovski Peak in the Pamir mountain range.

Historical Background. The history of the boundary between China and the Russian Empire dates back to 1689, when the Treaty of Nerchinsk established a line along the southeastern limits of Russia, up to the Pacific Ocean. In 1727 the Chinese and Russian governments carried their boundary westward to Mongolia. In the Treaty of Peking (1860), the boundary west of Mongolia was determined in general terms and in the Treaty of Chuguchak (T'ach'eng), signed in 1864, the boundary line was defined but not demarcated because of Muslim rebellions in the boundary region. In 1878 the Chinese occupied the disputed area and a new set of negotiations took place, resulting in the Treaty of Saint Petersburg in February 1881. Russia occupied the Turkistan and Tajikistan areas between 1879 and 1884, establishing its boundary with China in central Asia. The boundary itself was defined in five protocols. The final one, dated 22 May 1884, described the boundary that later became the northern section of the border between China and Tajikistan up to the Uch-bel Pass, while the southern section was never defined by a treaty. Russia became the Union of Soviet Socialist Republics (USSR) in 1917 and in 1924 Tajikistan was formed as a territorial entity from the Tajik areas of Bokhara and Turkistan. In 1929 it became a constituent republic of the USSR with the Chinese–Russian boundary of 1884 as its southeastern border. Tajikistan became an independent country in 1991, adopting the Chinese–Soviet Union boundary as its boundary with China with no formal agreement.

Present Situation. The boundary is situated in a rugged area, where no roads have been built and where there is no need for boundary pillars. Therefore, the line was never demarcated. The southern section of the boundary (191 miles; 307 km.) has never been determined by a treaty. Nevertheless, since 1884 there have been no boundary disputes in the area and since Tajikistan's independence there have been no conflicts concerning its alignment.

CHINA — VIETNAM The boundary between China and Vietnam runs 796 miles (1,281 km.) between the Gulf of Tonkin and the tripoint boundary with Laos. It is a section of the former boundary between French Indochina and China.

Geographical Setting. The China–Vietnam boundary line is not based on its geographical significance, but was adopted as a line of defense against bands of brigands attempting to cross from China to Tonkin, the former Vietnam. Following natural obstacles, such as mountains and rivers, it begins on the shore of the Gulf of Tonkin, between Dongxing (China) and Mong Cai (Vietnam), at 21°40'N and 108°E. It sets out westward, leaving the southern tributaries of the Yu River (Yu Chiang) in China. Near the Chinese city of P'ing-hsiang it turns northward and crosses the upper tributaries of the Yu River. Then changing direction toward the west it climbs into a mountainous area, crosses the eastern river of Vietnam—the Claire River (Song Lo in Vietnamese; Pan-lung Chiang in Chinese)—and reaches the border town of Lao Cai on the Red River (Song Hong in Vietnamese; Yüan Chiang in Chinese). Thence it traverses along the Red River for about 31 miles (50 km.), follows some local watersheds and runs westward, crossing the Black River (Song Da in Vietnamese; Li-hsien Chiang in Chinese) and reaches the border junction with Laos.

Historical Background. During the second half of the nineteenth century France expanded its holdings in French Indochina in Southeast Asia. During 1866–1867 the French realized that the Mekong

Mountainous region of the China–Vietnam border

River was not the main avenue for trade with the Chinese province of Yunnan and shifted their interests northward to the Gulf of Tonkin. A French force was sent to negotiate navigation rights on the Yu Chiang, the main river in southern China. Subsequently, fighting broke out and the city of Hanoi, then under the Kingdom of Annam, was captured by the French army. Clashes spread toward the Annam–China borderland in the Tonkin region, which eventually led to a treaty of peace and commerce between France and China in 1885. Commissioners were then appointed to identify and mark the boundary between them, followed by the signing of a boundary convention in June 1887, which carried the boundary as far as the Black River, near today's China–Laos–Vietnam boundary junction. However, problems concerning pirate and brigand activities soon led the Chinese to occupy certain areas allocated to the French, whereupon French officials undertook to define the boundary with greater care. With Chinese cooperation, the work was begun in 1892 and in June 1894 an exchange of maps and notes authorized the entire boundary line from the Gulf of Tonkin to the Black River, which was demarcated by 308 boundary pillars. In 1895 the line was extended eastward to the Mekong River. This extention added 18.5 miles (30 km.) to the China–Vietnam boundary, the rest of it following the present boundary between China and Laos.

Present Situation. The independence of Vietnam in 1954 did not affect the settled boundary line, which has thus been maintained as the present boundary. The Sino-French treaties that settled the boundary lines in this region are not challenged by China today and there has not appeared to be any need for China to negotiate its boundaries with Vietnam any further. Recent conflicts that led to clashes along the border were not related to the alignment of the boundary.

CHRISTMAS ISLAND This island is located in the southeast Indian Ocean and forms an external territory of Australia. The island's total land area is 52 sq. miles (135 sq. km.) and it has an estimated population of 2,300 (1994). Christmas Island has no land boundaries.

COCOS (KEELING) ISLANDS An archipelago located in the Indian Ocean, Cocos Islands is an external territory of Australia. With no land boundaries, its area is 5 sq. miles (14 sq. km.). Cocos Islands has an estimated population of 700 (1994).

COLOMBIA A South American country (area: 439,733 sq. miles [1,138,908 sq. km.]; estimated population: 34,900,000 [1994]), Colombia is situated in the northwestern part of the continent. It is bounded in the north by the Caribbean Sea, northwest by Panama (140 miles; 225 km.), west by the Pacific Ocean, southwest by Ecuador (367 miles; 590 km.), south by Peru (1,802 miles; 2,900 km.) and northeast by Venezuela (1,274 miles; 2,050 km.) and Brazil (1,022 miles; 1,644 km.). The capital of Colombia is Bogotá.

Over 200 years after the Spanish conquest in 1525 the *audiencia* (district) of Santa Fe de Bogotá, incorporated into the viceroyalty of Peru in 1559, was transferred to the viceroyalty of New Granada (1740), which was created by combining the land areas now comprising Colombia, Ecuador and Venezuela. South-American-born Creoles, feeling their prosperity threatened by continued subjugation to Spain, fomented early resistance to Spanish rule in the form of the Comunero Revolt of 1781. After independence was achieved in 1821, New Granada became the Republic of Gran Colombia, which lasted until 1830.

Continuing conflict between the Liberal and Conservative parties, which began in the latter half of the nineteenth century and continued into the mid-twentieth, had earlier resulted in an "alternating governments" agreement, restored in 1958. Colombian life, however, has been plagued by recent and continuing violence, in part political and in part related to international traffic in narcotics centered in the city of Medellín.

COLOMBIA — BRAZIL see BRAZIL–COLOMBIA.

COLOMBIA — ECUADOR Colombia and Ecuador are separated by a boundary that runs for 367 miles (590 km.) between the boundary junction with Peru on the Güeppi River in the east and the mouth of the Mataje River in Ancón Bay in the Pacific Ocean. It follows an internal division in the former colonial Spanish possessions in South America.

Geographical Setting. The eastern terminus of the boundary is located on the Güeppi River, west of the small town of Cabo Minacho (Ecuador). It follows the river downstream eastward to its confluence with

Colombia's boundaries

Tulcan, Ecuador, near the Colombia–Ecuador border

the Putumayo River and follows the main navigation channel of the Putumayo River upstream northwestward for about 65 miles (105 km.) to its confluence with one of its tributaries, the Cuhimbe River, in the small town of Cuembi. The boundary line leaves the river and runs for 15 miles (24 km.) in a straight line southward to the San Miguel River, west of the town of La Nueva Santa (Ecuador). It follows the main navigation channel of the San Miguel River upstream westward to its source. Then it runs westward for about 5 miles (8 km.) and reaches the Chingual River east of the Ecuadorian town of La Bonita. It follows that river upstream northward and then westward to its source near El Carmelo (Ecuador) and then runs northward for about 20 miles (32 km.) to the Carchi River, west of the Colombian town of Ipiales. The boundary follows the river upstream westward to its source on the volcanic cone of Chiles (15,630 feet; 4,764 m.), passes the peak from east to west and reaches the

source of the San Juan River. It follows the river downstream northwestward to its confluence with the Mira River in the small town of Tobar Donoso (Ecuador). It follows the Mira River northwestward for 20 miles (32 km.), leaves it and, in a short straight line westward, reaches the Mataje River. The boundary follows that river downstream to its mouth in Ancón Bay.

Historical Background. The Presidency of New Granada was established in the sixteenth century and was reorganized as the Spanish viceroyalty of New Granada in 1739, including the areas of today's Ecuador, Colombia, Venezuela and Panama. On 20 July 1810 Colombia declared its independence from Spain, becoming Great Colombia, but this was not assured until 1819. Ecuador also achieved independence, in 1822, and joined Great Colombia as "the Province of the Ecuador." In 1830 Great Colombia split up into the states of Venezuela, Ecuador and the republic of Great Colombia. On 29 February

1832 the boundary between Ecuador and Colombia was placed along the line established by Great Colombia on 25 June 1824, according to the last Spanish dividing line that had been established before independence, but for about 100 years Colombia and Ecuador could not agreed on the exact alignment of the boundary. Ecuador demanded all the areas of the former Spanish Ecuador westward to 74°W, in accordance with the principle of *uti possidetis*, but Colombia refused to accept Ecuador's demands. After long negotiations a boundary treaty was signed at Bogotá, Colombia, on 24 May 1908, establishing the line along the San Miguel and San Juan rivers. As this treaty was not ratified, a new treaty was signed at Bogotá on 15 July 1916, which defined the boundary line in great detail. Demarcation of the line was carried out between 16 July 1917 and 9 July 1919. Thus, the long dispute between the two states was calmed and the present boundary line established.

Present Situation. Since 1919 there have been no disputes concerning the alignment of the demarcated boundary, although in 1925–1931 Ecuador broke its diplomatic relations with Colombia, following a boundary treaty signed between Peru and Colombia which closed a section of the Ecuador–Colombia boundary on the Putumayo River.

COLOMBIA — PANAMA The boundary between Colombia and Panama runs for 140 miles (225 km.) between the Pacific Ocean in the north to the Caribbean Sea in the south, mainly along water partings. It is conceded to be the dividing line between Central and South America.

Geographical Setting. Situated on the isthmus connecting Central and South America, the boundary begins at Cabo Tiburón, in the Gulf of Darién, located on the shore of the Caribbean Sea. The line runs between boundary marks, follows small river watersheds and climbs to the crest of a local cordillera to Cerro Sande situated some 1,443 feet (440 m.) above sea level. It then descends and follows another watershed southward to a point 558 feet (170 m.) above sea level. It climbs up to Mount Tanela (4,642 feet; 1,415 m.) and then continues southeastward to Alto Limon and southwest to Mangle. Following the watershed it runs northward to Alturas de Nique and then runs southward to El

Cruce on the watershed between the Jurado (Colombia) and Tucuti (Panama) rivers, which eventually flow into the Pacific Ocean. The boundary travels southwest to the nearby Altos de Aspavé, a point of contention between Panama and Colombia for many years, and in a straight line south reaches Punto Equidistante, a point situated between two small towns—Jurado (Colombia) and Cocalito (Panama)—on the shore of the Pacific Ocean.

Historical Background. The history of this boundary line, like most of those in Latin America, dates from the Spanish colonial period. In 1740 a Spanish viceroyalty of New Granada included the provinces of Colombia, Panama, Venezuela and Ecuador. Early in the nineteenth century all these provinces declared their independence from Spain, uniting to create the independent state of Greater Colombia. In 1830, however, Venezuela and Ecuador withdrew, leaving only Colombia and Panama in the Republic of New Granada. The people of Panama failed in an attempt to establish the State of the Isthmus of Panama in 1841, but in 1855 the state of Panama was created as an autonomous province in Colombia, with boundaries similar to those existing today. In the second half of the nineteenth century, following changes in the integral organization of Colombia, Panama was further reduced to a department of Colombia.

Panama proclaimed its independence on 3 November 1903, placing itself under the protective power of the United States, which administrated the Panama Canal Zone. Only 11 years later, in April 1914, did Colombia, by a treaty with United States, recognize the independence of Panama, with a boundary that crosses the isthmus. A boundary treaty was signed on 20 August 1924, recognizing the line established back in June 1855. It took another 14 years to set and mark the boundary on the ground and on 17 June 1938 an exchange of notes marked the final stage of the boundary alignment between Panama and Colombia.

Present Situation. The boundary line covers a well-defined area and is demarcated by pillars along its entire length. There are no known disputes between Panama and Colombia concerning the location of the present boundary.

COLOMBIA — PERU This is one of the most

recently established boundaries in South America (1942) and it is still in dispute owing to Ecuadorian demands in the border area. The boundary is 1,802 miles (2,900 km.) long and runs from the boundary junction with Brazil in the confluence of the Javari (Yavari) and Amazon rivers in the southeast to the boundary junction with Ecuador on the Güeppi River in the northwest.

Geographical Setting. The southeastern terminus of the boundary line is located at 4°13'30.5"S and 69°56'33.7"W at the confluence of the Javari and Amazon rivers, between the towns of Tabatinga (Brazil) and Leticia (Colombia). From there the line follows the main navigation channel of the Amazon River upstream westward for about 80 miles (130 km.), leaves the river and runs in a straight line northeast for about 130 miles (210 km.). It reaches the Putumayo River in the town of Puerto Soccoro (Colombia) and follows its main navigation channel upstream westward for about 500 miles (800 km.) to its confluence with one of its tributaries, the Güeppi River. The boundary line follows that river upstream westward for about 25 miles (40 km.) and meets the boundary junction with Ecuador northwest of the small Colombian town of Cabo Reyes.

Historical Background. The territory of the republic of Colombia, which became independent in 1819, purported to include everything within the boundaries of the old captaincy-generals of Granada and Venezuela in the viceroyalty of New Granada. In 1821 Peru proclaimed the independence of all the intendancies that had formed the viceroyalty of Peru. The Treaty of Perpetual Union, League and Confederation between Colombia and Peru, signed at Lima on 6 July 1823, provided that the precise demarcation of the boundaries that should divide their territories should be arranged by a special convention. However, an internal Peruvian arrangement concerning its boundaries met with Colombian protest as the former included within its boundaries areas in the Mainas province, north of the Marañón River, which had formed part of the territory of New Granada since 1718. Although the states signed a treaty in 1823 by which both recognized the 1809 boundaries of the former viceroyalties of Peru and New Granada, Colombia never ratified it. The dispute led to war in 1828, which lasted until the Colombian victory in February 1829. A final peace treaty, signed at Guayaquil in September 1829, called for a boundary commission that would work in accordance with the 1809 colonial line.

Ecuador's independence from Colombia in 1830 led to new boundary disputes between Ecuador and Colombia on one hand and Ecuador and Peru on the other. However, the disputes between Peru and Colombia lapsed into occasional protests. The treaty of 23 October 1851 between Brazil and Peru concerning their boundary led to a Colombian protest that was repeated in 1866 and 1869. In 1894 a general conference was called by Peru to settle the boundaries between the four countries, but Ecuador refused to approve of the convention. To settle their boundary dispute, Peru and Colombia agreed on 12 September 1905 to bring the issue of the boundary in the 10,000-sq. mile (25,890-sq. km.) Putumayo region before the pope and the king of Spain for arbitration. This plan was never carried out and Colombia and Peru agreed (13 April 1910) to establish a boundary commission, but once again the motion came to nil. Only 12 years later, on 24 March 1922, was a boundary treaty that delimited the present boundary line signed and a demarcation boundary commission finished its work by 14 March 1930. A boundary treaty between Colombia and Brazil, signed on 19 March 1928, settled the disputed Tabatinga area of southeastern Colombia and a trapezium area of about 4,000 sq. miles (10,360 sq. km.), from the Putumayo River down to the Amazon River, which was formerly claimed by Peru, was delivered to Colombia. A dispute concerning the Leticia region, which led to some local fighting between Colombia and Peru in 1932–1934, was ended with the intervention of the League of Nations, which awarded the area to Colombia.

Present Situation. After about 100 years of negotiations, fighting and settlements, the Columbia–Peru boundary was established and from 1934 there were no more serious disputes concerning its alignment.

COLOMBIA — VENEZUELA This boundary primarily follows a Spanish colonial boundary that was established in 1810. The land boundary was reestablished in 1932, but the main disputed area between the two states, the maritime boundary in the Gulf of Venezuela, was settled only in 1982. The boundary runs for 1,274 miles (2,050 km.) between the boundary tripoint with Brazil on the Negro River in the southeast and the Gulf of Venezuela in the Atlantic Ocean in the north.

Geographical Setting. The Brazilian tripoint is located in the main navigation channel of the Negro River, southeast of San Jose Island, at 1°13'27.2"N and 66°50'54.2"W. It follows the Negro River upstream northward to a point near the Colombian town of Cejal, where the river becomes the Guainía River and runs westward into Colombian territory. In a straight line northeastward the boundary reaches the Atabapo River, follows it downstream northward to its confluence with the Guaviare River and continues northward to its confluence with the great Orinoco River. It follows the main navigation channel of the Orinoco River to its confluence with the Meta River, between the towns of Puerto Páez (Venezuela) and Puerto Carreño (Colombia). The line bears with the Meta River upstream westward for about 140 miles (225 km.) to Apostadero on the Meta and in a straight line heads northwest for about 70 miles (110 km.) to reach the Arauca River. Thence it follows the Arauca River upstream westward to its confluence with the Sarare River, which it follows to its confluence with the Oira River, and follows this to its head. Along the Tama ridge it reaches the head of the Táchira River, follows it to the Don Pedro ravine and reaches the mouth of the Garita River in the Zulia River. Thence the boundary runs along the Oro River to its source, trends across the watershed made up of the Perijá Ridge and the Oka mountains, running parallel to the shore of the Gulf of Venezuela, stretches along the Valledupar ridge and reaches its northern terminus in the Frailes hillocks on the La Guajira peninsula.

Historical Background. During the eighteenth century both states were constituents of Spanish New Granada in South America, but in 1819 Colombia (with today's Ecuador, Panama and Venezuela) became independent as Great Colombia, while Venezuela received full independence in 1830. Both states adopted the *uti possidetis* principle for their common boundary, which relied on the colonial divisions, but Venezuela claimed the entire area that was called the captaincy-general of Venezuela until 1810, while Colombia insisted on adopting the 1810 colonial line as its boundary with Venezuela. A friendship treaty of 14 December 1833 established

the boundary but Venezuela refused to approve of the treaty. Another treaty signed in Caracas (Venezuela) on 23 July 1842 provided for the institution of a boundary commission and a special conference dealt with four disputed areas in 1844. An agreement was reached concerning the northern section of the boundary but the southern area was not settled. In 1845 and 1872 Colombia suggested arbitration, only to be rejected by Venezuela, and in the 1870s diplomatic relations between the two states were broken several times. On 14 September 1881 it was agreed to submit the dispute for arbitration to the Spanish king, who accepted the office in November 1883 but died before reaching a conclusion. A detailed award signed by the queen regent of Spain on 16 March 1891 established the boundary between the two states, giving the entire La Guajira peninsula to Colombia. By a treaty signed in Bogotá on 24 April 1894 Colombia ceded to Venezuela certain territories—including settlements on the east coast of the peninsula, but the Colombian Congress refused to accept these changes. However, both states officially accepted the Spanish award in 1894 and a demarcation commission was appointed.

No further agreements concerning the precise location of the boundary line were signed until another round of talks that began in 1913 led to a convention in Bogotá (3 November 1916) which called for an arbitrator, named on 20 July 1917 as the Swiss Federal Council. An award was presented on 24 March 1922 defining the boundary line with a few minor modifications to the 1891 award. A Swiss commission demarcated the line between 1922 and 1924. Some minor problems concerning boundary markers were handled during the following years and the final boundary agreement was reached in 1932.

A new dispute arose in the 1920s with the discovery of oil resources in the area of the Gulf of Venezuela and Lake Maracaibo. Sovereignty over the water and resources of the Gulf of Venezuela and the area around the islands of Los Monjes (northeast of the La Guajira peninsula) was questioned and in 1953–1958 the area was occupied by Venezuela. During the 1970s several talks took place and an agreement was reached on 21 October 1980. The agreement confirmed that the islands belong to Venezuela but that Colombia has limited rights in the gulf. On 1 February 1982 a demarcation team established the maritime boundary between the two states.

Present Situation. In 1932 both states accepted the demarcation of the land boundary and following that there were no more land boundary disputes. The 1982 agreement solved the maritime boundary dispute and at present no other issues concerning the boundary's alignment are known.

COMORO ISLANDS (Comores/Al-Qumur) A republic consisting of three islands in the Indian Ocean, the Comoros are located between the southern African mainland and Madagascar. The republic has a total area of 863 sq. miles (2,235 sq. km.) and an estimated population (1994) of 510,000. It has no land boundaries and its capital is Moroni.

The Comorians voted for independence from France in a referendum conducted in 1974. Only the people of the southernmost island of Mayotte voted to remain part of France. Independence was declared unilaterally in 1975 for all the islands. Mayotte, however, is still governed by France, causing some tensions between the two countries.

CONGO A central African country (area: 131,977 sq. miles [341,820 sq. km.]; estimated population: 2,700,000 [1994]) situated on the equator, the Congo is bounded in the north by Cameroon (325 miles; 523 km.) and the Central African Republic (290.5 miles; 467 km.), east and south by Zaire (1,010 miles; 1,625 km.), southwest by Angola (125 miles; 201 km.) and the Atlantic Ocean and west by Gabon (1,183 miles; 1,903 km.). The capital of the Congo is Brazzaville.

The first contact of the Congolese with Europeans was as early as the fifteenth century. The Portuguese traded with them and tried to convert them to Catholicism, but their conversion was only superficial. Protestant missionaries who arrived in their region in the nineteenth century found only vague signs of Christianity. At first the Congolese joined the missions and became Protestants but later an independent church was formed by Simon Kimbangu, regarded by the Congo as a prophet. This is still the largest and most important independent church in Africa and most Congolese are members.

The Congolese gained their independence from the French in 1960. Since then the politics of the country have been characterized by ethnic divisions, mainly between the northern and southern peoples but also among the peoples of the north themselves. The first two presidents of Congo came from the south but after 1968 there were three northern presidents who gave priority to the development of the northern areas. Some of the northern peoples also felt that they had been neglected by the government. In 1990 popular resentment of the government and the severe economic crisis forced the president to agree to a democratization process. A national conference was formed and became a sovereign body.

CONGO — ANGOLA see ANGOLA–CONGO.

CONGO — CAMEROON see CAMEROON–CONGO.

CONGO — CENTRAL AFRICAN REPUBLIC see CENTRAL AFRICAN REPUBLIC–CONGO.

CONGO — GABON Running for 1,183 miles (1,903 km.) between the Atlantic Ocean and the boundary tripoint with Cameroon on the Ivindo (Ayina) River, the Congo–Gabon boundary follows a former French colonial boundary.

Geographical Setting. The boundary tripoint with Cameroon is located at the intersection of the Ivindo River and 2°10'20"N. The boundary line follows the Ivindo River downstream southward to its confluence with the Djoua River from the east. It follows the Djoua River upstream eastward for about 70 miles (110 km.), leaves it and continues eastward for another 10 miles (16 km.). It then changes its direction southward for about 60 miles (100 km.) to reach the town of Mbendze (Congo). From there the boundary runs southwest and then south toward the equator and after crossing the equator runs southeast for about 50 miles (80 km.) to reach the Haut Ogooué region of Gabon. Thence it continues southward for 145 miles (233 km.) and changes its direction westward. It runs for about 70 miles (110 km.) to the vicinity of M'binda (Congo) and turns north, west and south, leaving the northern tributary of the Kouilou River within Congo. The boundary reaches the northern tributary of the Nyanga River, follows it downstream southward for 30 miles (50 km.) and forms a straight line westward to the N'Gounie

River, the main river of southwestern Gabon. The line follows that river southwest and then northwest until it reaches the main road that links Loubomo (Congo) and Lambaréné (Gabon). It follows the road southeastward, crosses the northern tributary of the Nyanga River and then runs southward to leave the whole Nyanga region within Gabon. The southernmost sector of the boundary line runs southwestward, reaching the Atlantic Ocean at Point Chibobo, southeast of Mayumba (Gabon).

Historical Background. Both Congo and Gabon became French colonies in 1889 and in 1903 Moyen (Middle) Congo and Gabon became divisions of French Congo (which also included today's Chad and Central African Republic). On 11 February 1906 a decree was published in which the four colonies were defined separately in general terms. French Congo became French Equatorial Africa in 1910, which was reorganized in 1934, 1937 and 1941—defining the limits of the colonial possessions only in general terms each time. Gabon's borders were established in a series of sanctions between 1940 and 1946, while those of Moyen Congo were established in 1940. Congo became independent on 15 August 1960; Gabon two days later, on 17 August 1960. Without a formal agreement, both states assumed the undemarcated, general colonial division as their common international boundary.

Present Situation. Since 1960 no disputes concerning the boundary alignment have been reported. Early in the 1960s Congo made claims on the region of Haut Ogooué, but dropped them later on. The undemarcated boundary line led to some localized incertitudes regarding the alignment, but no serious problems arose.

CONGO — ZAIRE

The boundary between Congo and Zaire runs for 1,498 miles (2,410 km.) southward, from the Central African Republic tripoint in the Ubangi (Oubangui) River to the boundary tripoint with the Angolan exclave of Cabinda on the Chiloango River. It follows the former colonial boundary between Belgium and France in central Africa.

Geographical Setting. The northern terminus of the boundary line is located in the confluence of the Gouga and Ubangi rivers, at the boundary junction with the Central African Republic. Following the main navigation channel of the Ubangi River downstream southward for 290 miles (467 km.), the boundary reaches the river's confluence with the great Congo River. It continues along the Congo River downstream southwestward for about 500 miles (800 km.) to a point west of the Tombo Rapids. On its way the boundary crosses Stanley (Malebo) Pool, leaving Bemu Island within Congo. Departing from the Congo River east of Manyanga (Congo), the boundary turns northward to follow some local rivers and straight-line segments, until it reaches the Loungou River. It extends along that river upstream northwestward to its source and then runs north to the watershed between the Congo and Niari rivers, east of Mindouli (Congo). It trends across the watershed westward for about 60 miles (100 km.) and southwestward for about 50 miles (80 km.) to Kiama Peak, the source of the Chiloango River. The boundary then follows the Chiloango River downstream northwestward to the boundary tripoint with Angola.

Historical Background. The French entered the region north of the Congo River in 1880 and in 1882 established the colony of French Congo, which included Middle (Moyen) Congo. On 15 January 1910 French Congo became French Equatorial Africa. Belgium entered central Africa as King Leopold of Belgium established the Committee for Upper Congo Studies in 1878, which was later known as the International Association of the Congo. In the Berlin Conference of 1884–1885 the Association, which changed its name to Congo Free State, was recognized as a governing power on the Congo River. Congo Free State then reached an agreement with France to divide their possessions in the Congo region. This line was extended eastward in 1885 and 1887, and by a declaration of 5 February 1895 the boundary line in the Stanley Pool area was delimited.

In 1895 Congo Free State was submitted to Belgium, which accepted it only in 1908, when it became Belgian Congo. In 1903 a boundary commission detailed its boundary with Moyen Congo and a declaration signed on 23 December 1908 determined the exact line in the Chiloango River area. Belgian Congo became independent on 30 June 1960, changing its name to Zaire on 21 October 1971. French Congo became independent on 15 August 1960 and was renamed Congo. Both countries adopted the colonial boundary as their common international boundary, although no additional formal agreements were made.

Present Situation. The land sectors of the Congo–Zaire boundary are mostly demarcated and no current disputes are known concerning its alignment. However, the riverine sectors do present problems concerning the allocation of the many islands located in the Congo and Ubangi rivers. A dispute concerning navigation rights developed in 1970 and could arise again for lack of a clearly defined boundary in the Congo River.

COOK ISLANDS A self-governing overseas territory in free association with New Zealand, this group of islands is located in the South Pacific Ocean. Its total land area is 90 sq. miles (233 sq. km.) with an estimated population of 18,000 (1994). Its capital is Avarua and it has no land boundaries.

Over 90% of the Cook Islands' population are engaged in farming (coconuts, bananas and citrus) and fishing. In recent years tourism has become the most important source of national income.

COSTA RICA Costa Rica is a Central American country situated between the Caribbean Sea and the Pacific Ocean. It is bounded by Nicaragua (192 miles; 309 km.) in the north and by Panama (205 miles; 330 km.) in the northeast. Its area is 19,730 sq. miles (51,100 sq. km.) and it has an estimated population (1994) of 3,300,000. The capital of Costa Rica is San José.

About 95% of the population of Costa Rica inherit varying mixtures of the *mestizo* blend of Spanish conquerors and colonists with Indians, including some African roots. People of many other nationalities and cultures have immigrated to Costa Rica: between 1870 and 1920, 20–25% of the population growth could be attributed to immigration. Since 1920 its effect has been minor.

COSTA RICA — NICARAGUA The 192-mile (309-km.) boundary between Costa Rica and Nicaragua marks, with some modification, the former provincial boundary under the Spanish regime in Central America. It runs from east to west between the Caribbean Sea and the Pacific Ocean.
Geographical Setting. The boundary line begins on the shore of the Caribbean Sea near the Bay of the Harbor Head lagoon. It runs along the shore of the lagoon to the mouth of the San Juan River and follows the northern bank of the river for about 80 miles (130 km.) upstream to a point 3 miles (5 km.) below the Old Castle (El Castillo Viejo) at 10°59'38.924"N and 84°21'33.634"W, where boundary pillar no. 2 is erected. From there it runs in a series of straight lines to the shore of Lake Nicaragua and along the southern shore of the lake (at a height of 106 feet [32 m.]) to the Sapoa River. Again following straight lines, the boundary runs 108 miles (174 km.), crossing the Inter-American Highway to boundary pillar no. 20 and reaching a central point in Salinas Bay in the Pacific Ocean, which was fixed at 11°03'47"N and 85°43'52"W.

Historical Background. From 1540, Costa Rica and Nicaragua were administrative units of the Spanish Empire in Central America and the line dividing the two provinces was later to determine the political boundary between the two countries. Both became independent from Spain on 15 September 1821, but to resolve some territorial problems, Costa Rica and Nicaragua signed the Canas-Jerez Treaty on 15 April 1858, which confirmed the boundary between them. Over the next 30 years several new treaties were proposed in order to settle problems concerning the use of ports and waterways but none were ratified. Only in March 1889 was an arbitral award upholding the treaty of 1858 conferred by President Grover Cleveland of the United States. On 27 March 1896 an associated demarcation commission was appointed and five arbitration awards were made between 1897 and 1900 to determine the boundary as it reaches the Caribbean Sea, along the shore of the Nicaragua Lake and at Salinas Bay. The geographic coordinates of the boundary pillars were confirmed by an Inter-American Geodetic Survey team in 1965.
Present Situation. From 1900 onward there have been no known disputes concerning the location of the boundary, which is well demarcated.

COSTA RICA — PANAMA The boundary between Costa Rica and Panama is 205 miles (330 km.) long and, like the other four Central American boundaries, extends from the Caribbean Sea to the Pacific Ocean. Some 32 miles (51 km.) of the boundary follow a straight line while the remaining sections coincide with topographical features.

Geographical Setting. The northern point of the boundary line lies at the mouth of the Sixaola River in the Caribbean Sea near 9°30'N and 82°30'W. The line follows the main navigation channel of the river upstream in a generally westerly direction to its confluence with the Yorkin River. Following this river southward the boundary reaches Brákicha Point, where the Yorkin River intersects parallel 9°30'N. At this point the boundary leaves the river, runs for 7 miles (11 km.) in a straight line southeast and turns west to reach a point called Namu Uoki at 1,906 feet (581 m.) above sea level where it intersects meridian 82°56'10"W. It follows the meridian south for 27 miles (43 km.) until it reaches the Cordillera mountain range, which is the watershed between the Atlantic and the Pacific oceans, at a point located 7,899 feet (2,407 m.) above sea level. The boundary line follows the mountain range for 27 miles (43 km.) in a southeasterly direction, climbs to the highest point of the boundary on Cerro Echandi (9,500 feet; 2,895 m.), and reaches Mount Pando, which is the meeting point of the larger mountain range with a secondary range and constitutes the watershed between the Gulf of Dulce on the Costa Rican Pacific coast and Charco Azul Bay situated on the Panamanian Pacific coast. From that point the boundary line follows the watershed, passing through the Canoas Pass, crossing the Inter-American Highway and reaching the coast of the Pacific Ocean at Point Burica situated on the Cerro Burica peninsula.

Historical Background. After the abolishment of the Spanish Empire in Central America in 1821, a boundary was established between the Central American Federation and the Republic of Great Colombia. Thus, the present boundary between Costa Rica and Panama is, with some minor changes, the boundary between the Republic of Costa Rica, established in 1838 as an independent state, and the Republic of Colombia that was established a few years earlier.

During most of the nineteenth and the first half of the twentieth centuries controversies involving this boundary remained peaceful for the most part, reflecting the claims of the states concerned with the boundaries of their ancestral states. In November 1896 Costa Rica and Colombia agreed to French arbitration but Costa Rica later protested against a section of the line that was established in 1900, partly because of a lack of adequate geographical knowledge. In 1903 Panama became an independent state, inheriting the boundary problems of Great Colombia. In 1910 Chief Justice Edward D. White of the United States became an arbitrator but his 1914 award was not accepted by Panama. Only on 1 May 1941 did Costa Rica and Panama sign a treaty concerning their common boundary line and three years later, on 18 September 1944, the demarcation was completed and a final boundary treaty was signed.

Present Situation. The land boundary is demarcated with precision while the river section is very clear. The two countries being the most peaceful in Central America, no disputes concerning the boundary alignment are known.

CÔTE D'IVOIRE see IVORY COAST.

CROATIA (Hrvatska) A former republic of Yugoslavia that declared its independence in 1991, Croatia (area: 21,829 sq. miles [56,538 sq. km.]; estimated population: 4,850,000 [1994]) is situated in southeastern Europe, on the Balkan Peninsula. It is bounded in the north by Slovenia (283 miles; 455 km.) and Hungary (204 miles; 329 km.), in the east by Serbia (158 miles; 254 km.) and Bosnia (523.5 miles; 842 km.) and in the south and west by the Adriatic Sea. Croatia's capital is Zagreb.

In 1102 Croatia became part of the kingdom of Hungary by a personal union, but retained its autonomy under its own *Ban* (ruler). In the sixteenth century Croatia, as part of Hungary (both threatened by the Ottomans), became a Habsburg possession. By the early seventeenth century, the major part of Croatia was under Ottoman rule. Only a narrow strip in western Croatia remained under Austrian and Hungarian rule. However, the peace treaty of Karlowitz (1699) gave all of Croatia to the Habsburgs. Here, the Croats preserved until 1840 a measure of internal autonomy and used the Croatian language for official purposes, until an attempt to introduce Hungarian as the official language sparked off a revival of Croatian national aspirations followed by the emergence of a movement calling for the union of all southern Slavs. These were the aims of the 1848 rebellion, which was suppressed quickly. The late nineteenth century saw the steady growth of the movement striving for autonomy and for a southern Slav political entity.

In 1917 a Croatian Committee in Exile in London signed the Corfu Declaration with representatives of the Serbian government, which provided for the unification of the southern Slavs of Austria-Hungary with the independent states of Serbia and Montenegro. This led to the establishment in 1918 of the kingdom of Yugoslavia; however, the Croats were soon disappointed by their inferior role in the new kingdom. Croatian nationalism, led by Stjepan Radic and his Croatian Peasant Party, came out against Serbian ascendancy in the kingdom. Radic's assassination in 1928 deepened Croat antagonism to the Serbs.

In World War II the *Ustase*, a Croat fascist movement led by Ante Pavelic, utilized the German occupation of Yugoslavia in April 1941 to proclaim an independent Croatian state within the broadest possible borders. This state pursued a policy of expulsion and extermination of ethnic minorities, mainly Serbs, Jews and Gypsies. The *Ustase* were allied with the Germans and fought against both Yugoslav resistance movements: that led by the monarchist government-in-exile in London and the communist one led by Tito (himself a Croat).

In 1946 the People's Republic of Croatia was established as one of Yugoslavia's federated republics. Under Tito all nationalist movements were suppressed, but following his death in 1980 the long rivalry between the Serbs and Croats erupted again. In 1991 Croatia proclaimed its complete independence and seceded from Yugoslavia. The Serbs reacted by force, starting a war which led the major powers to recognize independent Croatia. In 1992, the Croats of Bosnia-Herzegovina became involved in a civil war between Croats, Serbs and Bosnian Muslims.

CROATIA — BOSNIA see BOSNIA–CROATIA.

CROATIA — HUNGARY

The Croatia–Hungary boundary is 204 miles (329 km.) long. It extends southeast and northeast from the tripoint boundary junction with Slovenia to the tripoint with Serbia. Croatia and Hungary have maintained the boundary that was established in 1920 between the former Republic of Yugoslavia and Hungary.

Geographical Setting. From the Slovenian tripoint on the Mura River, this boundary follows the river in a southeasterly direction, through the Pannonian plains. When it arrives at the mouth of the Mura River, which flows into the Drava River, it joins the latter to form the main part of the boundary. At certain points the boundary deviates from the present course of the river, its line based on the former riverbed. Thus, there are small areas of Croatian territory on the Drava's northern bank and Hungarian parcels on its southern bank. The eastern sector of the boundary cuts northeastward through the lowlands of the Baranya region. It then runs across the Danube River and meets the Serbian border on its eastern bank.

Historical Background. This boundary is one of the oldest European boundaries, as the Drava River has been used as a dividing line between the two countries for many centuries. Croatia and Hungary experienced many centuries of changing unions and federations (almost continuously from 1102 to 1918), although the Drava River functioned as their common boundary throughout. The first precise survey was carried out in 1763–1787 during the rule of Joseph II (a German king and Holy Roman emperor). The western section of boundary, on the Mura River, is the northern limit of the Croatian region of Medimurje which throughout history occasionally belonged to Hungary. In 1918, however, the region was finally reintegrated into Croatia. Only the easternmost sector of the boundary was delimited for the first time after World War I at the Paris Peace Conference. It cut through a former Hungarian region and divided the county of Baranya. The boundary as a whole was agreed upon by the Treaty of Trianon in 1920 as a section of the boundary between Hungary and the newly established Kingdom of Yugoslavia. It was confirmed by the Paris Treaty of 1947 between Hungary and federal Yugoslavia. Croatia declared itself independent in 1991 and accepted its northern border as a common international boundary with Hungary.

Present Situation. There are no known disputes concerning the boundary line.

CROATIA — SERBIA

Two separate land boundaries constitute the Croatia–Serbia boundary, which in all is 158 miles (254 km.) long. In the north is the

Croatia–Serbia boundary (149 miles; 239 km.), which extends from the boundary tripoint with Hungary southward to the tripoint with Bosnia. In the south the Croatia–Montenegro boundary (9 miles; 15 km.) runs from another boundary junction with Bosnia to the Adriatic Sea. The maritime boundary between Croatia and Serbia (Montenegro), in the Bay of Kotor, has not been delimited.

Geographical Setting. From the boundary tripoint with Hungary the boundary runs southward through the Pannonian plains. In principle it begins by following the course of the Danube River south and southeast, although there are several Croatian pockets on the left bank of the river and some small Serbian pockets on its right bank. Near the town of Ilok the boundary leaves the Danube and continues through the hills of Fruska gora and a flat area, cutting across the historical Croatian region of Srijem. It continues southwestward until it reaches the Sava River at the boundary tripoint with Bosnia. The southern section of the boundary runs from the second boundary junction with Bosnia, on the slopes of Orjen Mountain, across the Prevlaka peninsula to the Adriatic Sea in the Bay of Kotor.

Historical Background. The oldest section of the Croatia–Serbia boundary is the central line that follows the Danube River. It is the legacy of the Treaty of Karlowitz, signed between Austria and the Ottoman Empire in 1699.

The northern sector of the boundary was settled in 1945 as a boundary line between Yugoslavia's Croatian and Serb republics. Delimitation was carried out on the basis of an opinion provided by a special federal boundary commission (the Dilas' Commission, named after its chairman). The region of Baranya, on the right bank of the Danube, was allotted to Croatia on the grounds of possessing a larger Croatian community. Other deviations from the current riverbed of the Danube date back to the old municipal limits in the area. The commission also provided a proposal for the boundary line between the Danube and Sava rivers. The former Croatian region of Srijem was divided by the boundary line on the basis of the prevailing ethnic distribution of Croats or Serbs.

The southern boundary, between Croatia and Serbia (Montenegro), coincides with the border of the former independent Republic of Dubrovnik and was established in 1419 and 1426. From 1700 the same line was used as the boundary between the Republic of Dubrovnik and the narrow Bosnian exit to the sea. In 1815 this boundary was integrated with the Republic of Dubrovnik in the Austrian province of the Kingdom of Dalmatia. The exit to the Bay of Kotor was first held by the Ottoman regime, until 1878, when it was taken over to become part of Austro-Hungarian (1878–1918) Bosnia-Herzegovina. After World War II this section of the boundary became a dividing line between the republics of Croatia and Montenegro and extended to the Bay of Kotor.

Present Situation. The boundary is widely considered an international boundary, since Croatia was recognized as an independent state in early 1992, but it is disputed by Serbia. Since autumn 1991 the Croatian region of Baranya, as well as most of the Slovenian borderland along the Danube, have, in effect, been under Serb occupation and the Serbs consider it part of the self-proclaimed "Serbian Republic of Krajina." In March 1992 these areas came under international control as Sector East of the United Nations Protected Areas (UNPA) within Croatia. Despite the presence of peacekeepers and repeated UN Security Council resolutions confirming the integrity and boundaries of Croatia, there have been no moves toward reintegration of the areas into Croatia. Croatian borderlands near the Montenegro boundary were also occupied in 1991, but the Serb troops withdrew in October 1992. The boundary is disputed by Serbia, which claims the entire Bay of Kotor, including the Prevlaka peninsula. Due to this dispute there is no agreed maritime boundary.

CROATIA — SLOVENIA The boundary between Croatia and Slovenia runs for 283 miles (455 km.) from the boundary tripoint with Hungary on the Mura River, generally southwestward to the Adriatic Sea at the Bay of Piran; about 149 miles (240 km.) of the boundary run through rivers. A maritime boundary has not yet been delimited, although negotiations began in 1992.

Geographical Setting. From the Hungarian tripoint the boundary partially follows the Mura River and its former riverbed northwestward. It then turns south and heads through a hilly area to the Drava River, which is followed westward. When it leaves the river it runs through the Macelj mountains and

Croatia–Slovenia boundary crossing

reaches the Sutla River. This river is followed to its confluence with the Sava River northwest of Zagreb. South of the Sava River the boundary follows its tributary, Bregana, and the watershed on the Zumberak mountain. Then it bears southward until it reaches the Kupa River. The central part of the boundary follows this river and its tributary, Cabranka, southward and westward to Cabar. From there it runs through the mountainous area that divides the regions of Gorski kotar (Croatia) and Notranjsko (Slovenia). North of the Croatian port of Rijeka the boundary enters the region of Istria. It runs through the mountainous terrain of Cicarija and the hills of northern Istria, continuing westward to the Dragonja River and to the sea.

Historical Background. Most of the boundary between Croatia and Slovenia, and particularly its central section, is the old dividing line between the historical Slovenian provinces of Styria and Carniola to the west and Croatia to the east, which were established during the Middle Ages. From the sixteenth to the twentieth centuries it was maintained under the Habsburg rule. The northern sector of the boundary, north of the Drava River, is an old limit between the Croatian region of Medimurje (which occasionally belonged to Hungary) and Styria. Only the western sector of the boundary, on the Istrian peninsula, was delimited for the first time in the midtwentieth century. In 1947, after World War II, Yugoslavia controlled most of the peninsula and settled this section. The westernmost part of the peninsula boundary was delimited in 1954, when the free territory of Trieste was temporarily under the Allies and was divided between Yugoslavia and Italy. A minor boundary change in Istria was carried out in 1956 to Slovenia's benefit. Until 1991 it was the boundary between two federal republics of the former Yugoslavia and after the dissolution of Yugoslavia it was recognized as an international boundary.

Present Situation. Since 1992 a joint boundary commission has been demarcating the line. A few minor points and sections of the land boundary are disputed and are under negotiation; but the maritime delimitation is currently of greater importance.

CUBA   The island of Cuba is the largest of the Caribbean islands, situated 135 miles (217 km.) south of Florida. Cuba has an area of 42,804 sq. miles (110,861 sq. km.) and an estimated population (1994) of 11,000,000. Its capital is Havana and it has no land boundaries.

After several decades of Spanish colonization,

which began in 1494, most of the Indian population of Cuba had disappeared, due to epidemics, genocide and forced labor. Those who survived generally adopted Spanish culture after attaining freedom. Indian women often intermarried due to the shortage of women among the Spanish settlers.

The white population consisted initially of the Spanish *conquistadores* (conquerors), and the traffic of Spanish migrants to and from Cuba was constant ever since the conquest. These Spaniards were mainly from Andalusia, the Canary Islands and Asturia. The first black slaves from Africa came to Cuba in the early sixteenth century. Havana became an important slave market and by the mid-1800s blacks outnumbered whites. Black slaves came from West Africa, mainly from Senegal and also the Congo, but the largest and most influential African group in Cuba were the Yoruba, originally from southwestern Nigeria. The presence of the Yoruba in Cuban culture is still felt today through food, music and other national expressions.

The Revolution of 1959, led by Fidel Castro, introduced revolutionary changes; after about a year, the principal aim of the government to reduce social and economic inequalities was welcomed by the poor and working class majority but rejected by most upper and middle class people. As a result of this national conflict and the strong US sanctions against Cuba (including a long-lasting economic blockade), a massive exodus of primarily white upper and middle class Cubans started in the 1960s. These migrants were accepted as political refugees by the United States. More recent migrants from Cuba are representative of the island's population composition.

CYPRUS (Kípros/Kibris)   The eastern Mediterranean island of Cyprus became an independent state in 1960. However, in July 1974 Turkey invaded the island, occupying over one-third of its area and declaring its northern region independent on 15 November 1983. The United Nations, with the support of all the countries of the world except Turkey, refused to recognize the Turkish Republic of Northern Cyprus (TRNC) and declared all secessionist actions in Cyprus illegal. The area of the island is 3,572 sq. miles (9,251 sq. km.), the TRNC occupying 1,287.5 sq. miles (3,335 sq. km.) of it. Of

the total population (710,000 [1994]) some 136,000 live in the Turkish republic. Besides the unofficial line between the Cypriot republic and the TRNC, Cyprus shares boundaries with two sovereign bases of the United Kingdom, located on the southern and eastern coasts of the island. The Dhekelia Base boundary is approximately 64 miles (103 km.) long and the Akrotiri Base boundary covers some 30 miles (49 km.). The capital of Cyprus is Nicosia.

Cyprus was colonized by Greeks by 1000 B.C.E. or earlier. Other conquerors followed: Phoenicians, the Ptolemises and Romans. Christianized in the first century, Cyprus had its own independent patriarchate within the Byzantine empire. Cyprus came under Latin rule, first French, then Venetian, from the twelfth century to 1571, when the Turks took over. Muslims settled in lieu of the Westerners, in particular in the northeastern corner, but were much more tolerant toward their Orthodox Greek subjects than their predecessors had been. In the eighteenth century, the Orthodox *ethnarch* became responsible for taxation of the Greeks, thus starting the political and economic preponderance of the church which continues until today. As Greek nationalism awakened and inflamed Greek Cypriots as well, church leaders led the struggle for *enosis* (unification) with Greece; yet throughout most of the Ottoman period, peaceful coexistence between the communities was the rule, although social contact between Greek and Turkish Cypriots was limited. In 1878 Cyprus came under British administration (under continued Ottoman suzerainty) as a naval base against Russia. Turkey relinquished its claim to Cyprus in 1923.

After Turkish independence, thousands of Turkish Cypriots left for Turkey, changing Cyprus's demographic balance to its current ratio. Greek Cypriots welcomed the British in the hope that the latter would enable *enosis*; Turks in the hope they would prevent it, since *enosis* would transform the Turks into a vulnerable minority. However, from the 1930s, Britain faced an anticolonial struggle in Cyprus. Greek antifascist resistance in World War II inspired new *enosis* hopes. For the Greek Cypriots, Crete served as an example of a Greek island that had obtained *enosis* after a century of revolts. For the Turkish Cypriots, however, Crete exemplified the prospect of forced expulsion of Muslims. While the Greeks advocated the freedom of movement and settlement throughout the island, the Turks feared that such an arrangement would perpetuate their minority status; they therefore advocated ethnic segregation, and eventually *taksim* (partition). Radicalization of the Greek Right reached new levels in the 1950s with the election of the fiercely pro-*enosis* Michael Mouskos as Archbishop Makarios III, vying in pro-Hellenism with Giorgios Grivas's underground militant organization EOKA. Their intransigence made any constitutional compromise short of *enosis* unattainable. In 1960, the British decided to grant Cyprus limited independence; by then, however, too much blood had been spilt for either community to desire continued cohabitation with the other. A consociational constitution was adopted, but no Cypriot security force could be established. Community clashes broke out in 1963. The Turks, victims of violent Greek attacks, moved to fortified villages. Their enclaves were blockaded by the Greeks and they became economically dependent on mainland Turkey. Thus de facto partition started.

In 1974, a coup against Makarios encouraged by the Greek colonels, who aimed at annexing Cyprus, triggered a Turkish invasion. Mutual massacres and forced population removals ensued in factual partition: 62% of Cypriot territory is in the hands of the Greek Cypriots, 38% under the control of Turkish Cypriots who in 1983, unilaterally declared independence. Tens of thousands of Turkish Cypriots fled to North Cyprus; 200,000 Greek Cypriots to the Greek-held South. This development has transferred the problem from one of powersharing to the question of how to build federal links between two territorially separated ethnic communities. United Nations peace-keeping forces along a buffer zone monitor the split island.

The Greek sector is relatively prosperous, with a standard of living much higher than mainland Greece. Having integrated its refugees, the Greek Cypriot sector recovered in the 1980s, with a new tourist boom on which its economy largely depends. The Turkish Cypriot sector suffers from an international boycott, declining tourism and a stagnant economy; incomes here are four times lower than in the Greek Cypriot sector. Still, thousands of mainland Turks have settled in formerly Greek homes, raising the Turkish Cypriot population.

From 1976 the UN has sponsored peace talks. The Greek Cypriots demanded a strong bi-communal federation. The Turkish Cypriots seemed in no hurry. Negotiations continued throughout the 1980s, but were mostly deadlocked, and as time passes, partition is becoming entrenched.

CYPRUS — UNITED KINGDOM Occupying a total of 99 sq. miles (256 sq. km.), the Sovereign Base boundaries encompass two separate bases. The Akrotiri base, southwest of Limassol, comprises the peninsula that is the southernmost part of the island and a small coastal area north of Episkopi Bay and has a boundary of approximately 64 miles (103 km.). The Dhekelia base is on the northern shore of Larnaca Bay, northeast of the city of Larnaca, with a boundary of about 30 miles (49 km.). The boundaries are well demarcated by boundary pillars according to the Treaty of Establishment, which was part of the 1960 Independence Constitution.

Geographical Setting. The boundary of Dhekelia Base begins on the shore of Larnaca Bay, at approximately 38°42'57"E and bears north and then southeast. It crosses a dry-weather road, heads generally northward and follows the Pergamos road, leaving it at about 35°01'35"N to turn westward. Running northwest the boundary crosses another dry-weather road (from Pergamos to Arsos) at about 33°40'40"E and 35°02'30"N and proceeds generally northward for 1 mile (1.6 km.). It then turns generally northeastward and reaches a point at roughly 33°42'22"E and 35°03'40"N on a dry-weather road that links Lysi to the Pergamos road. Here the boundary forms an arc to rejoin the Pergamos road, follows its western side southward and, almost 0.5 miles (0.8 km.) from Pergamos, loops to the west, regaining the road less than 0.25 miles (0.4 km.) further south. It passes west and south of Pergamos and then follows the direction of a dry-weather road from Pergamos to the church of Arkangelo, continues past the church and reaches the fork in the road (where it branches to Makrasyka and Lysi). At this point the boundary runs southeast to the Dhekelia–Athna road, follows it to a bypass south of Athna and along this until the road turns northeast. Here the boundary progresses toward Avgorou, and due west of Avgorou turns southward to cross the dry-weather road from Xylophagou to the church of Alambronas, just southwest of the church, at approximately 35°N.

It runs east for 1 mile (1.6 km.), south for 1.25 miles (2 km.) and turning west again crosses the Xylophagou–Alambronas road. Then it turns southwest and crosses the Xylophagou–Ormidhia road and the line of wells south of it before turning sharply east, passing south of Xylophagou, and north to approximately 33°51'30"E and 34°58'10"N, from which point the boundary runs in a straight line to the Mediterranean coast at roughly 34°57'12"N.

There are also four small enclaves of Cypriot territory that fall within Dhekelia Base; of the two largest, one encompasses the settlement of Xylotymbou on the Dhekelia–Lamaca road, while the other surrounds the residential area of Ormidhia and a finger of land running northwest from it. The two smaller enclaves respectively lie to the north and south of the Ormidhia–Lamace road, which remains within Sovereign Base territory.

The boundary of Akrotiri Base begins at the coast of Episkopi Bay, at approximately 32°45'20"E and 34°38'45"N, runs in a straight line to the main road between Episkopi and Ktima and follows the road east to the footpath that skirts a local forest and runs west of and parallel to the Pharkonia River. It follows the footpath to its intersection with the water pipeline and then in a series of straight lines makes its way to approximately 32°49'35"E and 34°42'N. It then runs eastward to reach the dry-weather road between Sotira and the town of Episkopi, and follows it to the southern edge of a bridge. Here the boundary leaves the road and continues in a long curve to the southeast, across the Limassol road, passing south of the town of Episkopi to the dry-weather road that runs to the bridge over the Kouros River. At this point the line bears north and then follows the Limassol road, running south of it and skirting the southern edge of the town of Kolossi to approximately 32°59'26"E, where it turns south to meet and follow the road to Trakhoni. It passes north of Trakhoni, continues southwestward for 0.5 miles (0.8 km.) and then runs generally south to the Limassol road. The boundary passes west and south of Asomatos to the coast of Limassol Bay, at approximately 33°00'60"E.

Historical Background. The island of Cyprus was part of the Ottoman Empire from 1571 to 1878, when Britain joined Turkey in a defensive alliance and signed the Convention of 4 June 1878. Under the terms of the convention Turkey agreed to assign the occupation and rule of Cyprus to Britain, but not to cede legal possession of it. With the antagonisms created by World War I, Britain annexed the island outright on 5 November 1914, although Turkey did not recognize this until the Treaty of Lausanne in 1923.

The period between 1950 and 1960 experienced reemerging Greek nationalism (*enosis*), with Turkish Cypriots adamantly refusing to be colonized by Greece. Under the patronage of the Greek Orthodox Church, an underground organization (EOKA) began terrorist activities, while the Turkish Resistance Organization (TMT) came to fill the vacuum in Turkish Cypriot defenses. The ensuing intercommunal clashes eventually led to the London and Zurich Agreements, which laid the framework for the 1960 Independence Constitution. An independent Cyprus Republic was subsequently created on 16 August 1960. Within the constitution and the Treaty of Establishment, the two Sovereign Base areas (Akrotiri and Dhekelia) remained under the sovereignty of the United Kingdom and despite further changes in the political make-up of Cyprus, including the 1974 Turkish invasion and annexation of North Cyprus, their demarcation by boundary pillars remained intact. The extent of the Sovereign Base areas results from President Makarios's insistence that the land ceded to Britain must be less than 100 sq. miles (259 sq. km.).

Present Situation. The British Sovereign Area boundaries are not in dispute, although their future is very much interlinked with the territorial aspirations of both the Greek and Turkish Cypriot populations on the island.

CZECH REPUBLIC A landlocked country in Central Europe, the Czech Republic (area: 30,502 sq. miles [78,970 sq. km.]; estimated population: 10,426,000 [1994]) formed the western part of the former Czechoslovakia until 1993. It is bounded by Poland (382 miles; 615 km.) in the north, by Slovakia (122 miles; 197 km.) in the east, by Austria (285 miles; 456 km.) in the south and by Germany (507 miles; 815 km.) in the west. Its capital is Prague.

The Czechs are descendants of Slavic tribes that settled Bohemia and Moravia in the fifth and sixth centuries. Their name has been adopted from an eponymous tribe which inhabited central Bohemia. By the ninth century, tribal states emerged, of which the strongest, Great Moravia, was formed in the basin of the Morava River, through which runs a central trade route from the Baltic to the Adriatic Sea. It expanded all over Bohemia and Moravia, part of Slovakia, the southern part of today's Poland and the western part of Hungary. At that time the country was christianized, and after a long period of vacillation between Rome and Constantinople, it accepted Catholicism, first with a Slavonic and later with the Latin rite.

At the beginning of the tenth century, Great Moravia collapsed under the attacks of the Hungarians. It was the turn of the Pvemysl dynasty, who ruled the Czechs from their castle in Praha (Prague), to unite Bohemia and later Moravia as well under their rule. The Pvemysl rules (895–1306) tied Bohemia to the Holy Roman Empire, within which they received the title "King of Bohemia." They invited a large number of German settlers and made Prague into one of the greatest centers of culture and learning of that period.

With the extinction of the native dynasty, the kingdom of Bohemia was ruled by the House of Luxembourg (1310–1437). Karl, King of Bohemia, was from 1355 also Karl (Charles) IV, emperor of the Holy Roman Empire. He made Prague his capital, embellishing it and founded its university. After his death, however, the country became embroiled in the Reformation struggles. The execution in 1405 of Jan Hus, who had called for church reforms, split the country between Catholics and Hussites.

The election of Ferdinand I of Habsburg in the sixteenth century began almost 400 years of Habsburg rule (until 1918). During the Thirty Years' War the Habsburgs and Catholicism became entrenched in Bohemia and Moravia, followed by germanization of the country's cultural life.

Czech nationalism began to develop in the early 1800s, at first in cooperation with German nationalism, but during the revolutions of 1848 their ways parted, when the German constituent assembly in Frankfurt declared Bohemia and Moravia part of the German fatherland. During the nineteenth century Czech nationalist shifted their stress from autonomy within the Habsburg Empire to independence from

it. They also forged ties with the other Slavs of the empire, and especially with the Slovaks, which resulted in the creation of Czechoslovakia in 1918.

In this new state the Czechs, numbering twice as many as the Slovaks and more advanced socioeconomically, became the dominant element. This created strong resentment among the Slovaks. The presence of many Germans (some 2,500,000) and Hungarians under the democratic regime of Czechoslovakia (which granted free political expression to the diverse national elements) was used as an excuse by the Nazis for the dismemberment of Czechoslovakia following the Munich accord of 1938.

After World War II Czechoslovakia was reconstituted and the Germans were expelled. A communist regime was installed in Prague in 1948 and the country became part of the Soviet bloc. In 1968 the short-lived "Prague Spring" (an attempt to reform the communist regime along more liberal lines) was crushed by Soviet troops. Since then, until the regime's collapse in 1990, Czechoslovakia was one of the most rigidly Communist countries in Eastern Europe. In 1969 it was transformed from a unitary state into a federation of two republics. Following the end of communism and the rise of Slovak (and to some extent Czech) nationalism, the two component republics of Czechoslovakia decided to sever their federal links and became separate independent states in January 1993.

CZECH REPUBLIC — AUSTRIA see AUSTRIA–CZECH REPUBLIC.

CZECH REPUBLIC — GERMANY Running for 507 miles (815 km.) between the boundary tripoint with Austria in the Sumava mountains in the south and the tripoint with Poland on the Neisse (Nyssa, Nisa, Neise) River in the north, the boundary between the Czech Republic and Germany follows the boundary between Germany and the Austro-Hungarian Empire as it was established in the nineteenth century.

Geographical Setting. From the southern boundary tripoint on the Sumava Mountains in the Bohemian Forest (Cesky Les), between the peaks of Pfockenstein (4,520 feet; 1,378 m.) and Dreisessel (4,369 feet; 1,332 m.), the boundary runs northwestward, primarily along the watershed of the Bohemian Forest mountains. It crosses the road between Passau (Germany) and Praha (Czech Republic), reaches the Lusen peak (4,494 feet; 1,370 m.) and crosses the Zwiesel (Germany)–Klatovy (Czech Republic) and Cham (Germany)–Plzen (Czech Republic) roads. The line continues north-northwestward, through the Upper Pfalzer Forest (Oberpfälzer Wald), crosses the road and future highway between the A93 (E50) highway that runs in Germany and Plzen near Waldhaus (Germany) and then heads northward to reach the Gernzland Tower. There the line turns northwestward and crosses the Marktredwitz (Germany)–Cheb (Czech Republic) road before arriving at the northwesternmost point of the boundary, which is located west of Hranice (Czech Republic) and east of the German town of Hof. At this point the boundary line bears southeastward, leaves the town of As in the Czech Republic, reaches the Plauen (Germany)–Cheb road and then runs northeastward along the Erzgebirge (Krusnéhory) mountain range. It reaches the Chemnitz (Germany)–Karlovy Vary (Czech Republic) road south of the Fichtelberg peak (3,985 feet; 1,215 m.). Following the road northward the boundary meets a point north of Vejprty (Czech Republic), runs east-northeastward and crosses the Chemnitz–Chomutov (Czech Republic) road to reach and cross a confluence of the upper tributaries of the Zschopau River near Olbernhau (Germany). It follows one of the tributaries southeastward and then northeastward as to leave the village of Deatch-neudorf with Germany. The line proceeds east-northeastward, crossing the Dresden (Germany)–Teplice (Czech Republic) road and reaches the Elbe (Labe) River north of Decín (Czech Republic). Its turns northwestward in order to leave the area around the Czech town of Velky Senov within the Czech Republic and thence runs southeastward, reaching the Neisse (Laustizer Neisse) River, which it follows to the boundary tripoint with Poland on the southeastern corner of the German town of Zittau.

Historical Background. The area of today's Czech Republic (Bohemia) lost its independence in 1620 and only regained it in 1918. Its present boundary with Germany dates back to the establishment of the new map of Europe after World War I. According to the Treaty of Versailles, signed between Germany and the Allies on 28 June 1919, the boundary between Germany and the newly established state of Czechoslovakia was to trace the line that existed on 3 August 1914 (before the outbreak of World War I) between Austria and Germany, from its junction with the old administrative boundary separating Bohemia and the province of Upper Austria to a point north of the salient of the old province of Austrian Silesia, about 5 miles (8 km.) east of Neustadt (today the Polish town of Prudnik). The line follows the old boundary line between the Austrian Empire and Saxony in the northwest and between Austria and the kingdom of Bavaria in the southwest. Bavaria and Saxony became parts of the German Empire in 1871.

The 1918 line placed within Czechoslovakia the Sudetenland region, which was mainly inhabited by Germans at that time. After Czechoslovakia was granted a small parcel of Silesia in March 1921, the plebiscite which gave western Silesia to Germany in October shifted the boundary between Czechoslovakia and Germany eastward to the present Czech town of Bohumin. Changes made in the location of the boundary line in October 1938 (in accordance with the Munich Agreement) and in March 1939 were abolished after World War II and the former line was reinstated. Modifications in the Germany–Poland boundary that also took place after the war placed the eastern section of the Germany–Czechoslovakia boundary in Polish hands and the line was shortened to its present form. The division of Czechoslovakia into the Czech Republic and Slovakia on 1 January 1993 did not affect the boundary, its entire course only following the limits of the Czech Republic.

Present Situation. Since the reestablishment of the present boundary after World War II and the mass transfer of Germans from Czechoslovakia into Germany, there have been no disputes concerning the alignment of the boundary. The changes which took place in Eastern Europe in 1989 opened the boundary line, which is now one of the busiest international crossings in Europe.

CZECH REPUBLIC — POLAND   This is the western section of the boundary between Poland and the former Czechoslovakia as it was established after World War I. It is 382 miles (615 km.) long and

The Czech Republic–Poland boundary runs through mountain peaks

reaches from the boundary tripoint with Germany on the Neisse River, east of the German town of Zittau, to the tripoint with Slovakia in the Siaski mountains, west of the Polish town of Jaworzynka.

Geographical Setting. From the boundary's western terminus on the Neisse River it runs eastward for 9 miles (15 km.) and northward for 10 miles (16 km.), leaving the town of Bogatynia within Poland. The line heads eastward again, crosses the road and railway between Zgorzelec (Poland) and Liberec (Czech Republic) and bears southeastward to reach the source of the Jizera River. It follows the river downstream southeastward for 10 miles (16 km.) and leaving it the line parallels the Jablonec (Czech Republic)–Jelenia Góra (Poland) road northward. Crossing the road south of Jakuszyce (Poland) the boundary runs eastward along the watershed of the Sudetic Mountains, passing over the peaks of Brzenica (4,467 feet; 1,362 m.) and Snezka (5,254 feet; 1,602 m.) toward the Trutnov (Czech Republic)–Bolkow (Poland) road. After crossing the road the boundary runs southward, eastward and northward to leave the small town of Okrzeszyn within

Poland and then continues eastward along the watershed to a point located west of Nowa Ruda (Poland). Trending southwestward, it reaches the Hradec Kralové (Czech Republic)–Klodzko road and facing southeastward leaves the town of Kudowa-Zdrój within Poland. It reaches the Orlice River, follows it downstream, courses along the Gory Bystrzyckie Range and meets the Cervena Voda (Czech Republic)–Bystrzyca Klodzka (Poland) road. The line crosses this road and turns northeastward and northwestward, following the local watershed to a point south of the small Polish town of Zloty Stok. From there it runs eastward following ethnic divisions rather than the local watershed, crosses the Jeseník (Czech Republic)–Nysa (Poland) road and reaches the railway that links the Polish towns of Nysa and Kedzierzyn-Kozle. Leaving the railway within Poland the boundary line runs southeastward, reaches the Opava River and follows its course downstream in the same direction for about 5 miles (8 km.) to the north of the Czech town of Opava. It then runs eastward, reaching the Oder (Odra) River, follows it upstream eastward, leaves it (placing the town of Kanvina in the Czech Republic) and regains it to follow it upstream southward to the Czech town of Trinec. Running southeastward through the Velky Stozek peak (3,208 feet; 978 m.) the boundary between the Czech Republic and Poland reaches its junction with the Slovakian boundary west of the Polish town of Jaworzynka.

Historical Background. After World War I Czechoslovakia became independent (28 October 1918) and Poland a few days later. The boundary line between the two was established in July 1920, mainly along ethnic divisions, from the German boundary tripoint east of Neustadt (today the Polish town of Prudnik) to the Romanian tripoint in eastern Ruthenia. The plebiscite that divided Silesia (1921) between Germany and Poland placed the boundary tripoint east of the previous point, while a dispute concerning the region of Teschen had also established the boundary line in that area in July 1920. Poland occupied the Teschen area in October 1938 but it was returned to Czech hands after World War II. The new Germany–Poland boundary, which was established in August 1945, carried the Czechoslovakia–Poland boundary westward to the town of Zittau. The separation of the Czech Republic and Slovakia on 1 January 1993 left the Czech Republic with the western section of this boundary.

Present Situation. Since the reshaping of Europe after World War II there have been no disputes concerning this boundary alignment. The establishment of the independent Czech Republic in 1993 did not cause any changes to the boundary with Poland, which was adopted by both states without any formal agreement.

CZECH REPUBLIC — SLOVAKIA The most recent of European international boundaries, the border between the Czech Republic and Slovakia was established on 1 January 1993. It is 122 miles (197 km.) long, running from the boundary tripoint with Austria at the confluence of the Morava (March) and Dyje (Thaya) rivers in the southwest to the boundary tripoint with Poland in the northeast.

Geographical Setting. Beginning in the southwest at the confluence of the Dyje and Morava rivers, east of the Austrian town of Hohenau, this boundary follows the Morava River upstream northeastward for 20 miles (32 km.), crossing the Brno (Czech Re-

public)–Bratislava (Slovakia) highway, and reaches the Czech town of Hodonín. There the line leaves the river and bears eastward along the watershed of the White Carpathian Mountains (Bíle Karpaty), crossing the main railway between Bratislava and Uherské Hradiste (Czech Republic), and then continues northeastward, passing through Velka Javorina Monument (3,182 feet; 970 m.), reaching and crossing the Trencín (Slovakia)–Uherské Hradiste road and, running eastward, reaches the small Vlára River. The boundary crosses the river and the road and railway that follow the river and then bears northward to the Javorniky Range. It trends along the watershed along the ridge, leaving the high peak of Velky Javornik (3,135 feet; 1,071 m.) in Slovakia, and reaches the boundary junction with Poland close to the Polish town of Jaworzynka.

Historical Background. Until World War I both states were part of the Austro-Hungarian Empire— the Czech area (including the regions of Bohemia and Moravia) as part of the Austrian region and Slovakia under Hungary. The administrative boundary that divided the Czechs and Slovaks mainly followed watersheds and the Morava River. During the last year of World War I, the Czechs and Slovaks signed the Pittsburgh Treaty (30 May 1918), which called for the establishment of a united Czechoslovakian state. Following the collapse of the Austro-Hungarian Empire a Czech republic was established (28 October 1918), which Slovakia joined two days later, on 30 October 1918, to form the independent Republic of Czechoslovakia. Following the Munich Treaty of September 1938 Slovakia became an autonomy (October 1938), declaring its full independence on 14 March 1939. The areas were reunited after World War II, but on 1 January 1993 Slovakia left the republic once again and the independent Czech and Slovak republics were instituted. The old administrative line that dated back to the nineteenth century became the international boundary between these newly established states.

Present Situation. Since achieving independence both states have adopted the former administrative boundary line as their common international boundary. No disputes concerning the boundary's alignment are known and 10 boundary crossing points serve as land connections between Slovakia and the Czech Republic.

D

DENMARK (Danmark) A country in northwestern Europe (area: 16,633 sq. miles [43,079 sq. km.]; population: 5,200,000 [1994]), Denmark consists of the Jutland Peninsula and a number of islands in the Baltic Sea. It has only one land boundary, with Germany (42.5 miles; 68 km.) to the south of the Jutland Peninsula. The capital of Denmark is Copenhagen.

Modern Danes are said to descend from the tribe of Danes who, in the sixth century, arrived from Sweden and merged with the indigenous Jutes and Frisians. All Danish-speaking groups were unified in Denmark in the ninth century. Originally southern Sweden was part of this realm, which joined in expeditions of the Vikings who plundered the French and Spanish coasts and conquered Normandy and part of England. Danish seamen wreaked havoc on the Carolingian empire, and destroyed Celtic kingdoms in the British Isles (Danish was spoken in parts of England until the twelfth century). The pagan Germanic religion long subsisted among Danes. By the tenth and eleventh centuries, however, they finally gave in to Christianity.

In the late Middle Ages Danish power extended over Norway and Sweden as well as over Pomerania, Courland and Estland on the Baltic coast. Later, the ethnically half German Schleswig-Holstein duchies were united under the Danish crown. The loss of Sweden in 1523 started three centuries of Danish-Swedish enmity. The adoption of Lutheranism entrenched permanent German cultural hegemony. In the mid-seventeenth century, however, disastrous wars against Sweden destroyed Danish supremacy in the Baltic for good. Danes ceased being a great power, a decline not made good even by the Danish-Norwegian union in 1720.

The Danes lost Norway to Sweden in 1815. In the nineteenth century the southern duchies of Schleswig-Holstein became bound up with the Germans' nationalistic aspirations. While North Schleswig had remained Danish, Holstein was becoming predominantly German. Overall, the German element was growing at the expense of the Danish. The duchies' substantial and influential German minority sought autonomy from Denmark, while the Schleswig Danes wished to thwart the germanization process. In 1864 Denmark lost the whole of Schleswig-Holstein (representing 40% of its territory) to Prussia. The late nineteenth century was a period of deprivation for the Danes now included in Germany, which followed a policy of germanization. Tens of thousands migrated to Denmark or overseas.

After World War I only the Danish-populated zones of northern Schleswig reverted to Denmark after a referendum; Southern Schleswig joined Germany. Today the 50,000–60,000 (8–10%) Danish-identified citizens in South Schleswig are very well integrated.

DENMARK — GERMANY The boundary between Denmark and the Federal Republic of Germany is Denmark's only land boundary, running for 42.5 miles (68 km.) across the Jutland Peninsula.
Geographical Setting. The land boundary runs along a flat area in a series of straight lines, along streams and roads and around municipal and property boundaries. It is well documented, especially in the settled areas—such as the specification of a point that stands exactly 54 feet (16 m.) from a known road. The boundary runs along a line that had divided the old duchy of Schleswig and since this line did not separate two states, the present boundary sometimes dissects towns and villages. East of the bridge located west of Skomagerhus, the

Denmark–Germany boundary crossing

boundary line enters the sea, dividing the Flens-burger Förde (Fjord) between the two countries (32 miles; 51 km.) until it reaches the Baltic Sea. At that point, the two countries share a continental shelf boundary running 214 miles (342 km.) northwest of Kiel Bay, north-northeast of Fehmarn Island, and southeast of Lolland and Falster islands. Further eastward, the boundary runs in the Baltic Sea be-tween the Danish island of Bornholm and the Ger-man island of Rügen. West of the Jutland Peninsula, a maritime boundary runs northwest through the North Frisian Islands (18 miles; 29 km.) toward the North Sea. There, a maritime boundary of about 210 miles (340 km.) marks the sea limit between the two countries. These maritime boundaries, to the east and west of the land boundary, were created to con-trol navigation lines, fishery zones and, in the North Sea, areas of oil and gas exploitation.

Historical Background. For centuries, the land cor-ridor between Germany and the Jutland Peninsula, in which the duchies of Schleswig and Holstein were established in the Middle Ages, was a transi-tional region inhabited by both Germans and Danes. In 1460 the two duchies were joined under the Dan-ish crown; after the Napoleonic wars Holstein was transferred to the German Confederation. In the early nineteenth century Denmark attempted to re-assert control over both duchies, but a joint Austrian and Prussian force defeated Denmark. In the ensu-ing Treaty of Vienna (30 October 1864) Denmark renounced its claims to both duchies. In 1866 Aus-tria ceded its claims on the area to Prussia and the region was controlled by Germany until the end of World War I.

According to the Peace Treaty of Versailles, signed on 28 June 1919, Holstein was retained by Germany, while Schleswig was divided into two zones whose future status were to be decided by plebiscite. Southern Schleswig voted to remain part of Germany; but the northern half chose to join Den-mark. This was approved by the Allied Powers and Denmark. A boundary commission then demarcated the definitive boundary, which remains the present land boundary between the two countries.

Present Situation. As an open border, there are no alignment problems along the line.

DJIBOUTI   An east African country (area: 8,958 sq. miles [23,192 sq. km.]; estimated population: 410,000 [1994]), Djibouti is bounded in the north by Eritrea (68 miles; 110 km.), in the east by the Gulf of Aden and Somalia (36 miles; 58 km.) and in the south and west by Ethiopia (217 miles; 349 km.). Its capital is Djibouti.

Djibouti's history is one of internecine squabbles. The Issa, constituting almost 50% of the population, are closely related to the Somali, while the Afar with almost 40% of the population, are part of a larger group of Afar found in neighboring Ethiopia. Both countries have made territorial claims on Djibouti (since renounced). Other elements which further exacerbate the situation are the harsh climatic conditions in this small country: 90% of the land is uninhabitable desert and less than 10% is suitable for grazing cattle; its strategic location in the Horn of Africa and its invaluable port at the entrance to the Red Sea; and French colonial policy, which favored the Afar.

Colonization efforts by the French only began in 1862, continuing until 1900. Because of its strategic value Djibouti was long a major outpost of the French Foreign Legion, and in 1977 it became the last country in continental Africa to achieve independence. French and other European interests are still strong and almost 70% of the workforce is employed in providing services to French and other European nationals stationed in the country. Although the population has enjoyed a minor economic boom with the reopening of the Suez Canal in 1975, the territory shows little opportunity for serious economic development. Ethnic stability is maintained by a constitutional provision whereby the president must be an Issa and the prime minister an Afar, but drought, lack of development and conflict throughout the Horn of Africa threaten this country's stability and independence.

DJIBOUTI — ERITREA   The boundary between Djibouti and Eritrea runs for 68 miles (110 km.), from the mouth of the Oued (dry river) Weima in the Red Sea to the boundary tripoint with Ethiopia. It follows the colonial boundary between former French and Italian possessions in northeastern Africa.

Geographical Setting. The Red Sea terminus of the boundary is located in Ras (Cape) Doumeirah, at the mouth of Oued Weima. The boundary line follows the dry river upstream southwestward for about 30 miles (50 km.) and reaches boundary monument no. 100 (bis) of the former French–Ethiopian boundary located in Djibouti on the right bank of Oued Weima, at the dry river's confluence with Oued Gouagouya. This point stands opposite boundary monument no. 100, built at 12°211'4.2433"N and 42°42'02.2856"E on the left bank of Oued Weima. Thence the boundary runs southwestward for 37 miles (60 km.) in a series of eight straight lines, connecting boundary monuments and reaching the boundary junction with Ethiopia at 12°31'31.522"N and 42°27'42.340"E.

Historical Background. In 1862 France concluded commercial treaties with local chiefs of the African coast on the Gulf of Aden. This led to the establishment of a French protectorate in 1884–1885, which was named French Somaliland in 1896. Italy occupied the southwestern coast of the Red Sea in 1889, establishing the Italian colony of Eritrea. A border between the Italian possessions on the Red Sea and the French territory was described in general terms in a protocol on 24 January 1900. The precise alignment was prescribed in a further protocol on 10 July 1901. Italy occupied Ethiopia in 1936 but following its defeat in World War II it renounced the title by virtue of the Peace Treaty of 1947 and in 1952 Eritrea was placed under Ethiopian sovereignty. Two demarcation protocols for the boundary between Eritrea (under Ethiopia) and France were signed, on 16 January and 2 November 1954. The actual demarcation took place in 1954–1955, except for the sector between monument no. 100 (bis) and the coast. French Somaliland became independent as the Republic of Djibouti on 26 June 1977, while Eritrea gained independence in 1992. Both states adopted the colonial line as their common international boundary without a formal agreement.

Present Situation. In accordance with the policy of the Organization of African Unity, neither state has made any claims on the other's territory, and no dispute is known concerning the alignment of their common boundary.

DJIBOUTI — ETHIOPIA The Djibouti, Ethiopia and Somalia boundary tripoint is on Madaha Djalelo hill. From there it runs for 217 miles (349 km.) to the tripoint with Eritrea in the north. It follows the southern and western boundary between former French Somaliland and Ethiopia.

Geographical Setting. Setting out from Madaha Djalelo (1,614 feet; 492 m.), at approximately 10°59'55"N and 42°58'05"E, the boundary runs generally westward for 112 miles (180 km.), stretching through Rahale, mainly following straight lines and cliffs by dry streams, running south of Gobad (Djibouti) and north of Airoli (Ethiopia) and reaching the south bank of Lake Abbe. There the boundary line crosses the lake northward for 20 miles (32 km.) and then continues in a straight line northward for 19 miles (30 km.). In a series of straight lines it heads generally northeast for 66 miles (107 km.), connecting 39 boundary monuments. The boundary line places the small town of Ogag within Ethiopia and the towns of Balho and Daimoli in Djibouti. The boundary reaches boundary monument no. 92 of the old French–Ethiopian boundary, which is the location of the present boundary tripoint with Eritrea, at 12°31'31.522"N and 42°27'42.340"E.

Historical Background. France signed commercial treaties with local chiefs of the northeast African coast in 1862, and a French protectorate was established on the African coast of the Gulf of Aden in 1884–1885, known from 1896 as French Somaliland. Except for a short Italian occupation between 1936 and 1940, Ethiopia was the only African state that was not conquered by a European power, and its foreign relations were independent. The border between the French possessions and Ethiopia was established in general terms by a convention of 20 March 1897. On 3 June 1947, after the events of World War II (when Italy had occupied Ethiopia and the British liberated it), an exchange of letters delimited the boundary. Another exchange of letters (28 August 1948 and 29 October 1949) established the demarcation of the boundary line. On 26 June 1977 French Somaliland became the independent Republic of Djibouti and the French–Ethiopian boundary became an international boundary without any formal agreement.

Present Situation. Since Djibouti gained its independence and in accordance with the policy of the Organization of African Unity, neither state has raised any claims for changes in the boundary's alignment. The well demarcated boundary line serves both states peacefully.

DJIBOUTI — SOMALIA Connecting the Gulf of Aden in the northeast and the boundary tripoint with Ethiopia in the southwest, the boundary between Djibouti and Somalia runs for 36 miles (58 km.). In a straight line it follows the colonial boundary between the earlier British and French possessions in Africa's eastern projection.

Geographical Setting. On the shore of the Gulf of Aden at approximately 11°27'55"N and 43°15'45"E, the northeastern terminus of the boundary is located, east of the small town of Loyada (Djibouti). It runs in a straight line southwestward all the way to the boundary tripoint with Ethiopia, on Madaha Djalelo hill (1,614 feet; 492 m.), located at approximately 10°59'55"N and 42°58'05"E. It trends through the wells of Hadou and Abassouen, follows the caravan route as far as Bia-Kabouba and from Zeyla to Harrar and passes by Gildessa.

Historical Background. During the first half of the nineteenth century Britain concluded a number of commercial treaties with Somali chiefs located on the African coast of the Gulf of Aden. Shortly after, in 1862, France signed a treaty with Afar (Djibouti) chiefs, providing for the cession of the coastal plain of the Gulf of Tadjoura, north of the British sphere of influence. During 1884–1885 France extended its holdings in Djibouti by signing treaties with the local sultans and various chiefs. Meanwhile, Britain established the protectorate of British Somaliland in 1884.

France and the United Kingdom reached an agreement delimiting the boundary between their respective possessions in the area in February 1888. In 1896 the French territory became known as French Somaliland and was renamed (5 July 1967) the French Territory of the Afars and Issas. It became independent on 27 June 1977 as the Republic of Djibouti. British Somaliland became independent on 26 June 1960, merging with Italian Somaliland to form a united Somalia. Without any formal agreement Djibouti and Somalia adopted the colonial border as their common international boundary.

Present Situation. Although the boundary between

the two states was never demarcated, neither has disputed its alignment.

DOMINICA An island state in the Lesser Antilles in the Caribbean Sea, Dominica is situated between Martinique and Guadeloupe. Dominica's area is 290 sq. miles (751 sq. km.) and it has an estimated population of 88,000 (1994). It has no land boundaries and its capital is Roseau.

The island was first colonized by the French in 1727, who ceded it to the British in 1763. The majority of Dominica Islanders are descendants of African slaves brought to the island to work on the extensive coffee and sugar plantations established during French colonization. However, there also exists a significant community descended from the indigenous Carib Indian population, who have been able to preserve their identity through the establishment of a reserve where they are able to practice their traditional lifestyle. English is the main language, with a French patois also commonly spoken. About 90% of the population is Roman Catholic. Agriculture and tourism constitute the island's economic mainstays.

DOMINICAN REPUBLIC (República Dominicana) A country (area: 18,704 sq. miles [48,443 sq. km.]; population: 7,600,000 [1994]) occupying the eastern region of the Caribbean island of Hispaniola, the Dominican Republic shares a common boundary with Haiti in the west (222 miles; 358 km.). The capital of the Dominican Republic is Santo Domingo.

The history of the Dominicans has been marked by many periods of colonization and war. Columbus moved the administrative center of Hispaniola to Santo Domingo on the south coast in 1496. For one generation Hispaniola was the focal point of the emerging Spanish empire in the New World, but the streambank gold deposits were depleted by the mid-1500s. For several hundred years the population was small and economic development was negligible. When the Dominican Republic gained its independence from Spain in 1821, it was occupied by Haiti almost immediately (1822–1844). Spain annexed the island again in 1861, and a second War of the Restoration was fought to regain independence in 1865. As a politically weak country, the Dominican

Republic sought assistance from the United States, and even requested annexation to the United States in 1870. In fact, the United States did assume control of the the Dominican Republic on several occasions over the last century; from 1916 to 1924 United States troops governed the island, and as recently as 1965 US Marines intervened to install a friendly government.

Between 1930 and 1961 the Dominican Republic was ruled by the military dictator, General Rafael Trujillo; he encouraged a rapid build-up of the capital city Santo Domingo (temporarily renamed Ciudad Trujillo) and also shifted populations into designated rural areas and toward the Haitian border, where tension culminated in a massacre of over 10,000 Haitian squatters in 1937. Since Trujillo's assassination, Dominican politics have been dominated primarily by long-time President Juan Balaguer, who has held the office for most of the last three decades.

The Dominican population has grown rapidly in the twentieth century (at an annual rate of between 2 and 3%), and has shifted dramatically toward Santo Domingo. Until the 1930s the largest percentage of the population was in the central valley region, and Santiago was the largest city; today greater Santo Domingo has over 3,000,000 people, nearly half of the nation's total, and is five times larger than greater Santiago.

DOMINICAN REPUBLIC — HAITI The 222-mile (358-km.) boundary between the Dominican Republic and Haiti divides the Caribbean island of Hispaniola. Hispaniola is one of very few islands with dual sovereignty and the only one made up of two independent states. Approximately 65% of the island belongs to the Dominican Republic, while the remainder belongs to Haiti. The boundary generally runs in a north–south direction, dissecting the island's major mountain chains, while some 100 miles (160 km.) of the boundary run through rivers.

Geographical Setting. The boundary begins in the *thalweg* (the deepest navigable channel) at the mouth of the Dajabón River and runs along the course of that river to its confluence with the Capotille River. It then follows the Capotille River to its source on Mount Citadel. From that point it crosses the mountain chain, along peaks, plains and rivers to the Pedernales River. The boundary then runs along the *thalweg* of that river to the Caribbean Sea. Islands lying offshore to the northern and southern coasts of Hispaniola are the undisputed territory of the Dominican Republic.

Historical Background. In 1526 the island of Hispaniola (Española) was under Spanish rule. In 1625 French and English pirates established headquarters there and around 1630 a group of Norman adventurers overran the island. The governor-general of the French Antilles took control in 1641 and the French government sent a governor in 1665. In 1680 the French and Spanish governors amicably settled the Rebouc River as the boundary between their territories. The western third of the island was confirmed as French in 1697 and later became known as Haiti. In 1793 war broke out between France and Spain, and in the 1795 peace treaty Spain ceded to France the entire Spanish part of Santo Domingo. France did not occupy this territory until January 1801, after a slave revolt in Haiti. In 1804 Haiti became independent and promptly occupied the entire island.

Parts of the island were passed between the Spanish, French and English until 1822, when the entire island came under firm Haitian control and remained so until 1844, when a revolt in the city of Santo Domingo led to the expulsion of Haitian troops and the proclamation of the Dominican Republic in the former Spanish territory. Haiti made continuous attempts to reconquer its lost territory—until 1856, when Spain finally recognized the Dominican Republic's independence. France had recognized the independence of Haiti in 1825. Each country drew up successive constitutions that proclaimed their mutual boundary as the line dividing the former French and Spanish portions of the island, often identified as that specified by the Treaty of Aranjuez (3 June 1777). Only in 1874 did they negotiate a treaty that defined the boundary in general terms. This, however, was assailed in both countries as they disagreed on the meaning of a number of its provisions. An attempt at papal arbitration in 1895 failed and was followed by further attempts to settle the boundary in 1899 and 1901. This had yet to be accomplished when the United States began occupation of both countries in 1915.

After the Americans withdrew from the Dominican Republic in 1924, the Haitians and Dominicans negotiated a boundary treaty, which was signed on 21 January 1929. It provided, inter alia, that the boundary "starts from the *thalweg* of the mouth of the river Dajabón or Massacre, in the Atlantic Ocean" and continued to describe the course of the boundary in considerable detail, referring frequently to roads, towns, rivers, peaks and other landscape features in a similar fashion. It also provided for a mixed demarcation commission to "determine with the necessary precision the division line just described and to establish it on the ground with visible marks...." Boundary demarcation began in 1930 and was completed by the end of the decade. A second agreement was signed on 27 February 1935 to resolve five disputed points left undetermined by the commission, and on 9 March 1936 the two countries signed a protocol revising a number of provisions of the 1929 treaty. All three agreements allow for joint use of boundary lakes, rivers and roads, require demilitarization of the area within 6 miles (10 km.) of the border on each side and call for dispute settlement procedures.

Present Situation. The Haiti–Dominican Republic boundary itself is no longer in dispute; but the border zone, though guarded and patrolled only by police, remains tense. With numerous Haitians working (mostly as agricultural laborers) in the Dominican Republic, the Dominicans are anxious about another possible Haitian invasion and occupation. Cross-border trade is mostly local, except during unusual circumstances such as the United Nations economic sanctions against the Haitian military during the early 1990s, when the Dominican government permitted large quantities of embargoed goods to cross into Haiti.

The boundary is not marked by natural features or pillars, but by a sharp difference in vegetation on each side of the border. On the Dominican side much of the original forest cover has been left largely intact by the relatively sparse working-class population, while on the Haitian side the mostly poverty stricken dense population has almost denuded its third of the island of trees, right up to the border, in its struggle to survive.

E

ECUADOR A country in northwestern South America (area: 109,483 sq. miles [283,451 sq. km.]; population: 11,000,000 [1994]), Ecuador is bounded in the north by Colombia (367 miles; 590 km.), east and south by Peru (883 miles 1,420 km.) and west by the Pacific Ocean. Quito is the capital of Ecuador.

Nearly 80% of the population are Indians or *mestizo* (mixed Indian and European—mainly Spaniards). Ecuadorian coastal Indian tribes such as the Puna, Esmeralda and Huancavilca and their mountain counterparts, the Cara, Quitu and Puruha, preserved a certain measure of cultural identity within the Inca empire. In 1525 the Inca emperor Huayna Capac divided his realm between his two sons, Huascar, who received the south (the territories of modern Peru and Bolivia), and Atahualpa, who received the northern kingdom of Quito. Although Atahualpa won the ensuing civil war, he was captured and put to death by his allies, Spanish *conquistadores* under Francisco Pizarro, after having converted to Catholicism (1533). Atahualpa's death enabled the Spanish to assume control over the country and to establish themselves as the ruling classes. The city of San Francisco de Quito was founded in 1534 over Indian ruins; Guayaquil was founded in 1535. The *audiencia* (district) of Quito became part of the viceroyalty of Peru but in the eighteenth century its administration was transferred to the viceroyalty of Nueva Granada, centered in Bogotá.

Ecuadorian demands for independence were first heard in Quito in 1809. In the ensuing struggle against Spain the territory of Quito's *audiencia* was finally liberated by Bolívar's army in the Battle of Pichincha (1822) and incorporated as the southern department of the republic of Gran Colombia. In 1830 it seceded and became the republic of Ecuador.

Since then the Ecuadorians have suffered from a series of dictatorships, military interventions, political turmoil and limited democracy during most of the past century. Despite the separation of church and state, attained by the liberals at the beginning of this century, and a certain degree of modernization, socioeconomic cleavages still divide Ecuadorians. The Indians masses remain particularly indigent with many working small plots of land on large *haciendas* (farms), where they are paid very little.

Near the Ecuador–Colombia border

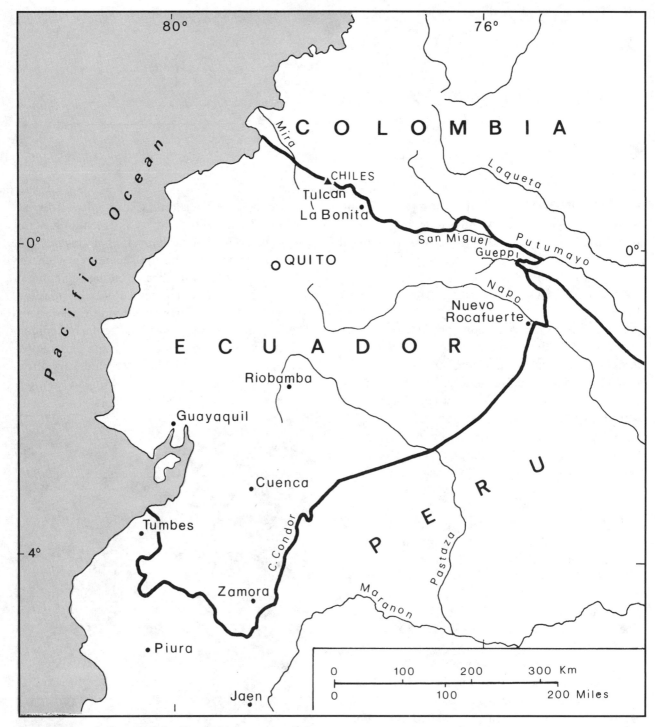

Ecuador's boundaries with Colombia and Peru

Even those who own some land in the Andes Mountains only subsist with difficulty. Free agricultural communities founded in colonial times own the least fertile lands, which have since become exhausted. Whereas some Indians migrate to the cities to improve their lot, they generally converge on the poorest urban sectors, furthering social and cultural problems. Modernization, agricultural exports (fruit, cocoa and coffee), mineral exploitation and petroleum have brought some prosperity to the country, but social pressures have produced populist politics and conservative and military reactions.

In 1979 Ecuador adopted a democratic constitution: elections have been held regularly since then. However, as in other Andean countries, the onerous combination of historic, ethnic and socioeconomic divisions have encumbered the emergence of a strong national identity.

ECUADOR — COLOMBIA   see COLOMBIA–ECUADOR.

ECUADOR — PERU   The present boundary between Ecuador and Peru is one of the most contested boundaries in the world, and the most problematic in South America. Ecuador never accepted a boundary agreement and the two countries have yet to solve their prolonged dispute. The 883-mile (1,420-km.) boundary covers rivers, watersheds and mountain ranges. The border gives Ecuador, which considers itself an Amazonian state, a small section of the lesser tributaries of the Amazon River.

Geographical Setting. The boundary between Ecuador and Peru begins in the Pacific Ocean, at the mouth of the Capones River. Then, following various rivers (including the Chira, Macará and Canchis

rivers), it continues generally southeastward until it reaches the confluence of the Chinchipe and San Francisco rivers. Turning northward, the line crosses the Andes Mountains, faces northeast and trends across the Cordillera del Cóndor and the watershed between the Zamora and Santiago rivers up to the confluence of the Santiago River with the Yaupi River. Following a generally north-northeast direction and a network of rivers (including the Curaray, Napo, Aguarico and Güeppi), the border finally reaches the tripoint of Colombia, Ecuador and Peru on a tributary of the Putumayo River, close to the equator.

Historical Background. The first European expedition to the Amazon River was probably organized in Quito in 1542 by its governor, Gonzalo Pizarro. This event, though disputed by Peru, became a foundation for Ecuador's claim to the entire region between the Pacific Ocean and the Amazon River. In 1563 Spain created Quito as a province of the viceroyalty of Peru. In 1717 it was transferred to the viceroyalty of New Granada. It was returned to Peru in 1723 and went back again to New Granada in 1740, when its southern boundary was fixed along a

River Napo crossing the Ecuador–Peru boundary

line from the Tumbes River, along the Marañón and Amazon rivers to an unspecified point on the western boundary of Portuguese territory (Brazil). Another decree in 1802 transferred the Maynas region in the eastern part of Quito back to Peru. Quito's boundaries were vaguely defined as the Marañón to the border of the Portuguese territory and along all the rivers that joined the Marañón from the north and the south, up to the head of each river's navigation channel. Peru has thus claimed that Maynas was under its administration when it became independent in 1821, but Ecuador claims that the 1802 decree only transferred certain military and ecclesiastical functions to Peru, while the land area remained a part of New Granada. In 1822 Quito was liberated from Spanish control and joined with Colombia and Venezuela to form the new republic of Greater Colombia.

In 1826 Peru claimed the whole of Maynas and two years later claimed Jaén. War broke out between Peru and Great Colombia in July 1828 and ended with a Colombian victory in February 1829. On 22 September 1829 the two countries signed the Treaty of Guayaquil, which attempted to settle the boundary dispute by recognizing their territorial limits as "those of the old viceroyalty." Venezuela seceded from Great Colombia in November 1829, leaving a much smaller country to sign the Mosquero-Pedemonte Protocol to the Treaty of Guayaquil on 11 August 1830. The protocol provided that the Marañón, Macara and Tumbes rivers were to constitute the definitive borders between the two countries. In the following month the three southern departments of Great Colombia (Ecuador, Azuay and Quito) seceded and became the Republic of Ecuador. The new country continued to rely on the Treaty of Guayaquil and its protocol as a foundation for its claim to the disputed areas, but Peru regarded the treaty as null and void. For more than a century the two countries continued in a state of varying degrees of hostility.

Major clashes broke out in the disputed border areas on 5 July 1941 and fighting continued until the two parties signed a cease-fire agreement on 2 October that year. On 29 January 1942 Peru and Ecuador signed the Protocol of Rio de Janeiro that established the boundary, which was subsequently recognized internationally and shown on most maps. De-

marcation of the boundary ensued and proceeded under extraordinarily difficult conditions for the next nine years. This effort was complicated by some ambiguities in the Rio Protocol and even more so by the discovery in 1947 of a hitherto-unknown river system—the Cenepa—running southward into the Marañón River between the Zamora and Santiago rivers, near the Cordillera del Cóndor. Ecuador claimed that this discovery invalidated the corresponding clause in the Rio Protocol and in 1951 suspended demarcation of the boundary, leaving 48 miles (78 km.) undemarcated. After various attempts to resolve this new dispute, Ecuador declared the entire Rio Protocol null and void in 1960. In January 1981 Ecuador occupied three Peruvian military posts (Paquisha, Mayayco and Machinaza) in the Cóndor area and was confronted with Peruvian retaliation. Fighting raged between 28 January and 2 February. Tensions have continued to rise sporadically since then, notably in 1984 and 1991. After the latter incident, Peru presented a proposal for the settlement of several outstanding problems to Ecuador, including completion of the demarcation of the last 48-mile (78-km.) stretch of the Rio Protocol boundary. Ecuador responded with cautious approval but insisted on complete rejection of the 1942 Protocol, while Peru continued to insist that any solution to the boundary problem should be sought within the protocol's framework.

Present Situation. Parts of the boundary between Ecuador and Peru are still disputed. As in most of Latin America, the problems are largely the result of Spanish colonial policies and practices, of different administrative boundaries being drawn for various purposes (judicial, civil, ecclesiastical, military, etc.) through unfamiliar, sparsely-populated areas far from major population centers, and of frequent changes in the numerous lines. The section of the Ecuador–Peru boundary that runs from the Pacific Ocean south-southeast high into the Andes, has two segments still in dispute, around the cities of Tumbes and Jaén. The remainder of the boundary region, called Maynas, from the eastern slopes of the Andes to the Amazon basin, the Marañón and Amazon rivers in the south and almost to the Putumayo River in the northeast, and including the major city of Iquitos, is the largest area in dispute, covering 125,000 sq. miles (323,500 sq. km.).

As of late 1994 the districts of Tumbes, Jaén and Maynas continue to be claimed by Ecuador and administered by Peru. No solution to the dispute is in sight. In February 1995 there were some military clashes in the border area between Ecuador and Peru, and the potential for further hostilities still exists.

EGYPT (Misr)   A Middle Eastern country (area: 386,560 sq. miles [1,001,190 sq. km.]; estimated population: 56,430,000 [1994]), Egypt is located in the northeast corner of Africa. It is bounded in the north by the Mediterranean Sea, in the northeast by Israel (165 miles; 266 km.), in the east by the Gulf of 'Aqaba (Gulf of Eilat) and the Red Sea, in the south by Sudan (791 miles; 1,273 km.) and in the west by Libya (690 miles; 1,100 km.). The capital of Egypt is Cairo.

Since the unification of Upper and Lower Egypt (c. 3100 B.C.E.) the country was ruled by a succession of 30 dynasties. These pre-Arab Pharaonic Egyptians spoke a Hamitic African language with strong Semitic influences. Their hieroglyphic script already appeared with the first dynasty.

After a long, rather self-contained history, Egypt finally succumbed to more powerful neighbors, in the last millennium B.C.E. Assyrians, Persians, Greeks and Romans each contributed to the current heterogeneity of the population as they conquered and settled the prosperous Nile region. Some communities were assimilated into the local culture; others, notably Greeks and Jews, formed important Diaspora communities in Alexandria and other cities.

The final decline of ancient Egypt's rich culture came with the advent of Christianity in the fourth century. Temples were closed, hieroglyphic texts were abandoned and Greek became the official and administrative language. Still, the language of ancient Egypt has been preserved until today in Coptic, used mainly as a liturgical language but still spoken in some remote villages in Upper Egypt and written in a variant Greek script.

With the division of the Roman Empire into eastern and western realms, Egypt found itself under the rule of the Byzantines. However, corruption, steep exactions of tax farmers from the peasantry, and persecution of monophysites, all nourished resentment against Constantinople. Most of Egypt's Christians

therefore welcomed the Arab conquest of the country in 641 as a means of liberating themselves from an oppressive regime.

The subsequent process of Islamization constituted the biggest rupture and cultural discontinuity in Egyptian history. The Mediterranean economic circuit was interrupted and Egyptian history became intertwined with that of the Muslim world. Large-scale immigration of the invaders stimulated steady arabization: Arabic became the official language in the eighth century; Coptic went out of daily use by around 1000.

Despite expectations to the contrary, taxation continued to be heavy during the Umayyad and Abbasid caliphates. But several Coptic revolts were harshly suppressed and Islam had established itself as the dominant religion by the eighth century, promoted, to some degree, by partial tax exemptions for Muslims. Under the Tulunid dynasty (868–905) Egypt enjoyed a brief spell of independence, but Egypt's heyday came under the Shi'ite Fatimid dynasty (969–1171), which founded Cairo as their administrative capital. Salah ad-Din (Saladin; 1137–1193), a Kurd who defeated Crusader kingdoms in Syria and Palestine, established the succeeding Ayyubid dynasty and restored Sunni orthodoxy. In 1250 Mamelukes (Turkish slave-praetorian soldiers) took power. Transit trade between Mediterranean Europe and the Red Sea was stimulated by the crusades, but suddenly ruined by the discovery in 1498 of the Cape of Good Hope route. In 1516, the Ottomans conquered Egypt, beginning three centuries of neglect during which the irrigation canals from the Nile fell into disrepair and the country was reduced to poverty.

Soon after Napoleon Bonaparte's invasion of Egypt in 1798, Muhammad Ali (1769–1849), a Macedonian general of Albanian descent, seized power and seceded, for all practical purposes, from the Ottoman Empire. He undertook an ambitious program of modernizing the administration, army, educational system and economy. Egypt's traditional agriculture, based on the inundation of fields with Nile waters, was progressively brought under control by a system of canals, permitting the introduction of cotton production and industries. He also laid the groundwork for the digging of the Suez Canal, but when it was opened (1869) the project's exorbitant cost had ruined Egypt's finances and brought the country under British influence. Nationalist anti-British incidents promoted by the military and intellectuals only served to entrench British hegemony; Britain occupied Egypt in 1882 to protect the flow of cheap Egyptian cotton to British textile factories.

Nonetheless, popular discontent continued to be expressed in the demands of the nationalist opposition for the departure of the British troops, the installation of a parliament, and independence. Although Britain officially suspended its protectorate after World War I, in effect it retained control, provoking further pan-Arab and Egyptian nationalism in the 1930s.

The defeat of the Egyptian army by Israel in 1948 undermined the prestige of the monarchy. In 1952 a group of Free Officers seized power, deposed the king and declared a republic. Under Gamal Abdel Nasser, Egypt acquired the trappings of a one-party system, but the nationalization of industries and businesses led to the emigration of large and economically important minority communities of Greeks and Jews. Having obtained the departure of British troops, in 1956 Nasser nationalized the Suez Canal, provoking a three-pronged attack by France, Britain and Israel. In the June 1967 war Egypt lost the Sinai peninsula to Israel; the ensuing war of attrition along the Suez Canal led to the wholesale depopulation of canal cities.

Nasser's successor, the pragmatic and pro-Western Anwar al-Sadat, opened war on Israel in October 1973; but later became the first Arab head of state to conclude a peace treaty with Israel as well. The Suez Canal, closed since 1967, was reopened in 1975, promising a brighter economic future for Egypt, but Sadat's peace accord with Israel earned him the enmity of other Arab states. He was assassinated in 1981 by Muslim fundamentalists. By the late 1980s, under Hosni Mubarak, ties with other Arab states were restored and the 1990–1991 Persian Gulf crisis enabled Egypt to regain its leading role in the Arab world.

EGYPT — ISRAEL   The boundary between Egypt and Israel is 165 miles (266 km.) long and stretches from the Mediterranean shore at Rafah in a line south-southeastward to the Gulf of 'Aqaba (Eilat) between Taba (Egypt) and Eilat (Israel).

Geographical Setting. The northernmost section of the boundary, between Egypt and the Gaza Strip (which is controlled partially by the Palestinian National Authority but the boundary is held by Israel) runs for 7 miles (11 km.) in a straight line, dividing the town of Rafah and then coursing through an arid dune-covered plain. The remainder of the border between Egypt and Israel, 158 miles (255 km.) in length, continues the generally straight line south-southeastward to the Red Sea coast at the head of the Gulf of 'Aqaba at Ras Taba, 6 miles (10 km.) directly west of the Jordanian town of 'Aqaba, or 9 miles (14 km.) along the coast from 'Aqaba. The line passes through the sparsely populated and arid Sinai desert. The boundary also traverses rugged terrain, particularly in its central and southern sections, which are associated with the foothills of the Mount Sinai massif and the Negev hills, reaching an altitude of 3,280 feet (1,000 m.) in the Mount Harif (Jebel Haruf) area. The boundary departs from its geometric orientation where steep topography and deep canyons proved inaccessible to the surveyors demarcating the boundary.

Historical Background. The present-day Egypt–Israel boundary is essentially the result of imperial rivalry between Britain and the Ottoman Empire. The first indication of the division of territory between Palestine and the Ottoman possessions of Egypt and Hejaz was an Ottoman map of 1841 that indicated a line from Han Yunes to Suez.

Britain gained control over Egypt in 1882. It subsequently became apparent that the 1841 Han Yunes–Suez line crossed the southern tip of the Suez Canal leaving 2–3 miles (3–4 km.) of the southern entrance of the canal in Turkish controlled territory. Following the Turkish sultan's decision in 1892 to reestablish his authority in Sinai, the British were particularly concerned that the 1841 boundary line advanced Ottoman power dangerously close to the strategically vital Suez waterway.

The British therefore resolved to push the Ottomans back to a Rafah–Taba line in 1906. The dispute over the boundary resulted in confrontation between British-Egyptian and Ottoman forces at 'Aqaba and Taba in January 1906 and brought them to the brink of war. Despite offering two alternative lines, negotiations came to nought and the Ottomans were faced with a British ultimatum in May. Bereft of German, French and Russian support and recognizing Turkish military weakness, the Ottomans were forced to accept the British Rafah–Taba line. The Turkish–Egyptian boundary agreement was accordingly signed at Rafah on 1 October 1906 and the boundary was demarcated between June and October the following year.

Following World War I and the dismemberment of the Ottoman Empire, Palestine became a British mandated territory. The Egypt–Palestine boundary then temporarily lost its international status to become an administrative boundary between two British controlled territories. Despite significant pressure, particularly in the 1920s, to redraw the limits between the two areas the boundary remained unchanged.

In the course of Israel's War of Independence (1948–1949) Egyptian forces initially occupied large areas of the Negev as far north as Beersheba but by early 1949 Israeli forces had recaptured the entire Negev with the exception of the Gaza Strip and had pursued Egyptian troops into the Sinai area, capturing a large parcel between Han Yunes and Nizana. Israel subsequently withdrew its forces from the Sinai and signed an armistice agreement with Egypt on 24 February 1949. The Egypt–Israel armistice line coincided with the Egypt–Palestine international boundary of 1906, with the exception of the Gaza Strip which remained under Egyptian control. The mixed armistice commission was headquartered at El Auja (Nizana), 2 miles (3 km.) within Israeli territory, and a relatively small triangular demilitarized neutral zone, covering less than 30 sq. miles (80 sq. km.), was established within Israeli territory around the headquarters. Israeli forces subsequently crossed the armistice line into the Sinai in the course of the 1956 Suez campaign and the Six-Day War of 1967. In 1956 the Sinai and

The oasis of Kadesh-Barnea near the Egypt–Israel border

Gaza Strip were occupied by Israel for a relatively brief period and were returned to Egypt by March 1957.

Following the Six-Day War Israeli forces again occupied the Strip and Sinai and fought a war of attrition along the Suez Canal for over 1,000 days. The stalemate prompted a surprise attack on Israel by Egypt and Syria in October 1973 (the Yom Kippur War) which resulted in Egypt recapturing 425 sq. miles (1,100 sq. km.) of the Sinai from Israel and Israel capturing 620 sq. miles (1,600 sq. km.) of Egyptian territory west of the canal before a cease-fire was declared. The 1973 war demonstrated the military parity between the two sides and thus encouraged them to seek peace. Israel conducted a phased withdrawal from the Sinai peninsula from March 1974. The United States brokered the Camp David Accords of 1978, providing the framework for peace and a peace treaty was duly signed between Egypt and Israel on 26 March 1979. Article I of the treaty stated that Israel would withdraw its forces to the international boundary between Egypt and mandated Palestine, a move that was finally completed (with the exception of the Gaza Strip) in April 1982. Article II of the treaty stipulated that the parties would recognize the border as inviolable (albeit without prejudice to the Gaza Strip issue). In 1981 Egypt and Israel began the task of demarcating their mutual boundary—a process which presented 15 points of dispute. While most of the disputes concerned minor alterations to small segments of the boundary and were easily resolved, one major dispute emerged over ownership of the Taba area on the Gulf of 'Aqaba, which amounted to 9,700 sq. feet (900 sq. m.) and included a resort and hotel. After several years of fruitless negotiations the two sides finally agreed to submit the Taba dispute to independent international arbitration in 1986. The arbitration was concluded in September 1988, its findings broadly in Egypt's favor. The decision was accepted by both parties and Israel withdrew from Taba.

Present Situation. While all disputes concerning the boundary line between Egypt and Israel have been resolved, the final status of the Egypt–Gaza Strip boundary remains an open issue. Although the majority of the Gaza Strip is controlled by the Palestinian National Authority (PNA), Israel has retained control over a narrow buffer zone along the bound-

ary with Egypt so that the Palestinian authority has no direct contact with Egypt. This situation could change should a fully independent Palestinian entity finally come into existence. In light of the Israel-Jordan Peace Agreement and progress in the Israeli-Palestinian peace process, there are prospects of enhanced transboundary cooperation, particularly between Egypt, Israel and Jordan along the Red Sea littoral.

EGYPT — LIBYA The international boundary separating Egypt and Libya extends southward from the Gulf of Salum on the Mediterranean Sea to the Egypt–Sudan–Libya tripoint at Jebel Uweinat, about 690 miles (1,100 km.) south of the Mediterranean, at 22°N and 25°E.

Geographical Setting. Northward from the tripoint, the boundary follows the 25th meridian for about 500 miles (800 km.) up to 29°14'N. From there to the sea the boundary consists of arcs connected by straight lines. Only the northern part, stretching 206 miles (330 km.), is demarcated.

The boundary traverses mostly uninhabited desert wastes characterized by large sand dunes and gravel beds. As it approaches the coast it runs through a rocky area between marshes and salt lakes.

Historical Background. The current line dates from 1841, when the Ottomans appointed Muhammad Ali as hereditary governor of Egypt. On a map accompanying the London Treaty of 1841, a line along the 29th meridian marked the boundary between Egypt and the Ottoman province of Libya. Tripoli was occupied by Italy in 1912; that same year Egyptian forces captured the coastal town of Salum. Whereas Britain controlled Egypt from 1882 to 1922, Tripoli and the neighboring province of Benghazi were incorporated as the Italian Colony of Libya. Attempts to formalize the boundary between British Egypt and Italian Libya first reached fruition in 1919, when the two countries signed an agreement placing the oasis of al-Jaghbub in Libya. An agreement concerning the remainder of the line was signed on 6 December, 1925. A chain of permanent beacons was erected in the northern sector of the boundary in 1938.

Present Situation. Following World War II, Egypt proposed moving the boundary westward to the 24th meridian, thereby attempting to gain control over

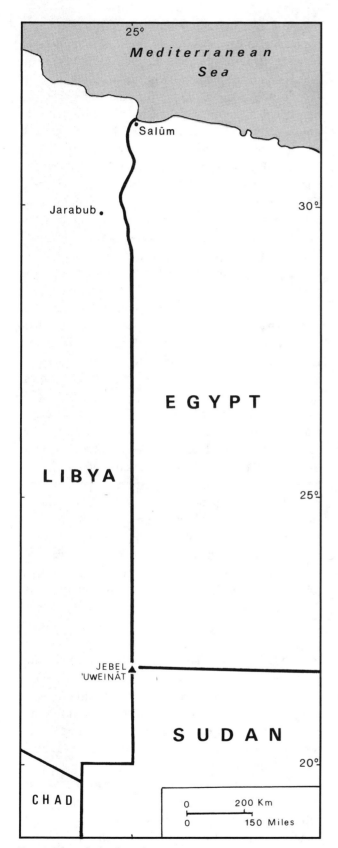

Egypt–Libya–Sudan boundaries

the town of Bardïyah and the al-Jaghbub oasis. The proposal was never answered and was eventually withdrawn. There are currently no disputes regarding the delineation of the border area.

EGYPT — SUDAN The Egypt–Sudan boundary is made up of two sections: the first, from the boundary tripoint with Libya to the Red Sea, is an international boundary; the second, from approximately 33°10'E to the Red Sea, is an administrative line. Apart from the Wadi Halfa salient to the north, the international boundary follows the 22nd parallel for 791 miles (1,273 km.), while the administrative line deviates above and below this parallel for 221 miles (355 km.). Both boundaries traverse arid desert surfaces, except for a thin ribbon of cultivation along the Nile. The international boundary originates from the Anglo-Egyptian agreement of 1899, while the administrative alignment appeared in 1902. Although delimited, both lines have remained undemarcated.

Geographical Setting. The international boundary runs eastward from the boundary tripoint with Libya at 22°N and 25°E. It trends over sandy surfaces for approximately 180 miles (290 km.), over rocky surfaces for about 140 miles (225 km.) and then again over sandy surfaces until it reaches the Nile Valley. At this point the Wadi Halfa salient, a small finger-shaped area, heads north of the 22nd parallel, until reaching its northernmost point at 22°12'12"N. The width of this salient does not exceed 8 miles (13 km.). The boundary line reaches Lake Nasser, runs along its western shore for about 10 miles (15 km.), crosses it from west to east and runs southward along its eastern shore to the intersection of the 22°N parallel with the lake. East of the Nile Valley the boundary continues along the 22nd parallel across sandy surfaces for another 160 miles (257 km.), and from there to the Red Sea the predominant terrain is rocky.

The administrative boundary, which trends to the south and north of the international boundary through a series of straight-line segments, initially heads southeastward from approximately 33°10'E for about 30 miles (50 km.) to Jebel Bartazuga. It then bears east-northeastward for 29 miles (46 km.) to Bir Hesmet Umar and turns north-northeast for 17 miles (27 km.) to meet the international boundary.

Continuing north-northeast for 15 miles (24 km.) it reaches Jabal al Deiga, where it again turns east-northeast for about 35 miles (55 km.) and passes Jabal Umm at Tuyur al Fawqani. Then, for a further 42 miles (67 km.), it trends north-northeast to Jabal Niqrub al Fawqani. For 17 miles (27 km.) the boundary runs southeastward to Bir Meneiga and finally stretching northeastward for 36 miles (58 km.) it reaches the Red Sea via Bir Shalatein.

Historical Background. In 1898 a joint Anglo-Egyptian military force brought an end to the revolution in the formerly Egyptian, administered Sudan. Following this Britain made a claim to a part in the administration of Sudan. On 19 January 1899 an Anglo-Egyptian agreement determined the international boundary between Egypt and Sudan and the administration of Sudan. The agreement also specified the creation of the Egyptian enclave of Suakin, a Red Sea port, in Sudanese territory. Two significant amendments were made to this initial agreement within the following five months: the Suakin enclave agreement was abrogated and the land returned to Sudan, and in the region of Wadi Halfa land was transferred from Egypt to Sudan, placing 10 Egyptian villages in Sudanese territory.

The administrative boundary was eventually incorporated to facilitate the accommodation of nomadic tribes along the international boundary and, in the process, to retain the continuity of certain tribal areas. It was first created by an edict on 25 July 1902 and was implemented by a decree on 4 November 1902; both of which established boundaries and enumerated the tribes and wells to be administered by each state. In delimiting the western segment of the administrative boundary, a straight line was drawn between Jebel Bartazuga, south of the 22nd parallel, and Korosko, north of the parallel and in the Nile region, which consequently left a large triangle of land free of administration. This was later eradicated, however, after confirmation of an agreement between the Egyptian Intelligence Service and the Egyptian Sirdar (military commander in chief) to shorten the western segment of this boundary.

The westernmost terminus of the Egyptian–Sudanese boundary, on the 22nd parallel, was not clarified until the Italo-Egyptian Agreement of 6 December 1925 provided for the delimitation of the

Egypt–Libya boundary terminus. This point was strengthened by the terms of the exchange of notes between Britain, Italy and Egypt on 20 July 1934, which delimited the Libya–Sudan boundary.

A dispute arose in 1958 as Sudan, a recognized independent state since 1 January 1956, prepared to hold elections in the area north of the 22nd parallel. Egypt made it clear in a note to the Sudanese government that the territories north of the 22nd parallel had never been part of Sudan, but fell under Egyptian sovereignty. Egypt accordingly prepared to hold a plebiscite, along with Syria and including the territory north of the parallel, to confirm the proposed United Arab Republic (Egypt and Syria). Sudan, however, pointed out that for the large part of the past half century the territory had been considered by both countries to fall under Sudanese administration. It noted that in two previous Sudanese elections held in the territories north of the 22nd parallel, Egypt had not protested, and similarly, in a previous Egyptian plebiscite these territories had been ignored.

Present Situation. Since 1958 both Egypt and Sudan have maintained their respective views on the sovereignty of the land in the administrative zones. Since 1992 the Red Sea border area of Halaib has become the focus of such a dispute, largely as a result of competing petroleum exploration concessions being awarded by both governments in the region. Egyptian military presence is reported to have been stepped up in the disputed triangle, although mediation and negotiation efforts continue and a joint committee is examining the boundary issue. The boundary's demarcation remains incomplete at present.

EL SALVADOR The smallest and most densely populated (area: 8,124 sq. miles [21,041 sq. km.]; population: 5,580,000 [1994]) of the Central American states, El Salvador is bounded in the north and east by Honduras (213 miles; 342 km.) and in the west by Guatemala (127 miles; 204 km.). The capital of El Salvador is San Salvador.

In 1524 Spanish *conquistadores* encountered culturally-advanced Indians of Nahua descent and the Pipil kingdom of Cuzcatlan. The Indians were completely subjugated by 1539, by which time what is now El Salvador (divided into San Salvador and

Sonsonate) became a subordinate territory of Guatemala. In 1811 San Salvador issued the first Central American declaration of independence. In 1821 El Salvador was incorporated into the Mexican empire until its fall in 1823, and in 1840 it was the last state to withdraw from the Federation of Central America. The country first experienced prolonged political turmoil, and then a succession of military dictatorships.

The Salvadoreans have suffered from profound economic inequality: until the emergence of the land reform movement in the 1980s, almost all the wealth was controlled by a few powerful families. The result has been extreme underdevelopment, associated unemployment (30–40%), educational deprivation (two-thirds of the population is illiterate), heavy dependence upon American aid, and political instability.

Demands for social justice have fueled guerrilla opposition to the government in a civil war, which began in the 1970s, and more than a decade of violence on both sides further oppressed the poverty-stricken people. In 1979 the government was ousted. A new constitution was adopted in 1983 and a civilian president freely elected in 1984.

EL SALVADOR — GUATEMALA The boundary between El Salvador and Guatemala runs northeastward for 127 miles (204 km.) from the mouth of the Paz River in the Pacific Ocean to the tripoint boundary of Honduras, Guatemala and El Salvador at Cerro Monte Cristo (elevation: approximately 3,950 feet [1,200 m.]) situated at 14°25'20"N and 89°21'28"W.

Geographical Setting. Most of the border between these two countries is comprised of rivers—the Paz, Hueviapa, Chingo, Cusmapa and Anguiatu rivers, as well as some smaller tributaries. Another segment of the boundary runs through Lake Guija. Altogether the common water boundary extends for some 106 miles (170 km.). Straight lines stretch overland connecting the river boundaries. The importance of rivers to form the boundary and the instability of such a line led the two countries to sign an agreement according to which the boundary, at the time of its demarcation, would remain unchanged, regardless of any natural or artificial change in the rivers' courses. Since the boundary runs through the

middle of rivers, each country reserved the right to exploit half of the water for agriculture and industry.

Historical Background. Both El Salvador and Guatemala gained independence from Spain in 1821, as regions of the Confederation of Central America. In 1839 the confederation was dissolved; El Salvador declared its independence in 1841. The two countries continued to rely on the old Spanish colonial boundaries for nearly a century. In August 1935, El Salvador and Guatemala agreed to reestablish their boundary and on 26 March 1936 Guatemala, Honduras and El Salvador agreed to accept the summit of Monte Cristo as the common tripoint boundary. The agreement was the first stage of an official demarcation process. On 9 April 1938, a further delineation agreement was signed and a demarcation team worked until September 1940 erecting 530 boundary pillars and markers along the agreed line.

Present Situation. There are no known disputes concerning the boundary between El Salvador and Guatemala. As the current boundary is relatively modern, care was taken in demarcating the land boundary that private lands would not be divided between the two countries. Both governments have taken into consideration any future problems that might arise by compiling a detailed agreement.

EL SALVADOR — HONDURAS Stretching southeastward for 213 miles (342 km.), the boundary between El Salvador and Honduras sets out from the boundary junction with Guatemala on Monte Cristo and ends at the Gulf of Fonseca on the Pacific Ocean. After 170 years of disputes, the exact location of the boundary line was established in 1992 by the International Court of Justice.

Geographical Setting. The boundary tripoint with Guatemala is located on the summit of Cerro Monte Cristo, at 14°25'10"N and 89°21'20"W. From there it runs generally eastward along local watersheds to the confluence of the Ciptesala and Pomola rivers and follows the median line of the Pomola River downstream to a point close to a boundary marker located at 14°24'51"N and 89°17'54"W. The boundary leaves the river and runs in straight lines to reach the summit of Zapotal Mountain (9,200 feet; 2,800 m.) and again in a series of straight lines to the head of the Copantillo River, following it southeastward for about 40 miles (65 km.) to its confluence with the Sumpul River. This river is followed to its confluence with the Chiquita (Oscura) River, the source of which is found in Honduras. Forming a series of straight lines that link local watersheds and riverbeds, the boundary runs in a southeasterly direction and meets the Lempa River, the main river flowing through El Salvador. It progresses through the center of that river downstream eastward and then southward to its confluence with the Torola River, which flows from the east. It follows the median line of the Torola River upstream eastward for about 30 miles (50 km.) to its confluence with a stream known as Arenal or Aceituno, and follows it to its source. Once again in a series of straight lines north, east and south, it reaches the Unire River and follows it downstream to a point known as Paso de Unire. There the line turns eastward and arrives at the Goascorán River at a point known as Los Amates. It follows the middle of the Goascorán River downstream southward to the point where it emerges in the water of the La Union bay in the Gulf of Fonseca. The boundary runs in the Gulf, dividing its islands between the two states such that the island of Tigra is left in Honduras and the island of Meanguera in El Salvador.

Historical Background. Until 1821 both El Salvador and Honduras were part of the Spanish colonial empire of Central America. In 1821 both gained independence and belonged to the Federal Republic of Central America until this was dissolved in 1838. Honduras claimed that its territory covered the Spanish colonial bishopric of Honduras, while El Salvador claimed some Spanish administrative areas, broadly defining its boundaries in 1841 as the Paz River in the west (with Guatemala), the Conchagua inlet in the east and the province of Chiquimula in the north (both with Honduras) and the Pacific Ocean in the south. Border disputes forced the two states to conclude a boundary treaty, signed at San Miguel (El Salvador) on 10 April 1884, delimiting the boundary from the Gulf of Fonseca to the Guatemalan tripoint. However, Honduras refused to ratify this treaty and another treaty that set up a boundary commission was signed in Tegucigalpa (Honduras) on 28 September 1886; yet only the Goascorán River section was agreed upon. On 19 January 1895 another round of talks regarding the

boundary took place, which brought about a treaty that was signed on 13 November 1897 determining some sections of the boundary. But neither state ratified this and no significant progress toward solving the border issue was made over the next 50 years.

Conflict concerning Salvadoran immigration into Honduras, football violence and border clashes led to the outbreak of a full-scale five-day war between the two states on 14 July 1969. The Organization of American States intervened, a truce was reached and during 1970–1971 a Uruguayan moderator tried to work toward solving the disputes. On 4 June 1970 a demilitarized zone 1.8 miles (3 km.) wide was established on each side of the border, but military clashes on the border led to more peace talks and after four years of negotiations a general peace treaty was signed in Lima (Peru) on 30 October 1980. Section IV of the treaty described the delimitation of the 140 miles (225 km.) of the border over which there had been no controversy and which were to be demarcated over the next five years. To delimit the disputed sections the case was submitted to the International Court of Justice (ICJ). In its decision of 11 September 1992 the ICJ defined the present course along the disputed land sections and ruled on the legal status of the islands in the Gulf of Fonseca.

Present Situation. Since 1992 no incidents or disputes concerning the boundary's alignment have been reported, both states having accepted the ICJ's decision. The boundary line was demarcated and 170 years of boundary disputes came to an end.

EQUATORIAL GUINEA (Guinea Ecuatorial)

A country in west Central Africa (area: 10,831 sq. miles [28,052 sq. km.]; estimated population: 390,000 [1994]), Equatorial Guinea is bounded in the north by Cameroon (118 miles; 189 km.) and in the east and south by Gabon (217.5 miles; 350 km.). Its capital is Malabo.

The political life of Equatorial Guinea has been characterized since the colonial period by sharp ethnic cleavages and regional conflicts mainly between the Fang of Rio Muni and the Bubi of Bioko. The Bubi, who are less numerous, underwent a process of westernization and modernization during the colonial period as a result of considerable investments by the Spaniards in the development of their region. As independence neared, the pro-Spanish

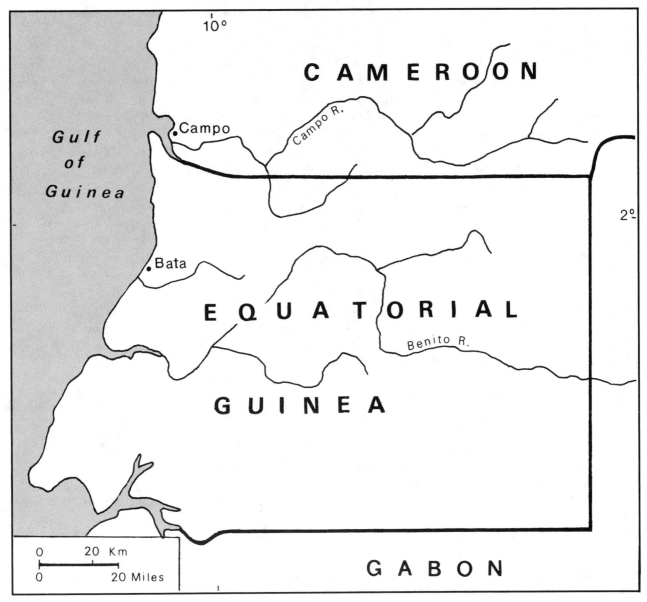

Equatorial Guinea's boundary with Cameroon

Bubi came to fear domination from the more politically active but underdeveloped Fang and formed a separatist movement. Their efforts to establish a separate state failed however, and in 1968 a leader of the Fang, Francisco Macias Nguema, became Equatorial Guinea's first president. During his brutal dictatorship, which lasted until 1979, about one-third of the population fled the country. Although the Bubi saw his rule as a Fang takeover, his persecutions were not aimed only at the Bubi, and many members of his own ethnic group suffered during his rule. Even after Nguema was deposed in a military coup, the Fang continued to dominate political life in the country. The regime, while somewhat more moderate, continued to be dictatorial.

EQUATORIAL GUINEA — CAMEROON see CAMEROON–EQUATORIAL GUINEA.

EQUATORIAL GUINEA — GABON The boundary between Equatorial Guinea and Gabon follows the former colonial boundary between the Spanish and French possessions in equatorial Africa. It runs for 217.5 miles (350 km.) from the boundary junction with Cameroon southward, then westward to the Atlantic Ocean.

Geographical Setting. The boundary line runs directly southward from the boundary junction with Cameroon, which is situated at 2°10'N and 11°20'E, along the meridian for 81 miles (130 km.) until it reaches 1°N. At this point the line forms a right angle, running westward along the 1°N latitude until it reaches the Muni River. The boundary then follows the main channel of the river to a large estuary at Corisco Bay and divides the estuary into northern and southern sections: Equatorial Guinea to the north, including the towns of Nsogobo and Puerto Ivadier; Gabon to the south. The boundary line ends at the mouth of the estuary, in the Atlantic Ocean's Mondah Bay.

Historical Background. Spanish interest in tropical Africa dates from 1778 when Spain installed a commercial station in Guinea. Later Spain established the colony of Spanish Guinea, which consisted of a continental parcel—Rio Muni—and the islands of Fernando Póo, Annobón, Elobey and Corisco. The French stationed themselves in tropical Africa during the nineteenth century, and until 1910 Gabon was part of French Congo, then becoming a unit within French Equatorial Africa. In 1885 and 1894 Germany (which had ruled the area known as Kamerun—today Cameroon—north of Spanish Guinea) and France formulated agreements that delimited their spheres of influence in Africa, whereby the French area was to include the area of Spanish interest on the coast. The territory under Spanish sovereignty was confirmed and delimited by the Franco-Spanish Convention of 27 June 1900 and in 1901 the boundary was demarcated.

On 17 August 1960 Gabon became independent and on 11 June 1966 signed a convention with Spain concerning the boundary between Rio Muni and Gabon. Equatorial Guinea became independent two years later, on 12 October 1968. In 1972 Equatorial Guinea and Gabon were in dispute regarding sovereignty over islands located in the Muni River estuary. Subsequently, an ad hoc commission of the Organization of African Unity confirmed that the Franco-Spanish Convention of 1900 determines the alignment.

Present Situation. Since 1972, no disputes have been reported regarding the delimitation of the boundary between these tropical African countries.

ERITREA An east African country (area: 36,177 sq. miles [93,662 sq. km.]; estimated population: 3,500,000 [1994]), Eritrea was a northern province of Ethiopia until 1993. It is bounded in the north by the Red Sea, in the east by Djibouti (68 miles; 110 km.), in the south by Ethiopia (651 miles; 1,047 km.) and in the west by Sudan (345 miles; 555 km.). The capital of Eritrea is Asmara.

The Eritrean People's Liberation Front (EPLF) fought a 30-year war for independence from Ethiopia, claiming a long legacy of self-government. This was true, to some degree, for the small population of the harbor city of Massawa, which since the late sixteenth century was loosely attached to the Ottoman Empire. However, a distinct Eritrean entity only emerged during the period of Italian colonization (1885–1942). Eritrea only became an Ethopian province in 1962; however, the Muslim and Tigrinya-speaking majorities did not acquiesce to the politics of Amhara cultural and political dominance, a factor which contributed considerably to Eritrean nationalism. Massive Ethiopian military offensives against Eritrean guerrillas between the years 1977 and 1978 caused more than 500,000 Eritreans to flee the region, mainly to the Sudan, and unwittingly popularized the national cause. In 1991 the EPLF, the EPRDF (Ethiopian People's Revolutionary Democratic Front) and the TPLF (Tigray People's Liberation Front) agreed on Eritrea's de facto independence, which was recognized by the Ethiopian government after a referendum in 1993.

ERITREA — DJIBOUTI   see DJIBOUTI–ERITREA.

ERITREA — ETHIOPIA Running for 651 miles (1,047 km.), the Eritrea–Ethiopia boundary extends from the boundary tripoint with Sudan on the Takkaze River in the northwest to the tripoint with Djibouti in the southeast.

Geographical Setting. The boundary begins in the Takkaze (Setit) River and follows it upstream, generally eastward, to about 14°20'N and 37°30'E. There it forms a straight line north-northeastward up to the Mareb River at its confluence with its tributary, the Ambessa River, where the districts of Serae and Western Tigre meet. It follows the Mareb River to its intersection with the Belesa River, which it follows southeast and south before turning east and then southeast to course along the Endeli River. Passing the town of Rendcoma, the boundary leaves the highlands and crosses the northern end of the Danakil depression and the Danakil plain, running some 35 to 40 miles (55 to 65 km.) inland from and roughly parallel to the coast. Thus it meets the border with Djibouti at the Weima River, 27 miles (43 km.) east-southeast of Mussali Mountain.

Historical Background. Eritrea was created as an Italian colony in 1889 and consists of parts of the ancient kingdom of Tigre and a coastal lowland strip that had intermittently come under the control of the Ottoman Empire and Sudan. The Italians attempted to increase their territory—but were opposed by Ethiopia under Emperor Menelik and were defeated at Adwa in 1896. Subsequently, the Treaty of Addis Ababa was signed on 26 October 1896, annulling the previous Treaty of Wechale, under which the Italians had sought to become the protectors of Ethiopia. The question of Eritrea's boundaries was postponed, but in a treaty signed on 10 July 1900 Eritrea was formally severed from Ethiopia and the boundaries were delimited between 1900 and 1908. During the Italian occupation of Ethiopia, from 1936 to 1941, the borders of Eritrea were expanded to create Greater Eritrea, but the pre-World War II boundary was restored when the country was liberated. After World War II Eritrea became a United Nations protectorate under British rule, until 1952 when it was federated to Ethiopia. In 1960 it became a province of Ethiopia and in 1993 achieved independence, with Asmara as its capital and adopting the 1908 boundary line.

Present Situation. Eritrea's common border with Ethiopia is recognized by both countries.

ERITREA — SUDAN

This boundary is 345 miles (555 km.) long and runs from the boundary tripoint with Ethiopia on the Setit River in the southwest to Ras Kasar on the Red Sea coast in the northeast. It follows a series of straight lines, mountain crests and peaks and is demarcated throughout by iron poles and masonry pillars.

Geographical Setting. On the right bank of the Setit (Takkaze) River, opposite the mouth of the Khor Royan, the boundary tripoint with Ethiopia is marked by an iron pillar. From there the border runs northward to another pillar and in a straight line to the summit of the western end of Jebel Nuwar, where a conspicuous tree is surrounded by a circle of stones and marked by an iron pillar on either side. The border then takes a straight line marked by four iron poles to the highest point of the eastern Korateib rocks. Iron posts were also placed on either side of this point. From Korateib the boundary runs in a straight line to the highest summit of the El Burai (Buruck) hills, where another iron pole is located. From here it forms another straight line up to the highest point of Jebel Abu Gamal and then to a point on the right bank of the Mareb (Gash) River and to the south of Jebel Gulsa. In a straight line indicated by two iron marks it reaches the peak of Jebel Anderaib, on which another iron pole was placed, and another line takes it to the crest of the ridge that lies on the southern side of the Kassala (Sudan)–Agordat (Eritrea) road. It crosses over the summit of Jebel Abun (Abeshkar) and is marked by 14 iron poles. The boundary passes Khor Sabderat to Quasana peak and to Jebel Eunice and Deberenis. Northward to Jebel Beneifer the boundary passes through a number of hills and then follows the watershed between the streams flowing east to the Baraka River and those flowing west to the Mareb and Langueb rivers. It follows the course of Khasm Dada from the foot of the Eskenie range southeast to its confluence with the Bakara River, which it then follows northward to its confluence with the Ambacta River. It runs northeastward to Jebel Aar through the undulating region of the watershed between the Ambacta River and the Loi torrent. From Jebel Aar it continues to the wells of Afta, past the Afta torrent to the summit of Hamet and along the northern edge of the Hagar-Nusch plateau to a point north of the Roribet peak and up to the Sciancolet hill. It heads eastward along the watershed between the Korora-Tabeh and Aitara-Arerib valleys, reaches Abbeindeu and Teffanait mountains and then follows the riverbed of the Karora River to the heights of Gaei-Helli and Halibai and from there continues to the Red Sea coast at Ras Kasar.

Historical Background. Eritrea's unification and the demarcation of its boundaries were achieved by the Italians in the 1890s. Before that the highlands were part of the Kingdom of Tigre, intermittently under Ethiopian rule, and the lowlands were variously controlled by Turkey, Egypt and Sudan. Eritrea became an Italian colony in 1889 and remained so until after World War II.

In the latter half of the nineteenth century most of present-day Sudan was part of Egypt, under the sovereignty of the sultan of Turkey. In 1882 the British military occupation of Egypt began and Anglo-Egyptian troops combined forces against the Mahdi, who had set up a state in Sudan. After the Sudan War of 1896–1899 the reconquered state became a condominium as Anglo-Egyptian Sudan. A treaty was signed on 15 May 1902 and an agreement reached on 6 December 1907, leading to a demarcation of the boundary in 1902–1903 and 1909 by Major Gwynn. This demarcation, however, was opposed by Ethiopia.

In 1947 Italy renounced all rights to Eritrea and a period under the United Nations Administrative Authority ensued, at the end of which Eritrea was made a federal part of Ethiopia with its own internal government. Gradually government passed entirely to Addis Ababa and in 1960 Eritrea became a province of Ethiopia. On 1 January 1956 Sudan became independent and on 3 January 1967 Ethiopia and Sudan issued a joint communiqué accepting the principles of the 1902 treaty. After further negotiations an exchange of notes took place on 18 July 1972, confirming the Gwynn line with some modifications.

Opposition to the 1960 status of Eritrea resulted in a long and destructive war for independence. In 1993 a referendum produced an overwhelming vote in favor of secession and in May 1993 Eritrea became independent. Both countries accepted the 1902 boundary as their common international border.

Present Situation. The boundary between Eritrea and Sudan is not in dispute.

ESTONIA (Eesti) A former republic of the Soviet Union, Estonia (area: 17,413 sq. miles [45,082 sq. km.]; estimated population: 1,620,000 [1994]) gained independence in 1991. It is bounded by Russia (180 miles; 290 km.) in the east, by Latvia (166 miles; 267 km.) in the south and by the Baltic Sea in the north and west. The capital of Estonia is Tallinn.

An ancient people, the Estonians are first mentioned by Tacitus. In the ninth century, Vikings raided Estonia on their way to Russia. Sweden, Den-

mark and Russia later tried to conquer and convert the Estonians in the eleventh and twelfth centuries, but only in the first half of the thirteenth century did the Estonians adopt Christianity. At that time southern Estonia and northern Latvia (then known as Livonia), were overrun by the Order of the Knights of the Sword (later part of the Teutonic Order); the Danish king conquered northern Estonia.

In 1346 the king of Denmark sold his part of Estonia to the Teutonic Order. Upon the Order's dissolution in 1561, Poland and Sweden vied for control of the Baltic countries, with the latter emerging victorious in 1629. By then, the three centuries of German rule had made a marked impact on the country. Bishoprics, estates, and later cities were established, creating a German nobility and a predominantly German class of burghers. Native Estonian peasants were pressed into serfdom.

In the Northern War of 1701–1721 the Swedes lost the Baltic provinces to Russia. Czar Alexander I (reigned 1801–1825) officially liberated the Estonian peasantry from serfdom, but only under Alexander II (reigned 1855–1881) were they granted rights such as freedom of movement and released from the jurisdiction of landowners and from compulsory unpaid labor. Industrialization and urbanization in Estonia generated enormous socioeconomic changes in the Estonian population which, with the spread of education and the revival of Estonian literature, created the infrastructure for an Estonian nationalism.

This nationalism, however, only fully matured in response to efforts at Russification during the reigns of Alexander III (1881–1894) and Nicholas II (1894–1917). At first Estonians were delighted that this Russification had enfeebled German culture and influence, but they soon became increasingly alienated from Russia as well. In the wake of the 1917 revolution, Estonia declared itself independent and enlisted foreign aid in resisting attempts at annexation by the Soviet regime. Following the Ribbentrop-Molotov Agreement of 1939, Estonia, like the other Baltic states, was forced to accept Soviet bases on its territory, the first in a rapid series of stages that led to its annexation by the Soviet Union, where it was given the status of a union republic.

During the Soviet period, a rapid industrialization of the northern part of the country was followed by urbanization and internal migration from the agricultural south. As a result, the overwhelming majority of Estonians now live in the north. Industrialization and efforts by the Soviet authorities also caused an influx of Russians into Estonia—ethnic Russians now constitute about 20% of the population.

In the liberal atmosphere of Mikhail Gorbachev's policies of *perestroika* and *glasnost*, Estonian nationalists struggled for secession from the Soviet Union and complete independence. Independence was achieved in 1991, upon the dissolution of the USSR.

ESTONIA — LATVIA With only minor modifications the boundary between Estonia and Latvia follows a line that was established after World War I. The length of the boundary is 166 miles (267 km.) and it runs from the boundary tripoint with Russia in the east to the Gulf of Riga in the Baltic Sea in the west.

Geographical Setting. The eastern terminus of this boundary line is located in a flat area about 12 miles (20 km.) northeast of the Latvian town of Aluksne. It heads westward, leaves the town of Ape in Latvia and reaches the Gauja (Gauya) River north of the Latvian town of Vireshy. It follows the river downstream northwestward for 20 miles (32 km.) and leaves it where the river turns westward. The boundary line continues northwestward, passes between Valga (Estonia) and Valka (Latvia) and reaches a point southeast of Moisakula (Estonia). Forming a curve south, west and northwestward, it leaves the entire Moisakula region within Estonia. The line runs southwestward for 35 miles (56 km.) and reaches the Gulf of Riga north of Ainazi (Latvia) after crossing the main highway between Riga and Tallinn, the capitals of Latvia and Estonia. The boundary runs across the Gulf of Riga, leaving the island of Runy with Estonia.

Historical Background. The present boundary between Estonia and Latvia dates back to the creation of modern Europe after World War I. Neither had ever been an independent political unit, although the Estonians and Latvians had constituted separate ethnic groups for centuries. Both were ruled by the Russian Empire from 1721 and only in the wake of the 1917 revolution did Latvia and Estonia proclaim their independence, which was recognized by the Versailles Peace Treaty of 1919. Both fought against the Soviet and German forces between 1919 and 1920 and in 1920 both achieved full independence. The boundary between the two states was established in July 1920 by means of arbitration and was based on the local ethnic division. In 1923 a treaty of friendship was signed between them whereby each recognized the arbitration line.

Following the Ribbentrop-Molotov agreement of 1939, Estonia and Latvia were forced to grant bases to the Soviet Union and were then annexed to the USSR in August 1940 as republics. After World War II, when the two republics had been occupied by Nazi Germany, some minor changes, mainly in the southeastern corner of the line, were made in the boundary. In 1991 Estonia and Latvia became independent states, adopting the existing division as their common international boundary line without a formal agreement.

Present Situation. Although no formal disputes are known concerning the boundary alignment, there are some groups that call for the restoration of the boundary to its pre-1940 position.

ESTONIA — RUSSIA From the boundary tripoint with Latvia in the south, this boundary runs for 180 miles (290 km.) northward to the Gulf of Finland. It follows the line that was established after World War I when Estonia became independent.

Geographical Setting. The Latvian tripoint is located 10 miles (16 km.) southeast of the small town of Rouge (Estonia) and from there the Estonia–Russia boundary traverses northward for 20 miles (32 km.) through a flat area and reaches the railway between Pskov (Russia) and Valga (Estonia) west of Pechory (Russia). It runs eastward for 6 miles (10 km.) and then northward to reach the southern shore of Lake Peipus (Chudskoye) south of Repyna (Estonia). The boundary crosses the lake northward and divides it between Russia and Estonia, such that one-third of the lake is left with Estonia. As the boundary meets a point in the lake 6.5 miles (10.5 km.) from its northern shore, it turns northeastward to leave the Narva (Narova) River, which runs between the lake and the Gulf of Finland, in Estonia. It runs parallel to the river to the town of Narva (Estonia), crosses the main road and railway between Tallinn (Estonia) and Saint Petersburg (Russia) and ends in the Gulf of Finland halfway between the mouths of the Narva (Estonia) and Luga (Russia) rivers.

Historical Background. During the late Middle Ages the Germans ruled the area known today as Estonia. In 1651 northern Estonia was annexed to Sweden, which also ruled southern Estonia (Livonia) from 1629. In 1721 the Russian Empire occupied Estonia and ruled until 1917, when, following the Russian Revolution of March 1917, northern and southern Estonia were united and after the Communist Revolution of November 1917 declared its independence, which was recognized by the Western Powers in May 1918. During 1919 both Soviet and German forces made abortive attempts to occupy Estonia and its independence was reestablished on 29 May 1919. On 2 February 1920 the Dorpat Peace Treaty between Estonia and the Soviet Union was signed, in which the Pechory region was left with Estonia.

Estonia came under the influence of the Soviet Union in accordance with the German-Soviet Agreement of 1939 and became a Soviet republic of the Soviet Union on 16 June 1940. It was occupied by Germany between 1941 and 1944 but was reoccupied by the Soviet Union, which ruled Estonia again until 1991. During that period some minor changes were made in Estonia's boundaries as the Pechory region was ceded to the Russian republic. Estonia became independent in August 1991, following the disintegration of the Soviet Union. The last internal boundary between the two Soviet republics became the international boundary line between the two independent states of Estonia and Russia.

Present Situation. Although both states adopted the former internal division and neither raised any formal claims to the other's territory, there are some informal disputes concerning the common boundary line. Some call for the creation of an independent Narva republic in northwestern Estonia or for Narva's secession from Estonia and reunification with Russia. On the other hand there are claims to return the borderland of the Saint Petersburg and Pskov districts (in the Pechory region) that are now under Russian rule to Estonia. Until these issues are solved, the boundary between Estonia and Russia cannot be stabilized.

ETHIOPIA (Ityopiya) A landlocked east African country (area: 471,800 sq. miles [1,221,500 sq. km.]; estimated population: 52,500,000 [1994]), Ethiopia is bounded by Eritrea (651 miles; 1,047 km.) in the north, by Djibouti (217 miles; 349 km.) and Somalia (994 miles; 1,600 km.) in the east, by Kenya (535 miles; 861 km.) in the south and by Sudan (1,380 miles; 2,221 km.) in the west. Ethiopia's capital is Addis Ababa.

In the political sense, the Ethiopians are the inhabitants of the state of Ethiopia as shaped during the reign of Emperor Menelik II (1889–1913). Its boundaries excluded the territory of the former Italian colony of Eritrea, which in 1952 formed a federation with Ethiopia; it was annexed as a province in 1962. In 1991, after 30 years of guerrilla and civil war, a new Ethiopian government acquiesced to Eritrean independence. However, in a cultural sense, many Eriteans share characteristics and historical legacies with the peoples of northern Ethiopia. Although Ethiopia is often identified with Christianity, the largest religious group is Sunni Muslim.

From the latter half of the nineteenth century, as a by-product of imperial expansion, political centralization, and the confrontation with European colonialism, attempts were made to popularize the idea of being "Ethiopian" and to develop a sense of patriotism and national identity distinguished from regional and ethnic loyalties. This idea of Ethiopian nationalism was bolstered among intellectuals and other politically minded people by Menelik II's victory over the Italians at Adawa (1896), and by resistance against the Italian efforts at colonization (1935–1941). It was hindered, however, by the injustices linked with imperial expansion and the obvious dominance of the Amhara. During the reign of Emperor Lij Yasu (1913–1916) an unsuccessful attempt was made to reconstruct relations between the competing ethnic groups and to incorporate the Muslim peoples of the south (Afar, Somali, Oromo). The Italians were later able to exploit this situation during their short colonial interlude.

During Haile Selassie's rule (1916–1974), attempts at "Amharization," particularly among the emerging middle class, were used to forge a core population identifying solely with Ethiopia. While Amharization became an integral part of the politics of modernization, it also elicited antagonism among

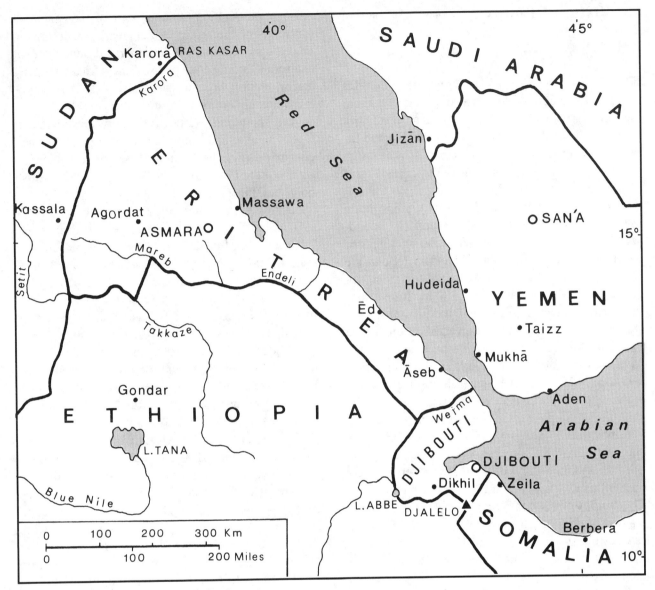

Boundaries of Ethiopia, Eritrea and Djibouti

non-Amhara peoples and encouraged them to assert their own identities. During the 1960s self-help organizations encouraged road-construction, literacy campaigns, education, etc., among the Tigray, Oromo, Gurage, Kambata and Hadiya. These networks of organized ethnicity would often provide the basis for "national movements," which began emerging in the 1970s.

The monarchy of Haile Selassie was overthrown in 1974 and a military government under Mengistu Haile Mariam assumed power. Under Mengistu, Ethiopia formally adopted Marxism-Leninism, animating earlier discussions of the "nationality question." Practical politics, however, favored further

centralization and cultural Amharization in the name of Ethiopian unity, and fueled simmering ethnic conflicts. In a short time the government found itself in conflict with national liberation movements fighting for increased government participation and even independence for Eritreans, Tigray, Afars, Oromo, Sidamo and Somali.

A coalition of many of these groups ousted Mariam in June 1991. The new Ethiopian government is currently claiming to favor decentralization and has encouraged the formation of ethnic organizations. At the same time, such organizations are sanctioned only insofar as they are linked to the umbrella organization of the EPRDF.

ETHIOPIA — DJIBOUTI   see DJIBOUTI–ETHIOPIA.

ETHIOPIA — ERITREA   see ERITREA–ETHIOPIA.

ETHIOPIA — KENYA

This boundary, 535 miles (861 km.) in length, is demarcated throughout. From the boundary junction with Somalia on the Dawa River it follows the lowest course of the riverbed for about 120 miles (193 km.), forms a number of straight-line segments and crosses Lake Rudolf (Turkana) for 24 miles (39 km.).

Geographical Setting. Starting from a point in the lowest channel of the Dawa River, opposite boundary pillar no. 1 (which is located on the right bank of the river), the Ethiopia–Kenya boundary follows the channel upstream generally westward to a point opposite a boundary pillar at Malca Mari. It then runs in a straight line to Eimole Diko, leaving it in Kenya, and leaving the Italian road to the Dawa River in Ethiopia. It then forms another straight line to the summit of Burduras, leaving the police post and local well with El Roba (Ethiopia). From the summit of Burduras it forms a straight line to the summits of Gamadda, Guf Dika and Faiyu, leaving Gagabba in Kenya. From there it follows the watershed between the Gadduduma and Adde valleys on one side and the valleys of the Bor and Dembi rivers on the other, to a point on the hill south of Dembi. The border continues along the watershed to the summit of Gaiyu and in a series of straight lines reaches the summits of Dimbi Dalarra and Yabello, the wells of Godoma remaining in Kenya. It runs along the valley east of the Harbor Police Station and trends along the bottom of the valley between the two Moyales to the summit of Gaferso. In another series of straight lines, the border reaches the summits of Ajali, Abo and Somai, dividing the local wells between Ethiopia and Kenya. The boundary then runs in more straight lines between summits, still dividing the region's wells, until it intersects the 4°27′N parallel and follows it to a point in Lake Rudolf, north of North Island (at approximately 36°3′E). Once again in a straight line westward, the boundary reaches the Todenyang (Kenya)–Namuruputh (Ethiopia) road at a point known as Consul's Rock. It then follows the road to the boundary tripoint with Sudan.

Historical Background. In 1887 the British East African Association obtained part of the mainland territories of the sultan of Zanzibar. The following year the association was incorporated under a royal charter as the Imperial British East Africa Company and in 1895 it became the British East Africa Protectorate under the administration of the British crown, including the territory between the Indian Ocean and the Rift Valley. On 1 April 1902 the eastern province of the Uganda Protectorate was transferred to the East Africa Protectorate by the British Foreign Office.

An Anglo-Ethiopian agreement of 6 December 1907 delimited a boundary between the East Africa Protectorate, Uganda and the Empire of Ethiopia from the confluence of the Dawa and Juba (Genale) rivers to a point northwest of Lake Rudolf. In 1920 the East Africa Protectorate was reorganized, creating the Protectorate of Kenya, which became a British colony. Jubaland, west of the Juba River, was ceded to Italy in 1925 and was incorporated into Italian Somaliland and the Ethiopia, Kenya and Italian Somaliland tripoint was shifted inland to the Dawa River, opposite Malca Rie. When the Rudolf province was transferred to Kenya in 1926 the eastern section of the Sudan–Uganda border (from Lake Rudolf to Mount Zalia) became the western section of the Kenya–Sudan boundary. An Anglo-Ethiopian agreement of 29 September 1947 provided for the redelimitation of the boundary and a boundary commission under Colonel Clifford completed its work during 1951–1955. However, the following year (1956) the Ethiopian government refused to ratify the Clifford line and on 15 November 1963 an Ethiopian-Kenyan agreement modified the 1947 settlement and provided for the subsequent redemarcation of several parts of the boundary. A treaty between Kenya and Ethiopia of 9 June 1970 superseded all previous agreements and determined the present boundary.

Present Situation. This boundary is recognized by both countries.

ETHIOPIA — SOMALIA

For 994 miles (1,600 km.) the boundary between Ethiopia and Somalia runs from the tripoint with Kenya on the Dawa River in the south to the boundary junction with Djibouti in the north. It follows *thalwegs*, topographical features and administrative lines.

Geographical Setting. The Ethiopia–Somalia boundary begins in the *thalweg* of the Dawa River, which it follows northwest to its confluence with the Ganale-Dorya at Dolo, where it begins to follow the provisional administrative line of 1950. This runs between detailed towns and villages to 'let (Somalia) and then continues northeast and east to a point 4 miles (6 km.) southeast of Gherou (Ethiopia). From here the boundary continues in a straight line northeast to 8°N and 48°E. Turning sharply west it follows the 8°N parallel to its intersection with 47°E, where it heads northwest in a straight line to 9°N and 44°E. From here it trends along hills and mountains to the boundary tripoint with Djibouti.

Historical Background. The Somali Republic consists of the territories that once constituted the Trust Territory of Somalia (formerly Italian Somaliland) and British Somaliland. After the Battle of Dogali in 1887, Italy and Ethiopia signed an agreement, the Treaty of Wichale, the terms of which were interpreted quite differently by each country. Ethiopia believed the treaty gave it the option of calling upon Italy for aid and advice in matters of foreign affairs; Italy believed that Ethiopia was placed under its protection.

In another conflict, in 1896 at Adwa, Ethiopia again frustrated Italian ambitions in the Horn of Africa and the subsequent treaty at Addis Ababa annulled the Wichale Treaty. Ethiopia modified its boundary with British Somalia, regaining most of the Haud region and establishing the southern limit of the protectorate. This latter treaty established part of the present border and provided the right of movement across the border for local inhabitants to graze their herds. It also specified a determination to agree on the border between Ethiopia and the Italian sphere of influence. This was apparently done in September 1897, but official texts were not exchanged and the map no longer exists. Furthermore the sovereignty of a large section below the 8°N parallel was left in doubt: Ethiopia fixed the tripoint with British Somaliland at 48°E, while Italy set it further inland, at 47°E. Although a convention of 16 May 1908 settled the Ethiopia– Italian Somaliland border, from Dolo to the British Somalia tripoint, reference was made to the ambiguous 1897 agreement. In 1910, 80 miles (129 km.) of the border were demarcated, from Dolo to 'let. During 1929

and 1930 the border between British and Italian Somalilands was demarcated and the line on the 8°N parallel, between 47°E and 48°E, was included. From 1931 to 1934 an Anglo-Ethiopian commission demarcated the Ethiopia–British Somaliland boundary. This was done only west of 8°N and 47°E, but the Ethiopian government reserved its rights to the area up to 48°E. After the Ethiopian-Italian war of 1936, Italy increased its possessions to include the Ogaden region and the upper parts of the Juba (Giuba) and Wabi Shebelle drainage areas. For a short period at the beginning of World War II British Somaliland was under Italian control. It was restored to British administration in 1941 and this was extended to Italian Somaliland, Ogaden and the Haud region. When the British withdrew from most of Ogaden in 1948, an Anglo-Ethiopian protocol described a provisional boundary. However, both Ethiopia and Italy expressed disquiet about the line. The United Nations Trusteeship for Somalia declared that its boundaries with Ethiopia should be those fixed by an international agreement and that those boundaries that were not yet fixed were to be established under the auspices of the General Assembly. In 1955 Ethiopia and Italy agreed that the 1908 convention would provide the basis for the boundary's location. Negotiations have since failed to obtain any agreement. When the British withdrew from the Haud region in 1954, they reserved the right of British Somalis to graze and water their livestock there. British Somaliland became independent on 26 June 1960 and on 1 July 1960 combined with the Trust Territory to form the republic. However, upon gaining independence Somalia declined to recognize the Anglo-Ethiopian treaty of 1897 and afforded only de facto recognition to all its boundaries with Ethiopia.

Present Situation. Since independence Somalia has claimed the Somali inhabited areas of the Ogaden region. The boundary alignment east of Dolo to the former tripoint with Italian Somaliland remains provisional and is a source of dissatisfaction to both countries. Cross-border tribal warfare broke out in the Borena district in 1991.

ETHIOPIA — SUDAN   From the boundary tripoint with Eritrea in the Setit River in the north, this boundary runs for 1,380 miles (2,221 km.) to the boundary tripoint with Kenya in the south. It is demarcated throughout by numbered beacons.

Geographical Setting. From the Setit (Takkaze) River, the boundary forms a straight line to beacon no. 1. From there it continues south-southwest along roads and summits and reaches beacon no. 9 on the Atbara River. The boundary runs south and then turns west to the boundary junction between Sudan, Eastern Sudan and Central Sudan. From there it continues south-southwest to beacon no. 18, at the crossing of the Dinder River. Passing beacons 19 to 22, it trends over rocks, hills and a main river channel, and at beacon no. 22 intersects the Blue Nile. The *thalweg* of the Blue Nile is the frontier to beacon no. 23, where it continues in a straight line to beacon no. 24 and then continues across watersheds. It turns northwest for a short distance and then again heads south-southwest. At beacon no. 32 the road from Kurmuk (Sudan) to Kutu (Ethiopia) crosses the boundary. Curving slightly to the east it then runs south and reaches the boundary junction between Central and Southern Sudan. The boundary then continues south until it bears westward past beacon no. 37 and meets the Baro River. Following the *thalweg* of the Baro River, the boundary goes to the mouth of the Pibor River, follows the *thalweg* of the Pibor southward to its confluence with the Akobo River and the *thalweg* of the Akobo southeastward to the village of Melile. From there the line travels to 6°N and 35°E and to 5°40'N and 35°15'E.

It follows 35°15'E to its intersection with 5°25'N and then continues generally southeast to the boundary tripoint with Kenya.

Historical Background. The modern history of Sudan began in 1821, when the area was conquered by Muhammad Ali, viceroy of Egypt for the Ottoman sultan. When the Mahdist revolution began in 1882 the Egyptian government, unable to suppress it, took the British advice to abandon all the territories south of Aswan if not Wadi Halfa. In 1885 The Mahdi captured Khartoum and set up a state that included all of Sudan except the towns of Suakin (on the Red Sea coast) and Wadi Halfa. The Mahdi and his successor ruled until 1898, when Kitchener led an Anglo-Egyptian force to victory at the Battle of Omdurman. There followed a period of condominium when both British and Egyptians held power in Sudan, but the British negotiated Sudan's borders. Following the treaty of 15 May 1902 and the agreement of 6 December 1907, the boundary was demarcated in 1902–1903 and 1909 by Major Gwynn. This demarcation was contested by Ethiopia and it was not until 3 January 1967 that Ethiopia and Sudan issued a joint communiqué accepting the principles of the 1902 treaty. After further negotiations an exchange of notes took place on 18 July 1972, confirming the Gwynn line with some modifications.

Present Situation. The boundary line that extends between Ethiopia and Sudan is fully recognized by both countries.

F

FAEROE ISLANDS (Føroyar)   Located in the North Atlantic Ocean, southeast of Iceland, this group of islands is a self-governing island region of Denmark. It has no land boundaries and its total land area is 540 sq. miles (1,399 sq. km.). Faeroe Islands has an estimated population of 49,000 (1994). Its capital is Tórshavn.

The inhabitants of the Faroe (Far Oer) archipelago are citizens of the Kingdom of Denmark. Their language is closely related to Icelandic. They engage in fishing, agriculture, sheep-herding and down-collecting.

FALKLAND ISLANDS   An archipelago in the South Atlantic Ocean, the Falkland Islands are situated east of the coast of Argentina. The islands are a United Kingdom crown colony with a total land area of 4,702 sq. miles (12,173 sq. km.) and an estimated population of 2,000 (1994). The capital of the Falkland Islands is Stanley. It has no land boundaries.

The inhabitants of the Falkland Islands are primarily British. Most engage in sheep-rearing, although there are indications that there are large oil and gas deposits in the region; these may alter the islands' traditional economy. Argentina, which calls the islands the Malvinas and claims them as its own, attempted to assert sovereignty by invading the islands in 1982. Britain recaptured the islands soon after, and there are currently over 4,000 British troops still stationed there.

FIJI   An independent archipelago, Fiji comprises some 332 islands, of which only 110 are inhabited. It is located in the South Pacific Ocean and has no land boundaries. The area of Fiji is 7,078 sq. miles (18,325 sq. km.) and it has an estimated population of 800,000 (1994). The capital of Fiji is Suva.

The Fiji group comprises four main islands: Viti Levu (where 70% of the population live), Vanua Levu, Tavaeuni and Kandavu. First settled approximately 3,500 years ago, the islands came to serve as a launching ground for exploration and settlement in the Pacific Ocean, toward the islands now known as Polynesia.

Native Fijians make up only about 48% of the archipelago's total population. Indians, descended from immigrants brought by the British colonial government to work in the sugarcane plantations, form another 46%. Native Fijians speak a Melanesian language with several regional dialects, of which Bau is considered the official. The majority are Christians, with Wesleyan Methodism being the leading denomination.

The traditional Fijian economy is agricultural and village-based, with taro, yams, cassava and sweet potatoes as staples. Copra is a major cash crop, especially on the smaller islands, and fishing is increasingly important.

The clan (*mataquil*) is the social division which formed the major landholding entity on the cession of the Fiji Islands to Britain. In recent years there has been migration from villages, especially in the periphery, toward urban centers and an increasing tendency to leave the communal village framework to work the land as independent farmers. Within villages commercial production is on the increase and a considerable number of the independent farmers cultivate sugar, the dominant cash crop in Fiji, which has been traditionally grown by Indo-Fijians.

The traditional institution of the Great Council of Chiefs is still influential in the political arena and even day-to-day life. At the same time, racial diversity, compounded by former British colonial policies, have left Fiji a legacy of ethnic unrest. Native

Fijians own over 80% of the land, while over 90% of the sugar cultivation, Fiji's largest export, is produced by Indians, most often on land leased from native Fijians. This ethnic division has taken political shape since independence. The government is dominated by Fijians and run by some of the highest ranking native chiefs; the opposition is dominated by Indo-Fijians. Tensions climaxed after the 1987 general election when the ruling government was defeated by an Indian-dominated coalition. A military coup ousted the coalition government and a new interim government was promptly formed. Under the new administration Fiji declared itself a republic and withdrew from the British Commonwealth. The influence of the army has decreased since 1991.

FINLAND (Suomi) A Scandinavian country (area: 130,552 sq. miles [338,000 sq. km.; estimated population: 5,020,000 [1994]) situated in the northeastern corner of Europe, Finland is bounded in the north by Norway (453 miles; 729 km.), in the east by Russia (816 miles; 1,313 km.), in the south and west by the Baltic Sea and in the northwest by Sweden (364.5 miles; 586 km.). The capital of Finland is Helsinki.

The common ancestors of the Volga-Kama-Ural Finno-Ugric peoples reached the Baltic coast before the first century. Between then and the eighth century, Finnish tribes of hunters and fishers migrated into present-day Finland. Here they separated into four tribes: the Kainulaiset (Kvanes), who settled east of the Gulf of Bothnia, the Hamalaiset (Tavastes), who chose the lake district, the Varsinais (Suomalaiset), who originally settled in southwest Finland, and the Karjalaiset (Karelians), living around Lakes Ladoga and Onega. In the process, the Finns forced the indigenous Lapps northward.

Finnish raids against the Swedes in the twelfth century, provoked the Swedes to call a "crusade" against the shamanist Finns. Upon conquering the country the Swedes introduced Catholicism and, from the thirteenth to eighteenth centuries, sent colonists to Finland. Swedish culture had a significant impact on the Finns but did not prevent the emergence of a rich local culture exemplified by the epic national poem, the *Kalevala*.

The expansion of Finnish areas of settlement northward in the fifteenth and sixteenth centuries

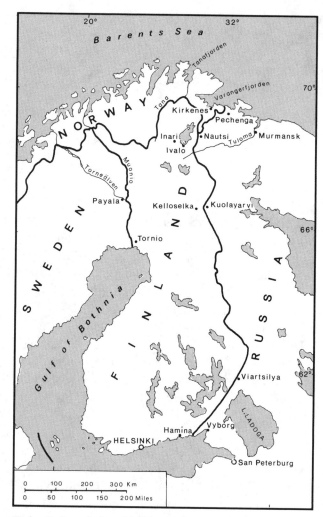

Finland's boundaries with Norway, Russia and Sweden

drove the Lapps even further from their original territory. This colonization of the north (a process which continues today) led to the introduction of feudalism. Around 1600 a peasant revolt, the "War of the Cudgels," was suppressed by the Swedes, who used the occasion to impose a new Lutheran ruling stratum. By the eighteenth century, however, Swedish influence weakened. The Finnish language, virtually abandoned by the ruling classes, once again became accepted.

During the Napoleonic Wars, Sweden's role was supplanted by Russia, which invaded Finland and annexed it in 1809. Reconstituted as a grand duchy, the Russian administration was at first mindful of preserving Swedish-Finnish institutions and privileges. However, the emergence of Finnish nationalism in the nineteenth century prompted attempts at forcible Russification.

This only augmented Finnish enmity toward Russia: the Russian Revolution of 1917 provided the occasion to declare Finland an independent republic .

In the post-World War I reshuffling of borders, Finland lost part of Karelia to the Soviet Union. After the secret Soviet-German pact of 1939, the Soviets forced the Finns to cede another piece of Karelia, causing them to seek the military backing of Nazi Germany. In punishment for siding with Germany, the Finns were forced to cede even more territory to the Soviet Union after World War II. Since 1917 they have lost 10% of their original territory, suffered massive destruction and loss of life, and were forced to absorb 500,000 Karelian refugees. Only absolute neutrality during the Cold War saved them from further Soviet encroachments.

Initially undertaken to pay off war debts to the Soviet Union, land reform and industrialization have allowed Finland to develop into a social-democratic capitalist society with a high standard of living.

FINLAND — NORWAY   The present boundary between Finland and Norway follows the boundary line established between Russia and Sweden in the early nineteenth century. It runs for 453 miles (729 km.) between the Swedish boundary in the west and the Russian tripoint in the east.

Geographical Setting. The boundary tripoint with Sweden is located at the head of Signal Valley (Signaldaled) on the watershed between the North Sea and the Baltic Sea. The line runs northeastward, along the watershed, reaching the Raisduoddar peak (4,477 feet; 1,365 m.). Keeping to the watershed, the boundary runs southeastward for about 55 miles (90 km.), reaching the Ur'devarri peak (2,158 feet; 658 m.), and then runs eastward, crossing the main road between Kemi (Finland) on the Baltic shore and Alta (Norway) on the Alta Fjord of the North Sea. Still on the main watershed, the boundary reaches the source of the eastern tributary of the Anar River. It follows the tributary downstream northward to its confluence with the Anar River and then follows the river downstream northward to its confluence with the Vall River. The boundary line follows the joined river, called the Tana River, downstream northward and northeastward to the small town of Polmak (Norway). Thence it leaves the river and runs east-southeastward to cross the

Naatamo River west of the small town of Neiden. In a series of straight lines the boundary runs southward, crossing the Munk River to reach the Russian tripoint at Krokfjell (Muotkavaara), east of the Pasvik River.

Historical Background. Both Finland and Norway were sections of larger states until the beginning of the twentieth century. From 1814 Norway was ruled by Sweden while Finland, which was previously ruled by Sweden, became part of the Russian Empire on 17 September 1809 by the Treaty of Hamina (Fredrikshamm). Russia and Sweden then established a new boundary between themselves, demarcating the line between 1810 and 1824. The Saint Petersburg Convention between Russia and Sweden, signed on 14 May 1826, established the present boundary lines between Norway and Finland, between Norway and Russia and between Sweden and Finland. Problems evolving from the 1824 delimitation were clarified in the Harpranda Convention of 15 September 1888 and the boundary line was surveyed and demarcated again in 1896. Norway became independent when the union with Sweden was dissolved on 26 October 1905. Russia recognized the new state, and the northern section of the former Sweden–Russia boundary line in Finland became the boundary between Norway and Russia. Finland became independent 6 December 1917 and its independence was recognized by Russia on 1 March 1918.

By the Treaty of Peace between Finland and the Russian Soviet Republic, signed on 14 October 1920 at Dorpat, the province of Petsamo (Pechenga) was transferred to Finland thereby enlarging the Norway–Finland boundary line up to the Varanger Fjord in the Barents Sea. Finland and Norway established their common boundary line by the final protocol signed at Christiana (Oslo) on 28 April 1924, according to which the boundary would remain that which was traced at the time of the last Swedish–Russian frontier delimitation and demarcation in 1896. On 15 October 1925 the boundary commission's maps and protocols were completed and signed. By the treaty of peace with Finland signed after World War II in Paris on 10 February 1947, the province of Petsamo was returned to the Soviet Union, thus establishing the boundary between Norway and Finland up to the Russian tripoint at

Moutkavaara (Krokjell). This boundary post was agreed upon on 18 December 1947 and a protocol regarding its maintenance was signed at Helsinki on 7 February 1953 by Finland, Norway and the Soviet Union.

Present Situation. Since 1826 no changes have been made in the boundary line, which was last demarcated in 1896. The establishment of the two states in the twentieth century did not change the boundary line determined between Russia and Sweden. Both Norway and Finland adopted the boundary line in 1924 and from then onward there were no disputes concerning its alignment.

FINLAND — RUSSIA

Today's Finnish–Russian boundary is the former Finnish–Soviet Union line, which stretches 816 miles (1,313 km.) from the Russia–Norway–Finland boundary tripoint in the north to the Gulf of Finland in the Baltic Sea in the south.

Geographical Setting. The boundary sets out northeastward from the Gulf of Finland, east of the Finnish city of Hamina and west of the Karelian Isthmus (Russia). It follows a series of straight lines for 38 miles (61 km.) to the Saimaa Canal, which connects Saimaa Lake with the former Finnish town of Vyborg, now in Russia. Crossing the canal, the boundary enters a lake-studded plateau, continuing northeast for another 175 miles (281.5 km.), again in a series of straight lines, only here and there following local creeks, until it reaches boundary mark no. 577, which is located in a woodland area about 60 miles (96.5 km.) northwest of Joensuu (Finland). The boundary then changes its direction and travels northwestward in a series of straight lines for about 300 miles (483 km.) in a hilly, uninhabited wilderness of forest and swamp. From a point between the towns of Kelloselkä (Finland) and Kuolayarvi (Russia), the boundary runs northeastward for 58 miles (93 km.) and enters the Arctic Circle. In the lowlands of the Arctic basin, east of Inari Lake, it runs northeastward again and in another series of straight lines, most of which average over 15 miles (24 km.) in length. Before reaching the Norwegian boundary tripoint at Krokfjell (69°03'N and 28°55'E), the boundary turns west for about 8.5 miles (14 km.) and then northwest for 2.5 miles (4 km.) to include the Jäniskoski power station in Russia. It then travels northeastward to the boundary tripoint with Norway.

Historical Background. As were most of the Eastern European boundaries, the Finnish–Russian boundary was formed in two stages: following World War I and following World War II. From the beginning of the nineteenth century Finland was a grand duchy belonging to the czarist empire of Russia and from 1809 to 1917 the Finnish–Russian border was an internal boundary of Russia. In December 1917, however, after the outbreak of the Russian Revolution, the Finns declared their independence and a mutually acceptable boundary was negotiated and delimited by the Treaty of Dorpat, signed on 14 October 1920. The treaty confirmed the existing boundary between the grand duchy of Finland and imperial Russia while transferring the northern Pechenga (Petsamo) region to Finland to allow Finland access to the Arctic Ocean. The boundary line then started from a point situated about 15 miles (24 km.) from the Soviet city of Leningrad and ran northward across Lake Ladoga. Until 1938 Finland and the Soviet Union surveyed and demarcated the entire boundary between the Arctic Ocean and the Baltic Sea.

During the early years of World War II, from November 1939 to March 1940, the Winter War between the Soviet Union and Finland took place after a Red Army attack on Finland. Subsequently, on 12 March 1940 the Finns were forced to sign an armistice agreement that led to the cession of eastern Karelia, the province of Salla and part of the Rybachi Peninsula of the Pechenga region. Finland lost about 10% of its population as well as its major port—Vyborg. In 1942, after the German attack on the Soviet Union, Finland regained its pre-1940 boundaries but in 1944 was forced to signed a second armistice agreement by which it not only returned to the 1940 boundary but it also lost the Pechenga area, thus returning to the pre-1920 boundary. Furthermore, as part of the postwar reparations, Finland ceded to the Soviet Union a hydroelectric power station at Jäniskoski, altering the section of the boundary near the Norwegian tripoint.

Present Situation. Since 1947 there have been no alterations made in the boundary line between Finland and Russia. The internal transformations of the Soviet Union did not have any effect on the Finland border region and there are no known disputes concerning this well demarcated boundary.

FINLAND — SWEDEN For its entire length this boundary line follows rivers and lakes and it is one of the oldest boundary lines, established early in the nineteenth century. It runs for 364.5 miles (586 km.) between the Norway boundary tripoint at the head of the Signal valley in the north and the mouth of the Torne River in the Baltic Sea in the south.

Finland–Sweden boundary

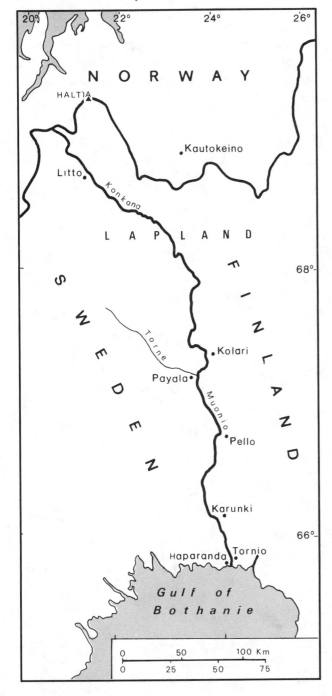

Geographical Setting. From the boundary tripoint on the watershed between the North Sea and the Gulf of Bothnia of Baltic the boundary line runs southeastward along a local stream, reaching the Kilpis Lakes. It crosses the lakes to the mouth of the Konkama River and follows the river to its confluence with the Lataseno River that flows from Finland, west of the Norwegian town of Karesuando. The boundary follows the joined river, the Muonio River, downstream southeastward to its confluence with the Torne River, which flows from Sweden, east of the Swedish town of Pajala. Thence it follows the Torne River downstream southward to its mouth in the Gulf of Bothnia in the Baltic Sea, between the towns of Haparanda (Sweden) and Tornio (Finland).

Historical Background. The area of today's Finland was occupied by Sweden in the mid-thirteenth century and its rule was recognized by Russia in 1323. The Finns and the Swedes then were united into one nation. Russia occupied Finland during the Northern War (1700–1721) but returned it to Sweden (except the southeastern province of Karelia). Russia occupied more Finnish territories in 1741–1743 and in 1808 the whole area of Finland was occupied by Russia. By the Treaty of Hamina (Fredrikshamm) of 17 September 1809, Sweden ceded Finland to Russia and a new boundary was established between the two states. The survey and demarcation of the boundary were accomplished in 1810 and 1824 and the Saint Petersburg Convention of 14 May 1826 established the boundary between Russia (including Finland) and Sweden (which at that time included Norway). It was to run along the Torne, Muonio and Kankama rivers northwestward and then along the watershed eastward. This protocol established the present boundary between Sweden and Finland. Problems evolving from the earlier delimitation were the basis for another survey and demarcation of the boundary line, which was completed in 1896.

Finland declared its independence on 6 December 1917 and its boundary with Sweden, which lost Norway in 1905, was established along the former Russia–Sweden boundary line from the Gulf of Bothnia to the Kilpis Lakes and the boundary tripoint with Norway.

Present Situation. Since 1826 no changes have

been made in the boundary's alignment. The boundary is very clear and no state has ever raised any claims concerning its neighbor's territory. This is one of the peaceful boundary lines that has never been in dispute.

FRANCE   A country in Western Europe (area: 212,860 sq. miles [551,307 sq. km.]; population: 57,600,000 [1994]), France is bounded in the north by Belgium (386 miles; 620 km.), in the northeast by Germany (280 miles; 451 km.) and Luxembourg (45 miles; 73 km.), in the east by Switzerland (356 miles; 570 km.) and Italy (303 miles; 488 km.) and in the south by Spain (387 miles; 623 km.), Andorra (37.5 miles; 60 km.) and the Mediterranean Sea. Along France's Mediterranean shore, close to the Italian boundary, it shares a common boundary with Monaco (2.7 miles; 4.4. km.). France also shares a boundary with the Netherlands in the small Caribbean island of Saint Martin. The capital of France is Paris.

From the seventeenth century, the French created one of the world's largest colonial empires; French settlers and cultural missions spread French language and culture around the world. As a result, about 90,000,000 people are French-speakers today. Besides being an official language in Belgium, Switzerland and Canada, French is widely spoken in the Val d'Aosta (Italy), in North Africa (the Maghreb), West Africa, Madagascar, the Caribbean, French Guiana, New Caledonia and the Pacific Islands. Most French are Catholic. Modern French descend from a mixture of populations, the oldest stratum being prehistoric Celts. In the second and first centuries B.C.E., the Romans conquered Gaul and exerted a culturally formative, although demographically negligible, influence. Germanic invaders (West Goths, Burgundians, Longobards, Alemans and Franks) were more numerous, but they too were absorbed into the Gallo-Roman culture. Infiltrating from the northeast and adopting Christianity in the sixth century, Franks became the dominant ethnic group and gave the French their name. However, a specific French consciousness did not appear until the twelfth century, when northern France was unified by a succession of kings who established their power over outlying provinces. Efforts to expel the English from western France during the Hundred

Years' War did much to institute a collective French identity. France went on to forge a centralized new entity, incorporating Normandy and eventually other provinces such as the Provence and Brittany. From the seventeenth century French kings attempted to assimilate the periphery by imposing linguistic and religious uniformity, becoming, in the process, Europe's foremost power. During the eighteenth century the social and intellectual influence of the bourgeoisie advanced; intellectuals criticized France's increasingly obsolescent *ancien régime*, which perpetuated the power of the aristocracy. The French Revolution (1789) abolished feudal particularism, achieved a high degree of unity, created a radically

France's northern and eastern boundaries

democratic regime and empowered the bourgeoisie. The empire of Napoleon Bonaparte (1804–1815) revolutionized the whole of Europe.

Throughout the nineteenth century the French continued to experiment with a variety of political arrangements. This was also an era of extraordinary cultural creativity. But while Paris remained the cultural capital of Europe, the French were demographically and economically overtaken by the more industrialized Germans. The catastrophic Franco-Prussian War (1870) ushered in the democratic Third Republic, but the loss of Alsace-Lorraine also fired French irredentism.

Although France emerged victorious from World War I, the disastrous consequences of the war fostered a defeatist attitude among many French; during World War II some collaborated with the Nazi occupation forces. At the same time, many French sought to restore their independence and integrity and formed several underground movements such as the *Maquis*, whose exploits against the Germans are now legendary.

Political instability and divisive colonial wars abroad marked the postwar era. It took the leadership of outstanding statesmen such as President Charles de Gaulle (1890–1970) to take drastic measures, such as ending French rule in Algeria, to provide a modicum of stability. Nonetheless, both the right and the left were dissatisfied with the turn of affairs in France—the May revolt in Paris (the "metaphysical revolution") of 1968 signaled the profound disillusionment of the young with the French government.

Past decades have witnessed the modernization of French economic and social life. Today France is quite industrialized, but most French remain small-town dwellers, with a strong rural element, making them one of Western Europe's most agrarian nations. After a long period of stagnation, the population is growing again, but France is still much less densely populated than most of its neighbors.

In recent years France has experienced the mass influx of immigrants from North Africa (1,500,000), as well as Portuguese, Spaniards (600,000), Italians (600,000) and Africans. The demographic weight (3%) and conspicuous presence of non-European Muslims on France's social map have nourished xenophobic nationalist movements.

French culture has become synonymous with a high quality of life. This achievement, however, has had its price with the "high" culture of court and capital affecting provincial and popular cultures. Whereas historically the center tried to gallicize peripheral regions such as French Flanders, Normandy, Provence and Alsace-Lorraine, such centralization has provoked regionalist reactions against Paris. Burgundy has retained an individuality reflecting its Middle Kingdom past and Swiss influence remains perceptible in the Franche Comte and the Jura; the proximity of Italy can be felt in Savoy and the Dauphine. Complete assimilation has clearly failed among the Bretons, Basques and Corsicans.

FRANCE — ANDORRA   see ANDORRA–FRANCE.

FRANCE — BELGIUM   see BELGIUM–FRANCE.

FRANCE — GERMANY   The boundary between France and Germany runs for 280 miles (451 km.) between a boundary junction with Luxembourg on the Moselle (Mosel) River in the northwest and the Swiss boundary on the Rhine (Rheine) River in the southeast. Its eastern section follows the Rhine River and the entire line mainly follows a nineteenth-century delineation.

Geographical Setting. From the northwestern terminus of the boundary line on the main navigation channel of the Moselle River, east of the small German town of Perl, the France–Germany boundary line runs southeastward for about 30 miles (50 km.), crossing the Nied River. It reaches the Metz (France)–Saarbrücken (Germany) railway north of the small French town of Bening and pursues it northeastward. Then the boundary runs eastward, south of Saarbrücken, to reach the Saar River. The line courses along the river upstream for 20 miles (32 km.), running southward, northeastward and eastward to a point northwest of the small French town of Bliesbruck. From there it continues eastward along the old boundary line of north Alsace, reaching the Lauter River east of the French town of Wissembourg. It follows that river downstream eastward to its confluence with the great Rhine River east of the small French town of Lauterbourg. The boundary then follows the main navigation channel of the Rhine River upstream southward for approximately 120 miles (195 km.) to the Swiss tri-point, which is located on the river, north of the Swiss town of Basel and east of Moningue (France).

Historical Background. The history of this boundary line marks the history of the last 1,000 years of French-German relations. In the Verdun Agreement of 843, the first boundary line was established on the Rhine River. In 880 the area of Lotharingia (Lorraine), between the Rhine and the Schelde rivers, became a German possession; that boundary held up until 1648, when the Peace of Westphalia, which ended the Thirty Years' War (1618–1648), placed the area of Alsace in French hands while the area west of the Rhine River was left under the rule of the Spanish Habsburg Empire. Under Louis XIV, France occupied all of Alsace up to the town of Strasbourg and even some territory east of the Rhine River (1681).

In 1738 the Austrian Empire, which gained control over the central European regions of the Spanish Empire after 1700, gave France the entire area of Lorraine, and the Aachen Peace of 1748 determined most of the present boundary between France and Germany. The Congress of Vienna, 1814–1815 reorganized Europe after Napoleon I formed the German Union (*Deutscher Bund*), reestablishing the boundary line as it had stood between France and the German states of Baden, Bavaria and Prussia in 1792. These states were united into the German Empire in 1870.

Three great wars between France and Germany between 1870 and 1945 (the 1870–1871 war, World War I and World War II) placed the region of Alsace-Lorraine in the hands of the victorious Germany in 1871 and during World War II while France gained control over it in 1918 and in 1945. However, the Treaty of Versailles of 1919 placed the boundary on the July 1870 line, which was reiterated after World War II. The French ruled the German Saar district from 1945 and only on 1 January 1957 did they withdraw from it.

Present Situation. Since 1957 there have been no disputes concerning the alignment of the France—Germany boundary. Once one of the more problematic European boundaries it is now one of the quietest boundary lines in the world.

FRANCE — ITALY The boundary line between France and Italy runs for 303 miles (488 km.) between the Swiss tripoint on Mount Dolent in the north and the Mediterranean coast east of Monaco in the south. Although it roughly coincides with the water divide separating the Rhone River basin (France) and the upper reaches of the Italian Po River, it leaves within France the historic Italian region of Savoy as well as the city of Nice (Nizza), once the center of Italian nationalism.

Geographical Setting. From the northern terminus of the boundary line, located on Mount Dolent (12,666 feet; 3,846 m.) in the northwestern Alps, the boundary runs southwestward, along the watershed between the L'Arve River (France) and the Dora di Ferret River (Italy). It reaches the peaks of Aig de Triolet (12,694 feet; 3,870 m.), Aig de Talefre (12,234 feet; 3,730 m.), Grandes Jorasses (13,802 feet; 4,208 m.) and Aig du Geant (13,163 feet; 4,013 m.) and passes the railway and tunnel between

France–Italy boundary crossing, on the Mediterranean coast

Chamonix-Mont Blanc (France) and Aosta. It then reaches Mont Blanc (White Mountain), the highest European mountain (15,767 feet; 4,807 m.), whose peak is located in France.

The boundary line continues westward, reaching the peak of Aig de Bionnassay (13,291 feet; 4,052 m.), and then runs southward, passes the Col da Bonhomme pass and reaches the Aosta–Bourg (France) road north of the Petit (Small) Saint Bernard pass. The boundary line continues to run southeastward along the watershed, passes through the Col du Mont pass (8,679 feet; 2,646 m.) and over the peak of Sassiere (12,320 feet; 3,756 m.) and reaches Mount Levanna (11,870 feet; 3,619 m.). Thence the boundary runs southward, reaches Rocciamelone Peak (11,601 feet; 3,537 m.), runs southwestward, through the Frejus tunnel, crossing the Torino (Italy)–Grenoble (France) railway, which runs in the Mount Cenis tunnel, and reaches the Frejus Pass (8,331 feet; 2,540 m.). The boundary heads southeastward, crosses the Briancon (France)–Cesano (Italy) road in the Mount Genevre pass, reaching Merclantaira Peak (10,798 feet; 3,292 m.), and passes through the Lacroix and Traversetta passes to arrive at Mount Viso (12,600 feet; 3,841 m.). Continuing southward, it crosses the Barcelonnette (France)–Cuneo (Italy) road and trends eastward along the watershed of the southern Alps, crossing the Nice (France)–Cuneo road. After reaching the upper valley of the La Roya River, it bears southward, crossing the La Roya River east of Piena (France) and reaches the Mediterranean coast between the commune of Mentone (France) and the commune of Ventimiglia (Vintimille, Italy).

Historical Background. Since the second century B.C.E. the north–south chain of the Alps between the Mont Blanc area and the Mediterranean has served as a "Natural frontier." Although the crest of the Alps was generally accepted as a boundary, many problems continued to arise in response to the placement and dominance of military installations, to human occupancy of the habitable land and to the routes across the mountain barrier or to remote settlements within it.

For many centuries the boundary line between France and Italy was shifted eastward and westward. France was organized as an independent state from the ninth century onward, while modern Italy be-

came independent only in the mid-nineteenth century. Treaties that determined the present boundary between the two states go back to the Treaty of Turin, signed on 24 March 1860. Under the terms of that treaty, the historic region of Savoy and the town of Nice were given to France, which helped the Italians in their war of independence against the Austrian Empire. A mixed commission was charged with the establishment of a boundary between France and Italy, although the subsequent convention of delimitation, signed at Turin on 7 March 1861, created a boundary that departed from the details of the originally projected alignment. Some ratifications were made in Italy's favor, the line having been shifted westward in places to follow artificial rather than natural features. As a result France was deprived of the heads of valleys in several places, as between the Col de Lunga and the Cime du Duable. In 1874 a small ratification of France's favor was made in the Mount Cenis railway tunnel near Modane.

During World War II Italy occupied an area in southeastern France, but at the conclusion of the war France took the opportunity to modify its boundary with the defeated Italy in such a way that it would generally coincide with the watershed. The Italian Peace Treaty of 10 February 1947 afforded the occasion to incorporate the changes long desired by France. Five areas, amounting to 268 sq. miles (694 sq. km.), were transferred from Italy to France in the Little Saint Bernard Pass, Mount Cenis plateau, Mount Thabor, Chaberton and the upper valleys of the Tintee, Vesubie and Roya rivers. Another change took place in November 1948, when a shift of 655 feet (200 m.) in the Little Saint Bernard Pass was made to the benefit of France.

Present Situation. Since 1948 there have been no changes in the French–Italian boundary and there are no disputes concerning its alignment. The border area is a peaceful one and for now, with the steps to unify Europe, the boundary is weakening its military activity.

FRANCE — LUXEMBOURG The boundary between France and Luxembourg runs for 45 miles (73 km.) between the boundary tripoint with Germany on the Mosel (Moselle) River in the east and the tripoint with Belgium on a tributary of the Chiers

France–Luxembourg boundary crossing

River in the west. It follows old administrative lines between local communities.

Geographical Setting. From the main navigation channel of the Mosel River at its intersection with the Saarburg (Germany)–Thionville (France) road, the boundary runs westward, reaching a northwestern tributary of the Mosel River, which it follows upstream westward for 2 miles (3 km.). It crosses the local road between Mondorf-les-Bains (Luxembourg) and Beyren (France) and then reaches the main highway between Luxembourg and Metz (France), south of Frisange (Luxembourg). The line follows a local stream for 1 mile (1.6 km.), runs southwest, crosses the railway between Luxembourg and Metz and meets the local road between Rumelange (Luxembourg) and Ottange (France), where one of the seven boundary crossings is located. Heading west for about 3 miles (5 km.) and then continuing northwest, the boundary reaches a junction point on the Esch (Luxembourg)–Aumetz (France) road, where it intersects the Alzette River. From there it bears northwest for about 10 miles (16 km.) to the boundary junction with Belgium. This terminus is situated on the main road between Luxembourg and Longuyon (France) where it meets with a northeastern tributary of the Chiers River, northeast of the French town of Longwy.

Historical Background. Luxembourg became a duchy in 1354 and was ruled by Spain and Austria from 1482. Along with Belgium, it was ceded to revolutionary France in 1797. In the Vienna Treaty of 1815 Luxembourg was established as a grand duchy, was placed under the rule of the king of Netherlands and its southern boundary with France was delimited. Belgium became an independent state in 1831, including most of western Luxembourg. The French boundary with what remained of the Grand Duchy of Luxembourg was delimited by the act appended to the peace treaty of 19 April 1839 between Belgium and Netherlands and was placed under the guarantee of the courts of Austria, Great Britain, France, Prussia and Russia. Luxembourg gained independence in 1848, dissolved its ties with the German Federation in 1867 and then declared itself a neutral state.

Present Situation. Despite the political history of Western Europe, which delimited its boundaries time after time, the France–Luxembourg boundary has not been changed since 1839. There are no disputes concerning its alignment and it is, in fact, one of the world's most peaceful boundaries.

FRANCE — MONACO This semicircular boundary between France and Monaco runs for 2.7 miles

France–Monaco boundary

(4.4 km.) running between two points located on the Mediterranean coast in southeastern France, near the Italian border.

Geographical Setting. Monaco is surrounded on three sides by the French department of Alpes-Maritimes, about 10 miles (16 km.) east of the French city of Nice. It is located around a natural port and within it there are three small towns, those of Monaco, Monte Carlo and La Condamin. The city of Monaco is situated on a rocky cape, La Condamin; north of the Monaco bay is the port and commercial area; and Monte Carlo, with its famous casino, is built on a cliff northeast of La Condamin, in the riviera. The eastern terminus of the boundary line, located on the coast east of Monte Carlo, runs northwestward, north of the town of La Condamin, and then heads southwestward to reach the Mediterranean Sea west of the cliff on which the town of Monaco is situated.

Historical Background. The Principality of Monaco (its name comes from the local temple built by the Greek to Herakles Monoykos), was established in 1070 under the Grimaldis. In 1297 it came under the patronage of Genoa and between 1524 and 1641 was under Spain. From 1641 Monaco remained under French suzerainty and was taken by the French Republic in 1793. In 1814 Monaco was given back to the Grimaldi family and was placed under the Kingdom of Sardinia. In 1861 it was placed under France again on the condition that it would be incorporated into France should the ruling prince have no children. Monaco's boundary never changed through the whole period.

Present Situation. There are no disputes concerning the alignment of the boundary, which is recognized by both states.

FRANCE — SPAIN   The boundary line between France and Spain runs along the Pyrenees mountains for a total of 387 miles (623 km.) in two sectors that are divided by Andorra. From the western Mediterranean Sea in the east the boundary runs to the mouth of the Bidassoa River in the Bay of Biscay in the west. This is one of the oldest stable boundaries in the world, established in the mid-seventeenth century and unchanged since then.

Geographical Setting. The easternmost terminus of the boundary is located on Cape Cerbère on the Mediterranean shore, between Banyuls (France) and Llansá (Spain). It heads westward, reaches the foothills of Monts Albéres and follows the watershed along it, between the Tech (France) and Ter (Spain) rivers. It crosses the main highway that links Perpignan (France) and Figueras (Spain) and continues westward along the watershed, to reach Donya Peak (8,902 feet; 2,714 m.). It then trends southwest along the watershed, reaching Puigmal Peak (9,551 feet; 2,912 m.), and northwest to the road between Mont Louis (France) and Puigcerdá (Spain). The boundary crosses the road and runs west for about 15 miles (25 km.) to reach the eastern Andorran tripoint, which is located west of Costabon Peak (9,557 feet; 2,914 m.).

Northeast of Puigcerdá, within the French boundary, is the Spanish exclave town of Llivia. Llivia was left in Spanish hands as it was a town rather than a village when the rural area of the province of Roussillon was transferred from Spain to France in 1659. A "peace road" connecting Spain with Llivia runs through French territory.

The western section of the boundary between France and Spain begins at the western tripoint with Andorra, south of the source of the Arieje River, which runs northward into France. The boundary follows the watershed of the central Pyrenees mountains northwestward, reaching Turgulla Peak (8,183 feet; 2,495 m.) and heading westward along the wa-

tershed, over the peak of Mount Rocuch (9,397 feet; 2,865 m.). It leaves the watershed, reaches the mountain pass of Pont du Roi on the Garonne River, which runs from Spain to France, and then arrives at Bacanere Peak (7,196 feet; 2,194 m.). At this point it turns and heads southward for about 15 miles (25 km.) and then continues westward along the highest section of the Pyrenees mountains, reaching the peaks of Port de Oo (10,214 feet; 3,114 m.) and Vignemale (10,817 feet; 3,298 m.)—the boundary's highest point. Running westward, it reaches Pourtalet Pass (5,888 feet; 1,795 m.), crosses the road between Sallent (Spain) and Laruns (France) and meets Somport Pass (5,379 feet; 1,640 m.), where a road and tunnel link Jaca (Spain) and Urdus (France). Thence the boundary runs northwestward, reaches Anie Peak (8,213 feet; 2,504 m.) and proceeds westward again, along the watershed of the western Pyrenees, reaching the main road between Pamplona (Spain) and Orthez (France). It runs south, west and north, leaving with France the villages of Urepel, Aldudes and Banca. While traversing north, the boundary line passes Mount Auza

France–Spain boundary crossing point

(4,277 feet; 1,304 m.), follows the watershed between the Bidassoa (Spain) and Nive (France) rivers, crosses the main road between Pamplona and Bayonne (France) and leaves the watershed to arrive at the Bidassoa River. For the last 5 miles (8 km.) the boundary follows the river downstream northwestward to its mouth in the Bay of Biscay, between the towns of Irún (Spain) and Behobie (France), on the highway between San Sebastián (Spain) and Biarritz (France).

Historical Background. The Pyrenees mountains have served as the boundary between France and Spain for many centuries. The Romans divided Gallia (France) and Hispania (Spain) along the range and later the Arabs, who occupied the Iberian Peninsula in the eighth century, retreated south of the Pyrenees after they were defeated in France. Between the ninth and seventeenth centuries, the Pyrenees became the boundary between France and Spain, although from time to time some areas south of the mountains were ruled by France, while toward the late sixteenth century Spain ruled the province of Roussillon, north of the eastern Pyrenees. During the Thirty Years' War (1618–1648) Spain lost some territories north and east of France (the Low Countries and the French Comte) and later France and Spain continued their struggle for European hegemony. The war ended with the Treaty of the Pyrenees, signed on 7 November 1659, in which it was agreed that the Pyrenees, which had anciently divided the Gauls (France) from Spain, be established as the division between Spain and France. France (under its king, who held the title Most Christian King) remained in possession of the entire Counties of Roussillon and Conflans, while Spain (under the Catholic King) held the county of Cerdagne and the principality of Catalonia. It was agreed that any area of Conflans south of the Pyrenees would belong to Spain, while any area belonging to Cerdagne and Catalonia situated north of the Pyrenees would remain in France. This was not the case, however, with Roussillon, which was placed as a whole under the French king. It was agreed in the treaty that within a month a special commission would define the Pyrenees mountains, which are about 40 miles (65 km.) wide, for the placing of the boundary line.

Thus, the boundary was established. Over the next 335 years, despite the major changes that formed and reformed the European nations in general and the political histories of France and Spain in particular, no changes in the location of the boundary line were made.

Present Situation. The 1659 boundary has been maintained to the present day and has been demarcated without modification several times since. There are no known disputes concerning the alignment of the boundary, which is familiar to the inhabitants of the region.

FRANCE—SWITZERLAND The boundary between France and Switzerland runs for 356 miles (570 km.) from the boundary junction with Italy at Mount Dolent in the Alps to the boundary junction with Germany on the Rhine River.

Geographical Setting. From the southern terminus of the boundary line between France and Switzerland at Mount Dolent (12,616 feet; 3,846 m.) it runs northwestward for 45 miles (72 km.) along the watershed between the Swiss part of the Rhone River and the French rivers of Arig and Drance until it reaches Lake Geneva near the city of Saint Gingolph. It enters the lake, running through it along the median line between the cities of Hermance (Switzerland) and Saint Gingolph. This section of the line was defined theoretically according to the locus of circle centers located between the Swiss and French banks, but for practical reasons it is superseded by a polygonal line of six sides, equally dividing the surface of the lake. From Hermance the boundary line runs southward and then westward in a semicircle to leave the city of Geneva in Switzerland, until it reaches the western part of the Rhone River. It then runs northward and eastward to reach a point situated east of the lake. Coursing northeastward through the Jura Plateau, the boundary line reaches the Doubs River, which is one of the main tributaries of the French Saône River, then following the median line of the Doubs River for about 25 miles (40 km.). Leaving the river, the boundary turns northward, then circling eastward to leave the valley of Porrentruy in Switzerland. Thence the line travels eastward and northeastward until it reaches the northern terminus of the boundary at the Rhine River near the city of Basel.

Historical Background. The boundary line

Crossing point on the France–Switzerland border

separating France and Switzerland is one of the oldest boundaries in Europe. Officially, it dates from the Second Treaty of Paris (20 May 1814), which recognized the independence of the Swiss Confederation with boundaries substantially as at present. This treaty, however, reconfirmed lines defined in numerous treaties previously concluded between the kingdom of France on the one hand and the prince-bishopric of Basel, the principality of Neuchâtel, the canton of Vaud (under the control of Bern) and the republic of Geneva on the other, dating between the sixteenth and the eighteenth centuries. The 1814 line was confirmed by a boundary convention signed at Bern on 9 July 1818 and a boundary demarcation team completed the demarcation of the line on 4 November 1824.

A strategic route in the valley of Dappes, a source of irritation between the two countries, was ceded to France on 8 December 1862 in exchange for a like territory immediately to the north.

After World War II, adjustments were necessary for clearing some minor boundary problems. On 25 February 1953 France and Switzerland signed two conventions. One of them deals with a minor modification of the boundary in the area between Basel

and the Doubs River, the other determines the boundary in Lake Geneva. Further adjustments were also necessary to keep the entire site of the expanded Geneva-Cointrin airport in Switzerland. Thus, on 3 December 1959 a new border document was signed between France and the Swiss canton of Basel-Stadt. With the expansion of the European Center for Nuclear Research in Geneva, however, the boundary line was simply ignored, the international boundary now passing through the middle of the site.

Present Situation. There are no disputes concerning the boundary alignment. At the time of delineation, French and Swiss farmers owned lands on opposite sides—Swiss farmers from the canton of Geneva still cultivate 2,260 hectares (5,582 acres) in the adjoining French area. In some areas the boundary line has created small enclaves entirely surrounded by the other state's territory; in other areas traditional local regions are divided by the border.

Legislation, treaties and agreements have been enacted to facilitate the lives of border inhabitants. Import and export of goods for everyday use and local agricultural products grown within a 6.3 miles (10 km.) radius of the customs crossing are duty free.

The pasturing of cattle on both sides of the border is regulated by an agreement signed on 23 October 1912. Free passage for inhabitants of border communities is controlled according to agreements dating from 1825 and 1938. The unrestricted right of passage for the Swiss military using the Swiss railway through French territory was determined on 12 May 1966. A similar agreement enables Swiss farmers from the canton of Basel to pass through French territory to reach their land and allows French farmers to do the same.

FRENCH GUIANA (Guyane française)

French Guiana is a French overseas department and an administrative region of France (area: 35,125 sq. miles [90,973 sq. km.]; estimated population: 129,000 [1994]), situated on the northeastern coast of South America. It is bounded in the west by Suriname (317 miles; 510 km.) and in the south and east by Brazil (418 miles; 673 km.). Its capital is Cayenne.

The interior of the country is sparsely populated: there are areas of Amerindian settlement in the Haut-Maroni and Haut-Oyapock. Half the population lives in Cayenne, the capital and chief port.

French Guiana has become infamous in popular lore as a French prison colony, especially because of the description of Devil's Island, in active use from 1859 through 1945, in Henri Charriere's novel *Papillon*. A less well-known, but more positive aspect of French Guianese history, was the pioneering clerical community at Mana, active from 1827 through 1846, which inaugurated formal education for freed black slaves and women.

In 1946 the colony became an overseas department of France. Political movements have arisen among the French Guianese for greater autonomy.

FRENCH GUIANA — BRAZIL

see BRAZIL–FRENCH GUIANA.

FRENCH GUIANA — SURINAME

The French Guiana–Suriname boundary is 317 miles (510 km.) long and reaches from the mouth of the Maroni River in the Atlantic Ocean in the north to the boundary tripoint with Brazil in the south. It follows a colonial boundary between Dutch and French possessions in northern South America.

Geographical Setting. The northern terminus of the boundary line is centered in the mouth of the Maroni River, which flows from south to north into the Atlantic Ocean. The line follows the main navigation channel of the river upstream southward to its confluence with the Lawa River near the town of Grand-Santi (French Guiana). It follows the Lawa River upstream southeastward to its confluence with the Itany (Litani) River and follows that river upstream southwestward to a point south of the town of Panapie (Suriname). There the boundary line leaves the river and runs along a small tributary southwest toward the boundary tripoint with Brazil, on the watershed between the northern tributaries of the Jari River, which runs into the great Amazon River (Brazil), and the Itany River.

Historical Background. Cayenne was founded by French traders in 1635 and subsequently small groups of colonists were sent from France by various companies. The territory became the property of the French crown in 1674. In 1667 Suriname came under Dutch rule and in 1688 France and Netherlands agreed that the Maroni River would constitute the boundary between their South American colonies, although neither had any knowledge regarding the upper course of the river. French Guiana was occupied by the Portuguese between 1809 and 1817, after which the colony became more prosperous, the interior was explored and more colonists arrived from France. Meanwhile, Dutch colonists were exploring and settling the area between the Tapanahoni and Lawa rivers, both tributaries of the Maroni. In 1836 the Dutch and French colonial governors agreed that the right bank of the Maroni to its source should be their boundary, but specified neither the Lawa nor the Tapanahoni as the source. In 1849 the Dutch government repudiated the agreement and the governors tried again in 1861 but failed to reach a conclusive decision.

In 1888 France and Netherlands agreed to submit the matter to Czar Alexander III of Russia for arbitration. The czar's award of May 1891 concluded that the Lawa River should be considered the upper course of the Maroni River and thus the boundary between the two colonies. Both parties accepted this decision, although the question of the boundary south of the Lawa River was left unanswered and became an important issue as settlement increased in the region. At a conference in The Hague in 1905, an agreement specified the Itany River as the boundary, but the agreement was never consummated. A decade later, on 30 September 1915, France and Netherlands signed a convention in Paris that accepted the Itany boundary, provided for a precise midriver alignment from one island to another and described various uses of the river.

Despite this agreement, the Dutch continued to claim the Marouini River (east of the Itany River) as the boundary and intermittent discussions failed to settle the matter. When Suriname became independent in 1975 it assumed the Dutch claim. Negotiations conducted in November 1975 and February 1977 produced a treaty between France and Suriname, by which Suriname recognized French sovereignty over most of the area in dispute, in exchange for 500 million francs as aid for joint development of any resources in the area. The treaty was initialled on 15 August 1977, but, despite further meetings in August 1978, it has not yet been signed. **Present Situation.** Since a military coup in Suriname in 1980, relations between the two countries have been poor and there has been no significant movement toward a final resolution of the dispute, the question remaining which of the upper tributaries of the Maroni River was originally intended to carry the boundary down to the Brazilian border. Surinamese maps show the disputed area as its own, while it is officially administered by France as a region of the overseas department of French Guiana.

No negotiations on the issue are currently underway or projected.

FRENCH POLYNESIA Constituted by a group of islands located in the South Pacific Ocean, French Polynesia has no land boundaries and its total land area is 1,545 sq. miles (4,000 sq. km.). Its capital is Papeete and the islands' estimated population is 210,000 (1994).

French Polynesia has been an overseas territory of France since 1957; it gained increased local autonomy in 1977. Although French law governs land tenure, in practice the old Polynesian system of joint land ownership still largely prevails today. Over 85% of the land is in Polynesian hands, a large amount of which is leased to the Chinese minority. The French government is responsible for conducting the external affairs of the territory, although by a constitutional settlement of 1990, the territorial government was enabled to enter into treaties with other Pacific states.

The economy of the islands is dominated by income from France. Agriculture and fishing provide most of French Polynesian exports. Coconuts and vanilla are the principal cash crops. Tourism is a main foreign exchange earner but it is currently affected by adverse environmental consequences from nuclear testing—underground nuclear tests have taken place on the island of Moruroa for more than 20 years.

G

GABON   A country in western Central Africa (area: 103,346 sq. miles [267,667 sq. km.]; estimated population: 1,210,000 [1994]), Gabon is bounded in the north by Equatorial Guinea (217.5 miles; 350 km.) and Cameroon (185 miles; 298 km.) and in the east and south by Congo (1,183 miles; 1,903 km.). The capital of Gabon is Libreville.

GABON — CAMEROON   see CAMEROON–GABON.

GABON — CONGO   see CONGO–GABON.

GABON — EQUATORIAL GUINEA   see EQUATORIAL GUINEA–GABON.

GAMBIA   The Gambia is a west African country (area: 4,127 sq. miles [10,689 sq. km.]; estimated population: 920,000 [1994]), located on the River Gambia, consisting of a strip of territory on both banks of the river. It is a narrow country, the widest area covering no more than 6 miles (10 km.), bounded on all sides by Senegal (460 miles; 740 km.) but open to the Atlantic Ocean in the west. The Gambia's capital is Banjul.

The people of the Gambia are divided among a number of ethnic groups, the principal of which are the Malinke, Fulani, Wolof, Diola and Soninke. Each has its own language, but the country's official language is English. About 85% are Muslims, the rest are mainly Christians, with a small number who adhere to traditional religions.

The Gambia is one of Africa's smallest states. It is a semi-enclave in Senegal, but Gambian history and colonial experience differ from those of the Senegalese. The Gambians became independent from colonial rule by the British in February 1965. The

Gambia–Senegal boundary

People's Progressive Party (PPP), the dominant party since independence, has tried to integrate all ethnic groups despite its initial identification with the Malinke. The Gambia's democratic and peaceful political life was interupted in 1981 by an attempted coup against the president, Dawda Jawara, which was averted with the intervention of the Senegalese army. As a result, the Senegambian confederation was established. It was dissolved in 1990, mainly because of Gambian fear of domination by the more numerous Senegalese.

GAMBIA — SENEGAL The boundary between the Gambia and Senegal extends for 460 miles (740 km.). It follows both sides of the Gambia River for about 200 miles (322 km.), from the Atlantic Ocean eastward, running parallel to the river at a distance of no more than 6 miles (10 km.) from it. The entire line is demarcated by pillars.

Geographical Setting. The northern sector of the boundary line begins at a point on the shore of the Atlantic Ocean, where it converges with Jinnak Creek, north of the mouth of the Gambia River. From that point the boundary follows parallel 13°36'N and runs for 68 miles (110 km.) to the point where the Gambia River forms a sharp bend and converges with Sarmi Creek. From here the boundary follows the northern bank of the river as far as Yarboutenda (Gambia) at a distance of 6 miles (10 km.) from the river.

The southern boundary line starts in the mouth of San Pedro River. It follows the bank of the river as far as 13°10'N and then continues along this parallel as far as Sandeng, which is located at the end of Vintang Creek. The line then runs northward toward the Gambia River, following the meridian that passes through Sandeng up to a point that stands at a distance of 6 miles (10 km.) from the river. Maintaining this distance, it runs parallel to the southern bank of the river as far as, Fatoto, south of Yarboutenda. The northern and southern lines meet at a point situated about 6 miles (10 km.) east of Yarboutenda, in the Gambia River.

Historical Background. In 1588 the British set up a commercial station at the mouth of the Gambia River and founded the city of Bathurst in 1826. During the same period the French established themselves in Senegal, north and south of the river. In

1843 the coastal region became a British colony, while the upper river area, around Georgetown, became a British protectorate. The Gambia was then disconnected from the neighboring French rule by an agreement signed on 10 August 1889 and boundary commissions demarcated the line in 1895–1896, 1898–1899 and 1904–1905. In 1904 Britain undertook to transfer the Yarboutenda area to France, but the conditions of the transfer were not clear and the boundary remained unchanged. In 1911, however, the demarcation of a small section of the boundary was modified.

Senegal became an independent state in 1960 and the Gambia achieved independence in 1965—both with the boundaries of 1889. The text of the 1889 agreement selected the small town of Yarboutenda as the center of a 6-mile (10-km.) radius that forms the extreme sector of the boundary line. This definition led to a delimitation problem concerning the sector, which remained unsolved until it was clarified in 1976.

Present Situation. The entire boundary line is now demarcated. Since the Heads of States Agreement of 18 January 1976 there have not been any disputes concerning the line between the Gambia and Senegal.

GEORGIA (Sakartvelo) Georgia (area: 26,911 sq. miles [69,700 sq. km.]; estimated population: 5,600,000 [1994]) became an independent country in 1991 after the collapse of the Soviet Union. Georgia is situated in the western part of the Transcaucasian area on the shore of the Black Sea. It is bounded by Turkey (156.5 miles; 252 km.), Armenia (102 miles; 164 km.) and Azerbaijan (200 miles; 322 km.) in the south and by Russia in the north (450 miles; 723 km.). Its capital is T'bilisi.

In the fifteenth century the Georgian kingdom was divided into several political units. In 1801 the east Georgian kingdom was abolished and Georgia was included in the Russian empire. Other parts of Georgia came under Russian rule between 1803 and 1878.

Georgia's independence was restored in the period 1917–1921, in the aftermath of the Russian revolution; in 1922 it became part of the Transcaucasian Socialist Federative Soviet Republic, and from 1936 it was a Soviet Socialist Republic. In 1991 Georgia

Georgia's boundaries

declared its independence. The capital of Georgia from the third to the beginning of the sixth century was Armazg-Mzcheta; since then the capital has been T'bilisi.

GEORGIA — ARMENIA   See ARMENIA–GEORGIA.

GEORGIA — AZERBAIJAN   see AZERBAIJAN–GEORGIA.

GEORGIA — RUSSIA   This undemarcated boundary line follows an internal boundary between two republics of the former Soviet Union. It is 450 miles (723 km.) long and runs from the Black Sea in the west to the boundary tripoint with Azerbaijan in the east.

Geographical Setting. The westernmost point of the Georgia–Russia boundary is located southeast of the city of Sochi (Russia), at the intersection of the Black Sea coast with the 40°E meridian. From there it runs northeast for about 15 miles (25 km.) to the main watershed of the Caucasus region. It follows the watershed southeastward—with three main exceptions. The highest Caucasian peak, Mount Elbrus (18,510 feet; 6,073 m.), which is considered by some the highest peak in Europe, and the peak of Dykh Tau (17,010 feet; 5,581 m.) are located in Russian territory, while Mount Kazbek (16,558 feet; 5,432 m.) is located in Georgia, placing the source of the Terek River in that country too. The third exception is in the eastern section of the boundary line, where the source of the east-flowing Andiyskoye River is located in Georgian territory. Apart from these deviations, the boundary line follows the main crest of the Caucasus mountains, reaching the boundary tripoint with Azerbaijan, on the watershed, east of the small Georgian town of Lagodekhi.

Historical Background. Georgia was an ancient kingdom that became a Christian country attached to the Russian Orthodox Church early in the Middle Ages. It was occupied by the Turks in the fifteenth century and by Russia in the nineteenth century. During World War I it became an independent state (28 May 1918) following the separation of the Georgian

Church and the Russian Church in 1917. On 3 March 1922 Georgia became part of the Transcaucasian Federation, which joined the Soviet Union on 6 July 1923. In 1936 Georgia was established as a constituent republic within the Soviet Union, and its boundary with the Republic of Russia was established by the central authorities in Moscow, initially by Georgia's most important politician, Joseph Stalin. Frequent changes were made along this boundary, based on national and religious factors, but it did not have the status of a state boundary. Georgia became an independent state in April 1991, while Russia, as a separate state, organized the Commonwealth of Independent States, which was not joined by Georgia. Both states adopted the last internal division as their common international boundary without a formal agreement.

Present Situation. Both countries have problems with local districts that seek independence along their common boundary. The Chechen Republic, on the Russian side of the boundary's eastern section; the Georgian province of Abkhazia, on the western side of the border; and the South Ossetian Autonomous Republic, on Georgia's eastern side; are all claiming independence. There are also some demands to transfer the southern area of Greater Sochi (Russia) to Georgia. However, since independence neither Russia nor Georgia has raised formal controversies concerning the alignment of their common boundary.

GEORGIA — TURKEY The present boundary between Georgia and Turkey is the northern section of the former Soviet Union–Turkey boundary. It is 156.5 miles (252 km.) long and extends from the Black Sea to the boundary tripoint with Armenia. The border region mainly crosses the Armenian plateau, with elevations averaging 5,000–7,000 feet (1,500–2,100 m.).

Geographical Setting. The Georgia–Turkey boundary begins on the Black Sea coast in the west, south of the Georgian village of Sarpi, which is located about 10 miles (16 km.) southwest of the Georgian capital of Batumi. It runs eastward in a woodland area, following a drainage divide for 9 miles (15 km.) until it reaches the Çoruh (Choroch) River. It then joins the river to the south on its western (Turkish) bank for 1.5 miles (2.5 km.), where it leaves the

river and travels eastward for 50 miles (80 km.), following the drainage channels up to Kanli Mountain (7,500 feet; 2,280 m.). From there the boundary runs northeastward for about 12 miles (20 km.) and another 12 miles (20 km.) eastward. Then trending generally southeastward, the line enters the Kura River and follows it upstream for 5 miles (8 km.). It leaves the river and continues eastward, reaching Hazapin (Khozapini) Lake and crossing it in a southeasterly direction. Thence the boundary runs eastward for another 18 miles (29 km.) until it reaches the tripoint border junction with Armenia.

Historical Background. As a section of the Soviet–Turkish boundary, which evolved from the original Turkey–Russia boundary, the background to the Georgia–Turkey border is a part of Transcaucasian history. After centuries of Ottoman rule, the Russians arrived in the border region at the beginning of the nineteenth century, gradually extending their boundaries southward at the expense of the Ottoman

The Turkish town of Rize, east of the Georgia–Turkey boundary

Empire. In 1878, by the Treaty of Berlin, Russia gained the provinces of Batumi, Ardahan and Kars from Turkey and established themselves south of the present boundary. In 1918, after Russia's withdrawal from World War I, Turkey retrieved these provinces, but negotiations between Turkey and the newly established Soviet Union reestablished the boundary along the 1878 line with the Soviet-Turkish Treaty of Moscow, signed on 16 March 1921. In 1936 Georgia became a separate constituent republic of the Soviet Union and later, in 1992, became independent Georgia.

Present Situation. Since March 1921 the boundary has remained unchanged. As it was delimited by officials from Istanbul and Moscow, the needs of the local inhabitants were never considered adequately, the line near the Black Sea running through the area inhabited by the Lazs, who are akin to the Muslims of Georgia rather than to the Turkish people. On that ground, Georgia suggested after World War II that an area stretching 180 miles (290 km.) along the Turkish Black Sea be annexed to Georgia. The Turks flatly refused and since then no disputes have been recorded concerning the location of the boundary line.

GERMANY (Deutschland) Germany is a country situated in Central Europe. In 1990 the German Democratic Republic (East Germany) was integrated into the Federal Republic of Germany (West Germany), becoming a united country (area: 137,818 sq. miles [356,950 sq. km.]; estimated population: 80,800,000 [1994]). Germany is bounded in the north by Denmark (42.5 miles; 68 km.) and the Baltic Sea, in the east by Poland (284 miles; 456 km.) and the Czech Republic (507 miles; 815 km.), in the southeast by Austria (487 miles; 780 km.), in the south by Switzerland (208 miles; 334 km.) and in the west by France (280 miles; 451 km.), Luxembourg (86 miles; 138 km.), Belgium (104 miles; 167 km.) and Netherlands (359 miles; 577 km.). The capital of Germany is Berlin.

The Germans descend from Indo-European peoples such as Franks, Saxons and Bavarians who, in the first centuries B.C.E., expanded along the North and Baltic Seas. Confrontation with the Romans was the first formative influence: Rhineland's ancient urban culture is a Roman contribution. Germany came into being in the ninth century in the eastern area of Charlemagne's partitioned empire, which eventually evolved into the Holy Roman Empire. However, German emperors failed to establish strong authority and their realm was fragmented into several power-bases. In the Middle Ages Hanseatic towns dominated northern Europe economically. From the thirteenth century population and economic growth led to commercial expansion into and colonization of Poland, Bohemia and Hungary. As Germans extended their hold over the eastern frontier, they Germanized and Christianized the local population. Of great importance was the colonization of the Baltic regions of Prussia under the Order of the Teutonic Knights.

In the sixteenth century Martin Luther and other Germans were among the vanguard of the Reformation, a formative moment of Germany's national consciousness. However, the Counter-Reformation succeeded in reclaiming southern Germany for Catholicism. Wars of religion, in particular the Thirty Years' War (1618–1648), left the country fragmented in hundreds of disconnected and weak principalities for centuries. The Napoleonic invasions destroyed feudalism and serfdom but simultaneously catalyzed a nationalist reaction led by Prussia, the dominant political and military power of northern Germany.

Mid-nineteenth century attempts to unify Germans by means of a liberal revolution fell through. It took another generation before Prussian chancellor Otto von Bismarck succeeded, around 1870, in imposing unity and welding together the different German regions (except for the Habsburg-dominated Austrian territories) into one empire. Rapidly industrializing and with a growing population, it became at once Europe's foremost political, economic and military power. German culture dominated European philosophy, social and natural sciences, and technology. Latecomers in the imperial race for colonies, they directed their energies toward Central Europe. World War I resulted in defeat, territorial losses and revolution. The 1920s' Weimar Republic lacked domestic legitimacy. In the early 1930s, the National Socialists came to power on a program of hyper-nationalism, and established a dictatorial regime led by Adolf Hitler. A combination of terror by state, party and security organs, as well as a corporate economy efficiently crushed all opposition. The Nazis launched Germany on a course of militarization and unlimited expansion.

After World War II Germany was laid waste and occupied by the Allied powers. They divided it into Western and Eastern zones, which soon matured into the Federal Republic of Germany (FRG) and German Democratic Republic (GDR), respectively.

After the war, 10,000,000 ethnic Germans—often centuries-old communities—were expelled from Central and Eastern Europe, throwing back the ethnic border between the Germans and the Slavs to the Oder-Neisse line: 7,000,000 from Posen, Silesia, Pomerania and East Prussia (now part of Poland), and another 350,000 from Poland in its prewar borders, 2,000,000 Sudeten Germans from Czechoslovakia, 200,000 from Hungary, 140,000 from Yugoslavia, 123,000 from Romanian Transylvania, 400,000 from the Soviet Union, in particular the Baltic republics. In addition, 4,000,000 GDR citizens fled west before the erection of the Berlin Wall in 1961. In the 1980s hundreds of thousands more Germans entered Germany from the GDR and Eastern Europe.

Two million Volga Germans in Russia remain in a category of their own. Deported en masse as collaborators in 1941–1942 to Kazakhstan and Saratov, they have been rehabilitated but not allowed to return to their former territory; 150,000 have migrated to Germany while the remainder have become assimilated into their immediate Russian-speaking surroundings.

The huge refugee population has been rather smoothly integrated. Germans rebuilt their society in two new countries. But while the Communist GDR never succeeded in fostering sufficient loyalty among its subjects, the capitalist FRG evolved into a viable polity, undergoing rapid economic growth in the 1950s and 1960s and creating once again one of the world's richest and most developed societies. In recent years the end of the Cold War, the fall of the Berlin Wall, and the reabsorption of the impoverished former GDR compel Germans to concentrate their energies nearer to home.

GERMANY — AUSTRIA   See AUSTRIA–GERMANY.

GERMANY — BELGIUM   See BELGIUM– GERMANY.

GERMANY — CZECH REPUBLIC   See CZECH REPUBLIC–GERMANY.

GERMANY — DENMARK   See DENMARK–GERMANY.

GERMANY — FRANCE   See FRANCE–GERMANY.

GERMANY — LUXEMBOURG   Most of the boundary between Germany and Luxembourg runs along rivers. It is 86 miles (138 km.) long and extends from the boundary tripoint with Belgium on the Our River in the north to the French tripoint on the Moselle (Mosel) River in the south.

Geographical Setting. The boundary tripoint with Belgium is located in the main navigation channel of the Our River, south of Outer (Belgium) and east of Weiswampach (Luxembourg). It follows the river downstream southward and southeastward to a point north of the town of Vianden (Luxembourg). There the boundary leaves the river and runs eastward for 2 miles (3.2 km.) to a point west of the small town of Geichlingen (Germany) and then runs southward to rejoin the Our River, southeast of Vianden. This leaves Vianden, which is located on the Our River, within Luxembourg. The line follows the Our River further southeastward to its confluence with the Sauer River, which flows from the west. Thence the boundary follows the main navigation channel of the Sauer River eastward and southward to its confluence with the Moselle River, which flows from the south. It follows the Moselle River upstream southward, reaching the boundary junction with France, located 2 miles (3.2 km.) southeast of the small town of Perl (Germany), on the Saarburg (Germany)– Thionville (France) highway.

Historical Background. Luxembourg, which was formerly a part of the Holy Roman Empire, became a separate duchy in 1354. It was later ruled by Spain and the Habsburgs of Austria, ceded to France in 1797 and made a grand duchy ruled by the Dutch king in the 1815 Treaty of Vienna. The limits of Luxembourg were first delimited by this treaty and the grand duchy (which was considered an independent state) had special relations with the German federation that shared its eastern boundary. In accordance with the Vienna Treaty, areas in eastern Luxembourg were transferred to Prussia (Germany) and the boundary was established along the rivers. In 1830 Belgium and Luxembourg revolted against Dutch rule; Belgium achieved independence and most of Luxembourg became part of it. The rest remained under Dutch rule and its boundaries were redelimited in the treaties of 19 April 1839. The area became independent in its own right in 1848. The severance of the German Confederation in 1867 led to the dissolution of ties between Luxembourg and Prussia and the dividing line became an international boundary between the two states.

Present Situation. Since 1867 no changes in the boundary line were made. The political changes that brought about major transformations in the Western European boundary lines never affected the Germany–Luxembourg line and it is one of the most peaceful boundaries in the world today.

GERMANY — NETHERLANDS The boundary between Germany and the Netherlands runs for 359 miles (577 km.) from the Ems-Dollart estuary in the North Sea to the tripoint boundary with Belgium in the south. Between the two points it passes over various natural and man-made elements found in the region's topography, such as moors, oil fields and rivers.

Geographical Setting. The northern terminus of the land boundary is found on the southeastern shore of the Ems estuary. The line runs southward for about 50 miles (80 km.) in the Boertanger and Nordhorn moors—an area covered with a thick growth of turf. The southern part of Nordhorn Moor is a gas and oil field, in which some 500 wells, located between Coevorden (Netherlands) and Meppen (Germany), are maintained in working order; these wells are almost equally divided between the two countries. West of Meppen the boundary line changes direction and travels along a stream westward for about 15 miles (25 km.) to a point south of the city of Coevorden and from there follows a zigzag southward for 10 miles (16 km.), crosses the Vechte River and joins a web of drainage channels. Thence it runs eastward for another 10 miles (16 km.) to the Dinkel River, crosses it and then trends southward, east of the

Germany–Netherlands border crossing

river and parallel to it, down to a point north of the small German town of Gronau. The line crosses the Dinkel River once again, west of Gronau and east of Enschede (Netherlands) and continues generally southwest along drainage canals, straight lines and village boundaries for 60 miles (96 km.) to the great Rhine River.

The boundary line enters the Rhine east of the town of Nijmegen (Netherlands), follows it for about 5 miles (8 km.) westward and then continues on land to a point about 2 miles (3 km.) east of Nijmegen. The line turns southeastward, parallel to the eastern bank of the Maas River for about 55 miles (88 km.), until it reaches the southern railway track that connects Düsseldorf (Germany) and Eindhoven (Netherlands). From there eastward and then southward, the line crosses the railway and continues southwest to its westernmost point, east of the small town of Sustaren (Netherlands). The last few miles of the southern boundary line travel southeastward, eastward and then southward to the boundary junction with Belgium, on an unnamed elevation east of the German town of Aachen, which peaks at 1,059 feet (322 m.)—the highest in the Netherlands.

Historical Background. The northern section of the boundary between Germany and the Netherlands, from the North Sea to the Rhine River, is one of the oldest boundary lines in Europe. The definition of the section was established in 1555, almost 100 years before the Netherlands became an independent state. The definition was achieved by the Peace of Augsburg, which ended the first round of the religious war between the Lutheran and the Catholic worlds, declaring the provinces of the Netherlands, which were mainly Protestant, separate from the Lutheran provinces of Germany. Essentially, this section of the line reflects, with only minor adjustments, the regional religious status quo that has prevailed since then. Following the Thirty Years' War of 1618–1648, the Netherlands was established as an independent state that adopted the 1555 boundary with Germany.

The area south of the Rhine underwent various changes as the Netherlands extended its sovereignty eastward and as Germany increased its influence westward to the city of Maastricht and other southern Netherlands regions over the years. The treaty between Great Britain, Austria, Prussia, Russia and the Netherlands, signed in Vienna on 31 May 1815, after the Napoleonic Wars, defined a new boundary in the southern Netherlands by dividing the claims of Prussia and the Netherlands, while the northern section was treated as an unchanged historical boundary. A detailed delimitation and demarcation description was included in the treaty between Prussia and the Netherlands that was signed in Aachen on 26 June 1816, and, in a boundary treaty between the Netherlands and Hanover (a German state), signed on 2 July 1824, a precise updated delimitation of the northern section was settled.

In 1839 the Low Countries were divided as the southern region became the independent state of Belgium, but the location of the boundary between the Netherlands and Prussia was not effected. Minor adjustments to the line were made in a later boundary treaty between the Netherlands and Prussia, on 11 December 1868, and the boundary line was thus maintained throughout the later part of the nineteenth century and the two World Wars. Following World War II, the Netherlands advanced territorial claims on Germany, concerning some 700 sq. miles (1,812 sq. km.) and over 100,000 inhabitants of the area. A demarcation commission agreed, by its final report issued in the Hague on 10 December 1949, to transfer only 26 sq. miles (67 sq. km.) and 487 acres (197 hectares) along with a population of 9,553, from Germany to the Netherlands. Negotiations then proceeded for an orderly and permanent settlement of the boundary. The main difficulty that arose was the creation of a water boundary through the Ems-Dollart estuary and north to the Frisian Islands. Albeit unable to resolve this dispute, the governments signed a final boundary treaty on 10 June 1963, according to which 43 minor adjustments in the boundary's location were made.

Present Situation. The 1963 agreement solved most of the boundary problems between the two states and there are no disputes concerning the land section of the line. The entire land boundary is demarcated. An agreement stands concerning the exploration and exploitation of the estuary, but the marine boundary has yet to be settled.

GERMANY — POLAND The boundary between Germany and Poland runs for 284 miles (456 km.) between the Czech Republic tripoint east of the

German town of Zittau in the south and the Oder Bay of the Baltic Sea in the north. It was established after World War II following mainly the Oder and the Neisse rivers.

Geographical Setting. The southern terminus of the boundary line is located on the Neisse (Nisa, Neise) River, in the southeastern edge of the German city of Zittau. It follows the median line of that river downstream northward for about 95 miles (155 km.) to its confluence with the Oder (Odra) River, passing by the eastern edge of the German towns of Gorlitz and Forst and dividing the German town of Guben and the Polish town of Gubin. From the confluence the boundary follows the main navigation channel of the Oder River downstream northward for about 110 miles (177 km.), passing by the eastern edge of the German town of Frankfurt on Oder and the western edge of the Polish town of Kostryzn. North of the small Polish town of Widuchowa the Oder River runs in two arms; the boundary follows the left (western) arm for about 12 miles (20 km.) to a point east of the small Polish town of Gryfino. Thence it leaves the river and runs north-northwestward to the Oder Lagoon, leaving within Poland the port city of Szczecin (Stetin). The boundary line crosses the Oder Lagoon from south to north, reaches the Usedom island, west of the central entrance to the lagoon, and crosses it, leaving the town of Swinoujscie (Swinemonde) in Poland. The boundary reaches its northern terminus in the Oder Bay of the Baltic Sea.

Historical Background. Poland lost its independence during the second half of the eighteenth century and in 1795–1796 its area was given to Russia, Austria and Prussia, which later became Germany. Only after World War I, in 1918, was Poland restored as an independent state. Its boundary with Germany was first established by the Treaty of Versailles, signed by Poland on 28 June 1919. However, that treaty left the main part of the country's boundaries undefined. Poland regained part of eastern Pomorze and almost all of Poznania, but in East Prussia (the area of today's Russian Kaliningrad) and Upper Silesia the Polish–German boundary was to be decided by plebiscite. Gdansk (Danzig) was to be a free city under the protection of the League of Nations. The plebiscite of East Prussia on 11 July 1920 voted to include the area within Germany, while Up-

per Silesia was divided between Poland and Germany by the Council of the League of Nations on 12 October 1921. This Germany–Poland boundary stood for less than 20 years, as Germany occupied Poland in September 1939, in the first move of World War II. The conclusion of that war led to a new Polish state with totally different boundaries. On 2 August 1945 in Potsdam, the United States, Great Britain and the Soviet Union issued a declaration establishing a new western boundary between Germany and Poland along the Oder and Neisse Rivers. Poland took over an area of 39,597 sq. miles (102,556 sq. km.) previously held by Germany to the east of the line, while East Prussia was incorporated into the Soviet Union. Gdansk was also turned over to Poland. On 6 July 1950 the Oder-Neisse boundary was recognized as final in a treaty signed by Poland and the German Democratic Republic (East Germany). West Germany never recognized that line. Only after the unification of Germany in 1991 was the 1945 line between the states accepted.

Present Situation. From 1945 there were no disputes concerning the alignment of the boundary line as both Poland and East Germany were under the Soviet Union influence. West Germany never recognized the Oder-Neisse line but had no land connection to that line. Only after the unification of Germany in 1991 did the 1945 line become their common international boundary and Germany accepted it without any claims concerning its alignment.

GERMANY — SWITZERLAND The Germany–Switzerland boundary runs for 208 miles (334 km.) between the boundary tripoint with Austria in Lake Constance (Bodensee) in the east and the French tripoint north of the Swiss City of Basel in the Rhine River in the west. Germany has an exclave around the town of Busingen inside Swiss territory, east of the Swiss city of Schaffhausen.

Geographical Setting. The boundary tripoint with Austria is located in the southeastern section of Lake Constance, 2 miles (3.2 km.) north of the Swiss town of Altenrhein. From there the boundary line runs through the lake in a northwesterly direction, reaching the mouth of the Rhine River where it enters the lake from the west. The boundary runs through the middle of the navigation channel of the river, between the German town of Konstanz and

Basel, near the Germany–Switzerland boundary

the Swiss town of Kreuzlingen up to the joint lake formed by Untersee Lake and Zellersee Lake. The boundary line runs through its southern section, leaving Reichenau Island in Germany, and through the middle of Untersee Lake to reach the mouth of the Rhine River at its westernmost point, east of the Swiss town of Stein a Rhine. Then the boundary line leaves the river and runs northward, crossing the road from Switzerland toward the German town of Singen, reaches the Schaffhausen–Singen road and turns southeastward and meets the Rhine River west of the small Swiss town of Rheinklingen. This section of the boundary line, about 15 miles (24 km.) in length, places five villages north of the Rhine River in Swiss territory. The boundary line then follows the main navigation channel of the river upstream westward for 4 miles (6.5 km.) to a point west of the monastery of Saint Katharine. There the line leaves the river and runs northward, circling for 53 miles (85 km.) the city and region of Schaffhausen to include it in Switzerland. The boundary line reaches the Rhine River south of the Swiss town of Neuhausen on Rhine and follows it upstream southward for 10 miles (16 km.), leaving the village and

the monastery of Rheinau within Switzerland. North of the small Swiss town of Elikon, the boundary leaves the river, circles the town and region of Rafz for 15 miles (24 km.), leaving it in Switzerland. It reaches the Rhine north of the Swiss town of Glattfelden and from there it follows the main navigation channel of the Rhine River upstream westward for about 35 miles (55 km.) up to a point north of the Swiss town of Birs-felden. Thence the line leaves the river, and runs east, north and west as to leave the town of Riehen in Switzerland. The boundary line runs along the northern suburbs of Basel (Switzerland) and runs once again to the Rhine River. There it reaches the boundary tripoint with France in the main navigation channel of the Rhine River.

Historical Background. Switzerland was developed as an independent state under the suzerainty of the Holy Roman Empire from 1291 onward. Between 1351–1353 the Zurich canton (district) joined the three original "Forest Districts," establishing a section of the present boundary between the Austrian province (*Kreise*) of Germany and Switzerland. With the occupation of the Aragu district by

Switzerland in 1415, its boundary with Germany was extended westward while the occupation of Thurgau in 1460 extended the line eastward to Lake Konstanz. During the last year of the fifteenth century (1499), the German Emperor Maximilian I attempted to occupy Switzerland but was defeated by the Swiss army. In the Basel Peace Treaty of September 1499, the independence of Switzerland was acknowledged by Germany. In 1501, after that victory, the districts of Basel and Schaffhausen joined Switzerland and the Appenzel district and the allied (*Zugewandte*) district of Saint Gallen joined it in 1513 (Saint Gallen became a full member of the Swiss Federation only in 1803), thereby establishing the entire boundary between Switzerland and the Grand Duchy of Baden, which later became part of Germany. Switzerland was occupied by Napoleon I in 1799 but was reestablished as a totally independent state (after the abolition of the Holy Roman Empire in 1806) by the Congress of Vienna of 9 June 1815, which also established its neutrality. The town of Busingen, which was part of the Baden Grand Duchy and is located east of the Swiss city of Schaffhausen, remains a German enclave that is still surrounded by Swiss territory.

Present Situation. Since 1815 the northern boundary of Switzerland has never been changed. The European history of the last 180 years, which created new states and boundaries all over Europe, did not affect the alignment of this boundary, which was repeatedly reconfirmed. There are no disputes concerning the alignment of this peaceful boundary.

GHANA   Ghana is a west African country situated on the Gulf of Guinea in the Atlantic Ocean. It is bounded in the west by Ivory Coast (415 miles; 668 km.), in the north by Burkina Faso (341 miles; 549 km.) and in the east by Togo (545 miles; 877 km.). The area of Ghana is 92,098 sq. miles (238,533 sq. km.) and it has an estimated population (1994) of 16,700,000. Its capital is Accra.

The Ghanaians were the first people in sub-Saharan Africa to become independent from colonial rule when they gained independence from the British in 1957. The main opposition to Kwame Nkrumah's party, the Convention People's Party (CPP), came from the Ashanti, who demanded autonomy and even secession. Nkrumah succeeded in creating a

Ghanaian identity and in minimizing ethnic conflicts. After his fall in a military coup in 1966, although Ghana's politics became very unstable and military coups followed periods of civilian rule, serious ethnic conflicts have been avoided. The Ashanti continued in opposition to most of Ghana's governments, but they acted in cooperation with other ethnic groups, and the demand for autonomy or secession grew weaker.

In the early 1990s demands for political reforms and democratization were raised by large segments of the Ghanaian people.

GHANA — BURKINA FASO   see BURKINA FASO–GHANA.

GHANA — IVORY COAST   The boundary between Ghana and Ivory Coast runs for 415 miles (668 km.) from the boundary tripoint with Burkina Faso on the Black Volta River to the Gulf of Guinea in the Atlantic Ocean. The present boundary follows the previous colonial boundary between the British and the French possessions in the region and is very well demarcated.

Geographical Setting. The northern terminus of the boundary line, which is the boundary tripoint with Burkina Faso, is located in the main navigation channel of the Black Volta River, at approximately 9°29'30"N. It follows the main navigation channel upstream southward, to reach a point on the right bank of the river, where a road between two villages crosses it. In a series of short straight lines and following a local river for a short distance, the boundary runs south to the Manzan River and follows it downstream southwestward for about 30 miles (50 km.) to its confluence with a local stream. Thence it follows that stream to a point where another local road crosses it. In another series of small streams and short straight lines, the boundary runs eastward and arrives at the Tanoé River north of Nougoua (Ivory Coast). It follows the Tanoé River downstream to the Ehi Lagoon and a small stream to the coast of the Gulf of Guinea, north of Half Assini (Ghana).

Historical Background. The British established the Gold Coast colony on 13 January 1886. The northern territories of the Gold Coast were made part of the colony in 1897 and in 1901 Ashanti was formally annexed to the Gold Coast. France established itself in the Gulf of Guinea in the nineteenth century, organizing French Sudan (1898), dissolving it on 17 October 1899 and forming the colony of Ivory Coast. The expansion of Britain and France in West Africa involved bilateral arrangements providing for the allocation of their spheres of influence, delimiting and demarcating their common boundaries between 1889 and 1905. The boundary between Gold Coast and Ivory Coast was first determined in 1889 and then in 1891, 1893 and 1898. The present boundary line was established by an agreement between the United Kingdom and France on 1 February 1903 and an exchange of notes on 11 and 15 May 1905.

Gold Coast became an independent state on 6 March 1957, adopting the name Ghana. Ivory Coast gained independence on 7 August 1960. Both countries adopted the colonial line as their international boundary. After independence it was found that some of the boundary pillars seemed to have disappeared, leading to local complications. In 1968 Ghana and Ivory Coast agreed to proceed with a joint demarcation operation, which took place in 1970–1973. The boundary line was redemarcated, cleared to the ground at a width of 25 feet (8 m.) and planted with teak trees.

Present Situation. Since the redemarcation of the line in the 1970s there have been no known boundary disputes concerning its alignment. It is one of the few finely demarcated boundaries in Africa.

GHANA — TOGO   The Ghana–Togo boundary follows a dividing line between the British and French mandate areas in the former German protectorate of Togoland. It runs for 545 miles (877 km.) between the boundary tripoint with Burkina Faso in the north and the Gulf of Guinea in the south.

Geographical Setting. The boundary tripoint with Burkina Faso is located east of the town of Bawku (Ghana) at about 11°8'33"N. It runs southeast for about 25 miles (40 km.), following local streams (Manjo, Konkumbo) and short straight lines that connect them and reaching the Oti River. The boundary follows that river downstream southward for about 60 miles (100 km.) to its confluence with the Kakassi River. Then running southward it follows a local tribal boundary to the Mo River, which

it follows downstream southwestward for 12 miles (20 km.). It leaves the river and follows a local watershed southward, dividing streams and villages between the two countries. In a series of straight lines, along watersheds, streams and tribal boundaries, the boundary runs south for about 160 miles (260 km.) to reach the intersection of 6°20'N and the Magbawi River. From there it runs in another series of straight lines to a boundary pillar located on the shore of the Gulf of Guinea on the road between Keta (Ghana) and Lomé, the capital of Togo.

Historical Background. Germany established a protectorate over the coastal area of the Gulf of Guinea on 5 July 1884. Britain captured the area west of Togoland (later Togo) in the second half of the nineteenth century, establishing the colony of Gold Coast (later Ghana) on 13 January 1886. Britain and Germany agreed on a boundary between their possessions and the allocation of their spheres of influence in the area in July 1886. The territories in the north of Gold Coast were made part of that colony in 1897 and the kingdom of Ashanti was formally annexed to it in 1901. Earlier, in 1890, and on 14 November 1899, Anglo-German arrangements for boundary delimitation took place and further delimitation and demarcation of the Anglo–German boundary took place by virtue of agreements on 26 September and 2 December 1901. During World War I the German Colony of Togoland, east of Gold Coast, was occupied by the British and French, who divided the area between themselves by a Franco-British Declaration of 10 July 1919. Togoland became a League of Nations trust area and Britain and France accepted mandates on the basis of the 1919 division. During 1927–1929 their boundary line was demarcated by boundary pillars. Following a plebiscite, the British section of Togoland was united with Gold Coast on 6 March 1957, when Gold Coast became independent under the name of Ghana. French Togoland became independent Togo on 27 April 1960. Both newly independent states adopted the mandate division but agreed to redemarcate the poorly marked boundary. In 1975–1976 Ghana and Togo redemarcated the boundary line and removed local obstacles.

Present Situation. Since 1976 neither state has challenged the boundary alignment and no disputes concerning it are known. There is, however, one major problem concerning the division of the Awe people, who inhabited northern Togoland and were divided by the British–French line of 1919, which later became an international boundary between two independent states. The Awes are calling for reunification, which may result in a change in the line.

GIBRALTAR A British colony (area: 2.5 sq. miles [6.5 sq. km.]; estimated population: 32,000 [1994]), Gibraltar is situated at the southern tip of the Iberian Peninsula in southwestern Europe. Gibraltar itself is a peninsula, bounded in the north by Spain (0.75 miles; 1.2 km.) and by the Mediterranean Sea from all other sides.

GIBRALTAR — SPAIN The border between Gibraltar and Spain is 0.75 miles (1.2 km.) long and runs from the Mediterranean Sea to the Atlantic Ocean. It is delineated by a fence that was initially erected in 1909.

Geographical Setting. This boundary was delimited unilaterally in 1909 and runs across the low sandy plain that separates the Rock of Gibraltar from the plains of Andalusia. It reaches from the west coast to the center of the peninsula and turns a few degrees south to meet the east coast north of Gibraltar's airfield.

Historical Background. Gibraltar is a narrow rocky peninsula rising steeply from the Andalusian lowlands of southwestern Spain at the eastern end of the Strait of Gibraltar. It is nearly 3 miles (5 km.) long. The promontory was first settled by the Moors in 711 and took its name from their leader, Tariq ibn Ziyad. Jebel el Tarik (Tarik's Hill) was later adjusted to Gibraltar. The territory was disputed by the Spanish and the Moors until the Spanish victory of 1462. During the War of the Spanish Succession, Gibraltar was taken by the Anglo-Dutch fleet and was ceded to Britain under the Peace Treaty of Utrecht of 1713. By this treaty Britain received "the full and entire propriety of the town and castle of Gibraltar, together with the port, fortifications and forts thereto belonging," and Spain was awarded first option should Britain ever wish to part with Gibraltar. The terms of the treaty were subsequently confirmed by the Treaties of Seville (1729), Vienna (1731), Aix-la-Chapelle (1756) and Paris (1763). After the Siege of Gibraltar (1779–1783), Spain agreed to withdraw

Gilbraltar, at the southern tip of the Iberian Peninsula

its claim to the peninsula in return for Minorca and Florida. The subsequent Treaty of Versailles, 1783, confirmed the previous treaties. At this time a band of neutral ground, some 0.9 miles (1.45 km.) wide, separated two opposing fortifications. The Spanish forts of La Línea were blown up in 1810, during the Napoleonic War, by the governor of Gibraltar, fearing the consequences of having them falling into French hands. In 1815, with the permission of the Spanish authorities, Gibraltar built a temporary fever hospital in the neutral zone and another outbreak of disease in 1854 gave rise to more buildings in the neutral zone, north of the first. In 1909 the British built an iron fence north of these buildings, annexing to Gibraltar land acquired by a process known as 'acquisitive prescription.' Spain disputes the legality of this interpretation of events, since the element of consent required by acquisitive prescription was confined to permission for temporary buildings in times of epidemic.

Since 1830 Gibraltar has been a crown colony and has, particularly since the opening of the Suez Canal, played an important part in the expansion of British interests around the world. It played a vital role in allied naval and military operations during both world wars and has since remained important to Britain and to NATO as a military base.

In 1964 the United Nations Committee on Decolonization invited Spain and Britain to find a diplomatic solution of the issue, but little progress was made. A referendum held in Gibraltar in 1967, in which nearly 96% of the population voted, showed an overwhelming majority preferring to remain British. The United Nations adopted a resolution requesting Britain to end Gibraltar's colonial situation by 1 October 1969. Spain closed the border and cut telephone and ferry links in an effort to bring about a settlement.

It was not until after 1975, with the death of General Franco and the restoration of democracy in Spain, that the diplomatic situation improved sufficiently to allow a resumption of talks and restoration of communications between Gibraltar and the mainland. In the Lisbon Declaration of 10 April 1980, Spain reaffirmed its intention to reinstate the territorial integrity of Spain and Britain reiterated its commitment to honor the wishes of the Gibraltarians. Britain and Spain have since signed a declaration on civil aviation and cooperate closely on matters of security and customs.

Present Situation. The border is still disputed and both parties accept that the question of sovereignty needs to be discussed.

GREECE (Ellás) A country in southeastern Europe (area: 50,949 sq. miles [131,958 sq. km.]; estimated population: 10,300,000 [1994]), Greece is bounded in the north by Albania (175 miles; 282 km.), Macedonia (153 miles; 246 km.) and Bulgaria (307 miles; 494 km.), in the east by Turkey (128 miles; 206 km.) and the Aegean Sea, in the south by the Mediterranean Sea and in the west by the Ionian Sea. The capital of Greece is Athens.

Greek tribes arrived in present-day Greece during the second half of the second millennium B.C.E. in several waves. From there they spread across the Aegean islands to the western rim of Anatolia. These areas, together with Crete and Cyprus, formed the classical Greek world, which developed a civilization that became the basis for the modern Western one. In later centuries the Greeks colonized parts of the Mediterranean, mainly southern Italy, eastern Sicily and the Black Sea shores.

The conquests of Alexander the Great at once widened the horizons of the Greek world and laid foundations for the fusion of civilizations into what became known as Hellenistic civilization, but at the same time pushed Greece itself to the margins of the new Hellenistic world. The marginalization of Greece was completed under the Roman Empire. With the partition of the Roman Empire, the eastern half gradually moved away from Latin to Greek, under the Byzantine Empire.

Greek was the first language into which the Bible was translated, and it was the main language of the early Christian church long before Latin. The Byzantine Empire developed a civilization of its own, one of the most illustrious in history, which was absorbed by many of the neighboring Slavic peoples (including the Russians). The end of the Byzantine Empire came with the fall of Constantinople to the Ottomans in 1453. However, with the Greek world under the Ottoman Empire the center remained in Constantinople/Istanbul. The Ottomans placed all the Eastern Orthodox Christians under the authority of the Patriarch of Constantinople and

Greece continued to be a marginal entity as before.

However, it was in Greece that in 1770 Russian-instigated uprisings against the Ottomans occurred. This had little to do with demands for independence, or with nationalism. By the 1820s, the situation had changed. The influence of nationalist slogans, the French Revolution, and the admiration for ancient Greece by European, and later Greek, Romanticists all created a national consciousness which, fed by the weakness of the Ottoman Empire, produced the revolt of 1821 and led to the Polar of Independence of 1821–1829, in which interventions by Britain, France and Russia created an independent little Greece on a small part of the territory inhabited by Greeks.

For the first time since the late fourth century B.C.E., mainland Greece, or more precisely Athens, became a center of the Greek world, although it remained for decades secondary to Constantinople. Greeks from outside Greece refused to come and serve the new kingdom. Many Greek diplomats and adminstrators continued to be in the service of the Ottoman Sultan. For most Greeks "inside," Constantinople remained the acknowledged center and its liberation their greatest aspiration.

Their hope (the *magali*, or "great idea") was to reunite all the territories regarded as the Greek homeland, forming classical (ancient) Greece as well as the Byzantine heartland. Many hoped for the reconquest of Constantinople, and the transfer of the capital to it from Athens: others hoped to reestablish the Byzantine Empire.

The leaders and rulers of the new Greek state did their best to expand its borders. In 1864 Britain transferred the Ionian islands to Greece. In 1881 Greece received Thessaly, to the north. Following the Balkan Wars Greece annexed Crete, almost all the Aegean islands (except the Dodecanese islands, annexed by Italy in 1912 and ceded to Greece in 1948), Epirus, and part of Macedonia, including Thessaloniki. Greece joined the Entente Powers in World War I in 1917, and gained Western Thrace as well as part of the Aegean coast of Anatolia, including the city of Smyrna.

In 1921 Greece, pushed by Britain, launched an offensive against the Turkish nationalists led by Mustafa Kemal Ataturk, but were defeated and thrown out of Anatolia, which became Turkish

Izmir. Following this disaster the monarchy was overthrown and a republic proclaimed. The monarchy was reinstated only in 1936. Following the Greco-Turkish War a general exchange of population was carried out, in which over 1,000,000 Greek Orthodox inhabitants of Turkey, many of whom did not speak Greek at all, were transferred to Greece, while a similar number of Muslim inhabitants of Greece were transferred to Turkey.

Following World War II, in which Greece was occupied by the Axis powers, British troops landed in Athens and restored the royal government. Simultaneously the Communists established their own regime in Thessaloniki. The civil war that followed ended only in 1949 and left deep wounds in the social and political fabric. The Left remained compromised for more than a generation, and once it started to gain in strength again, a military junta carried out a coup in April 1967. When the king opposed them, they sent him into exile and abolished the monarchy in 1973. In 1974 the junta lost control and democracy was restored to Greece.

The Greeks of Cyprus (then about 79% of the population), who had been passive through Ottoman and British rule (since 1878) started after World War II to demand British withdrawal and union (*enosis*) with Greece. From the mid-1950s this was backed by the armed activity of an underground led by a general from Greece. The Turkish minority objected to union with Greece, and in 1960 Cyprus was given independence as a binational republic, under guarantees from Britain, Greece and Turkey. However, as the Greeks did not give up their wish for *enosis* and the Turkish resolve to block it remained as strong as before, several crises, accompanied by rounds of clashes, occurred in the 1960s. In 1974 Greek extremists carried out a coup, backed, if not masterminded, by the junta in Greece, to unite with Greece. In response Turkey intervened militarily, forcefully divided the island, and established a Turkish Republic of Northern Cyprus.

GREECE — ALBANIA   see ALBANIA–GREECE.

GREECE — BULGARIA   see BULGARIA–GREECE.

GREECE — MACEDONIA   Macedonia gained independence in 1991, inheriting Yugoslavia's boundary with Greece. The boundary runs 153 miles (246 km.) through the center of the Balkan Peninsula in an east–west direction. Most of its length (140 miles; 225 km.) is a land boundary; the remainder runs through two lakes.

Geographical Setting. The boundary begins in the west at the boundary junction with Albania, in Lake Prespa, runs eastward to its shore and continues in the same direction through a mountainous area, about 6,000 feet (1,800 m.) above sea level. The boundary climbs the Pindar Mountains and follows the crest east and northeast to reach Gernavska Peak, situated 7,105 feet (2,165 m.) above sea level. It then continues to run in a generally easterly direction along the watershed. In the mountainous region the boundary reaches its highest elevation on Gareva Peak (7,755 feet; 2,363 m.), after having crossed some local roads. In a southerly direction, following the crest of the Baba Mountains, it reaches Koukov Peak (6,613 feet; 2,015 m.) and from there descends eastward. Covering a chain of local peaks, it then arrives at a point situated 2,475 feet (754 m.) above sea level. The boundary runs across a small plateau,

on which stands the Dragos monastery; the boundary touches the west wall that encloses the monastery buildings, leaving it within Greek territory. From the monastery it traverses eastward, still following the watershed, but descending to the plain. Turning northeastward, the boundary runs in a straight line from the base of the foothills across the plain, crossing the roads connecting Greece and Macedonia between Florina (Greece) and Bitola (Macedonia). Running eastward, the boundary crosses the Rakova River to a local crossroads. Turning southeast, it reaches a railroad track where it turns eastward to follow a series of straight lines and mountain crests. South of the Macedonian town of Gevgelija the boundary first crosses the main railroad between Salonika (Greece) and Skopje (Macedonia) and then crosses the Vardar River, the main river of the southern Balkans.

After crossing the river the boundary line runs eastward, changes its direction toward the south, and then again eastward following a local watershed and some straight lines until it reaches the southern shore of Lake Dojran. The boundary crosses the lake

Greece–Macedonia border

in a straight line northward to the Nikoliç Creek. Then following the course of the creek, the boundary runs to a local ridge, where it climbs northward along the ridge, and then forms a large curve to the east to reach the summit of Tumba Mountain, also known as Bélès or Pole Mountain (4,764 feet; 1,452 m.). The highest peak of this mountain marks the border junction of Greece, Macedonia and Bulgaria.

Historical Background. Although the area in which the border between Greece and Macedonia runs today has a long history of occupation and has had several delimitations, the present boundary has no foundation in delimitations made before the twentieth century. The current boundary was established by the final division of historic Macedonia between the Kingdoms of Serbia, Greece and Bulgaria at the end of the Balkan Wars of 1912–1913. The First Balkan War of 1912–1913 was ended after the joint forces of Bulgaria, Greece and Serbia defeated the Ottoman army, occupying most of the Balkan territory of the Ottoman Empire, including the province of Macedonia. In June 1912 Greece and Serbia peacefully concluded the delimitation of the boundary between them. A year later, in June 1913, Bulgaria attacked the Serbian and Greek armies along the Macedonian border. Greece and Serbia joined forces with the Ottoman Empire, Montenegro and Romania to fight the Bulgarian army, creating the Second Balkan War of 1913. The defeated Bulgars accepted an armistice in July 1913 and signed the Treaty of Bucharest with Greece and Serbia on 10 August 1913.

The boundary that was then established between Serbia and Greece from Lake Prespa to the boundary junction with Bulgaria is, with few exceptions, the present-day international boundary between Greece and Macedonia. The actual demarcation was completed in December 1913, although the line near the Macedonian town of Gevgelija, where the border crosses the Vardar River, was not demarcated following a dispute over the meaning of the phrase, "immediately north of the village of Sechevo," that was written in the boundary agreement. The Serbs interpreted it as meaning the houses of the village; the Greeks insisted that it referred to the entire village including the land that surrounds it. Only 14 years later, in 1927, after long negotiations between Greece and Yugoslavia, was the dispute settled with

a compromise. Since that time there have been no changes made in the boundary.

Present Situation. The former Yugoslav republic of Macedonia gained independence in 1991. Since then there have been problematic relations with Greece, but none of the disputes concern the boundary line between the two countries.

GREECE — TURKEY   The boundary between Greece and Turkey runs 128 miles (206 km.) in the southeastern extremity of the Balkan Peninsula. Mostly following rivers and covering only a very short section of land, the boundary line is very well demarcated.

Geographical Setting. The boundary begins at the tripoint boundary junction with Bulgaria on the Maritsa River, at about 41°42'N and 26°21'E. It follows the median line of the river downstream for 9 miles (14 km.) to its confluence with the Arda River. So as to leave the Turkish city of Edirne (formerly Adrianople) room to expand, the boundary follows the Arda River upstream for a little over 0.5 miles (1 km.), then leaves the river and runs over land southeast for 6.7 miles (10.8 km.) until it rejoins the Maritsa River. Two small Turkish towns, Bosna and Karaagaç, are located in the small Turkish enclave west of the river, as is part of the railroad connecting Greece and Bulgaria, which runs parallel to the Maritsa River. The land boundary is carefully demarcated by 23 intervisible boundary pillars. Upon returning to the median line of the Maritsa River, the boundary follows it southward for 19 miles (30 km.). All islands east of the line belong to Turkey; those west of the line belong to Greece. After dissecting a bridge (used by the Orient Express to reach Istanbul) the boundary reaches a river island designated "Q," and crosses it from north to south for some 2,600 feet (792 m.)—three boundary pillars are located on the island. It then returns to the river and runs southward for 71.5 miles (115 km.) to the point at which the Maritsa River separates into two branches. It then follows the eastern, main branch of the river for 21 miles (34 km.), finally reaching the Gulf of Enez in the Aegean Sea.

Historical Background. The Ottoman Empire lost most of its Balkan possessions in the nineteenth century. As a result of the First Balkan War (1912–1913), it was forced to accept a boundary line with

Bulgaria that ran in a straight line from the Black Sea city of Midye to the Aegean Sea city of Enez. However, in the Second Balkan War of 1913, Turkey pushed the boundary to the Maritsa River, restoring the historic city of Edirne to Turkey.

During World War I both Turkey and Bulgaria were allied with Germany and Austria-Hungary. Both countries suffered serious territorial losses as a result of their defeat: Bulgaria lost access to the Aegean Sea and Turkey lost what remained of its European possessions.

Although Bulgaria never recovered its lost territory, after three years of war (1919–1922) with Greece, Turkey managed to eject the Greek army from Asia Minor and Eastern Thrace. In the armistice agreement signed on 11 October 1922 it was agreed that Greece would immediately restore all of Eastern Thrace, as far as the Maritsa River, to Turkey. A peace treaty confirming this arrangement was signed on 24 July 1923 in Lausanne, Switzerland, whereby Turkey also received the parcel of land west of the river in order to facilitate future development of the city of Edirne. The treaty confirmed Greek sovereignty of the Aegean islands of Samothrace, Lemnos, Lesbos, Chios, Samos, Kos and Ikaria off the Turkish shoreline. Turkey was left with only the islands of Imroz and Bozcaada. An international boundary commission was then established to demarcate the line. Three years later, on 3 November 1926, the *Protocole de Conclusions de la Commission* was signed in Athens, ending a long history of boundary demarcations in the region.

Present Situation. Although there are no known disputes concerning the land boundary between Greece and Turkey, tensions between the two countries over their maritime boundary and Aegean Sea oil reserves almost led to war in the early 1980s. The dispute has yet to be settled.

GREENLAND (Grønland)   A self-governing island region of Denmark, Greenland is located in the North Atlantic Ocean. It is the largest island in the world, with an area of 840,004 sq. miles (2,174,770 sq. km.). The island has no land boundaries. Its estimated population (1994) is 58,000 and its capital is Godthab (Nuuk).

This former colony became self-governing after a referendum favoring home rule in 1979. With self-government came increased official usage of the Greenlandic language, an Eskimo-Aleut dialect.

GRENADA   An island in the Caribbean Sea, situated about 100 miles (160 km.) north of Venezuela. Its area is 133 sq. miles (344 sq. km.) with an estimated population (1994) of 90,000. Grenada's capital is St. George's and it has no land boundaries.

The inhabitants of Grenada are predominantly descendants of black African slaves, who worked the island's extensive sugar and spice plantations under British colonial rule. English is the official language and Roman Catholicism is the religion of 60% of the islanders; the rest are Protestants. Exports of agricultural products are the main source of foreign exchange. Grenada became independent in 1974. American military intervention following an internal military coup in 1983 led to the restoration of democratic government in late 1984.

GUADELOUPE   An overseas department of France, Guadeloupe is situated in the Caribbean Sea, between Dominica and Antigua and Barbuda. Its area is 687 sq. miles (1,779 sq. km.) with an estimated population of 418,000. The capital of Guadeloupe is Basse-Terre and it has no land boundaries.

The inhabitants are mainly descendants of black African slaves who worked on the island's sugar and banana plantations. The people are mostly Roman Catholic and a Creole dialect is widely spoken, although French is the official language. Sugar and bananas are the mainstays of the local economy, which is heavily dependent on trade with the French. There is increasing agitation for greater autonomy from France.

GUAM   The island of Guam is an unincorporated territory of the United States of America located in the Pacific Ocean. Guam has no land boundaries and its total area is 209 sq. miles (541 sq. km.). It has an estimated population (1994) of 145,000. Guam's capital is Agana.

GUATEMALA (Guatomala)   Guatemala (area: 42,030 sq. miles [108,857 sq. km.]; estimated population: 10,000,000 [1994]) is situated in Central America. It is bounded in the east and the north by Mexico (598 miles; 962 km.), by Belize (165 miles;

266 km.), Honduras (159 miles; 256 km.) and El Salvador (127 miles; 204 km.) in the west and by the Pacific Ocean in the south. The capital of Guatemala is Guatemala City.

Politically, the recent history of the Guatemalans has been characterized by violence, which has damaged the country economically through reductions in tourism and international investments. Their culture is mixed, belonging to both the Hispanic-American and ancient indigenous worlds, as described by Nobel prizewinner Miguel Angel Astiurias. Traditional dances, music, religious rites and games survive in Indian regions. The modern sector, however, does less well: despite free compulsory primary education, many children do not go to school, resulting in 50% illiteracy in the cities and 70% in rural areas. More than one-quarter of the population has no access to medical care.

For 2,000 years after the indigenous Guatemalans began to adopt sedentary agriculture, beginning about 2500 B.C.E., villages grew in size and sophistication. Guatemala and neighboring areas of Yucatan and Chiapas in contemporary Mexico were the cradles of the impressive Mayan civilization that lasted until the tenth century. Half a millennium after urban Mayan civilization began its decline, the descendants of the early Maya were conquered by the Spaniards beginning in 1523. During the colonial period, Guatemala's economy was reduced to agriculture, producing cocoa and indigo for export with the labor of Indians and blacks. After Central American independence from Spain was declared in 1821, Guatemalans briefly became part of the short-lived Mexican Empire. Since the collapse of the empire in 1823 Guatemalans have lived through a succession of authoritarian regimes, revolutions, and coup. The 1970s witnessed an escalation of political violence, coupled with the effects of a 1974 volcanic eruption and a 1976 earthquake. Rightwing terrorism decimated the rural Maya population, an act which led to global condemnation of Guatemala for human rights violations during the late 1970s and 1980s. Although the reestablishment of civilian government in 1986 was accompanied by the incorporation of human rights guarantees into the constitution, violence, at a lesser level, has continued.

GUATEMALA — BELIZE see BELIZE–GUATEMALA.

GUATEMALA — EL SALVADOR see EL SALVADOR–GUATEMALA.

GUATEMALA — HONDURAS The Guatemala–Honduras boundary is 159 miles (256 km.) long and runs from the Caribbean Sea inland southwestward to Cerro Monte Cristo, the boundary tripoint with El Salvador. It is demarcated throughout by pillars or rivers.

Geographical Setting. Where the boundary between Guatemala and Honduras runs along waterways and streams, it follows their median lines. From the tripoint with El Salvador, at Cerro Monte Cristo, the boundary runs north directly to the headwaters of the nearest tributary of the Frio (Sesecapa) River. It continues north along the tributary to its confluence with the Frio River, which it then follows to its confluence with the El Chaguiton creek. The line follows the creek upstream to its headwaters and then heads north to the summit of the watershed between the drainage basins of the Atulapa and Frio rivers. It heads east in a straight line to reach the southernmost and higher of the two peaks of Cerro Tecomapa, and continues some 1,310 feet (400 m.) to the confluence of two small creeks that form a tributary of the Tecomapa (Agua Caliende) creek. It traverses along this tributary downstream to its confluence with the Tecomapa creek, which it then follows to its confluence with the Olopa River. The border follows the Olopa River downstream to its confluence with La Brea creek, travels along La Brea upstream to a point 183 feet (56 m.) below its confluence with El Incienso creek and in a straight line eastward for 2 miles (3 km.) reaches the highest point of Cerro Oscuro. From there it runs east along the continental water divide to its junction with the watershed between the drainage basins of the Chanmagua and Blanco rivers, follows the watershed to its intersection with the watershed of the La Raya (Pezote) creek drainage basin and in a straight line north to the headwaters of the nearest tributary of the La Raya creek. It continues north to the tributary's confluence with the La Raya creek and to the La Raya's confluence with the Playon River. From here the border follows a number of rivers and after reaching the confluence of the Templador and Sulay rivers, it heads northwest in a straight line to the highest point of Cerro Ojo de Agua del Amate.

From this point the line continues in straight lines north to the summit of Cerro San Cristobal and northwest to the summit of Cerro Sepulturas and Bonete del Portillo. Running north again, it reaches Cerro Jute and there turns northeast to trend along the local crest to the watershed between the drainage basins of San Antonio and Tizamarte creeks. Generally north and northeast, the boundary then crosses a number of main and secondary watersheds, passes Palmichal and reaches the Managua River, which it then follows downstream to the mouth of the first creek north of the village of Aldea Nueva (Honduras). It then forms a straight line for 12 miles (19 km.) to a point on the Morja River, due east of the southeastern corner of the La Francia clearing, and bears northeast in another straight line for 24.4 miles (39.2 km.) to the junction of the secondary watershed between the Juyama and Encantado rivers with the main water divide between the Motagua and Chamelecón drainage basins. Once again the boundary joins the main and secondary local watersheds in straight lines and trends across them north and northeastward. In a straight line northeastward for 5.75 miles (9.25 km.) the line reaches the highest point of Cerro Escarpado, near the intersection of the secondary water divides between the Chiquito (Platanos), Nuevo (Cacao) and Chachagualilla river basins. Another two straight lines take the border northeast for 11.2 miles (18 km.) to the center of the Cuyamel railroad bridge over the Santo Tomas River and to the southernmost point on the right bank of the Tinto River, which flows from the Laguna Tinta. The boundary heads along the right bank of this river, at the mean high water mark, downstream to its confluence with the Motagua River. It then follows the latter river along its right bank at the high water mark downstream, to its mouth in the Gulf of Honduras. In the event of natural changes in these last two rivers, the boundary will follow the mean high water mark on the right banks of each.

Historical Background. Boundary disputes in this region concerning the location of its boundaries began shortly after the breakup of the Federation of Central America in 1843. Efforts made in 1845, 1895 and 1914 to resolve the problem of the Guatemala–Honduras boundary alignment were unsuccessful. Two treaties signed in Washington on 16

July 1930 provided for a Special Boundary Tribunal to delimit the boundary and for its subsequent demarcation. Taking as a starting point the boundary situation as it stood in 1821, when Honduras and Guatemala became independent from Spain, the tribunal was free to modify the boundary with respect to any significant interests held by the states as a result of their subsequent development. On 23 January 1933 the tribunal gave its opinion and award and the process of demarcation began. On 26 March 1936 a protocol was signed by Guatemala, Honduras and El Salvador, accepting Cerro Monte Cristo as the tripoint of their common boundaries.

Present Situation. This border is recognized by both Guatemala and Honduras.

GUATEMALA — MEXICO Demarcated by rivers and pillars throughout, this border is 598 miles (962 km.) miles long. It follows parallels and the courses of three rivers: the Suchiate, Salinas and Usumacinta.

Geographical Setting. The southernmost terminus of the boundary runs from a point three leagues from the mouth of the Suchiate River into and along its deepest channel, as far as 15°04'16.142"N and 92°03'37.93"W, 76 feet (25 m.) from the southernmost pillar of the customs house station at Talquian (leaving the customs house in Guatemala). At this point the river intersects a straight line that reaches the highest area of the volcano of Tacaná. From there the border forms a straight line until it intersects another straight line, at 15°15'35.153"N and 92°12'37.609"W, and follows it over the summits of Buenavista and Ixbul to a point that stands 2.4 miles (3.8 km.) beyond Ixbul Hill (16°04'32.21"N and 91°43'54.723"W). It then continues eastward along latitude 16°04'32.21"N until it meets Rio Chixoy (Rio Salinas), which it follows downstream northward to the middle of its deepest channel and to meet Rio Usumacinta. The border continues along the middle of the deepest channel of the Usumacinta northwestward until it arrives at the latitude 15 miles (25 km.) south of the center of the Mexican town of Tenosique in Tabasco. The boundary then follows this line until it meets the meridian that passes at a third of the distance from the center of the town square at Tenosique to the center of Sacluc. This meridian then carries the border to latitude

17°49'N, which is then followed east until it crosses Rio Hondo and reaches the boundary tripoint with Belize at 89°09'06.749"W.

Historical Background. Mexico, formerly the viceroyalty of New Spain, declared itself independent from Spain on 16 September 1810. The captaincy general of Guatemala had declared its independence from Spain 11 years later, on 15 September 1821. At that time Guatemala consisted of today's Guatemala, Chiapas (southeast Mexico), Costa Rica, El Salvador, Honduras and Nicaragua. Shortly afterward, Chiapas declared its union with Mexico and all of the provinces were briefly annexed to Mexico in 1822–1823. From 1824 to 1838 the five states were members of the Federation of Central America.

In 1877 a convention was signed providing for the survey of the Guatemala–Mexico boundary, but the survey was never completed. Nevertheless, a treaty delimiting the border was signed on 27 September 1882, by which Guatemala agreed to the incorporation of Chiapas into Mexico. A protocol of 14 September 1883 provided for the organization of a boundary commission under the 1882 treaty. The Salinas River section of the border was clarified by a convention on 1 April 1895, and by May of 1899 the whole boundary had been fully demarcated. Periodic flooding and the changing of river channels necessitated the canalization of the Suchiate River course, which was executed by an International Boundary and Water Commission and established by an exchange of notes dated 21 December 1961.

Present Situation. The position and legality of this boundary are undisputed.

GUINEA (Guinée)

A west African country, Guinea (area: 94,926 sq. miles [245,763 sq. km.]; estimated population: 7,700,000 [1994]) was formerly a part of French West Africa. It is bounded in the northwest by Guinea-Bissau (240 miles; 386 km.), in the north by Senegal (205 miles; 330 km.), northeast by Mali (533 miles; 858 km.), east by Ivory Coast (379 miles; 610 km.), south by Liberia (350 miles; 563 km.) and Sierra Leone (405 miles; 652 km.) and southwest by the North Atlantic Ocean. Guinea's capital is Conakry.

The Guineans gained their independence from the French in 1958. During decolonization the Fulani formed their own party. With the rise of the Parti Democratique de Guinée led by a Malinke, Ahmed Sekou Touré, the Fulani party lost most of its power. Sekou Touré led his country to independence. He tried to fight tribalism and accused the Fulani of keeping up ethnic conflicts. After independence his hostility toward the Fulani continued and in 1976 he arrested and executed over 500 Fulani in response to an alleged conspiracy against him.

The army has been in power since 1984, following Sekou Touré's death.

GUINEA — GUINEA-BISSAU

The ground sections of the 240-mile (386-km.) Guinea–Guinea-Bissau boundary are demarcated by boundary pillars. The line follows a colonial boundary between the French and Portuguese possessions in west Africa and extends southward from the boundary tripoint with Senegal to the Atlantic Ocean in the south.

Geographical Setting. The Guinea–Guinea-Bissau–Senegal boundary tripoint is located at approximately 12°40'30"N and 13°42'30"W. From there the boundary line runs southward to reach the Niamanka River, follows the river downstream southward to its confluence with the Tomine (Koliba) River and follows the Tomine westward to its confluence with the Corubal River, the main river in Guinea-Bissau. Thence the boundary runs westward along the Corubal River to its confluence with one of its smaller tributaries. It follows the tributary eastward to its source and then southward to reach another tributary, crossing it and reaching a third tributary, the Feliné River. The line follows the Feliné River upstream for 10 miles (16 km.) and as it departs from the river runs westward to boundary pillar no. 24 on the watershed between the Kogon River (Guinea) and the Corubal River (Guinea-Bissau). The boundary follows the watershed westward and southwestward until it reaches boundary pillar no. 1 on the Atlantic coast. The boundary continues in the sea, leaving Tristao Island with Guinea.

Historical Background. Guinea-Bissau was first reached by Europeans when the Portuguese arrived in 1446 and became a slave trading center. Until 1879 it was administered with the Cape Verde islands, but then became a separate colony under the name of Portuguese Guinea. The French established

Guinea's boundaries

themselves in Guinea in 1849 when they proclaimed the Boké region a French protectorate and then began its expansion eastward. The boundary between the French and Portuguese possessions in West Africa was established by a treaty signed on 12 May 1886, was demarcated between 1900 and 1904 and was confirmed in an exchange of notes dated 29 October and 4 November 1904. France established the colonial federation of French West Africa in 1904, in which Guinea was a separate unit that became independent on 2 October 1958. Portuguese Guinea became independent as Guinea-Bissau on 24 September 1974. Both newly established independent states adopted the colonial line as their international boundary without a formal agreement.

Present Situation. The present boundary was demarcated in the colonial era but it appears to lack clear definition in certain localities. However, no major doubts exist and since independence neither country has challenged its alignment.

GUINEA — IVORY COAST

The 379-mile (610-km.) boundary between Guinea and Ivory Coast runs in a north–south direction between the boundary junction with Mali in the north and the boundary junction with Liberia in the south.

Geographical Setting. There is no international agreement concerning this boundary and its alignment depends upon French administrative practice during the colonial period, the best evidence of this being found in maps. The boundary begins in the north, at the boundary junction with Mali. It runs southwestward to the Gbanhala River and follows its course upstream. Near its source, the boundary leaves the river, runs eastward to the Kourou Kelle River and follows it southward, west of the town of Bako (Ivory Coast). Then the line crosses the watershed between the great Niger River, which runs northeast, and the rivers flowing south, connecting two tributaries of the Sassandra River. The boundary runs south to the Feredougouba River, follows it upstream westward and continues along the Kouè stream. Departing from the stream, the boundary line runs to the Nimba Mountains (6,070 feet; 1,850 m.), reaching the upper source of the Cavally River at the boundary junction with Liberia.

Historical Background. Both Guinea (formerly French Guinea) and Ivory Coast were part of the large colonial French West Africa established in the nineteenth century. The French delimited administrative lines between their administrative units in principle in a decree of 17 October 1899. However, this decree, which determined the shape of Ivory Coast and Guinea as colonies, did not describe their precise limits. Guinea became independent on 2 October 1958 and Ivory Coast on 7 August 1960. Both

adopted the colonial line without signing an official agreement to this effect.

Present Situation. Some sectors of the boundary between these two west African countries are indefinite, especially along those areas where the watercourses are tortuous and branching. Nevertheless, since Guinea and Ivory Coast gained independence no disputes have been reported and there have been no objections to the principles of the alignment.

GUINEA — LIBERIA

The boundary between Guinea and Liberia runs for 350 miles (563 km.) between the boundary tripoint with Sierra Leone on the left bank of the Makona River in the northwest and the boundary tripoint with Ivory Coast at Mount Neun in the Nimba Range in the southeast.

Geographical Setting. The left (south) bank of the Makonda (Mao) River, at its confluence with the Dandogbia River constitutes the northwestern terminus of the boundary line. It follows the Liberian (south) bank of the Makonda River upstream eastward, to a point west of Macenta (Guinea). Thence the boundary line leaves the river and runs in a series of straight lines to the Nianda River, a tributary of the Saint Paul River. Leaving it within Guinea, the boundary follows its southern bank to its confluence with the Saint Paul River. Following the southern (Liberian) bank of the river, it follows it to its source. Leaving the river, the boundary runs southeastward in another series of straight lines, reaching the Mani (Mano/Saint John) River. It follows its southern bank to its source in the Nimba Mountains, which are divided by the boundary line. It reaches the Ivory Coast tripoint at Mount Neun (5,904 feet; 1,800 m.) in the Nimba Range.

Historical Background. French merchants established trading posts on the coast of today's Liberia in the late fourteenth century. In the fifteenth century the Portuguese established themselves in that region while the British, Dutch and French traded there in the seventeenth century. Liberia was established in 1820 by the American Colonization Society, which purchased some areas for the settlement of liberated black slaves from the United States. In 1822 the first permanent settlements of these slaves were established in Cape Mesurado (today Monrovia—the capital of Liberia). The area was named Liberia in 1838 and became independent in 1847. The French established themselves in west Africa in the mid-nineteenth century.

Guinea originated as a unit in the colonial federation of French West Africa. The territory acquired its present form in the French decree of 17 October 1899. Liberia expanded its territory inland toward the French area of Guinea but in 1910 was forced to leave an area of approximately 2,000 sq. miles (5,000 sq. km.) to Guinea. The agreement of 1910 established the present boundary, leaving the southern edge of the Nimba range within Liberia. On that side of the range one of the richest iron ore mines was found and from the 1950s Liberia shipped some 15 million tons of ore annually through the finest of west Africa's railways from the mine to the Liberian port near Lower Buchanan.

Present Situation. Guinea became independent on 2 October 1958, adopting its boundary with Liberia. Since independence there have been no disputes concerning the alignment of the boundary line. Its straight line segments are demarcated by pillars or monuments.

GUINEA — MALI

From the boundary junction with Senegal, the Guinea–Mali boundary runs west and southwest for 533 miles (858 km.) to the boundary tripoint with Ivory Coast. A large area of the boundary follows rivers and streams.

Geographical Setting. The boundary between Guinea and Mali was never described in a formal agreement and in the absence of an enactment the alignment relies upon mapped evidence. The western terminus of the boundary—the boundary junction with Senegal—is situated in the middle of the Balinko River. It runs southward, following the river's eastern tributary to its source and crossing a local watershed reaches the upper Falémé River. It follows this river northeastward to its confluence with its southeastern tributary and follows this stream to its source. Crossing a local watershed southeastward the boundary reaches the Bafing River, traverses along it downstream northeastward and reaches its eastern tributary. The line follows the tributary upstream to its source and, crossing another local watershed, it reaches the Bakoy River. Along the Bakoy River downstream, the boundary runs northeastward, then heads southeast, around the town of Niagassola (Guinea) and meets a northwest-

ern tributary of the great Niger River. The boundary crosses the Niger River and continues southeast along local rivers, including the Sakarani River, and a series of lines connecting them until it reaches the tripoint boundary junction with Ivory Coast.

Historical Background. From the middle of the nineteenth century onward the entire area of west Africa was a French colonial region under the name of French West Africa. The boundary between Guinea and Mali is based on an intracolonial boundary that was then established by the French administration. In principle Guinea has remained a unit as created by a French decree on 17 October 1899, with an administrative boundary line with French Sudan. On 2 October 1958 Guinea gained independence and Mali, part of the former French Sudan, became independent as the Republic of Sudan on 20 August 1960. A month later, on 22 September 1960, the Republic of Sudan became the Republic of Mali. Each state adopted the former colonial boundary line although no formal agreements were made.

Present Situation. This boundary appears to be undemarcated and certain areas of the line consist of wandering rivers and streams or run through large flood zones. However, since independence no disputes concerning the principles of alignment have been reported, although a certain degree of clarification and demarcation appear to be necessary.

GUINEA — SENEGAL

The Guinea–Senegal boundary follows the French administrative line between its possessions in western Africa. It is 205 miles (330 km.) long and extends from the boundary tripoint with Mali on the Balinko River in the east to the boundary tripoint with Guinea-Bissau in the west.

Geographical Setting. The eastern terminus of the boundary line, which is the boundary tripoint with Mali, is located on the Balinko River, a tributary of the Falémé River. It leaves the river and follows the Konkoniouma range westward for about 25 miles (40 km.). Crossing the Koila Kabe River, the boundary follows the Galendi range westward for 20 miles (32 km.) to the source of the Soudoul River. Coursing along that river downstream it reaches the Gambia River, crosses it, follows one of its small tributaries and then runs west along local rivers and short straight lines connecting them. This section of the boundary places named villages to the north (Senegal) and south (Guinea) of the line and reaches the Mitji River. The boundary line follows this river downstream westward to its intersection with 12°40'30"N and follows the parallel westward for about 25 miles (40 km.) to the boundary tripoint with Guinea-Bissau, at approximately 12°40'30"N and 13°42'30"W.

Historical Background. French settlers arrived in Senegal in the seventeenth century and from 1854 it came under the administration of a French governor. France established itself on the coast of Guinea in 1849 and expanded its territory over most of west Africa by the late nineteenth century. Guinea and Senegal were both units of the colonial federation of French West Africa, which also included today's Mauritania, Niger, Burkina Faso, Ivory Coast and Mali. The boundary between the Guinea and Senegal units was established by the French administration in 1898 and 1899. Some modifications were made on 27 February 1915 and on 13 December 1933. These boundaries were determined for the purpose of an internal organization of the French possessions, without international recognition. Guinea became independent on 2 October 1958 while Senegal, after a short period of being part of the Federation of Mali, became independent on 20 August 1960. Both countries adopted the administrative colonial line as their international boundary without any formal agreement.

Present Situation. The boundary line is generally delimited and is demarcated with only a few pillars. However, since independence, there have been no disputes concerning its alignment.

GUINEA — SIERRA LEONE

This boundary follows a colonial boundary between the former British and French possessions in western Africa. It runs for 405 miles (652 km.) from the boundary tripoint with Liberia on the Dandogbia River in the east to the North Atlantic Ocean in the west.

Geographical Setting. The boundary tripoint with Liberia on the Dandogbia River is located north of the small town of Koindu (Sierra Leone). The line follows the river downstream westward to its confluence with the Moa (Makona) River and follows the main navigation channel of that river upstream northward to its confluence with the Meli River.

Following the main navigation channel of the Meli River upstream northward, the boundary line reaches its confluence with the Uldafu River, which it follows to its source, where boundary pillar no. 11 was established. In a straight line, the boundary reaches boundary pillar no. 1, close to the source of the Tembikounda River, which is the source of the great Niger River. Then the line follows the watershed between the Niger River, which flows in Guinea northeastward, and the Little Scarcies River, which flows through Sierra Leone to the Atlantic Ocean southwestward. It reaches the 10°N parallel and follows it westward for 50 miles (80 km.) to its intersection with the Little Scarcies River. The boundary follows the river downstream for 6 miles (10 km.) and then runs in another straight line to the intersection of the Lolo and Kita rivers. It follows the Kita River westward to its source and to a boundary pillar. In a straight line southwestward the boundary reaches the Great Scarcies River, which is followed downstream southwestward to its confluence with the Great Mola River. There the boundary leaves the rivers and trends southwest along the watershed between the Mola and Scarcies rivers to reach the North Atlantic Ocean coast, northwest of the village of Kiragba (Sierra Leone).

Historical Background. The British established themselves in Sierra Leone in 1787 and almost a century later, in 1885, the colonies of Gambia and Sierra Leone were organized into the British West Africa Settlements. Two years later, however, Sierra Leone was established as a separate colony. In 1849 France settled on the Guinea coast and during the second part of the nineteenth century expanded eastward, establishing the French West Africa Federation, which included Guinea. The boundary between the British and French possessions in west Africa was then established in a series of agreements between 1882 and 1913. The demarcation of the boundary that was agreed upon in 1889 was carried out in 1895–1896, with some modifications in 1903 and 1912, and was finalized by the agreement of 4 September 1913. Guinea achieved independence on 2 October 1958 and Sierra Leone became an independent state on 27 April 1961. Without a formal agreement the newly established countries adopted the colonial line as their international boundary.

Present Situation. The boundary between the

French and British possessions was clearly marked on the ground after a survey determined its exact alignment. The ground sections, which constitute approximately half of the boundary, were marked by pillars, while the river sectors are distinctly defined. Since independence there have been no disputes concerning the boundary's alignment.

GUINEA-BISSAU (Guiné-Bissau) Formerly Portuguese Guinea, Guinea-Bissau is one of the westernmost African countries (area: 13,948 sq. miles [36,111 sq. km.]; estimated population: 1,050,000 [1994]). It is bounded in the north by Senegal (210 miles; 338 km.), in the east and south by Guinea (240 miles; 386 km.) and in the west by the North Atlantic Ocean. Guinea-Bissau is one of the poorest nations of the world. Its capital is Bissau.

Guinea-Bissau gained its independence from the Portuguese in 1974. During the colonial period the Portuguese brought to Guinea-Bissau a large number of Cape Verdeans to serve as work inspectors for local groups, mainly the Lanta. After independence these Cape Verdeans, who had educational advantages over the locals, dominated Guinea-Bissau's politics. This situation continued until 1980, when a Papel military coup supported by the Lanta, put an end to Cape Verdean domination. Since then a large number of Lanta, Papel and Manjaco have been appointed to high positions in the government and administration.

In 1991, following popular unrest, the regime declared a democratization process to be launched during 1993.

GUINEA-BISSAU — GUINEA see GUINEA–GUINEA-BISSAU.

GUINEA-BISSAU — SENEGAL For 338 miles (210 km.) the boundary between Guinea-Bissau and Senegal runs from the boundary tripoint with Guinea in the east to Cape Roxo on the shore of the Atlantic Ocean in the west. It follows the boundary line between the former French and Portuguese colonies in western Africa.

Geographical Setting. The eastern terminus of the boundary line, which is the boundary tripoint with Guinea, is located at approximately 12°40'30"N and 13°42'30"W. The boundary follows 12°40'30"N

westward for about 100 miles (160 km.) to its intersection with the 15°20'W meridian (17°30'W of the meridian of Paris), where boundary pillar no. 12 is located, 12 miles (19 km.) north of the town of Farim (Guinea-Bissau). From that point it follows the watershed between the Farim-Caheu (Guinea-Bissau) and Casamance (Guinea) rivers until it reaches the Atlantic Ocean in Cape Roxo.

Historical Background. The Portuguese established themselves on the western coast of Africa as early as 1446, establishing a colony in Guinea. The colony included the island of Cape Verde until 1879, when Portuguese Guinea was set up as a separate colony. The French established themselves on the west African coast in 1854 and a French governor ruled the area of Senegal, which became part of French West Africa in 1895. On 12 May 1886 France and Portugal concluded a treaty on the division of their possessions in western Africa, whereby the northern division determined the boundary between Portuguese Guinea and Senegal. The demarcation of the line was carried out during 1900–1905 and was confirmed by an exchange of notes in 1904 and 1906. Senegal became independent as part of the federation of Mali on 20 June 1960 and withdrew from the federation two months later to become independent Senegal. Portuguese Guinea remained a Portuguese possession until 24 September 1974, when it proclaimed its independence as Guinea-Bissau. Although no formal agreements were made, the newly established countries adopted the colonial boundary line as their international boundary.

Present Situation. Since Guinea-Bissau and Senegal gained independence no disputes concerning their common boundary's alignment have been reported. The entire length of the boundary line is well demarcated.

GUYANA A South American country (area: 83,032 sq. miles [214,969 sq. km.]; estimated population: 800,000 [1994]), Guyana is situated in the north of the continent. It is bounded in the north by the Atlantic Ocean, in the east by Suriname (373 miles; 600 km.), in the south and west by Brazil (695 miles; 1,119 km.) and in the west by Venezuela (462 miles; 743 km.). The capital of Guyana is Georgetown.

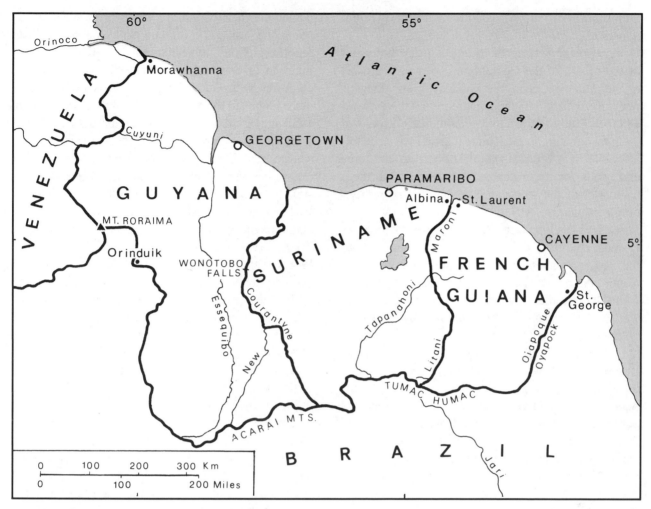

The boundaries of French Guiana, Guyana and Suriname

What eventually became British Guiana, and later Guyana, was first explored by Sir Walter Raleigh in 1595 and 1617. During the 1600s, Guyanese teritory was a subject of dispute among the Dutch, French and British, but following the Congress of Vienna (1814–1815), the land was divided into three colonies: British, French and Dutch. Plantation sugar, produced by black slaves, formed the economic base of Guyana well into the 1800s. After the abolition of slavery in the 1830s, the British began to import East Indians, at very low wages, to maintain plantation crop production. Discontent with British domination began about 1900, but did not reach serious proportions until the conclusion of World War II.

In 1953, in response to the Indian-led People's Progressive Party (PPP), Britain granted limited self-government; after the PPP's election victory,

Britain suspended the constitution, accusing the PPP of communist leanings. The PPP, which split along ethnic lines in 1955, managed in 1964 to return briefly to power under a new constitution, but was defeated by the largely black People's National Congress (PNC) in 1964. Following independence in 1966, the Guyanese established South America's first Marxist state, nationalizing much of its commerce and industry.

GUYANA — BRAZIL see BRAZIL–GUYANA.

GUYANA — SURINAME The boundary between Guyana and Suriname runs for 373 miles (600 km.) from the mouth of the Courantyne (Corantijn) River on the Atlantic coast in the north to the boundary tripoint with Brazil in the south. It follows the colonial boundary between the former

Dutch and British possessions in northern South America.

Geographical Setting. Setting out from the center of the mouth of the Courantyne River on the coast of the Atlantic Ocean, the boundary runs along its main navigation channel upstream southwestward and then southeastward to its confluence with one of its main tributaries, the Kutari (Cutari) River. It follows that river upstream southeastward to its source and heads for the watershed between the northern tributaries of the Amazon River and the rivers running northward.

Historical Background. Berbice, currently the easternmost county of Guyana, along with Suriname to the east, was Dutch territory from the mid-seventeenth century. In the late eighteenth century Suriname and Berbice disputed ownership of the land west of the Courantyne River and in 1794 the Dutch government ruled that Berbice extended to its west bank. In 1799 both territories were acquired by Britain, but the two Dutch governors were retained in office. They sought confirmation of the Courantyne boundary and a proclamation to this effect was published by the Governor and Councils of Berbice in 1800. Guyana (Britain) claimed that this proclamation did not actually constitute a boundary agreement. The Netherlands (later Suriname), however, maintained not only that the boundary was valid but that it had been confirmed by the Peace of Paris in 1815. The two countries similarly disagreed on sovereignty over the river itself. The Dutch regained control of the two colonies in 1802 but the British retook Berbice the following year and in 1831 the British united the colonies of Berbice, Essequibo and British Demerara into British Guiana.

In 1841 the British government commissioned an explorer to investigate the boundaries of the colony, who reported that the Curuni and Kutari rivers were the main tributaries of the Courantyne and mapped the British–Dutch boundary along them. This boundary was accepted by both the British and the Dutch, albeit the latter with some reservations.

In 1871 it was discovered that the New River was larger than the Curuni/Kutari, leading to a Dutch claim in 1899 that the New River should constitute the British–Dutch boundary. Britain rejected the claim, but the matter was not resolved.

In 1926 Brazil and the United Kingdom agreed to demarcate their boundary "along the watershed between the Amazon Basin and the basins of the Essequibo and Courantyne rivers as far as the point of junction or convergence of the frontier of the two countries with Dutch Guiana." The Dutch government reopened the boundary question in 1929 and in 1930 suggested a definition of the border as "the left bank of the Courantyne and the Cutari up to its source, which rivers are Netherlands territory." A treaty was drafted along these lines but was never signed due to the outbreak of World War II in 1939. In 1936, however, Britain, Brazil and the Netherlands agreed on a tripoint junction at the source of the Kutari River. The Dutch position hardened after World War II and in 1962 the government formally claimed the New River Triangle and began referring to the New River as the Upper Courantyne.

British Guiana became independent in May 1966 with its eastern (and western) boundary still unsettled. A meeting in London in June 1966 between representatives of Guyana and Suriname failed to settle the question. A serious dispute over the triangle territory broke out in December 1967, marked by a serious armed incident in August 1969. In 1970 Guyana and Suriname reached an agreement on a number of matters—but not on the boundary. Suriname achieved complete independence in November 1975 and continued to claim the triangle as its territory. Relations between the two countries waxed and waned thereafter and several agreements to reopen boundary negotiations remained unconsummated.

Present Situation. The boundary between Guyana and Suriname upstream from the confluence of the Courantyne River with the New River (Upper Courantyne) remains unsettled. Guyana continues to administer the triangle formed by these rivers and the Brazilian boundary and Suriname continues to claim it. Suriname also pursues its claim that the west bank of the Courantyne River below the New River constitutes the boundary, but de facto it continues to follow the *thalweg* of the river. No resolution of the problem is currently in sight.

GUYANA — VENEZUELA From the coast of the Atlantic Ocean in the north the boundary between Guyana and Venezuela runs for 462 miles (743 km.) to the boundary tripoint with Brazil on Mount Roraima in the south.

Geographical Setting. The northern terminus of this boundary is located at the intersection of the 60°W meridian with the Atlantic coast of northern South America. From there it runs southeastward for about 25 miles (40 km.) to a point west of the town of Morawhanna (Guyana) and turns southwestward to reach the Amacuro (Amakura) River. The line follows the river upstream southwestward to its source near La Horqueta (Venezuela), heads southwestward and then southeastward for about 90 miles (140 km.) along a local watershed and reaches the Cuyuni River, which is followed upstream westward to its confluence with the Venamo (Wenamu) River. It bears southward with that river to its source near Mount Venamo (6,200 feet; 1,890 m.). From Mount Venamo the boundary extends some 60 miles (100 km.) in a straight line southeastward, reaching the Brazilian tripoint on Mount Roraima (9,094 feet; 2,773 m.) in the Pakaraima Mountains.

Historical Background. The first European settlers arrived in northern South America from the Netherlands in 1581 and competed with Spain for control of the area west of the lower Essequibo River. In 1609 Spain withdrew from the contest under a 12-year truce with Holland. The Dutch remained the chief colonists through the seventeenth and eighteenth centuries. Between 1781 and 1814 the colonies of Berbice, Demerara and Essequibo were ruled alternately by the Dutch and British, but in the peace settlement following the Napoleonic Wars the British purchased the colonies from Holland and the territory remained British thereafter. In 1831 the three colonies were united into the colony of British Guiana, but Venezuela vigorously protested the inclusion of Essequibo, claiming that the Essequibo River was its "natural" eastern boundary and that Spain had discovered, explored and settled the region and had exercised political control over it. The British, on the other hand, claimed that the Dutch had controlled the region, including trade with the Indians through posts established on the Essequibo and other rivers. In 1841 the present western boundary of Guyana was surveyed by Robert Schomburgk and maps were prepared showing the boundary along the Amacuro, Cuyuni and Venamo rivers to the source of the latter, then in a straight line to Mount Roraima. In negotiations for a boundary treaty in 1844, Venezuela refused to accept a proposed boundary along such a line. Thereafter, the British and Venezuelan governments took steps to assert authority in the Essequibo region—until Britain formally proclaimed the Schomburgk line as the Venezuela–British Guiana boundary in 1886.

Venezuela broke diplomatic relations with Britain in 1887 and in 1894 asked the United States to intervene in what it claimed was a violation of the Monroe Doctrine. In 1895 the United States remonstrated with Britain and the following year Britain expressed willingness to make some concessions. In 1897 Venezuela and Britain agreed on arbitration and the arbitral tribunal determined in 1899 that the boundary should follow most of the Schomburgk line, but leave to Venezuela a strategic area to the south of the Orinoco River as well as two other parcels, which, in total was a loss of about 5,000 sq. miles (13,000 sq. km.) for British Guiana. The new boundary was demarcated and an agreement on the line was signed in 1905.

Venezuela reopened the boundary issue in 1951, questioning the validity of the 1899 arbitration award, and raised the issue again in the United Nations General Assembly in 1962, setting on record before British Guiana became independent that it did not consider the matter settled. Britain and Venezuela began discussions which led to the Geneva Agreement of 17 February 1966, establishing procedures for settling the dispute. Guyana became independent on 26 May 1966. The mixed commission established under the Geneva Agreement continued its work while many incidents soured relations between the disputants but failed to settle the dispute. On 18 June 1970 Britain, Guyana and Venezuela signed the Port of Spain Protocol to the Geneva Agreement, which placed a 12-year moratorium on the dispute, renewable for successive 12-year periods. However, Venezuela notified Britain on 11 December 1981 that it would not renew the moratorium when it expired.

Following a number of incidents in 1982, the question was returned to the UN General Assembly. Relations between Guyana and Venezuela improved beginning in 1984 and in March 1985 a special representative of the UN Secretary General visited both capitals and issued an optimistic report. Relations between the two parties continued to improve and the UN Secretary General was asked to provide good offices to help resolve the matter. In 1990 the distinguished scholar Alister McIntyre, vice chancellor of the University of the West Indies, was accepted by both states as the "good officer."

Present Situation. The largest territory disputed in Latin America is that between Venezuela and Guyana. The territory, known as the Essequibo, covers some 50,000 sq. miles (130,000 sq. km.), more than five times the area of Belize, and two-thirds of the present area of Guyana.

In late 1994 the dispute had yet to be resolved, but Dr. McIntyre was quietly continuing his work. It seems reasonable to expect that in due course the matter will finally be laid to rest, with the boundary roughly where it was established by the arbitration of 1899.

H

HAITI Situated in the Caribbean Sea, east of Central America, Haiti (area: 10,718 sq. miles [27,750 sq. km.]; estimated population: 6,600,000 [1994]) occupies the western region of Hispaniola Island. About three-quarters of Haiti is mountainous terrain. It is bounded in the north by the Atlantic Ocean, in the east by the Dominican Republic (222 miles; 358 km.) and in the west and south by the Caribbean Sea. Haiti's capital is Port-au-Prince.

Haitian society is divided into two cultures, Franco-Haitian and Afro-Haitian. The former dates back to the days of colonization. Many French customs were assimilated into Haitian culture, including language, education, religion (Catholicism), etiquette and cooking. Afro-Haitian culture characterizes the descendants of the slaves shipped in from Africa; it includes its own religion (Voodoo), language (French-based Creole), music, dance and cooking. These two cultures, when combined, form a composite Haitian culture; when separated, they divide Haiti into two social classes far removed from each other. In fact, Haitian society has always been divided into two groups: the small elite and the impoverished masses. The elite is made up of big business owners, including Haitian mulattoes, Arabs, some Europeans, Canadians and Dominicans. The poorer classes are mainly black.

Although Roman Catholicism is the official religion, Voodoo is the most practiced. It is based on the worship of family spirits (*loua*) which protect family members and bring them good fortune. Haiti is known for its art, particularly primitive painting and wood carving, much of which depicts Voodoo rituals.

The economy is largely based on agriculture; however, because of serious ecological problems such as deforestation and soil erosion, productivity has declined drastically. This has caused many Haitian farmers to leave their lands for the urban slums, or even to attempt the daring voyage to the United States in poorly made sailboats.

In 1804 Haiti earned the distinction of being the first black nation to acquire independence and abolish slavery, a great feat in view of the might of the army of the French. From independence to the ousting of the first democratically elected president, Jean B. Aristide, the military has been able to impose its will through a series of coups. Except for the oppressive 30 years of the Duvalier regime, the resulting government instability has crated an atmosphere of distrust for and discontent with the military and the chief executive officer. Since the early 1950s there has been neither an improvement in infrastructure nor the institution of a system to maintain living conditions and enforce zoning regulations. Today the Republic of Haiti is the poorest nation of the western hemisphere.

HAITI — DOMINICAN REPUBLIC see DOMINICAN REPUBLIC–HAITI.

HONDURAS A Central American country (area: 43,277 sq. miles [112,044 sq. km.]; estimated population: 5,240,000 [1994]), Honduras is situated between the Pacific Ocean and the Caribbean Sea. It is bounded in the west by Guatemala (159 miles; 256 km.), in the south by El Salvador (213 miles; 342 km.) and in the southeast by Nicaragua (573 miles; 922 km.). The capital of Honduras is Tegucigalpa.

Descendants of Jamaicans (about 2% of the population) brought to work in the local banana plantations live in the northern coastal area of the Caribbean Sea, where there are also whites of English stock, mainly Protestants, descendants of the

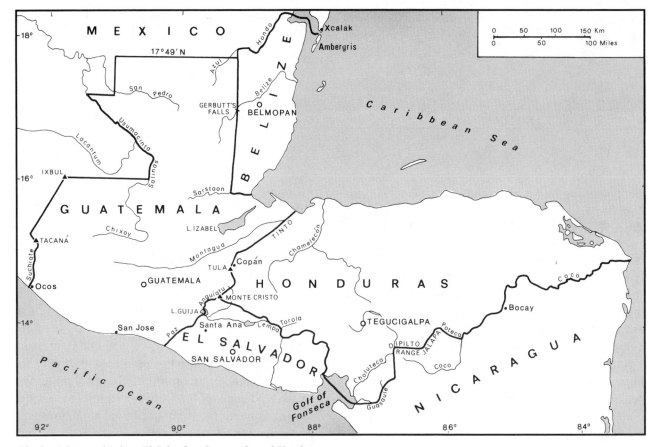

The boundaries of Belize, El Salvador, Guatemala and Honduras

settlers who developed the banana economy. The development of the plantation economy on the tropical coastal plains has caused a substantial migration from traditional settlement areas in the temperate mountainous regions.

Christopher Columbus arrived in Honduras in 1502, but no permanent Spanish settlement was established until 1522. Early struggles between indigenous Indians and Spaniards abated somewhat with the appointment of the first territorial governor in 1526, but major war between the colonists and the indigenes later broke out, lasting from 1537 through 1539. Honduras, never an independent colony, was part of Guatemala after 1570, at which time discovery of silver brought many new people, including the British, who threatened Spanish dominion over the country.

The Central American colonies separated from Europe in 1821 and, in 1823, Honduras, Guatemala, Nicaragua and Belize combined to form one country, called the United Provinces of Central America, from which Honduras withdrew in 1838. Early in

the twentieth century, the unstable Honduran government was increasingly controlled by Nicaragua, until the US sent Marines to protect US economic interests, particularly banana production. A succession of military dictatorships was followed by the reestablishment of civilian government in 1982. Of the two major Honduran political parties, the Liberals are actually conservative, while the right-wing National Party is closely tied to the military.

HONDURAS — EL SALVADOR   see EL SALVADOR–HONDURAS.

HONDURAS — GUATEMALA   see GUATEMALA–HONDURAS.

HONDURAS — NICARAGUA   The boundary between Honduras and Nicaragua runs from the Pacific Ocean in the west to the Caribbean Sea in the east, crossing the Central American isthmus. It is 573 miles (922 km.) long, of which 445 miles (716 km.) follow rivers. The land boundary is well demarcated.

Geographical Setting. The southwestern terminus of the boundary is located on the Pacific shore in the Gulf of Fonseca. In the gulf itself a 27-mile (43-km.) line has been delimited as the outset of the boundary. From the shore the boundary runs 15 miles (24 km.) in a straight line eastward to reach the Negro River in Amatillo. Following the median line of the river 6 miles (10 km.) upstream it then joins the Guasaule River for 16 miles (26 km.) northward. Then it enters the Torondano River, traveling along it to its confluence with the Quebrada Grande. The boundary continues along the bed of this ravine and then along its affluent, Pena Blanca, to its source on the La Botija ridge. Leaving the rivers it runs east-southeast along the ridge for 3 miles (5 km.). It turns northward for 32 miles (51 km.) in the hilly area in a line formed in accordance with local property lines until it reaches the Dipilto Range. The boundary follows the watershed of that range eastward and then the watershed of the Jalapa range northeastward to Portillo de Teotecacinte at 14°02'53.61"N and 86°08'09.01"W. The boundary line continues downstream along the center of the headwaters of the Limon River to its intersection with the boundary of Sitio de Teotecacinte. Along a series of eight straight lines and a short river channel eastward and then southward, the boundary line reaches the Poteca River. Then it courses along the main navigation channel of the river to its confluence with the Coco River. The line continues along the main navigation channel of the Coco River to its mouth at Cape Gracias a Dios on the shore of the Caribbean Sea. The line in these two rivers runs for a total of 387 miles (623 km.).

Historical Background. The settlement of the boundary between Honduras and Nicaragua was one of the most prolonged of Latin American boundary disputes. In 1821 Central America rose in revolt against Spain and formed the United Provinces of Central America in 1823. On 30 April 1837, however, Nicaragua declared itself independent and Honduras became independent two years later when the Union was dissolved. Only 50 years later, on 11 February 1888, did Honduras and Nicaragua negotiate a treaty concerning their common boundary based on the Hispanic colonial line. Between 1900 and 1904 a demarcation commission settled the western part of the line, from the Pacific Ocean to

Portillo de Teotecacinte, but could not agree on the eastern section. Both countries placed their claims before the king of Spain for arbitration and on 23 December 1906 the king proposed the present line along the Coco and Poteca rivers to Teotecacinte. Honduras accepted the arbitration but Nicaragua rejected it. The dispute continued for another 54 years until both countries agreed in 1960 to submit their claims before the International Court of Justice (ICJ). On 18 November 1960 the ICJ determined that the 1906 line suggested by the king of Spain should become the international boundary between the two countries. This time both countries accepted the judgment and a mixed Honduras-Nicaragua commission demarcated the boundary line. On 4 May and 5 August 1961 the two countries signed an agreement concerning the demarcation of the boundary line, by which 3,410 sq. miles (8,831 sq. km.) were transferred from Nicaragua to Honduras.

Present Situation. The boundary line between Honduras and Nicaragua is now a peaceful one. After the detailed demarcation of the line in 1961, no known disputes were reported and 140 years of boundary disputes came to an end.

HONG KONG A British colony that is due to become part of China in 1997, Hong Kong (area: 401.5 sq. miles [1,039 sq. km.]; estimated population: 5,900,000 [1994]) is situated in the Far East, southwest of Taiwan. Its only land boundary is with China (19 miles; 30 km.) in the west, while the South China Sea lies to its east, south and west. Hong Kong's capital is Victoria.

Hong Kong

HONG KONG — CHINA see CHINA–HONG KONG.

HUNGARY (Magyarország) A landlocked country (area: 35,934 sq. miles [93,033 sq. km.]; estimated population: 10,560,000 [1994]) in Central Europe, Hungary is bounded in the north by Slovakia (420 miles; 676 km.), northeast by Ukraine (64 miles; 103 km.), east by Romania (275 miles; 443 km.), south by Serbia (103 miles; 166 km.) and Croatia (204 miles; 329 km.), southwest by Slovenia (63 miles; 102 km.) and west by Austria (227 miles; 366 km.). The capital of Hungary is Budapest.

The Hungarians probably originated in the basins of the upper Kama and Volga rivers, and for unknown reasons migrated at an unestablished date to the steppes, where they adopted the culture of the steppe nomads. Although mainly of Finni-Ugric stock, they might have included a Turkic element which supplied their leadership. In the ninth century they were a federation of 10 tribes which roamed the steppes west of the Don River. Pushed west by the Pecheneg, they were led by their khan, Arpad, across the Carpathian Mountains. Here they established themselves in the plains of modern Hungary at the end of the ninth century and destroyed Greater Moravia in the following decade. Until defeated at Lechfeld by the emperor Otto I in 955, they were the terror of Germany, their raids reaching as far as France and Italy.

Arpad's great-grandson, Geza, converted to Roman Catholicism in 975, and his son, Saint Istvan (Stephen) was declared king of Hungary by the pope; tradition claims that he was crowned on Christmas Day, 1000. Hungary thus became part of Western Christendom and its defender in southeast Europe. Istvan's successors extended their borders to the Carpathians, annexing Slovakia and Transylvania. The kingdom of Croatia in the south was united with the Hungarian crown in 1102, although it retained its autonomy. In 1241 the Mongols devastated the country, reducing the population by almost half, but since the Mongols did not remain in occupation, Hungary survived as an independent kingdom and retained its status as a great power.

In 1301 the Arpad line became extinct, and from that time, with two exceptions, the country was ruled by foreign dynasties, the Angevins, Luxembourgs and Jagiellonians, all of whom were also rulers of other countries and thus involved Hungary in a web of internal and external struggles. In the mid-fourteenth century Hungary became involved in Balkan affairs, fighting the Ottomans; in 1396 a Hungarian-led crusade was defeated by the Ottomans at Nicopolis. In 1526 Süleyman the Magnificent defeated the Hungarian army in Mohács and occupied the Hungarian capital, Buda. In 1566 four decades of struggle between the Ottomans and the Habsburgs came to an end with the Habsburgs ruling the western fringe of Hungary and Croatia, as well as Slovakia, for which they had to pay tribute to the sultan; the bulk of Hungary (and Croatia) came under direct Ottoman rule, while an autonomous principality was established in Transylvania. Although under the suzerainty of the sultan, Transylvania played an active part in European politics and especially in the wars of reformation.

Following the second Ottoman failure to conquer Vienna (1683), the Habsburgs conquered most of the previous kingdom of Hungary, including Transylvania, and the territories were ceded to them by the Ottomans in the Peace of Karlowitz (1699). Hungary became part of the extended Habsburg Empire, centrally ruled from Vienna, and underwent a series of administrative reforms and germanization at a forced pace.

Partly in response to these policies and partly under the influence of ideas emanating from revolutionary France and Germany, a reform movement developed which, combined with a cultural revival, turned into a nationalist movement by the mid-nineteenth century. In 1848 Hungarian nationalists declared the independence of a restored Hungarian kingdom in its broadest scope. They were immediately crushed by the Russians in 1849. Following the Habsburg defeat in the Austro-Prussian war of 1866, a compromise was reached, which created a Great Hungarian kingdom in a dual Austro-Hungarian monarchy.

Throughout the nineteenth century the Hungarian nationalist movement had been at odds with the Croats, Slovaks and Romanians under its control, practicing a policy of repression which sought to enforce the assimilation of minorities into Hungarian culture. After World War I and the collapse of the dual monarchy, Hungary was forced to cede large territories to Czechoslovakia, Romania, Yugoslavia

Hungary—a landlocked country in Central Europe

and even to Austria, where great numbers of Hungarians lived. Thus, out of 10,000,000 Hungarians, 1,700,000 found themselves in Romania, 1,000,000 in Czechoslovakia, over 500,000 in Yugoslavia and 25,000 in Austria. This created strong irredentist pressures on Hungary's foreign policy. In World War II Hungary joined the Axis powers and was rewarded by Hitler and Mussolini with half of Transylvania and parts of Czechoslovakia and Yugoslavia. After the war Hungary was pushed back to its prewar borders, except for an additional strip it lost to Czechoslovakia. A hard-line Communist regime was imposed by the Soviet troops which occupied Hungary.

In 1956 Hungary's Stalinist regime was toppled and a new democratic government under Imre Nagy announced its withdrawal from the Warsaw Pact and declared Hungary's neutrality. This prompted the Soviets to crush the new government by military force and reimpose a Communist regime under Janos Kadar. However, Kadar's administration proved mild, enabling private-sector activities and bringing economic development to the country. By the late 1980s, Hungary was among the most prosperous and free countries in Eastern Europe and in 1989–1990 led the other eastern bloc countries in overturning the Communist regime through the electoral process.

HUNGARY — AUSTRIA   SEE AUSTRIA–HUNGARY.

HUNGARY — CROATIA   SEE CROATIA–HUNGARY.

HUNGARY — ROMANIA   The boundary between Hungary and Romania is 275 miles (443 km.) long and runs from the boundary junction with

Ukraine in the north to the boundary junction with Serbia in the south. The present boundary was established after World War I.

Geographical Setting. The northern terminus of the boundary is located on the Batar River, which is one of the southern tributaries of the Tisza (Tisa, Tissus) River, east of the small town of Halmeu, between the Tisza and Somesul (Szamos) rivers. The line runs generally south-southwest, roughly parallel to and west of the railway line between the Romanian cities of Satu-Mare and Arad, to facilitate railway connections between Romania and the former Czechoslovakian Republic. As the boundary was delimited such that all the Romanian people living in the border area would stay in Romania, it was delimited along village and town limits.

In its course the boundary cuts local rivers (Beretaul, Sebes Körös, Crisul Negru, Crisul Alb) and railway lines such as the Satu-Mare–Debrecen (Hungary), Oradea (Romania)–Szolnok (Hungary) and Arad–Szeged (Hungary) lines but keeps the villages of Kotegyan, Gyula, Ottolakan, Kevermes and Dombegyhaz undivided within Hungary. From a point 12 miles (20 km.) northeast of Arad, the boundary turns westward to reach the Muresul (Maros) River 0.6 miles (1 km.) south of the Nagyalak railway station. It follows the main navigation channel of the river downstream northwestward to a point about 2 miles (3 km.) upstream from the Makó (Romania)–Szeged railway bridge. It then follows a tributary of the Muresul River westward to a bend in its course, at about 46°10' N and 20°22' E, which is the boundary junction with Serbia.

Historical Background. The present Hungary–Romania boundary stems directly from the treaties and acts ending World War I. Before the war Hungary, as part of the Austro-Hungarian Empire, ruled a large area east of Hungary itself, including the entire Transylvania region. Romania had become an independent state in 1861, was recognized as such in the Congress of Berlin of 1878 and ruled the areas of Moldavia and Wallachia on the Black Sea. Romania extended its area southward after the Second Balkan War of 1913, but about 3,000,000 Romanians remained in the area ruled by Hungary. Romania entered World War I on the condition that the Allied Powers recognize its claims on all the areas lying east of the Tisza River. The defeated Hungary had to

accept the Treaty of Peace between the Allied and Associated Powers and Hungary and the declaration signed at Trianon on 4 June 1920. The boundary established in the treaty transferred to Romania 39,467 sq. miles (102,180 sq. km.) of Hungarian territory, with a population of 5,240,000, which included approximately 1,700,000 Hungarians. A demarcation team placed 4,500 intervisible markers on the ground and thus established the exact alignment of the boundary.

Between the two World Wars Hungary consistently but peacefully canvassed for a revision of the Trianon Treaty, especially the section concerning Transylvania. Allied with Germany and Italy during much of World War II, Hungary regained about 40% of the area in the Vienna Award of 30 August 1940. However, the Treaty of Peace with Hungary, signed on 10 February 1947, declared the Vienna Award null and void and the Trianon boundary was reinstated as the effective line between the two states.

Present Situation. The long-standing controversy between Hungary and Romania over the Transylvania region has been subordinated since the end of World War II. Neither country is openly pressing for boundary modifications and for now there are no open disputes concerning its alignment, although the basic issue persists.

HUNGARY — SERBIA This boundary follows a segment of the boundary between Hungary and the former Yugoslavia and was established after World War I. It runs for 103 miles (166 km.) between the boundary tripoint with Croatia in the Danube River in the west and the tripoint with Romania in the east.

Geographical Setting. The entire length of the Hungary–Serbia boundary runs through the lowlands of the Pannonian plains and has no perceptible natural features as its basis. The western terminus of the boundary is located in the Danube River, between the towns of Mohács (Hungary) and Batina (Serbia). It runs east-northeasterly along a line that separated Hungarian and Serb villages and reaches the Kigyos River about 2 miles (3 km.) east-south-east of Bacsmadaras Station. It follows the course of the Kigyos River but curves to the north of Ridica (Rigyicza), which is left within Serbia. The line continues east-northeastward, leaving Subotica within

Serbia, and reaches the Tisza (Tisa) River about 3 miles (5 km.) east-northeast of Hargos Station (Serbia). It follows the median line of the Tisza River upstream northward for about 3 miles (5 km.) and leaves it to run generally east toward the boundary junction with Romania, which is located 2.5 miles (4 km.) southwest of Kiszombor Station (Hungary) and about 10 miles (16 km.) southeast of the Hungarian city of Szeged.

Historical Background. The present boundary between the two states reflects only the last phase of over a century of boundary changes in the area. After 450 years of Ottoman rule, Serbia, which ruled most of the Balkan Peninsula in the fourteenth century, became an autonomous principality of the Ottoman Empire in 1817. Between the Ottoman and Hungarian regions lay a military zone that was ruled by the Austrian Empire. Serbia became an independent kingdom in 1878 while Hungary became a self-governing section of the Austro-Hungarian Empire that was reorganized in 1867. Until World War I the boundary between the two states ran along the Sava and Danube rivers, just north of Beograd (Belgrade)—but after the defeat of the Austro-Hungarian Empire in World War I major changes took place. Serbia, along with Croatia and Slovenia, Montenegro and Dalmatia, established the Kingdom of the Serbs, Croats and Slovenes in December 1918, later (1929) to become Yugoslavia, while Hungary's boundaries were redelimited by the Treaty of Trianon (4 June 1920) which established the independent Hungary. The boundary between Hungary and the new kingdom moved northward to include the whole Vojvodina province, including the city of Novi Sad, up to the outskirts of the Hungarian city of Szeged. This province was settled mostly by Hungarians and other non-Serbs but was attached to Yugoslavia. Until World War II Hungary never halted claims for the province and was reunited with it during 1941–1944. However, after World War II the 1920 boundary line was reestablished. Vojvodina's autonomy was abolished in 1989 and was divided between Serbia and Croatia, the constituent republics of the new Republic of Yugoslavia, leaving with Serbia the area east of the Danube River. After the collapse of Yugoslavia in 1991, Serbia (along with Montenegro) formed the independent republic of Serbia (which is sometimes still called

Yugoslavia), adopting its former boundary with Hungary as its international boundary in the north.

Present Situation. At present there is no open dispute between the two states concerning the demarcated boundary line. However, about 19% of Vojvodina's population in the 1981 census were Hungarians and the nationalist movement in Hungary is still pressing to reunite that province with Hungary. The Hungarian government insists that it is not responsible for such claims and that the 1920 boundaries are the officially accepted boundaries of present-day Hungary.

HUNGARY — SLOVAKIA Established after World War I and modified after World War II, this is the boundary between the former Czechoslovakian Republic and Hungary. It is 420 miles (676 km.) long and extends from the boundary junction with Ukraine in the east to the boundary junction with Austria in the west.

Geographical Setting. The junction of the Hungary–Slovakia boundary with Ukraine is located in the Tisza (Tisa, Tisia) River and from there the line runs generally westward. The demarcation team fixed the boundary between settlements, fields, railway lines, roads and other man-made features, thus establishing a well defined line between the two countries. Apart from two main river sections in the west, only a few minor areas follow natural lines, such as watersheds and rivers. While running westward, the boundary cuts railways and rivers (Bodrog, Hernád, Sajó), but leaves entire villages in Hungary or Slovakia.

About 90 miles (145 km.) from its eastern terminus, the boundary line turns southward for 20 miles (32 km.) to the confluence of the Sajó and Slana Rivers. Then it runs southwestward, crosses the Filakovo (Slovakia)–Salgótarján (Hungary) railway and continues northwestward to reach the Ipel' (Eipel, Ipoly) River about 1 mile (1.6 km.) south of Tesmag (Hungary). The boundary follows the Ipel' River downstream westward and departs from it near the Hungarian city of Tesa, leaving a local railway line with Slovakia. Returning to the Ipel' River, the boundary follows it southward to its confluence with the Danube River, near the city of Esztergom (Hungary). It follows the principal navigation channel of the Danube River upstream westward and northwestward for about 100 miles (160 km.) to a point on the right bank of the river, 2 miles (3.2 km.) east of the Rajka village church (Hungary). The boundary leaves the river, runs westward along the northern cadastral boundary of Rajka village and meets its junction with the Austrian boundary 2 miles (3.2 km.) northeast of the village church. By placing the boundary terminus at that point, the dam and spillway within the village limits remain in Hungarian territory.

Historical Background. The establishment of the Hungary–Slovakia boundary dates back to the reorganization of the European political maps after World War I. Before the war the entire area was part of the Hungarian section of the Austro-Hungarian (Habsburg) Empire and included an equal number (approximately 10,000,000) of Hungarians and non-Hungarians. With the collapse of the empire in 1918, its national minorities demanded complete independence while the Hungarians declared the establishment of an independent Hungarian state for all the Hungarians occupying a contiguous area within established boundaries. The newly established Czechoslovakian Republic, which was based on the areas inhabited by Czechs and Slovaks, was too narrow to have a defensive role while most of its railway systems ran through Hungarian-inhabited areas. The Czechs requested that the Danube River serve as their southern boundary while Hungary made claims for the area north of the Danube River, inhabited by some 750,000 Hungarians. The final Treaty of Peace between the Allied and Associated Powers and Hungary and the protocol and declaration, signed at Trianon on 4 June 1920, determined the boundary between Hungary and Czechoslovakia according to the Czech demands and Hungary was reduced to the plain, losing all of the northern mountainous area, as about 22% of its prewar territory was transferred to Czechoslovakia.

Hungary tried to regain some of its lost area and obtained a revision of the boundary with Slovakia in 1938–1939, but the peace treaty of 1947 restored the Trianon boundary. One modification was made in the Treaty of Peace with Hungary signed on 10 February 1947, which shifted the western terminus of the boundary to its present location.

Present Situation. The establishment of the independent Republic of Slovakia on 1 January 1993 did not cause any changes in the boundary's alignment. There are no known disputes concerning the boundary's location but there are many problems concerning the use of the Danube River for a planned hydroelectric power station to be built as a joint effort, which is currently rejected by the Hungarians. Moreover, the problem of a large Hungarian minority in Slovakia might be the cause of complications in the future.

HUNGARY — SLOVENIA   From the boundary tripoint with Austria in the northwest to the tripoint with Croatia at the confluence of the Mura and Krka rivers in the southeast, the Hungary–Slovenia boundary follows a segment of the line between Hungary and the former Yugoslavia and was established after World War I. The boundary is 63 miles (102 km.) long.

Geographical Setting. The northwestern terminus of the boundary line is located approximately 1 mile (2 km.) east of Tauka and about 10 miles (16 km.) northwest of the small Slovakian town of Hodos. The boundary runs eastward through the hilly Goricko region and along the watershed between the Rába and Lendava rivers for about 8 miles (13 km.) and then turns southward, passes east of Hodos, crosses the Krka River and reaches the westernmost extensions of the Pannonian plains. It runs southeastward, passes between Lenti (Hungary) and Lendava (Slovenia) and reaches the Lendava River. The line follows the river downstream southeastward to the boundary junction with Croatia, at the river's confluence with the Mura and Krka rivers, at a point 20 miles (32 km.) west of the Hungarian town of Nagykanizsa.

Historical Background. Slovenia, which was settled by the Slovenes in the sixth century, consisted of two separate provinces—Styria and Carniola—and belonged to the Hungarian section of the Austro-Hungarian Empire until the end of World War I. Along with Dalmatia, Bosnia, Montenegro, Serbia and Croatia it formed the Kingdom of the Serbs, Croats and Slovenes in December 1918, which later became the Kingdom of Yugoslavia (1929). Hungary became an independent republic on 24 November 1918 and its boundary with Yugoslavia was established by the Treaty of Trianon, signed on 4 June 1920. According to a detailed description, it was to run from a point on the watershed between the basins of the Rába and Mura rivers, about 1 mile (2 km.) east of Tauka, along the present southeastern boundary of Hungary. This line was demarcated in the early 1920s but was not accepted by Hungary. During World War II Hungary occupied the present-day Slovenian territory on the left bank of the Mura River, known as the Prekmurje (Transmura) region. However, after the war the 1920 line was reestablished, confirmed by the Paris Treaty in 1947 and thereafter never officially opposed by Hungary.

Slovenia became a constituent republic of prewar Yugoslavia and after a referendum of 23 December 1990 the parliament of the Republic of Slovenia declared its independence from Yugoslavia (25 June 1991) and accepted its existing boundary with Hungary in the northeast.

Present Situation. There are no official disputes concerning the alignment of the Hungary–Slovenia boundary line, although some Hungarians still support a reissue of the boundary question. Both sides of the border are inhabited with minority populations: nine mainly Slovenian villages are located in Hungary, north of the boundary, and Hungarians inhabit several villages in the southern part of the Prekmurje region.

HUNGARY — UKRAINE

The 64-mile (103-km.) boundary between Hungary and Ukraine extends from the boundary junction with Romania northwestward to the boundary junction with Slovakia. The line is marked by rivers and fixed boundary points.

Geographical Setting. The boundary line begins at the its tripoint with Romania, south of the Carpathian Mountains, on the Batar River east of a local village named Magosliget (Hungary) and follows the river's course downstream to its confluence with the Tisza (Tisia, Tisa, Theiss) River. It follows the Tisza River downstream to reach a local village called Darocz. Then the boundary forms a line that is fixed on the ground and separates Hungarian and Ukrainian villages. It meets the confluence of two small, local streams, again separating villages, and from there bears with the course of the Csaronda Stream to its confluence with the Tisza River. Rejoining the Tisza River, the line reaches a point east-southeast of the village of Tarkany and continues northwestward along the river to the boundary tripoint with Slovakia, west of the town of Chop (Ukraine).

Historical Background. The boundary between Hungary and Ukraine is the boundary between Hungary and the former Soviet Union, which was established after World War II and is part of the boundary established between Hungary and Czechoslovakia after World War I. Prior to 1918 the entire area was part of the Austro-Hungarian Empire, but with the collapse of the empire in 1918 its Hungarian territory was reduced. The Ruthenia region was detached from Hungary and was incorporated into the new Czechoslovak state, a transfer that was made to give Czechoslovakia a direct land connection with Romania and to withstand Hungarian pressure. The boundary was first delimited by the Committee for the Study of the Territorial Questions of the Paris Peace Conference in 1919. On 12 June 1919 the line suggested by the Commission on Czechoslovakia Affairs was approved by the main Conference and became part of the Treaty of Trianon, which established the boundaries of new Hungary, was signed on 4 June 1920 and came into effect on 26 July 1921.

The boundary between Hungary and Czechoslovakia was marked and measured on the ground by a delimitation commission during 1921–1925 and a convention for the settlement of boundary questions was signed in Prague on 14 November 1928. Pressure from Hungary, following its dissatisfaction with the Treaty of Trianon (a sentiment that still exists in Hungary today), led to a revision of the boundary line in Hungary's favor in 1938. But this lasted for only a short period.

With the collapse of Czechoslovakia in 1939, Hungary unilaterally occupied Ruthenia and additional parts of Slovakia. At the end of World War II Czechoslovakia ceded Ruthenia to the Soviet Union by the Moscow Agreement of 29 June 1945 and on 10 February 1947 Hungary signed the Treaty of Peace, by which it returned to its pre-1938 boundary. The treaty states that the boundary between Hungary and the Soviet Union was to stand along the former line between Hungary and Czechoslovakia as it existed on 1 January 1938. In 1991 Ukraine became an independent country and the former boundary between Hungary and the Soviet

Union became the boundary line between Hungary and Ukraine. Hungary still sees the Treaty of Trianon as an agreement that it was forced to sign in 1920. However, no border disputes are known to exist and the Hungarian government states that it holds no claims for a revision of the boundary line.

above: The Czech side of the Czech Republic–Poland boundary

below: Czech and Polish boundary control officers

274

above: Ipales—on the Ecuador–Colombia boundary

below: Denmark–Germany boundary crossing

above: France–Italy boundary in the Alps

below: The Rhine River follows the France–Germany boundary

Voges Mountain—a historic barrier between France and Germany

Gibraltar—a British territory in the Iberian Peninsula

The Danube River follows the Hungary–Slovakia boundary

The India–Nepal boundary region

above: The India–Myanmar boundary region

below: France–Spain boundary area

above: France–Switzerland boundary crossing

below: The Swiss checkpoint at the France–Switzerland boundary crossing

above: The Iraq–Turkey boundary area

below: The Tigris River, which follows part of the Iraq–Syria boundary

Israel–Jordan boundary in the Gulf of Eilat (Aqaba)

The westernmost point of the Israel–Lebanon boundary

above: A sand dune near the Jordan–Saudi Arabia boundary

below: The Lebanon–Syria border

above: A village near the Laos–Thailand border

below: Liechtenstein—a tiny landlocked European state

287

above: The road crossing the China–Nepal boundary

below: A Turkish village (Biblical Haran) near the Syria–Turkey boundary

Kilimanjaro Mountain on the Kenya–Tanzania border

I

ICELAND (Ísland) An island in the North Atlantic Ocean, Iceland is situated between the United Kingdom and Greenland. Its area is 39,769 sq. miles (102,962 sq. km.) and it has an estimated population (1994) of 270,000. Iceland's capital is Reykjavík and it has no land boundaries.

Iceland was first discovered in the eighth century by Celtic monks; from 872 it was colonized by Norse Viking rebels against the first attempts of Norway's monarchs to impose order, who brought their Celtic slaves with them. In due time Norway sent an elite class to Iceland, which established an original civilization dominating political life until the fourteenth century. While agriculture was hardly possible, pastures and fish fields abounded. There were no towns, only farms. The Icelanders' early history seems to have been peaceful and democratic. By the year 1000 they were Christianized, and slavery disappeared. However, the situation deteriorated in the thirteenth century. Unending vendettas brought the republic down, and subjected the island to Norwegian sovereignty.

By 1380 Icelanders passed under nominal Danish sovereignty. Volcanic eruptions, deterioration of the climate, the plague and the introduction of serfdom contributed to the islanders' ruin. In the sixteenth century Danish overlords imposed Protestantism. Epidemics and volcanic eruptions further decimated Icelanders in the eighteenth century. The nineteenth century witnessed gradual recovery, but many Icelanders escaped through emigration to Canada.

In 1904 Iceland became autonomous and parliamentarism was introduced. A new treaty in 1918 left only a personal union with Denmark. Total independence followed in 1944 as a result of World War II. In the Cold War, Iceland's importance as a prop for Western (North Atlantic Treaty Organization) bases often clashed with a popular tendency toward neutralism. The Icelanders were able to develop an extensive social security system, but in spite of recent prosperity, their economic basis, dependence on fishery, remains narrow and vulnerable. Extension of maritime zones has led to recent conflict with the British.

INDIA (Bharat) The second largest populated country in the world (after China), India (area: 1,269,212 sq. miles [3,285,989 sq. km.]; estimated population: 903,000,000 [1994]) is a south Asian country, situated between the Himalayas and the Indian Ocean. It is bounded in the north by China—in three sections (2,101 miles; 3,380 km.), Nepal (1,050 miles; 1,690 km.) and Bhutan (376 miles; 605 km.), in the east by Myanmar (909 miles; 1,463 km.), Bangladesh (2,519 miles; 4,053 km.) and the Bay of Bengal, in the south by the Indian Ocean and in the west by the Arabian Sea and Pakistan (1,810 miles; 2,912 km.). Its capital is New Delhi.

Bounded in the north by the Himalayan mountain chain, India can be more properly described as a subcontinent than a country. It has represented a cul-de-sac for the invasionary forces that have entered it from the northwest since time immemorial and its complex ethnic mix is primarily a result of successive groups of invaders remaining to intermingle with the indigenous population. While great kingdoms have flourished in different parts of the subcontinent over millennia (the civilization that built the cities of Moenjodaro and Harappa flourished in the Indus valley, in what is now Pakistan, some 4,500 years ago), India has been a single governmental entity for a relatively short time dating from the consolidation of British colonial rule in the first half of the nineteenth century.

India's northeastern boundaries run through the Himalaya Mountains

Since it gained independence from Britain in 1947, India has been a sovereign democratic republic, currently divided into 22 states and nine union territories. National government is centered in the capital, New Delhi.

INDIA — BANGLADESH see BANGLADESH–INDIA.

INDIA — BHUTAN see BHUTAN–INDIA.

INDIA — CHINA see CHINA–INDIA.

INDIA — MYANMAR The India–Myanmar (Burma) boundary is 909 miles (1,463 km.) long, running from the boundary tripoint with China in the northeast to the tripoint with Bangladesh in the southwest. It follows the colonial line between British India and British Burma, except for the southern section that today forms the boundary between Myanmar and Bangladesh.

Geographical Setting. This boundary mainly follows watersheds, rivers and streams. Its northeastern terminus, the boundary tripoint with China, is located in the Himalaya Mountains, south of the Chinese town of Zayu, between the northern tributaries of the Nami and Irrawaddy rivers (Myanmar) and the eastern tributaries of the great Brahmaputra River (India). The precise location of this tripoint is not yet settled and will remain so until India and China settle their boundary in northern Assam. The boundary runs southward along the Arakan Yoma mountain range, which forms the main regional watershed. About 50 miles (80 km.) south of the boundary tripoint, the line turns southeastward and passes through the Chaukhan Pass, leaving the Dihing River in India. Then it runs northwestward for about 40 miles (65 km.) to reach the Patkai Range, trends along the range southeastward, crossing the Pangsau Pass to Naga Hills, always keeping to the watershed, and runs southward, leaving the whole area of Manipur within India. South of the town of Tamu (Myanmar) the boundary turns eastward and runs in that direction for about 50 miles (80 km.). In its course it crosses the Manipur River, leaving its northern tributaries in India, while the main river runs in Myanmar and joins the Irrawaddy River, Myanmar's principal river. South of the Indian town of Kungnang the boundary changes its direction again, running southward to reach the Tyao River. It follows that river downstream southward to its confluence with the Boinu River and follows the latter upstream southward for about 45 miles (70 km.). Leaving the river, the boundary runs eastward, crosses its lower course, the Kaladan River, and reaches the tripoint with Bangladesh, which is located between the Lushai and Chittagong hills.

Historical Background. Until the early nineteenth century the border area between India and Burma was determined by many small and fierce tribes in the locality, who preserved their independence against larger states in the plains by raiding them from time to time. In the early nineteenth century the activities of these hill tribes created problems for the raided Burmese kingdom to the east, and the British East India Company in Assam and lower Bengal in the west, and contacts between British and Burmese forces led to the development of periodic friction. The Manipur basin and the fertile area along Logtak Lake were occupied by Burma in 1819, alarming the British, who then settled themselves in eastern Assam, and a war began in 1824. The Peace Treaty of Yandabu, which ended the war on 24 February 1826, established the British in the eastern provinces of Assam, asserted Manipur's independence and vaguely defined the boundary between British India and Burma along the Arakan ranges. The northern section of the boundary, between Assam and Burma, was settled in 1837 along the Patkai range. On 9 January 1834 the southern section of the boundary, south and east of Manipur, was established, leaving the region in British India. However, this section of the line created some problems as it divided the Khyens tribes and was defined again in 1881. Britain had acquired the adjoining area of Burma in 1886 after the third war between them and the boundary problem became an internal matter. The boundary east of Manipur was redefined in 1894 and demarcated in 1896. The southern seg-

ment of the boundary, through the territory of the Lushai people, south of Manipur, was settled in 1895 and demarcated in 1901 with some minor alterations in 1921 and 1922. The Government of India Act of 1935 separated Burma from India, an act that marked the final settlement of the colonial period. The intercolonial boundary became an international limit when India and Burma became independent in 1947 and 1948 respectively. Both states adopted the line as their common international boundary without a formal agreement, but the activities of some rebel tribes north of Manipur led to discussions between the two countries and a boundary agreement was concluded and signed in Rangoon (Burma) on 10 March 1967, defining the established boundary in detail. In June 1989 Burma became the Union of Myanmar.

Present Situation. Since 1967 there have been no known disputes concerning the boundary alignment. It is well established along watersheds, rivers, streams and a series of straight lines connecting boundary pillars that were erected in 1894.

INDIA — NEPAL The India–Nepal boundary runs for 1,050 miles (1,690 km.) and divides India's boundary with China. From the western border junction with China, near the intersection of 28°N and 81°E, it runs to the eastern boundary junction with China northwest of the Indian state of Sikkim.

Geographical Setting. The boundary between India and Nepal forms three sides of the Napalese rectangle; the short sides in the east and west, each approximately 120 miles (190 km.) long, and the long southern side, which is some 800 miles (1,290 km.) long. The northwestern corner, the western boundary junction with China, is in Barmdeo Mandi, northeast of the headwaters of the Kali River, west of the Urai (Pai-lin) pass and north of the Himalayan peak of Api (23,399 feet; 7,134 m.). It reaches the Kali River and follows its median line and then runs along the Sarda River southwestward until the latter enters the great Ganges plain at an altitude of approximately 660 feet (200 m.) above sea level. There it turns southeastward to form the southern section of the boundary, which generally coincides with the southern limits of the Terai, a forested tract, about 20 miles (32 km.) wide, located between the northern Nepalese foothills of the Himalayas and the

India–Nepal boundary

Ganges plain (India). It links the many rivers flowing between the Himalayas and the Ganges River with straight lines, separating farm and village lands and following rivers such as the Mohan to the west and the Narayani in the middle of the southern stretch. The boundary also crosses the Rapti and Gandak rivers, follows the Someswar range and regains the Terai region. East of the Indian town of Bhimnagar it crosses the Kosi River and runs eastward to reach the Mechi River north of the Indian city of Kishangani. The boundary turns northward, following the Mechi River to its sources in the Himalayas and then runs to the eastern boundary junction with China, north of the Himalayan peak of Kanchenjunga (28,146 feet; 8,581 m.), the third highest peak in the world.

Historical Background. The modern history of the boundary between India and Nepal originates in the late eighteenth century. Britain had established itself in India and had some commercial relations with Nepal, based on treaties signed in 1792 and 1801. In 1812 Nepal annexed over 200 villages from India,

some of which were under British protection. This led to a war between Britain and Nepal in 1814–1815. Nepal was defeated and agreed to a peace treaty that established the Kali and Mechi rivers as the eastern and western boundaries of Nepal, which have been maintained to the present. Britain annexed the Terai area between the Kali and Kosi rivers against a pension payment to the local chiefs. The Nepalese never accepted the British view that the entire Terai region ought to be placed in India and when the British realized that the disputed area was in fact lacking in commercial value they decided to return part of it to Nepal, thereby also saving the payment to the local chiefs. In a treaty signed in December 1816, the Terai area between the Rapti and Kosi rivers, in the central area of the lowlands, was submitted to Nepal and a survey commission demarcated the boundary line in 1817. This section of the line has also been preserved to the present day.

During the second half of the nineteenth century, the remaining areas of the Terai were given to

Nepal: in 1860 Britain returned its western section, between the Rapti and Kali rivers, and this part of the boundary was demarcated on the ground by stone pillars. In 1875 undemarcated boundary segments between the Rapti and Gandak rivers and between the Kosi and Mechi rivers were surveyed and the boundary line was positioned. No further changes were made in the boundary alignment.

Present Situation. The political changes in the Indian subcontinent which led to India's independence never changed the India–Nepal boundary location and the old colonial line, which was settled under different political circumstances, is fully functional. No boundary disputes are known to exist as India and Nepal mutually recognize their common boundary line.

INDIA — PAKISTAN   The India–Pakistan boundary runs for 1,810 miles (2,912 km.) between the Arabian Sea in the southwest and the Karakoram Range in the northeast. The boundary line of the disputed state of Jammu and Kashmir follows the "line of control" based on the 1972 consensus of both countries.

Geographical Setting. From the mouth of the Sir Creek in the Arabian Sea the boundary line follows it to a point on the 23°58'N parallel. It follows the parallel for 32 miles (51 km.) to its intersection with the 68°41'E meridian, which it follows northward for 30 miles (48 km.) to its intersection with 24°17'N. Then the boundary runs along the northern shore of the marshy area of the Rann of Kutch, leaving the small towns of Sadariaja Got, Baliari and Nabisar in Pakistan. At two points the boundary line leaves the northern shore, which was the historical boundary of the Sind region, and runs southward to give Pakistan the Sadariaja region and the area of Dhara Banni. Heading generally northward, the line leaves the Nagar Parkar area (including the small towns of Nagar Parkar, Kasbo and Vatawa) with Pakistan and reaches the boundary between the Indian state of Rajasthan (formerly the state of Rajputana) and the Hyderabad division (formerly Khairpur state) of the Sind province of Pakistan, west of the Indian town of Bakhasar. It traverses through the Thar Desert in a northwesterly direction for about 250 miles (400 km.), across the Jodhpur (India)–Hyderabad (Pakistan) railway. Thence it

runs northeastward for about 125 miles (200 km.), reaching a point located north of the Indian desert settlement of Kishangarh. Heading eastward for about 70 miles (110 km.), it continues crossing the Thar Desert along the line that divides the provinces of Bahawalpur (Pakistan) and Rajasthan (India) and thence runs northeastward for about 190 miles (300 km.), leaving the town of Fort Abbas with Pakistan and the town of Anupgath with India, and reaches a point east of the town of Bahawalnagar (Pakistan). Running eastward and then northward, the line reaches the Sutlej River and follows it upstream northeastward for about 60 miles (100 km.), separating eastern (Indian) and western (Pakistan) Punjab. East of the Pakistanian town of Kasur, the boundary leaves the river and bears northward, passing between Lahore (Pakistan) and Amritsar (India). As it reaches the Ravi River it joins its course upstream northeastward to its confluence with the Ujh River and follows that river upstream for 12 miles (20 km.). Leaving the river it runs northwestward, following the old southern boundary of Kashmir that crosses the Chenab River and reaches the Tawi River south of the town of Chhamb. From this point the boundary line used to run along the western boundary of Kashmir, but in 1972 a cease-fire line was delimited, dividing the region of Jammu and Kashmir between India and Pakistan. Thus, the present line runs from the Tawi River northward and northwestward, crosses the river and leaves the town of Chhamb with Pakistan. It then runs northward for 70 miles (113 km.) through Jangar and Mithidhara, reaches and crosses the Poonch River and leaves the town of Poonch in Indian territory. From there the line proceeds northward through the small towns of Jarni Gali, Uri (on the Jhelum River) and Kaiyan, crosses the Kishanganga River and reaches the town of Lunda. Turning eastward, it runs for about 220 miles (355 km.) through the peaks of Durmat and Karobai Gali, crosses the upper Indus River, trends through the Chorbat La Pass, climbs the Karakoram Range and reaches its junction with the Chinese boundary west of Karakoram Pass.

Historical Background. British India included the areas of today's India, Pakistan and Bangaladesh until the Indian Independence Act of 18 July 1947. According to this act the two western Muslim provinces became Pakistan on 15 August 1947 while on the same day the seven eastern Hindu provinces formed independent India. The province of Punjab (and the eastern province of Bengal) was divided between the two new states in accordance with its religious character. Major disturbances concerning the separation process led to a bloodshed that claimed some 500,000 lives and the transfer of approximately 17,000,000 between the two states. The boundary between the province of Sind and Indian Kutch was also disputed, leading to fighting along the boundary line during April–June 1965. An international tribunal provided an award on 19 February 1968, mainly in India's favor but with some benefits for Pakistan.

The boundary in the Jammu and Kashmir region however, is still in dispute. Jammu and Kashmir has an area of approximately 85,000 sq. miles (220,000 sq. km.) and is bounded by India in the south, Pakistan in the west, Afghanistan in the northwest and China in the north and east. In 1947 it had an estimated population of 4,000,000, of whom 77% were

Muslims. It was generally assumed that with the independence movement of 1947 Kashmir, a contiguous state with a predominantly Muslim population, would accede to Pakistan. However, its ruler, the Maharaja, hesitated in his decision to accede to Pakistan or India, or alternatively to seek to maintain Kashmir's independence, and proposed to both a standstill agreement with Kashmir. To prevent accession to India, a Muslim rebellion (October 1947), with the help of Muslim tribes from Pakistan, led to a war in Kashmir through most of 1948. The fighting continued until mediation efforts by a United Nations Commission led to a mutually accepted cease-fire line on 31 December 1948. A resolution to hold a plebiscite in the area was adopted by the UN Commission on 5 January 1949 and was accepted by India and Pakistan. However, the plan was never carried out and the concept was abolished in 1956. Unsuccessful negotiations between 1957 and 1965 led to a war in September 1965, but in a joint declaration made in Tashkent in January 1966 by the

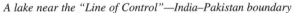

A lake near the "Line of Control"—India–Pakistan boundary

prime ministers of India and Pakistan they agreed to settle their disputes by peaceful means. Further discussions did not lead to any positive results. An Indo-Pakistani war over East Pakistan (Bangaladesh) was held in December 1971, leading to further armed disputes in Kashmir. At talks in Simla (India) between the two states it was agreed to establish "a line of control" based on the cease-fire of 17 December 1971. Further talks that aspired to achieve durable peace, including a final settlement of the Kashmir question, have taken place since then, but have failed to reach such results.

Present Situation. Besides the Kashmir area, both states accepted the alignment of the boundary as established in 1947 and by the award of the international tribunal of 1968 in the south. Neither state agreed on the Kashmir boundary, although both held to the cease-fire line of 1971—but never accepted its function as an international boundary. From time to time fighting occurs along the line, which is patrolled by United Nations forces and is one of the main land boundaries that awaits a final solution.

INDONESIA An archipelago in Southeast Asia, Indonesia (area: 752,410 sq. miles [1,947,989 sq. km.]; estimated population: 188,000,000 [1994]) is the largest Muslim country in the world—almost 90% of its population are Muslims. It is located between the Indian Ocean and the Pacific Ocean. On the island of Borneo, Indonesia has a land boundary with Malaysia (1,108 miles; 1,782 km.) and on the island of New Guinea it has a boundary with Papua New Guinea (510 miles; 820 km.). Indonesia's capital is Djakarta, on the island of Java.

Although different ethnic groups enjoyed considerable autonomy, early Indonesian history is dominated by the presence of several empires and sultanates such as Srivijaya, Majapahit, Ternate and Tidore. The Portuguese and the Dutch fought over control of the islands from the sixteenth to the nineteenth centuries, with the Dutch eventually gaining ascendancy and the Portuguese left only with the eastern half of the island of Timor. Dutch colonial rule was marked by corruption and harsh exploitation of the native population. In 1860, however, the publication of *Max Havelaar*, by Dutch author Multatuli (Edward Douwes Dekker), with its scathing condemnation of conditions under colonialism, led the Dutch to reconsider their position and improve conditions on the major islands.

Local nationalist sentiment increased between the world wars and many Indonesians viewed the Japanese occupation (1942–1945) and the nominal self-rule they then enjoyed as the first step toward independence. Nationalists led by Sukarno declared a republic; they continued to fight the Dutch after ousting the Japanese. Independence was finally granted in 1949. To counter the vast ethnic and geographic diversity of the country, Sukarno introduced a state ideology which called for the unity of Indonesia and appealed for the suppression of secessionist attempts.

Since independence, Indonesia has expanded to include western Irian, formerly western New Guinea (1963) and the former Portuguese colony of East Timor (1975). The East Timorese long resisted Indonesian rule. The Central Moluccas also attempted to establish an independent state but the revolt was quelled upon independence; some 40,000 refugees have fled to the Netherlands, where they continue to agitate for independence.

INDONESIA — MALAYSIA The land boundary between these countries runs across the island of Borneo and is 1,108 miles (1,782 km.) long. The line has been demarcated in only two small sections, most of its length being marked by mountain ridges and water divides.

Geographical Setting. The border region is composed of low folded mountains that are generally aligned from east to west. The boundary sets out from 4°10'N on the east coast of the Celebes Sea and heads westward, leaving the Simengaris River in Indonesia, to 117°E and 4°20'N. From there the boundary continues westward and trends along the line of ridges that form the main local watershed. Where the boundary crosses rivers, some deviations within a 5-mile (8-km.) radius were made to include small areas within Dutch (Indonesian) territory if the rivers emptied into the sea south of 4°10'N or within British (Malaysian) territory if they ran to the sea north of the parallel. The small island of Sebatik in the Celebes Sea was also divided along the 4°10'N parallel. The remainder of the boundary follows the line of the Iran Mountains southwestward and the main watershed between the principal rivers of the area as far as Cape Datu (Tandjoeng Datoek) in the South China Sea. Minor alterations along the watershed between the peaks of Api (110°04'E) and Raja (109°56'E) have been made to follow several small streams, paths and straight-line segments and 20 boundary markers are located in the region.

Historical Background. This boundary was delineated by Anglo-Dutch agreements before Indonesia and Malaysia gained independence and separated the Dutch Indonesian regions of East and West Kalimantan from the Malaysian states of Sarawak and Sabah. Borneo resisted and repulsed occupation for over two centuries although the Dutch, Portuguese, Spanish and English all tried to set up trading stations there and to exploit the strategic potential and resources of the island. The Dutch made four separate attempts to establish a viable base there, the last opportunity arising when the British East Indian Company aborted its attempts to set up factories and handed the management over to the Netherlands.

The British gained a foothold on the island in the first half of the nineteenth century, when James Brooke, the "Rajah of Sarawak," was rewarded with the sovereignty of that state for his part in quashing a rebellion. Although Brooke was a private explorer and the British disclaimed interest in Borneo, British naval support helped Brooke to control Dayak pirates. The Dutch, increasingly suspicious of British motives, offered protection to the sultanates along the island's eastern coast. However, by 1850 the Dutch accepted British occupation in the north of Borneo and after an eight-year rebellion in the Sultanate of Bandjarmas the Dutch had to rule from the island of Java, south of the Java Sea. The Sultanate of Sarawak continued to expand at Brunei's expense. The failure of the Sultanate of Sulu to control piracy led to Spanish action in Jolo, its capital. The Spanish had claimed an interest in Sulu in 1638 but had never occupied the archipelago. As Sulu influence waned in the north of Borneo traders displayed a renewed interest while Spanish traders gained sovereignty over Sabah for an annual payment. With a similar concession from the Sultan of Sulu for Sabah, the traders controlled about 30,000 sq. miles (77,500 sq. km.). A British commercial company canvassed for protection and Britain responded with a Royal Charter to the North Borneo Company in 1881. Spain's sovereignty in the Sulu archipelago

was recognized in return for relinquished claims to mainland Sabah. In 1889 the British and Dutch agreed on a common boundary and this was legalized by a convention in 1891. As geographical information improved, the original delimitation was amended in 1915, when four boundary pillars were placed on the 4°20'N parallel, where the Pentjiangan, Agisan and Seboeda rivers cross the boundary. On 26 March 1928 the last Anglo-Dutch boundary treaty was signed concerning a short section of about 18 miles (30 km.) between the Api and Raja peaks. Nationalists in Dutch East India declared independence on 17 August 1945 but the Republic of Indonesia was not declared until 28 December 1949. Sarawak became a British colony on 1 July 1946 and North Borneo on 15 July that year. On 16 September 1963 they both joined the Independent Federation of Malaya, which became Malaysia.

Present Situation. There is no boundary dispute at present, although both Indonesia and the Philippines have reservations regarding the incorporation of Sarawak and Sabah into Malaysia.

INDONESIA — PAPUA NEW GUINEA This 510-mile (820-km.) boundary runs from north to south across the island of New Guinea. It follows two meridians and the *thalweg* of the Fly River. The line is demarcated by 14 meridian monuments.

Geographical Setting. From the coast of the Pacific Ocean at 2°35'37"S in the north, this boundary courses directly southward along the 141°E meridian to its intersection with the *thalweg* of the Fly River. This northern section is marked by 10 pillars (MM1 to MM10). The boundary then follows the *thalweg* of the Fly River to its intersection with 141°01'10.2"E, which it then follows southward to 9°08'08"S at the mouth of the Bensbach River. This southern section is marked by four pillars (MM11 to MM14).

Historical Background. The Portuguese set up trading posts in what is now Indonesian territory during the sixteenth century, but from 1602 the Dutch established themselves in the islands that later became known as the Netherlands East Indies. In 1828 a declaration claimed the northwestern area of the island of New Guinea for the Dutch crown and it became a dependency of Tidore. In 1884 Britain established a protectorate along the southeastern coast of New Guinea and Germany annexed the northeastern coast, east of the Dutch region. The London Agreement of 1885 determined the border between the German and British lands by a series of lines from the north coast near Mitre Rock to the intersection of 5°S with 141°E. The Protectorate of British New Guinea was annexed by the British in 1888 and in 1895 the Dutch and British also agreed on a boundary along 141°E and joining the Fly River with the mouth of the Bensbach River. In 1899 the Imperial German government assumed control of German New Guinea. Following the Papua Act of 1905, British New Guinea became the Territory of Papua and was placed under Australian administration. After World War I the British government was awarded a mandate from the League of Nations to govern the Territory of New Guinea on behalf of the Commonwealth of Australia and the Papua and New Guinea Act of 1949 formally approved the referral of a mandate of New Guinea to the International Trusteeship system, confirming the administrative union of New Guinea and Papua under the title of the Territory of Papua and New Guinea.

Apart from Netherlands New Guinea (Irian Barat), the Netherlands East Indies became independent as Indonesia on 28 December 1949. By mutual agreement in 1962 Irian Barat was temporarily governed by the United Nations and the following year was placed under Indonesian administration. During 1969 the people of Irian Barat voted in eight consultative assemblies to remain in Indonesia.

In 1972 the name of the Territories of Papua and New Guinea was changed to Papua New Guinea. The present boundary was defined in 1973 and was established between Australia and Indonesia. It closely follows the boundaries settled between Britain and the Netherlands in 1895, which ran from the mouth of the Bensbach River to the *thalweg* of the Fly River along 141°1'47.9"E. The state of Papua New Guinea became fully independent on 16 September 1975, adopting the 1973 line as its land boundary with Indonesia.

Present Situation. There are no disputes concerning this border.

IRAN A southwest Asian country (area: 636,293 sq. miles [1,647,362 sq. km.]; estimated population: 61,660,000 [1994]), Iran is bounded in the north by Armenia (22 miles; 35 km.), Azerbaijan (380 miles; 611 km.), the Caspian Sea and Turkmenistan (617 miles; 992 km.), in the east by Afghanistan (582 miles; 936 km.) and Pakistan (565 miles; 909 km.), in the south by the Gulf of Oman in the Arabian Sea and the Persian (Arabian) Gulf and in the west by Iraq (906 miles; 1,458 km.) and Turkey (310 miles; 499 km.). The capital of Iran is Tehran.

The recent history of the peoples of Iran centers around the history of the Persians, the backbone of the Iranian state. The peoples of Iran are overwhelmingly Muslim and speak a variety of languages. While Iranian languages are spoken by the bulk of Iranian peoples, Turkic languages are spoken in the north in regions bordering with Azerbaijan and Turkmenistan. Arabic is spoken in the extreme southwest, near Iraq.

Since the 1930s, and especially after World War II, urban building has followed the European pattern. Reza Shah Pahlavi (1925–1941) enforced European-style dress including a modified French military kápi known as *kolah-e Pahlavi* (the Pahlavi head dress). This style and variations of it gradually became more entrenched among all strata of the population except for religious functionaries and for women, whose dress retained more traditional aspects. This tendency was reversed by the 1979 Islamic revolution, with men reverting to traditional dress and women wearing the traditional *chador* (long black robe and head-covering).

IRAN — AFGHANISTAN see AFGHANISTAN–IRAN.

IRAN — ARMENIA see ARMENIA–IRAN.

IRAN — AZERBAIJAN see AZERBAIJAN–IRAN.

IRAN — IRAQ The boundary between Iran and Iraq is 906 miles (1,458 km.) long and reaches from the Shatt-al-Arab River in the Persian (Arabian) Gulf to the boundary tripoint with Turkey on the Kuh-e-Dalanper. It is demarcated throughout by pillars or rivers.

Geographical Setting. Beginning in the Persian Gulf at Point R (29°51.20'N and 48°44.68'E), the boundary in the Shatt-al-Arab follows its *thalweg* for 65 miles (105 km.), "on a straight line joining at

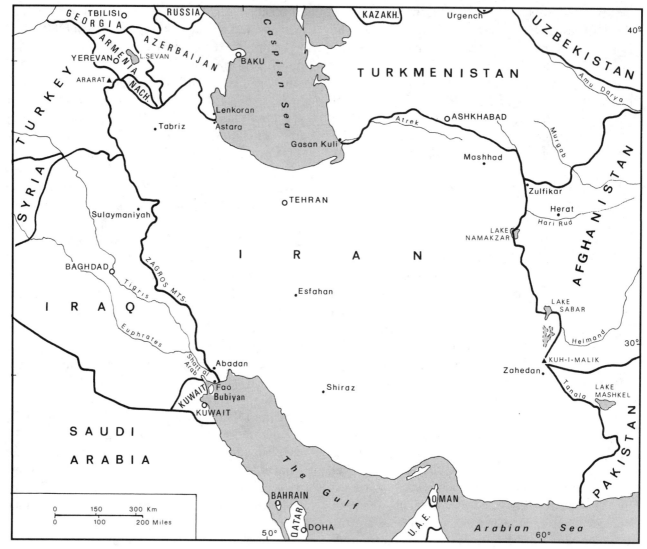

Iran and its boundaries

the astronomical lowest low water, the extremity of the banks at the mouth of the Shatt-al-Arab." It continues upstream, passing through additional points that indicate the course of the *thalweg*, until it reaches Point 59 (30°26.90'N and 48°06.62'E), which is at the confluence of the Shatt-al-Arab and al Khaiin River. From this point the boundary extends to boundary pillar no. 1 (30°27'13"N and 48°06'33"E) on al Khaiin River and follows the median line of this river northwestward for 5.56 miles (8.94 km.) to boundary pillar no. 2 (30°28'40"N and 48°01'27"E). Crossing a flat plain, the boundary continues northward in a series of straight lines for 35 miles (57 km.) to boundary pillar no. 12 (30°59'53"N and 48°01'56"E). It then turns west-

ward, continuing in short straight-line segments for 19 miles (31 km.) to boundary pillar no. 14-A (31°00'01"N and 47°40'54"E), and from this point it extends northward across a swampy plain, again in straight lines, to boundary pillar no. 14-B. Bearing northeastward in straight-line segments for 29 miles (46 km.), the boundary reaches pillar no. 5 (31°47'05"N and 47°51'57"E) at the eastern edge of the Tigris Valley. Northwestward from boundary pillar no. 15 the line follows the relatively low foothills of the Zagros Mountains, in some areas following the median line of Nahr al Tib and the Nahr Wadi, drainage divides and roads. It finally meets the boundary tripoint with Turkey at boundary pillar no. 125/12 (37°11'40"N and 44°46'E).

Historical Background. In the 1639 Zohab Treaty of Peace and Demarcation of Frontiers, Iran (Persia) and the Ottoman Empire, commonly referred to as Turkey (the predecessor state of Iraq in the area), delimited a common boundary in the territory between the Zagros Mountains and the Tigris River. Although this was disputed during the Turkish invasion of Iran in 1724, a peace treaty of 1746 reaffirmed the 1639 boundary. The Treaty of Erzurum of 1847 followed the Iranian-Turkish war of 1821–1822, stipulating that the 1746 boundary was valid. However, it also delimited a boundary in the Shatt-al-Arab for the first time, determining the boundary on the eastern bank of the Gulf, leaving the waterway under Turkish sovereignty—but allowing freedom of navigation. Work on the boundary prospered during 1848–1852 and by 1860 a collaborative map (Carte Identique) was produced to illustrate the boundary.

By the turn of the century, in an effort at stabilization, the United Kingdom and Russia had urged Iran and Turkey to agree to a detailed delimitation, which was completed in 1911. The so-called Constantinople Protocol of 1913 then provided for a further detailed delimitation of the entire boundary by a commission, which demarcated it in 1914. The protocol specifically stated that the Shatt-al-Arab, with the exception of certain islands, was to come under Turkish sovereignty; the demarcated boundary was to follow the low watermark on the Persian bank of the Shatt, except for the area around Khorramshahr, where the line was to follow the *thalweg*. In 1934 Iran (the name used for Persia from 1927) challenged the validity of both the Treaty of Erzurum and the Constantinople Protocol. There followed, on 4 July 1937, a frontier treaty between Iraq and Iran which reaffirmed the boundary established by the Constantinople Protocol and the minutes of the 1914 boundary commission, with the exception of the Abadan area, where, as in the Khorramshahr area, the boundary was moved from the low watermark to the *thalweg*. This change removed one of Iran's major grievances, but the country was still concerned about freedom of navigation and pressed for a *thalweg* boundary throughout the Shatt-al-Arab. Finally, on 6 March 1975, in a joint communiqué between Iran and Iraq, signed in Algiers, Iraq conceded a *thalweg* boundary along the length of the Shatt. In return Iran proposed to cease providing aid for Kurds in northern Iraq. However, in 1980 Iraq abrogated the Algiers Communiqué on the grounds that Iran had refused to restore to Iraq areas near Qasr-e-Shirin (which had allegedly been 'usurped' some 10 years earlier), and had allowed a Kurdish leader back into Iraq. Iran and Iraq entered a war that continued until 18 July 1988, when Iran accepted United Nations Security Council Resolution 598 which included calls for an immediate cease-fire and withdrawal to internationally recognized boundaries. It was not until the Iraqi invasion of Kuwait (1990) that Iraq accepted the 1975 Algiers agreement, although even then Iraq did not entirely and publicly accept Resolution 598.

Present Situation. The outstanding issues of the alignment of the international boundary between Iran and Iraq, control of land adjacent to the border and the status of the Shatt-al-Arab remain unsettled. UN Resolution 598 was only implemented to effect a cease-fire and partial separation of forces and the Iran–Iraq border question thus persists.

IRAN — PAKISTAN   The Iran–Pakistan boundary runs for 565 miles (909 km.) from Gwatar Bay in the Arabian Sea northward to the boundary junction with Afghanistan on Kuh-i-Malik-Siah. The border region is a desert, mostly inhabited by nomadic tribes.

Geographical Setting. The southern terminus of the boundary is located in Gwatar Bay, east of the mouth of the Dasht River (Pakistan). The line heads northward for 40 miles (64 km.) and then in a series of straight lines at right angles to each other, the boundary reaches the Dasht River north of the town of Ispikan (Pakistan). It follows the river upstream northward for 22 miles (35 km.) and eastward for 70 miles (115 km.). The boundary leaves the river and travels in a series of straight lines northward for 39 miles (63 km.) to reach the Mashkel River (Rud-e-Mashkid) River.

After crossing the Mashkel River, the boundary turns westward to trend along the watershed formed by the Siahan Range. Forming a right angle, the line heads northward again for 70 miles (113 km.) to the southwestern edge of the Hamun-i-Mashkel lake. It follows the western bank of the lake and thence heads westward to reach the Tahlab River, which it follows upstream northwestward for about 81 miles (130 km.) to a point where it becomes the Mirjawa River, between the towns of Mirjawa (Iran) and Padaha (Pakistan). In a straight line northwest, the boundary arrives at the closest point on the watershed of the Mirjawa range. It trends over the main watershed northward to Mazawad Peak (7,020 feet; 2,140 m.) on the Kacha Range and from there runs in a set of straight lines northwestward for about 40 miles (65 km.) to reach Malik-Siah Mountain (5,425 feet; 1,654 m.) at the border junction with Afghanistan, which is located at 29°51'31.950"N and 60°52'19.707"E.

Historical Background. British activities in the area close to the Iranian (then Persian) boundary with the British protected state of Kalat brought about a need to define the precise limits of the two authorities. In 1871 the line from the Arabian Sea up to the Mashkel River was defined by the British General F. J. Goldsmid by allocating the various local chieftaincies and small states to the British protectorate of Kalat or Persia along their already existing borders.

In 1895–1896 Britain established the boundary between British India and Afghanistan down to Malik-Siah Mountain. The boundary from that point to the Mashkel River was settled in an Anglo-Iranian agreement on 27 December 1895. It was demarcated by a boundary commission in the early months of 1896 and an additional agreement was signed on 24 March 1896. The boundary was determined along the main watershed of the Kacha Range up to the Padagi Peak, in a straight line to Kacha Peak (7,732 feet; 2,357 m.) and thence to the border junction with Afghanistan. Some problems concerning the exact location of the line were examined by the British in 1901 but no changes were made and in 1905 a new agreement confirmed the 1896 definition of the boundary. After Pakistan became independent on 14 August 1947, boundary negotiations with Iran were held and by 1957–1958 both governments settled the line on the basis of the previous agreements. On 6 February 1958 Iran and Pakistan signed an agreement in Tehran to clarify the precise alignment of the boundary. The demarcation of the line was carried out in 1958–1959 and on 8 December 1959 the final protocol was signed by the two governments.

Present Situation. Since 1959 no problems or disputes concerning the alignment of the boundary have been known.

IRAN — TURKEY The 310-mile (499-km.) boundary between Iran and Turkey runs southward from the confluence of the Aras (Araks) and Kara Su rivers, at the boundary tripoint with Azerbaijan (Nakhichevan), to the boundary tripoint with Iraq. The general location of the present boundary dates as far back as 1639, but the precise demarcation was not carried out until 1937.

Geographical Setting. The boundary sets out from the north, at the intersection of the Aras River with the Kara Su (Black River). It follows the *thalweg* of the Kara Su upstream northwestward for 15 miles (24 km.) and then turns southwest to form a straight line for 9 miles (14 km.) and to reach the foothills of the Little Ararat mountain. For 55 miles (88 km.) it curves east of the mountain, which is the lower peak of the Ararat (Agri Dagi) Massif, reaching the boundary's westernmost point south of the city of Dogubeyazit (Turkey). The boundary is crossed by the Sari Su and by the Dogubeyazit–Maku road and then follows mountain crests that form the watershed between the local eastward and westward flowing streams. For a distance of 4 miles (6 km.) the boundary follows a tributary of the Nazhi Chai and, as it was primarily delimited on a cultural rather than physical basis that was intended to separate villages and nomadic tribes, the line crosses some local eastward flowing rivers, especially in the vicinity of the Iranian cities of Khotur (Qutur) and Rizaiyeh. Heading toward its southern terminus, the boundary crosses the summit of Kuh-e-Dalamper and at the tripoint with Iraq boundary stone no. 99 of the Turkey–Iraq border is located.

Historical Background. The boundary between Iran and Turkey is one of the oldest and most stabilized boundaries in the world. Its roots were set in a 1639 Treaty of Peace and Frontiers that was signed between the Persian and Ottoman empires after 200 years of confrontation along their common frontiers. By this Treaty of Zohab a boundary reaching from the Aras River in the north to the Gulf in the south was established, dividing the Kurds who had settled the area 3,000 years earlier between the two powerful empires. The boundary line was determined by placing each village or tribe under the Persian or Ottoman regime, although these divisions were not demarcated on the ground. For over 200 years (until 1843) this physically undefined frontier remained unimplemented.

In the mid-nineteenth century, when the British and Czarist Russian empires became involved in the region, Iran (then called Persia) and Turkey (then the Ottoman Empire) agreed to stabilize its boundary conditions in a European fashion. Thus, in 1843 a commission including British and Russian representatives was appointed to adjudicate the Turkish–Persian boundary, a move that led to the signing of the second Treaty of Erzerum in 1847. This treaty vaguely defined the boundary between the two in accordance with the Zohab Treaty of 1639 and appointed a second mixed commission to delimit the boundary accurately. Only 50 years later, following the efforts of British and Russian experts and Persian and Ottoman diplomats, was the "Identical Map" (Carte Identique) produced in 1896 displaying a border zone 25 miles (40 km.) in width.

The Russo-Turkish war of 1877 led to the Congress of Berlin, where, on 13 July 1878, the Ottoman Empire agreed to cede the border area of Khotur to Persia—but later refused to implement the agreement. The 1847 Treaty of Erzerum was implemented by the Frontier Agreement of 21 December 1911 which provided for a mixed commission that included British, Russian, Persian and Ottoman delegates to establish a definite line between the two countries. On 17 November 1913 the Constantinople Protocol was signed. It provided a description of the entire boundary, from the Aras River to the Gulf, except for 40 miles (64 km.) in the Khotur area. Provision was also made for demarcation, carried out by a binational team using 227 boundary pillars during 1914.

An old Turkish palace near the Iran–Turkey boundary

Work on the boundary was halted with the outbreak of World War I and with the creation of the British mandate of Iraq in 1920 the border was shortened by about three-quarters of its length. The open question of Khotur and the Kurdish revolt against modern Turkey gave rise to a new definition of the boundary line. In the Angora Frontier Convention of 9 April 1929 Turkey and Persia established a detailed description of the boundary based on the 1914 demarcation. The Agreement Respecting the Fixation of the Frontier between Persia and Turkey of 23 January 1932 made some modifications and although the extent of each change was minor these areas had been a major irritant in terms of relations between Iran and Turkey. In the extreme north, the transfer of former Russian territory to Turkey by the Turkish-Soviet agreement of October 1921 also necessitated an extension of the boundary to the Aras River, which was accomplished by using the former Russo–Persian boundary along the Kara Su. Turkey gained some areas in the Little Ararat region when the mountain's eastern flank was placed within its borders. However, this led Kurdish tribes who had used the area in the past to organize uprisings against Turkey. In exchange for this parcel Persia was able to annex two areas in the central section of the line, around Khotur and Bajirge, to facilitate its control of the Persian Kurds. The boundary was again demarcated and a final agreement was reached on 26 May 1937. From then on, despite the political changes that changed the structure of the Middle East, no further changes were made in the boundary's location. The improved relations between Iran and Turkey since World War II were reflected in a 1955 agreement concerning the waters of the Kara Su and Sari Su, which rise in Turkey and flow into and along the border of Iran. The two countries were to have equal rights to the waters of the Kara Su while Turkey agreed to a minimum guaranteed supply of waters from the Sari Su to Iran.

Present Situation. There are no major points of dispute regarding the boundary alignment between the two countries. No territorial claims have arisen since 1937, although Kurdish separatist demands that have historically threatened both countries prevail with the current guerrilla war in Turkey.

IRAN — TURKMENISTAN Following the boundary between Iran and the former Soviet Union, of which Turkmenistan was a republic, the boundary between Iran and Turkmenistan extends for 617 miles (992 km.) from the boundary tripoint with Afghanistan on the Hari Rud River in the east to a point just south of the mouth of the Atrek River in the Caspian Sea in the west.

Geographical Setting. The eastern terminus of the boundary line is located on the Hari Rud River, north of the Afghan town of Zulfikar. The boundary follows the river downstream northward for about 100 miles (160 km.) to its confluence with the Tejend River, between the town of Sarakhs (previously in Turkmenistan; now in Iran). There the line leaves the river and runs northwestward along the foothills of the Hazar Masjed mountains, northeast of the Iranian city of Mashhad. South of the Turkmen town of Lutfabad the boundary climbs to the Kherbet Kopet mountain range, south of the Turkmen capital city of Ashkhabad. It follows its watershed to the source of the Sumbar River, which it follows downstream westward for about 30 miles (50 km.). Upon leaving the river it runs in a straight line southwestward, crosses a southern tributary of the Sumbar River and trends westward along a local watershed, reaching the Atrek River south of the Turkmen town of Chat (Sharlauk). The boundary line follows the Atrek River downstream southwestward for about 30 miles (50 km.) and leaves it to run parallel to it at a distance of about 10 miles (16 km.) south, to the Caspian Sea. This point is located south of the mouth of the Atrek River and the small Turkmen town of Gasan Kuli, and north of the Iranian town of Bandar-Torkman (Bandar Shah).

Historical Background. Turkmenistan, which was ruled by local Muslim emirs, was occupied by the Persian Nadir Shah in 1740, but Persia (Iran) lost it about 10 years later. In 1794 a Turkmen leader, Aga Mohamed, became the Persian Shah and his house ruled Persia until 1921.

The nineteenth century saw the advance of the Russian Empire into central Asia. The Russia-Persia war of 1825–1828 gave Russia part of Armenia in the west and some of the Kazakh and Turkmen areas were also occupied by Russia. From 1849 the Russians marched into south central Asia. In 1864 the area between the Black Sea and the Caspian Sea was occupied and in central Asia the Russians entered

Tashkent (1865), Bukhara and Samarkand (1868). In order to secure a safe passage from the Caspian Sea into the newly Russian areas in central Asia, the Russians needed to hold the area south of the Aral Sea through the territories of the emirates of Khiva and Mary. Thus, Russia occupied the emirate of Khiva in northeastern Persia in 1873, thereby establishing the boundary line east of the Caspian Sea up to Lotfabad along the traditional boundary between Persia and Khiva.

In 1879 Russia began its expansion into Kazakhstan and Turkmenistan, which was completed in 1884 by the occupation of Mary (Meru), east of the Hari Rud River, on which the boundary line was then established. Persia, which tried to occupy Afghanistan in 1837 and again in 1856–1857, was forced back by the British, who were afraid of the Persian expansion influenced by Russia. A buffer zone proposed by the British in central Asia was never accepted by Russia. The Russian advances were stopped on the Amu Daria River in the east but extended up to the northeastern Persian boundary without any protest from Persia.

After World War I the Soviet Union replaced the Russian Empire in central Asia and Turkmenistan became a constituent republic of it in 1925. Persia, which changed its name to Iran on 27 December 1934, recognized its northeastern border with the Soviet Union and no disputes were reported concerning the alignment of the boundary.

Present Situation. Turkmenistan became independent in 1991, adopting the Soviet Union–Iran boundary as its international boundary with Iran without a formal agreement. The line is well demarcated and, as it served as an international boundary for over 100 years, there are no claims to restore the boundary to any past line.

IRAQ (Al-'Iraq) A country in the Middle East, Iraq (area: 169,235 sq. miles [438,319 sq. km.]; estimated population: 20,700,000 [1994]) is bounded in the north by Turkey (219 miles; 352 km.), in the east by Iran (906 miles; 1,458 km.), southeast by the Persian (Arabian) Gulf, south by Kuwait (149 miles; 240 km.) and Saudi Arabia (502 miles; 808 km.) and west by Jordan (111 miles; 179 km.) and Syria (376 miles; 605 km.). The capital of Iraq is Baghdad.

The presumed ancestors of modern-day Iraqis cre-

ated some of the world's oldest cultures: Sumer, Babylonia and Assyria, which developed in the alluvial bed formed by the Tigris (Dijla) and Euphrates (Furat), the eastern leg of the Fertile Crescent. This is still the economic and cultural center of modern Iraq. In this "cradle of civilization," agriculture, domestication of animals, the wheel, cuneiform script and urban life were all first invented. Babylonia and Assyria were succeeded by the Persian, then the Greek and Roman, empires. Conquered by the Arabs in the year 633, the area was subject to much ethnic admixture over the following centuries. Mesopotamia once more became a world power under the Abbasid dynasty which founded Baghdad, until the Mongols devastated their capital in 1258 and again in 1393. The genocide they committed has left an enduring mark on Iraq. In 1533 the Turks took Baghdad and Iraq became a backward border province of the Ottoman Empire. In World War I Britain conquered the region.

Iraq as a modern state came only into being as a British mandate after World War I, but it has continued to suffer from internal disjunction. Created from three former Ottoman provinces, only its southern part (largely coextensive with ancient Mesopotamia) is Arab, while its northern mountainous part (Mosul Province) is Kurdish. Geopolitical juggling has created the preconditions of a longstanding feud of Iraqi Arabs with their Kurdish neighbours. The British imposed a Hashemite monarchy on Iraq and stimulated its integration into the world economy. In 1932 Iraq was the first mandate to graduate to independence. However, British influence remained preponderant in the 1930s and throughout World War I.

In the 1950s Iraq began to develop into an oil economy. State revenues rose but were unequally distributed. Anti-Western, nationalist and socialist impulses led in 1958 to a republican revolution, which was followed by nationalizations that broke up the landowner class. This ushered in a long period of instability, until the Ba'ath party consolidated its hold in 1968 by building a one-party state and taking full control over the army. Ever since, power has been the preserve of one clan stemming from the town of Tikrit.

At its outset, the secular Ba'ath regime still faced well-organized opposition parties: the Communists, strongest among the Shi'ites, and the Kurds in the north. After the Communists had been eradicated many Shi'ites turned to Islamic fundamentalism. The Kurds were decimated in repeated campaigns meant to eliminate any dream of autonomy. In 1979 Saddam Hussein al-Tikriti took power; by terrorizing and exterminating his opponents he transformed the Ba'ath party into an instrument enhancing his personal power. Iraq's succession of coups and countercoups progressively narrowed participation in the power elite, until it finally led to the current highly centralized and longlasting dictatorship resting on a combination of brutally coercing the masses, pampering its hundreds of thousands of armed clients, and in general distributing the economic benefits that have come with the post1973 oil boom (the Iraq Petroleum Company was nationalized in 1972).

Iraq's economy is now 90% based on oil exports; the petroleum bonanza has benefited mainly Iraq's traditional Sunni urban ruling class. It enabled the creation of a large services sector as well as a huge army of close to 1,000,000 soldiers. Rapid industrialization led to massive importation of foreign laborers, particularly from Egypt. Saddam Hussein's regime has needed external successes for domestic purposes, and Iraq was well endowed to fulfill his ambitions to become leader of the Arab world. Favorably located, with a large population, a rich agricultural base supplemented by enormous oil wealth, Iraq's geopolitical position is at once superb and vulnerable. In fact, Mesopotamia has historically been one of the Middle East's perennial power bases. Yet Saddam Hussein's adventurist foreign policies have squandered the country's resources and led the Iraqis from debacle to debacle. In the war against fundamentalist Iran, started in 1980, Iraq lost hundreds of thousands of soldiers, had its industrial infrastructure ruined and incurred a staggering war debt of $80 billion before agreeing to an inconclusive cease-fire in 1988. Within Iraq, the war served only to increase Shi'ite-Sunni antagonism.

The invasion and annexation in 1990 of Kuwait, Iraq's rich neighbor, although initially doubtless a popular move, led to the second Gulf War and unequivocal defeat for Iraq. The international embargo and bombings have caused widespread hunger and destruction. Still, Saddam Hussein was allowed to suppress ensuing Kurdish and Shi'ite rebellions, and

has maintained his (somewhat shaken) hold on power.

IRAQ — IRAN   see IRAN–IRAQ.

IRAQ — JORDAN   This boundary consists of six straight lines and extends 111 miles (179 km.) from the boundary tripoint with Syria near Jebel at-Tanaf in the north to the boundary tripoint with Saudi Arabia on Jebel (Mount) 'Anaiza in the south. Although the boundary is delineated on maps, there are no boundary markers on the ground.

Geographical Setting. The Iraq–Jordan boundary runs in an uninhabited desert area with no trace of human activity, apart from the main highway between Iraq and Jordan. Its northern terminus, which is the boundary tripoint with Syria, is located at 33°22'28.71"N and 38°47'36.97"E. The line runs south-southeastward in a straight line for about 59 miles (95 km.), crossing the Iraq–Jordan highway. It then turns and forms a series of four straight lines for 37.5 miles (60.5 km.). In another straight line southwestward, the boundary reaches the summit of Jebel 'Anaiza (Anazah) at the boundary tripoint with Saudi Arabia, at 32°09'15.24"N and 38°47'36.97"E.

Historical Background. The kingdom of Iraq and the emirate of Transjordan were both established as mandate territories of the United Kingdom after World War I. Neither state had ever been independent before and they had no common boundary between them. The emirate of Transjordan was established in 1922 but its eastern boundary was determined only 10 years later. In an exchange of letters between the countries' leaders (the Hashemite brothers: Abdallah of Transjordan and Faisal of Iraq) in 1932, it was agreed to draw the common boundary line from the Iraq–Nejd (later Saudi Arabia)–Transjordan boundary junction on Jebel 'Anaiza in a straight line to a point on the Iraq–Syria–Transjordan boundary junction near the summit of Mount Tanaf. The precise locations of these tripoints were later determined. In 1984, both countries agreed to modify the southern section of the boundary. Iraq gained an area east of the previous line and constructed a military airfield there while Jordan was able to extend its territory near the Saudi Arabian boundary.

Present Situation. The exchange of territory in

1984 was carried out for the benefit of both countries. There are no boundary disputes between them, although the new line has never been marked on the ground.

IRAQ — KUWAIT The first official demarcation of the Iraq–Kuwait boundary was only carried out after the defeat of Iraq by United Nations sponsored forces in the Gulf War of 1991, when it was recognized that the boundary was a primary, if intermittent, cause of regional instability. The line is 149 miles (240 km.) long, stretching from the boundary junction with Saudi Arabia to a northern outlet of the Persian (Arabian) Gulf.

Geographical Setting. The Iraq–Kuwait boundary commences at the tripoint with Saudi Arabia at 29°06'05"N and 46°33'19"E. From there it follows the *thalweg* of Wadi al Batin northeastward to boundary point no. 72 at 30°06'13.3181"N. It follows that parallel to boundary point no. 90 south of Safwan (Iraq) and forms a geodetic line to boundary point no. 106 on the shore of Khor az Zubair, just south of Umm Qasr. From this point the land boundary follows the line of low water springs on the Kuwaiti shore of Khor az Zubair, leaving the waterway predominantly with Iraq. It reaches boundary point no. 134 opposite the point selected as the junction of two *khor*s. The boundary then moves offshore to reach boundary point no. 135. Here the maritime boundary commences, traversing to a median point of the channel (boundary point no. 136) and following a median line down Khor Abdullah to the last point of the boundary (no. 162), which remains ill-defined.

Historical Background. Following Britain's secret treaty with the sheikh of Kuwait in 1899 and until its independence in 1961, Kuwait fell firmly within Britain's sphere of influence. Under the Anglo-Ottoman Convention of 29 July 1913, Britain secured Ottoman recognition of Kuwaiti autonomy and in November 1914 Kuwait was promised British recognition as an 'independent government under British protection.' However, due to the collapse of the 1913 Convention with the outbreak of World War I, the guarantee was never ratified and a legacy of disagreements ensued regarding the boundary's delimitation. The line was first defined in 1923 during the British mandate of Iraq, when diplomatic correspondence confirmed the rough delimitation of the boundary outlined by the 1913 convention. However, the northern sector of the boundary remained problematic, having been determined by an ambiguous "point just south of the latitude of Safwan"—indeed, the history of the boundary from 1932 to 1992 was dominated by attempts to locate this point. In 1951 Britain offered the Iraqi government an interpretation of this point as "1,000 metres south of the customs post at Safwan." Iraq demanded that Kuwait cede the mudflats at Warbah to exercise sole control over the access to its proposed port at Umm Qasr. Agreement between the two countries on the land boundary was close, but Iraq refused to ratify any agreement unless Kuwait agreed to cede or lease all or part of the Warbah and Bubiyan Islands.

After Kuwait achieved independence (25 June 1961), Iraq made a claim of Iraqi sovereignty over Kuwait, on the basis of historical Ottoman sovereignty, Kuwait having been part of the Basra province in the Ottoman Empire. However, subsequent to the change in the Iraqi regime in February 1963 the friction between the two countries was eased. The Iraqi prime minister, under the new president, and the Kuwaiti heir apparent signed an agreement that recognized Kuwait's independence, its boundaries as specified in the 1932 correspondence and its sovereignty over Warbah and Bubiyan. Nevertheless, it soon appeared that Iraqi recognition of Kuwait did not involve acceptance of the latter's frontiers. Iraq's primary interests lay in an imposition of its access to the Gulf by acquiring Warbah and Bubiyan, the importance of which had increased considerably in view of Iraq's development of the Rumaila oil field and expansion of Umm Qasr. Negotiations were stepped up and in May 1975 Iraqi officials announced that they had produced concrete proposals: Kuwait was to lease half of Bubiyan to Iraq for 99 years and cede sovereignty over Warbah in return for Iraqi recognition of Kuwait's land borders. Kuwait's acting minister of information, however, stressed in December 1976 that the two islands belonged to Kuwait as defined in the 1932 exchange of letters and in the 1963 agreement. Little progress was made over the following years in talks on delimiting the border, although the Iran-Iraq War ironically produced improved relations as Iraq became increasingly dependent upon Kuwait's assistance. By 1988, as Iraq was faced with numerous immense problems, its territorial claims on Kuwait were again a focus of attention. Iraq was left with a debt of $16,000 million to Kuwait after the 1980–1988 war, Kuwait had growing concerns over Iraq's apparent willingness to lose full control of the Shatt-al-Arab channel (thus emphasizing its expansionary plans at Umm Qasr) and Iraq was concerned with its belief that Kuwait was deliberately weakening its economy through continuous over-production of oil.

On 2 August 1990 Iraq invaded Kuwait. The United Nations Security Council immediately passed Resolution 660, which demanded that "Iraq withdraw immediately and unconditionally all its forces ... [and called] on Iraq and Kuwait to begin immediately intensive negotiations for the resolution of their differences." At the end of February 1991 a cease-fire was enforced and Iraq had backed out of Kuwaiti territory. A UN Iraq-Kuwait Observer Mission was set up to supervise the cease-fire and a de-militarized zone was established 10 miles (16 km.) north and 5 miles (8 km.) south of the border. Under the terms of Resolution 686, the UN set up a border commission which, after considering the historical evidence, established that a 2,132-foot (650-m.) strip of land along the northern boundary (controlled by Iraq) lay within Kuwait. This border placed 11 oil wells at the southern tip of the Rumaila oil field as well as the Umm Qasr naval base jetties in Kuwaiti territory. The boundary was delimited, de-marcated and accepted by Kuwait in 1993 and on 10 November 1994 Iraq decreed that it recognized both Kuwait and its borders.

Present Situation. It appears that the precise loca-tion of boundary point no. 162 is defined according to the location of the mouth of Khor az Zubair's main navigable channel. This floating boundary point and a delimited offshore boundary extending from it are likely to become issues of dispute. Addi-tionally, and more significantly, although the Iraq–Kuwait boundary is now fairly well defined, it continues to represent a source of tension between Iraq and Kuwait due to the dormant Iraqi claims of rights to Kuwaiti territory and Iraq's historical ambi-tions to gain a larger area of the Gulf coastline.

IRAQ — SAUDI ARABIA The boundary be-tween Iraq and Saudi Arabia runs for 502 miles (808 km.) between the boundary junction with Kuwait in the east and the tripoint with Jordan in the west. The boundary is composed of eight straight lines that connect wells located in the uninhabited desert.

Geographical Setting. The boundary line was es-tablished primarily to separate the Iraqi Muntafiq, Dhafir and Amarat nomadic tribes and the Saudi Arabian Shammar Nejd. The eastern boundary ter-minus stands at the junction with Kuwait at the con-fluence of Wadi Awja (Aujah) and Wadi al Batin (29°06'05"N and 46°33'19"E). The boundary runs westward for about 110 miles (177 km.) in a straight line to Bir al Ansab, thence turning northwest for about 75 miles (120 km.) to Birkat al Jumaymah, east of the Saudi town and airfield of Rafha'. The line travels northward for 52 miles (84 km.), passing Birkat al 'Aqabah, to the boundary point at Kasr Al 'Athamin. The boundary turns westward for about 40 miles (65 km.) to Bir al Lifiyah and then contin-ues northwest for 20 miles (32 km.) to Bir al Maaniyah and west-northwest for another 105 miles (169 km.) to Bir Judayyadit 'Ar'ar, northeast of the Saudi town of 'Ar'ar and the airfield of Badanah. In another straight line, for some 90 miles (145 km.), the line travels to Muqr an Na'am and from there 45 miles (72 km.) to Jebel 'Anaiza (Anazah). Here the western terminus of the boundary is located, at 32°13'51"N and 39°18'09"E.

Historical Background. For hundreds of years, the Middle East was ruled by the Ottoman Empire with no substantial internal or national boundaries. Thus, when the League of Nations accorded Britain the mandate to govern Mesopotamia on 24 April 1920 there was little understanding of the territorial limits of the region. The boundaries of modern Iraq were later established by the British in a series of agree-ments and treaties with Iran (Persia), Turkey, France (which held mandatory rule over Syria), Saudi Ara-bia and Kuwait.

At the turn of the eighteenth century the puritani-cal Wahhabi movement, backed by the ancestors of the present ruling Saudi family, established control of the sultanate centered in Riyadh in central Arabia. During the early years of the nineteenth century they managed to conquer most of northern Arabia and sacked towns in Mesopotamia, but their power was crushed by the Ottomans. Saudi power increased again in the early twentieth century and its area was expanded north and east up to the Persian Gulf, establishing its rule over most of the Arabian Peninsula. During World War I, Riyadh's ruler, Ibn Sa'ud, although officially neutral, aided the Arab revolt against the Turks by harassing the Turkish allies in Arabia. Britain recognized the Saudi power by the Treaty of Qatif of 26 December 1915. At the war's end there were no boundaries between Arabia, Kuwait and the newly established Iraq. The tribal rivalries and conflicts between the three main families of Arabia (the Hashimis of Hejaz—ancestors of the present King Husain of Jordan, the Rashidis of Mount Shammar and the Saudis of Riyadh) increased after the war. In 1919 the Saudis defeated the Hashimis at Turaba and by 1922 the Rashidis were also defeated and Ibn Sa'ud was able to extend his frontiers toward Iraq and the newly established Transjordan. Britain, which supported Ibn Sa'ud, confronted the threat to its other allies in the area and the British foreign office attempted to overcome the territorial problems: the British high commissioner for Iraq and Ibn Sa'ud signed the Treaty of Mohammerah (Khorramshahr of today) on 5 May 1922, which dealt with the future relations between the two countries.

The Saudis initially refused to accept the European concept of a boundary as an imaginary line in the open desert that might contain the movement of tribes who are accustomed to roam widely in search of pasture and water. They finally agreed to delimit the boundary on condition that the lives of the nomads would not be disturbed. In the Protocol of Uqayr of 2 December 1922, which delineated the boundary line, it was agreed that "the Iraqi Government pledges itself not to interfere with those Nejd tribes living in the vicinity of the border should it be necessary for them to restore to the neighboring Iraqi wells for water, provided that these wells are nearer to them than those within the Nejd boundaries." Thus, the grazing and watering practice traditionally conducted by tribes crossing the boundary would remain undisturbed.

Present Situation. In contrast to other Iraqi boundaries, there are no active disputes between Iraq and Saudi Arabia regarding the alignment of the boundary. The boundary was marked on maps but never physically demarcated. Those who live in or frequent the frontier region are familiar with the exact location of the line. Any potential disputes between Iraq and Saudi Arabia do not concern their common boundary line.

IRAQ — SYRIA   This boundary is 376 miles (605 km.) in length. The Tigris River is followed for 3.2 miles (5.1 km.) and less than 4 miles (6.5 km.) cross the Euphrates River; the remaining stretch of boundary is on land. Running generally southwestward from the boundary tripoint with Turkey to the tripoint with Jordan, it is delimited according to the 1932 League of Nations Report of Geneva, but is only partially demarcated.

Geographical Setting. Setting out from the Turkish tripoint at the confluence of the Tigris and the eastern Khabur rivers, this boundary follows the *thalweg* of the Tigris River, which is situated about 0.6 miles (1 km.) below Pesh Khabur, for 3.2 miles (5.1 km.). It leaves the river and heads in a straight line southwestward for about 68 miles (109 km.), first to Tell Dahrāyā (point 384) and then to Tell Khoda-ed-Deir (point 391). The boundary then trends southward for 153 miles (246 km.) in a series of straight-line segments and is divided into sectors. The Sinjar sector terminates at Tell Sfug (trig point 332) and the salt deposit sector sees the boundary through the Buarah sabkha until it reaches Jabal Bāghuz. Just beyond this point the line meets the *thalweg* of the Euphrates River near the northeastern extremity of Baghuz Island. It follows this *thalweg* upstream for a short distance before heading in a straight line to the Leachman boundary stone (point 169). From here the boundary forms a straight line toward a point situated 19 miles (30 km.) from the minaret of Abu Kemal and joins the minaret to a point 2 miles (3.2 km.) north of Tell Romah. It continues in this southwesterly direction to the Jordanian tripoint at approximately 33°22'29"N and 38°47'33"E.

Historical Background. The boundary between Iraq and Syria is essentially artificial and is a result of a division of British and French spheres of influence following the Allied victory over Ottoman Turkey in World War I. On 16 May 1916 the two colonial parties concluded a secret agreement commonly known as the Sykes-Picot Agreement. Key provisions within the agreement included the partition of the entire Fertile Crescent into several zones,

The Tigris River runs from Turkey to Iraq

which directly influenced the eventual delineation of the Iraq–Syria boundary. The signing of the Mudros Armistice on 30 October 1918 marked the complete Turkish defeat in Arab Ottoman lands and at the Paris Peace Conference it was decided that the Arab provinces should be wholly separated from the Ottoman Empire and that the newly conceived mandate system should be applied to them. The Conference of San Remo (24 April 1920) established the mandates: Syria and Lebanon under France, Palestine and Mesopotamia under Britain. This, in effect, became the manifestation of the 1916 Sykes-Picot Agreement.

The declaration of the mandates was rejected by Amir Faisal, who represented the Arab nationalists, and while both sides (Arab and French) prepared for war, the French issued an ultimatum that demanded unconditional acceptance of the mandate. The Franco-British Convention of 23 December 1920 defined the boundaries between their mandate areas in Lebanon and Syria (France), and Palestine and Mesopotamia (Britain), and provided for the demar-

cation of the frontiers by an Anglo-French boundary commission. However, it delimited the boundary only in general terms, subject to later demarcation. The League of Nations appointed a commission entrusted with the study of the boundary between Iraq and Syria, and the boundary as it stands today is based on this commission's report, published on 10 September 1932. Grazing and watering practices, traditionally conducted by tribes crossing the boundary, remained largely undisturbed. The potential for political disturbances, however, has persisted over the years since ethnic and tribal affinities are essentially identical on both sides of the boundary. On 3 October 1932 Iraq was admitted to the League of Nations as an independent state. The Kurdish conflict, for example, has continued with only brief respites since 1932; the Turkish incursion in March 1995 into northern Iraqi territory, cordoned off as a United Nations protection zone and an autonomous haven for the Kurds, exemplified the fragile state of coexistence along the northern sectors of the Iraq–Syria boundary.

Present Situation. There are no active disputes between Iraq and Syria regarding the specific alignment of the boundary.

IRAQ — TURKEY The Iraq–Turkey boundary is 219 miles (352 km.) in length and has been fully demarcated since the 1926 Treaty of Ankara. It runs from the boundary tripoint with Syria in the west to the boundary tripoint with Iran in the east.

Geographical Setting. Beginning on the *thalweg* of the Tigris River, at its confluence with the Khabur River and at an altitude of approximately 1,000 feet (305 m.), this boundary follows the *thalweg* of the eastern Khabur River eastward for 15 miles (24 km.), and then that of the Hezil River (Nahr al Hayzal), a tributary of the Khabur River, for another 21 miles (34 km.). To the west of the boundary, in Iraq, lies the province of Mosul and to the east, in Turkey, the vilayet (province) of Mardin. Climbing from a level of 3,000 feet (915 m.), the boundary proceeds northeast and then east for 29 miles (46 km.) up to an elevation of 7,000 feet (2,134 m.). There it leaves the Hezil River and eventually joins the upper Khabur river system. Continuing east-

ward, the boundary coincides with a drainage divide and continues for 22 miles (35 km.) to reach the Great Zab River, which flows from the north to join the Tigris River below Mosul. The boundary follows the Great Zab River downstream for less than 1 mile (1.5 km.), then meandering eastward for 13 miles (21 km.), and meeting the Av-i-Marik, a tributary of the Great Zab River, which it follows downstream for 3 miles (5 km.). Heading east again, the boundary crosses the highlands at elevations frequently above 7,000 feet (2,134 m.). At a distance of 80 miles (128 km.) from its confluence with the Great Zab River, the boundary meets the gorge of the Kuchuk River and for the remaining 42 miles (67 km.) follows the Hajji Bak to its intersection with Iran's boundary.

Historical Background. Conquered by Mongols in the thirteenth or fourteenth century, the town of Mosul was incorporated into the Ottoman Empire by 1534 and from then until 1879 was politically subordinate to the Turkish administration at Baghdad. In 1879 it became an independent vilayet (province), equal in status to Baghdad, with a largely Kurdish population. By 1920 Turkey (having lost the Basra

Iraq–Turkey border region

and Kirkuk areas of Baghdad) signed the Treaty of Sèvres which called for the establishment of a Kurdish state in the region, but this was never ratified. Article 27 defined Turkey's southern boundary as largely coinciding with the northern border of the province of Mosul. While Britain was led to support the incorporation of the area into Iraq after the discovery of oil in the region, Turkey renounced this treaty, insisting that the Kurds were not a separate nation. In 1923 the Treaty of Sèvres was replaced by the Treaty of Lausanne, which called for a friendly arrangement between Iraq and Turkey. With no such arrangement forthcoming, the League of Nations recommended, in June 1925, that a permanent border be established. The Brussels Line that was delimited almost exactly followed the northern border of the Mosul vilayet. Following a dispute, the matter was referred to the International Court of Justice which, in November 1925, recommended that Mosul be awarded to Iraq (i.e., using the Brussels Line). Iraq, Turkey and the United Kingdom signed the Treaty of Ankara on 5 June 1926, establishing the border in accordance with the League of Nations recommendation, except for a slight modification that allowed for a direct road between the Turkish villages of Animan and Ashuta. By September 1927 the entire border had been demarcated.

Present Situation. There have been no serious incidents along the boundary since 1927, although recent developments have complicated relations between the two countries. During the Gulf War of 1990–1991, strategic measures taken by Turkey were interpreted by Iraq as an illustration of Turkey's territorial ambitions. Although the 1926 Treaty of Ankara delimited the border between Iraq and Turkey, the Turkish president spoke of the need to redraw the map of the Middle East, mentioning the Turkish claims to Mosul and Kirkuk, and Turkish nationalists have never accepted the incorporation of the Mosul area into Iraq. Relations are also complicated by the existence of large Kurdish communities on both sides of the border. Each state allegedly manipulates rival Kurdish guerrilla groups against the other. This source of conflict seems set to continue for the near future.

IRELAND (Éire) A European country (area: 27,137 sq. miles [70,257 sq. km.]; estimated population: 3,600,000 [1994]), Ireland's only land boundary is with the United Kingdom (224 miles; 360 km.) in the north, which separates Ireland from Northern Ireland. The capital of Ireland is Dublin.

Gaels, the Iron Age Celtic forebears of the Irish, may have entered the island in the sixth century B.C.E. from Spain or southern France. After subduing the indigenous Picts, they built a hierarchical culture, religiously unified but divided by internal strife. In the fourth century C.E., the Celts adopted Christianity; the amalgamation of the Picts and the Celts gave rise to the Irish. The sixth to eighth centuries were the Golden Age of Irish civilization, which produced a very original and imaginative literature, architecture, manuscripts and sculpture. The Irish were at the time much more advanced than continental Europeans. They sent their monks to rechristianize the European continent.

Viking invasions in the ninth century broke Irish power. Scandinavians settled Dublin and established towns and commerce, until driven out by the Irish monarchy. After conquest by the English in 1171, Anglo-Norman landlords introduced feudalism, and from their castles and fortified towns reduced the Irish to serfdom. After a while, English nobles were assimilated and Irish culture revived. In the sixteenth century, however, the Tudors completed the English conquest of Ireland. A cruel campaign under Elizabeth I finally subdued the Irish.

The Reformation duplicated the ethnic English-Celtic contradiction with a Protestant-Catholic one. Most Irish remained Catholic, but English and Scottish colonization in the seventeenth century eventually turned Ulster into a predominantly British-Protestant region.

A Catholic Irish revolt in 1641 triggered the English civil war. The Irish were pacified by Oliver Cromwell and the original Catholic population dispossessed. Land grants were offered to any Englishman prepared to keep the rebels in check, while entrepreneurs drove out indigenous farmers and replaced them with colonists. Most of the Irish were reduced to poverty and survived as landless laborers for the English. Ireland became a British colony, sending wool to England, prohibited from weaving themselves, victims of programmed underdevelopment. That policy was also harmful to the Anglo-Irish Protestant establishment, which aspired to greater autonomy, and in the late eighteenth century obtained legislative independence. In 1800 Ireland was annexed to Britain, a step which resulted in the formation of revolutionary Irish movements throughout the nineteenth century.

The failed potato harvests in 1845 to 1847 led to catastrophe: famine killed 1,500,000 Irish, and millions more escaped to Britain and the United States, starting a process of depopulation. Since 1850 over 3,000,000 Irish have left Ireland.

Misery stimulated nationalism, federalist agitation

and rural guerrilla warfare by secret societies. British land liberalization and tenant security against eviction only provoked secessionist tendencies among Protestant ultras. Presbyterians and Tories conspired to torpedo Irish autonomy, but land reforms undertaken to preempt the independence movement ended the supremacy of the established aristocracy.

However, nationalist agitation was not to be contained. The early twentieth century was the era of Gaelic cultural renaissance. The Sinn Fein, which

Ireland's boundary with Northern Ireland (United Kingdom)

was established in 1905, boycotted colonial institutions. By World War I, England conceded Home Rule (although Protestants obtained promise of separate treatment for Ulster), but it was too late: in 1916, the Bloody Easter revolt broke out in Dublin, followed by a full-scale war of independence. Britain recognized the Irish Free State as an autonomous dominion within the British Empire, but imposed partition and negotiated a separate status for Northern Ireland. After a period of reconstruction in the 1920s, an economic crisis brought radical Eamon de Valera to power. In 1949 Eire (Southern Ireland) became a completely independent republic. The Irish remained, however, an overwhelmingly agricultural and poverty-stricken society of large families. From the 1950s a new, less ideologically-marked, generation came to power. Economic debates have since primed national ones. In the 1960s industrialization was successfully undertaken, as well as cautious rapprochement with Northern Ireland, although (at least officially) Eire maintains its claim over the whole of the island. Until entering the European Community in 1972, which put an end to isolationism, the southern Irish remained poorer than their northern brethren. The spillover effect of the civil war in Northern Ireland and global recession maintain them in a state of structural underdevelopment. The Irish live in a state where the Catholic church continues to wield old-style power over the private life of the citizen.

IRELAND — UNITED KINGDOM This boundary is 224 miles (360 km.) long, dividing the Republic of Ireland and Northern Ireland (United Kingdom). It runs from the western shore of the Lough (Lake) Foyle estuary on the northern coast of Ireland to Carlingford Lough on its western coast.
Geographical Setting. From the coast of Foyle Lough, southwest of Muff, the Ireland–United Kingdom border cuts into the Inishowen Peninsula to encompass Londonderry and its surrounding area (the 'Liberties'). It runs to the secondary road that travels to Belmont, follows it for almost 1.5 miles (2.4 km.) and turns northwest for about 9 miles (15 km.) before resuming its generally southwestern route. It runs southwest, southeast and south in an irregular line to the Foyle River at the division between Londonderry and Tyrone counties. The line follows the

median line of the Foyle River to a point just south of Clady, where it leaves the river and continues generally southwest to the Mournebeg River, which it then follows. The boundary reaches a woodland, runs through it at about 600 feet (180 m.) and heads south toward the Leaghany River. This river forms the boundary to its confluence with the Derg River, which then forms the boundary eastward. Curving southwestward, the line joins the Fermanagh county boundary, reaches Lough Erne and proceeds westward through smaller loughs. Heading generally south, the boundary joins the Erne River north of the town of Belleek (Northern Ireland), follows it south of Belleek, turns west, passes through Lough Melvin and Lough Macnean and south to Cuilcagh mountain. From here it follows a number of streams and weaves through the archipelago of Upper Lough Erne. Emerging from Lough Erne on the Finn River, the boundary leaves the river and bears northward to include in the Republic of Ireland an irregular pedicel of land that contains Drumslow and Lough Coleman. The boundary returns to the Finn River some 600 feet (180 m.) upstream and follows it northward through the maze of drumlins on the Monaghan (Republic of Ireland) border. After approaching Slieve Beagh the boundary turns northwest and then proceeds northeast and southeast along streams and loughs to join the Blackwater River. It follows the Blackwater River south to the junction with Armagh county (Northern Ireland) and keeps to the Armagh–Monaghan border southward. The line turns southwest and generally south along several small streams until it passes south of Carrickduff. There it heads northward to the southern bank of Tullynawood Lake and makes its way through the local drumlins, loughs and rivers. Eastward, it trends along the boundary between Armagh and Louth (Republic of Ireland), the highland north of Dundalk, to join the Newry Canal, which it follows into Carlingford Lough.
Historical Background. The boundary between Ireland and the United Kingdom was formed in 1920 when Ireland was partitioned in an effort to balance the aspirations of Catholic Irish nationalists for a free independent Ireland, and Protestant Ulster unionists, who wanted to remain British. The boundary commission was charged with the task of creating a border between Northern Ireland and the

area south and west of it "in accordance with the wishes of the inhabitants, so far as may be compatible with the economic and geographic conditions." However, in 1925, after a premature publication of the commission's intentions caused dismay to both sides, it was decided to leave the boundary as it stood at the time of partition. It separated the counties of Donegal (Republic of Ireland) from Londonderry, Tyrone and Fermanagh (Northern Ireland); Leitrim, Cavan and Monaghan from Fermanagh (Northern Ireland); Monaghan from Tyrone and Armagh; and Louth from Armagh. This meant that ancient county and parish boundaries were elevated to the status of international borders. It also cut through farms, settlements and even individual houses, ignoring the economic and social needs of the people on either side. The line has never been demarcated and provides every opportunity for both expedient and genuine confusion regarding its exact location.

Present Situation. This border has never been accepted by the Republic of Ireland, which includes in its constitution a determination to reunite the island.

ISRAEL   A Middle Eastern state located on the eastern shore of the Mediterranean Sea, its total land area is 8,019 sq. miles (20,761 sq. km.). Israel also rules occupied areas (the Golan Heights, Judea, Samaria and the Gaza Strip) with an area of 2,948 sq. miles (7,632 sq. km.). Its estimated population is 5,100,000 (1994), while the occupied areas' population is estimated at 2,100,000. Israel is bounded in the north by Lebanon (49 miles; 79 km.), in the northeast by Syria (47 miles (76 km.), in the east by Jordan (148 miles; 238 km.) and in the southwest by Egypt (165 miles; 266 km.). Israel's area and boundary lines are presently under discussion and may be changed in the near future.

The country was under Ottoman rule until World War I, after which the League of Nations awarded a mandate to Great Britain, which had promised to create a Jewish National Home without prejudicing the rights of the Arab inhabitants. The Jewish enterprise developed against a background of growing local Arab hostility and resistance, especially as Jewish nationalism evoked the emergence of a Palestinian Arab nationalism.

Palestine already had a large Arab population

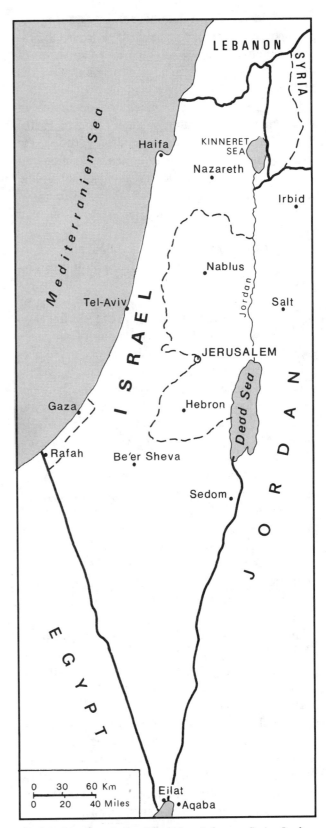

Israel and its boundaries. Clockwise: Lebanon, Syria, Jordan, Egypt and the Mediterranean Sea

when modern Jewish nationalism, or Zionism, began and the Arabs have continued to regard the establishment of the Jewish state as an invasion of their patrimony and as an alien intrusion in the Arab Middle East.

Arab anti-Jewish outbreaks, first occurring in 1920, grew in momentum in the 1920s and 1930s. When the United Nations decided on partition, the Arabs of the country rose in armed opposition and after the state was proclaimed were joined by the armies of six Arab states. In the battle that followed (the War of Independence), Israel's army emerged victorious.

Palestine was divided into Israel, areas annexed by the kingdom of Jordan, and the Gaza Strip, ruled by Egypt. As a result of the 1967 Six-Day War, in which Israel decisively defeated an alliance of Egypt, Syria and Jordan, the whole of historic Palestine fell into Jewish hands. The future of the areas taken over, with their large Arab population and burgeoning Palestinian nationalism, became a crucial issue. The problem polarized Israeli society between those who were determined that these areas would remain under Israeli control and those who were prepared to grant the Palestinians autonomy or even statehood.

While the war of 1973 (the Yom Kippur War) paved the way for a peace agreement with Egypt in 1978, the Palestinian question was exacerbated and put into even sharper focus by the outbreak in 1988 of an intensified Arab campaign of civil uprising (the *intifada*). Following the 1991 Gulf War, US pressure brought Israel, its Arab neighbors and Palestinians into talks on the possibility of a peace settlement.

The Jewish settlement developed a European ethos. After the establishment of the State this was gradually challenged by newcomers from Muslim lands, who at first had a difficult time finding their niche but nonetheless moved up the socioeconomic ladder and, with the immigration from North Africa in the 1950s, became numerically a majority. More recently the influx of immigrants from the former Soviet bloc has resulted in an approximate numerical parity between the immigrants of European origin and those coming from Muslim lands.

The relationship between religion and state is among the most controversial issues in Israeli politics. Religious Jews have established a number of political parties which, although representing only one-sixth of the voters, have occupied key positions in almost all governments as they held the balance between the right and the left blocs of parties. They have obtained many concessions, some of which effect the way of life of even the secular Jewish community (such as the exclusive application of religious law in matters of personal status, including marriage and divorce).

Israel is today a predominantly urban society, with only 5% employed in agriculture. Two-thirds of the population are concentrated in the lowlands. To sustain their military strength, the absorption of immigrants and high standard of living, Israelis remain heavily dependent on foreign subsidies from Jewish communities and other sources, particularly aid from the US.

ISRAEL — EGYPT see EGYPT–ISRAEL.

ISRAEL — JORDAN Until October 1994 there was no formally agreed Israel–Jordan boundary— only former colonial lines and post-1948 armistice, cease-fire and separation lines. However, following the peace treaty of 26 October 1994, the process of delimiting and demarcating the boundary between the two parties began. For 148 miles (238 km.) the boundary follows the Yarmuk and Jordan Rivers down to the Dead Sea and then to the Gulf of 'Aqaba (Gulf of Eilat) through Wadi 'Araba.

Geographical Setting. From the Israel–Jordan–Syria boundary intersection in the north, at a point where the unused railway line crosses the Yarmuk River above El Hamma (Hammat Gader), the boundary follows the middle of the main courses of the Yarmuk River downstream westward to its confluence with the Jordan River and thence follows the Jordan River downstream southward to the Dead Sea and the southern marshland that it bisects via the 'Araba (Arava) valley. It trends south-southwest to a point between the towns of Eilat (Israel) and 'Aqaba (Jordan), 2 miles (3 km.) west of 'Aqaba. The land boundary was demarcated in July 1995 and boundary pillars were placed at specific coordinates; in the Gulf of 'Aqaba the two countries are committed to concluding a delimitation of their maritime boundary.

Historical Background. Until 25 October 1994 there was no formally agreed Israel–Jordan boundary. The complexity of demarcating this line was not only due to the political and military developments since the establishment of the State of Israel in 1948, but was deeply affected by access to resources along the border and by the transformation of population which has taken place over the last seven decades. The present-day boundary originates from two distinct periods: colonial and post-1948. The Balfour Declaration of November 1917 stated that the British government viewed with favor the establishment in Palestine of a national home for the Jewish people. Consequently, the San Remo Conference of 1920 placed Palestine under a British League of Nations mandate and by 1922 the British govern-

ment had decided to separate Transjordan from Palestine. Accompanying the order in council that announced this separation, details of the delimitation were laid out. Nevertheless, except for 2.5 miles (4 km.) in the extreme south, from the shores of the Gulf of 'Aqaba northward that were demarcated in 1946, this boundary remained only vaguely marked on maps. In Wadi 'Araba (Arava Valley—the rift valley between the Gulf of 'Aqaba and the Dead Sea) the boundary was intended to follow the line of lowest points, but maps failed to reproduce this. Through the Dead Sea the boundary was to follow a line equidistant from its eastern and western shores; once again, however, due to inaccurate cartographic representation and the gradual drop in sea level that caused it to shrink, the Dead Sea remained poorly

The Israel–Jordan boundary follows the Jordan River

delimited. Along the Jordan River problems arose when significant shifts in channel direction made delimitation of the boundary along its central line of a temporary nature; the same was found in delimiting the Yarmuk River upstream. In 1927 it was decided that the boundary line would follow the middle of the Jordan River, always changing its location with the changing of the riverbeds.

Arab-Jewish conflict deepened under the British mandate and the failure to find any formula on the constitutional future of Palestine that would gain acceptance by both sides led Britain to pass the matter on to the United Nations in 1947, which subsequently recommended immediate independence, with partition between an Arab state, a Jewish state and Jerusalem under UN Trusteeship. The subsequent birth of Israel in 1948, the ensuing Palestine War (1948–1949) and the Six-Day War (1967) all resulted in the appearance of new boundaries in addition to those sections of the former colonial boundaries that remained in force. Following the armistice agreement between Israel and Jordan in 1949, a new boundary was delimited, partly made up of the former colonial boundary but also including the Green Line boundary across the central highlands of Palestine. Some 2,270 sq. miles (5,880 sq. km.) of territory to the west of the Jordan River, known as the West Bank, was annexed by Jordan, as was East Jerusalem. The West Bank was considered a key element to the land of Israel (Eretz Israel) by many Israelis, since its constituent parts, Judea and Samaria, were, according to the Old Testament, given to the Jews by God. This division of the West Bank and Jerusalem lasted until 1967 when, following collaborative military efforts by Jordan, Egypt, Syria and Iraq against Israel, the Israeli forces gained an area more than three times greater than the territory of Israel after the 1949 armistice. This included East Jerusalem and the Jordanian territory of the West Bank, placing the cease-fire line along the eastern boundary of British mandatory Palestine. Despite UN Security Council Resolution 242, which demanded withdrawal, Israel retained the territory and so intensified the Israeli-Jordanian conflict.

As the political atmosphere began to improve in the 1980s, peace negotiations continued. The notion of an autonomous Palestinian state received greater attention and on 31 August 1988 Jordan gave up rights to the West Bank and all of Jerusalem (except for the holy places) in favor of the Palestinians. Israel and Jordan eventually signed a peace treaty on 26 October 1994, which set out the principle of the boundary settlement (Article 3) and provided for a final demarcation of their common border by August 1995. The treaty provides for the border to follow the middle of the original main courses of the Yarmuk and Jordan rivers (except for the southern course of the Jordan River and the northern sector of the Dead Sea), and to run through the Dead Sea and the Arava Valley to the Gulf of 'Aqaba. Since the 1967 war, Jordan has argued that Israel occupied some 135–155 sq. miles (350–400 sq. km.) of territory on the Jordanian side of the Palestinian mandate boundary in Wadi 'Araba and in the Yarmuk area. The precise extent of this occupation was unclear, but the treaty appears to provide for all such territory to be returned to Jordan. There are also a number of plots of land which, although defined as Jordanian territory, can retain Israeli private land ownership, usership rights and property interests for an initial 25-year period, with the option of renewal for another 25 years.

Present Situation. The Israel–Jordan boundary is now open and the Israelis completed the final phase of withdrawal from Jordanian territory on 11 February 1995. However, a number of outstanding issues remain, not least of which is that should an independent Palestinian state emerge, a similar boundary agreement would have to be concluded covering the northern sectors of the Dead Sea and the lower course of the Jordan River. Moreover, the issue of Jerusalem, with which Jordan still feels it has a custodian role to play, has yet to be tackled. Although the 1994 treaty aims to resolve the crucial issues of riparian water rights, considerable flexibility is available to both sides in determining the consequences should the Yarmuk or Jordan rivers change course, naturally or artificially, thereby maintaining a potential for future disputes.

ISRAEL — LEBANON The boundary between Israel and Lebanon extends for 49 miles (79 km.) from the Mediterranean coast at En Naqura (Lebanon) generally eastward before diverting sharply northward in a salient as far as Metulla (Israel). Southeastward it then courses to a tripoint boundary junction with Syria on the Hasbani River.

Geographical Setting. The Israeli–Lebanese borderland represents a transitional area between the Lebanese mountains to the north with elevations reaching 10,000 feet (3,000 m.) and the lower, rolling Galileean hills to the south, which do not exceed 4,000 feet (1,250 m.). In the west, the boundary line runs along a series of low ridges, their elevations increasing toward the central sector of the boundary up to approximately 2,500 feet (800 m.). Also traversing through deep valleys and steep slopes, the boundary follows a rugged landscape. In the east, the line extends northward along the rim of the great Jordan Rift Valley before entering the valley at approximately 145 feet (53 m.), near its eastern terminus on the Hasbani River.

Historical Background. The Palestine (Israel)–Lebanon boundary is based on an Anglo–French line that stemmed from the scramble for former Ottoman territory in the wake of World War I. The proposed division of territory between the two imperial powers was determined in the secret Sykes-Picot Agreement of May 1916, which provided for the creation of three zones in the region: an international sphere under joint Allied control encompassing much of what was to become Palestine; a British sphere consisting of a coastal enclave that included the ports of Acre and Haifa; and a French sphere north of the international zone, comprising the whole of present-day Lebanon. The Sykes-Picot Agreement and Britain's Balfour Declaration of 2 November 1917 that favored "the establishment in Palestine of a national home for the Jewish people...," were at odds with Britain's secret commitments to the Arabs for the establishment of their own independent states in the region. Eventually, on 19 September 1918, the British established Occupied Enemy Territory Administrations to provide interim stewardship over the formerly Ottoman possessions. The new division of the territory marked a

A crusaders' castle near the Israel–Lebanon boundary

radical departure from that envisaged in the Sykes-Picot Agreement, such that the international sphere ceased to exist and the French zone was significantly eroded in favor of an expanded British area. Palestine's Zionists were anxious to secure the water resources of Upper Galilee (south Lebanon) within British Palestine and to ensure that the basis of the Jewish homeland should have readily defensible borders. However, their proposals to shift the northern boundary of the Palestine mandate significantly northward—to or even beyond the Litani River—met with little success. Finally, in June 1920, the British and French agreed to a compromise, whereby the boundary was shifted north of the Sykes-Picot line to En Naqura. From there the boundary was to proceed generally eastward, except for a northward salient in the east that would include Metulla and the Hula Valley, the northernmost Jewish settlements of the time, in Palestine. The Litani River was to remain entirely under French jurisdiction. On 23 December 1920 the proposal was fully accepted as the basis for the Palestine–Lebanon boundary by the British and French and a demarcation commission was established. In February 1922 the boundary commission submitted its final report and the Palestine–Lebanon Boundary Agreement was signed. It was ratified by the British government on 7 March 1923 and came into effect on 10 March 1923. The Zionists, however, viewed this line as a disaster, as it separated Palestine from key water resources north of the line and would prove difficult to defend, a point that was clearly demonstrated during the mandate period.

The first years of the line were quiet, as Britain and France were allied and the predominantly Arab local populations simply ignored the line, but during the 1936 Arab uprisings in Palestine it became clear that the infiltration of men and arms from north of the border could hardly be prevented. Britain made an abortive attempt to physically seal the entire length of the boundary with what became known as Tegart's Wall—a series of barbed wire fences backed by frontier posts. During Israel's War of Independence (1948–1949) a guerrilla force, the Arab Liberation Army, invaded Israel from Lebanon, but was swiftly defeated by Israeli forces who counterattacked into Lebanon and reached the Litani. Israel pulled out of Lebanon in exchange for a General Armistice Agreement that was signed at En Naqura on 23 March 1949.

The Israel–Lebanon Armistice Line coincides with the Anglo–French international boundary between Palestine and Lebanon. Both sides observed the agreement and as a result between 1949 and the Six-Day War of 1967 only six major incidents occurred on the border. Following Israel's comprehensive defeat of the Arab states in the Six-Day War, south Lebanon increasingly became the base for guerrilla attacks by Palestinians against Israel. Israel responded by an increasingly aggressive policy of intervention and pre-emptive raids into south Lebanon. After the outbreak of the Lebanese Civil War in 1975, Israel sought to create a buffer of friendly client militias north of the border by means of the Open or Good Fence policy from May 1976, thus ensuring the security of northern Israel from guerrilla attacks. In 1978 Israel invaded southern Lebanon and achieved the establishment of a buffer zone along the entire length of the Israel–Lebanon border. Despite the deployment of a United Nations Interim Force in Lebanon (UNIFIL), Israel refused to withdraw from all the territory occupied in Lebanon. Instead, a security zone 3–6 miles (5–10 km.) wide encompassing 190–230 sq. miles (500–600 sq. km.) was handed over to the Israeli-backed South Lebanon Army (SLA) and was bolstered by a permanent Israeli military presence. Since 1978 Israel has maintained a policy of intervention in south Lebanon, supporting the SLA in the security zone itself and carrying out frequent artillery barrages, air strikes and raids north of the zone against terrorist targets. In 1982 Israel invaded Lebanon as far north as Beirut in Operation Peace for Galilee, finally withdrawing to the security zone in 1985 after over 1,000 soldiers were killed and having ultimately failed to fully remove either the Palestinian or Syrian presence in Lebanon. From 1985 to the present Israel has reverted to maintaining border security through the buffer zone.

Present Situation. The Israel–Lebanon boundary remains a source of confrontation between Israeli and SLA forces and guerrilla groups, particularly those of the Iranian-backed Islamic Hezbollah. Incidents including rocket attacks on northern Israel and Israeli air raids and artillery bombardments against targets north of the security zone are commonplace.

There appears to be little disagreement between Israel and Lebanon over the actual alignment of the border, save for concerns over alleged unilateral Israeli micro-territorial adjustments to the line and persistent reports of significant Israeli abstraction of Lebanese waters, particularly from the Litani River (although no hard evidence to support this accusation has emerged). Nevertheless, negotiations have reached a stalemate over the issues of Israeli withdrawal from Lebanese territory and security guarantees for northern Israel.

ISRAEL — SYRIA The Golan Heights that constitute this border region and extend between Mount Hermon and the mouth of the Yarmuk River, have been Israeli-occupied Syrian territory since 1967. There are two almost parallel lines of separation, delimited and demarcated in 1974; the 47-mile (76-km.) western line is the actual boundary while the eastern line marks the limits of a demilitarized zone under United Nations supervision. The boundary runs generally southward from the boundary tripoint with Lebanon to the boundary tripoint with Jordan. The international boundary line runs westward, east of the Jordan River.

Geographical Setting. The Golan Heights is a plateau and escarpment region 30 miles (50 km.) long and reaching an altitude of 3,949 feet (1,204 m.). Overlooking Israel, it represents a significant strategic position—providing a panorama that includes the entire Hula (northern Jordan) depression and Lake Tiberias. The armistice line begins in the north at the intersection of the Hasbani River with the Lebanese–Syrian boundary and extends eastward about 3 miles (5 km.) to the base of the rift valley escarpment. From there it extends southward on the east side of the Jordan trench and Lake Tiberias to the Yarmuk River at El Hamma. The de facto boundary on the eastern side of the Heights runs almost parallel to the armistice line, at a distance of 5–14.5 miles (9–23 km.), from the Lebanese border, passing west of El Quneitra and meeting the Jordanian border.

Historical Background. During World War I, Britain and France planned to divide the Ottoman Empire between themselves according to the Sykes-Picot Agreement of 1916 and to create two independent Arab states. However, in 1917 British Foreign Secretary Arthur Balfour effectively supported the Zionist aim of creating a Jewish homeland in Palestine. As Jerusalem was captured by British forces in December 1917 and pressure from the League of Nations increased, the Balfour plan was gradually accepted by the British. By the Treaty of Sèvres (10 August 1920) the British and French effectively enacted the Sykes-Picot Agreement, whereby France established a mandate over Lebanon and Syria, and Britain over Palestine and Mesopotamia. In 1922 Transjordan was established as an autonomous entity by a boundary agreement between Britain and France, with a line separating the mandated territories as established on 5 March 1923, leaving the Golan Heights with Syria. Syria became independent in 1946. In December 1947 Britain declared that it would terminate its mandate on 15 May 1948 and consequently, on 14 May 1948, the Jewish National Council declared the new State of Israel, which was almost immediately invaded by Iraqi, Egyptian, Syrian, Lebanese and Transjordanian forces. The Armistice Agreements of 1949 terminated this Arab-Israeli war, established cease-fire lines along pre-existing boundaries and imposed others that delimited demilitarized zones between Israel and Syria along their common dividing line. This was an immediate cause of Israeli-Syrian confrontation as the status of three of these demilitarized zones, which were superimposed over territory allocated to Israel under the partition plan, remained under dispute. Contention frequently resulted from decisions of the United Nations Mixed Armistice Commission, essentially regarding military advantage, private rights and sovereignty in these zones. Between 1951 and 1953, for example, Israel embarked upon two important water projects, one of which involved a Jordan River diversion plan, which entailed work in the central demilitarized zone. The second project—to drain the Hula marshes—lay outside the zonal areas but required an access road to a drainage canal that would affect some 100 acres of Arab-owned land. The ensuing disputes and the gradual deterioration of security in the frontier areas led to the demise of the Mixed Armistice Commission by 1960, after which the frequency of incidents intensified, with water continuing to be a significant catalyst for conflict. On 5 June 1967, following the closure of the Strait of

The Israel–Syria boundary on Mount Hermon

Tiran to Israeli ships by Egypt (which also entered into a defence treaty with Jordan) Israel attacked Egypt, Syria, Jordan and Iraq simultaneously and by the end of the Six-Day War had gained control of the Golan Heights, the West Bank, East Jerusalem, the Gaza Strip and the entire Sinai Peninsula. After the Six-Day War and contravening United Nations Security Council Resolution 242 which demanded withdrawal, Israel refuted any future validity of the 1949 armistice lines and of demilitarized zones. It insisted on a definitive peace treaty that would establish a mutually agreed delimitation of territorial sovereignty with demarcated boundaries.

On 6 October 1973, frustrated by the loss of territory, Syria and Egypt attacked Israel (the Yom Kippur War), but by the time the war had ended, Israel had occupied an additional salient extending toward Damascus. Even though the United States Secretary of State mediated a disengagement agreement under

which Israel returned to the pre-October 1973 lines (including evacuation of the town of El Quneitra which constituted a minor territorial adjustment in Syria's favor), the northern front of the Golan Heights became a primary zone of constant military activity and confrontation. Occupation of the Golan plateau was strategically and economically important to Israel: it covered significant water resources for Lake Tiberias, Israel's main reservoir, and over the years Israel had established a civilian infrastructure worth several billion dollars. However, for Syria, as well as the topographic and agricultural advantages that the Israelis were now enjoying, the Israeli occupation of the Golan represented a standing threat to Damascus which lies only 25 miles (40 km.) from the front.

Present Situation. The inauguration of an Israeli Labor government in July 1992 saw moves toward peace with its Arab enemies, and with the Peace

Treaty of 26 October 1994 between Israel and Jordan, hopes of a similar settlement to the Israel–Syria boundary dispute were raised. However, recent events have shown little breakthrough in the peace process as both Syrian and Israeli stances have only hardened. While the Syrians demand a clear Israeli commitment to total and comprehensive withdrawal from the Syrian territory to the borders that existed prior to 1967, Israel is pushing for a limited withdrawal from half the occupied territory and an examination of normalized relations there before completing full withdrawal. Thus, as peace negotiations continue, the territory of the Golan Heights, which constitutes the border between Israel and Syria, remains very much in dispute.

ITALY (Italia) A southern European country (area: 116,324 sq. miles [301,163 sq. km.]; estimated population: 58,100,000 [1994]), Italy is a peninsula that reaches into the Mediterranean Sea. It is bounded in the northwest by France (305 miles; 488 km.), in the north by Switzerland (460 miles; 740 km.) and Austria (267 miles; 430 km.) and in the northeast by Slovenia (124 miles; 199 km.). Bounded within Italy are two tiny states, San Marino (24 miles; 39 km.) and Vatican City (2 miles; 3.2 km.). It is bounded by the Adriatic and Ionian Seas in the east, by the Mediterranean and Tyrrhenian Seas in the south and southwest and by the Ligurian Sea in the west. Italy's capital is Rome.

Italy formed the core of the Roman Empire which united the Mediterranean world 2,000 years ago: this was the Italians' first collective experience. Overstretched and weakened, Rome could not resist barbaric invasions in the first centuries C.E. Italy was divided among a number of successor monarchies of Germanic origin (viz. the Longobards in the sixth century). South and east Italy remained for some time outposts of the Byzantine Empire, but eventually were also swept away.

In the Middle Ages, Italian ports and artisan and merchant cities were among Europe's most advanced, and made Italy Europe's most prosperous (and coveted) region. From the eleventh century, the merchant republics of Venice and Genoa vied with each other to establish their dominion over the eastern Mediterranean. Florence, Siena, Milan and a host of other towns, thrived on manufacture and banking, while Rome exploited its status as a sacred city for temporal gain. The very advance of the North Italians enabled them to defeat the German emperor's attempts at centralizing power. Since then, the North Italians have remained the richest and most urbanized part of the Italian population. Pisa, Amalfi, Genoa, Venice, and later Siena, Florence and Milan were ruled by bourgeois bankers and entrepreneurs under whose patronage artists and intellectuals developed a wholly new culture: that of the Renaissance, which celebrated individualism and the heritage of the classical period.

However, the particularistic city-states also laid the base for the political fragmentation of the Italians that was to endure until the nineteenth century. After they had succeeded in defeating the ambitions of the German Hohenstaufen emperor to create a unitary state, in the sixteenth century Italy's competing and warring merchant republics succumbed to the more tightly disciplined armies of French and Spanish invaders, attracted by the prospect of rich booty. Ottoman expansion cut off traditional trade routes; the age of discoveries shifted commerce away from the Mediterranean to the Atlantic, sealing Italy's decline.

Thereafter, Italian unity and self-determination was only finally achieved in the 1860s, under the kingdom of Sardinia, by a combination of astute diplomacy and popular action, particularly Giuseppe Garibaldi's Expedition of the Thousand, which defeated the French Bourbon and papal forces. Plebiscites ratified the unification and established a monarchy.

However, after half a century of political crises capped by the miseries caused by World War I, the chasm between rich and poor in Italy very nearly brought about a socialist revolution. Upon its failure, Benito Mussolini installed a Fascist dictatorship. Restoring order and providing a modicum of economic progress bought the regime broad support, but the political capital was spent on grandiose foreign adventures, which dragged the Italians into World War II on the German side. After the war, a none-too-stable democratic republic replaced Fascism.

Since 1945 fast economic and social modernization frequently punctuated by fierce class struggles has transformed Italian society. Despite superficial westernizing fashions, family bonds remain very strong. Italians are a very urbanized people; even their villages often take an urban character. Contrast between regions remains the central fact of Italian life. Since World War II, the north has become heavily industrialized, while the south has remained relatively isolated, underdeveloped and poor.

Population growth has led to massive emigration. Between 1860 and World War I, over 2,000,000 migrated to the Americas and North Africa. After World War II 4,000,000 moved to Switzerland, France (600,000), Germany (450,000), Belgium (200,000) and other, mainly European, destinations.

Domestic migration waves have been even more massive—population moves from countryside to city, from mountain to coast, from island to continent and from south to north. With the influx of millions of southerners, the industrial and prosperous north not only imported a pool of cheap labor, but also a host of social problems. Current regionalist anti-southerner movements such as the Lombard League may represent the Italian version of the anti-foreigner Right in Germany, France and Britain, although today Italy itself has become an immigration country for 500,000 North Africans and Ethiopians.

ITALY — AUSTRIA   See AUSTRIA–ITALY.

ITALY — FRANCE   See FRANCE–ITALY.

ITALY — SAN MARINO   The Italy–San Marino boundary is 24 miles (39 km.) long. San Marino has an areal territory of only 24 sq. miles (61 sq. km.) that is completely surrounded by Italian ground.
Geographical Setting. San Marino is located on the western slope of Mount Titano (2,421 feet; 738 m.), in the eastern Apennines of Italy. From its northeasternmost point, on the Rimini (Italy)–San Marino highway, the boundary runs southward for 5 miles (8 km.) to reach the Marano River. It follows the river upstream southward for about 1 mile (1.6 km.) and meets the road between Montesqudo (Italy) and San Marino. It continues south toward the Mercatino Conca (Italy)–San Marino road and then runs westward, crosses the upper Marano River and arrives at the road that enters San Marino from the southwest. Thence the boundary runs northward,

reaching the road that enters San Marino from the west. The line heads northeastward for about 10 miles (16 km.), crossing the main Rimini–San Marino highway and regaining the northeasternmost spot of the boundary.
Historical Background. San Marino, which claims to be the world's oldest republic, was established by San Marinus in the fourth century. During the Middle Ages it was a city-state that constructed its castle in the tenth century. The Papal State attempted to occupy it several times but in 1740 recognized its independence. Napoleon I recognized San Marino's independence in 1797 and the Congress of Vienna did so in 1815. When Italy was united during the second half of the nineteenth century San Marino did not join it, but in 1862 it signed a treaty of friendship with Italy—which also recognized its boundary. During World War II San Marino remained neutral and was never occupied by external armies.
Present Situation. There are no disputes concerning the boundary between Italy and San Marino as Italy has officially recognized the independence of San Marino and its territorial area. There are no boundary checkpoints or barriers between the two states.

ITALY — SLOVENIA   The boundary between Italy and Slovenia runs for 124 miles (199 km.) between the Austrian tripoint in the north and the Gulf of Trieste of the Adriatic Sea. It follows the Italian–former Yugoslavia boundary that was established after World War II.
Geographical Setting. The northern terminus of the boundary is located on the peak of Petzen (Pec) (4,559 feet; 1,509 m.). From there the boundary line runs southward for about 10 miles (16 km.), passing the Pontebba (Italy)–Jesenica (Slovenia) road and boundary post, reaching the northern slope of Mount Jalovec (8,670 feet; 2,643 m.). Thence the boundary runs westward, reaching the Predel Pass and boundary post (3,792 feet; 1,156 m.) and following the local watershed it runs southwestward, crossing Mount Cergnala (7,688 feet; 2,344 m.) and Mount Canin (8,485 feet; 2,587 m.) and reaching Gran Monte (5,274 feet; 1,608 m.). It runs southeastward, reaching the upper Natisone River, and follows it downstream for about 6 miles (10 km.). Departing from the river, the boundary runs in a semicircle to

the south, leaving some Slovenian villages within Slovenia. The boundary reaches the Natisone River again, crosses it and runs east-southeastward for about 13 miles (20 km.), reaching the source of the Idrije River. It follows that river downstream southwestward for about 15 miles (25 km.), leaves it and runs southwestward and southeastward in a series of straight lines to Mount Sabstino (1,984 feet; 605 m.). Then the boundary line runs southward, crosses the Soca River, passes east of the Italian city of Gorizia, crosses the Isonzo River and meets a point about 2 miles (3 km.) from the small Italian town of Saint Giovanni, located off the Adriatic shore. The boundary line runs southeastward for about 20 miles (35 km.), parallel to the shore, about 5 miles (8 km.) inland, so as to leave the city of Trieste within Italy. From a point about 5 miles (8 km.) east of Trieste, it heads southwestward and westward, reaching the Gulf of Trieste south of the small Italian town and boundary post of Saint Bartolomeo.

Historical Background. Both Italy and Slovenia were part of the Habsburg Empire in the mid-nineteenth century. Italy became independent in 1861,

but its northeastern boundary was placed far west of the present line as the area around Venice was held by the Austrian Empire. During the nineteenth century Italy was expanded northeastward but had claims to the area of the eastern Adriatic shore, which has a mixed population of Italians and Slovenians. During World War I Italy signed the London Agreement of 26 April 1915, in which France, Great Britain and the Russian Empire agreed that Italy would receive the areas of Trieste, Gorizia, Istra and the Dalmatian coast down to Cape Palanka. The city of Fiume was not included in that agreement. After the war, Italy placed these claims, including the city of Fiume, before the Paris Peace Convention in February 1919. In the Peace Treaty with Austria signed in Saint Germain in September 1919, Italy gained Goriza, Trieste and the Istera peninsula populated with over 250,000 Slavs. The question of Fiume and the Dalmatian coast, however, remained open to negotiation.

The first Slovenian national program was formulated in 1848, but up to World War I it was ruled by the Austro-Hungarian Empire. The Slovenian leaders

Italy–Slovenia border crossing

collaborated in 1918 in the formation of the united Kingdom of Serbs, Croats and Slovenes, which later became Yugoslavia. Italian troops occupied Trieste on 4 November 1918. Italy and the newly established kingdom dealt with the boundary issues at a conference in Rapallo in November 1920. Italy waived its claims to Dalmatia except for the town of Zara (Zadar). A boundary was established which gave Italy the islands of Lagosta (Losinj) and Pelagosa (Pago), while both states recognized the independence of the free city of Fiume (Rijeke). Italy pressed for the inclusion of that city within it, a move that was carried out by the Pact of Rome of January 1924. Italy occupied Slovenia during World War II.

The Treaty of Peace, which was finally ratified in September 1947, gave Yugoslavia Fiume (now called Rijeke), Zara (Zadar), Pola (Pula) and Isteria (Istra), while the future of Trieste remained doubtful. Earlier, in February 1947, Trieste was proclaimed the Free Territory of Trieste, a small, neutral independent state. On 20 March 1948 the Western Powers suggested to include Trieste within Italy but the Soviet Union did not agreed to the proposal. The issue of Trieste was settled on 5 October 1954 by the partition of the territory between Italy and Yugoslavia. Italy acquired an area of 91 sq. miles (236 sq. km.)—including the city of Trieste—with a population of 310,000, of which 63,000 were Slovenians. Yugoslavia gained an area of 202 sq. miles (523 sq. km.) with a population of 73,000, that included 30,000 Italians. Thus, the 40-year dispute came to an end.

Present Situation. Slovenia became independent on 25 June 1991, adopting Yugoslavia's boundary with Italy as its international boundary without a formal agreement. There is no known dispute concerning the alignment of the boundary line, which is fully accepted by both states.

ITALY — SWITZERLAND

Mainly coursing through the Alps, the boundary between Italy and Switzerland runs for 460 miles (740 km.) from its western terminus on Mount Dolent, at the boundary junction with France, to Piz Lad at the boundary junction with Austria. The entire boundary is well demarcated.

Geographical Setting. Starting out on Mount Dolent, (12,616 feet; 3,846 m.). The boundary runs eastward along the watershed between the Swiss part of the Rhone River and the tributaries of the Italian Po River. The line passes by Mount Matterhorn (14,774 feet; 4,504 m.) and reaches Mount Rosa (15,217 feet; 4,639 m.), the highest mountain in Italy and the second highest peak in Europe. From Mount Rosa it runs generally northeastward along the watershed to Simplon Pass, which links Italy and Switzerland, and to Nefegen Pass at the northern end of Ossola Valley (Italy). From there the boundary runs southeastward, generally following the watershed and crossing drainage systems that feed the Alpine lakes. The boundary line reaches the northern section of Lake Maggiore and crosses it, leaving its northern part in Switzerland. The boundary runs eastward, southward and again eastward to Lake Lugano, mainly following cultural, rather then physical, lines. Then it runs in Lake Lugano from north to south, continues on land southward for about 6 miles (10 km.), turns east for about 5 miles (8 km.) and runs northward to meet Lake Lugano again. Here the boundary line creates two enclaves: the Swiss region of Mendrisio is surrounded by Italian territory in the east, south and west and its only means of direct access to the rest of Switzerland is through the lake; the small Italian town of Campione D'Italia, situated on the southeastern shore of the lake, is surrounded by Swiss territory.

The boundary line crosses Lake Lugano again from south to north and runs northeastward along the watershed to reach Splügen Pass. Thence it heads eastward to Valle (Valley) di Lei. It trends along the high range of the Bernina Alps east and southeastward for 60 miles (96 km.), reaching a tributary of the Italian Adda River north of the Italian city of Tirano. Northeastward along the local watershed the boundary reaches the Grego di Stalvio Pass and then proceeds northward to the boundary junction with Austria at Gruben Joch, near the northern slope of Piz Lad (7,155 feet; 2,180 m.).

Historical Background. The long history of the boundary between Italy and Switzerland has involved over 400 separate documents. The first demarcation of the boundary appears to have taken place as early as 1559. Over the following years boundary treaties were negotiated and then signed between the various kingdoms and republics of

Italy–Switzerland border at the Campione D'Italia enclave

northern Italy and the different prefectures and cantons of Switzerland. On 2 August 1752, a treaty for the regulation of the boundary between Lombardy and the prefectures of Lugano, Locarno and Mendrisio was signed by the Duchess of Milan, the Empress of Austria and the Helvetian League, all of whom were involved in the boundary negotiations. On 20 March 1815, following the Napoleonic Wars (1800–1814), the Eight Powers Declaration on the Affairs of the Helvetic Confederacy established new boundaries for Switzerland and fixed the current French–Italian–Swiss tripoint on Mount Dolent. In 1861 the Lugano Convention resolved some minor problems concerning the Ticino (Switzerland) boundary (which was fully demarcated during 1891–1895) and the convention of 27 August 1867 led to the demarcation of the eastern section of the boundary. At the beginning of the twentieth century, an exchange of notes determined the boundary at the main Alpine passes. Major changes took place after World War I, however, as the Tirol region was transferred from Austria to Italy by the Treaty of Saint-Germain, which was signed on 10 September 1919. This extended the boundary line between Italy and Switzerland by 33.5 miles (53.5 km.), from Cima Garibaldi to Piz Lad. It took about eight years to settle this part of the boundary, which was completed by exchanges of notes dated 3 October 1927 and 22 August 1927.

On 22 March 1929, a declaration resolved disputes in three water areas of the boundary. During World War II, on 24 July 1941, the Swiss Confederation and the Kingdom of Italy signed a convention on the determination of their common boundary, which led to the publication of 16 large-scale maps illustrating the line. Waterworks, tunnel construction and other operations along the border after 1949 created the need for further boundary modifications, which were carried out by a series of boundary agreements that took place between the countries.

The adjustments, although numerous, have resulted in only minor territorial transfers.

Present Situation. In spite of the harsh natural forces and the political changes that have taken place in the region, the Italian and Swiss governments—through constant maintenance, surveillance and mutual cooperation—have been able to preserve the boundary with only minimal difficulties. There are no known disputes concerning the boundary's alignment.

ITALY — VATICAN CITY Vatican City is surrounded by the city of Rome, the capital of Italy, and its boundary is 2 miles (3.2 km.) long.

Geographical Setting. Vatican City is located in western Rome, west of the Tiber River. Covering an area of 0.17 sq. miles (0.44 sq. km.) its eastern limits are marked by a wall and the open Saint Peters Square. From the northern edge of the square the boundary runs northward along the eastern wall of the Belaverde Palace for 1,000 feet (300 m.) and westward along its northern wall. Heading northward again for about 380 feet (115 m.) it bears along the walls of the Vatican Museum and then turns southwestward and follows this direction for about 0.6 miles (1 km.), along the wall of the Vatican Gardens. Running eastward and crossing the railway line, the boundary reaches the southeastern corner of Saint Peters Church. The line runs to Saint Peters Square and follows its oval line southward, eastward and northward, finally reaching its northern edge.

Historical Background. The secular rule of the Papal State, which in the Middle Ages held a large area in central Italy, was abolished on 13 November 1871 after the amalgamation of Rome with Italy in 1870. For 60 years the popes would not recognize the occupation and never accepted the loss of independence. On 11 February 1929 the Lateran Agreement, which was signed between Pope Pius XI and the king of Italy, reestablished the state of Vatican City, a zone that was declared a "neutral area," within the city of Rome. Italy then paid Vatican City a sum of $3.5 million for the loss of its territories outside of the city.

Present Situation. The 1929 pact was accepted by all governments of Italy and no disputes concerning the alignment of the Italy–Vatican City boundary line are known.

IVORY COAST (Côte d'Ivoire) A west African country, Ivory Coast (area: 124,518 sq. miles [322,377 sq. km.]; estimated population: 13,500,000 [1994]) is bounded in the north by Mali (331 miles; 532 km.) and Burkina Faso (363 miles; 584 km.), in the east by Ghana (415 miles; 668 km.), south by the Gulf of Guinea in the South Atlantic Ocean and west by Liberia (445 miles; 716 km.) and Guinea (379 miles; 610 km.). Its capital is Abidjan.

The Côte d'Ivoire gained independence from the French in August 1960. During the decolonization period, which started after the end of World War II, the Baule were the most active ethnic group in politics. A Baule chief named Félix Houphouet-Boigny founded in 1946 the PDCI (Parti Democratique de la Côte d'Ivoire). It was affiliated to the interterritorial party of French West Africa, headed also by Houphouet-Boigny, the RDA (Rassamblement Democratique Africaine). Although he himself was a member of the Baule, Houphouet-Boigny soon turned the PDCI into a party which represented all the ethnic groups in the country.

During the 1950s the PDCI became the only force in the Côte d'Ivoire, and Houphouet-Boigny was the uncontested leader. His speeches emphasized the ethnic diversity of the country and the importance of unity.

After independence, which was gained peacefully, Houphouet-Boigny became president, with the PDCI as the only party. No serious ethnic problems have emerged during his rule. However, the Baule play a dominant part in politics.

Since the beginning of the 1990s there has been popular pressure for democratization. The government has only partly responded, and full democratization has not yet occurred.

IVORY COAST — BURKINA FASO see BURKINA FASO–IVORY COAST.

IVORY COAST — GHANA see GHANA–IVORY COAST.

IVORY COAST — GUINEA see GUINEA–IVORY COAST.

IVORY COAST — LIBERIA The boundary between Ivory Coast and Liberia runs for 445 miles

(716 km.) between the mouth of the Cavalla River in the Atlantic Ocean in the southeast and the boundary tripoint with Guinea at Mount Neun in the Nimba Range in the northwest. For the most part it follows the Liberian banks of various rivers.

Geographical Setting. From the mouth of the Cavalla River, east of Cape Palmes and the Liberian town of Harper, the boundary follows the right (west) bank of the river upstream northward for about 305 miles (490 km.), to its confluence with the Bone River. It follows the Liberian bank of that river upstream for about 7 miles (11 km.) to its source and in a short (2 miles; 3.2 km.) straight-line segment it reaches the headwaters of the Dain River. The boundary runs along the western bank of the Dain River to its confluence with the Nimoi River and runs along that river downstream, covering a total of 16 miles (26 km.) over both rivers. The boundary reaches the confluence of the Nimoi River with the Neun River and follows the latter upstream for about 115 miles (185 km.) to the boundary tripoint with Guinea at Mount Neun in the Nimba Range.

Historical Background. Liberia was established by the American Colonization Society, which was established in 1816 in order to settle liberated black American slaves in Africa. In 1820 land was bought on the west African coast and in 1822 the first permanent settlement was established in Cape Mesurado, the site of today's Monrovia, the capital of Liberia. The area was named Liberia in 1838 and became an independent republic in 1847.

Côte d'Ivoire was once made up of several separate kingdoms. From the sixteenth century the Portuguese, French and British established trading centers along the coast, dealing in slaves and ivory. During the nineteenth century, France acquired the region by means of treaties with local leaders. Contact with Liberia was made in the Cavalla River. That river and its mouth near the navigationally significant Cape Palmas is the key, past and present, to the Liberia–Ivory Coast boundary. Black American settlers at the Maryland colony in East Liberia had what they believed to be valid claims to the coast east of the Cavalla River. Their long-standing interest, if based on nothing more that proximity, negatively impacted Franco-Liberian relations for most of the nineteenth century. The French concern was

for regional stability but that seemed always beyond the reach of the Maryland settlement. Of all the indigenous ethnic groups between Monrovia (Liberia) and Abidjan (Ivory Coast), none were more difficult to subdue than the Kru and Grebo people adjacent to the Maryland colony. By 1892 France signed a boundary treaty with Liberia, placing the boundary on the western bank of the Cavalla River. The agreement left the Maryland settlement area within Liberia, after years of fighting against the indigenous Grebo and Kru people. The shape of Ivory Coast as a French colony was generally fixed by the French decree of 17 October 1899, breaking up the former French Sudan. The Ivory Coast became independent on 7 August 1960, adopting the 1892 boundary line as its international boundary with Liberia.

Present Situation. There are no disputes concerning the alignment of the boundary line, but the instability of the region continues. At the time of the April 1980 military putsch, which was more of an ethnic revolution than anything else, the Cavalla boundary took on special significance because of family ties between the executed Liberian President Tolbert and the president of the Ivory Coast. Liberian soldiers sought to seal this border, often with force. Numerous incidents have been reported along the line since.

IVORY COAST — MALI   From the tripoint boundary junction with Burkina Faso on the Leraba River in the east to the boundary tripoint with Guinea on the Gbolonzo River in the west, the boundary between Ivory Coast and Mali stretches for 331 miles (532 km.).

Geographical Setting. This boundary has never been described in an agreement and its alignment is mainly based on maps. The eastern terminus of the boundary line, which is the boundary tripoint with Burkina Faso, is located at the intersection of the Bani and Leraba Rivers. Thence it runs westward for about 50 miles (80 km.), following some local streams and connecting them with straight lines. It reaches the Bagoé River and follows it downstream northward for about 40 miles (65 km.) to its confluence with the Kankèlaba River, leaving the small town of Tingrela with Ivory Coast. The boundary follows the Kankèlaba River upstream westward, southward and again westward to reach its source. Continuing westward and crossing some local rivers the line meets the Baoulé River north of Maninian (Ivory Coast). From there it follows the Baoulé River southwestward to reach the boundary tripoint with Guinea, located at approximately 10°24'N and 7°42'W.

Historical Background. Côte d'Ivoire and Mali were both units within French West Africa, which was established in 1895 and also included today's Senegal, Mauritania, Burkina Faso, Guinea, Benin and Niger. France reorganized the area several times but maintained the colony of Ivory Coast within its limits. In 1899 the area was divided into separate units without a description of their frontiers and only in 1902 was the boundary between Ivory Coast and the military zone north of it mentioned in an official decree, but the exact boundary line was never formally established. The Federation of Mali, which included Senegal and the Sudanese Republic, was dissolved in 1960 and Mali became independent. Ivory Coast became independent on 7 August 1960. Both states adopted the administrative colonial line as their common international boundary without a formal agreement.

Present Situation. No demarcation is known to have taken place along this border and certain sectors of the line still lack definite delineation. However, no disputes concerning the alignment have been reported since 1960.

J

JAMAICA An island state in the Caribbean Sea, Jamaica is situated south of Cuba. Its area is 4,244 sq. miles (10,988 sq. km.) and it has an estimated population (1994) of 2,523,000. Jamaica has no land boundaries and its capital is Kingston.

Jamaica, whose historically indigenous (later exterminated) Arawak people were encountered by Columbus in 1494, was disappointing to the Spaniards because it lacked gold, and was therefore largely neglected, falling to the British in 1655. It became a base for British pirates preying on Spanish shipping, and of the slave trade.

The latter, introduced by the Spanish, enabled the development of one of the most flourishing sugar plantation economies in the Caribbean, but also imported enough Africans to organize a continuing guerrilla movement to harrass the British during the seventeenth and eighteenth centuries. The plantation economy collapsed with the abolition of slavery in the 1830s and in 1866 Jamaica was designated a crown colony. Initiating moves toward self-determination in the 1930s, Jamaica became internally autonomous in 1959 and an independent Commonwealth member in 1962.

JAPAN (Nihon) A country in east Asia, Japan is located in the northern Pacific Ocean. It consists of four large islands (Hokkaido, Honshu, Shikoku and Kyushu) and many smaller islands. Japan's total land area is 145,870 sq. miles (377,657 sq. km.) and its estimated population (1994) is 124,900,000. It has no land boundaries and its capital is Tokyo.

The Japanese are known to have originated from a mixture of peoples who came to the Japanese islands at various times and from various places on the Asian continent and formed a group of tribes in the mid-first millennium B.C.E. Some time after 250 B.C.E., an influx of rice-growing people created the Yayoi culture which first flourished in western Japan before penetrating to the northeast. The Yayoi dominated the islands for five centuries; the first state, Yamato, founded in the fourth century, represented the Japanese transition from ancient tribes into a nationality.

Throughout their early history (third–tenth centuries), the Japanese developed a culture strongly influenced by the Chinese and the Koreans. Their first contact with Europeans (the Portuguese and the Dutch in particular) occurred during the sixteenth century, but was followed by 200 years of isolationism during the Tokugawa period. Contacts with the West were renewed following the arrival of Commodore Matthew C. Perry from the United States in 1853, and friendship treaties with the United States, Russia, Britain and the Netherlands soon followed. Strong internal resistance to opening Japan to foreign contacts was finally overcome after the ascension of Emperor Meiji in 1868; the Meiji Restoration, as it is known, signaled the end of Japanese feudalism and isolationism and marked the entry of Japan into the modern era.

Japan's victories in the Sino-Japanese (1894–1895) and Russo-Japanese (1904–1905) wars marked its emergence as a regional superpower; it was one of the Big Five powers at the post-World War I Versailles Peace Conference. Meanwhile, it rapidly transformed from an agricultural to an industrial nation. Japan's participation in World War II was ended by the destruction of Hiroshima and Nagasaki by US atomic bombs in 1945; this ushered in the Atomic Era, precipitated the unconditional surrender of the Japanese to the Allied Powers, and led to the institution of a parliamentary system of government based on the sovereignty of the people. The new constitution promulgated in 1946 also prohibited any political role for the emperor other than as titular head of state.

Japan's remarkable economic expansion in the postwar period (initially triggered by massive US aid and the economic boom consequent upon Japan's role as a major supplier during the Korean War) has made it second only to the United States among non-Communist nations in total value of GNP. Japanese export penetration into foreign markets, coupled with Japanese consumer loyalty to home-produced goods, has enabled the country to continue to register substantial trade surpluses.

JORDAN (Al-Urdun)   A country in the Middle East, Jordan (area: 35,135 sq. miles [91,000 sq. km.]; estimated population: 4,100,000 [1994]) is bounded in the north by Syria (233 miles; 375 km.), northeast by Iraq (111 miles; 179 km.), east and south by Saudi Arabia (461 miles; 742 km.) and west by Israel (165 miles; 266 km.). Jordan has a small outlet to the Red Sea from its port town of 'Aqaba in the south. The capital of Jordan is Amman.

Since the area of what is now Jordan never developed into an autonomous power center, it developed

to cope with the influx of Palestinian refugees. In 1950 Jordan annexed the West Bank, the area west of the Jordan river which had been earmarked for a Palestinian state, thus increasing its population by one-third. The monarchy (from 1953 under Hussein), initially only supported by the Beduin and a few well-to-do merchant families, has weathered many crises and seems gradually to be gaining broader legitimacy, hand in hand with the crystallization of a separate Jordanian identity. Following the loss of the West Bank to Israel in 1967, Palestinian guerrillas posed the most serious threat to the monarchy.

In the ensuing "Black September" of 1970, thousands of Palestinians in Jordan were killed; many more left for Lebanon. Still, the growth of Jordan's economy during the 1970s also benefiting the Palestinians while satisfying various East Bank constituencies.

After the outbreak of the *intifada*, Jordan in 1988 formally disengaged from the West Bank and initiated cautious democratization. Elections in 1989 led to massive gains for Islamic fundamentalists. The 1991 Gulf War crisis imposed a severe burden on Jordan's

Jordan–Israel–Saudi Arabia boundaries on the Red Sea

no specific regional identity until its establishment after World War I by Britain. In 1922 Transjordan was carved from the British mandate over Palestine, and created to compensate the emir (from 1946 king), Abdallah, for Hashemite efforts to aid the British during that war (the Hashemites had ruled over Hejaz in the Arabian Peninsula until expelled by the Saudis).

Following the 1948 war with Israel, Transjordan had

economy: its trade was disrupted by the anti-Iraq embargo, financial support by Saudi Arabia and the Gulf states was cut, and hundreds of thousands of its migrant workers, mostly Palestinians, were compelled to return home. Postwar recovery and the start of common Jordanian-Palestinian peace talks with Israel appear to have given Jordan new hope. A peace treaty with Israel was signed in 1994.

JORDAN — IRAQ see IRAQ–JORDAN.

JORDAN — ISRAEL see ISRAEL–JORDAN.

JORDAN — SAUDI ARABIA The Jordan–Saudi Arabia boundary, as defined following a bilateral agreement of 1965, measures 461 miles (742 km.) and runs from the boundary tripoint with Iraq at Jebel 'Anaiza (Anazah) to the Gulf of 'Aqaba. The southwestern terminus in the Gulf is not precisely determined to date, but lies approximately 11 miles (18 km.) south of the port of 'Aqaba.

Geographical Setting. From Jebel 'Anaiza the boundary proceeds southwestward in a series of straight-line segments, initially running to the intersection of 39°E and 32°N. It then forms a straight line to 31°30'N and 37°E, where it turns sharply southeastward to reach 30°30'N and 38°E. It then turns southwestward again, trending toward 30°20'N and 37°40'E, which stands 1.2 miles (2 km.) north of the well of Mashash Hadraj. From this point the boundary takes a south-southwesterly direction to

30°N and 37°30'E, where it turns southwestward to arrive at 29°52'N and 36°45'E just south of Al-Unab airfield (Jordan). From here to the Gulf of 'Aqaba the boundary forms three more straight-line segments, passing through 29°30'N and 36°30'E and through 29°11'N and 36°04'E, which is about 0.5 miles (1 km.) north of the old Hallat 'Ammar railway station. Before meeting the Gulf, the line passes the northeastern Al-Durra Police Post (Saudi Arabia), the precise location of which is not clear; consequently, the coastal terminus is also imprecise.

Historical Background. On 24 April 1920, Palestine (northwest of Jordan) was placed under British administration as a mandated territory, thereby formally terminating the Ottoman control of the region. However, upon dividing the mandate along the Jordan River–Wadi al-'Araba line for administrative purposes, the precise southern limits of Palestine were left undelimited. While Britain claimed access to the Gulf of 'Aqaba, Saudi Arabia contrastingly considered the northwestern terminus of their border at Ma'an, some 50 miles (80 km.) north of the

A dry river in Jordan, near the Jordanian–Saudi Arabia boundary

British coastal claims. Consequently, the 1920s witnessed a debate between the Arabian sultanates of the Nejd and Hejaz regions of Saudi Arabia in an attempt to delimit the southern boundaries of the Transjordanian and Syrian mandates. On 2 November 1925 the Hadda Agreement between the British and the sultan of Nejd delimited the central and eastern sectors. The disputed Kaf region was assigned to the Nejd, but the Hejaz in the western sector of Jordan remained undefined. Britain proceeded to delimit the boundary unilaterally to include within Transjordan a narrow outlet in the Gulf, a course of action that was rejected by the entire Kingdom of Saudi Arabia in an exchange of notes in May 1927. Both parties eventually reached an agreement to maintain the status quo pending a solution to the dispute.

The Treaty of London was signed on 22 March 1946, whereby Transjordan became independent as the Hashemite Kingdom of Jordan, adopting the 1925 Hadda Agreement boundaries, which remained unresolved. Following unsuccessful negotiations between 1961 and 1963, a mutually acceptable line was drawn up in the Amman Agreement of 9 August 1965, which came into effect on 7 November of that year. In accordance with this agreement Jordan ceded 2,700 sq. miles (7,000 sq. km.) to Saudi Arabia in the southeastern sector of the boundary line, while gaining 12 miles (19 km.) of coastline and 2,300 sq. miles (6,000 sq. km.) of territory mostly in the southern and northeastern sectors of the line. The boundary agreement also created an area where, should oil be discovered in the future, petroleum revenues will be shared equally.

Present Situation. Jordan's only maritime outlet is at the Gulf of 'Aqaba and therefore the country considers access to it of paramount importance. However, since the 1965 agreement to realign the boundary, there have been no significant disputes to threaten Jordan with such a loss.

JORDAN — SYRIA The Jordan–Syria boundary is 233 miles (375 km.) in length, delimited but not marked on the ground.

Geographical Setting. The boundary line begins in the Yarmuk River, about 12 miles (20 km.) from its confluence with the Jordan River at the Jordan–Israel–Syria tripoint above Al Hamma. The boundary runs eastward, following the river and its tributaries, Wadi Zayun and Wadi Mayddan, for about 24 miles (38 km.). Then in the vicinity of Paria the boundary leaves the river, runs southeastward for about 80 miles (130 km.) to a point close to the summit of Tall-Rimah and then turns northeastward and runs in a straight line for 129 miles (206 km.) to the Iraqi tripoint at 33°22'29"N and 38°47'33"E.

Historical background. The history of the boundary dates back to World War I. On 16 May 1916 Great Britain and France concluded a secret agreement, known as the Sykes-Picot Agreement, which delimited Ottoman territory into British and French spheres of influence. France assumed control of northern Syria while an area south of a line rather arbitrarily delineated on maps along the Yarmuk River and northeastward through the Syrian desert was assigned to be directly under British influence. After the war, France held the mandate for Syria and Lebanon while Britain held the mandate for Palestine and Mesopotamia. On 23 December 1920 Britain and France signed a convention that defined the boundaries between these mandate areas. It provided for the demarcation of the boundaries by an Anglo-French Boundary Commission but delimited the line only in general terms. The western part of the boundary, that of British Palestine and French Lebanon and Syria, was demarcated on 3 February 1922, with a final agreement made on 3 March 1923. The boundary between French Syria and British Transjordan, however, was never demarcated. On 31 October 1931 a protocol between France and Britain was signed in Paris, defining the exact location of the Syria–Transjordan boundary which later became the international boundary between these two states. The boundary is essentially artificial—apart from the 24 miles (38 km.) of the water line along the Yarmuk River.

Present Situation. In recent years there has been considerable political friction between the Jordanian and Syrian governments, partly related to the use of the Yarmuk river for irrigation. However, there are no active disputes between Jordan and Syria regarding the specific alignment of the boundary.

K

KAZAKHSTAN A landlocked republic in central Asia and a former republic of the Soviet Union, Kazakhstan (area: 1,049,156 sq. miles [2,717,300 sq. km.]; estimated population: 17,200,000 [1994]) is bounded in the northwest by Russia (4,255 miles; 6,846 km.), southwest by the Caspian Sea, Turkmenistan (236 miles; 379 km.), Uzbekistan (1,369 miles; 2,203 km.) and by Kyrgyzstan (653 miles; 1,051 km.) and east by China (953 miles; 1,533 km.). Kazakhstan's capital is Alma-Ata.

Historically, the area of contemporary Kazakhstan, as part of the great European chain of steppes and deserts, served as a corridor for the many migrations and invasions of nomadic peoples on their way from east to west. This continuous procession created powerful ethnic interaction among the indigenous

Kazakhstan and central Asia's boundaries

tribes and the tides of newcomers. By the end of the first millennium C.E. numerous Turkic tribes, among them Qypchaq, dominated the area. During the thirteenth and fourteenth centuries many Mongols were gradually integrated into local nomadic groups. Toward the beginning of the sixteenth century these tribes became consolidated into the Kazakh people, and for a short time a state, the Kazakh khanate, emerged, which later broke into three federations: The Great, the Middle and the Lesser Hordes (*Zhuzes*, lit. "parts"). During the eighteenth and nineteenth centuries these Kazakh federations gradually became part of the Russian Empire.

With the breakdown of this empire in 1917, a short-lived Kazakh autonomy headed by the Alash Orda national modernist party existed until 1919. The Russian Bolsheviks crushed it and established the Kirghiz Autonomous Soviet Socialist Republic (ASSR) in 1920 and renamed in 1925 the Kazakh ASSR within the framework of the Russian Federation. In 1936 it was given the status of a Soviet Socialist Republic (SSR). In 1991 Kazakhstan became an independent state within the framework of the Commonwealth of Independent States.

KAZAKHSTAN — CHINA see CHINA–KAZAKHSTAN.

KAZAKHSTAN — KYRGYZSTAN This boundary, which crosses predominantly mountainous terrain, only achieved international status in 1991, having divided two Soviet union republics since 1936.
Geographical Setting. The boundary meanders in a roughly east–west direction for 653 miles (1,051 km.) starting at the junction with the Chinese border immediately to the east of the 22,944-foot (6,995-m.) Pik Khan Tengri, and trending to the tripoint with Uzbekistan at the northern end of the Pskemskij mountain range. The eastern half of the border rarely falls below 6,560 feet (2,000 m.) above sea level, crossing to the north of Issyk-Kul' lake, but further west it descends to skirt the foothills of the Kyrgyz mountains. In its central section the border follows the Chu River in a northwesterly direction for approximately 93 miles (150 km.).
Historical Background. Until the Soviet period, there were very few clearly defined boundaries in central Asia. Toward the end of the eighteenth cen-

tury, much of the territory now occupied by the central Asian republics came under control of the rival Khanates of Bukhara, Khorezm (Khiva) and Kokand, which were brought under Russian control during the second half of the nineteenth century; however, no borders were formally defined during either period. Following the Russian Revolution of 1917, the Red Army rapidly consolidated control over Russian central Asia and the region was formally divided into discrete "national" units. The territories now known as Kazakhstan and Kyrgyzstan were initially designated as Autonomous Soviet Socialist Republics but were promoted to full union republics in 1936. When the Soviet Union collapsed at the end of 1991, the Alma-Ata Declaration which established the Commonwealth of Independent States elevated the existing republican boundaries to full international borders without any changes.
Present Situation. Although both governments have pledged to respect the territorial integrity of their neighbors, a number of territorial claims have been made by nationalist groups on either side of the border. In particular, there are border disputes and disturbances between Alma-Ata's Dzhambul Oblast (in Kazakhstan) and Bishkek's Talas Oblast (in Kyrgyzstan).

KAZAKHSTAN — RUSSIA This is one of the world's longest land boundaries, and although modified during the 1960s, it largely originates from the creation of the Autonomous Soviet Socialist Republic after World War I.
Geographical Setting. This boundary is 4,255 miles (6,846 km.) stretching from the Caspian Sea to the northern tip of China's Xingiang Autonomous Region in the Altai mountains. Although the border runs mainly through relatively low (less than 3,280 feet [1,000 m.] above sea level except at its easternmost end), even and sparsely populated terrain, the line it follows is largely circuitous, having been drawn according to Soviet nationality principles. At its western end it starts in the Volga delta and runs northwest through the Caspian lowland before drifting north, northeast and then east, crossing the Zhayyq and Ural rivers. Near Zhailma, west of the Torghay plateau, it heads in a generally northward direction for approximately 186 miles (300 km.) before resuming its eastward progression, crossing the

Tobol, Ishim and Irtysh rivers. South of Alferovka it turns southeast and runs in an almost straight line for about 310 miles (500 km.). At longitude 80°E it resumes its erratic course eastward, climbing into the Altai mountains toward the border with China.

Historical Background. The Russia–Kazakhstan periphery has long been a region of transition and a springboard for Russia to extend its geopolitical influence into central Asia. A major fortified Russian outpost was established at Orenburg in the early eighteenth century to facilitate the Russian advance from the steppes south and the territory now known as Kazakhstan was effectively under Russian rule for over 250 years until the breakup of the Soviet Union in late 1991. Modern Kazakhstan emerged as an autonomous political entity within Russia in 1920 and was elevated to a full Soviet Socialist Republic in 1936. Unlike most other interrepublic boundaries which have remained remarkably stable since the 1920s, the administrative boundary between Kazakhstan and Russia was modified during the 1960s but there have been no changes since. The boundary has been a full international border since the Alma-Ata Declaration of 21 December 1991 which formally established the Commonwealth of Independent States to replace the Soviet Union.

Present Situation. Around 37% of Kazakhstan's population are ethnic Russians. It is therefore not surprising that there are active Russian nationalist movements claiming large chunks of northern Kazakhstan as Russian territory including Aktyubinsk, Uralsk, Kustanay, Kotchetav, Tselinograd, a region east of the Irtysh River, and the mountainous area of western Siberia to the east of Semipalatinsk. In August 1991 Boris Yeltsin stated that Russia reserved the right to raise the issue of revision of borders with all contiguous republics except the Baltic states and, although the situation has improved with the signing of a Memorandum of Understanding on border cooperation, the threat of the annexation or secession of Russian dominated areas of Kazakhstan remains.

For their part, Kazakh nationalists claim that Kazakhstan's natural western frontier is the Volga river. Within this claim, the districts of Astakhan, Volograd and Orenburg are all included on various geographical and historical grounds. In the north, there is a Kazakh claim to a belt of territory from Kurgan and Omsk all the way to the Altai mountains in the northeast.

In response, Russian nationalists advance their own claims to large areas of northern Kazakhstan where ethnic Russians are in the majority. Complicating the problems created by nationalist territorial claims is the fact that the Kazakhstan–Russia border is largely unmarked. Meetings have been held to discuss its demarcation but there has been little practical progress.

One curiosity resulting from the breakup of the Soviet Union is worth noting. Since the Soviet space program was in all but name a Russian program, independent Kazakhstan has little use for the Baykonur Cosmodrome—the largest and most versatile of Soviet space launch sites—and in March 1994 the site was leased to Russia for 20 years. While under lease the Cosmodrome, which is located near the rail village of Tyuratam (about 100 miles [160 km.] east of the Aral Sea), will be considered as Russian territory, creating a short additional stretch of border between the two states.

KAZAKHSTAN — TURKMENISTAN This short international boundary divides two newly independent countries which border the eastern shoreline of the Caspian Sea.

Geographical Setting. At 236 miles (379 km.) this is by some way the shortest of the boundaries between the former Soviet republics of central Asia. The land border starts approximately halfway up the east coast of the Caspian Sea at Cape Suz, and then loops round the north of the Garabogazköl Aylagy (which is currently enlarging due to rising water levels in the Caspian Sea). It then turns southeast to trend along the southern flank of the Ustyurt Plateau until it reaches the tripoint with Uzbekistan.

Historical Background. Ruled by the Mongols from the thirteenth century, Kazakhstan came under Russian control from the eighteenth century. Inhabited by the traditionally nomadic but now largely sedentary Kazakh people, it joined the USSR as an autonomous republic in 1920 and became a full union republic in December 1936.

Kazakhstan was the site of Soviet leader Nikita Khrushchev's "Virgin Lands" agricultural extension program during the 1950s, which led to a large influx of Russian settlers, turning the Kazakhs into a minority in their own republic. Later, in December 1986, there were violent nationalist riots when the long-serving leader of the Kazakh Communist Party (KCP) was sacked by Soviet leader Gorbachev and replaced by an ethnic Russian.

Turkmenistan's nationalist movement was more muted than in other former Soviet central Asian republics: in August 1990 Turkmenistan's supreme soviet declared its "sovereignty"; however, in the USSR constitutional referendum of March 1991 the population voted to maintain the Union, and the anti-Gorbachev attempted coup in Moscow in August 1991 was initially supported by Turkmenistan President Niyazov. However, in the October 1991 referendum there was an overwhelming (94%) vote in favor of independence.

Therefore, as an international boundary, the border between Kazakhstan and Turkmenistan is very new, having been established in December 1991 following the eventual collapse of the Soviet Union and the creation of the Commonwealth of Independent States.

Present Situation. Formally the boundary is not under dispute; however, despite the formal agreements that have been reached, old conflicts have not only gone unresolved but have acquired a new urgency given the increase in republic authority. In Turkmenistan, for example, there is currently strong and powerful sentiment in favor of the claim for part of the Mangyshlak Oblast of Kazakhstan on the Caspian littoral.

KAZAKHSTAN — UZBEKISTAN

This boundary, which crosses diverse topographical environments—mountain, fertile plain, desert, plateau and the environmentally devastated Aral Sea—also crosses a diverse mix of nationalist feelings, and therefore, although formally recognized, it remains very fragile in nature.

Geographical Setting. This border is the lease circuitous of all the former Soviet central Asian republican boundaries, consisting mainly of straight-line segments, particularly in the west. It is also unique among the central Asian borders in that it has not been fully delimited: Running from east to west for 1,369 miles (2,203 km.), the border begins at the tripoint with Kyrgyzstan at a height of over 13,120 feet, (4,000 m.). Trending southwest, it passes to the

north of Tashkent and the Chirchik River until it reaches the agricultural region at the southern shores of Chardarinskoye Vdkhr. From here on it is largely delimited in straight-line segments; trending in a westerly direction, it passes to the north of Ozero Aydarkul' at a height of about 984 feet (300 m.), and then turns to head northwest into the Kyzylum Desert. On reaching the shores of the Aral Sea, where the shore has receded approximately 25 miles (40 km.) between 1960 and 1990 (due largely to the cataclysmic growth in irrigated agriculture), the land boundary continues on the emerging island of Vozrozhdeniya in the Aral Sea, splitting it in two. On the western shore of the Aral, the boundary then heads in a straight-line segment west-southwest for over 130 miles (209 km.), until it reaches a point on the Ustyurt Plateau. From there it trends due south for approximately 265 miles (426 km.) and meets the Turkmenistan border.

Historical Background. Kazakhstan and Uzbekistan became sovereign states in late 1991 following the breakup of the Soviet Union. When the Commonwealth of Independent States was established on 21 December 1991 it was agreed that the new states would respect the territorial integrity of the "national" republics created under the Soviet Union.

Previously, both states had been union republics. Kazakh people (called Kirgiz until 1925) are an ethnic mix of Turkish and Mongol tribes who speak a Turkic language, although the still-strong Slavic presence (concentrated in the north) and a general ethnic diversity make the Kazakhs a minority in their own republic. Most of the region now constituting Kazakhstan became an autonomous republic in 1920, and a full union republic in 1936. Uzbekistan became a constituent republic of the USSR in 1925, although guerrilla resistance continued for a number of years.

It is significant to note that in 1930 the region known as Karakalpak came under direct control of RSFR (previously part of Kazakhstan), but by 1936 it had been transferred to Uzbekistan. In 1956 and 1963 parts of southern Kazakhstan, including Hungary Steppe, were transferred to Uzbekistan, although in 1971 certain areas were returned. The Karakalpaks are now an indigenous group with an autonomous republic contained within the borders of Uzbekistan, lying along the western shores of the

Aral Sea and covering an area of 63,731 sq. miles (165,000 sq. km.). The Supreme Soviet of the autonomous republic of Karakalpak approved a new constitution on 10 April 1993, under which the autonomous republic became a sovereign parliamentary republic within Uzbekistan.

Present Situation. There remain a number of outstanding territorial claims from both Kazakhstan and Uzbekistan which although not formal, threaten to destabilize the present boundary in the future. Kazakhstan still supports the secessionist claims for Karakalpak sovereignty—Karakalpaks, the titular nationality of the autonomous republic in Uzbekistan, have been arguing for secession of their area from Uzbekistan since the latter gained independence. Similarly, however, Kazakhstan contains "hotspots": Uzbekistan holds aspirations for the southern part of the Chimkent region between the Syr Darya and Arys rivers, and secessionist claims are being made by Uigurs and ethnic Germans, the latter which make up nearly 5% of the population of Kazakhstan.

KEELING ISLANDS see COCOS (KEELING) ISLANDS.

KENYA An east African country and formerly a British colony, Kenya (area: 224,961 sq. miles [582,646 sq. km.]; estimated population: 27,900,000 [1994]) is bounded in the northwest by Sudan (144 miles; 232 km.), in the north by Ethiopia (535 miles; 861 km.), in the east by Somalia (424 miles; 682 km.) and the Indian Ocean, in the south by Tanzania (478 miles; 769 km.) and in the west by Lake Victoria and Uganda (580 miles; 933 km.). The capital of Kenya is Nairobi.

Kenya was declared a British protectorate in 1895. During the colonial era the British encouraged European settlement in Kenya, mostly on lands in the highlands which previously belonged to the Kikuyu. During the 1920s Kenyans, mainly from among the Kikuyu began to organize. During World War II the economic situation of the Kenyan farmers deteriorated while the European settlers prospered. This situation led in 1944 to the creation of the Kenya African Union. It was a coalition of several peoples, but its main support came from the Kikuyu, one of whom, Jomo Kenyatta, was its head.

During the late 1940s and early 1950s a Kikuyu guerrilla organization known as the Mau Mau launched a militant campaign against European settlers. This developed into a civil war between the Mau Mau and British-supporting Kenyans, which led to the death of about 13,000 Kenyans and a few dozen Europeans. As a result the Kenya African Congress was banned and Kenyatta was jailed. In 1960 the British opened the political arena to Africans and two main parties competed for power: Kenya African National Union (KANU), headed unofficialy by Kenyatta, who was still in prison, and supported by the Kikuyu, Luo and Teida peoples, and the Kenya African Democratic Union (KADU), which was supported by the smaller peoples of Kenya. KANU won the elections and Kenyatta led Kenya to independence in December 1963. He ruled the country until his death in 1978, kept close ties with the British, and invited the European settlers to stay in independent Kenya.

After his death he was peacefully replaced by Daniel arap Moi of the Kalenjin. Moi continued Kenyatta's policy but allocated more funds to the region of his own people. He declared Kenya a one-party state in 1982.

At the beginning of the 1990s protests and demonstrations of large scale erupted in Kenya demanding a multi-party democracy. Moi and his party won the multi-party elections of 1992, but his power was considerably reduced. The Kikuyu have been dominant in the government and civil service of the country since independence and remain the most powerful and influential people even after Moi's coming to power.

KENYA — ETHIOPIA see ETHIOPIA–KENYA.

KENYA — SOMALIA This boundary is 424 miles (682 km.) long and runs from north to south in a straight line, except for southwestern and southeastern sections in the north and south. In the north the boundary tripoint with Ethiopia is on the *thalweg* of the Dawa River and in the south the boundary extends to the Indian Ocean. It is demarcated by boundary pillars and consists entirely of a series of straight-line segments.

Geographical Setting. From the boundary tripoint with Ethiopia in the *thalweg* of the Dawa River and about 1,476 feet (450 m.) upstream from Malca Rie, this frontier runs in a series of straight lines southwestward to Damas (Dumasa) and from there to El Wak. It then follows longitude 40°59'44.34"E down to latitude 0°50'S and there turns southeast to reach a point where it heads south. The line meets pillar no. 29 and arrives at the coast of the Indian Ocean at Dick's Head, north of Kilang (Kenya). The line is marked on the ground by a lane about 13 feet (4 m.) wide that is cut through vegetation. It is also demarcated by cairns and 29 cemented pillars that are numbered consecutively from the north. During 1957–1958, the administrators of Kenya and the former Italian Somaliland collaborated in clearing and redemarcating the boundary with new pillars.

Historical Background. In 1887, the coastal region of Kenya was leased to the British East Africa Company, which then assumed control of a large area now included in modern Uganda and Kenya.

From 1889 Italy made various claims to the Indian Ocean coast of Somalia and the British East Africa Company sublet the Indian Ocean ports, which it held on lease from the sultan of Zanzibar, to Italy. In 1891 Italy, acting as protector of Ethiopia, reached an agreement with Britain on their respective spheres of influence and an Anglo-Italian treaty of 24 March 1891 delimited the border from the *thalweg* of the Juba (Giuba) River up to latitude 6°N. During 1895 the administration of Kenya was transferred to the British crown and became the British East Africa Protectorate. By another Anglo-Italian treaty (15 July 1924), Italian Somaliland was expanded, as some 36,000 sq. miles (93,200 sq. km.) of Jubaland, west of the Juba River, were ceded to Italy in accordance with the 1915 Treaty of London. The treaty also provided for the boundary's demarcation by means of an accurate survey and for the allocation of water resources in the border zone. The new demarcation, along 40°59'E, created an artificial division of the Somali peoples. In 1960, Italian Somaliland united with British Somaliland and became independent as Somalia. Kenya became independent in December 1963 and since then has not sought to alter its boundary with Somalia, although Somalia has raised the issue of the union of Somali peoples. In 1967 both governments declared their intention to respect the status quo and resort to pacific means of settlement.

Present Situation. Since 1967 a policy of reconciliation concerning the Somali peoples has prevailed. The Constitution of the Somalia Republic states that it "...shall promote, by legal and peaceful means the union of Somali territories...." There are no formal claims to one another's territories and both states adopted the colonial line without concluding a formal agreement concerning its exact alignment.

KENYA — SUDAN The 144-mile (232-km.) boundary between Kenya and Sudan runs from east to west along the 4°32'N parallel from 35°55'E to about 34°24'E and then southwestward to the boundary tripoint with Uganda.

Geographical Setting. Following a straight line that begins at a point on the shore of the Sanderson Gulf of Lake Rudolf (Turkana), this boundary runs directly eastward through the northernmost point of the northernmost crest of the long spur running north from Mount Lubur (Kenya) to the northernmost point of the northernmost crest of the long spur running northwest of Jebel Mogila. There the line turns southwest to trace a straight line to the southernmost point at the foot of Jebel Harogo and to the summit of Jebel Latome at the boundary tripoint with Uganda.

Historical Background. The area of the present boundary line between Kenya and Sudan was part of the British colony of Uganda, which had expanded much further north of its present limits in the early years of the twentieth century. In 1910, a transfer of territory from Belgian Congo (Zaire) to British Sudan formed a large wedge of Sudanese territory deep into Uganda. Administrative difficulties in this wedge prompted an exchange of lands between Uganda and Sudan and in 1912 an adjustment of their common boundary was agreed upon in principle after a joint commission. Unfortunately, the commission was unable to make a full investigation of the country and drew a straight line from a point near Jebel Mogila toward Lake Rudolf, which was wrongly assumed to run clear of the grazing grounds of the Turkana.

The wording of the subsequent order (21 April 1914) describes the section between Mount Lubar and Jebel Mogila as "a straight line, or such a line as would leave to Uganda the customary grazing grounds of the Turkhana tribe...." In 1914 this line

Lake Turkana (Rudolf) on the Kenya–Sudan boundary

was accepted by both countries. By the protectorate order of 1926, the Rudolf Province of Uganda was transferred to Kenya, which also inherited the boundary between Sudan and Uganda. In 1931 the provisional commissioner of the Turkana Province (Kenya) and the District Commissioner of the Eastern District of Mongala Province (Sudan) agreed on a delineation of the grazing grounds of Turkana. Known as the "Red Line" and at various times considered to be either the final boundary or a purely administrative convenience, it involves Kenya in an incursion into the "Ilemi Triangle," between the Red Line in the northwest and northeast on the one hand and the straight line along the 4°32'N parallel in the south on the other. There are no international agreements regarding this border, but in 1938 the Red Line, somewhat modified, was established on the ground. Neither Sudan nor Kenya has challenged the border since gaining independence (in 1956 and 1963 respectively). Modern maps show the 1914 border with the Red Line as an additional administrative, rather than international, division.

Present Situation. The difficulty of maintaining order in this area has resulted in a situation whereby

Kenya has control and administrative responsibility inside the territory of Sudan. Since the demarcation of the Red Line, a "Blue Line" has been proposed, lying even further north in Sudan, to offer strategic benefits not achieved by the Red Line. Kenya, with the permission of the Sudanese government, maintains several police posts between the Red and Blue lines and another post at Kibish, north of the Blue Line. The only legally defined border remains that of 1914.

KENYA — TANZANIA Except for an irregular central section that skirts the eastern and northern flanks of Mount Kilimanjaro, this border runs in a series of straight lines southeastward from Mohuru Bay on Lake Victoria to Ras Jimbo on the coast of the Indian Ocean. The line is 478 miles (769 km.) long.

Geographical Setting. From the boundary tripoint with Uganda in Lake Victoria (1°S and 33°56'E) the boundary line runs eastward to Mohuru Bay, on the shore of Lake Victoria, south of the Kenyan town of Karounga. Then the boundary line follows a line of pillars and crosses southwestward for 310 miles

(500 km.), passing along the northern edge of Lake Natron (Tanzania) and reaching to Kitenden on the northern edge of Mount Kilimanjaro (19,217 feet; 5,859 m.), leaving it with Tanzania. From there the boundary forms a straight line to Laitokitok and a series of straight lines to Lake Chala. It crosses through the center of the lake and trends up to the highest point of Chala Hill, where it turns to reach the highest point of a hill south of Lake Chala. It runs along the highest points of three more hills and heads south to enter the *thalweg* of the Losoyai River. The boundary heads along the river downstream to its confluence with the Ruvu (Bangani) River, upstream along the *thalweg* of the Ruvu to Lake Jipe (Yipe) and through Lake Jipe to the boundary pillar on its southern bank. From here the boundary line runs to the mouth of the Ngobwe River and along the northern bank of Jimbo Creek to Ras Jimbo on the coast of the Indian Ocean, between the town of Moa (Tanzania) and the small town of Vanga (Kenya).

Historical Background. From 1890 to World War I

(1914–1918), Tanganyika (later Tanzania) formed part of German East Africa. In 1922 it became a mandate later United Nations Trusteeship under British rule. Tanganyika became independent on 9 December 1963 and with Zanzibar, which also gained independence that year, formed the United Republic of Tanganyika and Zanzibar, which in 1964 became the United Republic of Tanzania.

Kenya belonged to the British East Africa Protectorate but achieved independence on 12 December 1963. Its boundary with Tanzania was largely established during the 1890s, when Britain and Germany sought to clarify their territorial claims. That Kilimanjaro was a gift from Queen Victoria to her grandson Wilhelm, later Emperor Wilhelm II of Germany, is untrue, but the story seems to have become popular after World War I, when European settlers hoped to include the mountain in Kenya. The border in this region actually reflects the competing claims of various treaties made with tribal leaders. The alignment from the tripoint with Uganda in Lake Victoria is the result of an Anglo-

Mount Kilimanjaro near the Kenya–Tanzania boundary

German instrument that was signed on 8 July 1906 but was not ratified. An agreement of 1914 using the same boundary description as that of 1906, from Lake Victoria to Lake Jipe, was subordinated by the outbreak of World War I. Nevertheless, section 4 of this agreement provided that the boundary pillars themselves would constitute the border in the event that their exact geographical coordinates were altered in future surveys. A mixed commission of 1914–1915 established the pillars which line the boundary line from Lake Victoria to Kitenden.

The section from Lake Jipe to the Indian Ocean was established by an Anglo-German protocol of 14 February 1900. In 1922 the line described in the 1914 agreement was accepted as valid by both governments and has been recognized by Kenya and Tanzania since independence. In 1957 demarcation was carried out by both states, between Lake Jipe and the coast.

A significant outcome of the delimitation is the division of the Masai tribe by the arbitrary boundary. During the period following World War II the British government received petitions from the Masai, who sought both unification and separate independence. In 1960 a Masai delegation requested that Britain remain in Masailand after the rest of Kenya became independent. This proposal came to nil and the boundary dividing the Masai remains.

Present Situation. The Kenya–Tanzania boundary is not disputed by either side. Although Masai national consciousness is at odds with the Organization of African Unity's 1964 commitment to nation-building, irrespective of tribal divisions, the tribe's longstanding objection to the border is apparently undiminished. Efforts made by the newly democratic Republic of South Africa to return tribal lands to their original ethnic occupants are likely to encourage existing movements for territorial and tribal integrity throughout the continent.

KENYA — UGANDA The boundary between Kenya and Uganda is 580 miles (933 km.) long and extends from the boundary tripoint with Tanzania in Lake Victoria in the south, northward to the boundary tripoint with Sudan, located at approximately 4°13'N and 33°58'E.

Geographical Setting. From the boundary tripoint with Tanzania at Lake Victoria (1°S and 33°56'E),

the line runs northward in a straight line reaching south of the westernmost point of Pyramid Island (Kenya). It then heads north in straight lines to the westernmost points of Pyramid Island, Ilemba Island and Mageta Island, all of which belong to Kenya. It turns northwest to reach the southernmost point of Sumba Island (Kenya) and follows its southwestern and western shores to its northernmost point. From there the boundary forms a straight line northeast to the center of the mouth of the Sio River, which it follows upstream to its confluence with the Sango River. It runs along the central channel of the Sango River to its source, where it is marked by boundary pillar X and a cairn. Forming a straight line on the true bearing of 40°56'08" for a distance of 502.7 feet (153.2 m.), the boundary reaches a stone and by a straight line on true bearing 40°58' after a distance of 933.6 feet (284.6 m.) arrives at boundary pillar Y near the Mumeris–Busia road. In another series of straight lines, each terminating at a boundary pillar, the line continues for almost 2 miles (3 km.) and meets the Alupe River at a point marked by boundary pillar no. 9. It follows the center of the Alupe River downstream to its confluence with the Kami River and follows the Kami to its intersection with the eastern edge of the Ugandan Mjanji–Busia–Mbale road. Following this road, the border runs north to its intersection with the Malawa (or Malaba, also known as the Lwakhakha or Lwagaga) River and takes the central course of that river upstream to its source at approximately 1°06'23"N. Eastward in a straight line, the boundary reaches the second highest summit (Lower Elgon) of Mount Elgon and there turns north to the Hot Springs, where a stream emerges from the mountain's crater. The boundary courses along the median line of the stream to its confluence with the Bukwa (Kibukwa) River and then bears northwest to follows a line of cairns and a small natural depression to the source of the Kanyerus River. From here the border continues to trend across mountains, rivers, hills and straight lines northwest and northeast. At Sagat Hill it sets out to form a series of straight lines, generally northward, and once again proceeds over hills and rivers in the same direction. Turning northwest, it reaches a beacon at the highest point of the Kariemakaris Ridge. The boundary line runs northward to the hillock of Lokuka, up to the top of the

Karamuroi (Karithakol) pass, west of the source of the Kanumuton River, down the center of the pass to the base of the Turkana escarpment, through a series of 180 boundary pillars, and along the base of the escarpment to the base of Mount Zulia, arriving at its intersection with the boundary tripoint with Sudan in the north.

Historical Background. Originally a division between the protectorates of Kenya and Uganda, this boundary was established in 1926 and amended in 1927, 1933 and 1936. It became an international boundary in 1962, when Uganda became independent. The protectorate of Uganda originally consisted of the Kingdom of Buganda, which became a British protectorate in 1894. The following year the British East African Protectorate was organized and included most of what is now Kenya; protection was also extended to lands around Buganda and the whole area was then known as Uganda. At that time its eastern boundary with the East Africa Protectorate cut through Lake Rudolf in the north and approached Lake Naivasha in the south. In 1902, a large area of eastern Uganda—the Eastern province, the southern region of the Elgon district and the southern region of the Rudolf province—was transferred to British East Africa. What remained of Uganda was the reduced Central province, the northern region of the Rudolf province, the Nile province, the Western province and the kingdom of Uganda. Britain had considered uniting the two protectorates but the idea was soon abandoned and in 1905 British foreign office supervision of Uganda was replaced by colonial office direction. In 1910, another part of the Elgon district (Central province) was transferred from Uganda and in 1926 the remaining territory of the Rudolf province was also assigned to Kenya.

The boundary across the crater of Mount Elgon was altered in 1936 and it was the resulting boundary that was inherited by Uganda upon achieving independence on 9 October 1962. Demarcation with boundary pillars took place in 1927 and 1933 along the line between the Sango and Alupe rivers. The section from the Kanumuton River to the boundary tripoint with Sudan was demarcated in 1959–1960; the section between the Bukwa and Kanumuton rivers, which constitutes 94 miles (151 km.) of the boundary, is not demarcated.

Present Situation. Kenya became independent in 1963. Both states adopted and recognized the colonial boundary line without reaching a formal agreement. There are no known disputes concerning the alignment of the line, which is only partially demarcated.

KIRIBATI An islands state, Kiribati is located in the central Pacific Ocean, around the point where the International Date Line intersects the equator. Its total land cover, which consists of 33 islands, is 313 sq. miles (811 sq. km.) with an estimated population (1994) of 72,000. Its capital is Tarawa and it has no land boundaries.

The Gilbertese, 30,000 of whom inhabit the island of Tarawa, are mostly Christians. They are not uniform in their social organization. The northern Gilbert Islanders have a traditional Polynesian social stratification while the southerners lack it. Their main economic resource until the end of the 1970s was valuable deposits of phosphate on Ocean Island. Now their economy relies on copra production and on foreign aid, with the government as the primary employer.

KOREA A peninsula on the eastern coast of Asia, Korea is divided into North Korea and South Korea. It is generally believed that the Korean people's ancestors were migrants from the north who moved to the peninsula 4,000 years ago. Their name is derived from the Koryo, a dynasty that ruled the peninsula from 913 to 1392. Since at least the seventh century, when the peninsula was politically unified, Koreans have shared a common history, language and culture. The Korean Peninsula is one of the few places in the world where no other sizable ethnic minority exists.

Although racially similar to the Chinese and Japanese, Koreans have a distinctive language with six major dialectic divisions, believed to have developed from a Tungustic prototype thousands of years ago. The most significant external influence on the language was Chinese, from which many words were borrowed. A mixed Chinese-Korean writing system, introduced in 1894, is still in use in South Korea.

The ancient religious beliefs of the Koreans included animism and shamanism. Buddhism reached

Korea between the fourth and sixth centuries, and Confucianism, which had a decisive influence on the peninsula, was Korea's state religion from the fourteenth to the early nineteenth centuries. Christianity, introduced in the nineteenth century, failed to win mass appeal.

Although contacts with the Chinese and Japanese have had a marked influence on Korean culture, and despite Japanese colonization in the early twentieth century, Koreans have maintained a separate and distinctive national identity. Following the Korean War (1950–1953), however, the peninsula was divided into two countries, one supported by the United States, and the other by the Soviet Union and China. North Korea has a Marxist ideology and an economy based on the doctrine of self-sufficiency, and is populated by 32% of Koreans; the 68% residing in South Korea have a capitalist system and an export-oriented economy. Korean is the official language of both countries, and the people share the same cultural heritage although, being more exposed to the outside world, South Korea is markedly more Westernized.

KOREA, NORTH (Choson-minjujuui-inmin-konghwaguk)

A country in eastern Asia, North Korea is bounded in the northeast by Russia (12 miles; 19 km.), in the north by China (881 miles; 1,417 km.), in the east by the Sea of Japan, in the south by South Korea (148 miles; 238 km.) and in the west by the Yellow Sea. Its area is 46,540 sq. miles (120,538 sq. km.) with an estimated population (1994) of 22,600,000. Its capital is P'yongyang.

KOREA, NORTH — CHINA   see CHINA–KOREA, NORTH.

KOREA, NORTH — KOREA, SOUTH

The boundary between North Korea and South Korea divides the Korean peninsula. It runs along the 38°N parallel for 148 miles (238 km.) between the Sea of Japan in the east and the Yellow Sea in the west.

Geographical Setting. Officially following the 38th parallel, the line has been modified somewhat, never having been declared an international boundary. Its eastern point in the Sea of Japan is located between the towns of Kansong (South Korea) and Kosong (North Korea), 47 miles (75 km.) north of the 38th parallel. It runs 31 miles (50 km.) southwest, then turning westward for about 50 miles (80 km.) to a point south of the town of Pokkye-ri (North Korea). This part of the boundary covers a mountainous region which has isolated peaks that reach over 5,550 feet (1,690 m.). From Pokkye-ri the boundary runs southwestward for 45 miles (72 km.), crossing the 38th parallel at a point south of the North Korean town of P'anmunjom. Running southward for 12 miles (19 km), the boundary turns westward along the Han River to its estuary in the Yellow Sea. The Han Estuary extends 38 miles (61 km.), its northern bank belonging to North Korea and its southern bank to South Korea. The Paengonyong-do Islands, situated close the North Korean shore, are held by South Korea. A demilitarized zone 2.4 miles (4 km.) wide was constructed along the entire boundary. It is an almost uninhabited area except for two villages, one on each side.

Historical Background. The boundary between North Korea and South Korea is a military demarcation line resulting from the arrangements made at the end of World War II and later from the armistice

North Korea's boundaries with China and South Korea

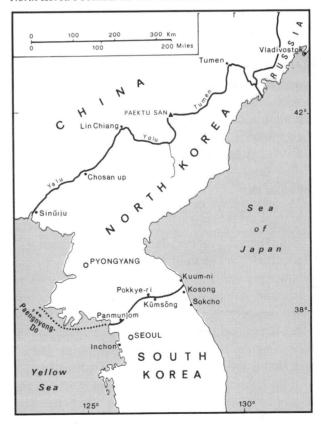

ending the Korean War of 1950–1953. Although between 1896 and 1904 the Russians and the Japanese, who divided Korea between themselves, used the 38th parallel as a military division, it was declared a boundary line only in 1945. It was agreed that the Soviet Union and the United States respectively would accept the surrender north and south of the 38th parallel. This line was chosen in haste and was not considered a permanent division, only being established for temporary military administration purposes. The Korean War confirmed the 38th parallel as the line between the two Korean states in the armistice agreement of 27 July 1953 but not as an official boundary line. From then on, as relations between the two countries deteriorated, the armistice line took on the character of a permanent international boundary.

Present Situation. There is no formal agreement between North Korea and South Korea concerning the location of the line although the armistice line is well demarcated and a demarcation team established 1,292 boundary pillars along it after the Korean War of 1950–1953. A similar line dividing North and South Vietnam, of 1954, has already disappeared, but the future of the Korean line will depend on the relations between the two countries and their patrons, the United States and China.

KOREA, NORTH — RUSSIA

The boundary between North Korea and Russia runs for 12 miles (19 km.) through the middle of the Tumen River, along the northeastern corner of North Korea.

Geographical Setting. The boundary line begins in the wide estuary of the Tumen River in the Sea of Japan, some 100 miles (160 km.) southwest of the Russian city of Vladivostok. The line follows the main navigation channel of the river for 12 miles (19 km.) to the tripoint boundary junction with China. There are no boundary markings in the river.

Historical Background. The North Korea–Russia boundary is part of the 1860 boundary between China and Russia. After almost two centuries of negotiations between the two countries, from 1689 to 1860, China and Russia settled the eastern section of their common boundary, placing it along the Amur and Ussuri rivers. The area south of Khanka Lake was declared a neutral zone in 1858 but in 1860 Russia occupied the region and in the Sino-Russian

treaty of that year the terminus of the boundary was placed in the Tumen River.

Japan occupied Korea in 1895 and forced China to grant independence to Japanese-controlled Korea, south of the Yalu River. In September 1909 a Sino-Japanese treaty placed the eastern part of the boundary with Korea in the Tumen River, establishing a boundary between Korea and Russia without any formal agreement. At the end of World War II, on 8 August 1945, the Soviet Union declared war against Japan and Russian troops landed in Korea, close to Vladivostok. By doing this, not only did Russia establish its boundary with Korea, but it enrolled itself as a partner in all future negotiations concerning the region. The establishment of independent North Korea left it with a direct land link with the Soviet Union, now Russia.

Present Situation. There is no known dispute concerning this boundary line, nor was it ever marked or officially agreed upon. Relations between North Korea and the former Soviet Union never favored such a discussion but the exact location of the boundary line will probably be concluded in the near future.

KOREA, SOUTH (Taehan-min'guk)

A peninsular country in eastern Asia, South Korea's only land boundary is in the north with North Korea (148 miles; 238 km.). In the east it is bounded by the Sea of Japan, in the south by the Korea Strait and in the west by the Yellow Sea. The area of South Korea is 38,230 sq. miles (99,249 sq. km.) with an estimated population (1994) of 44,200,000. Its capital is Seoul.

KOREA, SOUTH — KOREA, NORTH

see KOREA, NORTH–KOREA, SOUTH.

KUWAIT (Al-Kuwayt)

A country in the Persian (Arabian) Gulf (area: 6,880 sq. miles [17,818 sq. km.]; estimated population: 2,244,000 [1994]), Kuwait is bounded in the north and northwest by Iraq (149 miles; 240 km.), south by Saudi Arabia (138 miles, 222 km.) and east by the Gulf. Its capital is Kuwait City.

Kuwait was originally a small trading port in an otherwise desert area situated at the top of the Persian Gulf, at the nexus of an ancient caravan track and the sealane linking the Indus Valley and Mesopotamia. It was converted to Islam in the eighth century. In 1514 the Portuguese established a trading and staple station which, in 1756, fell into the hands of a dynasty originating from the Hejaz, the al-Sabahs, who are still in power. The British established a presence in 1793, and their influence grew throughout the nineteenth century. In 1853 Kuwait, squeezed by the Ottoman Empire, was forced to promise allegiance to Istanbul; it was attached to the vilayet Basrah, thus providing a basis for later Iraqi claims. Seeking protection for their territory, in 1899 the Sabahs negotiated a treaty with Britain, granting in return free navigation and supervision of Kuwaiti foreign affairs.

Before World War II, pastoralism supported a few thousand Kuwaitis. Fishing and boat-building constituted Kuwait's main sources of income; dhow-builders formed a Shi'ite guild. Pearling, Kuwait's traditional earner, suffered from competition with artificial Japanese pearls. Then, in 1938, oil was struck. Commercial exports led in the decade of World War II to rapid development. The population grew twelvefold, mainly through the influx of foreign workers: non-Kuwaitis formed 80% of the labor force.

In 1961 Kuwait became fully independent, and in the 1970s and 1980s it underwent rapid modernization and became one of the richest countries of the world. By 1980, it had nationalized its petroleum wealth. Indigenous Kuwaitis ("First Class Citizens") developed into a new class, an elite of merchant families who enjoyed free social services. In fact, the autocratic al-Sabah family tried to compensate for the lack of political participation by providing a wide array of free amenities. By contrast, most guest laborers did not share in the wealth. Denied political and economic rights, often living miserably and without the possibility of bringing over their families, the noncitizen second class majority depended on a first class sponsor for their residence permits, inducing a new form of dependence. That position was particularly galling to the Palestinians: preponderant in the press and mid-level management, they played a major role in the country's economic and cultural life, but were also a potential source of opposition. Troublesome noncitizen minorities were threatened with expulsion.

Kuwait holds enormous oil reserves, good for one century. Yet since the mid-1970s, as its technocrats realized how dependent it is on a single, depletable resource, Kuwait has started to reduce output. Attempts to diversify industry are, however, hampered by its small domestic market. By the 1980s Kuwaitis were living mainly on the interest on their gigantic foreign investments. The invasion by Iraq in 1990 ushered in seven months of occupation and systematic spoilation which has ruined Kuwait. Hundreds of thousands of guest laborers and 400,000 Kuwaitis (more than half the indigenous population) fled the country. Since the liberation of their land in the Gulf War of 1991, they have been returning only slowly.

KUWAIT — IRAQ see IRAQ–KUWAIT.

KUWAIT — SAUDI ARABIA The Kuwait–Saudi Arabia land boundary is 138 miles (222 km.) long and is demarcated throughout. It begins in the west, at the boundary junction with Iraq, and ends at the shore of the Persian (Arabian) Gulf in the west.

Geographical Setting. From the western boundary junction in the confluence of the dry rivers of Al Awja and Al Batuz the border follows a straight line east-southeast for a distance of 39.5 miles (63 km.) and meets the intersection of 29°N and 47°28'05.683"E. It then trends south-southeastward in straight-line segments for 28 miles (45 km.), to point 'H' at 28°31'26.526"N and 47°42'25.153"E, where it turns east and forms a straight line for 33.5 miles (54 km.). The boundary meets the coast at 28°32'02.488"N and 48°25'59.019"E, marked as point 'G' on the boundary map, south of the Kuwaiti port of Mina Saud.

Historical Background. Until their defeat in World War I, the Ottomans occupied part of the Arabian Peninsula. After the war the boundary between Kuwait—then a British protectorate—and the sultanate of Nejd (which together with the kingdom of Hejaz formed the kingdom of Saudi Arabia in 1932) was initially defined and delimited in the Uqair Convention of 2 December 1922. The 1922 agreement left an area of about 2,500 sq. miles (6,500 km.) unsettled, to be held jointly as a neutral zone pending a final settlement. After 1922, however, there was little interest in a more definitive settlement in the

'Neutral Zone'—until the discovery of oil in the Burqan fields a few miles north of the zone in 1938. With the probability of oil discovery within the Neutral Zone itself, concessions to private companies were granted by each government in 1948–1949. Later the two companies (Aminoil and the Pacific Western Oil Company) exploited the oil under a joint operating agreement. By 1958 both Kuwait and Saudi Arabia had granted the Japanese Oil Company separate concessions for offshore territories.

With the added administrative problems that new oil installations incurred, it was agreed that the Neutral Zone should be divided. After several years of initial discussions and survey work, the two governments signed an agreement (7 July 1965) to divide the zone geographically. The agreement stated that the boundary line between the two sections of the Neutral Zone was to be "the line which divides them equally into two parts and which begins from a point at the mid-eastern shore on the low-tide line and ends at the western boundary line of the zone," the northern section being annexed to Kuwait, and the southern section to Saudi Arabia. With regard to territorial waters adjoining both parts of the zone, each country would have the same rights as it had over the land areas of the zone, while "for the purpose of exploiting natural resources" it was agreed that "not more than six marine miles of seabed and subsoil adjoining the partitioned zone shall be annexed to the principal land of that partitioned zone." The northern boundary of the submerged zone adjoining the partitioned territory would be "delineated as if the zone had not been partitioned and without regard to the provisions of this agreement." If both sides agreed, they would "exercise their equal rights" in the area beyond the six-mile limit by means of "shared exploitation."

The new international boundary took effect with an exchange of instruments and the signing of a demarcation agreement in the city of Kuwait on 18 December 1969. Most of the apportionment and allocation of properties and facilities was completed by 20 May 1970, as agreed. Talks continued concerning the islands of Qaru and Umm el-Maradim, however, as the 1969 boundary agreement pertained only to the land boundary and not offshore boundaries. On the basis of an exchange of letters between Iraq and Kuwait in 1923 and 1932, both of these is-

lands belonged to Kuwait, but Saudi Arabia has historically contested their sovereignty.

Present Situation. Although Kuwait and Saudi Arabia reached an agreement on the partitioning of the Neutral Zone in the 1960s, the area's extensive oil reserves and difficulties relating to offshore boundaries, including the contested sovereignty of the Qaru and Umm el-Maradim islands, constitute possible sources of future territorial disputes between the two countries.

KYRGYZSTAN A landlocked country in central Asia (area: 76,640 sq. miles [198,414 sq. km.]; estimated population: 4,600,000 [1994]), Kyrgyzstan was a republic of the Soviet Union until its independence in 1991. Kyrgyzstan is bounded in the north by Kazakhstan (653 miles; 1,051 km.), in the east by China (533 miles; 858 km.), in the south by Tajikistan (541 miles; 870 km.) and in the west by Uzbekistan (683 miles; 1,099 km.). Kyrgyzstan's capital is Bishkek.

The first historical evidence of a Kyrgyz people dates back to the eighth century when they lived in the area of the Yenisey or the Irtysh Rivers in Siberia. They are first mentioned in the area of central Asia in the tenth century. After a number of migrations (at times forced) to and from the area of their present abode, they became its permanent inhabitants in the eighteenth century.

Traditionally, Kyrgyz tribes were built around three greater divisions which were composed of "wings" (right and left) and "branches." The memory of this tribal affiliation is still preserved. The Kyrgyz possess a very rich oral literature. Their *Manas* is probably the longest of world epics. Its two basic versions, written down only in the twentieth century, have 200,000 and 379,000 lines. It is a major repository of Kyrgyz collective memory, depicting the history, way of life and values of their ancestors. For centuries the Kyrgyz were nomads, moving with their herds in a yearly nomadic cycle from the plains to the mountains and back to find summer and winter grazing pastures. In the second half of the nineteenth century the Kyrgyz lands were conquered by the Russian Empire. Russian settlers expropriated much of the grazing land of the Kyrgyz, leading to many conflicts. In 1916 the Kyrgyz participated in the abortive revolt of central Asian

Muslims against the czarist Russian regime. Many lost their lands and many fled to China; nearly one-third of the people perished. In 1924 the Qara-Kyrgyz Autonomous Oblast (region), renamed in 1926 the Kyrgyz Autonomous Soviet Socialist Republic, was established within the framework of the Russian Soviet Federative Socialist Republic. In 1936 it was given the status of a Soviet Socialist Republic within the framework of the Soviet Union. Many Kyrgyz died during the forced sedenterization campaign and famine of the 1930s.

At the end of the 1980s there emerged a Kyrgyz movement of national awakening. In 1989 a law was passed making Kyrgyz the state language of the republic. In 1991 an independent Kyrgyzstan was proclaimed within the framework of the Commonwealth of Independent States.

KYRGYZSTAN — CHINA see CHINA–KYRGYZSTAN.

KYRGYZSTAN — KAZAKHSTAN see KAZAKHSTAN–KYRGYZSTAN.

KYRGYZSTAN — TAJIKISTAN

In contrast to other boundaries in central Asia, this border is relatively short (541 miles; 870 km.). However, this in no way lessens the significance of what is a widely disputed divide between numerous national peoples. As with other members of the commonwealth of Independent States, both Kazakhstan and Tajikstan are formally committed to observance of existing borders and to the principle of their inviolability by force. This commitment, however, has been continuously under threat since the two states gained independence in 1991.

Geographical Setting. Beginning at the tripoint with China, the boundary runs due west only to turn back on itself, and run north and then due east to a point where it meets the Uzbekistan border. Heading west, it passes along the Zaalayskiy mountain range, crosses the Kyzyl Suu river, and then traverses the Alasyskiy range before dropping below 16,400 feet (5,000 m.) and then turning north. It trends north for over 30 miles (48 km.), turns east, crosses the downstream section of a valley and then heads on to a point just south of the settlement of Gafurov. Trending east into the foothills of the Alay mountains the boundary meets one of three territorial enclaves; one which encompasses Voruhk and is administered by Tajikistan (the other two belonging to Uzbekistan). Circling to the south of Isfara, the boundary eventually meets the Uzbekistan boundary.

Historical Background. The border between Kyrgyzstan and Tajikistan is one of many former Soviet interrepublic boundaries which were elevated to the status of full international boundaries in December 1991, following the collapse of the Soviet Union and the creation of the Commonwealth of Independent States.

Kyrgyzstan is peopled by horse-breeding, mountain-dwelling nomads, the Turkic-speaking descendents of Mongol invaders. It was annexed by Russia in 1864, and was part of an independent Turkistan republic between 1917 and 1924. It then became a republic in its own right within the USSR and, from 1936, a constituent Soviet republic.

The Tajiks are also descended from the Mongol invaders, although once conquered by czarist Russia between 1877 and 1900, what is now northern Tajikistan was governed by Russia and southern Tajikistan by the emir of Bukhara. Eventually formed in 1924 from the Tajik areas of Bukhara and Turkistan, Tajikistan became a constituent republic of the Soviet Union in 1929. From the late 1980s there was a resurgence in Tajik consciousness and, on 31 August 1991, a declaration of independence was made. However, the gradual polarization of the regional and tribal affinities of the Tajik population led to the escalation of civil war in 1992, instigated by the conflicting forces of communism and Islamic fundamentalism. Examples of once-latent territorial aspirations can be found elsewhere in Tajikistan; what had been the Gorno-Badakhshan Autonomous Oblast during the Soviet era, in the southeastern sector of Tajikistan, declared itself an autonomous republic in December 1991 by a decision of the Oblast Soviet, and in April 1992 unilaterally converted itself into the Pamirs-Badakhshan Autonomous Republic—against the opposition of the Tajikistan government. As such, the eastern end of the border with Kyrgyzstan is fragile, as Gorno-Badakhshan expects more independence in its policies, although it is anticipated that it will remain in Tajikistan.

Present Situation. With the disappearance of the USSR in 1991, a number of border disputes were aggravated and revived on either side of this boundary. This is particularly the case where the border is awkwardly configured in its northernmost sectors. Kyrgyzstan has disputed territory on the northern slopes of the Alay and Zaalayskiy mountains (the northwestern border with Tajikistan), particularly in the vicinity of the cities of Badken and Isfara, near the tripoint with Uzbekistan. However, Kyrgyzstan itself claims the southern slopes of the mountains, the northern area of the Gorno-Badakhshan region in the Pamir mountains and the upper reaches of the Surkhob River valley.

KYRGYZSTAN — UZBEKISTAN Although cartographically appearing very short, this land boundary runs for 683 miles (1,099 km.). Achieving independence in 1991, both Kyrgyzstan and Uzbekistan are presently exposed to sociopolitical upheaval and regional demands for autonomy.

Geographical Setting. From west to east, this boundary loops around the north-pointing "finger" of the Pskemskij mountain ranges, at a height of over 13,776 feet (4,200 m.). Crossing the Chatkal River valley, it heads east-southeast over the Chatkal'skiy mountains and meanders down into Syr Darya River valley. Skirting the northern banks of this basin (known as the Fergana Basin), it meets the lake to the southwest of Uzgen, only to turn west-southwest toward Osh. The boundary then follows the southern banks of the Fergana Basin, and on meeting the Sokh River turns south for less than 10 miles (16 km.) until it meets the Tajikistan border. In southern Kyrgyzstan, in the foothills of the Alay mountains, there are three territorial enclaves of significance: two belonging to Uzbekistan, encompassing the settlements of Sokh and Iordan, and the other administered by Tajikistan.

Historical Background. As the challenges to Soviet power were finally crushed in 1925, in order to prevent the reemergence of pan-Islamic or pan-Turkic challenge to communism, Stalin divided Turkistan into five republics: Kazakhstan, Uzbekistan, Kyrgyzstan, Tajikistan and Turkmenistan. Closely related to the Kazakhs, the Turkic-speaking Muslim Kyrgyz were traditionally a nomadic hearding people, but during the Soviet era there was a compulsory abandonment of nomadic life and the replacement of individual farming with state collectiviza-

tion. Presently, ethnic Kyrgyz make up 52% of the population of Kyrgyzstan, and the largest minority is Russians at 22%—many of whom live in the capital of Bishkek where they are the majority ethnic group.

With the push toward democracy gathering speed in the 1920s, the eventual fall of the communist regime was characterized by multi-ethnic disturbances. The worst violence occurred between June–July 1990 in Kyrgyzstan, where over 300 people were killed in fighting between Kyrgyz and Uzbeks in the border district of Osh—an Uzbek-dominated city. However, on 20 June 1990, Uzbekistan declared sovereignty, and full independence was proclaimed on 31 August 1991; Kyrgyzstan, on the other hand, did not declare sovereignty until 12 December 1990—the last republic of the former USSR to do so. As with so many other independent central Asian states that emerged post-1991, Uzbekistan and Kyrgyzstan have witnessed the reemergence and growing significance of nationalistic, sociopolitical boundaries. Ethnic Germans and Uzbeks, for example, claim autonomy in Kyrgyzstan; two German districts previously dissolved by Stalin in 1942 were reestablished on 31 January 1992. They now have the right of juridical person, their own emblem, and are allowed to create a fund for social, economic and cultural development, and so potentially create a material base for national revival.

Present Situation. The border between Kyrgyzstan and Uzbekistan is the same as the former interrepublic boundary—which was particularly circuitous in design—and this has consequently done little to quell any dormant territorial aspirations. Relations between the two countries, which had remained tense, worsened in May 1993 after Kyrgyzstan introduced its own currency. On 24 May 1993, President Islam Karimov of Uzbekistan criticized the move, denouncing it as "political subversion directed against Uzbekistan," and proceeded to threaten "definite and strong measures in retaliation." Also, as indicated earlier, a particularly sensitive situation exists along the easternmost border with Uzebkistan, where certain groups are advocating the return of the Uzbek-dominated Kyrgyz cities of Osh Uzgen, Dzhalal-Abad and Karavan to Tashkent. Therefore, although formally recognized, in the light of these territorial claims, the boundary remains informally very much under dispute.

L

LAOS (Lao) A landlocked Southeast Asian country (area: 91,429 sq. miles [236,800 sq. km.]; estimated population: 4,600,000 [1994]), Laos is bounded in the north by China (263 miles; 423 km.), in the east by Vietnam (1,324 miles; 2,130 km.), in the south by Cambodia (336.5 miles; 541 km.) and in the west by Thailand (1,090 miles; 1,754 km.) and Myanmar (146 miles; 235 km.). The capital of Laos is Vientiane.

The original Lao state of Lan Xang lasted from the fourteenth to the eighteenth centuries. As colonial rulers, the French preserved the ancient dynasties ruling different regions of the country, with preference given to the dynasty ruling Luang Prabang. Upon independence, which was granted gradually in the 1950s, the ruling family of Luang Prabang was established as monarchs for the entire country, although certain sections were set aside for Communist insurgents known as the Pathet Lao, led by the king's half-brother. The Pathet Lao grew increasingly powerful and allowed the construction of the Ho Chi Minh Trail on its territory, connecting North and South Vietnam and Cambodia. A Pathet Lao regime was established throughout the country in 1975 and the monarchy was abolished.

Laos is one of the world's poorest countries. The population is 85% rural and much of the traditional village culture has survived.

LAOS — CAMBODIA   see CAMBODIA–LAOS.

LAOS — CHINA   see CHINA–LAOS.

LAOS — MYANMAR   This boundary runs for 146 miles (235 km.) southward and follows the *thalweg* of the Mekong River for its total length from the boundary tripoint with China at its intersection with the Nan-la Ho to the boundary tripoint with Thailand at the confluence of the Hok and Mekong rivers.

Geographical Setting. The Mekong River forms and demarcates this boundary, passing through deep, narrow valleys in densely forested and poorly populated country. The area is mountainous and the river flows through deep gorges cut into the sandstone and limestone bedrock of the southwest and northeast respectively. Rapids along the course of the river confuse the definition of the *thalweg* in places, although the area being sparsely populated and the river's use as a navigable waterway being limited due to the rapids reduce the likelihood of serious border violations.

Historical Background. The Laos–Myanmar boundary seems to have remained on or near the Mekong River since the twelfth century, when the Khmer empire ruled, and throughout the succession of Thai and Laotian control. European influence only began at the end of the nineteenth century, when France and Britain competed for influence in the region. The British tried to use Thailand (then Siam) as a buffer state between the two spheres of influence, fearing for its possessions in India. With the French expansion northward, Britain moved into the Shan States (eastern Burma) and finally agreed to a contiguous French–British border along the Mekong River, by an agreement on 15 January 1896, which is the only international act regarding this boundary line.

Present Situation. Since the Communist takeover of China, Nationalist guerrillas have operated from bases in northern Myanmar and Laos, many having now intermarried and settled in the region. The border region is not under the complete control of either Laos or Myanmar as ethnic insurgents occupy areas of the frontier on both sides. Nevertheless, there is no dispute concerning the position of the line.

LAOS — THAILAND
Extending 1,090 miles (1,754 km.), the boundary between Laos and Thailand runs from the boundary tripoint with Myanmar on the Mekong River in the northwest to the boundary tripoint with Cambodia at Preah Chambot pass in the southeast. It mainly follows watersheds and rivers.

Geographical Setting. From the boundary junction with Myanmar, at the confluence of the Hok and Mekong rivers at 20°22'N, the boundary runs south for 59 miles (95 km.) along the *thalweg* of the Mekong. At about 20°10'N and 100°36'E the boundary leaves the river to pursue the local mountain range to the west of the Kop River system. This range is a minor watershed separating the basins of several rivers flowing north and east to the Mekong River. After turning east around the Kop River system, the mountain range becomes the principal wa-

tershed between the Mae Nam (Thailand) and Mekong (Laos) river systems. This section of the boundary, along the several drainage divides, is about 286 miles (460 km.) long. At approximately 17°44'N and 98°39'E the boundary leaves the watershed and follows the *thalweg* of the Huang Nga River to its confluence with the Mekong River, 86 miles (138 km.) downstream. It follows the Mekong for the next 541 miles (870 km.), along the channel nearest to the Thai bank, thus placing the local islands in the Mekong in Laos. Due to seasonal variations in water levels in the Mekong River, at times these islands become attached to the Thai bank of the river; the boundary therefore leaves and rejoins the Mekong's channel, crossing the land between the islands and the bank. Approximately 4.5 miles (7 km.) east of the mouth of the Mun River, the boundary follows the watershed between the Mun and Mekong rivers, which runs generally south and southwest for 118 miles (190 km.), to the Cambodian tripoint at the headwaters of the Tonle Ropou.

A Thai village near the Laos–Thailand border

Historical Background. This border originated during the period of French colonialism in Indochina and developed against a background of Thai (Siamese) territorial expansion into Cambodia and French territorial gains west and north of Annam. The first treaty regarding the boundary (15 July 1867) returned the provinces of Battambang and Ankor, under French control since 1795, to Thailand (Siam) and in return the Thais recognized French claims to a protectorate in Cambodia. In a treaty of peace and convention between France and Siam, signed on 2 February 1894, Siam renounced its claims to the islands and the left bank of the Mekong River and agreed to the creation of a demilitarized zone over 15 miles (25 km.) wide on the river's right bank. Having thus gained half of Loungphrabang, a separate kingdom, the French pressed on to secure the second half and achieved enormous territorial gains under the convention signed at Bangkok on 7 October 1902. This convention was superseded by the ratification of 9 December 1904, which moved the Loungphrabang boundary to the watershed between the Mae Nam and Mekong river systems and required that Thailand renounce its suzerainty over Loungphrabang. A further treaty in 1907 returned a small section west of the Nam Huang to Thailand. The convention of 25 August 1926 established Laos's possession of all islands in the Mekong River—even in the event of the channel along the Thai bank drying up. During World War II the Japanese returned to Thailand the lands to the west of the Mekong, but this action was annulled and the border was reinstated on 17 November 1946.

Maps prepared by the Delimitation Committee in 1907 show some variations in the drainage pattern from that shown on modern maps. Since these maps were accepted and used by both the French and the Thais and figured in the Cambodian dispute with Thailand over the Preah Vihaer temple, it would seem that they held the potential to cause disagreement over some parts of the boundary. In 1975 Thailand closed its frontier with Laos after clashes with Lao Communist forces on the Mekong River. In 1987 the exact position of the border described in the 1907 Treaty was disputed and a war of some months duration ensued until peace was restored along the line.

Present Situation. The Laos–Thailand border is now recognized by both countries.

LAOS — VIETNAM The boundary between Laos and Vietnam runs for 1,324 miles (2,130 km.) between the tripoint with China in the northwest and the tripoint with Cambodia in the southeast. It follows an internal French colonial division but was not described by any formal agreements.

Geographical Setting. Most of this boundary follows the main watershed between the Gulf of Tonkin and the Mekong River. It runs in a mountainous area that has a tropical climate with an annual precipitation of 100 inches (2,540 mm.). The northern terminus of the boundary line, which is the boundary junction with China, is located between the Black River (Li-hsien Chiang in Chinese, Song Da in Vietnamese) and the eastern tributary of the Hou River (Nam Hou) that flows in Laos. From there the boundary runs southeastward for about 95 miles (150 km.) along the Pou Den Dinh ridge, which forms the watershed between the two rivers. It reaches the vicinity of Dien Bien Phu (Vietnam) and then crosses a local tributary of the Mekong River northward before turning southeast to follow the watershed between two branches of the Ma River (Song Ma). The boundary crosses the northern branch near their confluence and from there runs southwestward, reaching the upper tributaries of the Song Ca near the 104°E meridian. From that point, the boundary runs generally southeastward for about 450 miles (725 km.) along the main watershed of the Indochina peninsula (Châine Annamatique), between the South China Sea and the Mekong River and its southern tributaries. Here and there it leaves the watershed and runs in an upland area void of surface drainage, runs along a river (Se Pone River) for 37 miles (59 km.) and some straight lines. The boundary reaches the Ngoc Ang Plateau, which forms part of the watershed, and from there runs southward, leaving the main watershed and reaching the boundary junction with Cambodia, which is located between two tributaries that lead to the Srêpôk River. This boundary tripoint is situated about 30 miles (50 km.) west of Kontum (Vietnam) and about 50 miles (80 km.) southeast of Attopeu (Laos).

Historical Background. North and South Vietnam were ruled as a united dynasty from 1802. France

occupied Vietnam between 1858 and 1884 and settled itself east of the Mekong River area in 1894 by
a peace treaty with Siam (Thailand). French Indochina was established, including the areas of Vietnam, Cambodia and Laos (which had been an independent kingdom since the fourteenth century under
the Lao people from Thailand). The boundary line
between Laos and Vietnam was then reestablished
as an internal administrative boundary by French officials during the colonial period. After a series of
temporary changes took place along the internal
lines, Laos was created as a unified territory under
French rule (1899) and in 1904 the colonial division
east of the Mekong River assumed its present alignment. Both Laos and Vietnam became independent
in 1954, adopting the colonial line as their common
international boundary, although no formal agreement was made to confirm the mutual acceptance.
That year Vietnam was divided along the 17°N parallel into North Vietnam (a Communist republic)
and South Vietnam (a pro-West republic). They
were reunited in 1976 as the Socialist Republic of
Vietnam, regaining its whole boundary with Laos.

Present Situation. After 1976, Vietnamese troops
entered Laos and the border area between the two
states suffered border skirmishes between rebels
backed by Thailand from the south and by China
from the north. In the mid-1990s, the area became
calm and the Vietnamese troops returned to Vietnam. Despite the border clashes, no claims for
boundary changes were raised during that period
and the present boundary follows the line determined by the French at the turn of the century.

LATVIA (Latvija)   A northern European country
(area: 24,595 sq. miles [63,700 sq. km.]; estimated
population: 2,750,000 [1994]), Latvia was a republic of the Soviet Union until 1991. It is bounded in
the north by Estonia (166 miles; 267 km.), in the
east by Russia (135 miles; 217 km.), in the southeast
by Belarus (88 miles; 141 km.), in the south by
Lithuania (282 miles; 453 km.) and in the west by
the Baltic Sea. Its capital is Riga.

The Latvians take their name from the Latgallians
(Latgali), who originally lived in the northeast of
present Latvia and absorbed the Selonians (Seli), the
Semigallians (Zemgali) and the Couronians (Kursi).
Whether these were Latvian tribes or separate Baltic

peoples is the subject of debate. The Latgallians also
assimilated the Finnic Livs (or Livonians), who inhabited the northwestern part of present Latvia.

In the first century C.E. Tacitus testified to contacts
between the Roman world and the Baltic tribes,
based on the amber trade. In the ninth century the
Vikings crossed Latvia on their way to Russia. In
the tenth and eleventh centuries both the Swedes
and the Russians tried to conquer and baptize the
Latvians, but this was only achieved by the Germans in the first half of the thirteenth century; they
divided Latvia among the Teutonic Order, the bishopric of Riga and the free city of Riga.

The three centuries of German rule created profound change in the country. The country was westernized and both its nobility and its urban classes
germanized. Riga's joining the Hanseatic League
brought prosperity to the country, offset by the suffering inflicted on the population by constant wars

Estonia–Latvia–Lithuania boundaries

with, and among, the neighboring kingdoms of Sweden, Poland, Lithuania and Muscovite Russia.

Following the reformation, Poland and Sweden vied for the Baltic states, finally dividing Latvia in 1629. Vidrem (all territory north of Dvina) was annexed to Sweden, Latgale (the southeast) to Poland, and Courland became an autonomous duchy under the suzerainty of Poland. Following the Northern War, in 1721 Vidrem was annexed by Russia, to be followed by Latgale at the first Partition of Poland (1771) and Courland at the third (1795).

During the reign of Alexander I (1506–1825) the serfs were granted personal freedom, but only under Alexander II (1855–1881) were they given the right to own land. This, together with industrialization and urbanization, created a socioeconomic change among the Latvians, which together with the spread of education and the revival of Latvian language and literature created the infrastructure for Latvian nationalism. Nationalism, however, finally rose as a reaction to the policy of forced Russification pursued under Alexander III and Nicholas II.

The demand for a separate Latvian state was first made following 1905. In the wake of the 1917 revolutions Latvia proclaimed its independence, although it had to defend it (with foreign aid) against Soviet attempts at annexation. Following the Ribbentrop-Molotov agreement, Latvia was forced to grant bases to the Soviet Union and was then annexed to it in August 1940 as one of the Union republics.

During the first year of Soviet rule about 35,000 Latvians were arrested and deported to the Gulag, followed by almost 105,000 after the reconquest of Latvia from the Germans in World War II. About 65,000 Latvians fled to the West. The Soviet authorities initiated a policy of industrialization and Russification which resulted in the 1980s in the de facto transformation of Latvia into a binational state in which the Latvians accounted for no more than 60% of the population, while the Russians comprised almost 40%. Riga became an overwhelmingly Russian city.

In the late 1980s Latvian nationalists organized a struggle for separation from the Soviet Union and reinstatement of complete independence. After the dissolution of the Soviet Union in 1991, Latvia became an independent state. It had still to solve the great problems related to the large Russian population within its borders.

LATVIA — BELARUS   see BELARUS–LATVIA.

LATVIA — ESTONIA   see ESTONIA–LATVIA.

LATVIA — LITHUANIA   Following an internal division between two republics of the former Soviet Union, the boundary between Latvia and Lithuania runs for 282 miles (453 km.) between the boundary junction with Belarus in the east and the Baltic Sea in the west.

Geographical Setting. From the eastern terminus of the boundary, which is located about 15 miles (25 km.) south of the Latvian city of Daugavpils and about 15 miles (25 km.) east of the Lithuanian town of Zarasai, the boundary runs northwestward through a flat area. It crosses the Rokiskis (Lithuania)–Daugavpils road and the Kupiskis (Lithuania)–Jekabpils (Latvia) railway and reaches the Nyemenek River east of the Latvian town of Nereta. The boundary follows the river downstream northwestward and southwestward for about 50 miles (80 km.), leaving it at a point southeast of Bauska (Latvia). The line heads west, crossing the main railway between Kaunas (Lithuania) and Riga (the capital of Latvia) south of the Latvian town of Metene. Upon reaching a tributary of the Venta River, the line follows it westward for about 40 miles (65 km.) to its confluence with the Venta River, leaves it and runs southwestward for about 50 miles (80 km.), to cross the main road between Klaipeda (Lithuania) and Liepaja (Latvia). It reaches the Baltic Sea between the Lithuanian town of Sventoji and the Latvian town of Rucava.

Historical Background. Lithuania was established as an independent state in 1253 and during the Middle Ages (between the thirteenth and fifteenth centuries) controlled a large area in Eastern Europe, between the Baltic Sea and the Black Sea. In 1501 it joined Poland to form the largest European state of that time. The area of today's Latvia was ruled by the German Knights of the Teutonic Order. Russia annexed Latvia in 1721, most of Lithuania in 1795 and the entire area in 1815. These regions became constituents of the great Russian Empire without a formal dividing line between them. During World

War I the Germans occupied both areas but after the Russian Revolution and Germany's defeat the region was left in a political void. For two years different armies fought for that area: the Soviet Red Army, German troops, Latvian and Lithuanian forces, the British and the French.

As Latvia and Lithuania became fully independent in 1920, their common boundary was established by the Riga Treaty of September 1920 in accordance with the ethnic character of the border area. The Protestant Latvians held the territory north of the border while the Catholic Lithuanians remained to the south. The political changes that took place in the area during World War II (the Soviet annexation of 1940 and the German occupation of 1941–1944) did not change the boundary's alignment, which served as the internal boundary between the two Soviet republics until 1991. Latvia and Lithuania achieved independence from the USSR in August 1991, adopting their 70-year-old boundary line as their common international boundary without a formal agreement.

Present Situation. The boundary between these two states is one of the few boundaries of the former Soviet Union that are not disputed with regard to their alignment. Neither holds territorial claims against the other and each fully recognizes the line. Thus, the peaceful relations between the two independent states are reflected in the peaceful boundary line.

LATVIA — RUSSIA

The boundary between Latvia and Russia runs for 135 miles (217 km.) between the boundary junction with Belarus in the south and the junction with Estonia in the north. It follows the internal division between two republics of the former Soviet Union.

Geographical Setting. From the southern terminus of the boundary line, which is located 12 miles (20 km.) southwest of the Russian town of Sebej, the boundary runs northwestward across a flat area. It crosses the main Riga (Latvia)–Moscow (Russia) railway east of Zyluny (Latvia) and reaches the Velikaya River. It follows the river downstream northward for about 6 miles (10 km.) and leaving the river it runs northwestward and crosses the Daugavpils (Latvia)–Pskov (Russia) railway southeast of Pytalovo (Russia). Running northward for 60 miles (96 km.), it reaches the boundary tripoint with

Estonia about 15 miles (25 km.) northeast of the Latvian town of Aluksne.

Historical Background. Latvia, which is inhabited by an ethnically homogeneous group, gained independence for the first time in 1991. It was ruled by the Germans during the Middle Ages, by Sweden from 1621 and was annexed to the Russian Empire in 1721. Following the Russian Revolution of 1917 and the end of World War I, the Latvians declared their independence in November 1918. For two years Poland, the Soviet Red Army, a number of German units and local Latvian armies fought in Latvia and only in 1920 did Latvia make peace with the Soviet Union and Germany. The boundaries of Latvia were marked according to ethnic frontiers and were determined by the Riga Treaty signed between Latvia and the Soviet Union in March 1920. The German-Soviet Treaty of 23 August 1939 placed Latvia in the Soviet sphere of influence, which led to its occupation by the Soviet Union in June 1940 and its conversion into a Soviet republic on 5 August 1940. Latvia briefly came under German rule (1941–1944) but was regained by the Soviet Union and, following World War II, the boundary between the Soviet republics of Latvia and Russia was modified to Russia's benefit as it gained the town and district of Pytalovo. Latvia became independent in 1991, adopting its last internal division with Russia as its eastern international boundary.

Present Situation. There is no formal agreement concerning the alignment of the boundary line and Latvia holds an unofficial claim for the return of the borderland areas of the Pskov district from Russia. However, the boundary line is peaceful and remains undisputed.

LEBANON (Lubnan)

A Middle Eastern country (area: 4,015 sq. miles [10,400 sq. km.]; estimated population: 2,900,000 [1994]) on the eastern shore of the Mediterranean Sea, Lebanon is bounded in the north and east by Syria (233 miles; 375 km.), in the south by Israel (49 miles; 79 km.) and in the west by the Mediterranean Sea. Its capital is Beirut.

Lebanon's many ethno-religious communities reflect a history of geographical isolation and foreign intervention at one and the same time. Phoenicians (Canaanites), the presumed forerunners of the modern Lebanese, developed the natural ports of Tyre,

Sidon and Byblos until Greek conquests supplanted Phoenician trade preeminence. The region then came under Seleucid, Roman and then Byzantine control. The Muslim conquest changed its religious balance and language, but Christianity remained predominant in Mount Lebanon. Its fragmented coast and mountainous interior became a refuge for those fighting central authorities and/or dominant orthodoxies.

The late nineteenth century was an era of Maronite predominance and cultural revival spurred on by Western missionary efforts. Only the Maronites welcomed the French mandate after World War I. In 1920 the French added the predominantly Muslim regions to create "Greater Lebanon." The Syrians were outraged at this amputation. In its new borders, Lebanon's religious heterogeneity had significantly increased.

When Lebanon became independent in 1943, the leaders of its religious communities were forced to work out some formula for living together. The last census, of 1932, showing a slight Christian majority, became the basis for a carefully arranged power-sharing arrangement, whereby confessional identity determines allocation of parliament seats and of military and bureaucratic offices. Lebanese political culture came to be based on communal sectarianism.

Stability in the 1950s and 1960s made for prosperity, but also for a growing gap between rich and poor. A first civil war was fought in 1958 over Lebanon's adherence to conflicting political forces in the Arab world. In 1975 civil war broke out again, in the form of a power struggle between Maronite clans and Muslim Leftist-radicals supported by Palestinians. Effective central government broke down, to be restored only in 1989.

In that year Lebanon's leaders agreed to the Syrian backed Taif agreement, which called for a new equilibrium in Christian-Muslim relations, dissolution of all militias, and extension of state control over the whole territory. Controlled by a government of national unity, itself controlled by Syria, Greater Beirut has become a Syria-dependent city-state which is gradually extending its hold. Reconstruction has begun, but Lebanon's overriding question of identity still hangs over this heterogenous state.

LEBANON — ISRAEL   see ISRAEL–LEBANON.

LEBANON — SYRIA   The boundary between Lebanon and Syria follows waterways and mountain crests for its most part and covers 233 miles (375 km.) from the Mediterranean coast at Al 'Aridah to its intersection with Israel's boundary (on the Hasbani River).

Geographical Setting. From the Mediterranean coast in the north, the boundary follows the course of the Kebir River inland and around the northern edge of the Lebanon Mountains. It crosses the valleys of the Wadi Wasin, Wadi ash Sharbin and the Orontes River (Nahr Al-'Asi) east and south to encompass the Anti-Lebanon Mountains, reaching a height of 8,695 feet (2,650 m.), and Halimat Peak (8,082 feet; 2,464 m.). It trends along the ridge of the mountains south and southwest to Ram el Kebch. Here the boundary turns southeast to join a local road north of Tall Ftaya, follows the road to the wadi south of Tall Ftaya and then joins the wadi, running upstream into the mountains once more. Dropping southward into the valley south of the wadi, the boundary meets the crest of Satha Range. It follows this crest before crossing the deep valley of the Barada River between Maboun and Serghaya and rising to the southernmost peak of Mount Chmiss. From here the boundary crosses the valley to Mount Talle, courses along Mount Massayat to Makret al Loz and east to follow the road to Damascus as far as Mount Mazar, where it turns south. It regains the mountain crests, crosses the Ech Cheikh mountain (9,230 feet; 2,814 m.), which is the peak of Mount Hermon, and descends to the foothills to cross the valley to Mount Haurata. The line continues into the valley of the Hasbani River which it follows southward to its boundary junction with Israel.

Historical Background. Syria was part of the Ottoman Empire for some 400 years until 1918 and was governed by Turkish pashas in three provinces: Aleppo, Damascus and Tripoli. While Lebanon enjoyed a large measure of autonomy, whereby its native feudal lords were recognized, a lighter tribute was exacted and the country conducted its own foreign affairs, Ottoman oppression reduced Syria, once prosperous on its own trade and industry, to a poverty-stricken backwater. A treaty in 1740 placed all Christians visiting the Ottoman Empire under French protection and was the basis for the later French claim to protect all the Catholic Christians in

Lebanon–Syria border crossing

Syria—thus beginning the process that made French involvement in Syria inevitable after World War I. Lebanon's policy of free foreign trade and modern leadership as well as its modern roads, bridges, irrigation and farming methods made Beirut the gateway to Lebanon and Syria. The Turks, anxious to maintain their imperial integrity, kept the political situation volatile by destroying strong leaders and setting minorities against one another. In 1841 hatred between Druze and Christian elements, encouraged by Ottoman interests, resulted in a massacre of some 11,000 Christians in Lebanon. The French immediately occupied Lebanon. Syria's isolation ended in 1869 when the Suez Canal facilitated its return to a central part of world trade.

After World War I the Ottoman Empire was partitioned and France accepted the mandate for Lebanon and Syria, despite the local inhabitants' desire for autonomy and a well supported nationalist movement. The French treated Lebanon and Syria as two separate countries and Greater Lebanon was created in 1920 in an attempt to make the largely Christian Lebanon viable in terms of territory and resources. The boundary between Lebanon and Syria was created by the French in 1920, when the autonomous sanjak of Lebanon was expanded into modern Lebanon, then a French mandate territory, by the absorption of the entire littoral from the Palestinian border to Tripoli and of four districts of the interior. But the increase in size immediately altered the demographic situation, making the country overwhelmingly Muslim. In both countries French culture and language were imposed at the expense of Arab and nationalist opposition that was repressed with military strength. Anti-French sentiments were exacerbated when, in contravention of its mandate, France gave the Alexandretta province to Turkey (1939). During World War II the French high commissioner in Syria sided with the Vichy government and Syria became a battleground. As the British and Free French troops entered Syria in 1941, they declared the end of the mandate. Little changed until 1943, when the Nationalist Party dominated the republic, even though a new Syrian government declared its independent status. In an attempt to retain some of its privileges, France turned its military might on Damascus in May 1945 and only after British intervention was order restored.

On 12 April 1945 Lebanon and Syria were admitted to the United Nations as separate independent states. Both adopted the French division and the common international boundary followed the 1920 division between the two French mandates.

Present Situation. Since 1945 Lebanon has been troubled by internal political and religious friction and the presence of the Palestine Liberation Organization (PLO) forces have aggravated the internal situation from 1970 onward, attracting Israeli hostility. Syria (which never officially recognized Lebanon as a separate entity) invaded Lebanon in 1976, but the boundary alignment has been neither challenged nor disputed.

LESOTHO A landlocked southern African country (area: 11,725 sq. miles [30,355 sq. km.]; estimated population: 1,900,000 [1994]), Lesotho is surrounded on all sides by South Africa. The length of its common boundary with South Africa is 565 miles (909 km.). Its capital is Maseru.

LESOTHO — SOUTH AFRICA Lesotho is an enclave within eastern South Africa. The length of its boundary is 565 miles (909 km.) and it circumvents an area of high mountains, enclosing them within the state.

Geographical Setting. Clockwise from the confluence of the Orange and Makhaleng rivers in the south, the boundary follows the central line of the Makhaleng River northward through high ground. It leaves the Makhaleng after 15 or 20 miles (24 or 32 km.), turns west and northwest heading toward the mountain peak of Langeberg and up to the pillar of Jammerberg, where the boundary intersects the Caledon River. The course of the Caledon River is then followed northeastward to its source for 150 miles (241 km.). From there the boundary trends southeastward along the Maluti Mountains to the peak of Mont-aux-Sources (10,822 feet; 3,299 m.). It then follows the Drakensberg Mountains, crossing several peaks. At the source of the Umzimvubu

River, a southwesterly direction is taken to the source of the Tina River, again guided by mountain peaks. The boundary heads westward until it locates the source of the Telle River and follows its course in a northwesterly direction to its confluence with the Orange and Makhaleng rivers.

Historical Background. The Dutch ceded the Cape of Good Hope to Britain in 1814 and, to escape British rule, Afrikaner farmers moved northward (the Great Trek) to settle in the Orange Free State, Transvaal and Western Natal. Britain annexed Natal in 1843 as part of the Colony of the Cape of Good Hope and it became a separate colony in 1856. Transvaal gained independence in 1852 and later became the South African Republic. In 1848 the governor of the Cape of Good Hope declared British sovereignty as far north as the Vaal River and eastward to the Drakensberg Mountains. The Orange River Territory, north of the Orange River, established its own government in 1851 and on 23 February 1854 became the independent Boer Republic of the Orange Free State. Britain, during the Boer War of 1899–1902, annexed the Orange Free State as the Orange River Colony and the South African Republic as Transvaal. On 31 May 1910 the Union of South Africa, a British dominion, was created, consisting of the Cape of Good Hope, Natal, the Orange River Colony and Transvaal. It became a dominion in 1910, but became fully independent in 1931 and 30 years later was established as the Republic of South Africa (31 May 1961).

The Basuto (Suto) people lived mainly in the upper region of the Orange River basin and further north around the Caledon River. In 1843, the governor of the Cape Colony signed a treaty of friendship with Moshesh (Moshoeshoe), chief of the Basuto, Article III of the treaty describing the boundary between the Cape Colony and Basutoland, mainly consisting of the Orange and Caledon rivers. However, clashes ensued between the Basutos and British forces in the Orange River territories until the convention of 23 February 1854, which recognized the independence of Basutoland. Clashes between the Basuto people and the Orange Free State continued, with Basutoland asking for British protection on several occasions. On 12 March 1868 the governor of the Cape of Good Hope issued a proclamation declaring Basutoland British territory. In a treaty signed at Aliwal North on 12 February 1869 between the Cape of Good Hope and the Orange Free State, all the Basuto territory west of the Caledon River and the lands of Chief Molapo from the confluence of the Caledon and Putisani rivers north to the Drakensberg Mountains was ceded to the Orange Free State. This treaty also delimited the Basutoland–Orange Free State boundary. It was amended slightly by the British High Commissioner's Notice of 13 May 1870 and by Government Notice no. 74 of 6 November 1871. This replaced the territory of Chief Molapo within Basutoland and also delimited the sections of the boundary adjacent to Natal and the Cape of Good Hope. This line constitutes the present Lesotho–South Africa boundary. The British Commission was abolished on 1 August 1964 and Basutoland became independent as Lesotho on 4 October 1966.

Present Situation. Demarcation of the Drakensberg watershed technically raises a problem as the almost vertical escarpments of the range, which face outward from Lesotho, do not always constitute the drainage divide. Occasionally the escarpments and the drainage divide diverge, leaving grazing land between the boundary and the slopes of Drakensberg. The boundary has not been contested, but as recently as 1977 the Lesotho government reiterated claims to original Basuto lands that are now located in South Africa.

LIBERIA   A west African country on the shore of the Atlantic Ocean, Liberia (area: 38,265 sq. miles [99,067 sq. km.]; estimated population: 2,700,000 [1994]) is bounded by Sierra Leone (190 miles; 306 km.) in the northwest, by Guinea (350 miles; 563 km.) in the north, by Ivory Coast (445 miles; 716 km.) in the east and by the Atlantic Ocean in the south. Its capital is Monrovia.

Liberia was founded in 1847 by freed black slaves from the southern United States of America. The Liberians consist of a number of ethnic groups, including the Americo-Liberians, the descendants of the original settlers, who now constitute fewer than 2% of the population. Other groups are the Kpelle, Dan (Gio), Mano, Loma, Ghandi and Mende in the north of the country, the Kru, Bassa, Grebo, Krahn and Dei in the southeast, the Gola, Kissi and Vai in the southwest. More than 20% of the Liberians live around the capital of the republic, namely Monrovia.

The official language is English but the most widely spoken languages are Mande and Kru-Bassa. Liberia is officially a Christian state, although complete freedom of religion is guaranteed. Christianity and Islam are the two main religions but many Liberians adhere to traditional religions.

From the foundation of Liberia up to 1980 the Americo-Liberians formed the ruling elite and local ethnic groups were usually hostile toward them. In 1915 the Kru revolted against the Americo-Liberians, but the revolt was crushed with the help of the United States. In 1980 a military coup carried out by Samuel Doe, who belonged to the Krahn ethnic group, put an end to Americo-Liberian hegemony. He was in power for 10 years. In 1990 a civil war broke out between his ethnic group and the Dan, Mano and Kissi groups, during which he was killed. Despite efforts to end the war, it continues, disrupting the lives of all Liberians.

LIBERIA — GUINEA   see GUINEA–LIBERIA.

LIBERIA — IVORY COAST   see IVORY COAST–LIBERIA.

LIBERIA — SIERRA LEONE   From the boundary tripoint with Guinea on the south bank of the Makona River in the northeast to the Atlantic Ocean in the southwest, the boundary between Liberia and Sierra Leone runs for 190 miles (306 km.).

Geographical Setting. The southwestern terminus of the boundary line is located at the mouth of the Manne (Mano) River in the Atlantic Ocean. It runs northeastward, following the left (east) bank of the river to its confluence with the Morro River. It then follows the main navigation channel (*thalweg*) of the Morro River to its confluence with the meridian of approximately 10°26'18"W. It follows the meridian northward to its intersection with the Mauwa River and courses along the river northeastward to its confluence with the Magowi River, which it then follows through its main navigation channel upstream northeastward to its source. By short straight-line segments and various small rivers, it runs to the boundary tripoint with Guinea located on the intersection of the Dandogbia River with the left (south) bank of the Makona (Moa) river.

Historical Background. Both Liberia and Sierra Leone were first established as settlements for liberated slaves. Liberated slaves from the United States were settled by the American Colonization Society on the western coast of Africa from 1820 onward. In 1822, the first permanent settlement was established in Cape Mesurado, which is now Monrovia, the capital of Liberia. In 1838 the area was named Liberia and in 1847 it became an independent state. Sierra Leone ("the lion mountain") was settled in 1788 by liberated slave soldiers from Britain. Freetown, its capital, was established in 1791 and in 1808 Sierra Leone became a British Crown colony in which captured slaves that were freed by the British Navy were settled.

During the nineteenth century both Liberia and Sierra Leone expanded inland and Liberia held claims to the coastal area north of the Mano River as far as the Sherbro Islands in Sierra Leone, while the British did not establish a protectorate over the interior of Sierra Leone until 1896. Great Britain sought control of the coast as far as the mouth of the Mafa River, adjacent to the Cape Mount (Robertsport) settlement of Liberia. Liberia pressed to determine the boundary along the Moa River. The boundary dispute led to the 1887 treaty that placed the line from the mouth of the Mano River up to the boundary tripoint with Guinea on the Makona (Mao) River. The land segments of the boundary, especially along the 10°26'18"W meridian, were identified and demarcated in 1930.

Present Situation. Since 1887 the boundary line between these two states in western Africa has been secure. There are no known disputes concerning the alignment of the boundary, which was adopted by Sierra Leone as an international line upon gaining independence on 27 April 1961.

LIBYA (Libiya) A north African country (area: 679,184 sq. miles [1,759,086 sq. km.]; estimated population: 4,000,000 [1994]), Libya is bounded in the north by the Mediterranean Sea, east by Egypt (690 miles; 1,100 km.), southeast by Sudan (238 miles; 383 km.), south by Chad (656 miles; 1,055 km.) and Niger (220 miles; 354 km.) and west by Algeria (610 miles; 982 km.) and Tunisia (285 miles; 459 km.). Its capital is Tripoli.

After a confused history of successive conquests and colonizations by Phoenicians, Greeks, Romans, Byzantines and Arabs, the eleventh century invasions by nomad Arabs (the Bani Hilal) first created the core of the Libyan nation. An object of Spanish-Ottoman rivalry, Libya became a Turkish province in the sixteenth century. The Karamanli dynasty unified Tripoli, Cyrenaica and Fezzan in the eighteenth century, and became hereditary rulers under Ottoman suzerainty until the Ottoman Empire restored direct rule in 1835. In the same year, the religious leader Muhammad ben Ali al-Sanussi started a national-religious movement (Al-Sanussiya) based on autonomous oases. In 1890 his successors beat the Ottoman Turks but were unable to ward off Italian ambitions. In 1912 Italy conquered Libya and proceeded to destroy its tribal society. Colonization by Italians, mainly Sicilians and Umbrians, in the 1930s led to the displacement of the local population. During World War II the refugee King Idris supported the British against Italy, and after the war was restored to power.

Starting in the 1960s, massive oil revenues enabled Libyans to become independent from foreign aid and turned the country into a wealthy state. However, the oil boom profited a narrow elite whose conspicuous consumption patterns did little to endear it to other Libyans. A nationalist opposition of military, students and civil servants began to agitate against the monarchy, and demanded the evacuation of foreign military bases.

Modern Libyan history begins with the radical and antiroyalist revolution carried out in 1969 by Muammar Qadhafi and his "Free Officers." While the regime, initially, was dominated by the military, power shifted into civilian hands. However, Qadhafi's own role was only enhanced. Oil was nationalized in 1973; massive oil-derived revenues made possible a series of sociopolitical experiments which have thoroughly changed the Libyans' archaic social life.

Libya's economic policy is now "Islamic socialist." Officially the salaried class has been abolished in favor of producers' associations where no private gains may be realized, laborers own and manage expropriated factories, monetary exchanges are restricted, consumption is limited and private trade is abolished. In practice, Libyans needed foreign labor. By the end of the 1970s, one-third of their work force consisted of non-Libyan guest laborers, some of them later replaced by Libyans.

A one-party state was established. In the 1970s Qadhafi launched his "people's revolution," a cultural revolution to purge "ill elements." Direct democracy was institutionalized by directly-chosen revolutionary committees, established to ideologically activate the masses. Theoretically anarchist, Qadhafi's dictatorship of the revolutionary committees in practice transformed Libya into a police state, harshly suppressing any opposition—the most dangerous being radical Islamic fundamentalists. But in spite of internal crises, Qadhafi has always won, thanks to his symbolic function as victor over the monarchy and his power of mobilization.

In principle, Libya's leader has established a reputation for intransigence, adventurism and unpredictability. Libyans have initiated a number of failed fusion attempts with other Arab countries and have repeatedly confronted the West. Declining oil incomes in the 1980s provoked unpopular austerity measures. Disaffection by the army showed in coup attempts. After keeping a very low profile in the Gulf crisis, the Libyan leadership in 1990 risked a very circumspect domestic liberalization program, restraining the Revolutionary Committee's power and timidly allowing a private sector to reappear.

LIBYA — ALGERIA see ALGERIA–LIBYA.

LIBYA — CHAD see CHAD–LIBYA.

LIBYA — EGYPT see EGYPT–LIBYA.

LIBYA — NIGER This 220-mile (354-km.) boundary is delimited throughout and extends from the boundary tripoint with Algeria in the west, at about 23°30'54"N and 11°59'54.6"E, to the boundary tripoint with Chad, at approximately 23°N and 15°E, in the east.
Geographical Setting. The Libya–Niger boundary begins at the boundary tripoint with Algeria, known as reference point 1010 (which is its height in meters above sea level) at Garet Derouel El Djemel. It curves southeastward to Tummo and crosses a sandy waste with dunes for about 65 miles (105 km.) before the terrain becomes rocky and reaches an escarpment south of the oasis of Tummo. For the next 55 miles (90 km.) or so to the boundary tripoint with Chad the border crosses rocky desert country.
Historical Background. In 1911, the Cyrenaica, Fezzan and Tripolitania regions of northern central Africa were passed from Ottoman to Italian control and together were renamed Libya in 1934. Under the terms of the Italian Peace Treaty that followed World War II, Italy renounced its title to Libya (1947) and the country became independent on 24 December 1951.

Niger became an administrative subdivision of French West Africa in 1904. It was a military territory during 1912–1922 and was then reorganized as a civil entity, formally becoming a colony of French West Africa by a decree of 13 October 1922. On 3 August 1960 Niger became independent.

The border between Niger and Libya is delimited in two distinct sections. The first, from the Algerian tripoint to Tummo, was included in the Franco-Italian Arrangement of 12 September 1919. The second section, from Tummo to the boundary tripoint with Chad, is a conventional boundary based on the limits of the Turkish provinces (vilayets) of Tripoli and Barca from the days of the Ottoman Empire. The vilayet borders appear to have been accepted as an international boundary between Turkish and French territories by the Anglo-French Convention of 14 June 1898 and its supplement, the Anglo-French Declaration of 21 March 1899, concerning their respective spheres of influence in northern central Africa.

The western section, from Algeria to Tummo, is described in one sentence in an exchange of notes of 12 September 1919: *"De Rhat à Tummo, la frontière sera determinée d'après la crête des montagnes qui s'etendent entre ces deux localites, en attribuant toutefois à l'Itali les lignes des communications directes entre ces mêmes localités."* ("From Rhat to Tummo the boundary is to be determined along the peaks of the mountains that extend between the two points, assigning all of the direct communication lines between these points to Italy.") The Treaty of Friendship between France and Libya of 10 August 1955 confirmed the frontier as it stood then, but mentioned as a reference point only the Algerian tripoint. The eastern section of the boundary, from Tummo to Chad, is not described in any treaty or legal form; however, its location in practice was confirmed by the 1955 treaty. In 1935, an agreement was reached to adjust the section of the border toward the southeast—affecting Chad as well as Niger. However, although the agreement was drawn up and the adjustment found its way into many subsequent maps, it was never ratified and the previous boundary line remains in force.

Present Situation. This boundary is fully recognized by both countries.

LIBYA — SUDAN

The boundary between Libya and Sudan is 238 miles (383 km.) long and is situated in an empty desert area in northeastern Africa. It is an astronomic boundary, formed by latitudes and meridians, with no relation to the area's topographical or geographical features. It begins in the north at the boundary tripoint with Egypt and ends at the boundary junction with Chad in the south.

Geographical Setting. Starting at the border junction with Egypt on Jebel Uweinat, on the intersection of the 25th meridian east of Greenwich with 22°N, the boundary follows the meridian south as far as its intersection with 20°N. From this point it follows the 20°N parallel westward to meet the 24th meridian east of Greenwich, which it follows southward to reach the boundary junction with Chad.

Historical Background. Three colonial powers were involved in the creation of the boundary between Libya and Sudan: Italy, which ruled Libya between 1911 and 1947; Britain, which ruled Sudan (with Egypt) until 1956; and France, which ruled French Equatorial Africa and western Sudan. In 1898, Great Britain and France established their spheres of influence in the zones east and west of the Niger River but in 1899 the French military conquest of western Sudan was matched by a British reconquest of what is now called Sudan. The boundary between Egypt and Sudan was established along the 22°N latitude, while the northern terminus of the British–French boundary was fixed at 19°30'N and 24°E. Italy established itself in Libya in 1911 and claimed all of the Turkish Ottoman possessions in the area, especially the Serra Triangle south of 22°N, which, according to the British, had previously been part of Anglo-Egyptian Sudan. In 1934 the Serra Triangle was recognized as Italian on the basis of tripartite agreement which determined the boundary between the powers. Libya became independent on 24 December 1951; Sudan on 1 January 1956. Since their independence both Libya and Sudan have recognized the line established in 1934.

Present Situation. There are no known disputes concerning the delimitation of the Libya–Sudan boundary. The line is clearly defined but was never demarcated in the empty desert area.

LIBYA — TUNISIA

The Libya–Tunisia boundary is 285 miles (459 km.) in length, starting at the Mediterranean coast at Ra's Ajdir and ending at Fort-Saint in the Sahara. The boundary consists primarily of short-line segments connected by pillars, although in places the alignment is determined by wadis and ridges. It was delimited as a colonial boundary between the French and Turkish possessions in northern Africa in a convention in 1910 and was demarcated in 1910–1911.

Geographical Setting. The boundary sets out from the coast of the Mediterranean Sea and heads south, following the successive *thalweg*s of the Sabkhat al Maqta and the Khawi Smeïda. The boundary then follows a watershed southwestward to the mountains of Dehibat. It continues southwest through valleys and across rocky crests to Wadi Lorzot. The boundary follows the left bank of this wadi, turning south and southwest for another 19 miles (30 km.) to Bir Zar. It then proceeds south-southeast and southwest toward Ghudãmis (Ghadãmes) and along the northern bank of a channel between two salt marshes. Twisting west and then south, it arrives at the Algeria–Libya–Tunisia tripoint, between pillars 220 and 221 of the 1910–1911 demarcation, at about 30°13.5'N and 9°33.5'E.

Historical Background. In 1881 Tunisia was occupied by France and was proclaimed a French protectorate. In 1886 an agreement between France and Turkey delimited a boundary between Tunisia and the Turkish vilayet (province) of Tripoli. A more accurate delimitation was determined after a second agreement in 1892, extending it as far as Ghudãmis. Finally, on 19 May 1910, a Franco-Turkish convention delimited most of the present-day Libya–Tunisia boundary, which was then demarcated with pillars by a joint commission during 1910–1911. For the French this represented a successful transformation of tribal borders into definitive territorial boundaries, made possible by military pressure.

The demarcation process had some notable characteristics. Pillar no. 81 was never erected and, of the line that was demarcated between pillars 31 and 233, from Ra's Ajdir to Qãrat Hamil—located 9 miles (15 km.) southwest of Ghudãmis—the southernmost part has since become a section of the Algeria–Libya boundary.

In September 1911 Italy occupied the vilayet of Tripoli and the Treaty of Ouchy (12 October 1912) marked Turkey's recognition of Italian sovereignty in the area, which continued until World War I. From 1943 to 1951, the two Libyan provinces of Tripolitania and Cyrenaica were under British administration, while the French controlled the province of Fezzan. The 1947 Peace Treaty with the Allies heralded Italy's relinquishment of Tripoli to Libya.

On 21 November, the question of the final disposition of territory was eventually submitted to the United Nations General Assembly, which, in 1949, passed a resolution with the recommendation that Libya become independent before the end of 1951. Thus, on 24 December 1951, Libya declared its independence. Since then, Libya has been known successively as a kingdom, the Libyan Arab Republic and the Libyan Arab Socialist Jamahiriya.

Tunisia gained its independence on 20 March 1956, following the termination of the French protectorate, and by July 1957, the Tunisian Constitutional Assembly had voted to abolish the monarchy and established a republic.

Present Situation. Since independence, neither Tunisia nor Libya has questioned the boundary alignment, although it has been reported that the constrictive forces that have been placed on tribes in the area since the 1910 delimitation still result in confused patterns of transboundary land ownership.

LIECHTENSTEIN   A Central European country (area: 62 sq. miles [160 sq. km.]; estimated population: 30,000 [1994]), Liechtenstein is situated between Austria and Switzerland. It is bounded in the east by Austria (23 miles; 37 km.) and in the west and south by Switzerland (25.5 miles; 41 km.). The capital of Liechtenstein is Vaduz.

LIECHTENSTEIN — AUSTRIA   see AUSTRIA–LIECHTENSTEIN.

LIECHTENSTEIN — SWITZERLAND   Dating back to the fifteenth century, the boundary between Liechtenstein and Switzerland is one of the oldest established boundaries of the world. It runs for 25.5 miles (41 km.) between the northern boundary junction with Austria on the Rhine River and the southeastern junction with Austria on the Naafkopf Peak. Most of this line follows the Rhine River.

Geographical Setting. The northern terminus of the boundary line is located on the main navigation channel of the Rhine River, east of the E61 European highway, about 1 mile (1.6 km.) northeast of the Swiss town of Sennwald. It follows the Rhine River upstream southward for 20 miles (32 km.) to a point located east of Sargans (Switzerland) and west of Balzers (Liechtenstein). Leaving the river, the boundary heads eastward, crosses the road between Balzers and Maienfeld (Switzerland) and follows a local watershed. It trends over Falknis Peak (8,403 feet; 2,562 m.) and Grauspitz Peak (8,525 feet; 2,599 m.) and then reaches Naafkopf Peak (8,430 feet; 2,570 m.) at the southeastern boundary junction with Austria.

Historical Background. The Principality of Liechtenstein developed from the Roman province of Raetia and its history as a sovereign state began in 1342 when the County of Vaduz became a separate territory. Its eastern boundaries with the Toggenburg canton of Switzerland were established along the Rhine River as early as 1434. The counties of Vaduz and Schellenberg (north Liechtenstein) were united in 1719 and named the Imperial Principality of Liechtenstein. Its political independence was established after the Coalition War of 1806. Between 1815 and 1867 the principality joined the German Federation but its boundary with Switzerland was never changed.

Present Situation. Since 1434, the boundary between the two states has not been changed. It is one of the most peaceful boundaries in the world and no dispute concerning the undemarcated line has ever been known since its creation.

LITHUANIA (Lietuva)   A northern European country (area: 25,174 sq. miles [65,175 sq. km.]; estimated population: 3,820,000 [1994]) on the eastern shore of the Baltic Sea, Lithuania was a republic of the Soviet Union until 1991. It is bounded in the

The southern section of the Liechtenstein–Switzerland border crosses the Balzers–Maienfeld road

north by Latvia (282 miles; 453 km.), in the east and southeast by Belarus (312 miles; 502 km.), in the southwest by Poland (57 miles; 91 km.) and the Russian Oblast of Kaliningrad (141 miles; 227 km.), and in the west by the Baltic Sea. Its capital is Vilnius.

The Lithuanian principality expanded its rule over Russian provinces during the fourteenth century and by the end of that century had become the strongest power in eastern Europe. In 1569 the Lithuanians formed a union with the Poles, following which the Lithuanian aristocracy and urban population became in due time entirely polonized.

With the rise of Russia in the eighteenth century and following the division of Poland, the Lithuanians found themselves under the Russians. In the nineteenth century, especially after the Polish revolts of 1831 and 1863, the Russian authorities followed a policy of Russification. Thus, in 1863 Russian was proclaimed the sole official language and the Cyrillic alphabet was imposed on the Lithuanian language. Many Russians were settled among the Lithuanians. The Lithuanian national revival, a backlash to Russification, led to a nationalist movement which succeeded in proclaiming an independent state after World War I. Vilnius was occupied in 1920 by Poland, and Kaunas (Kovno) was pro-

claimed the capital of Lithuania in its stead. Following the Ribbentrop-Molotov agreement, Lithuania was occupied in 1940 by the Soviets and incorporated into the Soviet Union as one of its fifteen republics. Vilnius was then reinstated as Lithuania's capital. Between 1941 and 1945 it was occupied by the Germans. After World War II about 100,000 Lithuanians took refuge in Germany from the Soviets, while 200,000 others were exiled to the eastern parts of the Soviet Union. At the same time about 250,000 Russians were settled in the Lithuanian Soviet Socialist Republic. The Lithuanian diaspora in western countries has served since 1940 as a cultural and political center, keeping alive aspirations for independence.

In the late 1980s the nationalist movement gained in strength. In 1989 Lithuania proclaimed independence, which caused a prolonged, mainly non-violent, confrontation with Moscow. Following the disintegration of the USSR in 1991, Lithuania reclaimed its independence and was accepted as a member of the United Nations.

LITHUANIA — BELARUS   see BELARUS–LITHUANIA.

LITHUANIA — LATVIA   see LATVIA–LITHUANIA.

LITHUANIA — POLAND From its intersection with the Belarussian boundary west of a curve of the Nemunas (Neman) River in the southeast to its intersection with the Russian (Kaliningrad) boundary in the northwest, the Lithuania–Poland boundary follows a section of the border between Poland and the former Soviet Union as it was established after World War II. Today's line is 57 miles (91 km.) long.

Geographical Setting. From a point west of a curve in the upper Nemunas River, about 10 miles (16 km.) southeast of the small Lithuanian town of Kapciamiestis, the Lithuania–Poland boundary line runs northwestward, leaving the small town of Sejny in Poland and the small town of Lazdijai with Lithuania. Crossing the railway line that links Suwalki (Poland) and Alytus (Lithuania), the boundary heads west-northwestward, reaching the Vistytis Lakes, which are the source of the Pregel River. It follows the southern shore of the two main lakes, leaving them in Lithuania, and reaches the boundary tripoint with the Kaliningrad district of Russia west of the Lithuanian town of Vistytis.

Historical Background. From 1569 to 1776 Poland and Lithuania were united, forming the largest country in Europe at that time. Between 1772 and 1795 Poland lost its independence and its eastern section, together with Lithuania, became part of the Russian Empire. Only after World War I were Poland and Lithuania revived as independent states. After lengthy negotiations, a boundary between the two was determined by the Council of Ambassadors in March 1923. Although the line was primarily based on the states' ethnic features, the old Lithuanian capital, Wilno (Vilnius), was left in Poland. In October 1939, after the occupation of eastern Poland by the Soviet Union, the Vilnius region was transferred back to Lithuania, which became a republic of the Soviet Union in 1940. Poland was captured by Germany during World War II, reviving its independence in 1945.

A treaty between Poland and the Soviet Union, signed in August 1945 and ratified in 1946, established Poland's eastern boundary along the "Curzon Line," a small section of which was bounded by the Soviet Republic of Lithuania. When Lithuania became independent in 1991 both states adopted their common section of the existing boundary between Poland and Russia as an international boundary line.

Present Situation. No formal agreement has been signed concerning the alignment of the boundary line between Lithuania and Poland and both have unofficial claims to the other's territory. Some call for the creation of an autonomous Polish national territory in southeastern Lithuania (in the Lazdijai region), which was once ruled by Poland northward. Others seek a transfer of the Kaliningrad district from Russia to Lithuania, which would extend the boundary between Lithuania and Poland northward. Only a formal boundary agreement would solve such boundary disputes that arise with the political and international changes of the twentieth century.

LITHUANIA — RUSSIA Lithuania and the Russian Oblast of Kaliningrad share a boundary that runs for 141 miles (227 km.) between the boundary tripoint with Poland in the southeast and the Baltic Sea in the northwest. It follows an internal boundary that was established after World War II within the former Soviet Union.

Geographical Setting. The southeastern terminus of the boundary line is located in the Pregel River, west of the small Lithuanian town of Vistytis. The boundary runs northward to reach and cross the main railway between Kaunas (Kovno) in Lithuania and Kaliningrad in Russia. The line then follows a tributary of the Sesupe River downstream northward and near Naumietis (Lithuania) joins the Sesupe River downstream northwestward for 20 miles (32 km.). It leaves the river and runs in a straight line northwestward for 5.5 miles (9 km.) to the Neman River, which it follows downstream westward, leaving the town of Sovetsk (Tilsit) in Russian territory. Some 10 miles (16 km.) from the mouth of the Neman River, the boundary line departs from it and forms a straight line toward the shore of the Kursiu Marios lagoon. It crosses the lagoon in a straight line westward to its western shore and reaches the coast of the Baltic Sea south of the Lithuanian port town of Klaipeda (Memel).

Historical Background. Russian Kaliningrad (Königsberg) covers approximately 5,790 sq. miles (15,000 sq. km.) and has a population of about 871,000 (1993). The city of Königsberg in East Prussia was founded in 1255 by the Teutonic Knights. In 1525, the entire region surrounding the city was ceded to the Kingdom of Poland but was returned as an enclave to Prussia in 1660. In 1758–1762 it was under Russian occupation, although the city remained a Prussian territory and became part of the German state when it was formed in 1870. After World War I, Königsberg remained part of Germany but was severed from mainland Germany by the Polish Corridor, once again leaving the region isolated.

Lithuania, formerly under Russian administration, was established as an independent state in 1919 and its southern boundary with German East Prussia (the Königsberg region) was established along what is now its boundary with Russia.

During World War II, at the Tehran Conference (1943), the Soviet Union made demands on the region on the grounds that it needed to secure an ice-free port on the Baltic Sea. The area was captured by the Soviet army in April 1945 and was made a region of the Russian Federation. The area was then named Kaliningrad, the original German population was expelled and was replaced by almost 1,000,000 Soviet colonists, mostly laborors. Kaliningrad became a center for military entrenchment and housed a wide range of air, land and sea forces.

Lithuania's southern boundary, which had been established in 1919, was reestablished after the creation of the Kaliningrad region in September 1945 and after the Soviet Union had reincorporated Lithuania as one of its republics.

The collapse of the Soviet Union in 1991 and the official establishment of Lithuania as an independent state changed the status of its boundary line with Kaliningrad into an international boundary between Russia and Lithuania without any formal agreement.

Present Situation. Since Lithuania's independence, no official disputes concerning the alignment of the boundary have been reported. However, some Lithuanians demand a transfer of the Kaliningrad region to Lithuania, while others ask for a secession of the city of Klaipeda and the former Memel region from Lithuania. The future of the Kaliningrad region is presently insecure as about 220 miles (350 km.) of Lithuanian territory divide the Kaliningrad region and the Russian mainland.

LUXEMBOURG A landlocked Western European country (area: 998 sq. miles [2,584 sq. km.]; estimated population: 396,000 [1994]), Luxembourg is bounded in the north and west by Belgium (92 miles; 148 km.), in the south by France (45 miles; 73 km.) and in the east by Germany (86 miles; 138 km.). Its capital is Luxembourg.

The Luxembourgers form a population of mixed Celtic, Germanic and French origin. They have a collective identity, supported by a separate German dialect (Letzeburgish) which is their everyday language. Medieval Luxembourg supplied the Holy Roman Empire with several emperors before being absorbed by ambitious Burgundians and Habsburgs; thereafter, the Luxembourgers shared the fortunes of the Belgians until the Grand Duchy was created in 1815. After the Belgian revolution, the statelet was again split between Belgian and rump-Luxembourg, maintaining a personal union with Dutch kings.

Later in the nineteenth century, power passed to another branch of the Nassau dynasty (and soon evolved from absolutism to democracy), and Luxembourg became fully independent. Luxembourgers enjoy a high standard of living thanks to their heavy industry; long a fiscal paradise, one-quarter of their population is foreign.

LUXEMBOURG — BELGIUM see BELGIUM–LUXEMBOURG.

LUXEMBOURG — FRANCE see FRANCE–LUXEMBOURG.

LUXEMBOURG — GERMANY see GERMANY–LUXEMBOURG.

M

MACAO An overseas territory of Portugal (area: 6.6 sq. km. [17 sq. km.]; estimated population: 510,000 [1994]), Macao is to become a Chinese territory in 1999. It is situated on the southeastern coast of China. Macao's only land boundary is with China (0.21 miles; 0.34 km.) in the north, while its two islands (Taipa and Colôane) and peninsular area are surrounded by the South China Sea. Its capital is Macao.

MACAO — CHINA see CHINA–MACAO.

Macao–China boundary

MACEDONIA (Makedonija) A Balkan republic, Macedonia (area: 9,928 sq. miles [25,703 sq.km.]; estimated population: 2,200,000 [1994]) gained independence in 1991, upon the disintegration of Yugoslavia. It is a landlocked country, bounded in the north by Serbia (149 miles; 240 km.), in the east by Bulgaria (92 miles; 148 km.), in the south by Greece (153 miles; 246 km.) and in the west by Albania (94 miles; 151 km.). The capital of Macedonia is Skopje.

Macedonia was a part of the Ottoman Empire until 1912, but became part of Serbia in 1913 as a result of the Balkan War. Bulgaria claimed that the Macedonians were Bulgarians, while Serbia maintained that the Macedonians had been forcibly Bulgarized. The Serbs tried to assimilate the Macedonians immediately upon taking control of Macedonia.

After World War II the Communist regime in Yugoslavia under Tito established Macedonia as one of the constituent republics of Yugoslavia and made great efforts to develop Macedonian nationalism as a bulwark against Bulgarian irredentism among the Macedonians.

Following the disintegration of Yugoslavia and the subsequent war between Croatia and Bosnia-Herzegovina in 1991, Macedonia declared its independence. However, the new state had problems gaining international recognition, with the Greeks officially objecting to the use of the name Macedonia (on the grounds that it is also the name of a region in northern Greece that is intimately associated with ancient Greek history, having been the birthplace of Alexander the Great) and the Bulgarians repeating their longstanding claim to the region.

MACEDONIA — ALBANIA see ALBANIA–MACEDONIA.

MACEDONIA — BULGARIA see BULGARIA–MACEDONIA.

MACEDONIA—GREECE see GREECE–MACEDONIA.

MACEDONIA — SERBIA This boundary runs generally north-northeastward for 149 miles (240 km.) from the Albania–Macedonia–Serbia boundary tripoint to the Macedonia–Serbia–Bulgaria tripoint.

The boundaries of Albania and Macedonia

Geographical Setting. From the Albanian boundary tripoint the boundary follows the watershed on the Sar mountain, which divides the Drim River basin in the Kosovo region of Serbia and the Vardar River valley of Macedonia. East of the Sar mountain the boundary trends down to the Lepenac River valley and follows the river for a short distance. It then runs across the Crna mountain and east of the mountain cuts through the plain between the towns of Kumanovo (Macedonia) and Presevo (Serbia). It crosses the Pcinja River and follows the Kozjak mountain northward to reach the eastern boundary junction with Bulgaria at an altitude of 4,372 feet (1,333 m.).

Historical Background. Until 1913, the historical province of Macedonia (including the present-day state) was under Ottoman rule. Following the Balkan Wars (1912–1913), it was divided between Serbia, Bulgaria and Greece. (The present-day Macedonian state is almost the same territory as Serbia had gained from the partition.) The Serbian part was then incorporated into the Kingdom of Serbs, Croats and Slovenes, which later became Yugoslavia, and after World War II an internal boundary was established between Serbia and Macedonia, the two federal republics of Yugoslavia. It was the only republican boundary that had little basis in pre-Yugoslavian historical continuity. Only the easternmost section of the line coincides with the southern boundary of the Kingdom of Serbia, which was established by the Congress of Berlin in 1878. The rest of the boundary was agreed upon between republican leaderships in 1945 on the basis of a clear ethnic division and taking some physical features into account. However, sources and evidence of the line's delimitation are scarce.

Present Situation. The status of the boundary is not clear, as Serbia has not recognized the Macedonian state since the dissolution of Yugoslavia in 1991. Greater-Serbian nationalists regard Macedonia as "Southern Serbia." Several incidents were reported in 1993 and 1994, including violations of the boundary line by the Yugoslavian army. On the other hand, Macedonia is making claims for a boundary revision to gain possession of the Prohor Pcinjski monastery, located several hundred meters within the Serbian border. Since early 1993 the boundary has been observed by peacekeepers to prevent conflicts.

MADAGASCAR (Madagasikara) An island country, Madagascar is situated in the Indian Ocean, east of the southeastern coast of Africa. Its area is 226,658 sq. miles (586,818 sq. km.) and it has an estimated population (1994) of 13,000,000. Madagascar has no land boundaries and its capital is Antananarivo. It is generally believed that the Malagasy, the predominant population of Madagascar, first migrated from Indonesia some 2,000 years ago. Some may have reached the African coast where a hybrid Indonesian-African culture is thought to have flourished until it was obliterated during the Bantu expansion in the seventh and eighth centuries. Over the centuries, African and Arab immigrants intermingled with the Malagasy, but their contribution to the racial and ethnic makeup of the present population is still subject to debate.

A well-developed hereditary class system of nobles, commoners and slaves led to the emergence of numerous ministates. From the sixteenth to eighteenth centuries, the Merina began a series of conquests from which a unified kingdom emerged. Toward the end of the eighteenth century, Merina dominance waned. Madagascar became a protectorate of the French in 1885 and a colony in 1896.

Although Madagascar became an independent republic in 1960, dissatisfaction with continued French involvement in internal affairs led to a coup in 1972. The new Marxist government adopted many xenophobic policies, including the expulsion of foreigners, but this also led to a revival of Malagasy culture after years of French domination. In recent years, the government has rejected dogmatic Marxism in favor of economic and political liberalization. Ethnic politics still figure prominently in Malagasy politics. The Merina who, with 26% of the population, constitute the largest group, form the bulk of the middle class and still dominate the political arena.

MALAWI A landlocked east African country (area: 45,747 sq. miles [118,484 sq. km.]; estimated population: 9,700,000 [1994]), Malawi is bounded in the north and northeast by Tanzania (295 miles; 475 km.), in the east, south and southwest by Mozambique (975 miles; 1,569 km.) and in the west by Zambia (520 miles; 837 km.). The capital of Malawi is Lilongwe.

Malawi, which was a protectorate of the British, became independent in 1964 under the leadership of Dr. Hastings Kamuzu Banda's Malawi Congress Party. Banda's regime is known as one of the most conservative governments in Africa, and this is partly because at the time of independence it was heavily dependent on Rhodesia and the Portuguese territories for access to the sea; these territories were also its principal trading partners. As a result, Banda not only has maintained diplomatic relations with South Africa and the former colonial regimes of Portuguese Africa, but has also rejected requests for Africanization of the civil service. In addition, Banda has mobilized support from his own ethnic group, the Chewa. In 1966 Malawi became a one-party state with Banda as its president; in 1971 he became life president. He has consistently suppressed all opposition and as a result most of the opposition parties have had to operate outside the country, at one time or another claiming responsibility for raids and sabotage against government installations.

Since the early 1990s, two internal opposition movements, the Alliance for Democracy (AFORD) and the United Democratic Front (UDF), have led demands for a national referendum on the option of a multi-party system. Both groups are particularly strong in the north, where the Tonga and Tumbuka peoples live. These peoples have educational advantages over others further south, including the majority Chewa and other smaller ethnic groups, due to the north's superior mission schools. Dr. Banda has long campaigned against northern teachers, civil servants and students in the southern and central regions. The slow pace of Africanization of the civil service, army and police force has been attributed to attempts to prevent domination by northerners.

In June 1993 the Malawians voted in a referendum for a multi-party system.

MALAWI—MOZAMBIQUE

Demarcated throughout by beacons or natural features such as rivers, lakes and drainage divides, the 975-mile (1,569-km.) boundary between Malawi and Mozambique is delimited in accordance with the Anglo-Portuguese treaty of 11 June 1891. It extends from the boundary tripoint with Tanzania to the tripoint with Zambia.

Geographical Background. From the Tanzanian tripoint at the mouth of the Txuinde River on Lake Nyasa (Lake Malawi), at approximately 11°34'S, the boundary runs westward into the lake and reaches its median line. The line then heads south for approximately 205 miles (330 km.) to a point parallel to beacon no. 17, located on the eastern shore of the lake at 13°23'57.99"S, and runs eastward to touch the beacon. The islands of Chisumulu and Likoma on Lake Nyasa belong to Malawi. From beacon no. 17 (the last in a series of beacons demarcated for the Anglo-Portuguese treaty of 1891) the boundary follows a series of straight lines to beacon no. 11 on Lake Chiuta, then to beacons 7 to 7F on the eastern shore of Lake Chilwa and southward to beacon no. 1, which is about 195 miles (315 km.) from beacon no. 17, on the Malosa River. From here the boundary consecutively follows the *thalweg*s of the Malosa, Ruo and Shire rivers for approximately 150 miles (240 km.), passing the southern tip of the Elephant Marsh and following the western edge of the Eastern Marsh southward to beacon no. 52E near the confluence of the Nyamalikombe and Shire rivers. From beacon no. 52E, the boundary cuts westward in a straight line for about 15 miles (25 km.) to beacon no. 51A on the summit of Kancire Hill and then heads northwest across the Matundwe mountain range up to Zolou (Mozambique). The line runs northward parallel to the road between the Malawian towns of Necheu and Dedzu to the last beacon in the series, beacon no. 2. From there another series is demarcated crossing the Dzalanyama Range and reaching the Luia River. It follows the river downstream northwestward for about 25 miles (40 km.) and leaves it to follow the Lake Nyasa–Zambezi drainage divide to the Zambian tripoint at approximately 14°S and 33°14'E.

Historical Background. Portugal established trading posts along the coast of Mozambique in the sixteenth century and began exploring inland along the Zambezi River. A dispute arose with Britain over territorial claims in Delagoa Bay, which was submitted to President Mac-Mahon of France for arbitration. His award in 1875 assigned the bay and adjacent land to the south to Portugal. Nevertheless, disputes continued over the limits of Portuguese influence and in 1884 a conference was held in Berlin to examine territorial problems in central Africa. August 1887 saw Britain disputing the Portuguese claims on areas that were recognized under the Congress of Berlin as unoccupied territory. In response, three concessionary companies were formed during 1888–1893 to develop resources within Mozambique. The last of the companies' concessions expired in 1941 although Mozambique remained an overseas province or colony of Portugal until its independence on 25 June 1975.

During this time Dr. David Livingstone had explored Lake Nyasa in 1859 and set up missionary activities in the area. In 1878, an association of Scottish merchants formed the African Lakes Corporation, which merged with the British South Africa Company in 1893, and on 21 September 1889 and 14 May 1891 areas around lake Nyasa were declared British protectorates. Together they achieved independence as Malawi on 6 July 1964 and became a republic on 6 July 1966.

The boundary between Malawi and Mozambique was first delimited in Foreign Office papers of 13 February and 14 May 1891 after Nyasaland was declared a British protectorate. On 18 November 1954, a further Anglo-Portuguese agreement moved the border along Lake Nyasa from the Mozambique shore to the median line.

Present Situation. Considerable care has been taken in aligning the Malawi–Mozambique boundary. There have been numerous amendments to the demarcation over the years. No disputes have been record regarding the line, although Malawi has in the past made claims to areas of Mozambique that were part of the Malawi empire in the seventeenth century. There is, however, no tribal basis to the unification of such territories and no action has ever been taken. The beginning of 1992 saw the boundary between the two countries closed due to bandit activity in the area as Mozambique suffered several insurgencies.

MALAWI—TANZANIA Following the colonial boundary between the former British and German possessions in eastern Africa, the Malawi–Tanzania boundary runs for 295 miles (475 km.), from the boundary tripoint with Zambia in the northwest to the boundary tripoint with Mozambique in the southeast. Most of the line runs through Lake Nyasa and the alignment of this section is in dispute.

Geographical Setting. The boundary tripoint with Zambia is located at Nankumango (Nakungulu) Hill, where a boundary pillar was erected in 1898 and replaced in 1935 at 9°22'S and 33°E. The line heads eastward in a straight line for 3.5 miles (5.5 km.) to reach the Songwe River and follows it downstream southeastward to its mouth in Lake Nyasa. According to the colonial agreement between Great Britain and Germany, the boundary proceeds along the eastern, northern and western shores of the lake to the mouth of the Txuinde stream at approximately 11°34'30"S, south of Kiwindi (Tanzania). Tanzania never accepted this lake sector, claiming that the line should follow the median line of the lake, from the mouth of the Songwe River to a point in the lake that is located about 25 miles (40 km.) from its shore, opposite the mouth of the Txuinde stream, and from there form a straight line eastward to reach that mouth.

Historical Background. The Nyasa region was the subject of competition between European powers in the last quarter of the nineteenth century. The Portuguese established themselves in the area of Mozambique in the south, Germany developed an interest in eastern Africa in 1884 and established a protectorate east of Lake Nyasa in 1885 and British imperial activities constituted a British protectorate over the Nyasaland region on 14 May 1891. On 1 July 1890 an Anglo-German agreement had delimited their respective spheres of influence and determined the alignment in general between Lake Nyasa (Britain) and Tanganyika (Germany). On 22 February 1893, the British area was renamed as the British Central Africa Protectorate and as the Nyasaland Protectorate on 6 July 1907. In a protocol signed on 11 November 1898, the results of a joint boundary commission were set forth and the precise boundary delimitation was approved by both governments in an agreement signed on 23 February 1901. After World War I Tanganyika became a British mandate area, but no boundary changes were made. It became independent on 9 December 1961 and was renamed Tanzania on 29 October 1964. Nyasaland became independent as Malawi on 6 July 1964.

At first both states adopted the colonial boundary as their common international boundary, but no formal agreement was ever signed and a dispute developed concerning the boundary in Lake Nyasa, which was renamed Lake Malawi by Malawi legislation.

Present Situation. Since gaining independence, Malawi and Tanzania have been at odds over the boundary in the lake. The Anglo-German agreement of 1890, which delimited the spheres of influence, clearly described a boundary line along the shore of the lake, placing its entire northern sector in Malawi (then Nyasaland). Tanzania claims that there is evidence that prior to the establishment of the Mandate Territory of Tanganyika (1922) German sovereignty had governed up to the median line of Lake Nyasa. The dispute has not been settled but has lain dormant since 1967. The remaining segments of the boundary are clearly demarcated by the main navigation channel of the Songwe River and the short straight line that reaches the Zambian tripoint; no disputes are known concerning the alignment of these sections.

MALAWI—ZAMBIA

The boundary between Malawi and Zambia runs for 520 miles (837 km.) between the boundary tripoint with Tanzania in the north and the tripoint with Mozambique in the south. It follows the colonial boundary between the former British colonies of Nyasaland and Northern Rhodesia.

Geographical Setting. The northern terminus of the boundary is located on Nankungulu (Ngungulu) Hill, at 9°22'S and 33°E. It follows the watershed between the Luangwa River and its eastern tributaries which flow in Zambia, and the rivers and streams that run eastward toward Lake Nyasa, all of which are in Malawi territory. Along this watershed, the boundary runs southeastward to the source of the Luangwa River, placing the Ruwenya hills and the town of Chitipa in Malawi, and then leaves the Vipama hills within Zambia. The line continues southwest, between the Luwumbu and Lundavi rivers (Zambia) and the Rukuru, Dwangwa and Bua rivers (Malawi), and then south to the boundary tripoint with Mozambique, located at 14°S and 33°14'E, leaving the towns of Lundazi and Chipata within Zambia and the town of Mchinji in Malawi.

Historical Background. The area west of Lake Nyasa (Malawi), which was ruled by the local Malawi empire from the fifteenth century onward, became the British Protectorate of the Nyasaland Districts on 14 May 1891, following British commercial interests in the region that were led by the African Lakes Company. By an order in council on 6 July 1907, this became the Nyasaland Protectorate.

A general boundary line between the protectorate and other areas under British influence was established along the drainage that divides the basin of the Congo River from that of Lake Nyasa. The British-South African company attained a charter to exploit the area south of the Zambezi River (modern Zimbabwe) in 1889, and in 1891 expanded its activities north of the river—adopting the agreed line as its eastern limit. From 29 January 1900 the company held administration over the region, which was known as North-Eastern Rhodesia, while the British Colonial Office ruled the area from 1924.

The line between the two British possessions was never demarcated. Nyasaland became independent Malawi on 6 July 1964, while Northern Rhodesia became independent Zambia on 24 October 1964. Both newly established independent states adopted the settled colonial line as their common international boundary without any formal agreement.

Present Situation. Since achieving independence, neither Malawi nor Zambia has made any claims on the other's territory, and no disputes concerning the boundary alignment are known. The undemarcated boundary line is acknowledged and accepted by the two governments, as well as the local inhabitants who are involved.

MALAYSIA

A Southeast Asian country (area: 127,317 sq. miles [329,624 sq. km.]; estimated population: 19,050,000 [1994]), Malaysia is divided between the southern part of the Malaysia Peninsula and the northwestern part of Borneo island. Peninsular Malaysia is bounded in the north by Thailand (314 miles; 506 km.), while the Borneo region is bounded by Brunei (237 miles; 381 km.) in the north and by Indonesia (1,108 miles; 1,782 km.) in the south. Malaysia's capital is Kuala Lumpur.

Until the colonial period, there was no distinct Malaysian identity. Rather, 11 independent sultanates ruled the territory. By the early twentieth century, Great Britain had concluded a series of deals with the local sultans, giving it control over the area which controlled the strategic Strait of Malacca. In 1948, the 11 Malay states were united

Malaysian border crossing

into the Federation of Malaya; independence was granted in 1957. In 1963, plans were made to unite the country with the island of Singapore off its southern coast and three British colonies in northern Borneo (Kalimantan), North Borneo (Sabah) Brunei and Sarawak. Brunei withdrew shortly before the emergence of the new state of Malaysia, and Singapore withdrew from the federation in 1965. Today Malaysia is a constitutional monarchy with a king elected from among the nine hereditary sultans of mainland Malaysia for a five-year term. British interests are still important, as are increasing American interests. Islam plays an important role in affairs of state, and Islamic scholars are often consulted over points of law.

In the 1950s and 1960s Malaysia experienced a violent communist insurgency which threatened to sweep the country into civil war. The rebels were backed by Peking, leading many Malays to question the loyalties of the ethnic Chinese minority, about 30% of the population, and several racially-motivated riots erupted. In the 1960s Malaysia went to war with the Philippines, over possession of the province of Sabah on Borneo. Local government officials, in turn, were suspected of aiding Muslim Moro secessionists in the southern Philippines.

MALAYSIA — BRUNEI see BRUNEI–MALAYSIA.

MALAYSIA — INDONESIA see INDONESIA–MALAYSIA.

MALAYSIA — THAILAND This boundary extends from the Strait of Malacca in the west to the Gulf of Siam in the east for 314 miles (506 km.), across the Isthmus of Kra. The demarcated boundary follows watersheds in the west and center and the Golok (Kolok) River in the east.

Geographical Setting. Beginning on the northern bank of the Perlis River and then running generally northeast to the water divide between the Perlis (Malaysia) and Pujok (Thailand) rivers, the Malaysia–Thailand border links the Andaman Sea of the Indian Ocean with the South China Sea. Following the main watershed southward and then eastward, it passes the sources of Sungei (River) Pattani, Sungei Telubin (Khlong sai Buri) and the Perak River and reaches the source of the Pergau River. Leaving the main watershed to join the water divide between the Pergau River and the Telubin River, the line runs to Buket Lipae hill, which is the source of the main stream of the Kolok River. It then follows the Kolok River to the South China Sea at Kuala Tabar.

The line leaves the valleys of the Pattani, Telubin and Tanjung Mas rivers and the valley on the western bank of the Kolok River in Thailand, while the entire Perak River valley and the valley on the eastern bank of the Kolok River are left in Malaysia. The Pulau Langkawi islands, the islets south of the mid-channel between Pulo Tarutao and Langkawi and the islands south of Langkawi, are all Malaysian. Tarutao and the islets to the north of the mid-channel belong to Thailand. Of the islands close to the west coast, those north of the latitude where the northern bank of the Perlis River estuary touches the sea are in Thailand while those south of it are Malaysian.

Historical Background. This boundary owes its origins to Anglo-French agreements concerning their respective spheres of influence in Southeast Asia and the need to maintain peace and order in an area of British trade and development. British interest in the Isthmus of Kra was originally confined to the protection and supply of its trading fleet in the Strait of Malacca to and from the ports of Asia. Treaties with the Dutch and with local rulers gradually expanded the territory over which Britain held legal and administrative responsibilities and in 1826 the Straits Settlement was created. In the 1870s, this peace-keeping role extended inland with the creation of British residencies in the many small states of the isthmus, which together became the Federated Malay States in 1875, bordering states in the Thai sphere of influence. To secure its own territory, Britain reached an agreement with France dealing

Malaysia's boundary with Thailand

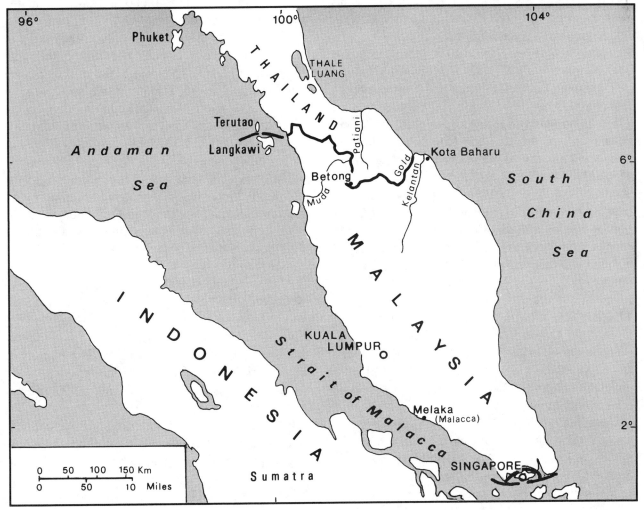

with those areas of Thailand upon which neither would encroach, thus establishing a border with Thailand along its loosely-allied southern states. Britain and France also elicited an agreement from Thailand not to cede any of its lands south of Bang Tapan to any other power. These southern states of Thailand (Kelantan, Trengganu, Perlis and Kedah) were not under full Thai rule and represented a potential danger to adjoining territories. In 1905 the Thai government sought foreign funding to build a railway from Bangkok to the Malay border and, fearing German involvement as much as French, the British renegotiated the border, incorporating the uncoordinated southern states in British territory. The new boundary was agreed upon in a treaty on 10 March 1909.

This border has stood unchallenged since, although the four southern states were briefly restored to Thailand by Japan during World War II (1939–1945) and repossessed at the end of it. Malaysia has been independent since 1957, adopting the 1909 line without a formal agreement.

Present Situation. Clashes took place along the boundary during 1948–1960 as Malaysian Communist forces attacked Malaysian and Thai territories from bases in the dense jungle of the border area.

Terrorism and smuggling cause problems along the border and the Thai and Malaysian authorities cooperate closely to maintain law and order. In 1991, Malaysia fenced off 19 miles (30 km.) of the border, from Perlis to Sinzok. In 1994, Thailand proposed a treaty for joint military action against border terrorism. Malaysia, however, rejected the proposal but gave assurances that terrorists would not find sanctuary in its borders. There are no disputes over the position of the line.

MALDIVES An island country in the Indian Ocean, the Maldives are located southwest of the southern tip of India. The republic's total land area is 115 sq. miles (298 sq. km.) with an estimated population (1994) of 240,000. It has no land boundaries and its capital is Male.

The Maldives were first settled by Tamil traders in about 1000 B.C.E. Their descendants, known as Giravaru, are today virtually indistinguishable from other Maldivians but nevertheless constitute a separate group. From the tenth century Sinhalese from Sri Lanka (Ceylon) began migrating to the islands and became the dominant ethnic group. Traditionally Buddhist, the islanders were converted en masse to Islam by Arabs in the twelfth century and Islam has since emerged as the dominant culture. An attempt at colonization by the Portuguese in the fifteenth century was short-lived and incidental. Colonization by the British beginning in the late nineteenth century similarly failed to leave a mark on the islanders. Independence was achieved in 1965 and the traditional sultanate was abolished in 1968.

Despite their importance in international trade, the Maldivians have been little influenced by the outside world and modernization has only recently been initiated. The low-lying islands have slowly begun sinking into the ocean, leaving the people's future in question.

MALI A landlocked west African country (area: 478,767 sq. miles [1,240,000 sq. km.]; estimated population: 8,750,000 [1994]), Mali is bounded in the northeast by Algeria (855 miles; 1,376 km.), in the east by Niger (510 miles; 821 km.), in the south by Burkina Faso (622 miles; 1,000 km.) and Ivory Coast (331 miles; 532 km.), in the southwest by Guinea (533 miles; 858 km.), in the west by Senegal (260 miles; 419 km.) and in the northwest by Mauritania (1,390 miles; 2,237 km.). The capital of Mali is Bamako.

The Malians gained their independence from the French in 1960 after a short-lived federation with the Senegalese, called the Mali Federation. Containing only two states with major cultural and historical differences made the federation highly unstable and caused it to collapse.

After independence the leader of Mali, Mobido Keita, abolished all opposition parties. In 1968 he was overthrown in a military coup by Mousa Traore. Since independence, the main ethnic conflicts in Mali are with the Tuareg, a nomadic people of Berber origin and the black African majority. Incidents between government forces and the Tuareg are quite frequent.

In 1991, following popular pressures for political reforms, Traore's regime was overthrown and a process of democratization was started.

MALI — ALGERIA see ALGERIA–MALI.

MALI — BURKINA FASO see BURKINA FASO–MALI.

MALI — GUINEA see GUINEA–MALI.

MALI — IVORY COAST see IVORY COAST–MALI.

MALI — MAURITANIA Generally following the intracolonial boundary in French West Africa with some modifications that were made after the independence of both states, the Mali–Mauritania boundary runs for a distance of 1,390 miles (2,237 km.) between the boundary tripoint with Algeria in the Sahara Desert in the north and the boundary tripoint with Senegal in the Senegal River in the southwest. Apart from its river sections, no other areas of the boundary line are indicated on the ground.

Geographical Setting. The southwestern terminus of the Mali–Mauritania boundary is located at the confluence of the Falémé River with the great Senegal River. From there it runs along the northern bank of the Senegal River upstream for 13 miles (21 km.) to its confluence with the Karakoro River. It follows the Karakoro River upstream northward for 101 miles (162 km.) to a point parallel to the town of Bilikouatè (Mali), leaves the river and runs 81 miles (130 km.) northeastward and southeastward to reach the confluence of the Tèrèkolè and Kolimbinè (Kolinbinè) rivers, leaving the villages of Tafara, Taskaye, Gueletie and Dovo in Mali. From this point the boundary follows the course of the Kolimbinè River upstream northeastward for 38 miles (61 km.), passing through some local lakes, and reaches Mael Mountain. From there, in a straight line that faces eastward, the boundary reaches Oueneibe (Gueneibe) and follows a diagonal line that passes the villages of Labidi, Gouguel and Bouioubi that are left in Mali. Reaching the 15°30'N parallel, the boundary runs along it for 253 miles (407 km.) to its intersection with the 5°30'W meridian. It then runs in a straight line northeastward for 57 miles (92 km.) to its intersection with 16°20'N and 5°20'W. It runs northwestward for 17 miles (27 km.) to reach the intersection of the 16°30'N parallel with a defined meridian that runs through the well of Agueraktem. The boundary line then follows this straight line for 595 miles (957 km.) north-northwestward through the Sahara Desert, passing through Agueraktem to its intersection with the 25°N parallel. After following the parallel eastward for 114 miles (183 km.) the boundary line reaches its tripoint with the Algerian boundary, located at 25°N and 4°50'W.

Historical Background. Both Mali and Mauritania were part of the French possessions in western Africa from the late nineteenth century. The French established the colony of French Sudan (today Mali) in 1893, although they gained control of the southern part of today's Mauritania along the Senegal River during the late eighteenth century. The area of Mali and Mauritania was incorporated into French West Africa in 1904. On 23 April 1913, the boundary between Mauritania (which became a French colony in 1920) and French Sudan was determined by a decree, but a later decree dated 5 July 1944 radically altered the line. This was followed by an order of the governor-general which defined the southern limits of Mauritania, transferring about 1,900 sq. miles (5,000 sq. km.) of French Sudanese territory to Mauritania. Mali became independent as the Republic of Sudan on 20 August 1960—two months after the establishment of the independent Federation of Mali, which included Senegal. On 22 September 1960 the Republic of Sudan was transformed into the Republic of Mali and Mauritania gained independence on 28 November 1960. Upon achieving independence, both states made claims on the other's territory and successful discussions led to the Kayes Treaty, which was signed on 16 February 1963, concluding a new boundary between the two states in general terms.

Present Situation. The Mali–Mauritania boundary is one of the few French intracolonial boundaries that were modified by an international agreement after the respective colonies achieved independence. The general descriptions of the 1963 delimitation led to bilateral talks between 1969 and 1970 and a joint technical commission was established to clarify some problems that are still in dispute. Since the Kayes Treaty, however, the boundary negotiations are peaceful and no hostile disputes are known.

MALI — NIGER The boundary between Mali and Niger is 510 miles (821 km.) long, reaching from the boundary tripoint with Algeria in the Sahara Desert in the north to the boundary tripoint with Burkina Faso west of the Niger River in the southwest. It follows a formerly French intracolonial division.

Geographical Setting. The Burkina Faso tripoint is located at about 14°59'30"N and 0°13'30"E, and from there the Mali–Niger boundary line extends eastward for approximately 55 miles (88 km.) along a series of short straight lines, crossing the great Niger River south of Labbèzanga (Mali) on an island in the river. The boundary reaches a point located at about 14°59'N and 0°58'E and then continues in a straight line northeastward for 30 miles (50 km.) to a point north of In Atés pond. Turning eastward it runs in a straight line for 79 miles (127 km.) to a point on the northern slope of Tiapsa peak. It continues in two straight lines, eastward and then northward, for 29 miles (46 km.), to reach the northwestern shore of a local pond south of Anderanboukane (Mali). Again the boundary runs in a straight line eastward for 31 miles (50 km.) toward a point in the Ahzar Amachkalo valley at about 15°21'18"N and 3°29'35"E. It heads northeastward, follows the valley and a dry stream for 94 miles (151 km.) and meets the intersection of 16°24'N and 4°12'E. From this point it extends northward along a straight line for 40 miles (65 km.), reaching the intersection of the 17°N parallel with the 4°13'E meridian. The boundary follows the 17°N parallel for about 1.5 miles (2.5 km.) to reach the 4°14'30"E meridian, which it follows northward for 152 miles (245 km.) up to the Algerian tripoint at about 19°08'30"N and 4°14'30"E.

Historical Background. Both Mali and Niger were parts of the French possession in western Africa organized in 1895 as French West Africa. Mali was organized as the French colony of French Sudan in 1890, while the whole of Niger was occupied by the French in 1904. Internal colonial boundaries were established in general terms in the ordinance of 20 March 1902, and a convention signed in Niamey on 26 August 1909 defined the boundary alignment between French Sudan and Niger in general terms. Some sections of the boundary were defined by the Ansongo Convention of 5 March 1928 and most of the southern line was defined in the Niamey-Gao Agreement of 3 April 1939. Nevertheless, no agreement provides a precise boundary description and no demarcation of the line has ever taken place, the alignment remaining one based upon mutual recog-

nition. Niger gained independence on 3 August 1960. Mali achieved independence as the Republic of Sudan on 20 August 1960 and on 22 September 1960 became the Republic of Mali. Both states adopted the colonial boundary as their international boundary, only a segment of which was agreed upon officially by a protocol signed at Gao on 27 February 1962.

Present Situation. This boundary was never demarcated and considerable clarification and delimitation seem to be required. Since independence, however, no significant disputes have been reported concerning the boundary's alignment and the colonial boundary is accepted as the international boundary.

MALI — SENEGAL   Most of the Mali–Senegal boundary line, which follows the former French intracolonial boundaries, follows the Falémé River. It runs for 260 miles (419 km.) between the boundary tripoint with Mauritania in the Niger River in the north and the boundary tripoint with Guinea on the Falémé River in the south.

Geographical Setting. The confluence of the Senegal and Falémé rivers, south of Diogountourou (Mauritania), constitutes the Mali–Senegal boundary tripoint with Mauritania and the northern terminus of the boundary. From there the line follows the Falémé River upstream southward for 35 miles (56 km.) to its confluence with an eastern tributary, the Sanon Kolè, near Nahè (Mali). The boundary follows the Sanon Kolè River upstream southeastward for 23 miles (37 km.) and leaving it the line heads southward for about 40 miles (65 km.) in a series of straight lines, reaching another eastern tributary, the Goumbamba. It follows the Goumbamba downstream southwestward for 10 miles (16 km.) to its confluence with the Falémé River north of Bountou (Mali). The boundary line then follows the Falémé River upstream southeastward for 168 miles (270 km.) up to its junction with the Balinko River. The boundary continues along the course of that river upstream southward for 7 miles (11 km.) to the boundary tripoint with Guinea at approximately 12°25'N.

Historical Background. European explorers first arrived in Senegal during the fifteenth century and French settlers entered the region from the seventeenth century onward. Senegal was administered under a French governor from 1854, and prior to 1880 the area east of the Falémé River constituted an integral part of Senegal. A decree of 6 September 1880 established the territory of Upper Senegal east of the river, which was named French Sudan in 1890. On 16 June 1895, France oversaw the federation of French West Africa, which included Senegal, French Sudan, Ivory Coast and French Guinea, describing a new set of boundaries in the Treaty of 24 December 1895 that was signed by the different members of the federation. A French decree (18 October 1904) organized the colony of Upper Senegal-Niger, which was renamed French Sudan on 4 December 1920.

The Federation of Mali, which included Senegal and French Sudan, became independent on 20 June 1960, but two months later, on 20 August 1960, Senegal withdrew from the federation and became a state in its own right, while French Sudan which became the Republic of Sudan and was renamed the Republic of Mali on 19 September 1960. Both states adopted the colonial boundaries as their common international boundary without any formal agreement. **Present Situation.** The land sector of the boundary between Mali and Senegal was never demarcated, while the precise location of the river boundary was never defined and according to varying opinions courses through the main navigation channel, the median line or the eastern bank on different maps. Moreover, the ownership of some islands in the Falémé River was not determined. However, no reports of disputes concerning the alignment of the boundary are known.

MALTA   The island of Malta is situated in the Mediterranean Sea, between Italy and Libya. Its area is 122 sq. miles (316 sq. km.) with no land boundaries. Malta has an estimated population (1994) of 380,000 and its capital is Valletta.

Malta was colonized by, successively, Phoenicians, Greeks, Carthaginians and Romans. In 870 Arabs from Tunis occupied the island, and converted its Christian population. The following centuries saw an influx of Arabs and Berbers. Malta became a pirate base and slave market. The Sicilian Normans conquered it in 1090, but by the thirteenth century there were still more Muslims and Jews than Christians. When Muslims were expelled, most opted for conversion to Christianity, but kept customs like seclusion and the veiling of women. Ruled by the houses of Anjou, then Aragon, Malta's importance grew as Ottoman maritime expansion threatened Spain.

After the fall of Rhodes, stronghold of the Order of the Knights of Saint John of Jerusalem, in 1522, Malta became a prime strategic outpost. In 1530 Charles V gave Malta to the order, henceforth known as the Knights of Malta. Repeated Turkish attacks necessitated the construction of fortifications which helped the Maltese withstand a siege in 1565. However, the Maltese population hated the Knights; their power was broken as a result of the French Revolution. In the nineteenth century, Britain turned Malta into a major naval base. Maltese trade became more significant after the opening of the Suez Canal. Population growth led to economic problems and to emigration to North Africa, the United States and Britain and its colonies.

After World War II the Maltese obtained autonomy and in 1964, full independence. In 1974 Malta became a parliamentary democratic republic. The last foreign troops left in 1979. In spite of close links with the Arab world, Malta seeks integration in the European Community.

MARIANA ISLANDS   SEE NORTHERN MARIANA ISLANDS.

MARSHALL ISLANDS   An archipelago in association with the USA, the Marshall Islands are situated in the North Pacific Ocean. Its total land area is 70 sq. miles (181 sq. km.) with an estimated population (1994) of 52,000. It has no land boundaries and its capital is Majuro.

In 1920 Japan was given a League of Nations mandate over the Marshall Islands, and began large-scale colonization, which was interrupted during World War II. Administered by the United States since 1947, the Marshallese voted in 1991 to form their own republic to be freely associated with the USA. The economy is based on copra, fisheries and tourism. The traditional society of the Marshallese consists of a complex system of matrilineal clans, socially stratified.

MARTINIQUE   An overseas department of France

in the Lesser Antilles in the Caribbean Sea, the island of Martinique is located between Saint Lucia and Dominica. Martinique has no land boundaries, its area is 425 sq. miles (1,100 sq. km.) and it has an estimated population (1994) of 380,000. Martinique's capital is Fort-de-France.

The island has a predominantly Roman Catholic population, most of whom are descendants of black African slaves. The economy is based on agriculture, with sugarcane and bananas as leading crops. French is the official language, but a Creole dialect is widely spoken. There exists a strong movement for independence from rule by the French.

MAURITANIA (Mauritanie/Muritaniya) A west African country, Mauritania (area: 395,956 sq. miles [1,025,130 sq. km.]; estimated population: 2,200,000 [1994]) is bounded in the north by Western Sahara (970 miles; 1,561 km.), in the northeast by Algeria (288 miles; 463 km.), east and south by Mali (1,390 miles; 2,237 km.), southwest by Senegal (505 miles; 813 km.) and west by the Atlantic Ocean. The capital of Mauritania is Nouakchott.

The Mauritanians became independent from colonial rule by the French in November 1960. Since then, Mauritanian political life has been dominated by the Maures and the black minority has suffered a great number of injustices and inequalities. Until 1980 slavery was legal in Mauritania, and only following the pressure of human rights movements was it abolished. However, it still exists in various parts of the country and the main sufferers are the black Mauritanians.

Following a dispute with Senegal in 1989, light-skinned Mauritanians living in Senegal were attacked while Senegalese and black Mauritanians were also attacked in Mauritania. About 48,000 black Mauritanians took refuge in Senegal. The conflict between Senegal and Mauritania has not yet been resolved.

MAURITANIA — ALGERIA see ALGERIA–MAURITANIA.

MAURITANIA — MALI see MALI–MAURITANIA.

MAURITANIA — SENEGAL The boundary between Mauritania and Senegal runs for 505 miles (813 km.), from the coast of the Atlantic Ocean north of Saint-Louis (Senegal) to the boundary tripoint with Mali at the confluence of the Niger and Falémé rivers, following a French colonial boundary.
Geographical Setting. The western terminus of this boundary is located on the shore of the North Atlantic Ocean near the mouth of the Senegal River and north of the city of Saint-Louis. The boundary crosses a sandy spit approximately 0.25 miles (400 m.) in width and leaves the island of Salsal with Senegal, passing through several water channels for 2.25 miles (3.6 km.) and reaches the Senegal River about 2.5 miles (4 km.) from the coast. Then, leaving the Ile aux Bois with Mauritania, the boundary runs eastward and from the town of Kaedi (Mauritania) southeastward it follows the northern bank of the Senegal River for 502.5 miles (808.5 km.) to reach the tripoint with Mali at the confluence of the Falémé and Senegal rivers.
Historical Background. French traders and settlers reached the western coast of Africa in the seventeenth century and in 1845 established the government of Saint-Louis (founded in 1658) in Senegal. On 6 September 1880, the territory of Upper Senegal (later renamed French Sudan and today the Republic of Mali) was created in the area east of the Falémé River.

France established itself in Mauritania in 1900 and a boundary between Senegal and Mauritania was created along the Senegal River by a decree on 25 February 1905. A finer description of the boundary between the two colonies was provided in another decree (8 December 1933), placing the line on the right bank of the Senegal River up to its confluence with the Falémé River. Senegal, as part of the Federation of Mali, became independent from France on 20 June 1960. It then seceded from the federation and declared its independence on 20 August 1960. Mauritania achieved independence three months later, on 28 November 1960. Both states adopted the French colonial division as their common international boundary without contracting an official agreement.
Present Situation. There are no known disputes concerning the alignment of this boundary. However, two minor issues appear to remain unsolved: the line's sector from the coast to the Senegal River, which is marked differently in different maps, and

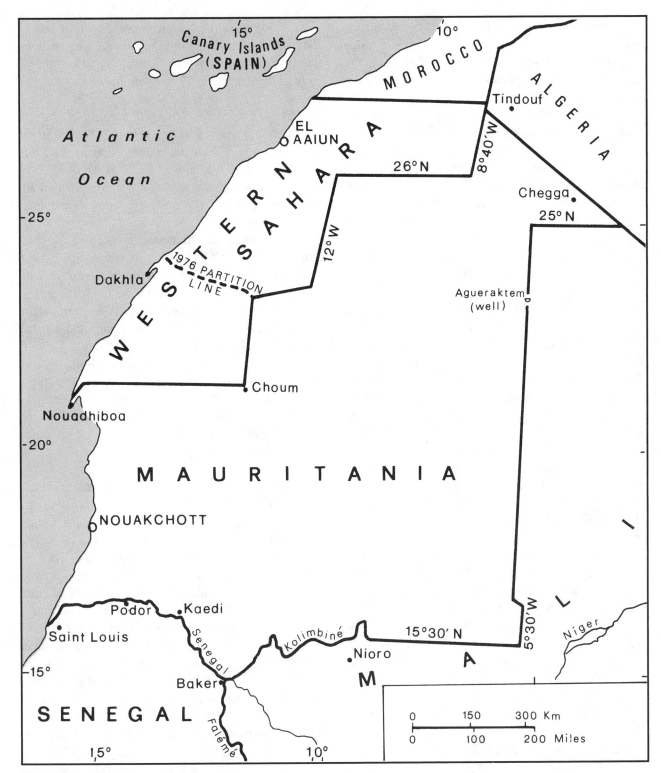

The boundaries of Mauritania and Western Sahara

the location of the tripoint with Mali, which could be on the right bank of the Senegal River or along its median line. The main boundary line on the right bank of the Senegal River has led Mauritania to re-

quest guarantees that it will continue to hold navigation and water utilization rights on the river.

MAURITANIA — WESTERN SAHARA   From

the boundary tripoint with Algeria the Mauritania–Western Sahara boundary runs for 970 miles (1,561 km.) to Capo Blanc (White Cape) on the shore of the Atlantic Ocean near the Mauritanian town of Nouadhibou (Port-Étienne). Western Sahara's present status is unclear, as the area was divided between Morocco and Mauritania by a partition that has never been internationally recognized.

Geographical Setting. The entire length of this boundary runs through the Sahara Desert and is an uninhabited area with no trace of human activity. The northeastern terminus of the boundary, which is the Algerian tripoint, is located at 27°17'40"N and 8°40'W, southwest of Tindouf (Algeria). It follows the 8°40'W meridian southward for about 100 miles (160 km.) to its intersection with the 26°N parallel. The boundary then heads westward for about 200 miles (320 km.) along that parallel to its intersection with the 12°W meridian, which it follows southward for about 190 miles (300 km.) to meet the Tropic of Cancer. In a series of straight lines linking some local high points, the boundary leaves with Mauritania the entire salient area of Ijil. Upon reaching 13°W and 21°20'N, the boundary follows the parallel westward for about 250 miles (400 km.) until it reaches the midpoint between the western and eastern coasts of the Capo Blanc peninsula. Thence it follows a line of midpoints to a location south of a monument erected on the cape. The monument itself stands in Mauritania.

Historical Background. The present boundary between Mauritania and Western Sahara is an outcome of the line delimited between the French and Spanish spheres of influence in western Africa. In 1884, Spain established its dominion along 622 miles (1,000 km.) of the Atlantic coast, a stretch known to the Spanish as Río de Oro (Golden River), opposite the Spanish Canary Islands. Mauritania was ruled by France from the mid-eighteenth century and was part of French West Africa, which was organized on 18 October 1904.

The southern and eastern limits of the Spanish possessions were set in general by a convention signed on 27 June 1900. On 3 October 1904 Spain extended its area north of the 26°N parallel reaching Morocco. France occupied Morocco in 1911 and confirmed the Spanish extension, Sequiet el Hamra, in the Franco-Spanish convention of 27 November 1912. Mauritania became independent on 28 November 1960, adopting the colonial line as its international boundary with Spanish Sahara without a formal agreement. In 1976 Spain handed its Spanish Sahara territory over to Morocco and Mauritania, and these two states arranged a partition along a straight line that extended from 23°N (Tropic of Cancer) and 13°W to the intersection of the 24°N parallel with the Atlantic Ocean, north of Dakhla. South of this line the area is under Mauritanian administration while the northern sector is administered by Morocco.

Present Situation. The boundary itself is not challenged but the 1976 accord, in which Spain gave Western Sahara to Mauritania and Morocco, was not recognized by many governments. Morocco has made claims to the northern areas of Western Sahara that it occupied in 1976. Due to such claims, the partition, and nationalist guerrillas fighting for self-determination, the political situation within Western Sahara is unstable. The United Nations is attempting to hold a referendum on the issue of sovereignty while violent conflicts are controlled under a United Nations cease-fire that has been in effect since September 1991.

MAURITIUS An island country, Mauritius is situated in the Indian Ocean, east of Madagascar. Its area is 788 sq. miles (2,040 sq. km.) and it has an estimated population (1994) of 1,100,000. Its capital is Port Louis. Mauritius has no land boundaries.

The island's first settlers were Arabs who arrived as traders in the tenth century but left shortly after. The Dutch discovered Mauritius in 1598 and introduced sugarcane, which accounts for almost 90% of the country's exports and 70% of the labor force. The French gained control in 1715 and brought African slaves to work the extensive sugar plantations. The Creole language developed from a fusion of French and African elements. In 1810 the British captured Mauritius and began importing Indians as laborers. Independence was granted in 1968.

Interethnic tensions, coupled with the decline in world sugar prices, have resulted in several violent clashes between the island's peoples. A state of emergency was declared in 1968–1970 and again in 1971–1978 after Africans and Muslims clashed over attempts to declare Creole the national language.

The Hindu Indian majority still dominates local politics, but ethnic political parties have some leverage in determining national affairs.

MAYOTTE A French territorial collectivity, Mayotte is situated in the Indian Ocean, between Madagascar and the African coast. Its area is 144 sq. miles (374 sq. km.) with no land boundaries. Mayotte has an estimated population (1994) of 87,000. Its capital is Dzaoudzi.

The inhabitants of Mayotte are of mixed Arab, Malagasy and African origin. Comorian, the common language, is a variant of Swahili heavily influenced by Arabic and written in Arabic characters. The people of Mayotte engage mainly in agriculture, growing vanilla, coffee and rice. Islam is the predominant religion. In both 1974 and 1976 the people of Mayotte voted overwhelmingly to retain their links with France rather than to join the independent Comoro Islands.

MEXICO A Central American country (area: 756,066 sq. miles [1,957,455 sq. km.]; estimated population: 91,600,000 [1994]), Mexico is bounded in the north by the United States of America (1,951 miles; 3,140 km.), in the east by the Gulf of Mexico, in the southeast by Belize (155.5 miles; 250 km.) and Guatemala (598 miles; 962 km.) and in the west by the Pacific Ocean. Its capital is Mexico City.

Spain came into conflict with the *criollos*, Spaniards born in Mexico, eventually precipitating a struggle for independence (1810–1821). Loss of territory to the United States in the late 1840s and occupation by the French during the brief reign of Maximilian in the 1860s were the result of the weakness of the early postindependence period. Stability was, however, restored during the administrations of Benito Juarez and Porfirio Diaz, although the latter established a dictatorship overthrown by what is now referred to as the Revolution, which began in 1910.

Since that time the Mexicans have established the most politically stable government in Latin America. While attempts to establish a correspondingly stable rural economy based on *ejidos* (agricultural cooperatives) have not met with much success, and with uneven industrialization, based largely on import substitution, the strong Mexican extended family, the central focus of Mexican cultural values, seems to have been able to weather all economic blows. Oil, nationalized in the late 1930s, is a powerful symbol of national self-determination and a non-negotiable item in attempts to establish a North American common market.

Some 25% of all Mexicans live, at an altitude of 8,000 feet (2,500 m.), in the capital, Mexico City. The population has burst beyond the municipal boundaries into the adjacent State of Mexico. During the pre-1980 economic boom, many impoverished rural peasants moved to the city where, they believed, life would be better for themselves and their children. Hospitals and schools were plentiful and government subsidies made buying food cheaper than producing it in rural areas.

Since Mexico's economic crisis, many of these migrants have been unable to find regular work and, consequently, suitable housing. As a result, they move in with relatives, one room sometimes sheltering as many as 10 people. Others construct makeshift housing of cardboard or corrugated, galvanized metal. Such settlements now form satellite towns around the capital. Mexico City is now the world's most unhealthy environment.

MEXICO — BELIZE see BELIZE–MEXICO.

MEXICO — GUATEMALA see GUATEMALA–MEXICO.

MEXICO — UNITED STATES OF AMERICA
The boundary between Mexico and the United States runs for 1,951 miles (3,140 km.), between the mouth of the Rio Grande River (Rio Bravo del Norte) in the Gulf of Mexico in the east and the Pacific Ocean in the west. The eastern section of the boundary mainly follows the Rio Grande River, to its intersection with El Paso.
Geographical Setting. The United States–Mexico boundary follows the middle of the Rio Grande (Rio Bravo del Norte) from its mouth on the Gulf of Mexico inland for a distance of 1,254 miles (2,018 km.) to a point just upstream from El Paso, Texas (United States) and Ciudad Juarez, Chihuahua (Mexico). Then it follows monumented overland alignment segments westward for a distance of 533 miles (858 km.) to the Colorado River. From that

point it follows the middle of the Colorado River northward for a distance of 24 miles (38 km.), and then it again follows an overland monumented alignment westward for a distance of 140 miles (226 km.) to the Pacific Ocean.

The region through which most of the boundary runs is characterized by deserts and rugged mountains. In sharp contrast with these conditions are the valleys of the Rio Grande and Colorado rivers, which provide life-giving water to the arid but level and often fertile land found along their banks. In recent years, more than 2,000,000 border region acres (810,000 hectares) along the rivers support irrigated agricultural enterprises. Rather than dividing the boundary, rivers and their basins serve as the region's natural focus. One of the most distinguishing characteristics of the border region along the United States–Mexico boundary are the 15 pairs of sister border crossing cities sustained by the needs of agriculture, the export-import trade and manufacturing, as well as tourism and other services. The population living in these sister cities and the smaller communities in the border region totals an estimated 7,000,000. The close proximity of these vigorously

growing communities gives rise to a host of trans-boundary air and water pollution problems. In the larger Mexican border towns assembly plants owned by Americans, known as *maquiladoras*, provide a large source of employment and foreign exchange. In both the American and Mexican press, the *maquiladoras* are often criticized as major sources of industrial pollution and the social problems stemming from rapid industrial development that plague border communities.

Historical Background. The original territorial limits of the United States were only vaguely defined by the treaties of 30 November 1782 and September 1783. The Texas annexation in 1845, the Mexican Cession of 1848 and the Gadsden Purchase from Mexico in 1853, provided the immediate historical backdrop for the determination of the United States–Mexico boundary as it now exists. In the early decades of the nineteenth century, American citizens moved rapidly west into Louisiana and across the boundary with Spain into Texas. The geography of Texas made it peculiarly susceptible to American invasion. It was shut off from Mexico by a wide belt of harsh desert but was open to the east.

A marker on the Mexico–US border

Many of the Americans took Mexican citizenship to better avail themselves of the rich agricultural lands of east Texas.

In 1819, James Long led a group of these settlers who proclaimed an independent Republic of Texas in anticipation of a Mexican revolt against Spain, which did occur in 1821. Although the government of the United States officially recognized Mexico's boundary on the Sabine River, an unruly tide of bellicose Americans continued to pour into Texas. Finally, in 1830, the Mexican government passed a law forbidding further American settlement west of the Sabine River. The Americans in Texas revolted and, in 1836, defeated the Mexican army. An independent Republic of Texas, set up in 1837, was guaranteed a future when the United States, Britain and France extended diplomatic recognition. It was not long before the annexation of the "Lone Star Republic" by the United States was widely subscribed to on both sides of the Sabine River while in Mexico annexation was considered an act of war. After annexation, the United States boundary followed the old administrative boundary of the Mexican state of Texas. The Texans themselves, however, claimed the area beyond this line to the Rio Grande. The United States supported them and made that river its border with Mexico. No longer able to tolerate these attacks on its sovereignty, Mexico engaged the United States in armed combat during 1846–1847. Suffering a conclusive defeat, Mexico was forced, in 1848, to cede to the United States all the area it claimed to the east of the Rio Grande and a line from the river's head to the boundary of the Oregon Territory as well as all the land north of the Gila River. This included the modern states of New Mexico, Colorado, Utah, Nevada, Arizona and California. In the Treaty of Guadalupe-Hidalgo that formalized this cession, the United States agreed to pay Mexico the sum of $15 million and to assume the liability of claims against Mexico not to exceed an additional $3.25 million. Much difficulty ensued, however, as boundary commissioners labored to follow the terms of the treaty and to demarcate the international line across the poorly mapped desert southwest. The problems were eliminated in 1853 with the Gadsden Purchase, which awarded Mexico $10 million in gold for a broad strip of land lying south of the Gila River in New Mexico and Arizona.

Whether viewed from the north or south, the border between Mexico and the United States soon came to be perceived as a major trouble spot. During the period from 1853 to 1920, a series of chronic transboundary encounters brought the two neighboring states to the verge of warfare on numerous occasions. Serious tensions continue to the present, although not at such heightened levels as those that preceded the 1920 Mexican Revolution.

Present Situation. The United States–Mexico international boundary is the responsibility of an agency known as the International Boundary and Water Commission, United States and Mexico (IBWC). The mission of the IBWC is to apply the rights and obligations which the governments of Mexico and the United States assumed under the numerous boundary and water treaties and related agreements through the years. In carrying out this mission, the IBWC is charged with seeking measures and procedures that will benefit the social and economic well being of the peoples on both sides of the boundary while improving relations of the two governments. The Mexican and United States Sections of the commission maintain their respective headquarters in the paired cities of Ciudad Juárez, Chihuahua and El Paso, Texas. The commissioners meet frequently—often weekly—and their offices are in daily contact. Treaty provisions that call for joint agreement or action are handled by the US Department of State and the Secretariat of Foreign Relations of Mexico. Once a project requiring funding is agreed upon, the two governments generally share the costs in proportion to their respective benefits. In cases of manmade works or operations in one country causing damage in the other, the costs are borne by the government in whose territory the problem originated.

Although there are no pending problems concerning the accurate location and physical maintenance of the present demarcated and monumented boundary, there are a number of problems growing out of its policing. In large measure this results from the wide economic disparity that exists between Mexico and the United States. Many Mexicans seeking better paying jobs available on the United States side continue to cross the boundary illegally. In the late 1970s the US Immigration and Naturalization Service (INS) began constructing fences along the boundary to stop illegal crossings, especially in the vicinity of the boundary zone sister cities. The fence proved to be easily breached and earned the derisive label "Tortilla Curtain" in the press. In 1984 President Reagan, in an apparently unguarded moment of exasperation, was quoted as remarking with reference to the United States–Mexico boundary, "the simple truth is that we've lost control of our own borders and no nation can do that and survive." Most recently the state of California has taken the lead in efforts to control illegal border crossings by passing legislation denying public welfare, education and health services to the illegal immigrants and their families.

MICRONESIA   An archipelago in the Pacific Ocean, Micronesia is situated north of Papua New Guinea. Its total land area is 271 sq. miles (702 sq. km.) and it has an estimated population (1994) of 104,000. Its capital is Kolonia. Micronesia has no land boundaries.

In the twentieth century the islands have been administered successively by Germany and Japan, and by the United States from 1947, as part of the United Nations Trust Territory of the Pacific Islands. In 1975, the islanders voted for a separated status as a US Commonwealth Territory.

MOLDAVA   A landlocked Eastern European country (area: 13,012 sq. miles [33,688 sq. km.]; estimated population: 4,500,000 [1994]), Moldava was a republic of the Soviet Union until 1991. It is bounded in the north, east and south by Ukraine (584 miles; 939 km.) and in the west by Romania (280 miles; 450 km.). Its capital is Kishinev.

The Romanian-speaking Moldavians were an integral part of Romania between 1918 and 1940. In the latter year the Bessarabian province of Romania was annexed by the Soviet Union and was established as the Moldavian Soviet Socialist Republic. The Soviets tried with little success to develop a distinct Moldavian nationality and language, for which a Cyrillic alphabet was adopted.

In 1991 Romanian-speaking Moldavians seceded from the Soviet Union and established an independent Moldava. The Russians and Ukranians (most of whom lived east of the Dniester River) and the Gagauz objected, fearing that the Romanian-speaking Moldavans would seek to merge with Romania,

an idea to which the Romanian state is known to be sympathetic. As a result, fighting broke out between Moldava's ethnic groups, threatening the territorial integrity of the region.

MOLDAVA — ROMANIA   The entire Moldava–Romania boundary, which is 280 miles (450 km.) long, runs along the Prut River between two boundary tripoints with Ukraine. It is part of the boundary between Romania and the former Soviet Union as it stood before the creation of Moldava as an independent country in 1991.

Geographical Setting. This boundary runs from north to south following the main navigation channel of the Prut River. It was agreed that the boundary line should shift in accordance with the natural changes in the position of the river's *thalweg*. It sets out at the northern border junction with Ukraine, south of the Ukrainian town of Lipkany. It runs south-southeastward and then southward to the southern border junction with Ukraine on the river.

Historical Background. The two Danubian principalities of Wallachia and Moldavia became independent between the fourteenth and sixteenth centuries but later fell to Turkish suzerainty. During the eighteenth century, Russian strength and interest in the area increased and in 1774 Turkey granted Russia the right to intervene in the affairs of the two principalities. Three years later Turkey ceded Bukovina, until then a part of Moldavia, to Austria but in 1812 Russia gained the territory of Bessarabia (between the Prut and Dniester rivers).

After the Crimean War of 1853–1856, the Great Powers guaranteed independent and local administration to both principalities under Turkish suzerainty. Lower Bessarabia was restored to Moldavia and Russia retained the northwestern area of the region. In 1861 both principalities combined to create the new state of Romania and its independence was recognized in the Congress of Berlin in 1878. The three districts of southeastern Bessarabia were restored to Russia, affording it access to the Delta of the Danube. No additional changes occurred along the northern boundary of Romania until 1918.

The collapse of Czarist Russia during World War I led to Romania's annexation of Bessarabia in 1918, but the newly established Soviet Union refused to recognize this act. In the early years of World War II Romania accepted Soviet ultimatums and returned Bessarabia and part of northwestern Moldavia on 28 June 1940. Approximately 19,500 sq. miles (50,500 sq. km.), with a population of about 3,400,000, were transferred from Romania to the Soviet Union accordingly. In 1940, the Soviets instituted the Moldavia Constituent Republic of the Soviet Union. The peace treaty with Romania signed in Paris on 10 February 1947 recognized the 1940 boundary and on 29 September 1949 the demarcation of the boundary between Romania and the Soviet Union was completed. The Moldavia Republic of the Soviet Union became an independent country (Moldava) in 1991 and the former Romania–USSR boundary on the Prut River became the Romania–Moldava boundary.

Present Situation. Romania was forced to accept the boundary of 1940 but never buried its claim to the area of Bessarabia and Bukovina. For the time being, however, no disputes are known concerning the boundary alignment.

MOLDAVA — UKRAINE
The boundary between Moldava and Ukraine runs for 584 miles (939 km.) between the two boundary junctions with Romania on the Prut River. It follows an internal boundary between two republics of the former Soviet Union.

Geographical Setting. The northwestern boundary junction with Romania is located on the main navigation channel of the Prut River, some 20 miles (32 km.) east of the Ukrainian city of Chernovtsy. It runs eastward for about 60 miles (95 km.), reaching the Dniester River south of the town of Sokireni (Ukraine). It follows the Dniester River downstream southeastward for about 40 miles (65 km.) and leaves it east of the town of Soroki (Moldava). Thence the boundary line runs southeastward and southward, leaving the Dniester River and the towns of Dubossary, Tiraspol and Dnestrovsa within Moldava. East of Tiraspol, the boundary line crosses the Odessa (Ukraine)–Kishinev (Moldava) highway and then follows a northern tributary of the Dniester River downstream southward to its confluence with the main river. It follows the Dniester southeastward again, leaves it about 5 miles (8 km.) from its mouth in the Black Sea and runs westward. North of

Bessarabia (Ukraine) the line bears southwestward, leaving the towns of Borodino and Bolgrad within Ukraine and the towns of Komrat, Chadir-Lunga and Tarakly in Moldava. The boundary line reaches the southern boundary junction with Romania north of the confluence of the Prut and Danube rivers, north of Reni (Ukraine) and north of the Romanian town of Galati.

Historical Background. Moldavia was a principality located on the eastern section of the Danube River, independent between the fourteenth and sixteenth centuries and then occupied by the Ottoman Empire. Today's Moldava is situated on the territory of Bessarabia, a southeastern European area that was annexed by Russia in 1812. During the Russian Revolution of 1917 Bessarabia broke away and joined Romania. The cession was confirmed by the Allies in the Paris Treaty of 1920, but was not ratified by the Soviet Union. The latter established the Moldavia Autonomous Socialist Soviet Republic east of the Dniester River in 1924. The Soviet Union reoccupied Bessarabia in June 1940 and in August 1940 the area was divided between the Soviet republics of Ukraine and Moldavia. The Prut River in the west and the Dniester River in the east constituted the boundaries of the new republic except for some areas east of the Dniester in the southeast. The southern part of Bessarabia, including the Black Sea coast, were annexed to Ukraine, only to be occupied by the German Army in 1941 and given to Romania. However, it was reoccupied in 1944 by the Red Army and the Moldavian republic was reinstated with some boundary modifications.

In the peace treaty of 1947, Romania recognized the latest annexation and the newly established Soviet Union–Romania boundary. Moldavia became independent as Moldava in August 1991 while Ukraine achieved independence in December 1991. Both states adopted the internal division as their common international boundary without a formal agreement.

Present Situation. As the modifications in the boundary line were made without consideration of the needs and wishes of the local inhabitants, there are some ethnic claims for further changes. Some call for the transfer of an area in northern Moldava to Ukraine while others call for the return of the Moldavan territory found on the eastern bank of the

Dniester River to Ukraine, or seek the creation of an independent Dniester republic in that region. The Bulgar people living in southern Bessarabia want an autonomous territory on the borderland of Ukraine and Moldava while the Budzhak and Gaguaz make claims for a dislocation of their territory in southern Bessarabia to create a federation of those peoples. These charges are still awaiting a formal agreement that will determine the exact alignment of the boundary between the two states.

MONACO

A tiny southern European country (area: 0.7 sq. miles [1.9 sq. km.]; estimated population: 30,000 [1994]), Monaco's only land boundary is with France (2.7 miles; 4.4 km.) in the east, north and west. Monaco is bounded by the Mediterranean Sea in the south. Its capital is Monaco.

The people of Monaco inhabit the smallest country in the world after Vatican City. Located in the French Riviera, near the Italian border, Monegasques have integrated both French and Italian cultural elements. French is the official language and the population is predominantly Roman Catholic.

Most Monegasques are employed in services, the tourism industry and in the world-famous casino in Monte Carlo.

MONACO — FRANCE   see FRANCE–MONACO.

MONGOLIA

A landlocked eastern Asian country (area: 604,829 sq. miles [1,566,500 sq. km.]; estimated population: 2,360,000 [1994]), Mongolia is bounded in the north by Russia (2,139 miles; 3,441 km.) and in the east, south and west by China (2,904 miles; 4,673 km.). Mongolia's capital is Ulan Bator.

Among the earliest inhabitants of Mongolia was a Mongolian people, the Huns, who created a nomadic empire and warred with the Chinese for centuries before dissolving in the fifth century. The Mongols became a major factor in world history in the early thirteenth century; under the leadership of Genghis Khan, the Mongol tribes were united and reached their zenith of power. Their empire was the largest the world has ever known, extending south to China, southwest to Turkistan, Iran and Iraq, and northwest to Russia. After Genghis Khan's death, the empire was divided among his sons, one of whom, Kublai Khan, later conquered China and founded the Yuan dynasty (1279–1368). The once powerful Mongol states had largely disappeared by the end of the fourteenth century, and the Mongols returned to their homeland in east and central Asia. They were later subdued by the Manchu who conquered China and founded the Qing dynasty (1644–1911), the last imperial dynasty in China's history. After the 1911 Chinese Revolution, Outer Mongolia declared its independence, and in 1924,

Mongolia's boundaries with China and Russia

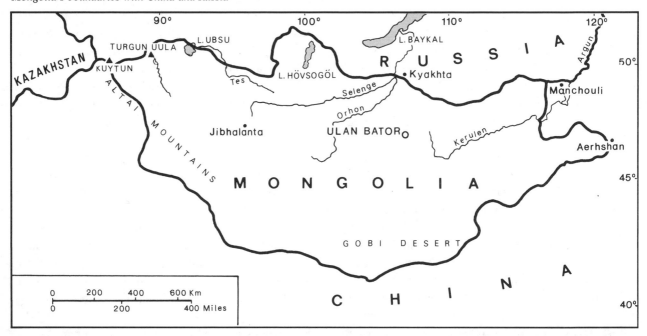

the Mongolian People's Republic was declared with Soviet support.

The Mongol language, a sub-family of the Altaic languages, is composed of nine major dialects, one of which, Khalkha, serves as the official language of Outer Mongolia. In the early thirteenth century, the Mongols adopted a script from the Turkic Uighurs which they retained until 1941, when the Mongolian government announced the adoption of a new phonetic alphabet derived from a modified Cyrillic script.

Traditionally, most Mongols practiced Tibetan Mahayana Buddhism, and that religion had a strong influence on Mongolian society. As a result of an anti-religious movement launched by the current government in the 1930s, about two-thirds of the people profess no religion or are avowed atheists.

The traditional economic occupation of Mongol society was nomadic animal husbandry. Even today, pastoral activities still dominate the economy, although farming has played an increasingly significant role. A distinctive feature of the Mongol dwelling is the *yurt* or *yer*, a cone-shaped, latticed structure used by herdsmen moving from pasture to pasture. The traditional society was based on blood relationship through the common male ancestor who gave his name to the clan. Marriage between members of the same clan was forbidden.

The Mongols in China are practically identical to the Mongols of Mongolia, but speak different dialects of the Altaic Mongolian language. Most Mongols can understand one another, although the written language, based on the Uighur script, has far fewer variants than the spoken language. Mongols in China have long been influenced by Han Chinese culture. Some now have Chinese names, speak Chinese and wear Chinese clothing.

During the Yuan Mongol dynasty, contacts with other countries were expanded and encouraged. The authorities also welcomed foreign religions such as Christianity and Islam, and encouraged Tibetan Buddhism. Numerous foreigners were employed by the state bureaucracy, among them Marco Polo, who returned to Europe to write the famous account of his travels in China. The Mongol Empire finally collapsed as a result of infighting among Mongol princes and extensive peasant uprisings.

Mahayana Buddhism was reintroduced from Tibet in the seventeenth century by Mongol princes attempting to unite their people. For centuries the religion was influential and widespread among the Mongolians.

MONGOLIA — CHINA see CHINA–MONGOLIA.

MONGOLIA — RUSSIA Following a segment of the boundary between Czarist Russia and the Chinese Empire that was established in the eighteenth century, the boundary between Mongolia and Russia runs for 2,139 miles (3,441 km.). It extends from the eastern boundary junction with China west of the Chinese Hu-lun (Dalai) Lake and the western Chinese tripoint located on Kuytun Mount (Hüyten Orgil) in the Altai Mountains.

Geographical Setting. This boundary line crosses one of the major drainage divides of central Asia, linking the headwaters of the Argun River (which flows eastward to the Amur River and the to Sea of Okhotsk in the Pacific Ocean) with the Yenisey River, which flows northward to the Arctic Ocean. The eastern terminus of the boundary line is located 55 miles (88 km.) west of the Russian town of Abagaytuy, which is located on a curve of the Argun River and west of the Chinese city of Manchouli (Manzhouli). The boundary runs westward for about 350 miles (560 km.) along an old Chinese boundary line, crossing some local rivers (the Rivers Uldz and Onon in Mongolia, Rivers Kyra and Ashinga in Russia), all of which run eastward to the Argun River. After crossing a southern tributary of the Chikoy River, the boundary runs northwestward, leaving the Bolshoy Uliley and other tributaries of the Chikoy River that flow to Lake Baykal within Russia. The boundary reaches a point located just south of the city of Kyakhta (Russia), where the boundary treaties were signed in 1727, and west of that town the line is defined by 23 points, principally mountain peaks and passes. The boundary line runs along a watershed that primarily follows the Sayan Mountains and the Yergak-Targak-Tayga, separating the upper Yenisey valley (Mongolia) from the main Yenisey tributaries, such as the Angara, Taseyeva Mana and Tuba (Russia). West of Kyakhta, the boundary line crosses the main road and railway between Ulan-Ude (Russia) and Ulan Bator (the capital of Mongolia). Heading westward, it reaches the

Russian town of Zakamensk and then runs northward and westward to Munku-Sardyk peak (11,453 feet; 3,492 m.) north of Hövsgöl lake, which is left in Mongolia. The boundary bears northwestward and reaches the Sayan Mountains. From the foothills of the mountains southward, it crosses the upper Bolshoi Yenisey River and reaching the 50°N parallel runs westward, passes south of Tsagan-Tologoy (Russia) and arrives at a point north of Lake Ubsu, which is within Mongolia. The line runs southwestward for about 280 miles (450 km.) along the watershed of the Altai Mountains and meets the western terminus of the boundary on Kuytun Mount, which is the source of the great Russian Ob River.

Historical Background. The boundary between Russia and Mongolia was first established in 1727 as a boundary between Imperial China and Czarist Russia. Mongolia, which was united by Genghis Khan in 1206 and by the end of the thirteenth century was part of the vast Mongol Empire, fell into ruin in the later years and became part of China in 1689. The August 1727 Bur Treaty between Russia and China established the central section of the boundary between the two states after the 1689 Treaty of Nerchinsk had determined the eastern sector up to Abagaytuy. The Bur Treaty defined the boundary east and west of Kyakhta in general terms and made provision for its demarcation, which was carried out along 1,690 miles (2,719 km.). The final Kyakhta treaty was signed in October 1727. The sector east of Kyakhta has been maintained to the present as the eastern sector of the Mongolia–Russia international boundary line. Mongolia, with the aid of the Soviet Union, became independent in 1921, adopting the former boundary as its boundary with the Soviet Union. It became an independent Soviet republic in 1924. After World War II, the Soviet Union annexed the Tannu Tuva region of western Mongolia, changed its name to the Tuvinskaya autonomus district and thereby moved the boundary southward to its present location. This act was never the subject of an international agreement but was accepted by the independent Soviet Republic of Mongolia. The collapse of the Soviet Union and the establishment of modern Russia had no effect on the boundary line.

Present Situation. The 250-year-old demarcation of the Mongolia–Russia boundary line still serves as the international boundary between the two states. There are no known disputes concerning its alignment and the new open Mongolian government never claimed for the return of the Tuva province from Russia.

MONTENEGRO see SERBIA (AND MONTENEGRO).

MONTSERRAT A Caribbean island, Montserrat has an area of 39 sq. miles (102 sq. km.). It is a dependent territory of the United Kingdom with an estimated population (1994) of 13,000. The capital of Montserrat is Plymouth. Montserrat has no land boundaries.

MOROCCO (Al-Magrib) A northern African country (area: 172,414 sq. miles [446,380 sq. km.]; estimated population: 27,000,000 [1994]), Morocco is bounded in the north by the Mediterranean Sea and two small Spanish territories (Ceuta [5 miles; 8 km.] and Melilla [6 miles; 10 km.]), in the east by Algeria (969 miles; 1,559 km.), in the south by Western Sahara (275 miles; 443 km.) and in the west by the Atlantic Ocean. Morocco's capital is Rabat.

Berbers doubtless were Morocco's original population. However, the coast was colonized first by Phoenicia, then by Romans, who ruled first through local Berber dynasties, then directly. In the seventh century North Africa was conquered and converted to Islam by Arabs: Berber tribes, previously divided in many minute realms, integrated into Arab armies.

In the ninth and tenth centuries Morocco fell prey to struggles between competing Arab dynasties, and was wrecked by the Hilali invasions. In the eleventh century, the Almoravids, a Berber tribe controlling trans-Sahara caravan routes, conquered Morocco, combining religious passion with ethnic and economic motives. Once in power, they built Marrakesh and went on to conquer Spain. After a while, religious zeal decreased and centrifugal tendencies reappeared: their place was taken by another Berber dynasty, the Almohads.

In the fifteenth century, Spanish expansionism cost Morocco a number of harbors. In the sixteenth century, the Sa'dians, another reformer dynasty, liberated the country in a holy war, and resisted Turkish advances in Algeria. Moroccan identity has since been anchored in the historical fact that they were never subdued by the Turks. The Alawite dynasty, which is still ruling today, came to power in the seventeenth century, and knew its heyday under Mullah Isma'il (1672–1727), after whose reign a decline set in. In 1856 the isolated kingdom was forcibly opened to European trade, and became an object of interest to the Spaniards, French, British and Germans. After temporarily delaying European penetration by playing off imperial rivals, early twentieth-century Moroccan kings were weakened by tribal revolts, while Moroccan economy was dislocated by European products. French claims were recognized in the 1906 Algeciras Treaty. From 1912 on, France imposed a direct protectorate. Spain obtained zones in the Rif mountains as well as Spanish Morocco. It took the French the better part of the 1920s to pacify the tribes and strengthen the *makhzen* (central administration): at first French authority was indirect and rested on the absolute monarchy. After Morocco was opened to European immigration and colonization, an anti-European revolt broke out in the Rif under Abdelkrim. After its suppression, colonization was facilitated by direct rule. From the 1930s, nationalist (partly pan-Arab) resistance originated with Morocco's urban elites, not from its mountain tribes any more. World War II put a stop to French colonization and renewed hopes for independence. France granted Morocco independence in 1956.

MOROCCO — ALGERIA see ALGERIA– MOROCCO.

MOROCCO — SPAIN The two enclaves of Ceuta and Melilla are claimed by Spain but are located on the Moroccan Mediterranean coastline. Ceuta is of major importance to Spain as it is located at the eastern entrance to the Straits of Gibraltar. The present land boundaries of Ceuta were determined by the Treaty of Larache in 1845, and those of Melilla by the Treaty of Tétouan of 1860 as well as the Moroccan-Spanish Convention of 1862. The land boundaries are short: 5 miles (8 km.) for Ceuta and 6 miles (10 km.) for Melilla.

Geographical Setting. Ceuta (7 sq. miles; 19 sq. km.) is located at the eastern entrance to the Strait of Gibraltar. It forms a peninsula that narrows to an isthmus and reaches Point Almina. Ceuta also has a coastal boundary of 12 miles (20 km.).

Melilla (5 sq. miles; 12 sq. km.), with a coastal boundary of only 2.4 miles (3.9 km.), lies south of the strategic Spanish island of Alborán, and is located 124 miles (200 km.) from Ceuta and 115 miles (185 km.) from Málaga. It is surrounded by a neutral zone, which is generally less than 0.6 miles (1 km.) wide.

Historical Background. The territorial disputes in this region are the legacy of the historical geopolitical organization of the area.

Spain claims these territories on historical grounds. Melilla was conquered by Spain in 1497, defeating the Islamic empire, although it subsequently witnessed many Muslim sieges, the most famous of which took place in 1774. Similarly, with the dissolution of the Iberian Union (Spain and Portugal) in 1640, Ceuta opted to remain under Spanish rule, although, like Melilla, it was also periodically subjected to Muslim sieges and attacks. Spain also stresses that the majority of residents in the two enclaves are Spanish and wish to remain under Spanish rule. In 1986 about 78% of Ceuta's population were Spanish, the majority of them traveling to mainland Spain for educational and career opportunities. In Melilla, Spaniards represent about 56% of the population. Spain further reiterates that Morocco has signed at least 12 legally binding bilateral treaties and conventions pertaining to the enclaves. The sovereign status of Ceuta and Melilla was confirmed by conventions in 1864, 1866, 1871, 1895 and 1910.

Morocco's principal claim to sovereignty over Ceuta and Melilla is based on their previous integration in the Islamic empire. Morocco holds that the Moroccan state has existed since the eighth century and that under Islamic law (*El Shari'a*), the two areas were an integral part of the Islamic kingdom before Spain eventually succeeded in gaining and reinforcing international de jure recognition of its sovereignty over the territories. They also claim that the Spanish presence is retarding the political and economic independence of Morocco; Moroccan independence in 1956 was only partial in that Spain did not withdraw from Ceuta and Melilla. The Moroccans also claim that the Spanish bases threaten Moroccan national security. In 1962, Morocco requested that the United Nations General Assembly recognize its rights over northern towns and islands

Morocco–Spain boundary checkpoint

occupied by Spain, and in 1975, in a memorandum to the UN, Morocco formally requested, albeit unsuccessfully, that the UN place the islands on the list of nonautonomous territories and apply Resolution 1514 on decolonization. Significantly, Morocco also stressed that there was a need for the restoration of Moroccan territorial integrity, especially as this concept forms the basis for Spanish arguments for the recovery of the British crown colony of Gibraltar.

A developing aspect of this boundary dispute has been the duplication of claims to the waters adjacent to the two areas. From a purely juridical point of view, both Ceuta and Melilla belong to the Spanish state and therefore Spain can enforce its maritime claims in accordance with the UN Convention on the Law of the Sea (UNCLOS) of 1982. These claims have great strategic significance, for were Gibraltar to be retroceded, Spanish territorial waters would be joined to those of Ceuta and the eastern entrance to the Strait would be entirely Spanish.

Present Situation. Both Morocco and Spain claim sovereignty over the two enclaves in northern Africa. Ceuta is a major center of export to other Mediterranean cities, while Melilla is less significant in this respect but is also a leading port. Both territories have belonged to the European Community since 1986 and to the NATO defence area since 1982, as they are legally an integral part of the Spanish state. Neither Morocco nor Spain has renounced claims to these territories and so the dispute over this boundary will continue to exist.

MOROCCO — WESTERN SAHARA   This boundary is delimited by a straight geometrical line 275 miles (443 km.) in length. It follows the 27°40'N parallel from the Atlantic seaboard to the 8°40'W meridian.

Geographical Setting. From the Atlantic Sea to 8°40'W the boundary travels through an arid wasteland. The first 15 miles (24 km.) inland from the coast cross dunes. The line then continues across a *sebkha* (salt marsh area) for approximately the same distance. The last and longest section of the boundary travels through an area characterized by wadis (dry streams), escarpments and dunes.

Historical Background. The boundary between

Morocco and Western Sahara dates back to the Spanish and French attempts to increase their spheres of influence along the Atlantic coast and inland between the Tropic of Cancer and the Tropic of Capricorn. The first Spanish claim was made by the 9 January 1885 Spanish Notification which indicated the Spanish sphere of influence along the coast between the 20°51'N and 26°8'N parallels. The notification was mainly for trade purposes and made no indication of any inland boundaries. French influence was mainly inland and the Moroccan kingdom stood between the two. The 1900 convention between France and Spain was the first attempt at forming inland and southern boundaries but failed to establish a northern limit between the Spanish sphere (Spanish Sahara) and the Kingdom of Morocco. The Franco-Spanish treaty of 3 October 1904 established the 27°40'N parallel as the boundary between Spanish Sahara and Morocco, ending at 8°40'W. This coordinate was to constitute the Algeria–Morocco–Western Sahara tripoint, but the Algerian–Moroccan boundary had not been agreed upon—hence the exact position of the tripoint is difficult to locate.

February 1976 saw Spain hand the territory of Western Sahara, formerly Spanish Sahara, to Morocco and Mauritania, which arranged a partition between them. A number of governments did not recognize the decolonization in this form and the political situation within Western Sahara is at present unstable due to the territorial claims by nationalist guerrillas and opposition to the partition.

Present Situation. To date, the unstable political situation between Morocco and Western Sahara has not been resolved. A United Nations-organized referendum on Saharan self-determination has been delayed due to concerns about Moroccan settlers in Western Sahara. A more recent Moroccan view is that if the Polisario Front (nationalist guerrillas) win the referendum, Morocco will pull out of Western Sahara. At this point the boundary will have to be revised and agreed upon by those in power.

MOZAMBIQUE (Moçambique) A southern African country, Mozambique (area: 308,642 sq. miles [799,074 sq. km.]; estimated population: 16,600,000 [1994]) is bounded in the north by Tanzania (470 miles; 756 km.), in the east by the Mozambique Channel in the Indian Ocean, in the south and southwest by South Africa (305 miles; 491 km.) and in the west by Swaziland (65 miles; 105 km.), Zimbabwe (765 miles; 1,231 km.), Zambia (260 miles; 419 km.) and Malawi (975 miles; 1,569 km.). Its capital is Maputo.

Mozambique became an independent state in 1975 following a long civil war led by the Liberation Front of Mozambique (FRELIMO). In 1977 FRELIMO declared itself a Marxist-Leninist vanguard party and embarked on a series of policies to establish a socialist state. One source of conflict was the violent actions of RENAMO (National Resistance of Mozambique). Supported by South Africa, it sought to challenge the regime, as peaceful political dissent was forbidden. RENAMO was not supported by any one ethnic group and has been accused of not adhering to any specific ideology other than the destabilization of the FRELIMO regime. The signing of the Nkomati Accord with South Africa in 1984 precipitated a series of peace talks which continued throughout the decade; in 1991 a timetable was set for discussions on the cessation of hostilities and the possibility of elections.

MOZAMBIQUE — MALAWI see MALAWI–MOZAMBIQUE.

MOZAMBIQUE — SOUTH AFRICA The boundary between these two countries is demarcated by pillars and rivers throughout its 305 miles (491 km.). The boundary falls into two sections, separated by the eastern border of Swaziland.

Geographical Setting. The northern section of the Mozambique–South Africa boundary begins at the boundary tripoint with Zimbabwe at the confluence of the Limpopo and Luvuvhurivier rivers. From there the boundary heads south and extends for approximately 255 miles (410 km.) in straight-line sections to the northern boundary tripoint with Swaziland at Mpundweni Beacon. This section roughly follows the eastern side of the Lebombo Mountains.

The second section of the boundary is approximately 50 miles (80 km.) long. It follows the Great Usutu River downstream eastward from the southern boundary tripoint with Swaziland for about 17 miles (27 km.) to its original confluence with the

Pongola River (physical changes have altered the course of the Pongola River so that its confluence with the Usutu River now lies within Mozambique). It then extends eastward in straight-line sections across a coastal plain to the Indian Ocean.

Historical Background. Portugal established trading posts along the coast of Mozambique in the sixteenth century and began exploring inland along the Zambezi River. A dispute arose with Britain over territorial claims in Delagoa Bay, which was submitted to President Mac-Mahon of France for arbitration. His award in 1875 assigned the bay and adjacent land to the south to Portugal. However, disputes continued over the limits of Portuguese influence and in 1884 a conference was held in Berlin to examine territorial problems in central Africa. August 1887 saw Britain disputing the Portuguese claims that had been recognized under the Congress of Berlin as the territory was not occupied. In response, three concessionary companies were formed during 1888–1893 to develop resources within Mozambique. The last of the companies' concessions expired in 1941 and Mozambique remained an overseas province or colony of Portugal until its independence on 25 June 1975.

The Cape of Good Hope was ceded to Britain by the Dutch in 1814. To escape British rule, Afrikaner farmers began to move northward (the Great Trek) and settled in the Orange Free State, Transvaal and Western Natal. Natal was annexed by Britain in 1843 as part of the Colony of the Cape of Good Hope and became a separate colony in 1856. Transvaal gained independence in 1852 and later became the South African Republic. In 1848, the governor of the Cape of Good Hope issued a proclamation declaring British sovereignty as far north as the Vaal River and eastward to the Drakensberg Mountains. In 1851, a government was established for the Orange River Territory covering the recently claimed territories north of the Orange River and on 23 February 1854 it became the independent Boer Republic of Orange Free State. Britain annexed the Orange Free State as the Orange River Colony and the South African Republic as Transvaal during the Boer War of 1899–1902. The Union of South Africa, a British dominion, was created on 31 May 1910, consisting of the Cape of Good Hope, the Orange River Colony, Natal and Transvaal. It became a

sovereign state in 1931 and a republic as South Africa on 31 May 1961.

On 29 July 1869, Portugal signed a treaty with the South African Republic establishing the northern sector of the Mozambique–South Africa boundary, from its northern tripoint with Swaziland northward to the Limpopo River. In 1888, a joint boundary commission representing Great Britain, Portugal, Swaziland and the South African Republic agreed that the southern terminus of the Mozambique–Swaziland boundary should stand on the Great Usuto River (Rio Maputo). On 6 October 1927, two Anglo-Portuguese exchanges of notes took place. One approved demarcation of the boundary up to the Limpopo River and the other fixed the northern tripoint with Swaziland at Mpundweni Beacon. The boundary tripoint with Zimbabwe was established by an Anglo-Portuguese exchange of notes on 29 October 1940.

Present Situation. Mozambique became independent on 25 June 1975, adopting its colonial boundary with South Africa as an international boundary without concluding a formal agreement to this effect. No disputes are known to have arisen concerning this boundary.

MOZAMBIQUE — SWAZILAND

This boundary extends northward from a southern junction with South Africa on the Great Usutu River to a northern junction at Mpundweni Beacon. It consists of straight-line sectors that connect beacons, roughly following the summit of the Lebombo Mountains. Its length is 65 miles (105 km.).

Geographical Setting. The line begins at the southern tripoint with South Africa, which is located, according to some maps, on the median line or *thalweg* of the Great Usutu River; available information does not indicate the precise position of the tripoint in relation to the river. From there the boundary heads north along straight lines demarcated by beacons, roughly following the summits of the Lebombo Mountains that rise from the coastal plain. The boundary ends at the northern tripoint with South Africa at Mpundweni Beacon.

Historical Background. In the sixteenth century, Portuguese traders set up posts along the coast of Mozambique and began exploring inland along the Zambezi River. Territorial claims in Delagoa Bay led to a dispute with Britain which was submitted to President Mac-Mahon of France for arbitration. His award (1875) allocated the bay and the area south of it to Portugal. Disputes continued over the limits of Portuguese influence, however, and in 1884 a conference was held in Berlin to examine the central African territorial problems. In August 1887, Britain disputed the Portuguese claims that had been recognized under the Congress of Berlin. As a result, three concessionary companies were organized (1888–1893) to develop resources in Mozambique. The last of the companies' concessions expired in 1941, although Mozambique remained an overseas province or colony of Portugal until its independence on 25 June 1975.

The Kingdom of Swaziland was subject to expansionist interest from Transvaal throughout the nineteenth century. To prevent Afrikaner encroachment, Britain protected Swaziland's independence, which was recognized in agreements between Britain and Transvaal on 3 August 1881 and 27 February 1884. At a convention in 1890, Britain and the South African Republic agreed to cooperate in administering the affairs of Swaziland, and a further convention in 1894 gave the South African Republic powers of protection and administration for Swaziland. Britain assumed these powers when it annexed Transvaal in 1900. In 1907, Swaziland came under the control of the British High Commissioner for South Africa, until the commission's dissolution on 1 August 1964. On 6 September 1968 the Kingdom of Swaziland became independent.

Portugal and the South African Republic signed a treaty, on 29 July 1869 that determined the southern limit of the Portuguese district of Lourenço Marques (Delagoa Bay) along the 26°30'S parallel inland from the Indian Ocean to the Lebombo Mountains, then running northward along the summit of the mountains. A joint commission (represented by Britain, Portugal, Swaziland and the South African Republic) demarcated the Mozambique–Swaziland boundary from the Great Usutu River northward along the Lebombo Mountains to the northern boundary intersection with South Africa (which was not precisely fixed) in 1888. This tripoint was settled by the erection of Mpundweni Beacon by a Portuguese-South African commission in 1894.

Present Situation. The boundary between Mozambique and Swaziland is demarcated throughout by beacons. A cordon fence also covers the length of the boundary according to Swazi maps, although it is not known whether it was erected unilaterally or on the basis of a joint agreement. Despite the fact that South Africa has established three Swazi homelands within its country, Swaziland has not made irredentist claims of any kind and no other disputes are known to exist.

MOZAMBIQUE — TANZANIA This boundary is 470 miles (756 km.) long and is demarcated throughout by streams, principally the course of the Ruvuma River, and a short section of pillars. It runs from the boundary tripoint with Malawi in Lake Nyasa to the mouth of the Ruvuma River on the coast of the Indian Ocean.

Geographical Setting. Beginning at the boundary tripoint with Malawi at the mouth of the Txuinde (Kwindi) River on the median line of Lake Nyasa at approximately 11°34'S, this line runs generally eastward to follow a series of 26 pillars to the confluence of the M'sinje and Ruvuma rivers. It then follows the *thalweg* of the Ruvuma River to the Indian Ocean—even when the position of the *thalweg* is altered by natural changes in the river's course. The line departs from the *thalweg* only to divide islands between the two countries such that all of the islands upstream of the confluence of the Ruvuma and Domoni rivers belong to Tanzania and all those downstream of the confluence to Mozambique.

Historical Background. The expansion of European possessions on the eastern coast of Africa progressed chiefly at the expense of the sultan of Zanzibar. German interest in east Africa began in 1884 and a German protectorate was established the following year. In an Anglo-German agreement in 1890, the region later to be known as Tanganyika gained recognition as a constituent of the German sphere of influence. In 1894, after the German invasion of Mozambique south of the Ruvuma River, from about 30 miles (50 km.) inland to the coast, Portugal ceded the land, the Kionga Triangle, to Germany. In 1886 this portion of territory had been declared by a procès-verbal (9 June) to belong to the sultan but had been seized the following year by Portugal. A League of Nations decision in 1919 restored it to Portugal and the boundary resumed its position as agreed in the 1886 German-Portuguese Declaration. In 1922, Tanganyika Territory became a League of Nations mandate under British rule and after 1946 it was a United Nations Trusteeship. Tanganyika became independent on 9 December 1961. Its boundaries were originally set out in the German-Portuguese Treaty of 1886 and in the 1891 Anglo-Portuguese Treaty, which delineated the parties' respective spheres of influence. It was modified by a joint German-Portuguese boundary commission in 1907, moving the Malawi tripoint southward by 0.3 miles (0.5 km.) to the mouth of the Txuinde River. The line had previously stood along the parallel connecting the shore of Lake Nyasa with the confluence of the M'sinje and Ruvuma rivers, a very arbitrary and evidently unfair line. During 1936 and 1937, a series of British and Portuguese notes established the sovereignty of various islands in the Ruvuma River, delimited the boundary in detail and determined the rights of the people of Tanzania and Mozambique for navigation, drawing water, fishing and salt extraction along the river.

Present Situation. Mozambique became independent on 28 June 1975. Both states adopted the colonial boundary as their common international boundary without a formal agreement and it is fully recognized by both.

MOZAMBIQUE — ZAMBIA The full length of this boundary is 260 miles (419 km.), of which 48 miles (77 km.) follow the Luangwa River. Thereafter it is demarcated by a series of 38 beacons situated upon eminences, bluffs and hills. It runs from the boundary tripoint with Zimbabwe in the southwest to the boundary tripoint with Malawi in the northeast.

Geographical Setting. From the confluence of the Luangwa and Zambezi rivers, the Mozambique–Zambia boundary follows the center of the main channel of the Luangwa River, passing west of the island of Niakatenga at 15°29'S, at the head of the Lupata gorge. It follows the main channel, passing west of the sand island of Niazawe and east of the sand islands of Ngoza and Kapondoro at 15°4'S, to the main channel's intersection with 15°S and 30°13'6"E. It then forms a straight line to beacon no. 1, which is a dry-stone pile with a cemented top, on the left bank of the Luangwa River at 14°59'58"S

and 30°13'23"E. Henceforth the border consists of a series of straight lines, tending northeast and linking the remaining beacons, which consist of cement masonry pillars—except for nos. 4, 7, 21, 23, 28 and 37, which are dry-stone constructions with cemented tops. Bearing northeastward for 0.2 miles (0.3 km.), it reaches beacon no. 2 on a bluff above the Luangwa River. The border reaches beacon no. 3 on the summit of a small conical hill. Beacons 4 and 5 are on the summits of Chikongoro Hill and Nyamiseje Hill respectively and 6.3 miles (10 km.) further on the border reaches beacon no. 6, on a hill summit 1 mile (1.6 km.) east of Ucha River. Beacon no. 7 is at the summit of Loriasoro Hill and beacon no. 8, which is 8.2 miles (13 km.) away, is located on a very low hill. On the highest northern summits of Kassekete Hill and Fingue Hill are beacons 9 and 10. Beacon no. 11 is on a low rocky hill called Iniawaro and a distinctive conical rock called Longwi is the site of beacon no. 12. The low rock, Kasuche, is the location of beacon no. 13; beacon no. 14 is on a low flat rocky ledge, Chongoni, close to and south of the village of Mwanjawantu. Two distinctive rocks, Chifisi and Sonzori, hold beacons 15 and 16, and beacons 17 and 18 occupy the highest points of Mount Mpinduka and of the low ridge Seza. Beacon no. 19 is on the top boulder of the highest, northern summit of the rocky Mzunje hill and 7.4 miles (12 km.) onward beacon no. 20 occupies the summit of the southernmost of the Kalunga hills. The summits of Tukakula and Bambe mountains have beacons 21 and 23, with beacon no. 22 between them on the southernmost spur of Mount Longa, close to the left bank of the Kapoche River. Beacon no. 24 occupies the highest boulder of the southernmost of the low Kampini hills and beacon no. 25 lies 1 mile (1.6 km.) further on, on the west side of the road leading from Chipata (Zambia) to Tete (Mozambique). Continuing another 7 miles (11 km.), the line meets beacon no. 26 on the split boulder which is the summit of Mount Barazia, the precipitous peak on the western side of the Mbizi Hills. The boundary then passes to beacon no. 27 on the lower southern summit of the ridge running south from Mangurro Hill and to beacon no. 28 on the summit of a peak. Beacon no. 29 lies at the northeastern spur of Mount Zonampeni, in the Viruli mountain range, and the boundary line runs 36 miles (58 km.) from there to beacon no. 38, at the intersection of 14°S with the Nyasa–Zambezi watershed. The border then follows the crest of the watershed in a southeasterly direction to the Chorasanu peak. Beacons 30 to 37 lie along the 36-mile (58-km.) line from beacon 29 to beacon 38.

Historical Background. Zambia, which became independent on 24 October 1964, had previously been known as Northern Rhodesia, which had been part of the Federation of Rhodesia and Nyasaland. That region of central Africa below the Congo and German Tanganyika remained free of European occupation until quite late in the nineteenth century. Then, in 1887, it became clear that Portugal wished to link its coastal possessions—Angola in the west and Mozambique in the east—by expanding its influence through the center of Africa. Britain at the time began to secure its own interests with a treaty in 1887 between the South African Republic and the Matabele king. A convention of 20 August 1890 between Britain and Portugal remained unratified but formed part of the subsequent agreement of 14 November 1890, which in turn led to the treaty of 11 June 1891. This treaty effectively confined Portugal to Angola and Mozambique, and an Anglo-German agreement of 1 July 1890 assured Britain that Germany had no ambitions in the area. In 1889 the British South Africa Company, headed by Cecil Rhodes, who had secured mineral concessions in Matabeleland, was chartered and received many of the powers of the British government. In 1893, the British South Africa Company seized Matabeleland and a subsequent order in council giving the company powers in Matabeleland referred to all the territories subsequently known as Southern Rhodesia. From 1891, the field of operations was extended to the lands under British influence north of the Zambezi River and south of the Congo and Tanganyika, but excluding Nyasaland (Malawi); these territories subsequently became Northern Rhodesia. After 1896, Northern Rhodesia was constituted as a colonial protectorate which status it retained when the British South Africa Company lost its charter in 1923. In 1964, Northern Rhodesia became an independent republic as Zambia. Mozambique achieved independence in 1975.

Present Situation. Both independent states adopted the colonial line between them as their international boundary without a formal agreement. Thus, the border is fully recognized by both countries and no disputes concerning its alignment are known.

MOZAMBIQUE — ZIMBABWE From the boundary tripoint with Zambia at the confluence of the Zambezi and Luangwa rivers to the tripoint with South Africa at the confluence of the Limpopo and Luvuvhurivier rivers, this boundary extends 765 miles (1,231 km.).

Geographical Setting. From the boundary tripoint with Zambia to the Mkumvura River, the boundary mainly consists of straight-line sectors between beacons running due south until it meets the 16°S meridian. This meridian is generally followed eastward as well as the *thalweg*s of some minor streams and rivers (Inyarumanu, Angwa, Karamwe, Msengezi). The boundary then follows the *thalweg*s of the Mkumvura River, returning to straight-line sectors up to the Mazoe River. The *thalweg* of the Mazoe River is then followed in an easterly direction until the boundary extends southward in straight lines to the Gairezi River. It then follows the central channel of the Gairezi southward to its confluence with the Jora River, also following the central channel of this river southward. Passing east of the Inyanga Mountains, the boundary continues southward to the Honde River along straight-line sectors, then to the Ruera, Púngoè and Mombezi rivers and skirts Mount Zaramira. The boundary then courses along the center of the Honde River westward to its confluence with the Ngarura River. From this point the boundary extends southward in straight lines between beacons, also utilizing the *thalweg*s of the Inhamgamba and Penbi rivers and passing along the Chimanimani Mountains to the Sabi River. From there the boundary runs in a straight line southwestward to the South African tripoint on the Limpopo River.

Historical Background. Exploration inland of the Mozambique coast along the Zambezi River began after Portuguese trading posts were stationed along the coast in the sixteenth century. A dispute arose with Britain over territorial claims in the Delagoa Bay region, but was subsequently submitted for arbitration to President Mac-Mahon of France. His award of 1875 assigned the bay and the land immediately south of the bay to Portugal. The limits of

Portuguese control continued, however, and in 1884 a conference was convened in Berlin to review the territorial issues in central Africa. Britain disputed the Portuguese claims again in 1887, claims that were recognized under the Congress of Berlin, as the territory in question was unoccupied. As a result the Portuguese government formed three concessionary companies (1888–1893) to develop resources within Portuguese Mozambique. The last of the concessions expired in 1941 and Mozambique remained an overseas province or colony of Portugal until its independence on 25 June 1975.

The area to the east and north of Bechuanaland, later to become Southern and Northern Rhodesia, was proclaimed a British sphere of influence in 1888. In 1889, Cecil Rhodes's British South Africa Company was granted a charter to operate in an imprecisely defined area between the Zambezi River and Bechuanaland. The boundary between Mozambique and Southern Rhodesia, which later became independent Zimbabwe, was first established in the Anglo-Portuguese treaty of 11 June 1891. By an order in council of 18 July 1894, the British South Africa Company also became responsible for the administration of Matabeleland. Some areas of Bechuanaland were also transferred to the company in 1895, between the Shashi and Macloutsie rivers, but these transfers were rescinded after objections from some Tswana chiefdoms. In the administrator's proclamation of 1 May 1895, which defined the boundaries of provinces and districts under the administration of the British South Africa Company, a substantial part of the northern sector of the boundary was established as the Pandamatenga (Hunter's) Road.

The charter of the British South Africa Company was abrogated in 1923 and Southern Rhodesia was annexed by Britain as a self-governing colony. From 1 August 1953 to 31 December 1963 it belonged to the Federation of Rhodesia and Nyasaland. On 11 November 1965 it made a unilateral declaration of independence, which was not recognized by Britain. Only after the establishment of a black majority regime in April 1980 did Zimbabwe become fully independent.

Present Situation. Since 1891, any territory disputes have been arbitrated as they have arisen and such areas finely demarcated. After achieving independence, both states adopted the colonial boundary as their common international boundary without a formal agreement. There have been no significant disputes regarding the boundary. Incidents of insurgency in the region and counter-insurgency operations by forces of the Salisbury (Zimbabwe) regime during 1972–1977 have not led to any questioning of the boundary.

MYANMAR (Burma) On 19 June 1989 Burma changed its name to the Union of Myanmar. It is an Asian country (area: 261,228 sq. miles [676,577 sq. km]; estimated population: 43,500,000 [1994]) situated in the southern part of the continent. Myanmar is bounded by China (1,358 miles; 2,185 km.) in the north and east, by Laos (146 miles; 235 km.) and Thailand (1,119.5 miles; 1,800 km.) in the east, by the Indian Ocean in the south, by Bangladesh (120 miles; 193 km.) in the west and by India (909 miles;

The boundaries of Bangladesh, Bhutan and Myanmar

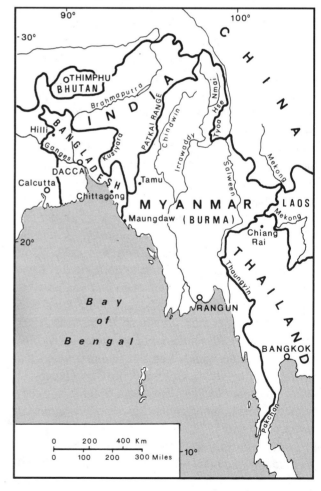

1,463 km.) in the west and north. Myanmar's capital is Rangoon.

The Burmans migrated south from Yunnan approximately 3,000 years ago. The first monarch, Kin Anawratha, set up a Burman kingdom in the eleventh century and made Theravada Buddhism the official religion of his kingdom. Two centuries later Kublai Khan's rule in the north shifted Burmese rule to its present location.

After three Anglo-Burman wars, Burma became a province of India under the British. During world War II, the Japanese conquered the country; in 1948 Burma became an independent state. The Union of Burma, now known as Myanmar, has been divided by ethnic strife and political unrest since gaining independence.

Currently, a military government maintains strict control over the country's fifteen states and provinces despite elections, which gave a majority of votes to the opposition.

MYANMAR — BANGLADESH   see BANGLADESH–MYANMAR.

MYANMAR — CHINA   see CHINA–MYANMAR.

MYANMAR — INDIA   see INDIA–MYANMAR.

MYANMAR —LOAS   see LOAS–MYANMAR.

MYANMAR — THAILAND   For its most part, the Myanmar–Thailand boundary follows mountain crests and *thalweg*s and has been demarcated. It runs 1,119.5 miles (1,800 km.) from the boundary junction with Laos on the upper Mekong River southward to the west coast of the Malay Peninsula.

Geographical Setting. Except for the Nam Kok Valley near the tripoint boundary junction with Laos and the Salween (Thaungyin) valley, the Myanmar–Thailand border is largely a mountain frontier. From the boundary junction in the northeast, the border follows the Nam Kok westward to its confluence with the Mai Sai, which it then follows west to the ridge that divides the drainage system of the Nam Mae Kham. The boundary then courses along a minor drainage divide between tributaries of the Nam Mae Kok, crossing the main river at about

The Myanmar–Thailand border follows mountain crests

20°04'03"N and 99°21'E. Continuing westward, the boundary joins the Salween–Mekong watershed. At the ridge line that forms the boundary between the Thai *changwad*s (provinces) of Chiang Mai and Mae Hong Song, the boundary departs from the main divide to follow a minor divide between the Salween and Nam Mae Pai rivers. At Loi Kangmong peak (5,280 feet; 1,610 m.), the boundary turns southward along the same minor watershed to cross Nam Mae Pai at approximately 19°13'30"N and 97°50'E. Continuing southward along the watershed, the boundary rejoins the major watershed near Doi Pratu Wiang. It then turns westward to join the Salween River at the northern limit of Karen State (Myanmar). For 81 miles (130 km.) to the confluence of the Salween River and Nam Mae Moei, the *thalweg* of the former constitutes the border. Then the *thalweg* of the Moei River is the border for 240 miles (386 km.). At its source, the main ridge of the Pa-wan Range serves to carry the border to the main watershed which is in turn followed southward to Mugadok Taung (Khao Mu Gatu) peak. The boundary is demarcated by eight straight-line vectors as it crosses the valleys of the Haugtharow and Megathat Chang. After rejoining the water divide, the boundary projects westward in a very narrow triangle to include the temple of Pra Ched Ong in Thailand before regaining the water divide. The ridge forms the Malay Peninsula's watershed as far south as Khao Daeng in the Chumphon province (Myanmar). Here the boundary bears southwestward to join the headwaters of the Pakchan River, which forms the boundary to the Andaman Sea.

Historical Background. The modern boundary between Myanmar and Thailand was created after the wars between British India and Burma between 1824 and 1886. With the incorporation of the Shan States in 1890, the whole of Burma became British. A convention between British India and Siam, ratified on 3 July 1868, defined the border of Siam and Tenasserim from the Salween River to the Andaman Sea. This was demarcated in 1892. Between 1889 and 1890 the border of the trans-Salween tract and the small states was laid down provisionally and demarcated as far as the Mekong River. The entire border was accepted by Siam in 1892 and, after final delineation and demarcation, recognized maps were exchanged (17 October 1894). In the 1930s the *thalweg* principle was applied to the sections of the border following the midstream of the Mae Sai and Pakchan rivers.

Two small parcels of detached territory on each side of the boundary were exchanged: Klong Wan and Wang Tow to Myanmar and Lan Kwai and See Sok to Thailand. In 1941, the Mae Sai river changed course and the *thalweg* of the new channel was accepted by both countries, provision being made for the boundary to remain along the *thalweg* in the event of future changes. The *thalweg* principle was also applied to the Mae Ruak (Nam Kok). In 1992, the National Legislative Assembly of Thailand approved a memorandum of understanding with Myanmar on a fixed boundary along the Mae Sai and Mae Rauk rivers as a permanent border line. This was ratified on 12 March 1992.

Present Situation. The border area is occupied by Karen guerrillas and is also the site of the Thai government's struggle against drug trafficking. The line itself is not disputed and plans were made in 1993 to open three border trading passes.

N

NAMIBIA A south African country (area: 317,939 sq. miles [823,144 sq. km.]; estimated population: 1,550,000 [1994]), Namibia is bounded in the north by Angola (855 miles; 1,376 km.) and Zambia (145 miles; 233 km.), in the east by Botswana (845 miles; 1,360 km.), in the east and south by South Africa (600 miles; 966 km.) and in the west by the Atlantic Ocean. Namibia also shares a boundary junction with Zimbabwe and, until 1994, had a South African enclave (Walvis Bay) on its Atlantic shore. The capital of Namibia is Windhoek.

Until World War I Namibia, which was then called South-West Africa, was under German colonial rule. In 1920 it became a mandate of the Union of South Africa. Following World War II the United Nations contested South Africa's continued control of the territory and opposed its integration into South Africa in the late 1960s. After a lengthy guerrilla war Namibia became independent in 1990. SWAPO (the South-West African People's Organization), a political force that emerged from the Namibian liberation movement, won the multi-party elections and formed the new state's government.

NAMIBIA — ANGOLA see ANGOLA–NAMIBIA.

NAMIBIA — BOTSWANA see BOTSWANA–NAMIBIA.

NAMIBIA — SOUTH AFRICA The boundary between Namibia and South Africa is 600 miles (966 km.) long and consists of a sector following the Orange River and a straight-line sector following the 20th meridian. It was demarcated by a joint Anglo-German boundary commission appointed in 1898. The boundary of the Walvis Bay enclave (within Namibia), which was surveyed and demarcated in 1885 and was 69 miles (111 km.) long, was abolished in 1994.

Geographical Setting. The Namibia–South Africa boundary begins at the mouth of the Orange River on the Atlantic seaboard. From there it follows the northern bank of the Orange River eastward inland for 348 miles (560 km.) until it reaches the 20°E meridian. The boundary then heads northward, following the meridian through the southern half of the Kalahari Desert for 253 miles (407 km.) until the boundary tripoint with Botswana is reached at the intersection of 20°E and the Nossob River.

Historical Background. In 1814 the Cape of Good Hope province was ceded to Britain by the Dutch. As a colony it was extended northward and eastward during the nineteenth century. Natal was made a separate British colony in 1857 and the Orange Free State and South African Republic (Transvaal) which had become independent were annexed as colonies during the Anglo-Boer war in 1900. On 31 May 1910 the Union of South Africa was created from the Cape of Good Hope, Natal, Transvaal and the the Orange Free State colonies. It became a sovereign state in 1931 and, after a referendum, was declared a republic on 31 May 1961.

In 1833, a German merchant obtained land concessions from a local chief on the coast of south-western Africa at Angra Pequena (Lüderitz), which extended from the northern bank of the Orange River to the 26th parallel and 20 miles (32 km.) inland. Germany claimed a protectorate over this area on 16 August 1884 and on 8 September 1884 also declared the coast north of the 26th parallel to Cape Fria to be under German protection, with the exception of the Walvis Bay area. Further expansion inland soon increased German South-West Africa to the present size of Namibia.

Germany ceded rights in its colonies to the Allies in the treaty of Versailles after World War I and on 17 December 1920 the administration of South-West Africa was mandated by the League of Nations to South Africa. After World war II and the dissolution of the League of Nations, the United Nations (UN) refused South Africa permission to annex South-West Africa, but South Africa refused to place the territory under a UN trusteeship agreement, claiming that the UN did not automatically replace the League of Nations. On 27 October 1966, the UN terminated South Africa's mandate, making South-West Africa a direct responsibility of the UN. By a UN resolution (12 June 1968), South-West Africa's name was changed to Namibia and in 1971 South Africa's presence there was declared illegal. On 7 August 1884 the Walvis Bay area (434 sq. miles; 1,124 sq. km.) was annexed by the Cape of Good Hope colony, remaining part of the Cape of Good Hope province and thereby eventually becoming part of South Africa. Laws were drafted in late 1993 to enable the Walvis bay area to be reintegrated into Namibia and the transfer took place in 1994.

Present Situation. The boundary between Namibia and South Africa has not been the subject of any claims.

NAMIBIA — ZAMBIA This boundary runs for 145 miles (233 km.) along the northern border of the Caprivi Strip from the quadripoint with Zimbabwe and Botswana in the east to the tripoint with Angola in the west. Roughly half of the boundary follows the Zambezi River and the rest is a straight-line sector.

Geographical Setting. From the boundary's quadripoint junction with Botswana and Zimbabwe at the confluence of the *thalweg* of the Chobe River with the Zambezi River, the boundary line runs west along the *thalweg* of the Zambezi to the center of the Katima Mulilo rapids. The islands of the Zambezi River, from the Chobe confluence upstream, are allocated such: Kankuma, the small island near it and Mpalela to Namibia; Nuntango to Zambia; Nansansi to Namibia; Ibozu, Kasuma, Lombe, Liabwelwa and Sipalandwe to Zambia; Kakomwe to Namibia; Kasange and Masulamini to Zambia; Nantungu to Namibia and the unnamed island opposite it to Zambia; Mabala and Kachila to Namibia; Nambezo to Zambia; Kasuntula and the unnamed island

near it to Namibia; Silombe, Mutonga, Kamili Muliata, Mangonda and Kampengule to Zambia; Kaytoya-ka-Musisanyane, Sikachila and the nameless island below it, Ngolongo and Likunganeno to Namibia; Lesser Isolionke to Zambia; and Greater Isolionke and Samasikili to Namibia. At the Katima Mulilo rapids, the point where the boundary leaves the river is marked by beacon no. 1 and seven further beacons mark the straight line that leads the boundary to beacon no. 9 at the Kwando River, where the boundary tripoint with Angola lies.

Historical Background. The Anglo-German Agreement of 1 July 1890 determining their respective spheres of influence in Africa limited German South-West Africa's eastern expansion to a line following the 18°S parallel until it met the Cuando (Kuando) River, which it then followed to the Zambezi River. This gave Germany access from South-West Africa to the Zambezi River by a strip of territory not less than 20 miles (32 km.) wide. This agreement established the southern border of the Caprivi Strip. Its northern edge was created in the German-Portuguese Declaration of 30 December 1886, which drew a straight-line from the borders of the Andara (Namibia) village on the Okavango River eastward to the Katima Mulilo rapids. The border between the Portuguese and British lands was established in the treaty of 11 June 1891, but at that time the western limits of Barotseland (British) were unknown. The line from the Katima Mulilo rapids was ascertained when the border between Zambia and Angola was moved west, from the Zambezi to the Kwando River to accommodate Barotseland, by an arbitral award of 1905, and from 1930 to 1931 a joint boundary commission surveyed and demarcated the straight line between the Zambezi and Okavango rivers. The resultant delimitation was approved in the tripartite (British-German-Portuguese) agreement signed on 16 August 1931.

Sovereignty of the islands in the Zambezi river in the sector downstream from the Katima Mulilo rapids was determined by a joint commission from Northern Rhodesia and South Africa according to the *thalweg* of the river and the consequential allocation of islands. German South-West Africa was administered under a League of Nations mandate by South Africa from 1920. When South Africa's request to incorporate South-West Africa was rejected by the United Nations General Assembly, South Africa refused to enter into a trusteeship with the UN and in 1949 stopped drawing up mandate reports. Growing international concern for the status of Namibia and the rise of organized protest inside the country forced the UN to terminate South Africa's mandate in 1966 and to place Namibia under its own immediate control. The situation was complicated by South African involvement in Angola, but by 1989 Namibia was able to hold elections in which the SWAPO Party gained a majority. The country achieved independence on 21 March 1990 and on 28 February 1994 Walvis Bay was returned to Namibian sovereignty.

Present Situation. Both Namibia and Zambia adopted and recognized the colonial boundary without dispute.

NAURU (Naoero)   An independent South Pacific island, Nauru is located north of the Solomon Islands. Its area is 8.1 sq. miles (21 sq. km.) and it has an estimated population (1994) of 10,000. Nauru has no land boundaries. Its capital is Yaren District.

A Micronesian-speaking people of mixed Micronesian, Melanesian and Polynesian descent inhabit Nauru. Formerly a joint trust territory of Australia, New Zealand and the United Kingdom, Nauru won independence in 1968. The island contains some of the richest and most highly developed phosphate deposits in the Pacific Ocean, but these are expected to be exhausted in the near future, and the current decline in production is the islanders' most significant economic problem.

NEPAL   A landlocked Asian country (area: 56,827 sq. miles [147,125 sq. km.]; estimated population: 20,400,000 [1994]), Nepal is bounded by China (768 miles; 1,236 km.) in the north and by India (1,050 miles; 1,690 km.) in the east, south and west. Nepal's capital is Kathmandu.

Having successfully resisted British colonization in the early nineteenth century, Nepal remained relatively closed to international influence until the 1950s, with the opening of borders to trade and travel.

Despite legislation in 1963 abolishing the Hindu caste system, caste hierarchy remains a dominant factor in the socioeconomic life of the Nepali. Many

occupations, such as haircutting, butchering and goldsmithing continue to be carried out by traditional lineage groups. The Newari (who are not a caste but a distinct Nepali ethnic group) continue to dominate in crafts based on a technique of metal casting originally developed by them.

NEPAL — CHINA   see CHINA–NEPAL.

NEPAL — INDIA   see INDIA–NEPAL.

NETHERLANDS (Nederland)   A Western European country (area: 16,139 sq. miles [41,785 sq. km.]; estimated population: 15,200,000 [1994]), Netherlands is bounded in the east by Germany (359 miles; 577 km.), in the south by Belgium (280 miles; 450 km.) and in the west and north by the North Sea. It also shares a boundary with France in the small Caribbean island of Sint Maarten. It has two capitals: Amsterdam and the Hague.

The Dutch descend from three West Germanic populations, Frisians, Franks and Saxons, who in the eighth century adopted Christianity. The Dutch remained an undefined collection of fiefs of the Holy Roman Empire until attached, in the fifteenth century, to the Burgundians' burgeoning territories. Under the Habsburgs, absolutism, religious persecution of Protestants and economic exploitation triggered a successful anti-Spanish revolt which gave rise to the United Provinces, the Dutch political entity, in 1579.

The Dutch built their prosperity on mercantile shipping in Scandinavia and profited from the shift of trade routes from the Mediterranean to the Atlantic to create a network of colonies in the East and West Indies. The influx of a Flemish cultural elite helped make the seventeenth century Holland's Golden Age, when art, science and tolerant humanistic thought flourished despite Calvinist intolerance.

Spain succeeded in restoring Catholicism to the southern Dutch provinces, which became part of the Netherlands in 1648. The Rhine-Meuse delta has since remained a major divide between the Catholic south and the Protestant north.

By the end of the seventeenth century the Dutch had lost their great power status. Economic revival later in the nineteenth century precipitated internal social tensions. Together with the emancipation of the Catholics, these developments gave birth to a

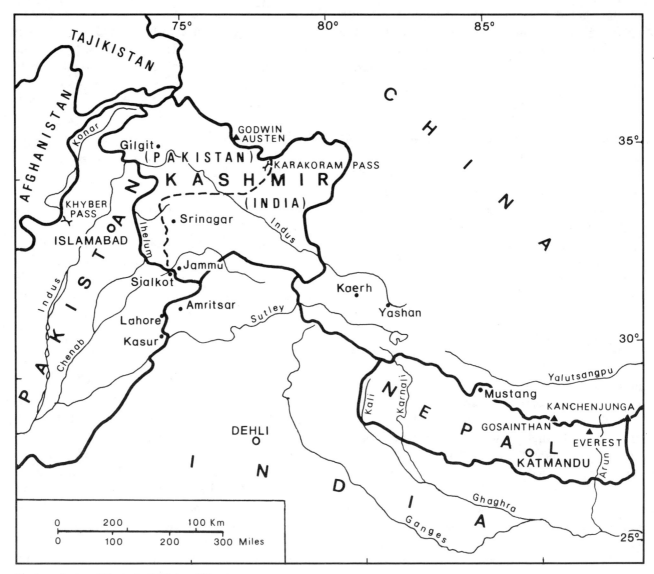

The boundaries of Kashmir (India) and Nepal

unique arrangement of four "pillars": Protestant, Catholic, liberal and socialist, which were in fact complex, closed subcultures, each with its separate parties, schools, trade unions, media, etc. Cross-contact was minimal, and allocations were decided by negotiations and compromises between each pillar's elites. This power-sharing system survived until the 1960s.

The 1970s saw the influx of 500,000 foreign workers, who created a conglomerate of minorities. Although racist antiforeigner movements such as those manifested in neighboring countries have hardly taken root among the indigenous Dutch, integration cannot be said to have been very successful to date.

NETHERLANDS — BELGIUM see BELGIUM–NETHERLANDS.

NETHERLANDS — GERMANY see GERMANY–NETHERLANDS.

NETHERLANDS ANTILLES (Nederlandse Antillen) A group of islands that form a self-governing Dutch territory, Netherlands Antilles is situated in the Caribbean Sea. Its total land area is 309 sq. miles (800 sq. km.) with an estimated population (1994) of 200,000. It has no land boundaries. The capital of Netherlands Antilles is Willemstad.

The Spaniards landed on Curaçao in 1499, and had also claimed Aruba and Bonaire, then inhabited

The Netherlands is bounded by Belgium, Germany and the North Sea

by peaceful Arawak, by 1527. The Dutch, who had set up colonies among the less peaceful Carib inhabitants (subsequently exterminated) of the Windward Islands, did not arrive in Curaçao until 1643; their hold over the "ABCs" was not fully consolidated until 1845, when the Netherlands Antilles came into formal existence. Curaçao, a Caribbean center of the slave trade, suffered a severe economic downturn when, in 1863, Holland decreed emanicipation in its colonies. Netherlands Antilleans did not recover until the discovery of oil in Venezuela in the early 1900s turned Aruba and Curaçao into important refining and transhipment centers. Refining Venezuelan oil was the major base of the islanders' economy until very recently. The people of these islands, who became an integral part of the Netherlands in 1954, have been assuming increasing autonomy in domestic decisions since the occurrence of severe, partly racial, internal disturbances in the 1970s and 1980s.

NEW CALEDONIA   A South Pacific island, New Caledonia is a French overseas territory. Its area is 7,175 sq. miles (18,576 sq. km.) with no land boundaries. New Caledonia has an estimated population (1994) of 180,000 and its capital is Nouméa.

New Caledonia became a French possession in 1853 and a French overseas territory in 1946. Since then the local Kanak have made numerous attempts to achieve independence, resisted by French settlers who remain loyal to the French republic.

New Caledonia has been strongly influenced by the presence of large scale mining enterprises of nickel, cobalt and chromium, discovered on the islands in the nineteenth century. New Caledonia has the largest known nickel deposits in the world, accounting for about 30% of the world's known reserves. After mining, tourism is the most important sector of the economy. The New Caledonian economy benefits from its status as a French overseas territory in association with the European Economic Community.

NEW ZEALAND   A country in the South Pacific Ocean, New Zealand has an area of 103,562 sq. miles (268,122 sq. km.) and an estimated population (1994) of 3,400,000. Its capital is Wellington. New Zealand has no land boundaries.

New Zealand underwent various waves of settlement before officially becoming part of the British Empire in the 1840s. The ever-increasing demand of European settlers for land was a major factor in promoting conflict between the local Maori and the Europeans during the nineteenth century. The 1840 Treaty of Waintangi between the British and most major Maori chiefs acknowledged, without really protecting, Maori land rights.

New Zealand played an increasingly important role in the South Pacific Islands after joining the South Pacific Commission as a founder member in 1947. It administered the United Nations Trust Territory of Western Samoa until the latter's independence in 1962 and assisted the Cook Islands in achieving self-government. New Zealand has a say in the affairs of Niue and Tokelau, and provides economic and administrative support to the tiny British territory of Pitcairn Island.

Traditionally the economy relied on a narrow range of primary export products, including dairy products, meat and wool. In 1990–1991 agriculture accounted for more than 60% of New Zealand's total exports. Manufacturing employs about 20% of New Zealanders, one-fifth of whom work in processing primary products.

NICARAGUA   A Central American country, Nicaragua is bounded in the north by Honduras (573 miles; 922 km.), in the east by the Caribbean Sea, in the south by Costa Rica (192 miles; 309 km.) and in the west by the Pacific Ocean. Its area is 50,054 sq. miles (129,640 sq. km.) and it has an estimated population (1994) of 4,200,000. The capital of Nicaragua is Managua.

Nicaragua was discovered by Columbus in 1502 on his last voyage to the New World, but permanent settlements were not founded by the Spaniards until 1524. With the end of the War of Independence in 1821, Nicaragua was annexed to the Mexican empire under Emperor Augustin Iturbide. In 1823, when the empire collapsed, Nicaragua formed a political union with Costa Rica, Honduras and El Salvador, which lasted only until 1838, when Nicaragua gained political independence. In the early twentieth century, however, Nicaragua became effectively an economic dependency of the United States, which supported the Somosa family dictatorship until Sandinista forces took power in the late 1970s after sustained civil war. Initially favorable to the new regime, which achieved world renown for its remarkable literacy campaign and efforts at land reform, the United States turned against the Sandinistas, supporting Somocista and counter-Sandinista forces (called "Contras") throughout the 1980s. The Sandinistas were ousted in free elections at the end of that decade.

NICARAGUA — COSTA RICA   see COSTA RICA–NICARAGUA.

NICARAGUA — HONDURAS   see HONDURAS–NICARAGUA.

NIGER   A landlocked west African country (area: 494,920 sq. miles [1,281,350 sq. km.]; estimated population: 8,500,000 [1994]), Niger is bounded in the north by Algeria (594 miles; 956 km.) and Libya (220 miles; 354 km.), in the east by Chad (730 miles; 1,175 km.), in the south by Nigeria (930 miles; 1,497 km.) and Benin (165 miles; 266 km.), in the southwest by Burkina Faso (390 miles; 628 km.) and in the west by Mali (510 miles; 821 km.). Niger's capital is Niamey.

The people of Niger gained independence from the French in August 1960. In the decolonization period two main parties competed for power: the Parti Progressiste Nigerien led by Hamani Diori eventually gained control of the new state and banned all opposition parties. Diori was overthown in a military coup in 1974.

Since independence there have been a series of ethnic incidents in the Tuareg region in the north of the country.

In 1984 a large number of Tuareg were expelled from Niger. In 1990 ethnic unrest resurfaced following the return to Niger of many Tuareg who had migrated to Libya and Algeria in the early 1980s to escape the drought. These incidents were caused by Tuareg dissatisfaction with the fact that the leader who came to power in 1987, Ali Saibou, did not fulfill his promise to rehabilitate the Tuareg who returned to Niger.

NIGER — ALGERIA   see ALGERIA–NIGER.

NIGER — BENIN   see BENIN–NIGER.

NIGER — BURKINA FASO   see BURKINA FASO–NIGER.

NIGER — CHAD   see CHAD–NIGER.

NIGER — LIBYA   see LIBYA–NIGER.

NIGER — MALI   see MALI–NIGER.

NIGER — NIGERIA   Demarcated by pillars and by the Komadugu/Yobe River, this boundary runs 930 miles (1,497 km.) from the boundary tripoint with Benin to the tripoint with Chad.

Geographical Setting. From the boundary tripoint with Benin, at the median point in the Niger River, the border crosses to the Foga (Dallau Mauri) valley through several points located on international roads. Then it runs northeast and north parallel to and 6 miles (10 km.) east of the road from Bengu to Matankari. (In 1910 it was found, at beacon no. 32, that the village of Kauara had been administered from Matankari and the boundary was moved south to leave it in Niger. An area of 83 sq. miles [216 sq. km.] was included in Nigeria and marked by beacons 33 and 34.) At a point 6 miles (10 km.) east of the cairn on Budu Hill, the boundary follows four straight lines before following a line parallel to and 3 miles (5 km.) south of the road from Bazaga to Malbaza, passing through Massalata, Birni-N'Konni (Niger), Tierassa and Sarnawa to a point 3 miles (5 km.) south of Malbaza. It runs straight via beacons 52 to 55 to a point 3 miles (5 km.) north of Antudu on the road from Wurnu to Sabon Birni and then reaches a point 6 miles (9 km.) from the center of Sabon Birni. At beacons 58 and 59, an area of 17 sq. miles (43 sq. km.) was annexed to Nigeria to include three small villages that were dependent upon Sabon Birni. The demarcation committee found no direct road, as described in the convention, between Sansanne-Aisa and Chibiri and so set that section of the boundary equidistant between them, creating a deflection of 110 sq. miles (285 sq. km.) and marked it with beacons 61 and 62. The boundary runs south of the Sultanate of Maradi in three straight lines without extending south of the 13°N parallel and crosses the Maradi–Katsina road halfway between Kandavai and Katsina. It then continues in a straight line to a point on the road from Katsina to Tessawa equidistant from Gida N'Duma and Yenkeisga. From a point on the Gallo-Raffa road, the boundary heads toward a point 3 miles (5 km.) southwest of Regia Mata, where it follows a line parallel to and 3 miles (5 km.) southwest of the road from Regia Mata to Zango as far as a point 4.3 miles (7 km.) west of the center of Zango. Then the line bisects the Zango-Gemi and Zango-Dumbi roads and continues to pass through points 5 miles (8 km.) northeast of Sara, 8 miles (13 km.) northeast of Shadere, 6 miles (10 km.) northeast of Dasha, 4.9 miles (7.8 km.) north of Baoure, 4.3 miles (6.9 km.) north and then 4.3 miles (6.9 km.) northeast of Bure, 3 miles

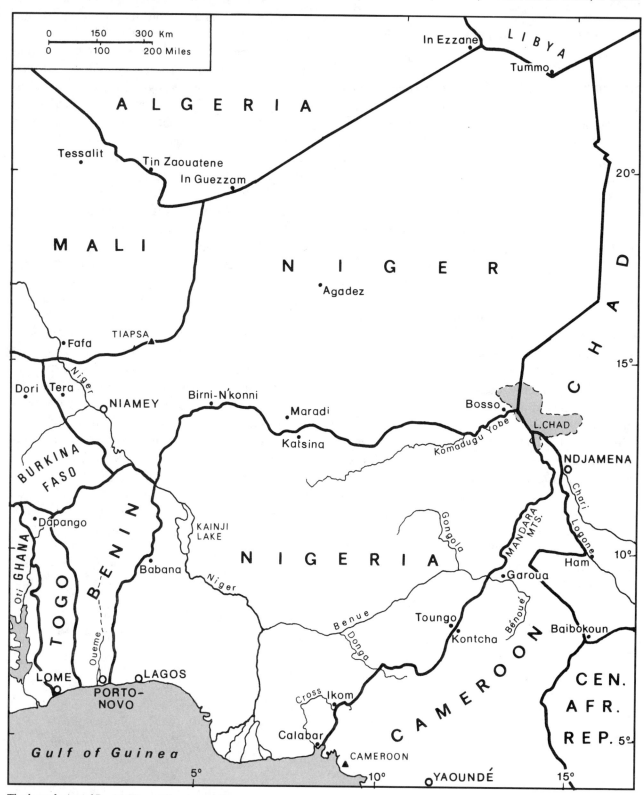

The boundaries of Benin, Niger, Nigeria and Togo

(5 km.) south of Karagua (at about 12°48'N and 9°37'E) and then 3 miles (5 km.) east of it and 3 miles (5 km.) west of the center of Bilamgari. Between beacons 93 and 101 various small deflections were made, allocating Angua Dala to Nigeria and Danchalci to Niger. The boundary then bisects a number of specified roads and runs to a point 3 miles (5 km.) south of Zumba. From there the boundary forms a line parallel to and 3 miles (5 km.) south of the road from Gurselik to Adabur until it meets the *thalweg* of the Komadugu/Yobe River, which it follows to Lake Chad. From the mouth of Komadugu/Yobe straight to 13°42'N and 13°38'20"E the boundary meets its terminus, east of the town of Bosso (Niger) at the boundary tripoint with Chad.

Historical Background. On 5 August 1890, the French and British established their respective spheres of influence in northwest Africa in a declaration that drew a boundary between them from Say on the Niger River in a straight line to Lake Chad. This was modified in 1898, beginning much further south on the Niger River and forming arcs and astronomical parallels. When the Royal Niger Company surrendered its charter in 1899 the British government assumed control, annexing the company's territorial acquisitions in the south to the Niger Coast Protectorate. This was renamed the Protectorate of Southern Nigeria. The company's holdings to the north became the Protectorate of Northern Nigeria. In 1901, the French created the military territory of Niger in French West Africa with its headquarters in Zinder. An Anglo-French convention of 8 April 1904 revised the boundary and, although the line was subject to changes in both the convention of 29 May 1906 and the agreement of 19 February 1910, was substantially the foundation of the modern boundary. On 1 January 1914, the two British protectorates were united to create a single state called the Colony and Protectorate of Nigeria. However, the Federation of Nigeria was proclaimed on 1 October 1954 and in 1960 Nigeria became independent. Niger became a colony in 1922, an overseas territory in 1946, an autonomous member of the French Community in 1958 and an independent state on 3 August 1960.

Present Situation. Niger and Nigeria adopted the colonial boundary as their common international boundary without a formal agreement.

NIGERIA   The most populated African country (area: 356,669 sq. miles [923,416 sq. km.]; estimated population: 92,800,000 [1994]), Nigeria is situated in western Africa and is bounded in the north by Niger (930 miles; 1,497 km.), northeast by Chad (54 miles; 87 km.), east by Cameroon (1,050 miles; 1,690 km.), south by the Gulf of Guinea in the South Atlantic Ocean and west by Benin (480 miles; 773 km.). The present capital of Nigeria is Abuja; Lagos served as its capital until recently.

The Nigerians became independent from British colonial rule in October 1960. During the colonial period the British divided Nigeria into three regions. The north, in which the Hausa-Fulani were the main ethnic group, was the largest and dominant region. The British did not allow missionaries to act among the Hausa-Fulani, and so Islam remained strong in the region. However, as the missions were the only way of receiving western education the Hausa-Fulani lagged behind the two other major ethnic groups of Nigeria, the Yoruba in the west and the Ibo in the east.

During decolonization the political parties in Nigeria were formed along ethnic lines and the political struggle soon became ethnic. After independence the Hausa-Fulani dominated Nigerian politics, but they feared competition with the southern people, especially the Ibo, who arrived in the north in large numbers to seek jobs. As a result discriminatory measures were applied. These ethnic tensions intensified during the 1960s and in 1966 some 30,000 Ibo were massacred in the north by the Hausa-Fulani. Following the massacre 2,000,000 Ibo, who had been dispersed all over Nigeria, fled to their original homeland in the southeast. In May 1967 the Ibo declared independence from Nigeria and their region became the Republic of Biafra.

This act resulted in a war that lasted two and a half years, during which thousands of soldiers on both sides were killed and about 1,000,000 Ibo died of starvation in Biafra. The war ended in 1970 with Biafra becoming part of Nigeria again.

After the war there were attempts to weaken the ethnic tensions in Nigeria by dividing the existing regions into smaller units that would cut across ethnic lines.

In 1968 Nigeria adopted a federal structure comprising 12 states; in 1976 seven more states were added, and another two were added in 1987. Although Nigeria's ethnic problems were not completely solved, the new federal structure contributed greatly to the lessening of ethnic conflicts. At the beginning of the 1990s the Nigerian government started a hesitant democratization process, allowing the creation of a two-party system. In order to ease ethnic tensions before the elections, nine more states were added in 1991, making a total of 30 states. The president denied allegations that the real purpose of this move was to postpone the elections.

NIGERIA — BENIN see BENIN–NIGERIA.

NIGERIA — CAMEROON see CAMEROON–NIGERIA.

NIGERIA — CHAD see CHAD–NIGERIA.

NIGERIA — NIGER see NIGER–NIGERIA.

NIUE The South Pacific island of Niue has free association with New Zealand. Its area is 14 sq. miles (36 sq. km.) and it has an estimated population (1994) of 1,600. Niue has no land boundaries and its capital is Alofi.

The islanders are mainly Protestants. Niue Island possesses a limited amount of natural resources, and copra, tropical fruits and high quality honey constitute its most important products.

NORFOLK ISLAND This island, located east of Australia, is an external territory of Australia. Its area is 14 sq. miles (36 sq. km.) and its estimated population (1994) is 2,700. The capital of Norfolk Island is Kingston and it has no land boundaries.

NORTHERN MARIANA ISLANDS The Northern Marianas is an archipelago in the Pacific Ocean that forms a commonwealth in union with USA. The islands have a total land area of 184 sq. miles (477 sq. km.) and an estimated population (1994) of 23,000. The Northern Marianas' capital is Saipan and it has no land boundaries.

The economy of the Northern Mariana Islands is dominated by tourism; agriculture is based on small holdings and the important crops are coconuts, breadfruit, tomatoes and melons.

NORWAY A northern European country (area: 149,469 sq. miles [386,975 sq. km.]; estimated population: 4,300,000 [1994]), Norway is bounded in the northeast by Russia (122 miles; 196 km.) and Finland (453 miles; 729 km.), in the east by Sweden (1,006 miles; 1,619 km.) and in the south and west by the Atlantic Ocean. The capital of Norway is Oslo.

In the eighth century petty kings commanding oligarchies of peasants-landowners colonized the mountainous regions of coastal Scandinavia. The first unified monarchy was established in the ninth century. However, limited arable land resulted in overpopulation, the peasantry was displaced by an emerging aristocracy and the new aristocrats were dissatisfied with the monarchy. These factors, combined with technical advances in shipping, caused many Norwegians to embark on Viking expeditions of conquest and discovery. England and Scotland were terrorized by Viking raiders; in northern France and Sicily they established Norman rule. In expeditions to the east, the Faeroe Islands, Iceland and Greenland were settled.

In 1030 the Norwegians officially adopted Christianity. Soon after, they became implicated in a series of inter-Scandinavian conflicts, in which independence was asserted and a strong hereditary monarchy was established. In 1397 the Union of Kalmar united Norway with Sweden and Denmark, creating what appeared to be a major power in northern Europe, but the ensuing period was catastrophic. Plague decimated the population, while the combined onslaught of the Danish monarchy and German merchants virtually eradicated the local aristocracy. Large numbers of Danes settled the country, establishing their own aristocracy there.

Growing European demands for shipping timber permitted some economic growth in the sixteenth century, while throughout the following centuries, urban entrepreneurs profited from fishing and whaling. In order to export their wood and fish, Norwegians started building their own merchant marine— it was to grow into the world's third largest. Denmark's implication in the Napoleonic Wars finally opened the way to dissolve the Union of Kalmar in 1809; despite a clamour for independence, however, the Norwegians were forced into a union with Sweden.

Throughout the nineteenth century economic expansion continued to fuel the Norwegians' longing for total independence, while the emergence of a national literature emancipated the Norwegian language from Danish influence. From the middle of the nineteenth century tensions mounted as the independence movement became more vocal. The Kingdom of Norway was proclaimed in 1905, but by then some 700,000 Norwegians migrated to North America. Despite its declaration of neutrality, Norway was occupied by Nazi Germany in 1940; following World War II a vast reconstruction program was begun and social-democratic governments developed an extensive social security system. From the 1970s, exploitation of North Sea oil further enriched the Norwegians. At the same time progressive redistribution policies remained in force.

Only in the 1980s did inflation and unemployment erode the Norwegian welfare state, enabling the conservatives to take over the reins of government.

NORWAY — FINLAND   see FINLAND–NORWAY.

NORWAY — RUSSIA   The boundary between Norway and Russia served for many years as one of the most strategic international boundaries, as it was one of only two boundaries that the Western World had in common with the Soviet Union (the second being the Turkey–Soviet Union boundary). Only 122 miles (196 km.) long, it was used by NATO forces to maintain direct communication with mainland USSR.

Geographical Setting. The boundary extends from the Finnish tripoint at Krokfjell and the Varanger Fjord in the Barents Sea in the Arctic Ocean. From the tripoint in the south it runs 4 miles (6.5 km.) southeastward across the Pasvikelv River, giving Norway control over both banks of the river in that area. Then turning northeastward, the boundary runs 67 miles (108 km.), joining the *thalweg* (the main navigation channel) of the Pasvikelv River. The river's islands are allocated to Russia or Norway by their positions to the east or west of the *thalweg*, respectively. The boundary departs from the river westward, to include in Russia the former Russian mission station in the village of Boris Gleb, and circumventing the village for about 6 miles (9.5 km.) the line allots both banks of the Pasvikelv River in

that area to Russian control. Continuing southeastward and then eastward in a series of straight lines for 16.5 miles (26.5 km.), the boundary crosses small lakes, local streams and marshes to reach the Jakobslev River. Joining the *thalweg* of that river, the line follows it for 26.7 miles (43 km.) to its mouth in the Varanger Fjord at boundary pillar no. 415 (69°47'46.16"N and 30°49'9.85"E).

Historical Background. One of the oldest stabilized boundary lines in Europe, the Norway–Russia boundary was established in 1826 by the Convention of Petersburg between Sweden, then holding Norway, and Russia. The circumvention of Boris Gleb dates directly from this convention. In 1885, the Haparanda Convention between Sweden and Russia clarified some of the problems that had evolved from the 1826 delimitation. The establishment of Norway as an independent state in October 1905 did not change the location of the boundary; nor did the transfer of the border area into independent Finland in 1918 or its return to the USSR in 1944. The final Soviet-Norwegian protocol, signed

Norway's boundary with Russia

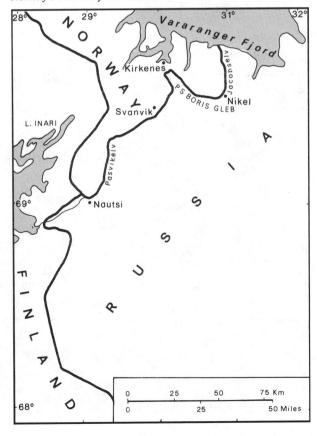

in Moscow on 18 December 1947, constitutes an agreement for the demarcation of the state frontier. Boundary marks, 415 in number, were detailed and the modern boundary, with only a few modifications of the 1826 boundary, was created. This protocol came into force on 23 May 1949 by an exchange of notes between the two states. In accordance with a protocol signed on 24 December 1963, land in the Soviet Union has been made available for use by Norway at two sites for the operation of a power station, while land in Norway, near Boris Gleb, has been made available for the Soviet Union for the same needs.

The creation of modern Russia in 1991 did not change the line either, and the boundary still held to its 1826 position.

Present Situation. There are no known disputes concerning the location of the boundary between the two countries.

NORWAY — SWEDEN One of the oldest boundary lines, still existing from the mid seventeenth century—this boundary is 1,006 miles (1,619 km.) long. It extends from the boundary tripoint with Finland at the head of the Signal valley in the north to

Idde Fjord in the Skagerrak Strait between the North Sea and the Baltic Sea.

Geographical Setting. From the boundary tripoint at the head of the Signal valley, the Norway–Sweden boundary runs southwestward and mainly follows the watershed between the Atlantic Ocean in the west and the Baltic Sea in the east. It runs about 25 miles (40 km.) westward and 60 miles (100 km.) southward and then courses parallel to Torne Lake (Sweden) to reach and cross the Narvik (Norway)–Malmberget (Sweden) railway. It runs southward for 40 miles (65 km.), passes east of the Storsteinspeak of Norway (6,209 feet; 1,893 m.) and continues southwestward along the watershed. It passes through Rago Peak (4,264 feet; 1300 m.) and passes east of Suliskongen Peak (6,255 feet; 1907 m.), which is the highest point along the boundary line. Continuing southwestward, the boundary line follows the watershed up to Jetnam Peak (4,962 feet; 1,513 m.) and then traverses east of the watershed, crossing some of the upper tributaries of the rivers that run toward the Baltic Sea, mainly to place the Lierne region within Norway. Thus, the Muru and the Lenglingen lakes and the Ingendola Rivers of the Baltic Sea river system belong to Norway.

Norway–Sweden border crossing point

The boundary crosses Rengen Lake, which is the source of the Swedish Indols River, and runs through some other small lakes in that area, northeast of the Norwegian city of Trondheim. South of Lierne region the boundary heads southward, following the watershed up to the Femund Lake area east of Roros (Norway).

All the Femund Basin, which runs eastward along the Trysilelva River into Sweden, is left with Norway. The boundary continues its southern direction along the watershed between the Glama River, the main river in south Norway, and the rivers that run in Sweden toward the Baltic Sea. Here and there it leaves the watershed and bears eastward so as to leave within Norway some areas inhabited by Norwegian people. Thus Rogden Lake, which runs into the Baltic Sea, and Makern Lake, are left in Norway. The boundary line crosses the Arvika (Sweden)–Kongsvinger (Norway) railway and in the far south it crosses the Store Le lake as well as a small lake located north of the Norwegian town of Komsjo. South of that town the boundary turns westward, to meet the river that runs into the Idde Fjord, follows it to the fjord south of the Norwegian town of Halden, and runs through the center of the fjord up to Skagerrak Strait so as to leave the island of Hvaler with Norway.

Historical Background. Norway, which up to the fourteenth century was an independent state, was united with Sweden and Denmark by the Union of Kalmar in 1397, to the east of the Skagerrak and Kattegat straits. In the peace treaty with Denmark, which was signed in 1660, the present boundaries between Denmark (including Norway) and Sweden were established. Sweden occupied Norway in January 1814.

The Norwegians resisted but the Swedish army forced them to accept a union with Sweden, although the Norwegians held to their territory and internal affairs. Norway became independent by leaving Sweden peacefully in 1905. Sweden accepted the separation and demilitarized the boundary line, which was never changed.

Present Situation. The boundary that was established in the mid-seventeenth century still exists. It was not demarcated, but the 330 years of stability established a well known line, which is respected by both sides.

There are no disputes concerning the alignment of the boundary, which is quite peaceful.

O

OMAN ('Uman) A Middle Eastern country (area: 82,061 sq. miles [212,457 sq. km.]; estimated population: 1,650,000 [1994]) in the Arabian Peninsula, Oman is bounded in the northwest by the United Arab Emirates (336 miles; 540 km.), in the east and south by the Arabian Sea, southwest by Yemen (179 miles; 288 km.) and west by Saudi Arabia (420 miles; 676 km.). Its capital is Muscat.

In the fourteenth and fifteenth centuries, Omani merchants traded caravan goods overseas from the port of Suhar. From 1508 to 1650, Muscat (Masqat) was in the hands of the Portuguese, who used it on their way to Goa. In the eighteenth century Ibn Saud consolidated Arab power in Zanzibar and on the east African coast. The slave trade brought Oman prosperity, and an alliance of traders and rulers was able to transform Muscat into a major Indian Ocean power and the leading port of the Persian Gulf. During the zenith of Oman's power (1800–1860) many Omanis migrated to Zanzibar, and for a time, the island was the center of Oman's commercial empire. In 1856, however, it lost Zanzibar and the slave islands off the east African coast, while Britain's proscription of the traffic in slaves and arms led to prolonged economic depression.

In the 1930s Oman's rulers tried to prevent social unrest by imposing medieval isolation on the state. In 1970, when a Dhofar secessionist movement, supported by South Yemen, threatened the country's integrity, the sultan cautiously opened up his country to outside influence.

The rebels were defeated in 1973; that same year Oman experienced a boom in oil production. Reserves, however, are meager and alternative sources of future income are uncertain.

OMAN — SAUDI ARABIA The Oman–Saudi Arabia boundary is 420 miles (676 km.) long, arching southeastward and southwestward from the boundary tripoint with the United Arab Emirates to the tripoint with Yemen.

Geographical Setting. The boundary between Oman and Saudi Arabia takes the form of three straight lines. From Umm az Zumul at the boundary tripoint with the United Arab Emirates in the north, which is at 22°42'30"N and 55°12'30"E, the boundary runs to the intersection of 22°N and 55°40'E. Then it reaches the intersection of 20°N and 55°E and ends at the intersection of 19°N and 52°E at the boundary tripoint with Yemen.

Historical Background. Oman has been an independent sultanate since the ninth century but was under Persia from the thirteenth to sixteenth centuries and conquered by the Portuguese in 1508. After expelling the Portuguese in 1650, the sultan went on to seize Portugal's east African territories north of Mozambique. Oman and the fortified city of Muscat had enormous strategic power at the height of the Indian and Far Eastern shipping trade with Europe. From 1891 it was a British protectorate and a military presence was maintained there until 1977. In 1970 Muscat and Oman changed its name to Oman.

During the sixteenth century the Ottoman Empire ruled Arabia, although it permitted a degree of local autonomy. One of the most powerful and prestigious local rulers was the sherif of Mecca. He governed as far south as Yemen and, in 1914, was promised independence by Lord Kitchener (in return for the sherif's support against the Turks). Thus, the Kingdom of Hejaz became an independent entity under the Treaty of Sèvres in 1920. Meanwhile, on the other side of the peninsula, the authority of Ibn Saud, ruler of the Nejd, was fully recognized by the government of India. War between the two kingdoms resulted in the victory of IbnSaud in 1926. In 1932 the combined countries were named the United Kingdom of Saudi Arabia. The discovery of oil in the region necessitated definition and demarcation of boundaries through the country, which was sparsely populated. The Buraimi Oasis on the frontier between Saudi Arabia and Oman was claimed by Saudi Arabia in 1949 and occupied in 1952. Saudi Arabia's claim was primarily on the grounds that the inhabitants of Buraimi had paid the *zakat* tax to Saudi rulers, an act that in itself constituted an acknowledgment of sovereignty. Arbitration of an agreement in 1954 was broken by British military action and relations between Saudi Arabia and the British occupiers of Oman deteriorated further after the British suppression of an Omani rebellion. Upon gaining independence, Oman's relations with Saudi Arabia improved and on 23 February 1982 Oman and Saudi Arabia signed a security pact—putting aside their territorial disputes, including the Buraimi Oasis issue. A border agreement between these countries was signed on 24 Sha'ban 1410 (21 March 1990) at Hafr al-Batin, providing for the survey and demarcation of the boundary by an independent specialist company under the supervision of a joint committee. It further provided for signs, border authorities and the rights of local inhabitants to nomadic migration, pasture and water resources.

Present Situation. From 1990 onward this demarcated boundary has not been in dispute.

OMAN — UNITED ARAB EMIRATES

OMAN — UNITED ARAB EMIRATES This boundary, in total 336 miles (540 km.) long, is divided into two sections. One crosses the Musandam peninsula from the Persian (Arabian) Gulf to the Gulf of Oman while the other, forming the western border of mainland Oman, extends from the Gulf of Oman some 10 miles (16 km.) south of Kalba to the boundary tripoint with Saudi Arabia at Umm az Zumul. There are also enclaves of the sultanate within the United Arab Emirates and of the United Arab Emirates within Oman.

Geographical Setting. The Musandam peninsula boundary separates it from the Emirate of Ras al Khaimah. From the Gulf of Oman in the southeast it follows the watercourse that separates Dibah al-Hisn from Dibah al-Bayah and turns west to follow the route from Dibah to Khatt and Ras al Khaimah until it reaches the country of the Habus people. There it heads northward and leaving the Habus country to the west, in the United Arab Emirates, crosses the slopes above Rams, Khur Khuwair, Ghalilah and Sha'am. It then turns west, enclosing a group of Dhahuriyins before arriving at the Gulf at the headland of al-Qir.

The eastern boundary of Oman proper, between the sultanate and the emirates of Ajman, Dubai and Abu Dhabi, includes the enclaves of Hatta (Dubai) and Masfut (Ajman). The boundary of Hatta was agreed upon in May 1959 and runs from Jabal Mussaya to Jabal Hajarain, then east across Wadi Qima to the east of the Qima village and to the base of Jabal Gimha, which is included in Dubai territory. It crosses the wadi mouths at Hasat al Ghara, al-Akhbab and Lawshaht and trends across Wadi Wayaya to the west of Oman's border post. It then meets and follows the watershed between the Qur and Hatta wadis and at Jabal Ghallas turns south to find Jabal Mussaya once again.

The Madha enclave in the United Arab Emirates is on the Dubai–Hatta road in the emirate of Sharjah and covers approximately 29 sq. miles (75 sq. km.). Within the Madha enclave is another enclave (Nahwa) belonging to Sharjah. The boundary of the Madha enclave was settled in 1969.

The boundary with Abu Dhabi runs from a point north of Shaab al Ghaf westward, through the Sabkah Thuwaimah, leaving Naqa al Hauz in Abu Dhabi. It then bears northward to the Husn Siqqiya and continues in straight lines westward to the Jizaat Daali woodland, Ghaf Sanuta, Hiyaira and to the top of the highest dune in the Muhanna group. Here the boundary turns southeastward, leaving Raqaat Yaariba in Abu Dhabi, and reaches a point between Raqaat al Aradh and Sih Gnaiyyar, where it turns south to pass west of Raqaat al Salli and arrive at the summit of Naqa Sulaima. The line continues southward to the dunes of Ramlat Saham and then to a point just north of Shantut. In a straight line it proceeds to a large sand dune 15 miles (24 km.) west of Tawi al Augan and reaches the eastern edge of the Urq al Rahail dune range. The boundary then heads toward a point halfway between the dunes of Mdairum and Raqaiyat and then forms a straight line that runs east of Ghadda bul Abbas and west of

Khur Umm al Aush to al-Ghuwaifah in Sihawaiyya. Through an astronomical point at Sihal Haira and through the center of eastern Kharimat Gharaidha the line reaches the narrowest part of western Sih Salil, east of Sabkha. The boundary then runs directly to a point just east of the astronomical point at Naqa Naif, southward along low sand ridges to Nabgha al Hussainiyaht and between Raadat al Hadh to the west and Diaithir to the east to the summit of Naqa Zahar, passing west of Khur Manahil. The boundary then runs in a straight line to its tripoint with Saudi Arabia at Umm az Zumul.

Historical Background. The Sultanate of Muscat and Oman had been a separate sovereign state since the ninth century. In 1508 it was conquered by Portugal, but by 1650 had expelled the Portuguese, become one of the most powerful influences in the region of the Arabian Sea and subsequently seized some of Portugal's east African possessions north of Mozambique. From 1891 Muscat and Oman was a British protectorate. In 1970 Muscat was dropped from the country's name.

The United Arab Emirates have been independent since 2 December 1971. Six emirates united in 1968 and were joined by Ras al Khaimah on 10 February 1972. They were known as the Trucial States from 1892, after Britain imposed its protection on the coast in order to ensure safe passage of its ships to India and the Far East.

Efforts to agree upon a border between Oman and the Trucial States began in 1934, principally due to the discovery of oil in the area, which made fixed borders politically desirable for the first time. Previously the hold over physical territory was less significant than the acknowledgment of interior leadership. This system allowed areas adjacent to oases lying between Oman, the United Arab Emirates and Saudi Arabia, such as Buraimi, to remain neutral territory. Buraimi, however, lost its neutral status when oil was discovered nearby and was fiercely disputed territory until 1982, when a series of security pacts with Saudi Arabia shelved this and other territorial disputes in the Arabian Peninsula. However, Oman's boundaries intersect those of Abu Dhabi at Al'Ayn and at Buraimi; of Sharjah and Fujairah at Dibah al-Hisn; of Ajman at Masfut; and of Dubai at Hatta. Oman's sovereignty over the Musandam peninsula was established after 1864 when

Britain, having set up a telegraphic station on the peninsula, needed to know whom to hold responsible for its safety. Nevertheless, there have been disputes as to the boundary's exact position.

Present Situation. Large sections of these boundaries are not delimited and differences of opinion as to their correct locations often arise.

OMAN — YEMEN Extending 179 miles (288 km.) from Ras Dharbat 'Ali on the Gulf of Aden coast to the tripoint with Saudi Arabia, the Oman–Yemen boundary follows a straight line except for a detour to divide the town of Habrut between the two countries.

Geographical Setting. The boundary between the Republic of Yemen and the Sultanate of Oman begins at the Arabian Sea coast at point no. 1, known as Ras Dharbat 'Ali, which stands at the intersection of 16°39'03.83"N and 53°06'30.88"E. It runs in a straight line to point no. 2 at the intersection of 17°17'7.91"N and 52°48'44.22"E and in another straight line to the intersection (point no. 3) of 17°17'40"N and 52°44'45"E. It likewise continues to 17°18'06.93"N and 52°44'33.50"E (point no. 4), to 17°18'08.87"N and 52°44'34.24"E (point no. 4a) and to 17°18'08.42"N and 52°44'35.57"E (point no. 4b). These last three points run along the western and northern sides of a fort in Oman. The boundary then reaches point no. 5 at the intersection of 17°18'15"N and 52°45'05"E, point no. 6 at 17°18'21"N and 52°45'02"E and point no. 7 at 17°20'59.4"N and 52°46'55.83"E, ending at the boundary tripoint with Saudi Arabia at the intersection of 19°N and 52°E.

Historical Background. The border between Yemen and Oman is largely based upon the tribal territories of the Mahra in Yemen and the Qara and other tribes of Dhufar in the sultanate. Yemen was twice occupied by the Turks, the second time from 1872 to 1918. Following the end of World War I and the Armistice of Mudros in 1918, Imam Yahya took power in the Yemen Arab Republic (the northern part) and refused to recognize the previous Anglo-Turkish agreements. Aden became a British colony until the independence movement of the National Liberation Front and the Front for the Liberation of Occupied South Yemen reached their goal. In 1967, a republican government took control in the north and in south Yemen the Yemen Democratic People's

Republic was formed. There was intermittent warfare between the two through the 1960s and into the 1970s, but in 1990 they merged to form the Yemen Republic.

Oman had severed ties with Britain after the 1798 Treaty of Friendship and became a protectorate in 1891; British military forces remained there until 1977. Border negotiations between Oman and Yemen began in 1982, their progress eased considerably by the unification of Yemen in 1990. On 3 Rabi al-Thani 1413 (1 October 1992) the Sultanate of Oman and the Republic of Yemen signed an agreement in San'a (Yemen), which demarcated the boundary between them, provided for the institution of border authorities and defined the rights to nomadic migration, pasture lands and water resources for the inhabitants of the border areas. Article 3 of the agreement provided for the survey and demarcation of the boundary line and the installation of signposts.

Present Situation. No disputes concerning this boundary line have been recorded since the 1992 agreement between the Sultanate of Oman and the Republic of Yemen.

P-Q

PAKISTAN A southwest Asian country (area: 307,491 sq. miles [796,095 sq. km.]; estimated population: 122,400,000 [1994]), Pakistan is bounded in the north by Afghanistan (1,510 miles; 2,430 km.), northeast by China (325 miles; 523 km.), east by India (1,810 miles; 2,912 km.), south by the Indian Ocean and west by Iran (565 miles; 909 km.). Pakistan's capital is Islamabad.

Islam arrived in the area of present-day Pakistan in the eighth century with the conquering armies of the Umayyad Caliphate. The Muslims ruled the area of northern India (of which Pakistan was a part) until the British established colonies in the nineteenth century. In the long struggle for independence from British rule, Muslim groups founded the All-India Muslim League in 1906, and by the 1930s there were calls for the establishment of an independent Muslim state detached from Hindu-dominated India. In August 1947, Pakistan, split by the large expanse of India into East and West, gained independence.

A track in the Afghanistan–Pakistan boundary

above: "Welcome to Bolivia"—Argentina–Bolivia boundary

below: "Welcome to Paraguay"—Argentina–Paraguay boundary

above: Austria–Czech Republic boundary crossing

below: Italian boundary post—France–Italy boundary

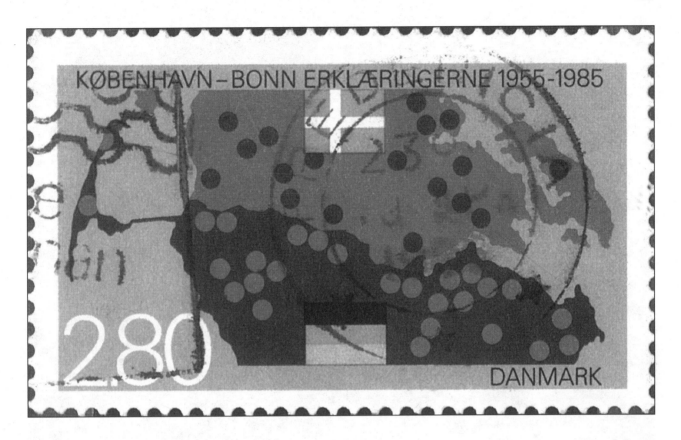

above: The Denmark–Germany boundary on a Danish postage stamp

below: Memorial stone on the former Denmark–Germany boundary

Canada–United States boundary in Champlain Lake, at the Quebec–Vermont border

"Peace Gate" on the Canada–United States border

Canada–United States boundary—the longest boundary in the world

above: The border area between Norway and Sweden

below: Norway–Sweden boundary crossing

The border region between Portugal and Spain

The Afghanistan–Pakistan boundary region in the high Pamir Range

above: The mountainous area of the Ecuador–Peru boundary

below: Pentazel swamps—Brazil–Paraguay boundary

above: A boundary pillar on the Egypt–Israel border

below: The India–Pakistan boundary region in Kashmir

428

Southeast Morocco—near the boundary with Algeria

The Morocco–Western Sahara boundary region

Maya ruins, near the Guatemala–Mexico boundary

Massai Mera reserve, north of the Kenya–Tanzania boundary

above: Colorado Lake, near the Bolivia–Chile boundary

below: A Lapp tent near the Norway–Finland boundary

In 1971, civil war broke out in East Pakistan, and with the help of India the independent state of Bangladesh was created there. Modern Pakistan ("land of the pure") is now comprised of what was West Pakistan.

PAKISTAN — AFGHANISTAN see AFGHANISTAN–PAKISTAN.

PAKISTAN — CHINA see CHINA–PAKISTAN.

PAKISTAN — INDIA see INDIA–PAKISTAN.

PAKISTAN — IRAN see IRAN–PAKISTAN.

PANAMA A Central American country, Panama is bounded in the north by the Caribbean Sea, in the east by Colombia (140 miles; 225 km.), in the south by the Pacific Ocean and in the west by Costa Rica (205 miles; 330 km.). The area of Panama (including the Canal Zone) is 29,761 sq. miles (77,081 sq. km.) with an estimated population (1994) of 2,510,000. Its capital is Panama City.

The first European expedition arrived in Panama in 1501. Panama rapidly became the point of embarkation for expeditions to Peru. The Panamanians enjoyed relative autonomy until Spain entered a period of political and economic decline in the mid-1700s; in 1740, the area became part of the territory of New Granada, now Colombia.

Upon achieving independence in 1821, Colombia, Ecuador and Venezuela formed the Republic of Gran Colombia; when it dissolved after nine years, Panama remained part of Colombia. In 1903 the Colombian government refused to allow the United States to build a canal across Panama and the Panamanians, with considerable North American assistance, revolted, declared independence and promptly leased the Canal Zone to the United States "in perpetuity."

The US proceeded to exert total sovereignty over the Canal Zone, administering it essentially as a colony. Although this arrangement was a source of political embarrassment to the Panamanians, they were economically dependent upon the Americans who were living there, and public opposition to US sovereignty did not erupt until after World War II. In 1979 the United States formally returned the Canal Zone to Panama. This symbolic victory over US domination, however, did not resolve Panama's continuing problems: Panamanians have since had to contend with political instability.

The boundaries of Panama and Costa Rica

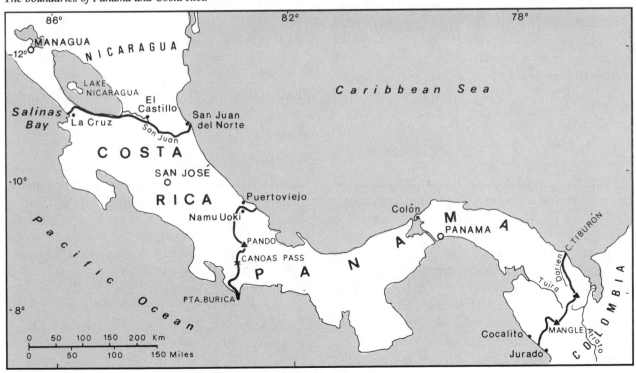

PANAMA — COLOMBIA see COLOMBIA–PANAMA.

PANAMA — COSTA RICA see COSTA RICA–PANAMA.

PAPUA NEW GUINEA Situated on the island of New Guinea, the second largest island of the Pacific Ocean, Papua New Guinea's only land boundary is with Indonesia (510 miles; 820 km.) in the west. Its area is 178,772 sq. miles (462,840 sq. km.) and it has an estimated population (1994) of 3,900,000. Its capital is Port Moresby.

The island of New Guinea was visited by European navigators from the early sixteenth century, but exploration and colonial settlement did not begin until the mid-nineteenth century. In 1884 Papua, the southern part of eastern New Guinea, and adjoining islands, was proclaimed a British protectorate, and the northern part of eastern New Guinea came under German administration. Australia formally administered Papua from 1906. From 1945 Papua and the former German New Guinea, administered since World War I by Britain (except for a brief period of Japanese occupations during World War II), became the Territories of Papua and New Guinea. As the Australian administration was extended into the interior, the country's largest population concentration was discovered, and by the 1950s all groups were brought under administrative control. Papua New Guinea attained independence in September 1975. Although it inherited from the Australian authorities a highly centralized administration, the heterogenous and fragmented nature of the country and its society resulted in the introduction of decentralization. By 1978 all 20 provinces had been granted provincial government status.

More than two-thirds of the working population are engaged in subsistence and semi-subsistence agriculture. The rest are engaged mainly in commercial agriculture in which the principal export cash crops are coffee, cocoa, coconuts, palm oil, rubber and tea. Since independence, copper, gold and silver have taken over as principal export commodities. More recently substantial deposits of chromite, cobalt, nickel and quartz have been discovered, all of which attract labor to the mining areas. Tourism is another expanding sector.

PAPUA NEW GUINEA — INDONESIA see INDONESIA–PAPUA NEW GUINEA.

PARAGUAY A landlocked country in central South America, Paraguay (area: 157,107 sq. miles [406,752 sq. km.]; estimated population: 4,600,000 [1994]) is bounded by Brazil (802 miles; 1,290 km.) in the northeast, by Bolivia (466 miles; 746 km.) in the northwest and by Argentina (1,168 miles; 1,880 km.) in the southwest, south and southeast. Its capital is Asunción.

The Guarani are the indigenous people of Paraguay. During the sixteenth century, their territory spread to the Andean foothills, the Brazilian frontier and the Amazon basin. The Spaniards arrived at Rio Paraguay in 1524. The capital city of Asunción was founded in 1537 on the Day of the Assumption of the Virgin. Later, members of the Jesuit and Franciscan orders founded agricultural colonies. They became both protectors and teachers of the indigenous peoples, instructing them to develop their skills, achieve relative autonomy and avoid exploitation. This angered the European colonists, anxious to increase their labor supply through the enslavement of the Indians, and resulted in the expulsion of the Jesuits from the New World. Paraguayans initiated a rebellion against Spain in 1810: the last Spanish governor left in 1811.

PARAGUAY — ARGENTINA see ARGENTINA–PARAGUAY.

PARAGUAY — BOLIVIA see BOLIVIA–PARAGUAY.

PARAGUAY — BRAZIL see BRAZIL–PARAGUAY.

PERU A South American country (area: 496,098 sq. miles. [1,284,893 sq. km.]; estimated population: 22,900,000 [1994]), Peru is bounded in the north by Ecuador (883 miles; 1,420 km.) and Colombia (1,802 miles; 2,900 km.), east by Brazil (970 miles; 1,560 km.) and Bolivia (560 miles; 900 km.), southeast by Chile (100 miles; 160 km.) and west by the Pacific Ocean. Its capital is Lima.

Pre-Columbian civilizations developed in Peru as far back as the end of the third millennium B.C.E. Establishment of the Inca Empir—an empire that controlled Peru and also parts of Ecuador, Bolivia,

Peru–Bolivia boundary in Lake Titicaca

northern Argentina and Chile in the fifteenth century was proceeded by the Chavin, Nazca and Tiahuanaco cultures.

The country was conquered by the Spaniards in 1531. This brought about the destruction of the Inca Empire, the foundation of Lima (1535) near the Pacific coast, in order to facilitate naval communications and transport with Panama and Spain, and the establishment of the viceroyalty of Peru. Spanish colonization lasted until the end of 1824, when the Peruvians, with the aid of Simon Bolívar, finally routed the Spanish armies and subsequently became fully independent.

After independence, Peru was dominated by the army and fought, together with Bolivia, two wars against Chile (1836–1839 and 1879–1884), losing both. The first war reasserted Peruvian national identity. The Chilean invasion of Peru during the Pacific War (Lima was occupied by the Chileans from January 1881 until the beginning of 1884) brought about fierce Peruvian resistance in the Sierra, which consolidated Peruvian nationalism and embedded patriotic feelings.

The ethnic and socioeconomic divisions within Peru have led to frequent historical and political discussions on the problems of Peruvian national identity. Some praise the historical role of Spain in Peru and hold that the nation's future will depend upon Peruvians of European descent, those able to lead the modernization of their society and economy. Others look for solutions based on a fusion of the European and Indian components of the nation. The left-wing Alianza Popular Revolucionaria Americana (APRA) was in favor of regenerating the indigenous Indian society through land reform. The guerrilla movement *Sendero Luminoso* (Shining Path) violently rejects Western liberal democracy and culture as well as the capitalist organization of the economy and attempts to impose an agrarian collectivist model of Marxist-Maoist revolutionary principles.

After a 12-year populist-military dictatorship that tried to impose land and economic reforms without much success, Peru returned to democracy in 1980. Since then, right and left wing policies have been unsuccessful in the effort to stabilize Peru's social development and economy. Both rural and urban guerrilla warfare complicate the situation by introducing further divisive elements. In 1990 a Peruvian of Japanese descent, Alberto Fujimori, was elected to the presidency. His government has applied strong neo-liberal economic adjustment policies and perpetrated a self-coup d'etat in 1992. This was done in order to fight guerrillas more effectively and to apply effective policies without parliamentary blockage.

PERU — BOLIVIA see BOLIVIA–PERU.

PERU — BRAZIL see BRAZIL–PERU.

PERU — CHILE see CHILE–PERU.

PERU — COLOMBIA see COLOMBIA–PERU.

PERU — ECUADOR see ECUADOR–PERU.

PHILIPPINES A country consisting of a group of islands in the western Pacific Ocean, the total land area of the Philippines is 115,831 sq. miles (299,886 sq. km.). It has an estimated population (1994) of 65,000,000; its capital is Manila and it has no land boundaries.

The ancestors of the Malay peoples of the Philippines most probably migrated from Southeast Asia. The Filipinos were mostly hunters, fishers and shifting cultivators at the time when they first came into contact with the Arabs, who came as traders and introduced Islam to the region in the fourteenth century. Ferdinand Magellan, a Portuguese-born explorer working for Spain, was the first European to discover the islands, which were then conquered and controlled by the Spaniards by 1571. Sporadic Filipino agitations for independence were boosted by the successful rebellions of the Spanish colonies in the Americas in the 1820s. Filipino opposition to colonial rule by Spain culminated in the unsuccessful revolt of 1896–1898, at the end of which the Spaniards sold the Philippines to the Americans; Filipino demands for independence continued.

American rule of the islands lasted nearly 50 years. During that period, the Philippines were used as a supplier of raw materials to and buyer of goods from the United States. During World War II, the islands were the major theater of military operations in the Pacific and were occupied by the Japanese between 1942 and 1945, when they were recaptured by the Americans.

The islands became a fully independent republic in 1946. However, the United States has maintained a significant naval and military presence in the region. The new state faced a difficult period of reconstruction after the damage the region incurred during the war. The government of the Philippines also faced insurrection by the Hukbalahaps, Communist guerrillas whose revolutionary demands included calls for land reform. President Marcos quelled renewed Hukbalahap activity in 1969, but was then faced by Muslim rebel groups, including the MNLF (Moro National Liberation Front), whose strongholds were in the southern islands; their armed opposition to his regime was used to justify the imposition of martial law in September 1972.

Corruption and human rights abuses lost Marcos the support of the Roman Catholic church and led to popular discontent. The rigging of elections in 1986 precipitated an uprising against him, resulting in his flight to Hawaii. Corazon Aquino became president. She quickly instituted land reforms designed to transfer ownership of land into the hands of the tenant farmers who work it. However, Communist insurgency, widespread poverty, a weak economy and the power of the military to influence internal affairs continue to pose problems for the people of the Philippines.

PITCAIRN ISLAND An island located in the South Pacific Ocean, Pitcairn Island is a dependency of the United Kingdom. Its area is 19 sq. miles (49 sq. km.) with a population of 60. Its capital is Adamstown and it has no land boundaries.

The population of Pitcairn Island are of Anglo-Tahitian stock, descendants of the Bounty mutineers who landed on the island in 1790 with six Tahitian men and 12 Tahitian women. In 1937 the population reached its peak of 233, and since then has declined, due to migration. All Islanders are members of the Seventh Day Adventist Church.

Two-thirds of Pitcairn's revenue is derived from the sale of postage stamps.

POLAND (Polska) An Eastern European country

(area: 120,628 sq. miles [312,683 sq. km.]; estimated population: 38,500,000 [1994]), Poland is bounded by the Baltic Sea and the Russian Oblast of Kaliningrad (269 miles; 432 km.) in the north, by Lithuania (57 miles; 91 km.) in the northeast, by Belarus (376 miles; 605 km.) and Ukraine (266 miles; 428 km.) in the east, by Slovakia (261 miles; 420 km.) and the Czech Republic (370 miles; 595 km.) in the south and by Germany (284 miles; 456 km.) in the west. Its capital is Warsaw.

Slavic tribes seem to have inhabited the area of today's Poland since the early centuries C.E. In the ninth and tenth centuries tribal states were formed, the strongest of which was that of the Wislanie that ruled over most of Lesser Poland. A second state evolved in Slask (Silesia). However, the tribe which

Poland's boundaries

Poland–Czech Republic boundary on Mount Izerae

established Poland as a state was that of the Polanje under the Piast dynasty. The name "Pole" is derived from their name (lit. "forest clearing dwellers").

Mieszko I (963–992) conquered Pomerania, Silesia and Lesser Poland. In 966 he converted to Roman Catholicism: Poles date the foundation of their country from that year. His son, Boleslaw I (992–1025), expanded the Polish domain westward and eastward into the basins of the Bug and Sam Rivers. He was the first crowned king of the Poles. Boleslaw III (1102–1138) divided Poland among his sons: the country, although officially one kingdom, remained divided for the following two centuries until it was reunited by the last Piasts, who forged an alliance with Hungary and Lithuania. Under the Jagiello kings (1385–1572) the United Kingdom of Poland-Lithuania reached its zenith as one of the major powers in Europe, extending over a huge territory from the Baltic to the Black Seas, and from the Odra River to about 50 miles (80 km.) west of Moscow.

As a major power, the kingdom was involved in the affairs of far removed areas and frequently had to fight the Ottomans, the Muscovites, the Swedes and other regional powers to the southeast, north and west. Internally, the country evolved into a parliamentary monarchy of the aristocracy with the Sejm (Diet) being convened regularly after 1493. In 1569, lacking an heir to the last Jagiello ruler, the Sejm formed the Union of Lublin, Poland, Lithuania, Prussia and Livonia, a *rzeczpospolita* (unified and indivisible commonwealth). This commonwealth, however, could only survive while it had a powerful monarch, such as the Vasa kings (1587–1668), or Jan III Sobieski (1674–1696). Under weak or corrupt rule it became a battlefield for its neighbors, whose strength was increasing. Following the rule of Peter the Great in Russia, and especially after the Northern War, Poland became a de facto Russian protectorate, and was finally partitioned among Russia, Prussia and Austria in 1772, 1793 and 1795.

After the Napoleonic Wars, in which a Duchy of Warsaw was created, Poland was redistributed among its neighbors. A kingdom of Poland was carved out by the Congress of Vienna and united with the Russian empire, while Krakow (Cracow) was made a free city. The Polish nobility and gentry had waged a struggle for the reinstatement of Polish independence from the first partition. Many now joined the French revolutionaries and Napoleon. In 1830 the Poles revolted but were crushed in 1831 by the Russians and Prussians. In 1846 an insurrection in Krakow resulted in the city's annexation to Austria. A second revolt in Poland in 1863 again took more than a year to be crushed by Prussia and Russia. This time the Russian authorities took steps to prevent the Polish nobility from revolting again.

After 1864 all three divisions of Poland underwent rapid industrialization and urbanization, which caused in their turn great social changes and the emergence of modern nationalism. During World War I both coalitions courted the Poles. After the war a Polish republic (the Second Commonwealth) was created by reuniting the areas which had belonged to Austria, Germany and Russia. The new Polish state had to fight for survival, annexing large territories in the east. As a result more than one-third of Poland's inhabitants belonged to minority groups, almost all of whom (the notable exception were the 3,000,000 Jews) continued to remain loyal to their previous nationalities. Internally unstable and externally a target for irrendentism, Poland became a dictatorship. Having defied Hitler's territorial demands, Poland was invaded by Germany in 1939, sparking off World War II and leading to Poland's being partitioned between Germany and the Soviet Union.

After the war Poland's borders underwent a drastic change. The eastern territories inhabited mainly by Ukrainians, Byelorussians and Lithuanians were annexed to the Soviet Union. In compensation the Poles received all the German territories east of the Oder-Neisse Rivers line as well as the southern part of East Prussia. Some 4,000,000 Germans escaped before the Soviet army's arrival in the country; after the war another 3,300,000 Germans were expelled.

By 1947 Poland, like the rest of Eastern Europe, was ruled by a Communist regime; unlike in other Communist states, however, the Catholic church maintained a powerful political position and gave significant support to the anti-communist opposition. During its 42-year existence the Communist regime underwent several major crises, all involving food riots and strikes by well-organized industrial workers. In August 1980 there was a widespread strike in the shipyards and coal mines. This time, however, circumstances had changed. A Polish cardinal had been elected pope, lending moral and political strength to the Polish opposition. Under the church's wing a free trade movement was formed, called *Solidarnosc* (Solidarity). Following the collapse of Communist regimes in Eastern Europe Solidarity came to power and its leader, Lech Walesa, was elected president. Since then the Poles have been struggling to build a democratic regime with a viable market economy.

POLAND — BELARUS   see BELARUS–POLAND.

POLAND — CZECH REPUBLIC   see CZECH RE-PUBLIC–POLAND.

POLAND — GERMANY   see GERMANY–POLAND.

POLAND — LITHUANIA   see LITHUANIA–POLAND.

POLAND — RUSSIA   The boundary between Poland and Russia (Kaliningrad) runs for 269 miles (432 km.) between the boundary tripoint with Lithuania in the east and the Baltic Sea in the west. Kaliningrad is an oblast of the Russian Federation separated from the Russian mainland by Lithuania and some 220 miles (350 km.).

Geographical Setting. The eastern terminus of this boundary line, which is at the junction with the Lithuanian boundary, is located on the Pregel River, west of the small town of Vistytis (Lithuania). The line follows the river downstream westward for about 5 miles (8 km.) and then leaves the river to run in a straight line westward, always keeping the Pregel River north of the boundary. On its way it crosses the Wegorapa River, passes south of the small town of Allenburg (Russia), which is located on the Lava (Lyna) River, crosses that river and reaches the shore of the Vislinski Zaliv (Zalew Wislany) lagoon, north of the Polish town of Braniewo and east of the 20°E meridian. The boundary line crosses the lagoon in a straight line westward and arrives at the coast of the Gulf of Danzig (Gdansk) in the Baltic Sea, south of the small town and fort of

Baltisk, which is located at the mouth of the lagoon.
Historical Background. The Russian region of Kaliningrad (Königsberg) covers about 5,790 sq. miles (15,000 sq. km.) and is populated by approximately 871,000 people. The city of Königsberg in East Prussia was founded in 1255 by the German Knights of the Teutonic Order. The region was ceded to the kingdom of Poland in 1525 but in 1660 it was returned as an enclave to Prussia. During 1758–1762 the region came under the occupation of Russia, but the city remained a Prussian territory and became a constituent of the German state when it was established in 1870. After World War I, Königsberg remained part of Germany but was dislocated from mainland Germany by the Polish Corridor and the region was isolated once again. During World War II, at the Summit of Tehran, the Soviet Union demanded the region on the grounds that it needed to hold an ice-free port on the Baltic Sea. The Soviet army captured the area in April 1945 and it was made a region of the Russian Federation (rather than linking it to the new Baltic satellite states). The area was named Kaliningrad, the original German population was ousted and replaced by close to 1,000,000 Soviet colonists, mostly laborers. Kaliningrad was then developed as a center for military entrenchment, holding a wide range of land, sea and air forces.

Kaliningrad's boundary with Poland was drawn as a straight line without consideration for the area's geographical features. Poland and the Soviet Union signed a boundary treaty in September 1945, which included the Kaliningrad line. Thus, an international boundary was established along the northeastern corner of Poland. The collapse of the Soviet Union and the establishment of the Baltic States and the independent states of the western region of the former USSR in 1991 left the Kaliningrad region in a unique position as a Russian exclave that shares a boundary with Poland.

Present Situation. There are no known disputes concerning the alignment of the boundary line between Poland and the Russian oblast of Kaliningrad, but the future of the Kaliningrad region has yet to be determined. Germany, which held the area until 1945, has no designs upon it, but there is a demand for the creation of a German republic (in Russia) on the territory. Some Poles hold claims on the area while others ask for the creation of a Polish autonomous territory there, although no official claims have ever been announced. Russia remains the "owner" of Kaliningrad at present, maintaining its common international boundary with Poland.

POLAND — SLOVAKIA Following the eastern section of the former Poland–Czechoslovakia boundary that was established after World War I, the boundary between Poland and Slovakia runs for 261 miles (420 km.). It extends from the boundary tripoint with the Czech Republic in the west to the boundary tripoint with Ukraine in the east.

Geographical Setting. The western terminus of this boundary line is located in the Beskids mountains, west of the Polish town of Jaworzynka. From this point the boundary line runs southeastward, reaches the Velka Raca peak (4,064 feet; 1,239 m.) and trends eastward to a peak located 3,792 feet (1,156 m.) above sea level. Then heading northeastward along the local watershed, the line reaches the Babia Gora (Babia Hora) peak (5,659 feet; 1,725 m.) and runs southeast toward Orava Lake. It crosses the lake, leaving its northern section in Poland while most of the lake lies within Slovakia. It continues southeast along the watershed of the Tatra Mountains, reaching an altitude of 6,767 feet (2,063 m.) on Volovec Peak and continuing eastward along the watershed to the Rysy peak (8,197 feet; 2,499 m.). The boundary turns northward to reach the road between Nowy Sacz (Poland) and Poprad (Slovakia) and northeastward to the Dunajek River south of Sromowce Wyzen (Poland). It follows that river downstream eastward for approximately 6 miles (10 km.), reaching a point west of the small Polish town of Szczwnica and then runs eastward down to the Poprad River.

The boundary line follows the river upstream southeastward down to a point northeast of the small Slovakian town of Lubotin. Leaving the river, the boundary line runs northeastward and then eastward along the watershed of the Zachodnie mountains. Crossing the Dukla (Poland)–Svidnik (Slovakia) road and the Dukliansky–Priesmyk boundary crossing point, the boundary arrives at the western Carpathian Mountains and runs along their watershed to the boundary junction with Ukraine on a peak that stands 4,005 feet (1,221 m.) above sea level, south of the small Polish town of Brzegi Gorne.

Historical Background. The present boundary between Poland and Slovakia was established after World War I. Slovakia, which was part of the Hungarian section of the Austro-Hungarian Empire, was united with the Czech Republic on 30 October 1918 to form modern Czechoslovakia. Poland, which until World War I was divided between Russia, Austria and Germany, became an independent state in late 1918. The boundary between the newly independent Czechoslovakia and Poland was defined in July 1920, mainly along ethnic lines. The political and territorial changes that characterized Europe before and after World War II did not affect the boundary line, which was reestablished after the war along its former alignment. The easternmost section of the line was placed within the Soviet Union (now within Ukraine) in August 1945, thereby shortening the boundary between Poland and the Slovakian region of Czechoslovakia. The independent state of Slovakia was constituted on 1 January 1993. No changes were made along the boundary line at that point, and both states adopted the 1920 line as their common international boundary without a formal agreement.

Present Situation. There are no known disputes concerning the alignment of the Poland–Slovakia boundary line. Neither state has ever raised claims to the other's territory and the boundary region is peaceful.

POLAND — UKRAINE A section of the boundary between Poland and the former Soviet Union that was established after World War II, the boundary between Poland and Ukraine runs for 266 miles (428 km.) from the tripoint boundary junction with Belarus on the Bug River in the north to the tripoint junction with Slovakia in the south.

Geographical Setting. The northern terminus of this boundary line is located on the Bug River, east of the town of Wlodawa (Poland). It follows the Bug River upstream southward for about 70 miles (115 km.) and reaches a point north of the small town of Belz (Ukraine). Thence it runs in a straight line southwestward for about 90 miles (145 km.), crossing the Lvov (Ukraine)–Lublin (Poland) and Lvov–Przemysl (Poland) railways, and reaches the

San River southeast of the small Polish town of Leska. The line follows the San River upstream southeastward for about 30 miles (50 km.) to its source in the Carpathian Mountains northeast of Uzhok (Ukraine). It then runs westward, leaving the entire Uzhgorod–Lvov railway in Ukraine and reaching the Slovakian boundary about 10 miles (16 km.) southeast of the Polish town of Baligrad.

Historical Background. Modern Poland was established as an independent state in 1918, after World War I. Its boundary with the newly organized Soviet Union was proposed by the territorial commission of the Versailles Peace Conference of 1919 to be based on the eastern limit of the area predominantly inhabited by a Polish population. Lord Curzon, then the British foreign secretary, suggested the "Curzon Line" on 8 December 1919 and later pressed the Poles to retire to it, giving the Soviet Union an opportunity to conquer more territories in 1920. The Polish and Soviet armies fought back and forth in Ukraine during 1920–1921 and, by the Riga Peace Treaty of 18 March 1921, a boundary line was established 125 miles (200 km.) east of the Curzon Line, deep inside Ukrainian territory.

During World War II eastern Poland was occupied by the Soviet Union (1940–1941) but later was held by Nazi Germany (until 1945). After the war, the Soviet Union and Poland, which was liberated by the Red Army, established a new boundary between them (September 1945), setting Poland's eastern boundary along the Curzon Line of 1919, with some minor modifications for the benefit of Poland. Poland thereby lost to the Soviet Union some 70,000 sq. miles (181,250 sq. km.) in the east, although it gained 39,000 sq. miles (101,000 sq. km.) from Germany in the west. The southern section of the new Poland–Soviet Union boundary line marked the eastern boundary of the Soviet Republic of Ukraine, which was established in 1936, gained a vote in the United Nations in 1945 even though it was not an independent state and became fully independent in 1991. The changing boundaries within the Soviet Union did not affect the international boundary line with Poland—which became the Polish–Ukrainian international boundary without a formal agreement.

Present Situation. Since 1991 there have not been boundary disputes as both states adopted the 1945

line as their common international boundary. Although there are some ethnic territorial conflicts within Ukraine that could affect its boundary with Poland (such as the demand to create a Galician autonomous territory in western Ukraine or to institute a Transcarpathian republic in southwestern Ukraine) there are no contentions between the two concerning its alignment.

PORTUGAL A European country (area: 35,516 sq. miles [91,950 sq. km.]; estimated population: 10,450,000 [1994]), situated in the southwestern corner of the continent, Portugal's only land boundary is with Spain (755 miles; 1,214 km.) in the north and east, while it is bounded in the south and west by the Atlantic Ocean. Portugal's capital is Lisbon.

The Portuguese are believed to descend from the Lusitan tribe who, in the third century B.C.E., entered into a compact with Rome. During the first millennium C.E., however, Portugal as such did not exist. The country was overrun first by the Suevi and West Goths, Germanic invaders from the north, then conquered in 711 by Muslim Moors. A long process of *Reconquista* against the North African rulers ensued: the Portuguese nation was shaped in this crucible. The process of reconquest was completed by the mid-thirteenth century, rounding off the territorial basis of Europe's oldest nation-state. The influence of the Arabs has remained stronger in the south, but the overall Arab imprint is less strong on the Portuguese than on the Spaniards.

The next episode in the crystallization of the Portuguese nation was the era of exploration and the establishment of the first worldwide seaborne empire in the fifteenth and sixteenth centuries. Portuguese mariners opened the Atlantic and established colonies from the African coast to insular Southeast Asia, China and Brazil. Behind the establishment of this immense empire lay not only economic interests but the aspiration to spread Christianity.

Portugal's period of glory was brief and was followed by a long era of decline. In 1578 the last Portuguese king mysteriously disappeared. The Spaniards occupied the country, and during the next decades the Portuguese lost most of their overseas empire to the Dutch and English. In 1640 they regained their independence. Emphasis was placed on the colonization of Brazil and the exploitation of

sugar, cotton and tobacco from plantations cultivated by imported African slaves.

Attempts at creating an industrial base in the eighteenth century failed. Portugal was practically a British colony, trading local wines for English textiles. By the nineteenth century, the Portuguese had become isolated from European currents and lost Brazil. Civil wars between the peasants and the bourgeoisie shook the country. After the establishment of a radical anticlerical republic early in the twentieth century, a confused period of coups and

Portugal's boundary with Spain

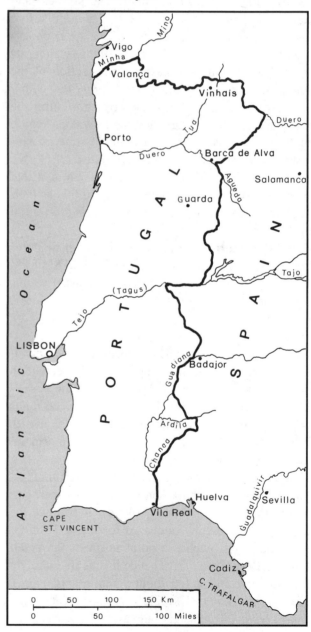

Portugal–Spain crossing point

countercoups exhausted the country's resources. This deepened the economic crisis and undermined the legitimacy of politicians, so that in 1926 a fascist military coup led by Oliveira Salazar was hailed as providing a measure of stability. Although the regime managed to provide some material progress, the army and secret police dominated the country and imposed isolationism on the people. Salazar became all-powerful from 1933.

Portugal has been a perpetual reservoir of cheap manpower: from the sixteenth century the dearth of arable land stimulated emigration. Between 1820 and 1935, 1,500,000 Portuguese immigrants colonized Brazil. Post-World War II emigration was directed toward France and other European countries. By the middle of the twentieth century the Portuguese were among Europe's poorest and least developed peoples. However, the migrants' experiences, along with Portugal's growing mobility and urbanization, began to change outlooks, and destabilized the regime. 1968 was the end of the Salazar era. His technocratic successors failed to modernize the economy and liberalize the political structure.

Unpopular colonial wars in Africa were the catalyst of the April 1974 Revolution of Carnations, which liquidated Portugal's colonial heritage. A parliamentary democracy was institutionalized. From the 1980s, mass tourism, the beginnings of industrialization and integration into Europe have brought about the rapid modernization of Portuguese society.

PORTUGAL — SPAIN   The boundary between Portugal and Spain, one of the oldest existing boundaries of the world, runs for 755 miles (1,214 km.) between the mouth of the Minha River in the Atlantic Ocean in the northwest and the mouth of the Guadiana River in the Gulf of Cadiz in the south.

Geographical Setting. The boundary line runs generally eastward for 130 miles (210 km.) and thence southward. Its northeastern terminus is the mouth of the Minha River near the small Portuguese town of Vila Nova de Cerveira. From there the boundary line follows the main navigation channel of the Minha River upstream northeastward for about 40 miles (65 km.). It runs southward, crosses the Limia River and reaches the Geres Range. Following the range eastward, the boundary reaches an artificial lake on a tributary of the Limia River, crosses it and continues eastward to Mount Larouco (5,002 feet; 1,525 m.). Leaving it within Portugal, the boundary line runs eastward and crosses the Tamega River and the Verin (Spain)–Chaves (Portugal) road. Continuing eastward, it crosses the upper tributaries of the Tua River and then reaches Mount Corraes (4,185 feet; 1,276 m.). Leaving it within Portugal, the boundary reaches the Culebra Range near the Pane Mira Peak. Then the boundary line changes its direction and runs in a generally southerly direction. It reaches the Sabor River and follows it downstream southward for 15 miles (25 km.). It leaves the river and runs southeastward, passes the Santa Luz Peak (2,991 feet; 912 m.) and meets the Douro River. The boundary follows the median line of the Douro River downstream southwestward for about 55 miles (90 km.) to its confluence with the Agueda River, near the small Portuguese town of Barca d'Alva. It follows the Agueda River upstream southeastward to its confluence with a southern tributary, follows that tributary southward for about 20 miles (32 km.) up to the small Spanish town of Fuentoes de Onoro, and then follows the watershed of the Gata Range. It passes through the Mezas Peak (4,143 feet; 1,263 m.) and runs southwestward to the Erjas River. It follows that river downstream southward to its confluence with the Tajo (Tejo) River, the main Iberian river. The line follows the main navigation channel of the Tajo River downstream westward for about 30 miles (50 km.) to its confluence with the Sever River. It follows that river upstream southeastward for about 30 miles (50 km.), leaves the river and runs southeastward to cross the Cacares (Spain)–Santarem (Portugal) road. It then continues in that direction, crosses the Badajoz (Spain)–Lisboa (Portugal) road and reaches the Guadiana River. Following it downstream southwestward for about 35 miles (60 km.), it reaches a point 3 miles (5 km.) north of the small Portuguese town of Mouro. Thence the boundary leaves the river and runs southeastward along a local watershed, reaching the Ardila (Ardilla) River. The boundary follows that river upstream eastward for about 10 miles (16 km.). Thence running southward, it reaches the Aroche Peak (2,355 feet; 718 m.).

Leaving it with Spain, the boundary runs westward, crosses the Beja (Portugal)–Aracena (Spain) road and reaches the Chanca River. It follows that river downstream southwestward to its confluence with the Guadiana River and follows that river downstream southward to its mouth in the Gulf of Cadiz, between the Portuguese town of Vila Real de Santo Antonio and the Spanish town of Ayamonte.

Historical Background. The area south of the Douro River was, in ancient times, the area of the Lusitanians. The city of Portus (today Oporto) was established by the Romans, and from the fifth century the area around it was called Terra Portuscalense, from which the modern name of Portugal was created.

Both Spain and Portugal were under Muslim rule from the eighth century. Portugal became independent in 1143 and during the thirteenth century reoccupied the Algavre province in south Portugal, completing the evacuation of the Muslims from Portugal. It took Spain another 250 years, until 1492, to completely free the Iberian Peninsula of the Muslim rule.

The Treaty of Alcanies of 1297 established Portugal's boundary with Castile in the Algavre, and the Peace Treaty of 1411, signed after a 28 years of war, established another boundary with Castile. Another round of wars for the hegemony of the Iberian Peninsula led to the Treaty of Alçacovas (1479), in which Portugal waived its claim to the Castilian throne. Castile was united with Aragon to became Spain in 1492 and the present boundary between the two states was established in detail. Spain occupied Portugal between 1580 and 1640. On 1 December 1640 Portugal became independent again but Spain only recognized it officially by the Treaty of Lisbon that was signed early in 1668, reconfirming the boundary between the two states. Portugal joined the War of the Spanish Succession (1701–1713) and the peace treaty of 1715 reestablished the former boundary between the two states.

The Treaty of San Ildefonso (1777), which determined the boundary between the Portuguese and Spanish possessions in South America and other parts of the world, did not change the Iberian boundary, which was left intact. Portugal was occupied by Napoleonic Spain in 1807 but was restored as an independent state in 1815 and from then on both states were independent, accepting the 1479 boundary as their common international boundary.

Present Situation. The changes in the political history of Spain and Portugal in the nineteenth and twentieth centuries never affected the boundary line. In fact, since 1668 and for the last 330 years, no changes were made in the boundary line and no disputes concerning its alignment are known.

PUERTO RICO A Caribbean island, Puerto Rico is a commonwealth in association with the USA. Its area is 3,460 sq. miles (8,959 sq. km.) and it has an estimated population (1994) of 3,600,000. Puerto Rico has no land boundaries and its capital is San Juan.

Of the permanent inhabitants of this mountainous island, most are concentrated in the coastal lowlands, with almost half in the San Juan metropolitan area. Roman Catholicism is the predominant faith among Puerto Ricans, who were ruled by the Spaniards for several hundred years. In spite of heavy North American influence since 1898, when the island was occupied by the US in the Spanish-American War, Puerto Ricans have retained much of their own mixed Spanish, African and American Indian culture; attempts by the USA to impose English as the official language failed early in the present century, and Spanish was subsequently restored.

To some extent, it is the mountain peasant, or *jibaro*, depicted with a guitar in one hand and a field machete in the other, who has symbolized the island's culture to its own people. The mountain music is less well-known than the renown coastal *salsa*, but it is the combinaton of the two, together with a unique pattern of dances and celebrations partly shared with Cuba, that give Puerto Rican culture its character.

Puerto Rico's economy is more industrialized than that of any other Caribbean island, dependent to a considerable extent upon labor-intensive manufacturing complemented by trade enterprises and financial services. While agriculture, dominant until the 1940s, has declined considerably, plantation sugarcane and distilled rum are still important products.

QATAR A Middle Eastern country (area: 4,416 sq. miles [11,433 sq. km.]; estimated population: 510,000 [1994]) that forms a small peninsula in the Persian (Arabian) Gulf off the Arabian Peninsula, Qatar is bounded in the south by Saudi Arabia (25 miles; 40 km.). Its capital is Doha.

In 1860 the currently reigning ath-Thani family took control in the shadow of growing Ottoman and, later, Saudi power in the Gulf region. In 1916 Qatar became a protectorate of the British. Save for Britain, it is unlikely that the Qataris would have escaped absorption into Saudi Arabia, the fate of most other neighboring Arabs.

In 1971 Qatar became independent from Britain. In 1972 a bloodless coup brought Khalifah bin Hamad ath-Thani to power, who allowed a very limited broadening of political participation, and installed a comprehensive social security system for Qatari nationals. Oil was nationalized in 1976. In 1981 Qatar became a member of the Gulf Cooperation Council. The regime maintains a strict Wahhabite Muslim lifestyle.

QATAR — SAUDI ARABIA Precise details of this boundary, which separates the Kingdom of Saudi Arabia from the peninsula of Qatar, remain unclear as a result of much secrecy over the agreements that were drawn up. The boundary is 25 miles (40 km.) long.

Geographical Setting. Although details of the 1993 boundary agreement remain unpublished, it is possible to briefly describe the geographical setting of this boundary. Approximately 19 miles (30 km.) northeast of Salway, on the cost of Dawhgat Salwah, the boundary trends in a southeasterly direction, intermittently over *sabkhats* (salt lagoons), until meeting a point approximately due west of the island of Dalma (in the Arabian Gulf) and half way across the base of the Qatar peninsula. From there it heads east-southeasterly over sandy desert for approximately 22 miles (35 km.), before turning northeasterly and heading in a straight line to meet the coast at Khawr al-Udayd to the west of Jabal al-Udayd.

Historical Background. The earliest defined boundary between Saudi Arabia and Qatar was the "Blue Line" of the 1914 Anglo-Turkish Convention, which marked the frontier of Ottoman rule, running due south from the head of the bay opposite Zaknuniyyah and Aden. In the 1920s, Saudi Arabia grew territorially under the increasing power of Ibn Saud, who developed considerable influence over

Qatar, then a protectorate of Britain. In 1932, with the creation of the Kingdom of Saudi Arabia and the need to establish ownership of oil resources, there was significant impetus to clearly define the Saudi Arabia–Qatar boundary.

In 1935, an agreement was signed between Britain, Qatar and the Anglo-Persian Oil Company, in which Qatar's territory was defined by the Blue Line. Ibn Saud, however, refused to accept this border on the basis that the 1914 Convention had never been ratified, that it had been drawn up after Ibn Saud had occupied the province of Hasa, and that the Ottomans had never exercised extensive authority in Hasa during their period of occupation there.

In response, various alternative borders were proposed: Saudi Arabia proposed the "Red Line," which claimed Jabal Nakhsh, the southern tip of Jabal Dukhan on Qatar's west coast, and Khawr al-Udayd; in contrast, Britain proposed the "Riyadh Line," which gave Saudi Arabia much of the Rub al-Khali but retained Jabal Nakhsh as being within Qatar and Khawr al-Udayd as part of Abu Dhabi.

Pressure increased to solve the boundary disputes as oil companies' interests in the area grew. The 1935 Riyadh Line proposed by Britain had been withdrawn, although legally Britain never renounced the Blue Line, and after World War II informal negotiations with the US Department of State took place with few conclusions. The last formal British declaration about the boundary was made at the Damman Conference in 1952. Even so, as the oil reserves of both Qatar and Saudi Arabia began to be recognized and exploited, the two parties became involved in economic and social development, subordinating territorial disputes.

Eventually, in 1965, a full agreement was initiated between the respective rulers and ratified by Saudi Arabia that year (although details were released only in late 1992). This agreement was at the cost to Abu Dhabi of Khawr al-Udayd and its validity was consequently challenged by the British on their behalf. However, it was suggested by the British Foreign Office that Saudi Arabia and Qatar had probably reached an understanding on their boundary a full 20 years before this treaty was concluded. It is possible that at some time during the early 1940s Ibn Saud agreed to stop claiming Jabal Nakhsh (the lo-

cality having been discovered by this stage to overlie no substantial oil deposits) in return for recognition from the Qatari ruler for unlimited access to Khawr al-Udayd.

The stability of any kind of boundary between Saudi Arabia and Qatar worsened in the early 1970s when, in parallel, discussions were beginning on formally delimiting Saudi Arabia's boundary with the new federation of the United Arab Emirates. The exact outcome on these negotiations, which is believed to have given (among other concessions) Saudi Arabia an outlet to the Gulf west of Sabkhat Matti, was to have profound implication on any future territorial developments in the eastern sector of the boundary. In 1990, for example, Saudi Arabia established a new border post close to what was assumed to be the Saudi–United Arab Emirates–Qatar tripoint. Similarly, in September 1992, an alleged Saudi attack on the Qatari frontier post at Khafus prompted further dispute, as Saudi Arabia claimed that the incident was within Saudi territory and refused to acknowledge official responsibility for the attack. Eventually the Qatari cabinet decided to sever the 1965 agreement and called for the formation of an international committee to investigate Saudi territorial claims and so recommence negotiations to agree on the final border.

In 1993 the renewed border dispute was addressed in an accord ratified by both parties, with Egypt as guarantor. Although details were not released, it was revealed that the deal provided for border demarcation, based on an agreed but unpublished map, within one year, and the accord reportedly maintains Qatari sovereignty over Khafus in exchange for territorial concessions in favor of the Saudis elsewhere, and Qatari acknowledgment of Saudi sovereignty over the corridor of land acquired from the United Arab Emirates to the southern Gulf.

Present Situation. The border remains in doubt if only as a consequence of the secrecy surrounding the details of the 1993 boundary agreement and the 1974 delimitation agreement between the United Arab Emirates and Saudi Arabia. In addition, several alleged armed incidents between March and October 1994, reported by Qatar but denied by Saudi Arabia, have exacerbated the fragile state of this boundary line.

R

RÉUNION An island in the Indian Ocean, Réunion is an overseas department of France. Its area is 969 sq. miles (2,509 sq. km.), with an estimated population (1994) of 630,000. Réunion has no land boundaries and its capital is Saint-Denis.

The population is predominantly Roman Catholic although there is also a significant Muslim community. Sugar is the single most important cash crop, but coffee, tropical fruits and geraniums are also grown, the latter providing oil for the manufacture of perfumes. Many islanders provide services to the extensive French naval presence on the island.

ROMANIA A southeast European country (area: 91,699 sq. miles [237,400 sq. km.]; estimated population: 23,200,000 [1994]) in the Balkan Peninsula, Romania is bounded in the north and east by Ukraine (330 miles; 531 km.), east by Moldava (280 miles; 450 km.) and the Black Sea, south by Bulgaria (378 miles; 608 km.), southwest by Serbia (296 miles; 476 km.) and west by Hungary (275 miles; 443 km.). Romania's capital is Bucharest.

The ancient inhabitants of modern Romania were the Dacians, who were conquered by the Romans under Emperor Trajan in the first years of the second century. Roman rule was followed by massive colonization, and it is now a maxim in Romanian historiography that the Romanians are the descendants of this fusion. This is, however, difficult to prove as settled life came to a halt for more than a millennium after Roman withdrawal from Dacia in 270, and the land was conquered by consecutive waves of nomads. According to Romanian scholars, the Latinized population found shelter in the Carpathian Mountains and Transylvania, and their counterparts south of the Danube River found shelter in the Pindus Mountains, where they are known as Vlachs.

Some Western scholars hold that the Romanians are descendants of Vlachs who crossed the Danube northward in the early thirteenth century, while others try to connect their origin to Romance-speaking crusaders.

In the last decade of the thirteenth century and over the following 50 years, the two principalities of Wallachia (known in Romanian as Muntenia, or Tara Romaneasca [Romanian land]) and Moldavia (Moldova) were founded southwest and northwest of the Carpathians by Romanian *voivodes* (princes) from Transylvania. These grew in strength and territory, alternately fighting off and submitting to strong neighbors: Wallachia to Hungary and Moldavia to Poland. In 1417 Wallachia accepted Ottoman suzerainty and almost a century later, in 1513, Moldavia followed suit. This lasted, not without occasional conflict, until 1878. The Ottomans moved the capital of Wallachia to Bucharest and that of Moldavia to Iasi (Jasi). The treaty of Kucuk Kaynarca (1774) between Russia and the Ottomans and subsequent treaties made both principalities a de facto Russian protectorate. After the Crimean War, the Peace of Paris (1856) placed the principalities, still under formal Ottoman suzerainty, under the collective guarantee of the European powers, but the two were not allowed to unite. In response, both principalities elected the same prince in 1859 and with the assent of the powers, including the Ottomans, they merged into a single Romania.

The Congress of Berlin, following the Russo-Ottoman War of 1877–1878, granted the Romanians independence and in 1881 they formed a kingdom. In 1913 Romania took part in the Second Balkan War and gained southern Dubroja from Bulgaria. In World War I Romania joined the entente powers and gained Transylvania and Bukovina from Austria-

Hungary, and Bessarabia from the Russians. This fulfilled Romanian nationalist demands, but the incorporation of Hungarians, Germans, Ukrainians and Russians now gave rise to animosity and irredentism. During World War II, Romania stayed neutral at first, which cost it dearly. In June 1940 the Soviet Union recaptured Bessarabia. In August Hitler and Mussolini forced Romania to transfer the northern half of Transylvania to Hungary and in September the Germans forced Romania to return southern Dobruja to the Bulgarians. Following that, and after an internal coup in Bucharest, Romania joined the Axis powers. It took part in the invasion of the Soviet Union in 1941 and was rewarded with Bessarabia and further territories east of the Dniester River as far as the Ukrainian city of Odessa.

In 1944 Romania was occupied by Soviet forces.

By 1948 sovietization was complete and a Communist regime was in power in Bucharest. Under the peace treaty Romania gave up southern Dubroja to Bulgaria, and Bessarabia and Bukovina to the Soviet Union, but was returned Transylvania. In 1965 Nicolae Ceausescu came to power, which he retained until 1990. He enforced a large, oppressive, apparatus of terror and brought the Romanians to the verge of starvation. In 1990 a popular uprising and coup toppled Ceausescu, and he and his wife were executed.

ROMANIA — BULGARIA see BULGARIA–ROMANIA.

ROMANIA — HUNGARY see HUNGARY–ROMANIA.

ROMANIA — MOLDAVA see MOLDAVA– ROMANIA.

Romania's boundaries

ROMANIA — SERBIA The boundary between Romania and Serbia runs for 296 miles (476 km.) between the Hungary tripoint on the Muresul River in the northwest and the Bulgarian tripoint at the mouth of the Timok River in the Danube River in the southeast.

Geographical Setting. From its northwestern terminus, the boundary line runs southeastward for 150 miles (240 km.), crosses the Aranca River, the Kikinda (Serbia)–Timisoara (Romania) railway, the two Bega Canals, the Timis River, the Birzava Canal and the Vrsac (Serbia)–Timisoara railway, reaching the Gornovat River. The line follows the river southwestward for 6 miles (10 km.), running eastward to the Nera River and follows that river downstream westward to its confluence with the great Danube River south of Bela Crkva (Serbia). Thence for about 146 miles (256 km.) the boundary follows the main navigation channel of the Danube River downstream southeastward. The Danube islands in the vicinity of the Romanian town of Moldova Noua belong to Romania, while the island southeast of Orseva (Romania) belongs to Serbia. The island south of Drobeta (Romania) as well as the islands of Ostrovu Corbului and Ostravu Mare are Romanian territory while other islands of the Danube River were allocated according to the course of the navigation channel. The Bulgarian tripoint is located at the confluence of the Timok River with the Danube River, near the small Romanian town of Pristol.

Historical Background. Both Romania and Serbia were ruled by the Ottoman Empire from the fifteenth century. The Wallachia province north of the Danube River became an autonomous province in the Adrianopol Treaty that was signed between Russia and the Ottoman Empire in 1829. It joined the autonomous Moldavia province in 1859 to become autonomous Romania in 1864. Serbia became an autonomous province in 1817. The Russian–Turkish War of 1877 led to the establishment of independent Serbia by the Peace Treaty of San Stefano signed on 3 March 1878, while the Congress of Berlin (1878) established the independence of Romania a few months later.

The boundary between the two newly independent states was determined on the Danube River, thus establishing the present eastern section of the boundary line. The conclusion of World War I placed with Romania, by the Peace Treaty of Trianon signed on 4 June 1920, the area of Transylvania, while at the same time it placed within the newly established Kingdom of the Serbs, Croats and Slovenes, established in December 1918, the province of Voivodina, north of the Danube River. Thus, the boundary between Romania and the Kingdom of the Serbs, Croats and Slovenes, later (1929) Yugoslavia, was extended northwestward up to the tripoint of modern Hungary. Changes in the line that took place during World War II were abolished and the present boundary was restored after the war. When the Republic of Yugoslavia was demolished in 1991 Serbia became an independent state, adopting the eastern boundary of former Yugoslavia as its international boundary with Romania without any formal agreements.

Present Situation. Although the area and boundaries in former Yugoslavia are in disorder, there is no known dispute concerning the alignment of the boundary, which is recognized by both states. The land section of the line is well demarcated, while the river section, including the allocation of the river's islands, is known and accepted by both states.

ROMANIA — UKRAINE The boundary between Romania and Ukraine is divided into two sections—northern and southern. Between the two, along the Prut River, lie the boundaries between Moldava and Romania to the southwest and between Moldava and Ukraine to the northeast. The length of the northern sector is 225 miles (362 km.) while the southern sector is 105 miles (169 km.) long. Both sections, along with the Romania–Moldava boundary, are the former international boundary line between Romania and the Soviet Union.

Geographical Setting. The northern section of the Romania–Ukraine boundary begins at the border junction with Hungary, north of the Romanian town of Satu-Mare. The line then runs eastward to the Tisza (Tisa) River and follows it to the foothill of the eastern Carpathian Mountains, south of the Ukrainian city of Rakhov. The boundary climbs the mountain range eastward and enters the Moldavan-Bessarabian plateau. Crossing the Siret River, the boundary runs northeast toward the Prut River. It then courses through the middle of the navigation channel of that river to the northern boundary junction with Moldava.

The southern section is a river boundary. It begins at the southern border junction with Moldava on the Prut River, north of the Romanian city of Galati. The line follows the main navigation channel of the Prut River to its confluence with the Danube River, east of Galati. It then follows the main navigation channel of the Danube River to its delta, where the boundary coincides with the Kilia arm to Vilkovo (Ukraine) and then the Old Stambul arm to the Black Sea.

Historical Background. The present boundary between Romania and Ukraine is the outcome of 200 years of Russian and Soviet Union activities in the Balkan and northwestern Black Sea regions. During the nineteenth and early twentieth centuries the Balkans were a buffer zone between the Slavic state of Russia and the western and central European states. During the fourteenth and fifteenth centuries two local principalities, Moldavia and Wallachia, became independent, but the two fell to the Turkish Ottoman Empire late in the fifteenth century. In the late eighteenth century the power of the Ottoman Empire waned as the strength of both Russia and Austria increased. In 1777 Austria annexed Bukovina (now in Ukraine), until then a part of Moldavia, by the Treaty of Peace between Russia and Turkey of 23 June 1812. Russia annexed Bessarabia (now partly in Moldava, partly in Ukraine) while the Wallachia and Moldavia regions were restored to Turkish administration.

The Crimean War of 1853–1856 brought some changes to the boundary line. In order to block the Russian march into the Balkan region, the Western powers guaranteed national administration to both principalities under Turkish suzerainty and lower Bessarabia was restored to Moldavia. Both principalities joined together to form the new state of Romania in 1861, which declared itself independent of Turkey in 1877. The Congress of Berlin, which was convened in 1878 after the war between Russia and Turkey, recognized Romania's independence but the three districts of southeastern Bessarabia were restored to Russia, which also gained access to the Delta of the Danube.

The next change that took place in the boundary's location was carried out during the last months of World War I. The collapse of the Czarist Russian Empire brought about a union between Bessarabia and Romania, which was signed on 27 March 1918. A treaty signed in 1920, with final ratification in 1927, between the Allied Powers and Romania, confirmed the union while the Soviet Union maintained that the action was illegal and never recognized it. At the same time Romania incorporated Austrian Bukovina. The Peace Treaty of Versailles, signed with Austria on 10 September 1919, that came into effect on 16 July 1920, also covered that annexation.

The boundary between Romania and Czechoslovakia (part of today's Romania–Ukraine boundary) was based on the Versailles Peace Treaty. It ran for 133 miles (214 km.) between the Hungarian boundary in the west and a junction with the Polish border in the east. It was demarcated between 1923 and 1930 and a convention was signed on 15 July 1930. The Ruthenia region was attached to Czechoslovakia in order to give it direct boundary contact with Romania.

Another section of today's boundary between Romania and Ukraine was the boundary between Romania and Poland, which was settled on 17 May 1935. The 33-mile (53-km.) line ran from the boundary junction with Czechoslovakia northeastward to the boundary junction with the Soviet Union. In 1922, the Soviet Union established the constituent republic of Ukraine which was bounded in the west by Romania.

During World War II, on 28 June 1940, Romania—under the joint pressure of the Soviet Union and Germany—returned all of Bessarabia, northern Bukovina and the Herta district of northwestern Moldavia, to the Soviet Union, transferring an approximate total of 19,500 sq. miles (50,500 sq. km.) and 3,400,000 people. The Soviet Union established the constituent republic of Moldavia in Bessarabia while Bukovina became part of Ukraine.

Major changes took place after World War II. On 29 June 1945 Czechoslovakia gave Ruthenia to the Soviet Union, disconnecting itself from Romania by doing so. Similarly, Poland ceded a large eastern parcel to the Soviet Union, also severing itself from Romania. The Treaty of Peace with Romania, signed in Paris on 10 February 1947, restored the June 1940 boundary between Romania and the Soviet Union along a line that was demarcated and the final document was signed in September 1949. For about 45 years the boundary line between the two countries was maintained without any changes. In 1991, with the collapse of the Soviet Union and the establishment of Ukraine and Moldavia (Moldava) as independent countries, the former division became the sectioned boundary between Romania and Ukraine.

Present Situation. During the incorporation of Romania into the Soviet sphere of influence after World War II, Romanian disagreement with the precise alignment of the boundary was never expressed publicly. During the late 1970s and early 1980s, however, Romania raised the question of Bessarabia and Bukovina, although there appears to be no open disagreement concerning the boundary. Since 1991 no boundary disputes between Romania and the new countries established along its eastern border have been known, but could be raised in the future.

RUSSIA Located partly in Eastern Europe and partly in northern Asia, Russia (area: 6,592,849 sq. miles [17,068,886 sq. km.]; estimated population: 150,000,000 [1994]) is the largest country in the world, even after the collapse of the Soviet Union in 1991. It is bounded by the Arctic Ocean in the north, by the Pacific Ocean in the east, by North Korea (12 miles; 19 km.), China (2,265 miles; 3,645 km.), Mongolia (2,139 miles; 3,441 km.), Kazakhstan (4,255 miles; 6,846 km.), Azerbaijan (176.5 miles; 284 km.) and Georgia (450 miles; 723 km.) in the south, by Ukraine (980 miles; 1,576 km.) in the southwest and by Belarus (596 miles; 959 km.), Poland (269 miles; 432 km.), Lithuania (141 miles; 227 km.), Latvia (135 miles; 217 km.), Estonia (180 miles; 290 km.), the Baltic Sea, Finland (816 miles; 1,313 km.) and Norway (122 miles; 196 km.) in the west. Russia's capital is Moscow.

The ethnonym "Russian" comes from Rus, the name by which the Eastern Slavs, following their Finnic neighbors, called the Scandinavian Vikings. It was the Vikings who organized the Russians and established the Kievan state in the late ninth century. These Rus, under the leadership of descendants of Prince Rurik of Jutland, soon became slavicized as their names testify. Vladimir (972–1015) gave Kievan Rus its territorial extension, the watersheds of all the rivers leading to the Baltic, Black and Caspian Seas, its first code of law and its dynastic seniority system. But most important, in 989 he converted his people to Orthodox Christianity, thus linking the Eastern Slavs culturally to the rich Byzantine civilization but isolating them from the Catholic West and from the neighboring Western Slavs.

His son Jaroslav (1019–1054) started the "Golden Century" when Kievan culture reached its zenith, which afterwards influenced all its successor states and peoples. Soon after his death, however, the Kievan state was divided into a growing number of principalities, and the center moved from Kiev to Vladimir. This change reflected the moving of the demographic, economic-commercial and cultural center of Kievan Rus to the northeast where the forefathers of the Russians were beginning to emerge as a separate people.

After the Mongol invasion of 1238–1240 the princes ruling in the central Russian lands were subjugated to the *khans* of the Golden Horde for about 240 years, while those in the west were gradually absorbed by Lithuania and Poland. It was through loyalty to the *khans* that the princes of Moscow (originally a small peripheral principality of Vladimir) managed to annex much territory. The process of "regathering the Russian lands" became part of the official ideology in the mid-fifteenth century under Ivan III, the first Muscovite ruler to declare himself "czar" (Caesar) as a demonstration of independence from and claim of overlordship over the Tatars. He was also first to claim to be the head of the Christian world as the heir to the Byzantine Empire.

Under Ivan IV, the Russians conquered Kazan (1552) and Astrakhan (1556) and began the expansionary process that brought them to the far eastern areas of Okhotsk within a century. In the middle of the seventeenth century under Alexis Romanov the eastern Ukraine was annexed. Peter the Great conquered the Baltic provinces and turned the Russians toward rapid westernization, but at a terrible cost in lives. Catherine the Great completed the "regathering of the Russian lands," in the eighteenth century by acquiring Lithuania and parts of Poland. In another direction she annexed the northern coast of the Black Sea and the Crimea and started expansion into the Caucasus. In the nineteenth century the czars rounded off their empire by conquering the Caucasus (in a lengthy and very costly war), central Asia and the Russian Far East.

The Russians spread through large parts of their expanding empire through colonization and assimilation, mainly of Finno-Ugric, Turkish non-Muslim and various Siberian groups. This assimilation was frequently facilitated by these groups' conversion to Russian Orthodox Christianity. The participation of Byelorussians and Ukrainians, in the colonization of newly conquered lands facilitated in many cases both their own Russification and the assimilation of the native population. In the second half of the nineteenth century, however, with the spread of nationalism, the Russian empire found itself sharing the predicament of other multi-national empires and used the same remedy: forced assimilation. This was also connected with the regime's attempt to divert grievances arising from social, economic, demographic and educational changes which found no adjustment in the political structure, by encouraging a development of Russian chauvinism.

World War I and the 1917 Revolution brought down the czarist regime and, following a bitter civil war, the Soviet Union was established on the principles of Marxism and recognition of the rights of all ethnic groups. Nevertheless, the Russians soon proved to be the dominant people of the Soviet Union as they had been in czarist Russia. The Russian Soviet Federated Socialist Republic (RSFSR) was the strongest and largest in population and area and was, in fact, the core of the Soviet Union. If in the first years of the new regime there were attempts to put down the centrality of the Russians, during Stalin's long rule it gradually became a principle, and the Soviet Union was proclaimed "a happy family of peoples, led and guided by the elder brother: the Russian people."

Accordingly, a policy of assimilation was carried out using different means, not all subtle. These included wholesale registration of ethnic groups as Russians; failure to provide small ethnic groups with alphabets, thus assimilating them by making Russian their literary language; and migration, both forced and encouraged. The subtlest and most widespread method was the creation of a "Russian-speaking population" through making Russian the only language of education. At the same time, the various officially-recognized national languages were subjected to creeping Russification of their alphabet, vocabulary and even grammar.

Following the dissolution of the Soviet Union the RSFSR separated from the other 14 republics. It was officially renamed the Russian Federation, but has come to be known as "Russia" around the world. This, however, did not seem to resolve the problems resulting from the country's remaining under the dominance of the Russians. In addition, 25,000,000 Russians found themselves living outside Russia, including 11,000,000 in the Ukraine alone.

RUSSIA — AZERBAIJAN see AZERBAIJAN–RUSSIA.

RUSSIA — BELARUS see BELARUS–RUSSIA.

RUSSIA — CHINA see CHINA–RUSSIA.

RUSSIA — ESTONIA see ESTONIA–RUSSIA.

RUSSIA — FINLAND see FINLAND–RUSSIA.

RUSSIA — GEORGIA see GEORGIA–RUSSIA.

RUSSIA — KAZAKHSTAN see KAZAKHSTAN–RUSSIA.

RUSSIA — KOREA, NORTH see KOREA, NORTH–RUSSIA.

RUSSIA — LATVIA see LATVIA–RUSSIA.

RUSSIA — LITHUANIA see LITHUANIA–RUSSIA.

RUSSIA — MONGOLIA see MONGOLIA–RUSSIA.

RUSSIA — NORWAY see NORWAY–RUSSIA.

RUSSIA — POLAND see POLAND–RUSSIA.

RUSSIA — UKRAINE The boundary between Russia and Ukraine follows the internal division between two republics of the former Soviet Union. It runs for 980 miles (1,576 km.) between the tripoint with Belarus west of the Snov River in the northwest and the Gulf of Taganrog in the eastern section of the Sea of Azov in the southeast.

Geographical Setting. From the Belarussian tripoint, located north of Shchor (Ukraine) and west of a curve in the Snov River, the Russia–Ukraine boundary line runs southeastward, reaches the Snov River and follows it upstream eastward for about 30 miles (50 km.). Running northward, it crosses the Shostka (Ukraine)– Novozybkov (Russia) railway. It then runs eastward, reaching and crossing the Desna River southeastward, crossing the Kiev (Ukraine)–Moscow (Russia) highway east of Glukhov (Ukraine). Thence it runs southward and after crossing the Seim River it heads eastward, crosses the Konotop (Ukraine)–Kursk (Russia) railway and the Psiol River and bears southward. After crossing the Sunry (Ukraine)–Belgorod (Russia) railway and the upper tributaries of the Vorskla River, the boundary line changes its direction and runs eastward for about 220 miles (360 km.), reaching the Kalitva River. The boundary follows that river downstream southward for about 25 miles (40 km.), leaves it and runs southwestward to reach the Derleu River, which it follows downstream southward to its confluence with the Donets River, east of Voroshilovgrad (Ukraine). It then follows the latter river downstream southeastward for about 40 miles (65 km.) and leaves it to form a straight line southward for another 40 miles (65 km.) to a point south of the Rostov on the Don (Russia)–Kharkov (Ukraine) highway, west of Novoshakhtinsk (Russia). Finally running southwestward for about 100 miles (160 km.), the Russia–Ukraine boundary reaches the sea at the Gulf of Taganrog west of the Ukrainian town of Novoazovsk.

Historical Background. Until 1991 Ukraine ("The frontier land" in Russian) had never been an independent state. In the Middle Ages Kiev, its capital, was the capital of Russia, but from 1240 until 1360 it was occupied by the Mongols. Later, the area of today's Ukraine was ruled by Lithuania, Poland and, from 1654, by Russia. Ukraine declared its independence in 1917, after the Bolshevik Revolution, but this was abolished by Soviet Russia, which occupied Ukraine in 1920 and established the Social Republic of Ukraine as part of the Soviet Union. The boundary between the Soviet republics of Russia and Ukraine was determined as an internal line in 1936. Changes in the area of Ukraine following World War II did not affect the internal division, which

served the needs of the Soviet Union until 1991. At that time Russia and Ukraine became independent states, adopting the 1936 line as their common international boundary line without making a formal agreement.

Present Situation. The boundary line that served as an internal division in the Soviet Union was not established in accordance with ethnic or geographical considerations. As an internal line such applications were not important, but when the republics gained independence both realized that these issues affected the line and many unofficial claims for each other's territories developed. Ukraine wants control of the area southeast of the Russian Gomel district as well as the southwestern part of the Russian Rostov district. Russia, on the other hand, calls for Ukrainian withdrawal from Crimea and its return to Russia. Although these claims are unofficial, only a formal agreement concerning the alignment of the boundary line will calm both states.

RWANDA A central African, landlocked country (area: 10,169 sq. miles [26,327 sq. km.]; estimated population: 7,700,000 [1993]), Rwanda is bounded by Uganda (105 miles; 169 km.) in the north, by Tanzania (135 miles; 217 km.) in the east, by Burundi (180 miles; 290 km.) in the south and by Zaire (135 miles; 217 km.) in the west. The capital of Rwanda is Kigali.

Colonized by the Germans in the late nineteenth century, the region, along with neighboring Burundi, was conquered by the Belgians in World War I. Initially Belgium favored the Tutsi, but Catholic missionaries eventually persuaded the colonial authorities to transfer their support to the majority Hutu shortly after World War II. The Tutsi king was deposed, and in 1962 Rwanda became an independent state. Characteristic of the independence movement was marked opposition by all parties to unite the country with neighboring Burundi as a single political entity.

In 1963, Tutsi refugees who had fled to Uganda attempted to invade Rwanda and reestablish their hegemony. The Hutu responded by massacring 12,000 Tutsi. By 1964 as many as 150,000 Tutsi fled Rwanda; they are still living as refugees along the border. The remaining Tutsi still form a sizable proportion of the educated elite, however, and Hutu resentment is still characteristic of relations between the two groups. Following the 1970s there have been continuing bloody clashes between the two groups and many more Tutsi have fled the country.

A small group, known as the Tussi, mostly refugees from Rwanda, live on the border with southwest Uganda, although some have lived in that area since the days of British rule. They speak a Southern Lacustrine Bantu language called Lunyarwanda. In 1990 they started an invasion of Rwanda under the leadership of military officers who had defected from Uganda, where the bulk of the Rwandan Patriotic Front fighters were born.

RWANDA — BURUNDI see BURUNDI–RWANDA.

RWANDA — TANZANIA Demarcated throughout by the Kagera River and by pillars, this border runs from the boundary tripoint with Burundi to the tripoint boundary junction with Uganda for 135 miles (217 km.).

Geographical Setting. From the boundary tripoint with Burundi at the junction of the *thalweg*s of the Mwibu and Kagera rivers, the Rwanda–Tanzania boundary runs northward along the *thalweg* of the latter to its intersection with the straight line that joins boundary beacon 59A and boundary beacon 59B. It then forms a series of straight-line sectors through the marshes and river channel, linking intervisible stone pillars that are located on prominent headlands or on islands in the Kagera Valley. When these lines cross terra firma, the boundary is determined by the shore of the headlands (the shore is taken to be the limit of dry land at extreme low water)—from the point where the straight line between pillars crosses the shore on departure from the marsh to the point where it or another straight line next crosses the shore on re-entering the marsh. When boundary pillars are situated upon islands, the boundary runs by the shortest possible route along the shore of the islands, from the point where a straight line between pillars first cuts the shore on leaving the marsh, to the point where the next straight line between pillars last cuts the shore on regaining the marsh. From the intersection described above, the straight lines reach the intersection of the *thalweg* of the Kagera River with the line between pillars 72A and 72B. Between these points the bor-

der reaches pillar no. 60 on the southwestern end of the Island of Zinga, continues to pillar no. 61 on Nyakagasha at the northern end of Kagoma and pillar no. 62 on Kaliba at the northeast end of Kayinya (Kagnigna) and arrives at pillar no. 63 at the southwestern end of the Island of Kyabalelwa (Tschabalelwa). Boundary pillar no. 64 is found on Luterana on the eastern side of Kageyo (Kageo); no. 65 on the western end of Mwoga; no. 66 on the western end of Gitaga; no. 67 on the northeastern end of Ndalama (Rurama); no. 68 on Magashi on the northeastern edge of Mubari; no. 69 on the southern point of Gabiro; no. 70 on Kitobelaho northeast of Nyakishoz; no. 71 on Gashoza at the northeastern end of Kamakaba. The boundary then reaches the *thalweg* of the Kagera River, where it cuts the line between pillars 72A on Ryanyawanga and 72B on Akanyo at the northern end of Kamakaba. It follows this *thalweg* to its junction with the *thalweg* of the Kagitumba River at the boundary tripoint with Uganda.

Historical Background. Between 1885 and the end of World War I Rwanda and Tanzania were part of German East Africa and were divided by an internal administrative boundary. By Article 119 of the Treaty of Versailles, Germany renounced its overseas possessions and German East Africa was administered by the League of Nations, Belgium being responsible for Ruanda-Urundi and the United Kingdom for Tanganyika. Under the provisions of the Milner-Orts Agreement of 1919, Belgium ceded the Kisaka (Gisaka) territory west of the Kagera to Tanganyika; the transfer took place on 21 March 1921. This gave the British a route from Tanganyika to its protectorate of Uganda and the new boundary was designed to accommodate the construction of a railway line between the two countries. However, by 1923 the detachment of the Kisaka territory was seen to have been detrimental to its people and the boundary was moved eastward once again to the Kagera River; on 1 January 1924 the territory of Kisaka returned to Belgian control. An Anglo-Belgian protocol of 5 August 1924 described the boundary between Rwanda and Tanganyika from the tripoint boundary junction with Urundi down the Kagera River to the boundary junction with Uganda. The midstream of the river was to constitute the boundary and a survey was to fix, provisionally, the position of the midstream point of the Kagera. Due to the swampy conditions and many meanders in the river, the 1924 protocol did not delimit the boundary accurately.

In 1934, a further Anglo-Belgian treaty aligned the present boundary and it was demarcated by pillars relative to the course of the Kagera River. Where the river itself is used, the *thalweg*, not the midstream, is the boundary. An additional agreement signed in London on the same day (22 November 1934) established water rights along the boundary. The Burundi tripoint was determined officially from an ordinance of the vice governor of Ruanda-Urundi that delimited the country's boundary in 1949. Prior to this a traditional line was used. The Ugandan tripoint is at the junction of the *thalwegs* of the Kagitumba and Kagera rivers and connects with a boundary established by an Anglo-German Agreement of 14 May 1910 that was reached to clarify those countries' respective spheres of influence. Ruanda-Urundi became two separate independent states, Rwanda and Burundi, on 1 July 1962. Tanganyika, independent from 9 December 1961, formed a United Republic with Zanzibar on 27 April 1964 and became the United Republic of Tanzania on 29 October 1964.

Present Situation. Both Rwanda and Tanzania adopted the colonial division as their common international boundary without a formal agreement.

RWANDA — UGANDA This 105-mile (169-km.) border runs between the boundary tripoint with Zaire on Sabinio peak and the tripoint with Tanzania. The line is demarcated throughout by streams or pillars.

Geographical Setting. The boundary between Rwanda and Uganda follows the watershed that stretches from the highest point of Sabinio Mountain through the highest points of Mgahinga (Gahinga) and Muhavura (pillar no. 1), where the road from north to south of the volcanoes crosses it between Sabinio and Mgahinga. It then runs to the Mulemule-Mussongo spur, then to the summit of Nyarubebsa hill and boundary pillar no. 2 between the Nyarubebsa and Mussongo hills. It bears along the road leading southward to the top of Mussongo, which is marked by a direction pillar, and along the crest to the summit of the hill marked by pillar no. 3. A curved line, marked by pillars 4–8, leads to

pillar no. 9 and a straight line from there climbs to the top of a hill marked by pillar no. 10. Another straight line takes the boundary to the southern summit of the Wugamba range (pillar no. 11) and it continues along the crest of this range to Kanyaminyenya hill, which is marked by pillar no. 12, and trends via several direction pillars to pillar no. 13 on the northernmost point of the range. Passing more direction pillars to pillar no. 14 on the Mabaremere hill and pillar no. 15, which lies due west of the confluence of the Vigaga (Kirurumi) and Mugera (Narugwamby) rivers, the boundary takes a straight line to that confluence, which is marked by pillar no. 16. It follows the *thalweg* of the Kirurumi River to its source at pillar no. 17 and then forms a straight line to pillar no. 18, located 2.5 miles (4 km.) northwest of the summit of Gwassa hill. The boundary takes straight lines to the top of Akasiru hill, which is marked by a direction pillar, and to pillar no. 19 at the top of Sanja hill. It then heads straight to pillar no. 20 on the path running from east to west in the valley east of Sanja hill and to pillar no. 21 on the top of Kisivo hill. From the spur of Kisivo hill east-northeastward and marked by direction pillars, the border reaches a conspicuous knoll at its foot, marked by pillar no. 22, a direction pillar on the edge of the swamp, and pillar no. 23 at the foot of a prominent spur. It follows the crest of this spur, which is marked by a direction pillar, to pillar no. 24 on its summit and continues along the crest to the top of Kavimbiri hill where pillar no. 25 is located. Along the crest of this hill the line meets boundary pillar no. 26 and, in a straight line marked by a direction pillar in the valley, reaches the summit of a small conspicuous hill (Nyakara), also marked by a direction pillar. Another straight line leads to the summit of Kitana hill and takes the boundary along its crest and its northern and northeastern spurs to a conspicuous knoll in the valley, which is marked by a direction pillar. Once again in a straight line to a direction pillar on a spur of Nebishagara hill, the boundary trends along the crest of this spur to its top, marked by boundary pillar no. 27. It continues along the crest and long spur of this hill to pillar no. 28 on the top of Magumbizi hill, thence along the water parting to pillar no. 29 on top of Kivisa hill, along the spur of this hill to its northern end and straight toward a direction pillar in the valley. It follows another straight line to pillar no. 30 on the southern summit of Ndega hill, runs to a hill on the western bank of the Muvumba River and then heads straight to pillar no. 31 on the top of another small hill. A series of straight lines, marked at each change of direction and by pillars 32 to 35 on prominent spurs, takes the boundary along the eastern slopes of the Mushuri range, around the slopes of the valley between the Mushuri range and the spur ending Kitoff hill and around Kitoff hill to pillar no. 36 on a spur at its southern end. It then reaches spurs on its southeastern and eastern edges and, passing a knoll at the foot of the last spur, it reaches the saddle between Kitoff and Mawari (Mabare), marked by pillar no. 37. Northeastward to the source of the Lubirizi River (pillar no. 38), the boundary then follows its *thalweg* to the Chizinga (Muvogero) River, courses along the *thalweg* of that river to its confluence with the Kagitumba River and finally bears with the *thalweg* of the Kagitumba River to its confluence with the Kagera River at the boundary tripoint with Tanzania.

Historical Background. In 1890, Germany and Britain divided between them the territory west of Lake Victoria as far as the Congo Free State. Initially the border was to run across Lake Victoria in a straight line to the Congo border, only deviating to encompass Mount Mufumbiro should it lie south of the 1°S parallel. Later Mufumbiro was found to be a volcanic region lying south of 1°S. In 1910, an Anglo-Belgian-German conference in Brussels agreed that Sabinio peak would be the tripoint of the territories of the three states and on 14 May 1910 the present boundaries between Rwanda and Uganda and between Tanzania and Uganda were delimited in an Anglo-German agreement. Details of the final delimitation and demarcation of the boundary from Sabinio peak and of the source of the southwestern branch (the Lubirizi) of the Muvogero River were provided in an Anglo-German protocol signed at Kamwezi on 30 October 1911.

The Tanzanian tripoint is derived from the administrative boundary between Ruanda–Urundi and Tanganyika within German East Africa. The tripoint at the *thalweg* junction of the Kagitumba and Kagera rivers was enshrined in the Anglo-Belgian Treaty of 1934. Uganda, a vaguely defined area which changed shape and size dramatically over the

years, was declared to be within the British sphere of influence by an Anglo-German agreement of 1 July 1890. The area was a protectorate from 1894 and in 1902 an order in council defined some of its borders; on 9 October 1962 Uganda became an independent state.

Present Situation. Both states adopted the colonial boundary as their international division in the 1960s and at present the line is undisputed.

RWANDA — ZAIRE From the boundary tripoint with Burundi at the confluence of the Ruzizi and Luhwa (Ruwa) rivers, this border runs northward and westward for 135 miles (217 km.) to Mount Sabinio at the boundary tripoint with Uganda. It follows streams, crosses Lake Kivu, is marked by pillars between Lake Kivu and Mount Hehu and thereafter forms straight-line sectors between mountain peaks.

Geographical Setting. The Rwanda–Zaire boundary extends generally northward from the boundary tripoint at the confluence of the Ruzizi and Luhwa (Ruwa) rivers, along the *thalweg* of the former into Lake Kivu. It crosses Lake Kivu northward, from the mouth of the Ruzizi River to a point on the northern shore halfway between Goma (Zaire) and Kisengyi (Rwanda), which is designated by boundary marker no. 1. Through the lake the line passes among the islands, leaving Iwinza, Nyamaronga, Kwidjwi and Kitanga to Zaire and Kikaya, Gombo, Kumenie and Wau (Wahu) islands to Rwanda.

From here the boundary is marked by a further 20 boundary markers and proceeds in a series of straight lines. It leaves the northern shore of Lake Kivu and runs to a point about 1,300 feet (400 m.) north (boundary marker no. 2) of the first marker and continues in the same direction until it meets the Kisengyi railway (boundary marker no. 3) and runs to a mound (boundary marker no. 4) about 100 feet (30 m.) west of a continuation of the same line. From that hill it trends toward the small Maheshi hill (boundary marker no. 5) near the village of Musangania and just over 1,310 feet (400 m.) north of the last marker, and then proceeds to boundary marker no. 6, which is located northwest of Kabuga village. It heads toward the hill crest near the intersection of two railways (boundary marker no. 7) and, at a point (boundary marker no. 8) that stands near Lumeniambra village, the line turns northeast to reach a small hill known as Ruwadsi (boundary marker no. 9) and continues to a mound (boundary marker no. 10) near the Kissegnies–Buschwaga railway. It reaches boundary marker no. 11 near a large tree at Imana Kiwumo and boundary marker no. 12 on a lava crest about 3,000 feet (900 m.) north of marker no. 11; marker no. 13 is found on top of a small hill and marker no. 14 about 2,000 feet (600 m.) northeast of it. The boundary proceeds to two small elevations in the lava plain east of Iwuwiro (boundary marker no. 15), to a point east of Kitimba hill (boundary marker no. 16) and on to marker no. 17 southeast of Tchabgato (Niakawanda) hill. Boundary marker no. 18 is at a point where the line of Tchabgato hill cuts the large depression between the slopes of the Ninanongo and Karisimbi. The boundary then bears north-northeast, following the depression to boundary marker no. 20, opposite Mongomane (Bihira); the intermediate marker, no. 19, stands at a point in the depression approximately 4,000 feet (1,200 m.) from no. 18. From boundary marker no. 20, where the line of Mongomane cuts the large depression between the slopes of Ninanongo and Karisimbi, the boundary forms a straight line northeastward, up to Kabuanga hill (boundary marker no. 21) and reaches the northern summit of Mount Hehu. It then runs straight to the summits of Karisimbi, Vissoke (Kishasha) and Mount Sabinio, following the crests of the chain of small volcanoes that runs between them.

Historical Background. The historic kingdom of Rwanda fell within the German sphere of influence from 1898 and was administered as part of German East Africa. After World War I, however, Germany renounced its overseas territories and German East Africa was governed under the League of Nations. Belgium was mandated to hold the northwestern area of German East Africa, then known as Ruanda-Urundi. The eastern limits of the Congo Free State were originally described in a declaration of the administrator-general of its Department of Foreign Affairs (1 August 1885), but were altered when the alignment was determined by the Belgian-German convention of 11 August 1910. A more precise delimitation of the line from the northern shore of Lake Kivu to Mount Hehu was approved by a protocol signed at Goma on 25 June 1911. Ruanda-Urundi became independent as two separate nations on 1 July 1962; Ruanda was renamed the Republic of Rwanda. In 1960 Zaire (formerly the Congo Free State and Belgian Congo) had also gained independence. As independent states, both accepted the exisiting boundary alignment, although no formal agreement was made to this effect.

Present Situation. In April 1994 civil war in Rwanda sent hundreds of thousands of refugees into Zaire. The border was closed temporarily on several occasions as Zaire sought first to impose order on the mass immigration and later to encourage Rwandans to return home. Zaire is threatened by the overspill of violence as the civil dispute is carried on in refugee camps, and by the pressure on its resources created by such a huge and sudden influx of people.

S

SAINT CHRISTOPHER-NEVIS see SAINT KITTS
AND NEVIS.

SAINT HELENA An island located in the South
Atlantic Ocean, Saint Helena is a dependent territory of the United Kingdom. Its area (including islands that are uninhabited dependencies) is 121 sq.
miles (314 sq. km.) with an estimated population
(1994) of 8,000. Its capital is Jamestown and it has
no land boundaries.

SAINT KITTS AND NEVIS An islands state,
Saint Kitts and Nevis is located in the West Indies,
in the Caribbean Sea, east of Puerto Rico. It consists
of three islands—Nevis, Saint Christopher (Saint
Kitts) and Sombrero—and its total land area is 104
sq. miles (269 sq. km.). It has an estimated population (1994) of 44,000. Its capital is Basseterre and it
has no land boundaries.

The country was first colonized by the British in
1623 and became independent in 1983. English is
the main language and the people are predominantly
Christians, with three-quarters of the population pro-
fessing Protestantism. The sugar industry generates
over 50% of total revenues, but tourism is also a significant income earner. Nevis recently seceded from
the federation.

SAINT LUCIA An island country, Saint Lucia is
situated in the West Indies in the Caribbean Sea. Its
area is 238 sq. miles (616 sq. km.) and it has an estimated population (1994) of 160,000. Its capital is
Castries. Saint Lucia has no land boundaries.

The island was ceded by France to Great Britain in
1814 and achieved full independence (after a 12-
year period of self-government) in 1979. Nearly
90% of the population is descended from black

Africans brought as slave laborers for the sugar, tobacco, ginger and cotton plantations established in
the seventeenth and eighteenth centuries.

**SAINT MARTIN (France) — SINT MAARTEN
(Netherlands)** Like Hispaniola but few others in
the world, this island is partitioned into two political
units. In this case (as formerly in Timor), the two
units are non-self-governing territories of European
countries. Once an important producer of salt, sugar
and cotton, this low volcanic island in the Lesser
Antilles is now chiefly a tourist destination.

Georgraphical Setting. The boundary divides the
island into nearly equal northern and southern
halves, passing in mostly gentle curves over low
hills and a large lagoon. The line is scarcely noticeable on the ground, being marked, for example, beside one transborder road by a small stone pillar and
a small sign, and along another road by a larger sign
reading (in English, the lingua franca of the island),
"Welcome to the French Side."

Historical Background. Columbus visited the island on his second voyage, but Europeans did not
settle there for almost a century and a half. The seventeenth and eighteenth centuries were a period of
intense rivalry among European countries for island
and mainland possessions around the Caribbean Sea
and few remained in the hands of a single metropolitan country throughout the colonial period. The island has been shared by two of these former rivals—
France and the Netherlands—from early in the
seventeenth century to the present, except for a brief
occupation of the Dutch portion by Spain during
1633–1648.

The first Frenchmen arrived in 1629 and, apparently unaware of this, Dutchmen settled on the south
side of the island in 1631. It seems that the two

The French–Netherlands border on the island of Saint Martin

colonies expanded and met without any notable friction and worked out a modus vivendi between them. This arrangement was formalized by the Treaty of Concordia (1648), modeled after a similar but relatively short-lived treaty between France and England in respect of the nearby island of Saint Kitts. After its signing in 1648, the Dutch West India Company became the first formal government in the south, to be replaced later by the government of the Netherlands. There has apparently been no significant controversy over either the sharing of the island or the boundary between the two portions.

Present Situation. Each part of the island is a dependency of other dependencies, probably a unique situation in the world. Saint Martin is a unit of the French West Indies, administered from Guadeloupe, an overseas department of France. Sint Maarten is a unit of the Netherlands Antilles, constitutionally an equal partner of the Netherlands in the kingdom, administered from Willemstad in Curaçao.

Since the metropolitan countries are members of the European Union, the entire island is a common market and there are no customs or immigration controls whatsoever. The boundary, then, serves purely local functions such as delimiting jurisdictions for taxation, planning and zoning, and administration of justice.

SAINT PIERRE AND MIQUELON This is a group of eight islands located in the Atlantic Ocean, south of Newfoundland (Canada). It is a French territorial collectivity with a total land area of 93 sq. miles (242 sq. km.) and an estimated population (1994) of 6,750. Saint Pierre and Miquelon has no land boundaries and its capital is Saint-Pierre.

SAINT VINCENT AND THE GRENADINES An islands country, Saint Vincent and the Grenadines is situated in the Caribbean Sea. It consists of the northern Grenadines islands and Saint Vincent island, and its total land area is 150 sq. miles (388 sq. km.). It has an estimated population (1994) of 115,000 and its capital is Kingstown. It has no land boundaries.

Located in the Windward Islands in the Caribbean Sea, the island of Saint Vincent controls about half of the Grenadines, a chain of more than 100 small islands scattered between Saint Vincent and Grenada to the southwest. Some three-quarters of the inhabitants of the country are descendants of

Africans brought to work as slaves during occupations by the British and the French. Perhaps 20% of the population is of mixed origin, with a small minority of European descent and a community of around 1,000 Black Caribs, descendants of the intermingling of Native Americans and runaway African slaves from other islands that predate the European colonization.

SAN MARINO   A tiny landlocked European country (area: 24 sq. miles [61 sq. km.]; estimated population: 24,000 [1994]), San Marino is situated in the Italian peninsula. It is bounded on all sides by Italy (24 miles; 39 km.). Its capital is San Marino.

SAN MARINO — ITALY   see ITALY–SAN MARINO.

SAO TOME AND PRINCIPE   A republic consisting of two tiny African islands in the Gulf of Guinea, Sao Tome and Principe has a total land area of 372 sq. miles (964 sq. km.) and an estimated population (1994) of 130,000. Its capital is Sao Tome and it has no land boundaries.

The islands became independent from the Portuguese in 1975. Since the mid-1980s, the government of Sao Tome and Principe has inclined toward democratization and capitalism and in 1991 multiparty elections were held.

SAUDI ARABIA (Al-'Arabiyah as-Su'udiyah) A Middle Eastern country (area: 830,316 sq. miles [2,149,690 sq. km.]; estimated population: 17,500,000 [1994]) in the Arabian Peninsula, Saudi Arabia is bounded in the north by Jordan (461 miles; 742 km.), Iraq (502 miles; 808 km.) and Kuwait (101 miles; 162 km.), in the east by the Persian (Arabian) Gulf, Qatar (25 miles; 40 km.) and the United Arab Emirates (364 miles; 586 km.), southeast by Oman (420 miles; 676 km.), south by Yemen (906 miles; 1,458 km.) and west by the Red Sea. Its capital is Riyadh.

It is with the sudden emergence of Islam around the holy places, Mecca and Medina, in the early seventh century that Arabia, the area of modern-day Saudi Arabia, became globally important. Arabs spread their religion and language, and in time mingled with the populations they conquered. When, in the late seventh century, political power passed from

Arabia to Damascus and thence to Baghdad and Cairo, Arabia became once more an isolated and fragmented tribal frontier. From 1517 on, it fell under Ottoman protection, at least nominally.

The modern history of Saudi Arabia began in the eighteenth century with the emergence of the Saudi tribal dynasty in Nejd. It allied itself with the puritanical Wahhabi reform movement, which demanded strict obedience to the tenets of the Koran. The Saudi dynasty conquered neighboring tribes and imposed a righteous lifestyle on them. By 1800 they had overrun most of the Arabian Peninsula. In the nineteenth century the Saudis established their capital in Riyadh. In 1925 they defeated the Hashemite rulers of the Hejaz (including the holy city, Mecca) and established the kingdom of Hejaz and Nejd. In 1932 the kingdom of Hejaz and Nejd was renamed Saudi Arabia.

In 1938 oil was discovered and production started. Until 1981 Saudi exports met ever rising oil demands. But proven reserves grew even faster: the Arabian Peninsula contains 45% of the world's proven oil reserves, and the Saudis control the single largest part of it. The past decades have seen the creation of a huge petrochemical infrastructure. Development was especially rapid from the 1960s until the early 1980s, but the Saudi economy suffered from a chronic lack of skilled labor (Saudi women have been largely excluded from social and economic life).

Foreign laborers were therefore hired. However, Saudi policy has been to limit to the utmost the impact of foreigners on the mores and political expectations of the population. Expatriates live in segregated communities and their movements are strictly controlled. Iraq's occupation of Kuwait in 1990 and the ensuing Gulf War brought about the enforced departure of foreign workers, including 800,000 Yemenis.

SAUDI ARABIA — IRAQ   see IRAQ–SAUDI ARABIA.

SAUDI ARABIA — JORDAN   see JORDAN–SAUDI ARABIA.

SAUDI ARABIA — KUWAIT   see KUWAIT–SAUDI ARABIA.

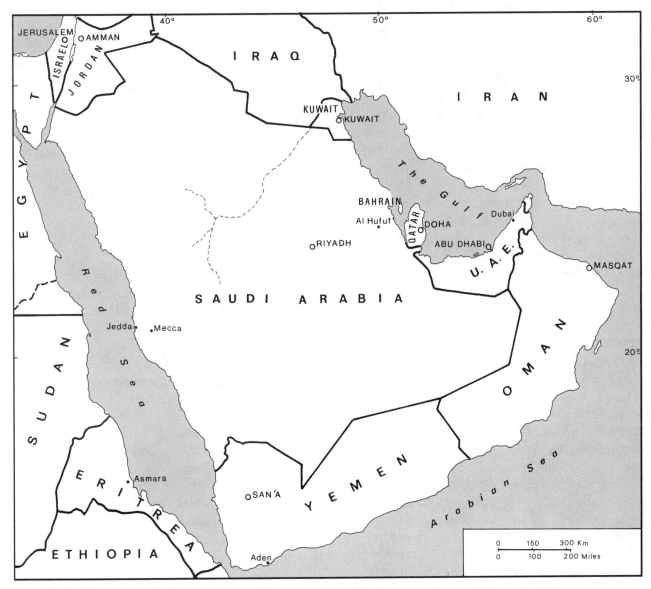

The Arabian Peninsula's boundaries

SAUDI ARABIA — OMAN see OMAN–SAUDI ARABIA.

SAUDI ARABIA — QATAR see QATAR–SAUDI ARABIA.

SAUDI ARABIA — UNITED ARAB EMIRATES Details of the boundary separating Saudi Arabia and the United Arab Emirates have only recently begun to emerge. The boundary is a division defined in the 1974 agreement between the two countries, although it is believed a further, if minor, amendment to the boundary may have been made in

1977. From the Persian (Arabian) Gulf, the line extends 364 miles (586 km.) southeastward and east-southeastward to its junction with Oman's western boundary.

Geographical Setting. From the Persian Gulf shore (24°14'58"N and 51°35'26"E) to the east of Duwaihin, the Saudi Arabia–United Arab Emirates boundary heads due south in a straight-line segment to 24°07'24"N and 51°35'26"E. There it turns southwest and trends directly to 22°56'20"N and 52°35'E in another straight line. At this point it heads in an east-southeasterly direction for the longest stretch of the boundary until it meets 22°38'N and 55°08'30"E, from where it continues on to Umm az Zumul (22°42'30"N and 55°12'30"E), where the boundaries of the United Arab Emirates, Saudi Arabia and Oman meet.

Historical Background. Traditionally, territorial boundaries were of little significance in this region; tribal allegiance defined political relationships. The alignment of boundary lines, however, necessitated by the search for oil and the birth of modern states, created significant territorial disputes. Negotiations between Abu Dhabi (subsequently part of the United Arab Emirates) and Saudi Arabia were no exception, lasting 40 years and involving oases, tribes and oil fields. In 1932 the dual kingdom of Hejaz and Nejd became the Kingdom of Saudi Arabia, established by ibn-Saud. Abu Dhabi, which, until the United Arab Emirates was formed in 1971, was represented by Britain, consequently became a focal point of Anglo-Saudi negotiations. Britain maintained that the only legal boundaries of its protectorate states with Saudi Arabia and Yemen were the Blue and Violet Lines that were laid down in the Anglo-Ottoman Conventions before World War I. The Blue Line defined the limit of the Ottoman territory in the Gulf, while the Violet Line defined the limit of the Ottoman territory in Yemen. However, between 1925 and the mid-1950s a number of other lines were proposed: in 1935 Saudi Arabia proposed a Red Line as Britain proposed the Riyadh or Ryan Line; later, in 1949, Ibn Saud laid claim to 80% of Abu Dhabi territory, while in 1952 Abu Dhabi put forward its own boundary with the Saudis. For lack of a strict delimitation, the situation was fragile. Indeed, the long-standing dispute between Saudi Arabia and Abu Dhabi and Muscat (subsequently part of Oman) over the oil-rich Buraimi Oasis led to the occupation of the oasis by Saudi Arabia. In 1955 a British-led force comprising troops from Abu Dhabi and Muscat evicted the Saudi occupying force, and in the absence of any agreement with Saudi Arabia, laid down a boundary on behalf of Abu Dhabi.

The question of the Saudi Arabia–Abu Dhabi boundary was therefore left unsettled at the time of the British withdrawal from the Gulf in 1971, when the United Arab Emirates formed a federation of the emirates of Abu Dhabi, Dubai, Sharjah, Ajman, Fujairah, Umm al-Qaiwain and Ras al-Khaimah (which acceded in February 1972). Saudi Arabia made it clear that while its territorial demands upon Abu Dhabi remained unsatisfied it would not recognize the existence or legitimacy of the United Arab Emirates. Occasional exchanges over the issue took place between 1972 and August of 1974, when an agreement eventually resolved three of the most controversial and difficult disputes: the Buraimi Oasis, the area of Khur al-Udaid at the base of the Qatar peninsula and the rich Zararah oilfield in the southern part of Abu Dhabi. The agreement was signed using the 1955 alignment as a guideline, and although versions of the boundary were shown on published maps in 1990, details have never been made public by either side. Saudi Arabia ceded six of the nine villages in the Buraimi Oasis area to the United Arab Emirates and in return received the Zararah oil field and Khur al-Udaid, which isolated the United Arab Emirates from Qatar, and won a 9–12-mile (15–20-km.) window to the sea.

After 1974 relations between Saudi Arabia and the United Arab Emirates improved and developed internal security, although it appears that the issue of international security was not finally settled. In 1976 the construction of a new highway to link Abu Dhabi with Qatar was halted as it reached Sila, when the Saudis claimed that the company was working in their territory. This resulted in renewed negotiations on the boundary in the winter of 1976–1977 and a new agreement was eventually reached in 1977; once again its details were not disclosed. Nevertheless, an oil-concessions map published by the United Arab Emirates ministry of petroleum in June 1977 (without an accompanying explanation) depicted the Saudi Arabia–United Arab Emirates boundary as starting on the coast some 20 miles (30 km.) west of Sabkhat Mati and following a course similar to that of the 1935 Saudi Red Line.

Present Situation. As a consequence of the historically fragmented solutions to numerous territorial disputes, as well as the secrecy surrounding the 1974 and 1977 agreements, this boundary does not have full international status although it is respected in practice by the signatory states. Despite the fact that it has become a widely accepted de facto boundary, full agreement has yet to be reached.

SAUDI ARABIA — YEMEN The Saudia Arabia–Yemen boundary extends 906 miles (1,458 km.)

from the Red Sea to a tripoint with Oman. Of this length some 75% is clearly disputed between the two states, representing one of the world's longest undefined boundaries and one of the most serious boundary disputes in the Middle East.

Geographical Setting. The western section of the boundary, governed by the Treaty of Taif, starts from the Red Sea coast at Oreste Point just north of the Yemeni town of Midi and extends over approximately 215 miles (345 km.). The boundary adopts a predominantly north-northeast trend for 131 miles (210 km.) from Oreste Point. The orientation then abruptly shifts to a broadly east-west trend for a further 84 miles (135 km.). The boundary includes four straight sections, the longest of which is 12.5 miles (20 km.) in length at the eastern extremity of the Taif line. On US Defense Mapping Agency (DMA) maps two gaps, of 7.5 miles (12 km.) and 22 miles (36 km.), are recorded together with a 5.5 mile (9 km.) section labeled "area under dispute." In contrast, Saudi maps show a continuous line, generally marginally to the Yemeni side of the DMA charted border.

The boundary traverses the coastal plain, foothills and mountain chain as it proceeds inland to the edge of the interior drainage basin. The topography exhibits a broadly north-south trend so that the essentially east–west boundary line cuts across the grain of some spectacularly rugged landscape, resulting in a complex delimitation.

From the terminus of the Taif line south and eastward there is no agreed boundary between the parties up to the tripoint with Oman. The boundary between Saudi Arabia and the former Yemen Arab Republic (YAR—North Yemen) is commonly shown on Yemeni maps as running south and southeast from the end of the Taif line for approximately 210 miles (340 km.). Saudi maps, however, diverge substantially from this line, trending significantly westward into Yemeni territory from the terminus of the Taif line before turning southwestward to a point 30 miles (48 km.) north of the Yemeni town of Marib, where it joins the southernmost point of the claim of Saudi 1935 (see below). These Saudi–former Yemen Arab Republic boundary claim lines pass through a semi-arid zone of transition between the relatively well watered and densely populated Yemeni highlands to the west and the sparsely inhab-

ited, arid lowlands and desert expanses of the Rub al Khali ("The Empty Quarter") desert to the east.

Further east, the boundaries between Saudi Arabia and the former Peoples Democratic Republic of Yemen (South Yemen) are usually shown on Yemeni maps as following straight lines as claimed by Britain when it held the Aden Protectorate. These straight lines are based on the Anglo-Ottoman "Violet Line" of 1914, stretching approximately 240 miles (390 km.) northeast from the end of the Saudi–former YAR boundary to a point at approximately 48°45'E and 18°17'N, where it joins the Riyadh Line and proceeds eastward for about 220 miles (350 km.) to the tripoint with Oman. Saudi Arabia has never accepted the Violet and Riyadh lines and Saudi-claimed lines lie significantly further to the south, are of 1935 vintage, and were reaffirmed in Saudi Arabia's claim of 18 October 1955. The eastern sectors of the Saudi Arabia–Yemen boundary run through some of the world's most inhospitable desert terrain—the Rub al Khali. At its extreme eastern end, the disputed zone consists mainly of sand dunes, which would make any demarcation problematic.

It should be noted that both Saudi Arabia (in 1990) and Yemen (in 1992) signed boundary agreements with Oman specifying the Saudi–Yemeni–Omani tripoint at 19°N and 52°E.

Historical Background. The Treaty of Taif line emerged after a period of instability and military conflict in the 1920s and 1930s between the Saudi (Nejdi) Kingdom and the Imamate of Yemen over control of the Asir region to the north of the current boundary. The Saudis gradually expanded their influence in Asir at the expense of its semi-independent ruler and the Yemeni Imam, culminating in the formal Saudi annexation of Asir in October 1930. The former ruling family took refuge in Yemen and used Yemeni territory as a base for staging crossborder attacks against the Saudis. The situation in the border zone continued to destabilize, resulting in the Saudi-Yemeni War of 5 April–12 May 1934—comprehensively won by the Saudis. Eight days after the cessation of hostilities, the two sides signed the Saudi-Yemeni Treaty of Islamic Friendship and Brotherhood (the Treaty of Taif) which definitively placed Asir and Najran (the eastern end of the line) on the Saudi side of the boundary. The Treaty of

Taif line was subsequently delimited and demarcated by a mixed Saudi-Yemeni commission in 1935–1936. In all, 239 boundary points were identified by the commission, 200 of which were demarcated by stone pillars. Many of these markers have reportedly been either moved or destroyed over the years. Since 1936 there have been recurrent calls by Yemeni nationalists for the return of the "lost provinces" of Asir and Najran.

In contrast to the agreed, delimited and demarcated Taif line, the Saudi–Yemeni boundary further to the east, either between Saudi Arabia and the former Yemen Arab Republic or Peoples Democratic Republic of Yemen, has never been the subject of international agreement. Indeed, many modern atlases and maps give no indication of where the boundary lies or mark it as "indeterminate" or "in dispute." The Yemeni claim in the Saudi–former Yemen Arab Republic sector closely follows the tribal division line approximated by the great Arabian traveller H. St. J. B. Philby in 1936–1937, the legitimacy of which rested on the contention that the Dahm tribe belonged to Yemen whilst the Saiar tribe did not. Saudi Arabia has consistently contested this line and put the boundary considerably further west in claims of 1935, 1955 and 1986. At the time, and to a certain extent to the present day, it could be argued that the control exercised by either party in the region was tenuous at best and the tribes concerned frequently regarded themselves as independent.

From the terminus of the Philby line, Yemen inherited two straight-line claims from the British–the Anglo-Ottoman Violet Line of 9 March 1914 and the Riyadh Line of 25 November 1935. The Riyadh Line was in fact a British response to Saudi Arabia's refutation of the Violet Line and proposal of the Hamza Line of 3 April 1935. The Riyadh Line was rejected by the Saudis within 24 hours but remained the maximum concession to the Violet Line which Britain was prepared to formally offer the Saudis. Britain subsequently reaffirmed the Violet and Riyadh lines as the northern limit of the Aden Protectorate in December 1954. For its part Saudi Arabia reaffirmed its 1935 Hamza Line claim in its territorial statement of October 1955 and subsequent maps including military surveys of 1986. Thus the two sides have remained as far apart as ever despite long-running negotiations.

Over the years the border zone has, however, been host to numerous military incidents and skirmishes, predominantly related to smuggling on the fringes of the former Yemen Arab Republic and to the confrontation between Saudi Arabia and the Marxist former PDRY. The discovery of oil in close proximity to the disputed area, particularly in Yemen's Marib basin area, has also provided an added incentive for the two sides to pursue their claims to the full. Indeed, in 1992 Saudi Arabia warned off six western oil companies operating under Yemeni licensees, claiming they were operating in Saudi-claimed territory.

In recent years the issues do not appear to have significantly changed. Curiously, however, the existing lines contrive to leave a wedge of territory, approximately 2,000 sq. miles (5,200 sq. km.) in area, currently unclaimed by either side. A series of meetings were held from 1992 onward, but little progress was apparent until the outbreak of the Yemeni civil war of mid-1994, in which Saudi Arabia played a prominent part in support of the ultimately defeated southern forces, perhaps with a view to securing territorial concessions.

Present Situation. Following a period of escalating tensions between the two claimants in late 1994 and early 1995, including frequent Yemeni accusations of Saudi troop build-ups in the vicinity of the boundary and reports of skirmishes between the two sides' security forces, bilateral relations took an upward turn with the signature of a Memorandum of Understanding on 26 February 1995. It confirmed the legitimacy and binding nature of the Taif accord and provided for a redemarcation of the Taif line, the establishment of joint committees for the demarcation of the remainder of the disputed land boundary (with arbitration in the event of disagreement) and for negotiation regarding a sea border and a military committee to ensure the prevention of incidents along the boundary.

SENEGAL   A west African country (area: 75,951 sq. miles [196,637 sq. km.]; estimated population: 7,900,000 [1994]), Senegal is bounded in the north by Mauritania (505 miles; 813 km.), in the east by Mali (260 miles; 419 km.), in the south by Guinea (205 miles; 330 km.) and Guinea-Bissau (210 miles; 338 km.) and in the west by the Gambia (460 miles;

740 km.) and the Atlantic Ocean. Senegal's capital is Dakar.

Senegal became independent in 1960. Leopold Sedar Senghor, a member of the Sparer and first president of the country, ensured that his party would represent all ethnic groups by merging it with all other parties and creating a single-party state. His 1974 democratization process was continued by his successor Abdou Diouf after Senghor's resignation in 1980.

In 1982 the Senegambian (Senegal–Gambia) confederation was established after the Senegalese army saved Gambia's president from a military coup. The confederation was created as a result of the close ethnic relations between the two countries, separated only by colonial borders: Gambia was a British colony but the same ethnic groups live in it. Despite cultural and linguistic connections, the confederation was dissolved in 1990 as a result of severe disagreements between the two countries. Until 1980 ethnic factors almost did not affect Senegalese political life. Since the early 1980s, however, the emergence of a separatist movement among the Diola in the southern province of the Casamance region, separated from the rest of the country by the Gambia and subject to some neglect, has periodically presented the government with considerable security problems.

SENEGAL — GAMBIA   see GAMBIA–SENEGAL.

SENEGAL — GUINEA   see GUINEA–SENEGAL.

SENEGAL — GUINEA-BISSAU   see GUINEA-BISSAU–SENEGAL.

SENEGAL — MALI   see MALI–SENEGAL.

SENEGAL — MAURITANIA   see MAURITANIA–SENEGAL.

SERBIA (AND MONTENEGRO) (Serbija)   Situated in the Balkan Peninsula of southeastern Europe, Serbia (area: 98,766 sq. miles [255,705 sq. km.]; estimated population: 10,500,000 [1994]) was formerly a constituent republic of Yugoslavia. It is bounded by Croatia in two sectors, in the north and in the south (158 miles; 254 km.), north by Hungary (103 miles; 166 km.), northeast by Romania (296 miles; 476 km.), east by Bulgaria (198 miles; 318 km.), south by Macedonia (149 miles; 240 km.) and Albania (178 miles; 287 km.) and west by Bosnia (328 miles; 527 km.). Serbia's capital is Belgrade.

Slavic tribes settled the present-day Serbia and Montenegro in the sixth and seventh centuries. By the ninth century they formed separate tribal states ruled by chiefs (*zupans*). The Zupan Mutimir converted in 879 to Eastern Orthodox Christianity, but until the mid-twelfth century the Serbs were under the overlordship of the Byzantines and/or Bulgars. The Neumanja dynasty established Serbia as an independent kingdom and founded, under Saint Sava, the Serbian Orthodox church. Serbian power reached its zenith under the rule of Stephen Dusan (1331–1355) who conquered Macedonia, Albania, Epirus, Aetolia and Thessaly and crowned himself czar of the Serbs and Greeks. The last Serbian king, Lazar, was captured and beheaded by the Ottomans at the battle of Kosovo (1389) and the Serbs came under Ottoman rule. Some Serbs fled into Hungary to continue to fight the Ottomans from there but were subdued during the Ottoman conquest of Hungary in 1527.

The only Serbs who never submitted to Ottoman rule were the Montenegrins, who as vassals of Venice kept fighting the Ottomans. Between 1516 and 1855 the Montenegrins were ruled by elected *vladikas* (bishops), although after 1697 the election was limited to the Petrovic Njegos family.

Ottoman defeats in the wars against Austria and Russia during the late seventeenth into the eighteenth centuries, the advancement of the Austrian border into Serbian lands, and encouragement by Russian and Austrian agents, helped to ignite a Serbian rebellion in 1804. By 1806, the rebels succeeded in occupying most of Serbia, including Belgrade, but following the Russo-Ottoman War of 1806–1812, the Serbs were defeated and in 1813 the Ottomans reentered Belgrade. A second rebellion in 1815 was more successful and by 1830 the Ottomans officially declared Serbia an autonomous principality under their suzerainty. Following the Balkan crisis of 1875–1878 Serbia gained independence and enlarged its territory, although territorial continuity with Montenegro was prevented by the Austrian occupation and administration of Bosnia-

Herzegovina and the district of Novi Pazar. In 1882 Serbia was proclaimed a kingdom.

Between autonomy and World War I, Serbian internal politics were characterized by the ongoing feud between the houses of Karageorge and Obrenovi, which influenced Serbia's foreign orientation to either Russia or Austria. Its foreign policy was based on the idea of a general uprising of the Christians against the Ottomans and the creation of a large South Slav state under Serbian leadership. According to the accusations of other southern Slavs, it was under the guise of a South Slav union that the Serbs had been continuously and singlemindedly trying to create a Greater Serbia at the expense of neighboring peoples and to dominate the other southern Slavs. Thus, for example, when Bulgaria united in 1885, Serbia, perceiving a threat to its supremacy among the southern Slavs, was quick to try and undo the union by use of force; it was the only party to make such an attempt.

After the Crimean War Serbia's autonomy was guaranteed by the Great Powers. In the 1860s and 1870s Serbia entered into a series of treaties with Greece, Romania, Montenegro and the Bulgarian revolutionary committee, thus creating a precedent for the Balkan League of 1912.

In the 22 years preceding World War I, a competition developed between the dynasties of Montenegro and Serbia over overall leadership of the Serbs. Under Nikolai (1860–1918), the Montenegrins

Bosnia, Croatia, Macedonia, Serbia and Slovenia's boundaries

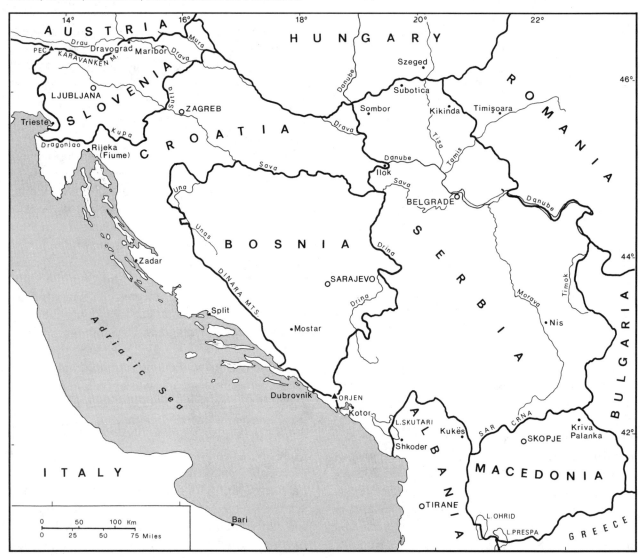

managed to double their territory and have Montenegro's independence recognized at the Congress of Berlin (1878); in 1910 it was proclaimed a kingdom. The timing of the outbreak of the First Balkan War (1912) was greatly influenced by the Serbian-Montenegrin competition. Both Serbia and Montenegro gained large territories in the Balkan Wars, and had now, in addition, a joint border.

In World War I Serbia and Montenegro fought on the side of the Entente Powers and were occupied by Austro-Hungarian forces. In November 1918, after their withdrawal, representatives of the Slavs of the regions of Dalmatia, Croatia, Slavonia, Slovenia and Bosnia-Herzegovina proclaimed the union of their territories with Serbia and Montenegro in one state of Serbs, Croats and Slovenes. The Serbs of Vojvodina joined Serbia, and the Grand National Assembly of Montenegro, under Serbian bayonets, voted unanimously to depose Nikolai and join Serbia too.

The Serbs were, from the start, the dominant element in the new South Slav state. Croat and Slovene disappointment at Serb dominance in the new kingdom, which in 1929 changed its name to Yugoslavia, led to separatist movements developing, mainly among the Croats. In World War II Yugoslavia was partitioned among Germany, Italy, Hungary and Bulgaria. An independent Greater Croatia led by Croat fascists was created by the Germans, while the Serbs remained under direct German occupation.

Liberated by its own Communist-led partisans under Josip Broz Tito, Yugoslavia was reinstated under a Communist regime and proclaimed a federation, with Serbia, Montenegro, Macedonia, Bosnia-Herzegovina, Croatia and Slovenia as its constituent republics. Nevertheless, communist Yugoslavia continued to be dominated by the Serbs, despite the fact that Tito himself was a Croat. Following the death of Tito, the rise of nationalism among the different groups in Yugoslavia and a mounting economic crisis caused relations among the republics and peoples of Yugoslavia to become increasingly strained. Relations became polarized between Slovenia and Croatia, which were pursuing an open market economy and political democratization, and Serbia, which was promoting Serbian nationalism and clinging to an orthodox Communist economy.

In 1991 Slovenia and Croatia seceded from Yugoslavia and proclaimed their independence. The Serbs living in Croatia, assisted by the predominantly Serbian Yugoslav army and air force, rebelled, starting a civil war which spread to Bosnia-Herzegovina. In this war the Serbs, more than the Croats and Bosnian Muslims, were accused of pursuing a policy of ethnic cleansing, of war crimes and of rape and slaughter on a massive scale, aimed mainly against the Bosnian Muslims.

SERBIA — ALBANIA see ALBANIA–SERBIA.

SERBIA — BOSNIA see BOSNIA–SERBIA.

SERBIA — BULGARIA see BULGARIA–SERBIA.

SERBIA — CROATIA see CROATIA–SERBIA.

SERBIA — HUNGARY see HUNGARY–SERBIA.

SERBIA — MACEDONIA see MACEDONIA–SERBIA.

SERBIA — ROMANIA see ROMANIA–SERBIA.

SEYCHELLES A country consisting of a group of islands in the Indian Ocean, east of Africa, Seychelles has a total land area of 175 sq. miles (453 sq. km.). It has an estimated population (1994) of 80,000 and its capital is Victoria. Seychelles has no land boundaries. The Seychelles Islands became independent from Great Britain in 1976.

SIERRA LEONE A west African country (area: 27,925 sq. miles [72,300 sq. km.]; estimated population: 4,400,000 [1994]), Sierra Leone is bounded in the north and east by Guinea (405 miles; 652 km.), southeast by Liberia (190 miles; 306 km.) and west by the Atlantic Ocean. Its capital is Freetown.

Sierra Leone became independent from British colonial rule in 1961. Since then the country's political life has been highly unstable and characterized by an incessant ethnic struggle for power between the Temne and the Mende.

At the beginning of the 1990s popular demands for political reforms and democratization were raised. Sierra Leone became involved in the civil war in Liberia which began in 1990, and during which around 125,000 Liberians took refuge in Sierra Leone.

SIERRA LEONE — GUINEA see GUINEA–SIERRA LEONE.

SIERRA LEONE — LIBERIA see LIBERIA–SIERRA LEONE.

SINGAPORE Situated in Southeast Asia, Singapore is an island below the southern tip of the Malay Peninsula. The area of Singapore is 240.6 sq. miles (623 sq. km.) and it has no land boundaries. It has an estimated population (1994) of 2,800,000 and its capital is Singapore.

Singapore joined with the British colonies of Malaya, Sarawak and Sabah to form the Federation of Malaysia in 1963. Ethnic tension between predominantly Chinese Singapore with its western-oriented, urban and mercantile culture, and the Malay-dominated remainder of Malaysia resulted in the amicable secession of Singapore from the Federation in 1965. As an independent nation with one of the world's largest ports, Singaporeans have fared

well. Ethnic tensions between the various communities are minimal although there has been some trouble, particularly with Malay Muslim fundamentalists. Under Lee Kuan Yew, Singaporeans developed a "clean cut" society with strict penalties for any infringement on what became defined as the national character. Behavior such as smoking and chewing gum in public is penalized by stiff fines and tourists have been turned away for having long hair. At the same time, Singaporeans live in the wealthiest country in Southeast Asia with the highest standards of education, health, and welfare.

SLOVAKIA Until 1993, Slovakia (area: 18,919 sq. miles [49,000 sq. km.]; estimated population: 5,334,000 [1994]), a landlocked country, was an eastern constituent republic of the former Czechoslovakia. Slovakia is bounded in the north by Poland (261 miles; 420 km.), east by Ukraine (56 miles; 90 km.), south by Hungary (420 miles; 676 km.), west by Austria (56 miles; 90 km.) and northwest by the Czech Republic (122 miles; 197 km.). The capital of Slovakia is Bratislava.

Slavic tribes settled the area of modern Slovakia

The boundaries of the Czech Republic and Slovakia

in the sixth–seventh centuries. However, unlike the Czechs, the Slovaks never managed to establish their own state. After being ruled by the Avar in the seventh century and by Greater Moravia in the tenth century (when they adopted Christianity), the Slovaks became part of Hungary and thus shared all the vicissitudes of the Hungarians. The nobility and burghers were or became Hungarian and so did the many peasants who, due to overpopulation, moved into the Hungarian plain. In 1526 the Slovaks came under the Habsburgs.

Slovak nationalism emerged at the beginning of the nineteenth century, first as part of Czech nationalism and later separately. The factor which marked separate Slovak conciousness was the development in the 1840s of the Slovak literary language, based on a dialect of central Slovakia. After suppressing the Hungarian revolution in 1849 the ruling Austrians facilitated the growth of Slovak nationalism by putting the Slovak-settled region under a de facto separate regime which favored the Slovaks over the Hungarians. However, after the establishment of the dual monarchy of Austria-Hungary in 1867, the Slovak region reverted to the control of Budapest, which pursued a policy of forced assimilation. This only helped drive Slovak nationalists to demand independence and to cooperate with other Slavs, mainly the Czechs.

In 1918, following World War I, the Slovaks joined the Czechs in establishing Czechoslovakia. However, the Czechs, being stronger numerically and more developed economically and socially, took the leadership of the new state. This led to growing resentment among the Slovaks, which found its expression in a strong autonomist movement. After the Munich agreement of 1938, Slovakia proclaimed its autonomy and was forced by Nazi Germany and Italy to surrender territories inhabited mainly by Hungarians to Hungary. Following the occupation of the Bohemia and Moravia regions by the Germans, Slovakia was granted independence under German protection.

After World War II Czechoslovakia was reconstituted under a Communist regime and many of the Hungarians living in the Slovak part of the country were expelled. Despite efforts by the Communist regime to industrialize Slovakia, the Slovaks remained generally less developed than the Czechs

and their standard of living, lower. In 1969 Czechoslovakia was made into a federation and a Slovak Socialist Republic was established alongside a Czech one. After the collapse of the Communist regime in 1990, Slovakia experienced a strong growth of nationalist demands to separate from the Czech republic. In 1992 the two component republics of Czechoslovakia reached an agreement on separation, and on 1 January 1993, Slovakia became an independent, sovereign state.

SLOVAKIA — AUSTRIA see AUSTRIA–SLOVAKIA.

SLOVAKIA — CZECH REPUBLIC see CZECH REPUBLIC–SLOVAKIA.

SLOVAKIA — HUNGARY see HUNGARY–SLOVAKIA.

SLOVAKIA — POLAND see POLAND–SLOVAKIA.

SLOVAKIA — UKRAINE This boundary was established after World War II between the USSR and Czechoslovakia. The detachment of Ukraine from the Soviet Union in 1991 and the establishment of Slovakia as an independent state on 1 January 1993, left them with a common boundary, which runs for 56 miles (90 km.) in Central Europe's Ruthenia region, from the tripoint boundary with Poland in the north to the tripoint with Hungary in the south.

Geographical Setting. The boundary begins at the tripoint with Poland on Mount Kremenec in the north, runs southwest, crosses the small Stuzica River and then runs south for 0.6 miles (1 km.) to join the main ridge of the Salinka range. Continuing southward, it crosses the Ulicka stream, always leaving the area's main railway and road on the Ukrainian side of the boundary. Generally southward, it follows the local watershed, passing Mount Popricny (3,300 feet; 1,000 m.) and reaching a point situated 3.75 miles (6 km.) north of the city of Uzhgorod (Ukraine), where it enters the Ruthenia plain. Running west of the city, it reaches the River Uh, east of the small town of Lekart (Slovakia). South of Lekart, the boundary travels southward and follows a series of straight lines, until it reaches the border junction with Hungary in an abandoned channel of the Tisza River, south of the Ukrainian city of Chop.

Historical Background. The collapse of the Austro-Hungarian Empire during World War I brought about the creation of a new map of Central Europe—and the establishment of independent Czechoslovakia in 1918. With this, Czechoslovakia acquired a common boundary with Romania and Poland in the east and gained the long disputed Ruthenia region. Hungary annexed Ruthenia after the German entry into Prague in March 1939, but the area was occupied by the Russians during the last stage of World War II. Czechoslovakia and the USSR acquired a common boundary when Ruthenia and parts of Romania and Poland were ceded to the Soviet Union. On 6 June 1945 the Moscow Agreement between Czechoslovakia and the USSR was signed, by which Ruthenia was transferred into the Soviet Union, with only a few minor deviations from the former provincial boundary north of Lekart.

However, south of this small city the boundary moved westward from the provincial line to include another area of some 58 sq. miles (150 sq. km.) in the Soviet Union. The final act was reached on 2 April 1946 when Lekart itself was placed within Czechoslovakia.

Present Situation. The political changes in Eastern and Central Europe from 1946 onward had no influence on the location of the boundary line. Ukraine inherited a section of the former western boundary with the Soviet Union, while Slovakia inherited the eastern boundary of Czechoslovakia, which remained unchanged. No disputes are known concerning the location of the boundary between the two new states in modern Central Europe.

SLOVENIA (Slovenija)   Until 1991, Slovenia (area: 7,819 sq. miles [20,243 sq. km.]; estimated population: 2,000,000 [1994]), a Central European country, was a constituent republic of the former Yugoslavia. It is bounded in the north by Austria (163 miles; 262 km.), northeast by Hungary (63 miles; 102 km.), east and south by Croatia (283 miles; 455 km.) and west by the Adriatic Sea and Italy (124 miles; 199 km.). Slovenia's capital is Ljubljana.

Slavic tribes, the ancestors of the Slovenes, settled in the territory of present-day Slovenia and further north in the sixth century. They were subjugated by the Bavarians in the mid-eighth century and formed part of the Carolingian empire, being divided among the marks of Carinthia, Carniola and Styria. The ascent of the Hungarians at the beginnning of the tenth

Slovenia–Italy boundary crossing point

century and German colonization of present-day Austria separated them from the Czechs.

German colonization assimilated most of the Slovenes north of the Drava River. From the thirteenth century onward Slovenia formed part of the Habsburg lands of contemporary Austria and shared their historical destiny. The fact that the Slovenes withstood acculturation is due exclusively to an intensive educational work by native Catholic priests who used Slovene as a literary language.

The origins of Slovene nationalism date back to the Napoleonic era when territories inhabited by Slovenes formed part of the Illyrian provinces of the French empire (1809–1814). The French encouraged the use of Slovene as an official language as part of their policy favoring Slovenes over Germans. In 1848 Slovene nationalists demanded for the first time an autonomous province within the Austrian empire.

In the second half of the nineteenth century Slovene nationalism was replaced by the idea of a union of all the southern Slavs within the Habsburg Empire. Following World War I, the Slovenes joined the Croats and Serbs in establishing the Kingdom of the Serbs, Croats and Slovenes, which in 1929 changed its name to Yugoslavia. Serb domination in Yugoslavia aroused some resentment among the Slovenes, but it never reached the intensity and proportions of that of the Croats.

In World War II, Slovenia was divided between Italy, Germany and Hungary. After the war it again became part of Yugoslavia and a Slovene republic was established as one of the five federated republics of Yugoslavia. In the 1980s with the economic deterioration and the general rise of nationalism among the various peoples of Yugoslavia, the demand grew for Slovenia's separation from Yugoslavia. This demand was based on the feeling that Slovenia, the most prosperous among the five republics, contributed much more to Yugoslavia than it received in return. In 1991, following an electoral victory of the nationalists, Slovenia proclaimed its independence from Yugoslavia, which was achieved almost without bloodshed.

SLOVENIA — AUSTRIA see AUSTRIA–SLOVENIA.

SLOVENIA — CROATIA see CROATIA–SLOVENIA.

SLOVENIA — HUNGARY see HUNGARY–SLOVENIA.

SLOVENIA — ITALY see ITALY–SLOVENIA.

SOLOMON ISLANDS The Solomon Islands is a country situated in the South Pacific Ocean. The total land area of this group of islands is 10,954 sq. miles (28,360 sq. km.) and it has an estimated population (1994) of 370,000. Its capital is Honiara and it has no land boundaries.

The Solomon Islands were a British protectorate since the late nineteenth century. During World War II Japan occupied the main islands and the group became a theater of war. In 1978, the islands became an independent state within the British Commonwealth.

SOMALIA (Somaliya) An African country (area: 246,201 sq. miles [637,414 sq. km.]; estimated population: 8,000,000 [1994]), Somalia forms the pointed projection of the eastern coast of the continent. It is bounded in the northwest by Djibouti (36 miles; 58 km.), in the north, east and south by the Indian Ocean and west by Kenya (424 miles; 682 km.) and Ethiopia (994 miles; 1,600 km.). Its capital is Mogadishu.

The independent Somali Democratic Republic was formed in 1958, out of the British colony of Somaliland in the north, and the Italian colony of Somalia in the south. The unification of Somalia with the Somali in Djibouti (former French Somaliland), southern Ethiopia and northern Kenya, was long a strategic aim for the leading political strata of Somalia. This encouraged several wars with Ethiopia (1963, 1977–1978) and continuous guerrilla activities in south Ethiopia and north Kenya. Internal friction after the fall of President Siad Barre (1969–1990) led to a de facto division of Somalia, and to the self-proclamation of a northern republic of Somaliland (1991). Clan-based politics proved crucial for these developments, although this was officially discouraged in favor of nation-building during Siad Barre's reign.

Since the 1960s, the Somali living inside Ethiopia (1,600,000 [1984]), have been known as Western Somali. They mainly live in the Haud (bordering northern Somalia) and Ogaden (Hararge, southern

Bale, south Sidamo) regions. They are Sunni Muslims. Most are nomadic pastoralists (camel and cattle-breeders), but there are also traders, drivers and mechanics.

The main Somali clans inside Ethiopia are the Issa, Gadabursi, Ishaaq, Ogaden (Darood) and Hawiya. In the Shaballe valley live the Reer Bare (acculturated Bantu agriculturalists). In the vicinity of the towns of Harar and Diredawa live mixed Oromo-Somali populations (Gurgura, Jarso). Culturally mixed groups in the southern Sidamo region are the Garri, Gurra, Gerri, Gerri-Mero (agriculturalists in the Juba valley) and Sakuye (Ajuran). Muslim Somali preachers played an important role in the Islamization of the southern Oromo region. Mutual adherence to an Islamic saint (the famous sanctuary of Sheikh Hussein in Bale) sometimes provided a focus for political alliances.

SOMALIA — DJIBOUTI see DJIBOUTI–SOMALIA.

SOMALIA — ETHIOPIA see ETHIOPIA–SOMALIA.

SOMALIA — KENYA see KENYA–SOMALIA.

SOUTH AFRICA (Suid-Afrika) The southernmost African country, South Africa (area: 435,380 sq. miles [1,127,200 sq. km.]; estimated population: 42,500,000 [1994]) is bounded in the north by Namibia (600 miles; 966 km.), Botswana (1,144 miles; 1,840 km.) and Zimbabwe (140 miles; 225 km.), in the east by Mozambique (305 miles; 491 km.) and Swaziland (267 miles; 430 km.), southeast and south by the Indian Ocean and west by the Atlantic Ocean. Landlocked within South Africa is Lesotho (565 miles; 909 km.). South Africa has two capitals, Cape Town and Pretoria.

South Africa's history is one of alternating periods of conflict and cooperation between its various peoples. The Khoikhoi (Hottentot) and the San (Bushmen), known jointly as the Khoisan, were the earliest inhabitants of South Africa. At some time between 500 and 1000, Iron Age migrants of Negroid Bantu-speaking peoples crossed the present northern border of South Africa. From their ancestral homeland in the Nigeria-Cameroon area, these Bantu-speakers came to populate virtually all areas of central and southern Africa. Traditionally the Bantu-speaking Nguni lived in the areas of the eastern Cape, Natal and parts of Transvaal; the Sotho lived in the areas of Transvaal, the Orange Free State and the northern Cape; the Venda in the area of the Soutpansberg; and the Tsonga in the coastal area from the Mozambique border to Saint Lucia Bay in Natal.

Prior to the late eighteenth century, most of these groups (with the notable exception of the San, who were organized in small family-based bands) were organized into a number of politically independent chiefdoms. Many of these were ethnically mixed, and modern scholarship has argued for the irrelevance of ethnicity in early South African history.

White settlement in South Africa began in 1652 with the establishment of a refreshment station at the Cape under the Dutch East India Company. These early Company settlers were the forefathers of the present day Afrikaners. In 1820, in an attempt to alleviate the chronic labor shortages, the British, who then ruled the Cape Colony, settled a group of English in the area of Algoa Bay (present-day Port Elizabeth). These early settlers form part of the ancestry of present-day white European English-speaking South Africans.

Slave-labor was resorted to at an early date. In addition to locally-captured slaves, others were imported into the Cape Colony from the East Indies and India, beginning almost from the inception of white settlement in the mid-seventeenth century. These were later supplemented with African slaves. The present-day colored population of South Africa emerged in consequence of settler-slave/Khoi/Bantu mixing and intermarriage from an early time. South Africa's present-day Asian population is descended from indentured laborers, Indians and Chinese, brought into South Africa from the second half of the nineteenth century.

Since the mid-sixteenth century, people in South Africa were plagued with political-military conflict and epidemic disease. The first military disputes between the Dutch and the Khoikhoi began in 1659 and sporadic conflict between the two continued until 1802. In 1779 the first armed confrontation began in what has been called the Hundred Years' War between the Xhosa and the white colonists.

In 1815, the *Mfekane* erupted. This was a series of dramatic political-military upheavals originating in the northeast sector of South Africa, which destroyed many of the existing African polities in the area and scattered peoples over half of the African continent.

Modern scholars are divided in their interpretations of these events. One school posits the view of a revolution in military tactics among the Zulu under King Shaka, who then went on a genocidal rampage against all neighboring polities, each of which followed with like rampages outward from the Zulu epicenter. A more recent school locates the origin and momentum of the *Mfekane* in accelerated slave-raiding expeditions by the Portuguese from the northeast and white settlers from the south; expedi-

tions which created havoc and prompted the emergence (and location) of the particular ethnic groups found in modern South Africa.

These dramatic events were enacted against the background of waves of epidemic human and bovine diseases. In 1713 a smallpox epidemic devastated the Khoisan population; and from the 1850s to the early 1900s plagues of locusts and cyclical cattle epidemics afflicted Bantu and European agriculture alike.

South Africa's unitary political system was constructed in 1910, following the loss of independence of Khoikhoi and Bantu chiefdoms and states by the end of the nineteenth century, and the defeat of the

South Africa's boundaries

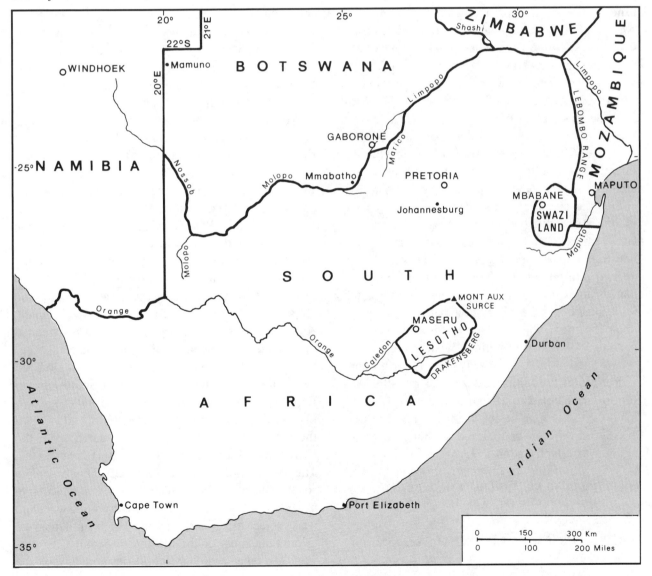

independent Afrikaner Republics in the Anglo-Boer War of 1899–1902. Racial segregation and discrimination became progressively more rigid under successive white administrations, culminating in the formal institution of apartheid in 1948 under the Afrikaner Nasionale Party. In 1961 South Africa withdrew from the British Commonwealth and declared itself a republic.

Under the scheme of apartheid, which aimed at the creation of 10 independent tribal homelands for South Africa's Bantu peoples, four such independent republics were established between 1976 and 1981: the Transkei and Ciskei (which divide the Xhosa between them), Bophutatswana (for the Tswana) and Venda (Venda). In addition, there were six self-governing states (which declined independence): Lebowa (for the Pedi), Gazankulu (Shangaan-Tsonga), Qwaqwa (Southern Sotho), Kwa Zulu (Zulu), Kwa Ndebele (Ndebele of the Transvaal) and KaNgwane (Swazi). All of South Africa's Bantu peoples were considered de jure citizens of one or another of these homelands. However, the Restoration of South African Citizenship Act of 1988 has requalified some of these peoples for South African citizenship. The future political settlement in South Africa will no doubt affect the fate of these homelands as quasi-separate territories.

Since the late 1980s violent clashes between the Inkatha party and the African National Congress have dominated Bantu politics in Natal and in the industrial Witwatersrand region in Transvaal. There are two interpretations of these clashes. One sees them as an expression of ethnic conflict between the Zulu Inkatha and the Xhosa-dominated African National Congress. The second sees this violence as an outcome of conflicting political visions for the future of South Africa: Inkatha is fighting for a South Africa in which traditional authorities and ethnicity form the basis of national politics; the African National Congress fighting for a supra-ethnic and unitary South African nationhood. A black majority regime was established in 1993.

SOUTH AFRICA—BOTSWANA see BOTSWANA–SOUTH AFRICA.

SOUTH AFRICA — LESOTHO see LESOTHO–SOUTH AFRICA.

SOUTH AFRICA — MOZAMBIQUE see MOZAMBIQUE–SOUTH AFRICA.

SOUTH AFRICA — NAMIBIA see NAMIBIA–SOUTH AFRICA.

SOUTH AFRICA — SWAZILAND The boundary between South Africa and Swaziland forms an irregular semicircle westward from the northern and southern tripoints with Mozambique at Mpundweni Beacon and on the Great Usutu River. The length of the boundary is 267 miles (430 km.) and it is demarcated along straight-line sections between peaks or along ridges, by pillars and rivers.

Geographical Setting. Beginning at the northern tripoint with Mozambique at Mpundweni Beacon, the boundary first heads southwest in a straight line to the Managa point in the Lebombo Mountains. Then another straight line is followed for 34 miles (55 km.), crossing the Komati River and reaching the Kamhlabane (Mandendeka) pillar. From this pillar the boundary heads in a southwesterly direction down through the Makonjwa mountain range and continues through the Silotwane Hills in a southerly direction until it reaches the source of the Ndhlozane River. The course of this river is followed for a short distance before the line heads southeast toward a point beyond the eastern shore of a lake fed by the Pongola River. From this point the boundary heads northward until it intersects the Great Usutu River, which is followed up to the tripoint with Mozambique on the river.

Historical Background. In 1814, the Cape of Good Hope province was ceded to Britain by the Dutch. As the Cape of Good Hope Colony, it was extended northward and eastward during the nineteenth century. Natal was made a separate British colony in 1857 and the Orange Free State and South African Republic (Transvaal) were annexed as colonies during the Anglo-Boer war in 1900. On 31 May 1910 the Union of South Africa was created from the Colonies of the Cape of Good Hope, Natal, Transvaal and the Orange Free State. This became a sovereign state in 1931 and, after a referendum, a republic on 31 May 1961. The Kingdom of Swaziland was subject to expansionist interest from Transvaal throughout most of the nineteenth century. To prevent Afrikaner encroachment, Britain undertook the protection of Swaziland's independence, which was recognized in agreements between Britain and Transvaal on 3 August 1881 and 27 February 1884. In a convention in 1890, Britain and the South African Republic agreed to cooperate in administering the affairs of Swaziland, and a further convention in 1894 gave the South African Republic powers of protection and administration for Swaziland. Britain assumed these powers when it annexed Transvaal in 1900. In 1907 Swaziland came under the control of the British High Commissioner for South Africa, until the commission's dissolution on 1 August 1964. On 6 September 1968 the Kingdom of Swaziland became independent.

The sector of the South Africa–Swaziland boundary, from the southern Mozambique tripoint southward to the northern point of the N'yawos Hills, is adjacent to Natal and was established by a proclamation of the governor of Zululand, annexing the Transpongola territories in 1895, although this gave no detailed description of the boundary. However, the Swaziland Report of 1908–1909 states that the boundary had been surveyed and beaconed in accordance with an agreement with the Natal government.

The rest of the boundary is adjacent to Transvaal, and was established in the Pretoria Convention of 3 August 1881 and the London Convention of 27 February 1884 between Britain and the South African Republic, was based on cessions by the Swazi kings to the Dutch.

Present Situation. The boundary between South Africa and Swaziland is demarcated throughout. It has not been the subject of serious dispute, but the Swazi rulers continue to claim the return of lands ceded to South Africa under colonial rule.

SOUTH AFRICA — ZIMBABWE

The boundary between these two countries is 140 miles (225 km.) long and runs for its entire length along the Limpopo River.

Geographical Background. From the tripoint with Botswana at the confluence of the Limpopo and Shashi rivers, the median line of the Limpopo is followed for the entire length of the boundary to its tripoint with Mozambique at the river's confluence with the Luvuvhurivier River. The only man-made feature that crosses the river boundary is a single road and rail bridge at the Beitbridge border crossing point.

Historical Background. The Cape of Good Hope province was ceded to Britain by the Dutch in 1814. As the Cape of Good Hope colony, it was extended northward and eastward during the nineteenth century. Natal was made a separate British colony in 1857 and in 1900 the Orange Free State and the South African Republic (Transvaal) were annexed as colonies during the Anglo-Boer war. These colonies were combined to create, on 31 May 1910, the Union of South Africa, becoming a sovereign state in 1931 and, after a referendum, a republic on 31 May 1961.

The present South Africa–Zimbabwe boundary was established by the Pretoria Convention between Britain and Transvaal on 3 August 1881. It was restated in the London Convention of 27 February 1884. The area to the east and north of Bechuanaland, later to become Southern and Northern Rhodesia, was proclaimed a British sphere of influence. In 1889, Cecil Rhodes's British South Africa Company was granted a charter to operate in an imprecisely defined area between the Zambezi River and Bechuanaland and by an order in council of 18 July 1894 the company became responsible for the administration of Matabeleland. Some areas of Bechuanaland were also transferred to the company in 1895, between the Shashi and Macloutsie rivers, but these transfers were rescinded after objections from some Tswana chiefdoms. The charter of the British South Africa Company was abrogated in 1923 and Southern Rhodesia was annexed by Britain as a self-governing colony.

From 1 August 1953 to 31 December 1963 Southern Rhodesia belonged to the Federation of Rhodesia and Nyasaland. On 11 November 1965 it made a unilateral declaration of independence which was not recognized by Britain, which revoked Rhodesia's self-governing status, declaring it to be a colony. Britian's attitute was supported by the United Nations Security Council, under which economic sanctions were prescribed. At the end of 1979 Britain resumed control and after 15 years of external pressure and internal strife Rhodesia became independent as Zimbabwe on 18 April 1980.

Present Situation. The boundary between South Africa and Zimbabwe has not been disputed. It is unclear, however, whether the boundary follows the median line or the *thalweg* of the Limpopo River.

SOUTH GEORGIA AND THE SOUTH SANDWICH ISLANDS

Together these two groups of islands located in the South Atlantic Ocean constitute a territory of the United Kingdom. Their total land area is 1,450 sq. miles (3,755 sq. km.). They do not have a permanent population. South Georgia and the South Sandwich Islands have no land boundaries.

SPAIN (España)

A European country situated in the southwestern corner of the continent (area: 194,934 sq. miles [504,880 sq. km.]; estimated population: 39,200,000 [1994]), Spain is bounded by France (387 miles; 623 km.) and Andorra (40 miles; 64 km.) in the north, by Gibraltar (0.75 miles; 1.2 km.) in the south and by Portugal (755 miles; 1,214 km.) in the west. Situated on the Mediterranean coast of Morocco are two small areas, Ceuta and Melilla, that are under Spanish administration, forming a common boundary with Morocco too. Spain's capital is Madrid.

In antiquity, the prehistoric ancestors of the Spaniards underwent Phoenician, Greek and Celtic influences before the Romans conquered the Iberian Peninsula in the last centuries B.C.E. The next invaders were the Germanic Visigoths and Vandals, not particularly numerous and hardly mingling with the indigenous population, but creating the first specifically Spanish civilization. The Muslim-Moorish conquest in the eighth century, lasting until the fifteenth, left deep and permanent marks (on Spanish culture and language). Asturias, Navarre and part of the Pyrenees in northern Spain were the only regions left untouched. From here started the *Reconquista*, a long crusade during which Castilian supremacy affirmed itself. Zones abandoned by Muslims were repopulated by Christian settlers. Those who stayed, the industrious *mudejars* (conquered Muslims) and Jewish merchants and financiers, were originally left in peace. However, under the impact of a series of hardships in the later Middle Ages, religious tolerance declined severely. The Inquisition created a sharp split between Christians and others. Under the unifying ideology of staunch Catholicism, the monarchs of Castile and Aragon attained control over the whole Iberian Peninsula: Spain's final unification in 1492 coincided with the forced baptism or expulsion of all remaining Jews and Muslims (*moriscos*). The Jews took their Spanish heritage (including language) with them throughout the Balkans, North Africa and the Levant. Those who stayed and converted remained suspect and persecuted. The expulsion of the Jews was an economic blow for trade; that of the Muslims for agriculture.

In the sixteenth century, the Spaniards under the Habsburg dynasty became the dominant European and world power, controlling Sicily, southern Italy and the Netherlands. The discovery of the Americas, the urge to extend the Catholic faith and lust for precious metals soon resulted in an overextended empire encompassing the greater part of Latin America and the Philippines. Within a century, this superpower was economically ruined and politically marginalized. Epidemics in the seventeenth century hastened the decline. Spain first lost its European dominions and then, in the nineteenth century, its American empire. This was an unstable era for Spain, plagued by a series of military coups and by the struggle between absolutists and liberals. Political tranquility returned when a constitutional monarchy was installed in 1874, but a corrupt oligarchy soon deprived parliamentarism of any legitimacy.

The twentieth century witnessed the establishment of modern industry in Catalonia; the rest of the country remained primarily agricultured. The misery of agrarian laborers in the south led to violent revolts, nourished a strong anarchist movement and strengthened regionalist and labor movements. The Second Republic (1931–1936), dominated by the Left, initiated agrarian, federal and anticlerical reforms, but revolutionary rhetoric frightened the propertied classes and alienated conservative peasants. The traumatic Civil War (1936–1939), part Catholic crusade, part reassertion of centralism against regionalists and part ideological class struggle, was won by the fascist Phalanges led by Francisco Franco, whose reign survived into the 1970s. His dictatorship, based on army and church, epitomized the supremacy of Castilians over the more outward-looking and economically more advanced Castilians and Basques.

After the mid-1950s, Catholic technocrats (Opus Dei) undertook a program of modernizing Spain's economy: opening Spain to foreign investment and importing technologies finally brought the industrial-revolution to hitherto rural Castile. Gradually, the old contradiction between the underdeveloped center and the advanced periphery lost its edge. A rural exodus inflated the urban population and reduced the number of peasants, rendering the question of agrarian reform less significant. In the cities a modern entrepreneur class emerged. The mass export of cheap manpower (mainly to France, Germany and Switzerland) masked unemployment. Tourism, work abroad, the media and European influences introduced modern and democratic values. Eventually even the church rallied the anti-authoritarian opposition. Franco's death in 1975 made possible a peaceful transition to a liberal, federal democracy. In the 1980s regional decentralization was begun, and Spain moved to become a growing industrial power.

SPAIN — ANDORRA   see ANDORRA–SPAIN.

SPAIN — FRANCE   see FRANCE–SPAIN.

SPAIN — GIBRALTAR   see GIBRALTAR–SPAIN.

SPAIN — MOROCCO   see MOROCCO–SPAIN.

SPAIN — PORTUGAL   see PORTUGAL–SPAIN.

SRI LANKA   An Asian island, Sri Lanka is situated in the Indian Ocean, south of India. Its area is 25,331 sq. miles (65,582 sq. km.) and its estimated population (1994) is 17,800,000. The capital of Sri Lanka is Colombo and it has no land boundaries.

The Sinhalese were the first settlers in Sri Lanka, arriving in the sixth century B.C.E. from northern India. Buddhism first entered the island in the second century B.C.E. The Sinhalese civilization was destroyed by civil war and the establishment of an invading Tamil kingdom in the north of the island. The first Europeans arrived in the early sixteenth century.

The Portuguese, having introduced Christianity and opened the island to the west, were defeated by the Dutch, who built up trade and established a colonial administration. The British, coming after the Dutch in the early nineteenth century, established a highly centralized colonial state which introduced education among other welfare benefits. Today more than 80% of the population is literate.

In 1948 Ceylon, as it became known, gained independence; in 1972 it was renamed Sri Lanka. The centralized nature of the political system has created strife between the Buddhist Sinhalese and the Hindu Tamil. The Tamil have been fighting for an independent state in northern Sri Lanka since 1983. Their battle escalated in the late 1980s when India attempted to negotiate a settlement but found itself on the offensive against Tamil rebels. By the early 1990s the situation was worsening.

SUDAN (As-Sudan)   A country in eastern Africa, Sudan (area: 967,500 sq. miles [2,505,813 sq. km.]; estimated population: 29,250,000 [1994]) is bounded in the north by Egypt (791 miles; 1,273 km.), northeast by the Red Sea, east by Eritrea (345 miles; 555 km.) and Ethiopia (1,380 miles; 2,221 km.), south by Kenya (144 miles; 232 km.), Uganda (270 miles; 435 km.) and Zaire (390 miles; 628 km.), southwest by the Central African Republic (724 miles; 1,165 km.), west by Chad (845 miles; 1,360 km.) and northwest by Libya (238 miles; 383 km.). Its capital is Khartoum.

Since the late nineteenth century Sudan was nominally an Anglo-Egyptian territory, but the British character of the regime became evident when in 1924 all Egyptians were evacuated from Sudan. The British ruled the Sudanese indirectly through sheiks and chiefs. As a result, tribalism, which had been greatly weakened in the late nineteenth century, was revived and encouraged.

Sudan became independent in 1956. Since then Sudanese political life has been very unstable. Civilian parliamentary governments were often replaced by military regimes. The governments under all these regimes faced two major problems: Sudan's economic dependence on one cash crop, cotton; and the ongoing rebellion in the south. The war between the south and the north had started even before independence, as a result of the political frustrations of the southern population. The Sudanese, mainly those living in the south, have suffered greatly in recent years from the civil war and natural disasters. It is estimated that hundreds of thousands have died of starvation since 1986.

SUDAN — CENTRAL AFRICAN REPUBLIC

see CENTRAL AFRICAN REPUBLIC–SUDAN.

SUDAN — CHAD see CHAD–SUDAN.

SUDAN — EGYPT see EGYPT–SUDAN.

SUDAN — ERITREA see ERITREA–SUDAN.

SUDAN — ETHIOPIA see ETHIOPIA–SUDAN.

SUDAN — KENYA see KENYA–SUDAN.

SUDAN — LIBYA see LIBYA–SUDAN.

SUDAN — UGANDA
This boundary is 270 miles (435 km.) long and has tripoints with Kenya and Zaire. Some 180 miles (290 km.) of the boundary are delimited by straight-line segments; the rest is mostly demarcated by rivers.

Geographical Setting. From the boundary tripoint with Kenya at about 4°13'N and 33°59'30"E, north of Mount Zulia, this boundary runs in a straight line to the southernmost point at the bottom of Jebel Harogo (Urungo) in the Didinga Hills. From there the boundary follows the southern limit of the Tereteinia area, first in a straight line to Jebel Lobyile and then west to the southernmost tip of the Tereteinia Mountains. It passes in a straight line to Module and then forms a series of straight lines, joining the peaks of Jebel Hala, Jebel Aggu and the northernmost point of the bottom of Jebel Matokko (Batogo or Atokko) before running southwest toward Lokai village as far as its intersection with the *thalweg* of the Assua River. It then follows the river to its intersection with a straight line. The boundary trends straight to the summit of Jebel Ebijo, then west in a straight line to the *thalweg* of the Unyama River and along its *thalweg* to its intersection with the *thalweg* of the Bahr el Jebel (White Nile). The boundary then continues west to the bottom of the foothills of the escarpment running northwest from Jebel Elengua. It follows these foothills to the northwest, so as to exclude the riverain people below Nimule, as far as the westernmost point of the foothills. The boundary heads northwest to the *thalweg* of Khor Kayu (Aju) and follows its *thalweg* to its confluence with the *thalweg* of Khor Nyaura

(Kigura), which it then follows upstream to its source. From here the boundary runs along the southern boundary of the Kuku tribe to the *thalweg* of the Kaia River, which it then follows to is source in a re-entrant of the Congo–Nile watershed 9 miles (14.5 km.) west-northwest of Kegui village and 11 miles (17.7 km.) south of Bangali village. In a straight line the boundary reaches the nearest point on the Congo–Nile watershed at about 3°27'40"N and 30°50'30"E, which is the location of the Sudan–Uganda–Zaire boundary junction.

Historical Background. In 1894, Britain leased to the Belgian King Leopold II, sovereign of the Congo Free State, the territories in the western drainage area, mostly the Bahr al Ghazal, of the White Nile. This land extended from the western shore of Lake Albert to the then Congo border, at 30°E, along the Congo–Nile watershed to the parallel of 25°E, up to the parallel of 10°N, along that parallel east to a point north of Fashoda and back to the western shore of Lake Albert along the *thalweg* of the Nile. The area leased was annulled in 1906, however, except for the Lado Enclave (until 1910) around the port of Lado, about 10 miles (15 km.) north of Juba on the Nile, and the Mahagi Strip (its southeastern part later to become part of Congo) west of Lake Albert.

After the creation of the Uganda Protectorate in 1894 Britain began to define its boundaries, which had always been vague. In 1910 the Lado Enclave became part of Sudan; its southern part (south of Nimule) being transferred to Uganda as the West Nile District in 1912. In exchange, Sudan gained the Bari-Lotuka area in the northeast. East of the Nile and north of Nimule, as far as Gondokoro, also became Sudanese after having been administered from Uganda. An Anglo-Belgian Commission of 1912–1913 settled the tripoint with Sudan during a redelimitation of the Congo–Uganda border and in 1913 a Sudanese-Ugandan commission also tried to delimit the border from this tripoint to Lake Rudolf. This delimitation became official on 21 April 1914.

In 1926, Uganda ceded an area to Sudan north of Madi Ipei near the Tereteinia Mountains in order to reunite tribal groups separated by the 1914 boundary, and the Rudolf Province was transferred from Uganda to Kenya. Uganda had thereby achieved its final shape and area. Sudan became independent on

1 January 1956 as the Republic of Sudan and Uganda achieved independence as the Republic of Uganda on 8 September 1967.

Present Situation. This boundary is recognized by both countries. Both adopted the colonial boundary as their common international boundary without any formal agreement.

SUDAN — ZAIRE Extending 390 miles (628 km.), this border follows the drainage divide between the Congo and Nile river systems, between the boundary tripoint with the Central African Republic in the northwest and the tripoint boundary junction with Uganda in the southeast.

Geographical Setting. From the Ugandan tripoint at about 3°27'40"N and 30°50'30"E, the boundary follows a generally high level watershed toward the northwest, with many streams issuing on either side. The boundary passes Libogo and the streams of the Limbaso, Atua and Lemvo, which are tributaries of the Dungu that run to the southwest while those of the Kobwa, Menzi, Bandama, Aou and Angafu, which are tributaries of the Yei, run to the northeast. As the boundary curves westward, the tributaries of the Akka River run to the southwest and those of the Merida, Ibba and Sue run north. The boundary passes over the top of Mount Baginzi, a bare, steep dome of rock with deep clefts, from one of which the source of the Sue river issues. Passing south of the old fort at Nambia, the boundary crosses Zingadi Hill and, some 25 miles (40 km.) further on, Barawa Hill, and continues past the sources of the Wo, Yebbo, Singbi, Puru and Lingassi streams to the Khor Bombuka, which is the border between the Sudanese districts of Yambio and Tembura. Along the southern side of the watershed, the upper reaches of the Akku, Burere, Baiyan, Tau, Makussa and Werre rivers flow close and parallel to it. This tendency is a feature noticeable all along the boundary but is most marked in the central and northern sections. A heap of stones that stands about 16 feet (5 m.) high, at 5°01'10"N and 27°14'52"E, marks the boundary tripoint with the Central African Republic.

Historical Background. For most of the nineteenth century Sudan was administered by Egypt as a Pashalic (province) of the Ottoman Empire, but from 1882 it was occupied by British forces and from 1899 became a condominium of Egypt and Britain as Anglo-Egyptian Sudan. From 18 December 1914 to 28 January 1922 Egypt (including Sudan) was a British protectorate. When it became apparent that Britain was unwilling to take on new territory recently explored by Stanley, King Leopold II of Belgium took his chance to gain an overseas colony and promoted an International Association for the Commercial Development of Congo. This, despite its name, was entirely his own enterprise and Leopold used the political anxieties of Britain and Portugal to gain their support for his colonial ambitions.

At the Berlin Conference on West Africa in 1884–1885, the association's treaties with African chiefs were accepted. In 1885 King Leopold was proclaimed sovereign of the Congo Independent State; in Belgium he was a constitutional monarch, in Congo he was an absolute ruler. On 12 May 1894, the British and King Leopold made an agreement delimiting their spheres of influence but by 1896 his abuse of power in the Congo had become an international scandal and a vigorous campaign for the reform of its government was mounted in Britain and America. On 15 November 1908 Belgium annexed the Congo Independent State and the process of reform began. A further agreement of 9 May 1906 had established the principle of the alignment of this boundary along the Nile–Congo watershed. Since then no agreement has described the alignment and there has been no demarcation. The boundary tripoint with French Congo, now the Central African Republic, was established in a Franco-British agreement of 21 January 1924. The Ugandan tripoint has not been demarcated and it is referred to in the Uganda Constitution of 1967 as "a point about 0.3 km. south of the source of the River Kaia (Kaya)." Sudan became independent on 1 January 1956 and on 25 May 1969 the name of the state was changed to the Democratic Republic of Sudan. The Belgian Congo became independent on 30 June 1960 as the Republic of the Congo; its name was changed on 1 August 1964 to the Democratic Republic of the Congo and on 27 October 1971 to the Republic of Zaire.

Present Situation. Both Sudan and Zaire adopted and recognized the colonial boundary as their common international boundary without reaching a formal agreement.

SURINAME   Located in northern South America, Suriname (area: 63,251 sq. miles [163,820 sq. km.]; estimated population: 415,000 [1994]) is bounded in the north by the Atlantic Ocean, in the east by French Guiana (317 miles; 510 km.), in the south by Brazil (371 miles; 597 km.) and in the west by Guyana (373 miles; 600 km.). The capital of Suriname is Paramaribo.

Although what is now Suriname was sighted by Columbus in 1498, the Native South American Indians repelled successive colonization attempts by waves of Spaniards, Dutch, British and French until British planters and their slaves from Barbados established the first European settlement in 1651. Suriname, extensively settled by Dutch sugar-, coffee-, cotton- and cocoa-planters driven out of Brazil, passed into Dutch hands in 1610 and remained primarily a plantation economy. Slaves were in the majority during the early part of this period: of the white minority, a third were Jews and the remainder French, Germans and British. After emancipation, Chinese were brought in as contract laborers, followed by East Indians and Javanese between 1873 and 1939. Mining, first of bauxite and aluminium, supplanted planting in importance early in the twentieth century.

The Surinamese, who achieved internal autonomy in 1954, were soon beset by interethnic strife between East Indians and Creoles. European, American and Dutch aid was suspended in 1983, three years after military seizure of power, in the wake of the execution of civilians. In 1986 military forces confronting the Surinamese Liberation Army raided Bush Negro villages in the interior, killing many people and driving thousands into exile in French Guiana: the increasingly unpopular military government was defeated in elections a year later.

SURINAME — BRAZIL   see BRAZIL–SURINAME.

SURINAME — FRENCH GUIANA   see FRENCH GUIANA–SURINAME.

SURINAME — GUYANA   see GUYANA–SURINAME.

SWAZILAND   A southern African landlocked country (area: 6,704 sq. miles (17,357 sq. km.); estimated population: 835,000 [1994]), Swaziland is surrounded by South Africa (267 miles; 430 km.), except for its eastern boundary with Mozambique (65 miles; 105 km.). The capital of Swaziland is Mbabane.

The Swazi people trace their ancestry to a small group of the Embo-Nguni, led by the dominant clan of the Damini, who lived in the area of Delagoa Bay in the sixteenth century. The Damini are still dominant in Swaziland. When the proto-Swazi split from the Embo nucleus in the eighteenth century and moved into the area of present-day Swaziland, they were led by King Ngwane III, who gave this people one of their names: the KaNgwane. The Swazi emerged as a coherent and homogeneous nation in the nineteenth century under Kings Sobhuza I and Mswati II; their name derives from the latter king. His death in 1868 ended both the era of Swazi territorial expansion and the process of assimilation of various local Nguni and Sotho groups into the Swazi people.

In April 1973 the constitution was changed from a Westminster-type system to a traditional one in which the king has unlimited power. The king functions as executive, legislative and judicial head, and succession is governed by Swazi law and custom. In 1986 King Mswati III was crowned.

The present Swazi political system is characterized by tensions between modernists and traditionalists which erupted during the 1970s in labor actions and violence. These were suppressed in autocratic fashion, sometimes violently. Both traditionalists and modernists are also to be found within the traditional aristocracy.

SWAZILAND — MOZAMBIQUE   see MOZAMBIQUE–SWAZILAND.

SWAZILAND — SOUTH AFRICA   see SOUTH AFRICA–SWAZILAND.

SWEDEN (Sverige)   A country located in northern Europe, Sweden (area: 173,732 sq. miles [449,964 sq. km.]; estimated population: 8,700,000 [1994]) is bounded in the northeast by Finland (364.5 miles; 586 km.) and in the west by Norway (1,006 miles; 1,619 km.). Sweden's capital is Stockholm.

The Swedes participated in Viking expeditions; Viking traders (*vareges*) established merchant

Norwegian customs office at the Norway–Sweden border

colonies in Letland, in the ninth century, then sailed down Russian rivers to trade furs and slaves with the Byzantines and Arabs, creating settlements in the process. However, they soon assimilated into the Slavs.

The Swedes resisted exchanging their Germanic deities in favor of Christianity until the thirteenth century, when a medieval Christian civilization evolved. However, the 1397 Union of Kalmar, superficially uniting Sweden with Norway and Denmark under Danish hegemony, provoked revolts of peasants and miners. Cooperation with Denmark became impossible after the 1523 "Stockholm bloodbath" massacre of the Swedish leadership. The Swedes regained their independence (save for the southernmost province, Scania) and soon embarked on a program of expansion. Under the Vasa dynasty, Sweden became a Lutheran monarchy; free peasants were its mainstay. From 1611 to 1721, the Golden Age of Sweden, it became a great power, leading wars against Poland and Denmark and dominating the Baltic region. In the late seventeenth century the power of metallurgy and armaments manufacturers

increased, Sweden's economy grew and Scania was incorporated back into Sweden. However, this extensive territory, gained within a brief period of time, was lost just as quickly. A disastrous Nordic War against Poland, Russia and Denmark ended Sweden's great status of power. Defeat in the Napoleonic Wars led to the loss of Finland in 1808 (Sweden was compensated by the addition of Norway, a union that lasted until 1905) and marked the last occasion in which Sweden participated in an armed conflict.

The nineteenth century was the heyday of Swedish liberalism; a constitutional monarchy was established. Swedes saw neutralism as a guarantor of their prosperity. But agricultural expansion and, after 1870, industrialization could not keep up with population pressure: 1,000,000 Swedes migrated to North America.

From the 1930s social-democrats built a welfare state based on agricultural cooperatives, high salaries, social contracts and extensive social security. This has led to the highest living standard in the world, paid for by the world's highest taxes, and, lately, unbalanced budgets. The 1970s–1980s crisis has affected the "Swedish model": industrial decline, coupled with the growth of public consumption (which finances educational expenses and social employment policies), deficits, growing inflation and an unfavorable balance of trade have resulted in a conservative backlash. In 1990 the Swedes took their first steps away from the welfare state and toward a freer market.

SWEDEN — FINLAND   see FINLAND–SWEDEN.

SWEDEN — NORWAY   see NORWAY–SWEDEN.

SWITZERLAND   A landlocked Central European country (area: 15,943 sq. miles [41,292 sq. km.]; estimated population: 7,000,000 [1994]), Switzerland is bounded in the north by Germany (208 miles; 334 km.), northeast by Austria (102 miles; 164 km.), east by Liechtenstein (25.5 miles; 41 km.), southeast and south by Italy (460 miles; 740 km.) and west by France (356 miles; 570 km.). Its capital is Bern.

The Helveti, a Celtic tribe conquered by Julius Ceasar in 59 B.C.E., were the first inhabitants of Switzerland (Helvetia). Switzerland became part of the Holy Roman Empire. Harsh domination resulted in the formation, on 1 August 1291, of the "eternal alliance" between the three forest cantons, the first step toward the Swiss Confederation. By 1353, five other cantons had joined the confederacy. All these allies were called Swiss.

From the sixteenth century on, overpopulation stimulated emigration: mercenary soldiers became the main export. Their remittances were responsible for economic growth and prosperity throughout the seventeenth and eighteenth centuries, along with banking and industrialization. This was the aristocratic-oligarchic era: cantons were ruled by paternalist patrician elites. Geneva became one of the intellectual capitals of the Enlightenment. Meanwhile social tensions caused by oppression of the peasants exploded in revolts. Revolutionary currents influenced by the French Revolution led to a brief French occupation and democracy, until Napoleon restored

Switzerland's boundaries

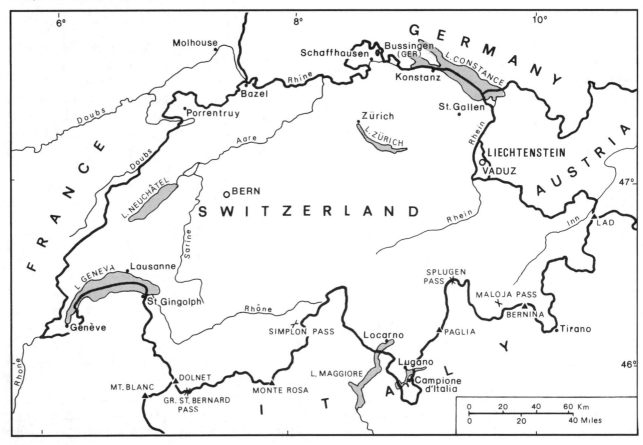

Swiss boundary marker

the Confederation. By the mid-nineteenth century, power passed to the liberal bourgeoisie, and Switzerland turned into a liberal democracy.

Thanks to a second industrial revolution based on hydro-electricity, tunnels, watchmaking and tourism, the later nineteenth century was an era of prosperity and stability for the Swiss; this has continued throughout the twentieth century. Since 1864, when the Red Cross established its headquarters in Switzerland, the country has become famous as a location for international organizations, and a refuge for the politically and religiously proscribed, as well as for capital fleeing the taxman. Switzerland remained neutral in both World Wars and ever since. Lately its isolationism has become an obstacle to its integration in Europe. The Swiss example represents an unusual achievement on three levels: first, they are made up entirely of heterogeneous and unconnected linguistic and religious minorities, yet judicious powersharing has permitted coexistence without major disruptions in one state. In spite of a certain rivalry between its multiplicity of subcommunities, federal government is carefully shared by representatives of various religions, tongues and cantons. Direct participatory democracy, referenda and other instruments maintain the citizens' influence on the polity. Secondly, thanks to a tradition of studious neutrality, they have managed to stay out of all international conflicts over the past 500 years (with one exception); still, the Swiss feel besieged and threatened. All adult males serve in the citizen reserves' army. Lastly, devoid of natural resources, the Swiss economy sustains one of the world's highest living standards, based on advanced industry and services. The Swiss nowadays share their land with numerous foreign workers (some 1,000,000 foreigners forming a quarter of Switzerland's labor force): mainly Italians and Spaniards who, even if born in Switzerland, cannot become citizens.

SWITZERLAND — AUSTRIA see AUSTRIA–SWITZERLAND.

SWITZERLAND — FRANCE see FRANCE–SWITZERLAND.

SWITZERLAND — GERMANY see GERMANY–SWITZERLAND.

SWITZERLAND — ITALY see ITALY–SWITZERLAND.

SWITZERLAND — LIECHTENSTEIN see LIECHTENSTEIN–SWITZERLAND.

SYRIA (Suriyah) A Middle Eastern country (area: 71,498 sq. miles [185,180 sq. km.]; estimated population: 13,500,000 [1994]), Syria is bounded in the north by Turkey (511 miles; 818 km.), in the east by Iraq (376 miles; 605 km.), in the south by Jordan (233 miles; 375 km.) and in the west by Israel (47 miles; 76 km.), Lebanon (233 miles; 375 km.) and the Mediterranean Sea. Its capital is Damascus.

Many Syrians probably descend from pre-Arab civilizations which occupied the western portion of the Fertile Crescent, such as Ugarit, Mari, the Aramaeans (who spoke a North Semitic language related to Hebrew) and others. In 636 Christian Byzantine Syria, weakened by Byzantine-Sasanid wars, fell prey to the Arabs and shortly afterwards

became the center of the first Umayyad dynasty. Arabic supplanted Aramaic and most Syrians embraced Islam. From 1516 to 1918 it was part of the Ottoman Empire.

At the beginning of the twentieth century, nationalism in Syria, organized in secret associations, was pan-Arab as well as Greater Syrian. Syria as a modern state was created by the French, who ruled the country under a League of Nations mandate (1920–1946) and delineated its current borders. The French, first detaching Syria from Lebanon, then gave autonomy status to Druze and Alawite areas and ceded the Iskenderun (Alexandretta) region to Turkey in 1939. Iskenderun is still claimed by the Syrians.

Syria's boundaries

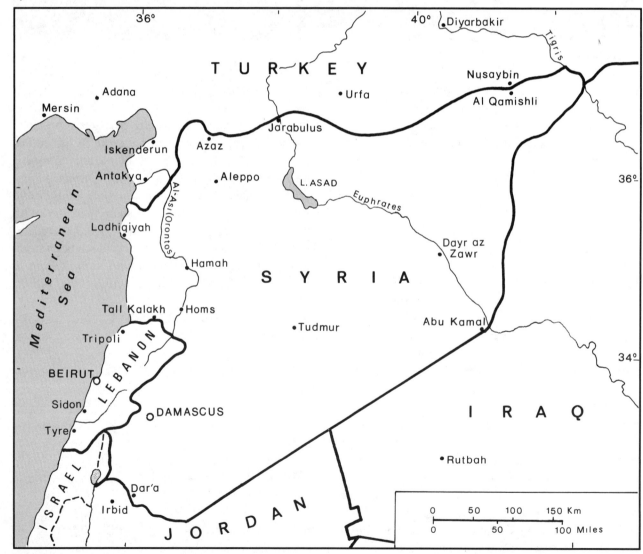

After independence in 1946, parliamentarism failed, and coup followed coup. Syria's recent political history is one of the progressive narrowing of the social base of its regime, which correspondingly increases the need for harsher repression. The upshot of this prolonged crisis was a strengthening of an antiliberal, state socialist, military-based regime. Political stability was only imposed after 1970 by the authoritarian military regime of Hafiz Assad who concentrated power in his hands and has meanwhile grown into one of the Middle East's longest surviving rulers.

In 1976 Syria first opposed Maronite hegemony in Lebanon, then invaded it in an attempt to forestall the victory of a leftist-Palestinian block. The Syrian economy suffered from the military occupation of Lebanon, and an arms race which absorbed a large portion of the budget. Discontent in the late 1970s fed support for the Muslim Brothhood among the Sunni middle class in Aleppo, Homs and Hama. Assad responded to the challenge with unprecedented brutality, razing parts of Hama in 1982 and massacring thousands.

For years, Syria dug itself into the role of spoiler of the Israeli-Arab peace process, striving to impel Israel to return to Syria the Golan, lost in the Six-Day War in 1967. The collapse of Soviet military

aid and the 1991 Gulf crisis combined to give Syrians the opportunity to mend fences with the West, to consolidate their hold over Lebanon, and to join the Arab-Israeli peace process.

SYRIA — IRAQ see IRAQ–SYRIA.

SYRIA — ISRAEL see ISRAEL–SYRIA.

SYRIA — JORDAN see JORDAN–SYRIA.

SYRIA — LEBANON see LEBANON–SYRIA.

SYRIA — TURKEY The boundary between Syria and Turkey runs for 511 miles (818 km.) between the Mediterranean Sea in the west and the boundary junction with Iraq, at the confluence of the Tigris and the Khabur Rivers in the east. The line is demarcated and established with boundary pillars.
Geographical Setting. The boundary line begins on the Mediterranean shore, where the Kara Dourane River reaches the sea, west of the Syrian city of Kassab. It then follows through the middle of the Kara Dourane River eastward, reaching a small ravine north of Rachourte, following it northeasterly up to a height of 3,313 feet (1,010 m.), then leading to a point 1 km. (0.62 miles) north of a ruined castle.

Syria–Turkey border crossing point

Eastward, across mountainous topography, the boundary line reaches the Orontes River (Nahr Al-Asi) and follows the median line of that river northward for about 19 miles (30 km.), until it converges with the Afrine River. Following the median line of that river for a short distance, the boundary then forms a large semicircle and runs northward, on the plain east and southeast of the Amik Lake, until it reaches the Qareh Su River. Thence it follows the median line of the river upstream for about 13 miles (21 km.) to a point near the railway station situated north of the Syrian city of Maydan Ikbiz (Meidan-Ekbes in Turkish). This section of the border line places the Hatay province and the Nur Mountains in Turkey.

From Maydan Ikbiz the boundary line runs eastward in a series of straight lines, following railway tracks, coursing through small rivers, covering crest lines and crossing the Afrine and the Quwaya rivers until it reaches the town of Chobanbey. (This town is placed in Syria while the railway station is left with Turkey.) From here the boundary line follows the Baghdad railway, placing the track within Turkish territory as far as Nusaybin (Nisibin). The boundary line crosses the Euphrates River north of the Syrian city of Jerablus, the stations and sidings of this section of the railway and all the installations also belong to Turkey. From Nusaybin the boundary line runs eastward to Cizre on the Tigris River and follows a series of 30 straight lines: some crest lines and some local tracks. The boundary enters the Tigris River and follows the median line of this river downstream to its confluence with the Khabur River, the junction border point with Iraq.

Historical Background. The Ottoman Turkish Empire ruled the entire area of the Middle East until the end of World War I. The empire was dissolved in 1918 and the area of Turkey was reduced to the Anatolia Peninsula. A boundary between Turkey and Syria (placed under French mandate) was delimited by article 27, part II of the Treaty of Sèvres of 10 August 1920. Then the boundary started at a point on the Mediterranean shore, about 35 miles (56 km.) north of the city of Alexandretta (Isk-enderun) and ran eastward to the city of Maydan Ikbiz (Meidan-Ekbes), about 11 miles (18 km.) north of the Baghdad railway up to the Tigris River, leaving today's Turkish provinces of Urfa and Mardin to Syria. A special administrative autonomous regime was established in the province of Alexandretta, claimed by Turkey but located within French Syria. In a later Turkish agreement of 20 October 1921, the boundary east of Maydan Ikbiz was placed in its present location, enlarging the Turkish territory to the south. The exact delimitation of the boundary line was proclaimed by the Franco-Turkish Convention of 30 May 1926 and again in the Protocol of Delimitation of the Turco-Syrian Frontier of 22 June 1929.

During the 1920s and 1930s, Turkey constantly made claims for the province of Alexandretta on the basis of the Turkish population that lived there. Finally, in 1938, Turkey retrieved Alexandretta from France and a new line was demarcated by The Franco-Turkish General Staff Agreement of 3 July 1938. Small changes were made in the alignment of the boundary by an agreement of 23 June 1939 and the whole province of Alexandretta (today the Turkish province of Hatay) was transferred to Turkey a month later.

Even though Syria had refused to agree to the transfer, Alexandretta was not retrieved and no changes were made in the boundary location when Syria became independent in 1944.

Present Situation. Turkey and independent Syria never signed any agreement concerning the boundary location. Syria refused to agree publicly to the changes made in 1938–1939 concerning the western part of the boundary. Relations between Turkey and Syria are influenced by the border disagreement but no active boundary dispute is known, both countries endeavoring to calm the situation. Turkish waterworks near the border region and problems concerning the management of the water of the Euphrates River, which flows from Turkey to Syria through the boundary line, have recently intensified the boundary problem and have left no sign of a possible agreement.

T

TAIWAN An Asian island country, Taiwan is situated in the Pacific Ocean, east of China. The area of Taiwan is 13,900 sq. miles (35,987 sq. km.) and it has an estimated population (1994) of 21,000,000. Taiwan's capital is Taipei. It has no land boundaries.

Taiwan is currently governed by Chinese mainlanders who opposed communism and fled to the island, where they formed the government of Nationalist China, which they claim to represent all of China—a claim not recognized by the mainland Chinese. Officially there is a state of war between mainland China and Taiwan. At the same time, the Taiwanese economy has boomed; Taiwan now boasts one of the highest annual economic growth rates in the world. Many young Taiwanese have begun advocating a form of independence that would put an end to the current totalitarian government and establish Taiwan as an entity distinct from the Chinese mainland, thus ending the longstanding state of war between the two countries and bring about foreign recognition of the island.

TAJIKISTAN A landlocked central Asian country, Tajikistan (area: 55,251 sq. miles [143,045 sq. km.]; estimated population: 5,700,000 [1994]) was a republic of the Soviet Union until 1991. It is bounded in the north by Kyrgyzstan (541 miles; 870 km.), in the east by China (257 miles; 414 km.), in the south by Afghanistan (750 miles; 1,206 km.) and in the west by Uzbekistan (722 miles; 1,161 km.). Tajikistan's capital is Dushanbe.

In 1924 the Tajik Autonomous Soviet Socialist Republic was created within the framework of the Uzbek Soviet Socialist Republic. The latter included the cities of Bukhara and Samarkand, which contained large populations identified as Tajiks, as well as a flatland area with a considerable Tajik popula-

tion. In effect, large numbers of Tajiks, whose main center was the town of Khujand, remained excluded from Tajik autonomy. In 1929, after heavy political bargaining, Tajikistan, now including the Khujand region, was elevated to the status of a Soviet Socialist Republic. During the decades of Soviet rule, a massive effort was made to rewrite Tajik ethnic and political history according to new ideological standards. Their emergence as a separate people was dated from the ninth–tenth centuries. The central Asian Khorasian state of the Samanid dynasty (864–999) was thus seen as the first Tajik state. In the same way Tajik cultural history was created by retroactively adopting political and cultural heroes of the region.

Soviet rule introduced drastic educational, political and economic changes, established new occupations, and paved the way for the emergence of a versatile, modern, indigenous intelligentsia. On the other hand, it brutally exterminated the pre-Soviet economic, political and cultural elites, created sharp antagonism between Tajiks and Uzbeks and aggravated the tension between the northern (flatland) Tajiks and those of the mountainous south. The latter claim that the former exercise political and cultural domination.

In the late 1980s new political-cultural trends came to the fore. One of these, associated with groups of the intelligentsia, emphasized the need to revise Tajik history during the Soviet period, focusing on the plight of Tajiks in neighboring Uzbekistan, who were losing their ethnic identity and were being reclassified as Uzbeks. The movement advocated changes in the Tajik language, bringing it closer to Iranian Farsi and Afghan Dari. The other trend, supported mostly by southerners, favored a return to traditional aspects of Tajik identity, including

Islamic values and the virtues of rural society, as opposed to the vices of modern secular life. A third trend, supported by the former political elite, centers upon a somewhat revised view of Tajik identity as it emerged in the former Soviet Union.

The proclamation of independence in September 1991 did not eradicate the deep cleavages between these groups. The breakup of the Soviet Union accelerated the eruption of civil war which resulted (up to 1993) in the loss of 50,000–80,000 lives. The Afghan Tajiks actively participated in resisting the 1979 Soviet invasion and were one of the main forces which led to the fall of the Soviet government in 1992.

TAJIKISTAN—AFGHANISTAN see AFGHANISTAN–TAJIKISTAN.

TAJIKISTAN — CHINA see CHINA–TAJIKISTAN.

TAJIKISTAN — KYRGYZSTAN see KYRGYZSTAN–TAJIKISTAN.

TAJIKISTAN—UZBEKISTAN This boundary achieved its international status following the collapse of the Soviet regime in 1991, when all previous inter-republic borders were simply retitled. Parts of this boundary are, however, under dispute.
Geographical Setting. Beginning in the agricultural region lying to the east of Termez, at its junction with Afghanistan, the boundary runs for 722 miles (1,161 km.) before meeting the Kyrgyzstan border on the southern banks of the Fergana Basin. Along its path it crosses the mountain ranges of Fissarskiy, Zeravshanskiy and Turkistanskiy and the rivers of Kofarnihon, Surkhonaaryo and Zervshan, continuing north to a point west of Khodzhent. From here it meanders northeast, up onto the Kurdminskiy mountains which overlook the Kayrakkumskoy Vdkhr. Rather than continuing northeast into the heart of the Fergana Basin, the boundary trends south until it meets the Syr-Dar'ya river which it follows downstream. At the mouth of the river in the Kayrakkumskoy Vdkhr, the Tajikistan–Uzbekistan boundary loops southeast before finally meeting the Kyrgyzstan border.
Historical Background. Conquered by Russia in the nineteenth century, what was then called Turk-

istan came under Bolshevik rule after World War I. Reorganized along the lines of ethnic and national territories, five Soviet republics were created in the central Asian region, including Tajikistan and Uzbekistan.

The Tajiks are unique among the major central Asian ethnic groups in that they are not Turkic; descending from Persian-speaking Iranians and, living in the valleys protected by such a high-mountain region, they have been able to preserve their distinct ethnicity, culture and language in the face of successive Mongol and Turkic conquests of the region. In their western valleys, however, Tajiks became closely mixed with Uzbeks, and the Soviet partition of the region in 1924 failed to segregate the two nationalities with accuracy. Consequently, Uzbeks make up one-quarter of the population of Tajikistan—many Uzbeks live in Leninabad Oblast in northern Tajikistan, and, in turn, many Tajiks live in Uzbekistan's Fergana Basin.

On 25 August 1990, Tajikistan declared its sovereignty, and later declared independence on 9 September 1991—19 days after Uzbekistan. While under Soviet rule, local communist leaders were able to maintain a false concept of territorial stability, but when the two republics became sovereign entities in 1991, territorial aspirations re-emerged.
Present Situation. As agreed in the Alma-Ata Declaration of 21 December 1991 which created the Commonwealth of Independent States, the international border between Tajikistan and Uzbekistan followed the same line as the old inter-republic boundary in the former Soviet Union. This inevitably creates potential for strife and parts of the common border are contested. Tajik nationalists resent inclusion of Samarkind, Bukhara and other historic Tajik-populated cities of the Zeravshan valley into Uzbekistan. Some also lay claim to the Surkhan-Darya region southwest of Dushanbe.

The continuing armed unrest in Tajikistan has alarmed Uzbek authorities in Tashkent, since Uzbeks comprise 24% of Tajikistan's population. There are, however, Uzbek nationalists who recall that the Fergana valley towns such as Khodjent, Isfara and Kanibadam had been excluded from the Tajik Autonomous Soviet Socialist Republic created in 1924 and were only included when it was made a full republic in 1929.

TANZANIA An east African country, Tanzania (area: 364,900 sq. miles [944,726 sq. km.]; estimated population: 28,200,000 [1994]) is bounded in the north by Uganda (246 miles; 396 km.) and Kenya (478 miles; 769 km.), in the east by the Indian Ocean, in the south by Mozambique (470 miles; 756 km.), Malawi (295 miles; 475 km.) and Zambia (210 miles; 338 km.) and in the west by Zaire—along Lake Tanganyika (305 miles; 490 km.), Burundi (280 miles; 451 km.) and Rwanda (135 miles; 217 km.). Its capital is Dar es Salaam.

The country was formed in 1964 as a result of the union of mainland Tanganyika (a British mandate and later a trustee territory; it achieved independence in 1961) and the former sultanate of Zanzibar (a British colony, 1860–1963), which includes the islands in the Indian Ocean of Zanzibar and Pemba.

TANZANIA — BURUNDI See BURUNDI–TANZANIA.

TANZANIA — KENYA See KENYA–TANZANIA.

TANZANIA — MALAWI See MALAWI–TANZANIA.

TANZANIA — MOZAMBIQUE See MOZAMBIQUE–TANZANIA.

TANZANIA — RWANDA See RWANDA–TANZANIA.

TANZANIA — UGANDA From the Rwandan tripoint in the west, this border runs 246 miles (396 km.) east to the boundary tripoint with Kenya in

Tanzania's boundaries

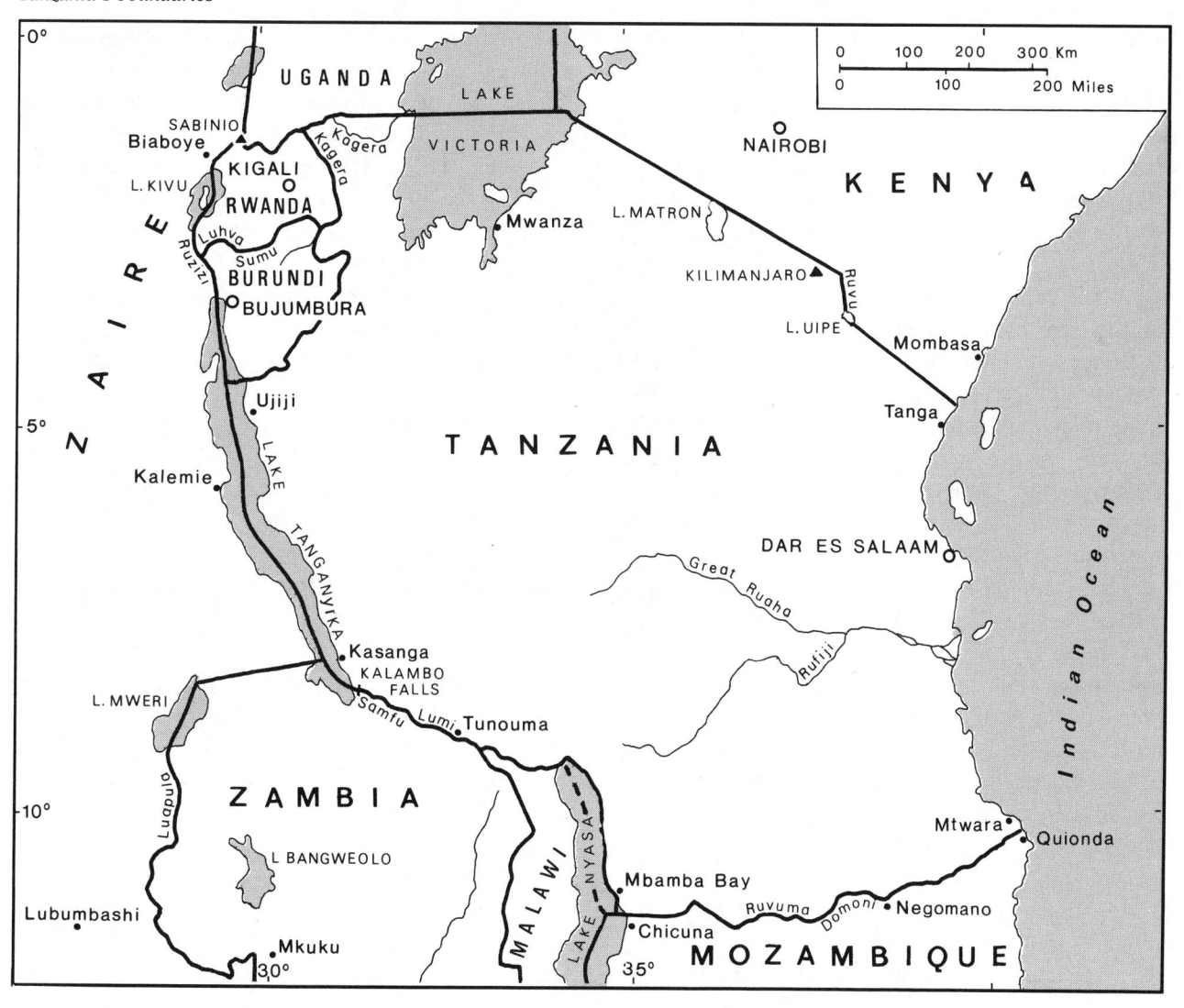

Lake Victoria. It follows the *thalweg* of the Kagera River and the 1°S latitude.

Geographical Setting. This boundary follows the *thalweg* of the Kagera River from the boundary tripoint with Rwanda as far as its second crossing of the 1°S parallel, between boundary pillars 26 and 27. The line then follows the series of boundary pillars positioned along the 1°S parallel as far as its intersection with the Kenyan tripoint at approximately 33°56'E.

Historical Background. In 1886, the British and German spheres of influence in East Africa lay respectively to the north and south of a line which ran from Vanga, on the coast of the Indian Ocean, to the eastern shore of Lake Victoria at a point where it is intersected by the 1°S parallel, which is just north of the lake port of Shirati. This line was extended westward, by the Anglo-German Treaty of 1 July 1890, to the border of the Congo Free State. It was not until 1910 that a treaty between Belgium, Germany and Britain established the Congo tripoint at Mount Sabinio. Prior to the 1890 agreement, Britain had claimed an area south of Lake Victoria extending to Lake Tanganyika, and Germany had claimed a swathe of territory through the Kingdom of Buganda, which would have given it an access route to the Nile valley. The boundary was modified by an Anglo-German agreement on 14 May 1910, from the Congo tripoint, along what is now the Rwandan border to the confluence of the Kagera and Kakitumba rivers, and from there to the Kagera River's second crossing of 1°S. An Anglo-Belgian protocol of 1924 located the Rwandan tripoint at the confluence of the *thalweg* of the Kakitumba River and the midstream of the Kagera River.

After World War I, German East Africa, consisting of Rwanda-Urundi and Tanganyika, was administered under League of Nations mandates with Belgium responsible for Ruanda-Urundi (later to become the two separate independent states of Rwanda and Burundi) and Britain administering Tanganyika until its independence in 1961. Tanganyika became Tanzania in October 1964. The Protectorate of Uganda, which largely consisted of the Kingdom of Burundi and other client kingdoms and attached territories, dates from 1894. Britain was anxious to protect its trade through the vital Suez Canal and future markets in Africa. Interest in Egypt meant interest in the whole Nile valley, even as far as Uganda. Control of Uganda also promised a huge expansion of trade throughout eastern Africa and between eastern Africa and India. Despite this, the Colonial Office was reluctant to undertake the expense of a new colony. The British government granted a Royal Charter to the Imperial British East Africa Company, which, refused government subsidies for administration and a railway, threatened to withdraw from Uganda in 1891. In 1894 the British government was persuaded to make Uganda a protectorate. Uganda became independent on 8 September 1967.

Present Situation. Tanzania and Uganda adopted the colonial boundary as their common international boundary without any formal agreement. It is recognized by both countries and no disputes concerning its alignment are known.

TANZANIA — ZAIRE The border between Tanzania and Zaire follows the median line of Lake Tanganyika, on which the tripoints with the Burundi and Zambia borders are located. It is 305 miles (490 km.) long. The exact position of the Zambian tripoint is inexact because of the indefinite status of the Zaire–Zambia boundary between Lake Mweru and Lake Tanganyika.

Geographical Setting. This boundary has not been subject to any precise determination, the position of the median line of Lake Tanganyika being accepted by custom and usage.

Historical Background. As a consequence of an exchange of declarations on 23 February 1885, the Belgian government recognized the International Association of the Congo within the limits prescribed by treaties with France and Portugal. The country was renamed the Independent State of Congo with King Leopold II of Belgium as its sovereign. In fact the territory was virtually a personal possession of the king and it was not until 1908 that it became a colony of Belgium. The Belgian Congo gained independence on 30 June 1960 as the Republic of Congo, becoming a democratic republic in 1964 and adopting the name the Republic of Zaire on 21 October 1971.

From 1890 Tanganyika was part of German East Africa. After World War I Germany renounced its overseas territories and Tanganyika became a mandate under the League of Nations, administered from 1922 to 1946 by Britain. Tanganyika became independent on 9 December 1961 and on 27 April 1964 formed, with Zanzibar, the United Republic of Tanganyika and Zanzibar, this being renamed the United Republic of Tanzania on 29 October 1964.

The border alignment between the two has not been a particular subject of any international agreement, although a variety of items of evidence support the median line principle. It is specified in the Declaration of the Administrator-General of the Department of Foreign Affairs of the Congo Free State of 1 August 1885 and in the Declaration of Neutrality of the Congo Free State of 28 December 1894. It is also referred to as the alignment in the convention concluded between Belgium and Germany on 11 August 1910 and in the protocol between Belgium and Britain of 5 August 1924.

Present Situation. Both states adopted, without a formal agreement, this de facto colonial boundary. The line has not been disputed since.

TANZANIA — ZAMBIA The boundary between Tanzania and Zambia reaches from its tripoint with Malawi for 210 miles (338 km.) to its tripoint, in Lake Tanganyika, with Zaire. Some 41 miles (66 km.) of the boundary run through Lake Tanganyika; from its shore to Malawi the boundary is demarcated by streams and pillars.

Geographical Setting. The boundary tripoint with Malawi is marked by boundary pillar no. 2 on top of Nakungulu Hill, and from there the boundary runs along the watershed past boundary pillar no. 3, about 4 miles (6.5 km.) from Nakungulu, to boundary pillar no. 4 opposite the source of Mpemba Stream. Here it leaves the watershed and follows the Mpenba downstream to boundary pillar no. 5 on the left bank, 390 feet (119 m.) north of Tontera village. From this point it forms a straight line to the true west to boundary pillar no. 6. It follows the watershed between the Nkana River and its affluents to the north and Karunga River and its tributaries to the south past the following boundary pillars: on Kumbi Hill (no. 7); about 2 miles (3 km.) north of the English station Fife (no.8); about 1,312 feet (400 m.) south of the source of the Ntakimba stream (no.9); between the old and new Stevenson Road (no.10); about 5,576 feet (1,700 m.) from the Nombwe village (no. 11); and about 5,576 feet

(1,700 m.) from Kissitu village (no. 12). At boundary pillar no. 12 the line leaves the water divide and heads in a straight line to boundary pillar no. 13, about 3,936 feet (1,200 m.) northwest of the English station Ikomba and thence in a straight line to boundary pillar no. 14 in the Suwa (Zuwa) Forest, about 2.2 miles (3.5 km.) south of Karimansire village, which is also on the water divide. It then follows the watershed past boundary pillar no. 15, about 2,296 feet (700 m.) west of the village of Shovere (Chowere); no. 16 on Dundundu Hill; no. 17 about halfway between Membwe and Mssungo; and the three boundary pillars in the neighborhood of the English station Mambwe (nos. 18–20). The last of these pillars is at the point where the watershed intersects 32°E. The boundary then progresses in a straight line to the source of the Massiete Stream and follows this downstream to its junction with the Masia Stream at boundary pillar no. 21. It then runs in a straight line to boundary pillar no. 22 on the left bank of the Ipundu, south of the ruins of Ipundu village, and in another straight line to the confluence of the Saissi River with the Kassokorwa Stream (boundary pillar no. 23). It follows the Saissi River upstream to its junction with the Rumi (Lumi) stream, follows the Rumi to its intersection with the Mkumbaw stream and follows this up to its source. From here the boundary goes in a straight line to the middle of the narrow saddle between the sources of the Mosi (Mozi) and Kipoko (Chipoko) streams and from there courses in a straight line to the southeastern source of the Safu (Samfu) Stream; it follows this downstream until it runs into the Kalambo River, which it follows downstream to its mouth in Lake Tanganyika. The boundary tripoint with Zaire in Lake Tanganyika is indefinite.

Historical Background. A division of spheres of influence that was agreed upon between Germany and Britain on 1 July 1890 included a delimitation of the territory between Lake Tanganyika and Lake Nyasa, most of which now comprises the border between Tanzania and Zambia. The agreement was made without any detailed knowledge of the geography of the area and only in 1898 was the boundary surveyed by an Anglo-German boundary commission. The *thalweg*s of the local streams were to form the boundary except where they could not be distinguished, in which case the boundary was to course along the middle of the stream bed. The alignment was fixed by an agreement on 23 February 1901. In 1889 the British South Africa Company received a Royal Charter and later was allowed to extend its operations north of the Zambezi River. By an order in council of 28 November 1899, provision was made for the administration of Barotseland—Northwestern Rhodesia, and another order of 29 January 1900 regulated the administration of Northeastern Rhodesia. This responsibility passed from the British South Africa Company to the Colonial Office in 1924. In 1953, the Federation of Rhodesia and Nyasaland was formed, each retaining its constitutional status. The federation was dissolved in 1963 and Northern Rhodesia became independent as Zambia on 24 October 1964.

Present Situation. This boundary is mutually recognized by Tanzania and Zambia. Tanzania became independent on 9 December 1961, adopting the name Tanzania on 29 October 1964. Both states accepted the colonial boundary as their common international boundary with no formal agreement to attest the recognition of the line.

THAILAND (Prathet Thai)   A Southeast Asian country (area: 198,115 sq. miles [513,115 sq. km.]; estimated population: 58,300,000 [1994]), Thailand is bounded in the northeast by Laos (1,090 miles; 1,754 km.), southeast by Cambodia (499 miles; 803 km.), south by Malaysia (314 miles; 506 km.) and west by Myanmar (Burma) (1,119.5 miles; 1,800 km.). Its capital is Bangkok.

The Thai people originated in the Chinese province of Yunnan. They began migrating to their present home in 1050, establishing a kingdom centered at Sukothai in the mid-thirteenth century. As the population gradually moved south, the capital was reestablished in several locations, the last being Bangkok in the late eighteenth century. From early in its history, Thailand was open to western influence. It was, however, the only country in the region not subject to colonial rule, allowing the indigenous culture to flourish. Although the king relinquished absolute power in favor of democracy in 1932, in 1976 a military coup gained virtual control of the country and curtailed political rights. This has resulted in several violent protests in the early 1990s, led by students, for a more democratic government.

The people of Thailand have faced several armed threats in recent years. Chief among these was a penetration from Cambodia of Vietnamese in search of rebels, the war against opium growers and drug lords in the infamous Golden Triangle, Muslim insurgents in the south and north and ethnic Meo insurgents along the Laotian border. Despite these problems, the country has adopted a decidedly pro-Western attitude which has resulted in considerable aid being granted to encourage development.

THAILAND — CAMBODIA   see CAMBODIA–THAILAND.

THAILAND — LAOS see LAOS–THAILAND.

THAILAND — MALAYSIA   see MALAYSIA–THAILAND.

THAILAND — MYANMAR   see MYANMAR–THAILAND.

TOGO   A west African country (area: 21,925 sq. miles [56,764 sq. km.]; estimated population: 4,100,000 [1994]), Togo is bounded by Burkina Faso (78 miles; 126 km.) in the north, by Benin (400 miles; 644 km.) in the east, by the Gulf of Guinea in the south and by Ghana (545 miles; 877 km.) in the west. Toga's capital is Lomé.

The territory of Togo was ruled by the Germans until World War I. After the defeat of Germany it was divided between France and Britain as a mandate. The larger eastern part was entrusted to the French, while the western, smaller, part became a British mandate, which joined Ghana when that state became independent in 1957.

The Togolese of French Togoland gained their independence in April 1960. During decolonization two main parties emerged. The Commite de l'unite togolaise (CUT), led by Sylvanus Olympio, began its political course by campaigning for the unification of the Ewe in both parts of Togo with the Ewe of Ghana. Toward independence, however, this goal was abandoned and the CUT demanded independence for French Togo. The French tried to encourage an opposition party, but it was Olympio's party that led Togoland to independence. In 1963, Olympio was overthrown in a military coup by Etienne

(Gnassingbe) Eyadema, whose support came mainly from his own ethnic group, the Kabre. The northern ethnic groups generally supported the coup because their region remained underdeveloped by the CUT government. When Eyadema gained power, the army was predominantly northern, but in order to avoid ethnic discontent in the south, he kept some southerners in top military and government posts.

In the beginning of the 1990s violent protests erupted in the capital demand of political reform. Eyadema, who feared the situation might develop into an ethnic conflict between the Ewe and the Kabre, promised a new constitution and a multi-party system. The democratization process started in

The boundaries of Benin, Burkina Faso, Ghana and Togo

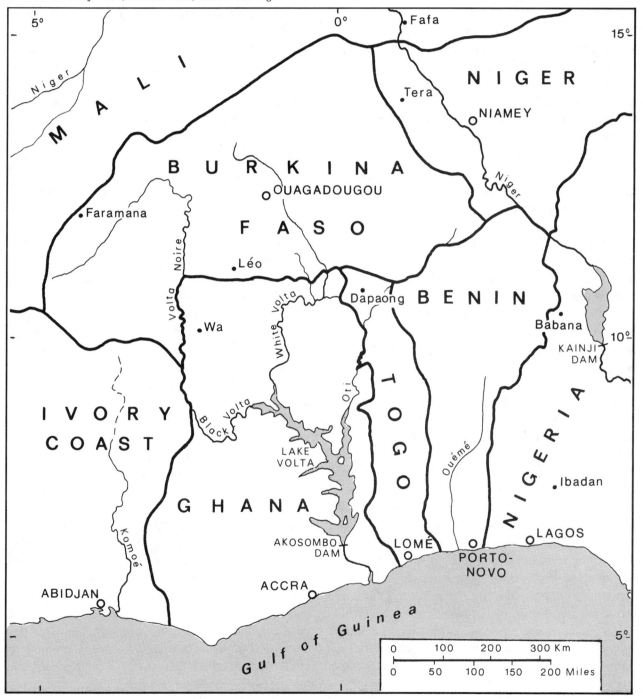

1991 but was halted by an outbreak of seriously violent incidents.

TOGO — BENIN   see BENIN–TOGO.

TOGO — BURKINA FASO   see BURKINA FASO–TOGO.

TOGO — GHANA   see GHANA–TOGO.

TONGA   An islands country situated in the South Pacific Ocean, Tonga's total land area is 290 sq. miles (750 sq. km.), with an estimated population (1994) of 105,000. Its capital is Nuku'alofa and it has no land boundaries.

Over one-half of the population of Tonga resides on the largest island, Tongatapu, where the capital, Nuku'alofa, is situated.

Tonga is a kingdom that became independent from Britain in 1970. Fishing and agriculture are the traditional and principal economic activities and 90% of the population farm their own plots. The government is the main employer. Tourism is on the increase.

TRINIDAD AND TOBAGO   Trinidad and Tobago is a country made up of two islands situated in the Caribbean Sea. It has no land boundaries, its total land area is 1,980 sq. miles (5,126 sq. km.) and it has an estimated population (1994) of 1,300,000. Its capital is Port of Spain.

When the islands were visited by Columbus in 1498, Trinidad was inhabited by the Arawak and Tobago by the Carib: these peoples were subsequently worked to death by the Spaniards.

The islands were neglected Spanish possessions until 1797, when they surrendered to a British naval expedition. Slaves were imported to cultivate tobacco and, later, cocoa. Tobago was acquired by the British in 1802 and adminstratively combined with Trinidad in 1889; prior to this time, after the abolition of slavery, Britain was already subsidizing the immigration of plantation labor from India. The inhabitants were granted self-government in 1925, entered the Federation of the West Indies in 1958, gained independence in 1962 and became members of the British Commonwealth, as a parliamentary republic, in 1976. Recent legislation has granted considerable autonomy to Tobago.

TUNISIA (Tunisie/Tunis)   A north African country (area: 63,170 sq. miles [163,610 sq. km.]; estimated population: 8,600,000 [1994]), Tunisia is bounded in the southeast by Libya (285 miles; 459 km) and in the west by Algeria (600 miles; 965 km.). Its capital is Tunis.

Berbers may have been the original Tunisians, but the first great civilization (Punic) was imported by Phoenicians in the ninth and eighth centuries B.C.E. Punic was still spoken in the Tunisian countryside in the fifth century C.E. Two centuries later, Arab invaders overran the Tunisian Berber tribes, leading to gradual but complete Islamization and arabization. In the eleventh century, the Fatimid rulers of Egypt launched the Bani Hilal against the Berbers, resulting in large parts of the North African Maghreb laying waste. Cities declined and many Tunisians reverted to nomadism. In the sixteenth century Tunisia became entangled in Spanish-Ottoman rivalry, and from 1564 it was an Ottoman province ruled by Mamelukes. In the seventeenth century Tunisia became semi-autonomous.

In the nineteenth century Tunisians increasingly came under European influence: France and Italy vied in their designs on them, resulting, in 1881, in the establishment of a French protectorate.

French administration left little power to indigenous Arabs. Tunisian nationalist agitation broadened after World War I into a campaign for a constitution, but was preempted by the gradual introduction of reforms. Habib Bourguiba, who was subsequently to mold modern Tunisia, established the Neo-Destour party in the 1930s. Since the French were not responsive to local demands, riots broke out in 1938. Bourguiba was exiled but returned in the 1950s to fan the fires of national revolt. In 1954 a guerrilla movement forced France to grant the Tunisians autonomy; full independence followed in 1956.

As the only active pre-independence political party, the Neo-Destour assumed power. At first a trade union tendency toward a state-controlled economy carried the day. However, in the 1970s the country was threatened with an agricultural crisis and a liberal economy was restored. Despite talk of political liberalization, however, the Neo-Destour party maintained control. Discontent erupted in 1978, when workers' and students' strikes demanding the abolition of the one-party system threatened the regime. A controlled experiment in democratization and multiparty politics was begun and Bourguiba lost power.

Throughout the 1980s the intellectual elite seemed unable to stop the emergence of the fundamentalist Islamic movement, which boycotted the 1990 elections. However, the Gulf crisis in 1991 split the fundamentalists, and the government introduced harsh repressive measures against them; the An-Nahda Islamic Movement was disarmed without provoking massive protests. Economic growth has since permitted some relaxation of social tensions.

TUNISIA — ALGERIA see ALGERIA–TUNISIA.

TUNISIA — LIBYA see LIBYA–TUNISIA.

TURKEY (Türkiye) Turkey (area: 300,870 sq. miles [779,253 sq. km.]; estimated population: 60,900,000 [1994]) is situated in two continents—Asia and Europe. Anatolia lies in Asia (291,771 sq. miles; 755,687 sq. km.) and Thrace in Europe (9,175 sq. miles; 23,763 sq. km.). The majority of Turkey's population are Muslim Turks. It is bounded in the west by the Aegean Sea and Greece (128 miles; 205 km.), in the north by Bulgaria (149 miles; 238 km.) and the Black Sea, in the east by Georgia (156.5 miles; 252 km.), Armenia (167 miles; 267 km.), Azerbaijan (5.5 miles; 9 km.) and Iran (310 miles; 499 km.) and in the south by Iraq (219 miles; 352 km.) and Syria (511 miles; 818 km.). Turkey's capital is Ankara, while its largest city is Istanbul.

Until 1,000 years ago, the territory of what is today Turkey was settled by populations unrelated to the Turks: Hittites and Urartu (claimed for ancestors by the Armenians), Phrygians and Lydians, Romans and Parthians. It was also home to some of the earliest Christian communities, and subsequently became the heart of the Byzantine Empire. However, between the eleventh and the fifteenth centuries, it was conquered and settled by a nomadic people that

Turkey's southern border with Syria

was driven from its ancestral homes in central Asia: the Turks.

From the tenth century, Turkish soldiers and slaves adopted Islam. Before long they took over the authority of their Arabic and Persian masters and founded realms of their own based on Sunni Islam, Arab-Iranian culture and the Arabic alphabet. Seljuq Turks pushed through Iran and Iraq into North Syria. In the eleventh century, they conquered and settled the larger part of Byzantine Anatolia. The invaders succeeded in thoroughly Islamicizing and Turkifying the larger part of Anatolia, in the process submerging Armenian and Greek culture. Only the Aegean area remained predominantly Greek until the 1920s.

However, the thirteenth century saw the weakening of the Seljuqs, who had established their capital in Konya. A new, dynamic tribe appeared on the scene: the Ottoman Turks, or Osmanlis, who completed the conquest of Anatolia and from there established the Ottoman Empire, which at its peak encompassed the Balkans, Arabia and North Africa.

The Ottoman Turks conquered Constantinople in 1453 and named it Istanbul, thereby finishing off the moribund Byzantine Empire. Subsequently, all of Arabia, North Africa and the Balkans were brought under Turkish rule. The Ottoman Empire reached its apogee under Sultan Suleyman the Magnificent (1520–1566) who laid siege to Vienna. The empire rested on an impressive administration and a formidable army. From the seventeenth century on, the empire gradually shrank under the impact of attacks by Christian states and the rising nationalism of minorities within the empire, as well as internal corruption.

Efforts at centralization and modernization of the empire came too late. The last sultans stifled efforts at parliamentarism and restored absolutism in 1877. From the army, the only thoroughly modernized institution of the empire, came in 1908 the Young Turks revolution. Originally Ottomanist in intent, it soon lapsed into vain attempts at imposing Turkification on the empire's mixed nationalities. As a result of the failure of Ottomanism, a narrow Turks nationalism retrenched itself in the Anatolian heartland. It attempted to Turkify the motherland by suppressing non-Turkish minorities. The massacres of the Armenians continue to cloud relations between the two peoples. Turkey chose the losing side in World War I. The Arab peoples shook off the yoke. Just as the victors intended to carve up the empire, Mustafa Kemal succeeded in galvanizing the Turkish masses: the invading armies were thrown out. The Turkish war of independence in 1922–1923 resulted in the establishment of a republic, and led to the uprooting of millennial Greek communities and wholesale population transfers between Greece and Turkey.

The significance of Mustafa Kemal Ataturk ("Father of the Turks") in restoring pride to his people and in forcing upon them drastic modernization cannot be overstated. He abolished the sultanate and the khalifate, instituted a one-party republic, and endeavored to thoroughly secularize social life, granting equal rights to women, prohibiting the veil, and imposing Western clothes (the visored cap is still the favored headgear of Turkish men), introducing the Latin alphabet and family names, purifying Turkish of Arab and Persian accretions and starting industrialization. The republic's capital was shifted from cosmopolitan Istanbul (Constantinople) to inward-looking Ankara.

After World War II, Turkey became a democracy with competing political parties—although the army, standardbearer of Kemalism, has repeatedly taken power. Mechanization of agriculture led to a mass migration to the slums around the big cities and to Western Europe.

The military coup of 1980 was widely applauded because it addressed the generalized sense of insecurity. Socially, the generals tended to steer Turkey into a disciplined hierarchical society. A restricted democracy was restored in 1982.

Turkey's role in the region is bound up with national questions, in at least three directions. First, continued suppression of the restive Kurds at home has failed to prevent the reopening of the Kurdish file internationally. The 1990 Iraqi crisis also reawakened feelings toward the province of Mosul. Secondly, the fragmentation of the former Soviet Union has created a power vacuum that invites Turkey to involve itself with its Turkic relatives in Azerbaijan, Turkmenistan and other new republics rife with ethnic conflict. Lastly, the explosion of Yugoslavia carries with it the risk of dragging the Turks down into civil strife.

TURKEY — ARMENIA see ARMENIA–TURKEY.

TURKEY — AZERBAIJAN see AZERBAIJAN–TURKEY.

TURKEY — BULGARIA see BULGARIA–TURKEY.

TURKEY — GEORGIA see GEORGIA–TURKEY.

TURKEY — GREECE see GREECE–TURKEY.

TURKEY — IRAN see IRAN–TURKEY.

TURKEY — IRAQ see IRAQ–TURKEY.

TURKEY — SYRIA see SYRIA–TURKEY.

TURKMENISTAN   A landlocked central Asian country, Turkmenistan (area: 188,456 sq. miles [487,900 sq. km.]; estimated population: 4,000,000 [1994]) is bounded in the north by Kazakhstan (236 miles; 379 km.), in the east by Uzbekistan (1,008 miles; 1,621 km.), southeast by Afghanistan (462 miles; 744 km.), south by Iran (617 miles; 992 km.) and west by the Caspian Sea. Turkmenistan's capital is Ashkhabad.

Historically, the Turkmen are direct descendents of the Oghuz, who entered central Asia from the east in about the tenth century. They were gradually converted to Islam and absorbed some pre-Oghuz, mostly Iranian, inhabitants of the area of present-day Turkmenistan. Although formally dominated at various times by Iran and the central Asian principalities of Khiva and Bukhara, they remained virtually independent for centuries until they were subdued by the Russian empire in the 1870s and 1880s. In 1924 the Soviet authorities promoted the creation of the Turkmen Soviet Socialist Republic. Since 1989 the Turkmen of the former Soviet Union have experienced a process of political and national awakening, and the awareness of Turkmen roots has become strongly stressed. In 1991 Turkmenistan proclaimed its sovereignty, but with the collapse of the Soviet Union it remained within the framework of the CIS (Commonwealth of Independent States).

TURKMENISTAN — AFGHANISTAN see AFGHANISTAN–TURKMENISTAN.

TURKMENISTAN — IRAN see IRAN–TURKMENISTAN.

TURKMENISTAN — KAZAKHSTAN see KAZAKHSTAN–TURKMENISTAN.

TURKMENISTAN—UZBEKISTAN   The founding Minsk and Alma-Ata declarations of the Commonwealth of Independent States on 8 and 21 December 1991, lay down the principles to which the member states must adhere. They were committed to the observance of existing borders within the ex-USSR and to the principle of their inviolability by force. Although there are no official boundary disputes between Turkmenistan and Uzbekistan, there are, however, a number of informal ethno-territorial claims that make this border characteristic of many other boundaries in central Asia.

Geographical Setting. For a large part of its 1,008-mile (1,621-km.) route the boundary follows the path of the Amu Darya (central Asia's largest river) en route to the Aral Sea. At its junction with the Afghanistan border, the boundary crosses the Amu Darya to head north up Kugitangtau mountain (16,289 feet; 4,966 m.), before turning northwest and gradually heading down onto land below 656 feet (200 m.). At the end of a straight-line segment, passing to the north of Chardzhou, the boundary again meets up with the Amu Darya, just north of Kabakly. It follows the course of this river to Gaz-Achak, where it circles to the south of the settlements surrounding Urgench. The boundary then again returns to the increasingly fan-like course of the Amu Darya, only to gradually meander south-westward, and then due south at the lake of Saryskamiskoje. Just before meeting the Krasnovodsk–Urgench road, the boundary heads west in a straight-line segment to meet the Kazakhstan border on the 56°E line of longitude.

Historical Background. In the late nineteenth century the rule of Imperial Russia was extended to what is now Turkmenistan, but on seizing power in late 1917, the Bolshevik regime deposed the remaining khanate and emirate forces, and their lands became people's republics. Toward the end of 1924 the Bolsheviks began to make more definitive territorial units based on ethnic and national compositions. Turkmenistan and Uzbekistan were both established in October 1924 as socialist republics of the USSR.

The new boundaries of the Soviet Republic varied greatly from old ones, and in several cases traced ethnic demarcations with circuitous complexity. The former territory of the Khiva khanate was divided between Uzbekistan, the Karakalpak autonomous Soviet socialist republic, Kazakhstan and Turkmenistan. The Kokand khanate was apportioned between Uzbekistan, Tajikistan, Kazakhstan and Kyrgyzstan, while the Bukhara emirate was divided between Uzbekistan, Turkmenistan and Tajikistan.

Turkmenistan declared its independence on 27 October 1991, having declared its sovereignty on 22 August 1990. The people of Turkmenistan have strong tribal loyalty which is reinforced by dialect and cultural and religious practice, and with the exception of the major cities and some Uzbek-populated eastern and northern pockets (most notably the Dashhowuz region), ethnic Turkmen are the majority, making up 73% of the total population. In central Asia, Uzbekistan is the most populous country and the Uzbeks are by far the largest ethnic group. Uzbekistan declared its independence on 21 August 1991.

Present Situation. Although there are no official boundary disputes between the two states, there are several nationalist and secessionist claims on both sides of the border. Uzbek nationalists claim the strip of territory southeast of Chardzhou between the existing border and the Oxus part of the Tashauz region of northern Turkmenistan. Turkmen nationalists, however, lay claim to an area of Uzbekistan south of Bukhara, even up to the city itself.

TURKS AND CAICOS ISLANDS   A British colony, the Turks and Caicos Islands are situated in the Atlantic Ocean, east of the Bahamas. Consisting of two groups of islands, the colony's total land area is 193 sq. miles (500 sq. km.) with an estimated population (1994) of 11,000. Its capital is Cockburn Town and it has no land boundaries.

The Turks and Caicos Islanders were under Bahamian authority until 1874, when their territory was annexed to the Jamaican colony. Independence efforts were initiated in the 1980s, but have thus far achieved neither resolution nor firm results.

TUVALU   An archipelago in the South Pacific Ocean, Tuvalu's total land area is 10 sq. miles (26 sq. km.) and it has an estimated population (1994) of 10,000. It has no land boundaries and its capital is Funafuti.

The Ellice Islands were declared a British protectorate in 1892 and linked adminstratively with the Gilbert Islands. In a 1974 referendum over 90% of the voters favored a separate status for the atoll group and, in 1978, Tuvalu became independent as a special member of the British Commonwealth.

U

UGANDA A landlocked east African country, Uganda (area: 91,343 sq. miles [236,487 sq. km.]; estimated population: 19,000,000 [1994]), most populated in the southwest and southeast, is bounded in the north by Sudan (270 miles; 435 km.), in the east by Kenya (580 miles; 933 km.), south by Tanzania (246 miles; 396 km.) and Rwanda (105 miles; 169 km.) and west by Zaire (475 miles; 765 km.). The capital of Uganda is Kampala.

It is estimated that the Bantu peoples arrived in their present settlement areas in southern Uganda at least 1,000 years ago. Present-day ethnic identities emerged with the formation of kingdoms. This openness to adaptation and change is a feature not unique to Bantu groups; it is also found among Nilotic- and Sudanic-speakers. From about 1500, groups of Western Nilotic-speakers (Luo) moved southward, founding the Bito dynasty in Kitara and

The Turkana tribe near the Kenya–Uganda boundary

imposing themselves in most of the Bantu areas as a cattle-herding aristocracy, out of which several kingdoms emerged. Nevertheless, they were linguistically assimilated by the Bantu majority. In northern Uganda the Luo settled in areas in which today they are the sole inhabitants. The most important of the Luo-speakers are the Acholi, but Western Nilotic-speakers are also to be found in southeast Uganda, which is inhabited by a number of small ethnic groups of Bantu and Nilotic origin.

Further to the east the more arid areas were settled by the Eastern Nilotic-speakers who, more than the Western Nilotes, adhered to an economy relying almost exclusively on cattle-herding. The only exception are the Teso, who early showed an eagerness to adapt to the new circumstances and economic possibilites provided by colonial rule. The Eastern Nilotic-speakers split up into several groups known collectively as the Karamojong. The Lango, one of the largest ethnic groups in the north, are probably the result of a fusion between Eastern and Western Nilotic groups, as are the smaller Kuman and the ethnic groups of the Labwor. Until the eighteenth century much of what is today Uganda was controlled by the kingdom of Kitara Bunyoro, a stratified society of Hima cattle-herding aristocracy and Bantu agriculturalists. The decline of Kitara Bunyaro coincided with the ascent of Buganda which developed out of its core area on the northern shore of Lake Victoria to become the most powerful kingdom in Uganda at the time of the arrival of the British.

The British established a protectorate over Buganda in 1894, after a short interlude of Imperial British East Africa Company rule during the years 1888–1893. The British were interested in the area of the Nile sources for strategic reasons. The kingdom subsequently became the base for colonial expansion, a process in which the Ganda themselves played a prominent role. They were not only instrumental in conquering territories, like that of the Teso, but also as agents of administrative penetration. For that reason Buganda always retained a special status within Uganda, and political developments in Uganda during the following decades centered to a certain extent around the Ganda and their kingdom. The conquest of Bunyoro proved difficult, and only after a prolonged war were the British able to impose their rule. The areas in the north were incorporated only later, and it took until 1914 for Uganda to assume the approximate borders it has today. Even then the Karamojong were not yet brought under the administrative system taken over by the British from the Ganda. This system was changing the traditional pattern of society, most notably among the segmentary societies in the northern part of the country, by introducing chiefs.

Uganda was, in terms of administration, by no means uniform, due to the special role conceded not only to Buganda but also to the kingdoms of the Nyoro, Toro and Soga. The British government succeeded in streamlining the system of colonial rule in 1900, when it divided Uganda into four provinces, one of which was Buganda. The British restricted the autocratic rule of the king by strengthening the role of a council of chiefs.

In the following decades the colonial system was slowly democratized, giving Africans more say in the central administration. Political differences in colonial Uganda were largely formulated along religious affiliations, especially Catholic or Protestant, but the separatist tendencies of the Ganda always played a major role.

In 1962 Uganda became independent under Milton Obote. In 1967 the kingdoms were abolished and dismembered into districts. Obote, himself a Lango, was deposed in a military coup led by Idi Amin in 1972. During Amin's dictatorship over 300,000 Ugandans were killed by his army, and the entire Asian population was expelled from the country. Moreover, the role of the south, the area of the main cash crop production, was strengthened. When Amin was deposed in 1979, Obote came back to power. His heavy dependence on support from the Lango and the Acholi, especially in the army, resulted in internal strife which developed into civil war. Yoweri Museveni, a southerner, started a guerrilla war, which brought him to power in 1986.

UGANDA — KENYA   see KENYA–UGANDA.

UGANDA — RWANDA   see RWANDA–UGANDA.

UGANDA — SUDAN   see SUDAN–UGANDA.

UGANDA — TANZANIA   see TANZANIA–UGANDA.

UGANDA — ZAIRE This boundary is 475 miles (765 km.) long, extending from the boundary tripoint with Rwanda in the south to the tripoint with Sudan in the north.

Geographical Setting. From Mount Sabinio in the east, the boundary proceeds in straight-line sectors along the southern extremity of Mdagana ridge, across its watershed to its highest point and then to summit of Chieshire (Tshieshire) knoll. Heading toward the confluence of the Nyarugando and Kanga rivers and following the *thalweg* (main navigation channel) of the former to its source the boundary then runs straight to the highest point of Gisko hill. It follows the watershed between Gisko hill and Lubona hill and further to a point 1,312 feet (400 m.) northwest of the summit of Lubona hill. Then, following the crest of the spur running northwest to the Sinda River, the border crosses to the crest of the opposite spur, which it follows to the summit of Kirambo hill. It trends along the crest of a spur running from Kirambo hill in a northeasterly and then northerly direction to the northernmost elbow of the Kako (Rutshuru) River and straight across the river to the mouth of the Kasumo River. It follows the *thalweg* of the Kasumo River to its source and then trends straight to the lowest point of the valley northeast of the northernmost elbow of the Kako River. The boundary then heads straight to the confluence of the Kiarakibi and Murungu rivers, following the latter downstream to its confluence with the *thalweg* of the Chango (Tshonga) River. Then the boundary runs to the summit of a hill about 2,296 feet (700 m.) north-northeast of this confluence and in straight lines reaches the summits of Chikomo (Deko South) hill, Deko North hill and a hill about 2 miles (3 km.) north of it. Then the line arrives at the point where the Kayonsa road crosses the Ivwi River and continues on to a prominent spur of the Nkabwa-Salambo massif about 0.6 miles (1 km.) to the north. It follows the crest of this spur and the watershed of the Nkabwa-Salambo massif to the summit of Nkabwa and follows the parallel of latitude of that summit eastward to its intersection with the *thalweg* of the Manyaga (Muniaga) River, which it then follows downstream to its intersection with the *thalweg* of the Ishasha River. It follows this to its mouth at Lake Edward. The boundary crosses Lake Edward in a straight line to the mouth of the

Lubilia-Chako River and follows its *thalweg* to its source, heads straight to the highest point (Margharita Peak) of the Ruwenzori range and runs on to the source of the Lami River, 3.3 miles (5.4 km.) northwest of the Kalengili peak and 12.4 miles (20 km.) southwest of the top of Karangora hill. It courses along the *thalweg* of the Lami River to its confluence with the *thalweg* of the Semiliki River, which it also follows to its mouth in Lake Albert. By a succession of straight lines, the boundary passes through the points midway between the shore of Lake Albert on the 1°30'N, 1°45'N and 2°N parallels and arrives at a point midway between the shores of the lake on latitude 2°07'N. From here the boundary runs northward to the intersection of 2°07'N with the extension of a straight line that reaches from the summit of Kagudi hill to the summit of a knoll, on the escarpment overlooking the western shore of the lake about 1 mile (1.7 km.) southeast by east of the summit of Kagudi hill. From this intersection, the border forms a straight line to the summit of Kagudi hill and a straight line toward the summit of Biet hill as far as its intersection with another straight line that joins the summit of Milia hill and the confluence of the Nashiodo and Alala rivers. The boundary continues in a straight line to this confluence and there enters the *thalweg* of the Nashiodo River and follows it to its source nearest the summit of Keresi hill. From there it runs in a straight line to the summit and follows the watershed of the Sido basin to the summit of Aminzi hill and up to the top of Monda rock. Again in a straight line, the boundary finds the confluence of the Narodo and Niabola rivers and follows the *thalweg* of the latter to a point nearest to the summit of Agu hill, to which it then runs. It traverses over the watershed of the Aioda river basin to the summit of Sisi hill and then follows the watershed of the Leda river basin to the summit of a knoll 2.6 miles (4.2 km.) southeast by east of the summit of Cho hill. Following the watershed between the Niagiaki river basin and the tributary that joins the Niagiaki River just below the confluence of that river and the Ammodar River, as far as a point nearest to that confluence, the boundary then runs straight to that confluence. It then follows the *thalweg* of the Ammodar River to its junction, 5,248 feet (1,600 m.) southwest of the summit of Akar hill, with the *thalweg* of its tributary originating near a knoll on the Congo–Nile watershed, 3.5 miles (5.6 km.) south-southeast of the summit of Ham (Utzi) hill and 3.8 miles (6.2 km.) west-southwest of the summit of Akar hill near the source of the Imithameri River. The boundary then follows the Congo–Nile watershed northward and meets its tripoint with Sudan about 0.2 miles (0.3 km.) south of the source of the Kaia River.

Historical Background. The limits of the Congo Free State (later Belgian Congo) had been set in general terms in 1885, but Britain and Germany were not then committed to a precise eastern boundary. The Anglo-German Agreement of 1 July 1890 fixed the north–south division of their spheres of influence and in 1910 Belgium, which ruled Belgian Congo from 1908, and Germany agreed upon their border south of the Mount Sabinio tripoint. A complicated series of leases along the Congo border with British territory was ended in 1910 and the section north to Mount Nkabwa was delimited on 14 May 1910. The rest of the boundary was agreed upon on 3 February 1915. Belgian Congo became independent on 30 June 1960, changing its name to Zaire on 21 October 1971. Uganda became independent on 8 September 1967. Both states adopted the colonial boundary without a formal agreement.

Present Situation. The Uganda–Zaire boundary line is not in dispute.

UKRAINE (Ukraina) An Eastern European country (area: 233,090 sq. miles [603,700 sq. km.]; estimated population: 52,000,000 [1994]), Ukraine was a republic of the Soviet Union until 1991. It is bounded by Belarus (554 miles; 891 km.) in the north, by Russia (980 miles; 1,576 km.) in the east, by the Black Sea in the south and by Romania (330 miles; 531 km.), Moldava (584 miles; 939 km.), Hungary (64 miles; 103 km.), Slovakia (56 miles; 90 km.) and Poland (266 miles; 428 km.) in the west. The capital of Ukraine is Kiev.

East Slavic tribes settled in the area of present-day Ukraine in the sixth–seventh centuries. From the ninth to thirteenth centuries they were part of Kievan Russia. It is in the centuries that followed invasions by the Mongols (1238) that the Ukrainians, like the neighboring eastern Slavic peoples, were formed. Unlike them, however, the ethnogenesis of the Ukrainians, their part in the inheritance of Kievan Russia and their status vis-a-vis the Russians were all subject to heated dispute, which gave rise to a wide range of theories. One of the more extreme of these holds that the Ukrainians were the original people of Kievan Russia while the Russians were descendants of frontier settlers who intermingled with a variety of other peoples. The other theory holds that the Ukrainians were not part of Kievan Russia but lived west of it, and only settled their present areas following the destruction and depopulation of Kiev by the Mongols.

While Kiev was, indeed, destroyed and depopulated by the Mongols, other principalities west and north of it survived. These were gradually absorbed by Poland and Lithuania. After the dynastic union between the two (1386) the Ukraine became part of Poland. In that period the term *Ukraina* (lit. "borderland") originated; it was Poland's southeastern frontier against the Crimean Tatars and the Ottomans.

The western and northern parts of the Ukraine were subjected to a strong Polish and Catholic influence. A Polish nobility enserfed the peasants, who largely retained their East Slavic speech and Slavonic service in the church (whether Russian Orthodox or Uniate). In the more turbulent borderlands beyond the Dnieper River, fugitives from the Polish border formed the Cossack bands which created the *Zaporizhska Sich* and, at the beginning of the sixteenth century, were strong enough to be mobilized by the Polish kings to protect them from Tatar raids.

In spite of this, inherent social, national and religious contradictions existed between the Cossacks and the Polish state. They erupted in a series of rebellions, the most powerful and famous of which was led in 1648 by Bohdan Khmielnycki. In 1654 he appealed to the Russians for help and swore allegiance to the czar, an event celebrated in the Soviet Union as the "Union of the Ukraine and Russia." A Polish-Russian struggle followed. Although the two partitioned the Ukraine along the Dnieper River in 1667, Ottoman and Swedish involvement prolonged the struggle until 1709.

In 1775 Catherine the Great suppressed and disarmed the Zaprozhian Cossacks and brought the Ukraine under regular Russian administration. At the second partition of Poland (1793) a large part of the Ukraine was added to the Russian Empire.

During the last two decades of the eighteenth and the first half of the nineteenth centuries, the Ukraine went through rapid socioeconomic changes and the steppe belt was developed and colonized, making the Ukraine the center of gravity of the Russian empire's economy first as the main grain producer and exporter and then as an important mining and industrial center. This rapid economic development was followed by great demographic, social and socioeconomic changes, which produced a revival of Ukrainian literature and the use of the Ukrainian language in education and scholarship during the middle of the nineteenth century. Among the leaders of this process were Taras Shevchenko (1819–1860) the national poet, and Mykola Kostomariv (1817–1885) and Panteleimon Kulysh (1819–1897), the founding fathers of Ukrainian historiography. In 1846 the short-lived "Secret Society of Saints Cyril and Methodius" was established in Kiev, an event which is commonly regarded as marking the birth of Ukrainian nationalism.

The Russian authorities regarded the Ukrainians (as well as the Byelorussians) as part of the Russian people. They even banned the name "Ukrainians," replacing it with the old term *Malorussy* (Lesser Russians). Alarmed at the growing use of the Ukrainian language in education and publication, they banned it in 1876 and started a campaign of forced Russification, which ended only after the revolution of 1905. During these years the center of Ukrainian nationalism, literature and scholarship moved to Austro-Hungarian Lvov, and then transferred to Lemberg.

Following the revolution of 1917, a national Ukrainian congress proclaimed in Kiev a "free sovereign" Ukrainian republic. In a countermove the Bolshevik regime formed a Ukrainian Soviet government in Kharkov. After the civil war most of the Ukraine remained under Soviet rule and was one of the founding republics of the Soviet Union. Western Ukraine came under Polish rule. During World War II the Ukraine was conquered by the Germans, who

The boundaries of Moldava and Ukraine

enjoyed the cooperation of some Ukrainian nationalists. Following the war, the western Ukraine, Transcarpathia (Carpathorus), Bukovina and southern Bessarabia were annexed to the Ukrainian Soviet Republic from Poland, Czechoslovakia and Romania. In 1954 the Crimea was annexed to the Ukraine as part of the celebration of the tricentennial of the "unification of the Ukraine and Russia."

While the Ukraine underwent further industrial development and became a crucial part of the Soviet economy (its economic far surpassing its demographic weight), the Ukrainians suffered great losses (in the millions) in the civil war, the collectivization and famine that accompanied it, and then again in World War II and during the incorporation of western Ukraine into the Soviet Union.

In addition, during the entire Soviet period the Ukrainians were under strong, albeit generally subtle, pressure to Russify, which further decimated their numbers (in one such case the Soviet authorities changed the nationality of the Kuban Cossacks in 1929 from Ukrainian to Russian, thus depriving the Ukrainians and adding to the Russians 2–3 million people).

Following the dissolution of the Soviet Union the Ukraine became a fully independent state. Although it joined the Commonwealth of Independent States (CIS), being the strongest member after Russia, it was an extreme advocate of keeping the CIS as loose an organization as possible.

UKRAINE — BELARUS see BELARUS–UKRAINE.

UKRAINE — HUNGARY see HUNGARY–UKRAINE.

UKRAINE — MOLDAVA see MOLDAVA–UKRAINE.

UKRAINE — POLAND see POLAND–UKRAINE.

UKRAINE — ROMANIA see ROMANIA–UKRAINE.

UKRAINE — RUSSIA see RUSSIA–UKRAINE.

UKRAINE — SLOVAKIA see SLOVAKIA–UKRAINE.

UNITED ARAB EMIRATES (Al-Imarat al-'Arabiyah al-Muttahidah) A Middle Eastern country situated in the Arabian Peninsula, the United Arab Emirates (area: 32,300 sq. miles [83,625 sq., km.]; estimated population: 2,600,000 [1994]) is bounded in the north by the Persian (Arabian) Gulf, in the east by Oman (336 miles; 540 km.) and in the south by Saudi Arabia (364 miles; 586 km.). Its capital is Abu Dhabi.

Until the 1700s there were only fishing, pearling and smuggling villages in the region, without known resources, yet strategically controlling the entrance to the Gulf. For this reason, the British signed a series of treaties giving them exclusive control over maritime relations but leaving the tribal sheikhs control over land. In 1892 the relationship was formalized in protectorate treaties. The sheikhs received subsidies in return, but were forced to (officially) suppress slave traffic.

After the 1950s oil exports created a boom, particularly in Abu Dhabi, causing explosive development and the highest per capita income in the world. Moderate amounts of oil were later found in Dubai, Sharjah, and Ras al-Khaimah.

As Britain prepared to leave in 1971, the emirates united in a confederation. They created an army with British support. Nevertheless each state maintains its own emir and princely families, and remains internally an absolute monarchy, with little mutual coordination. Abu Dhabi, five times bigger than the other emirates together and with the largest population and immense oil reserves, dominates politically. Competing against it is Dubai, until 1825 considered a dependency of Abu Dhabi. Its wealth was first based on smuggling gold, but Dubai and Sharjah are now developing as a shipping and commercial center. Throughout the emirates there are some agricultural oases; industrialization has been lagging due to water and labor shortages. Economic development transformed the sparse indigenous population into an upper class enjoying free education and medical services. As in other Gulf states, this situation has also made them extremely dependent on migrants, who constitute 80% of the labor force. The foreigners are concentrated in Abu Dhabi City and Dubai-Sharjah, there forming a powerless underclass whose political aspirations are feared. In Dubai alone there were 30,000, mostly Shi'ite, Iranians out of a total population of 210,000 (1983). The recession following the fall of oil prices in the 1980s led to attempts at repatriation.

UNITED ARAB EMIRATES — OMAN   see OMAN–UNITED ARAB EMIRATES.

UNITED ARAB EMIRATES — SAUDI ARABIA   see SAUDI ARABIA–UNITED ARAB EMIRATES.

UNITED STATES OF AMERICA   A North American country, the United States (area: 3,787,425 sq. miles [9,805,643 sq. km]; estimated population: 257,000,000 [1994]) is bounded in the north by Canada (5,525 miles; 8,893 km.), including the 1,538 miles (2,477 km.) between Canada and the American state of Alaska. This is the longest land boundary in the world. The United States is also bounded in the east by the Atlantic Ocean, in the south by Mexico (1,951 miles; 3,140 km.) and in the west by the Pacific Ocean. Its capital is Washington, in the District of Columbia.

The first Americans are believed to have settled in the present United States some 30,000 years ago. They fanned out across the diverse geographical regions, creating tribal societies and nations. The arrival of the first Europeans to the United States has also been the subject of some speculation although the first of the modern settlements were established only after Christopher Columbus's voyages to the western hemisphere in 1492. Four nations, Britain, France, Spain and the Netherlands, vied for control of the region, Britain becoming the dominant power on the eastern seaboard. Many of the first settlers, such as those known as the Pilgrims of Plymouth Rock, were refugees fleeing religious persecution; others were traders and merchants who recognized the vast wealth of this unexploited region. With the influx of European settlers, particularly in New England and Virginia, came a certain degree of self-rule.

Mexico–United States boundary

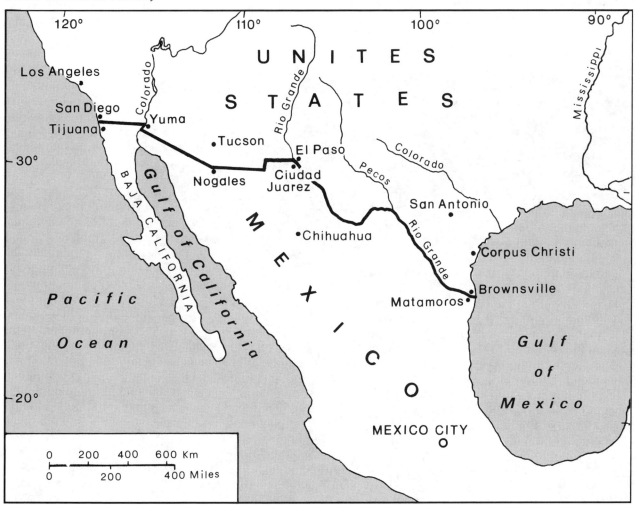

What were initially peaceful relations with the indigenous peoples occasionally became hostile as the burgeoning immigrant population made encroachments on their land and livelihood.

In the South, large plantations were established based on the exploitation of imported African slave laborers. While the first settlers were English, Scottish and Irish, there was also an influx of French, Germans and other Europeans. In the southwest, then under Spanish control, settlers intermingled with slave laborers and the native population, forming the core of the current Hispanic component of Americans.

With increased prosperity came a sense of distinction from Europe. Despite local political autonomy, the colonists considered themselves exploited by Britain, and sought to administer the colonies themselves. As tensions increased, so did the call for independence by thinkers such as Thomas Paine, Benjamin Franklin and Thomas Jefferson, who sought to create a federal republic out of the colonies. Gath-

ered together in 1775–1776 in the Continental Congress, they resolved that "These colonies are, and of right ought to be, free and independent states." Two days later, on 4 July 1776, they issued the Declaration of Independence, sparking the Revolutionary War which led to the formation of the United States of America.

The following years saw the split of American opinion among Liberals, Radicals and Conservatives, each with its own vision of the type of government to be adopted by the infant state. A compromise was reached in the Constitution of 1788 which still remains the basis of American political life. Written to "form a more perfect union, establish justice, ensure domestic tranquility, provide for the common defense, promote the general welfare, and to secure the blessings of liberty to ourselves and our posterity," it failed to liberate the millions of enslaved African-Americans. In 1791, 10 amendments were made ensuring such liberties as freedom of religion, speech, the press and the right to trial by jury.

The United States' international border crossing into Canada, Washington State

Known as the Bill of Rights, they were later echoed in the liberal constitutions of other countries but were not always put into practice in the United States. Expansion into lands inhabited by Native American peoples continued and the African-American population remained largely enslaved. Another question debated was regionalism and the rights of states against the federal government, matters which eventually erupted in the Civil War of 1861–1865.

Nonetheless, Americans prospered and expanded to the west. New immigrants poured in from Europe as more territories were annexed, including the Louisiana Purchase, Texas and California. As new territories were opened to settlement, the indigenous inhabitants were largely ignored and their rights violated. Waving the banner of "Manifest Destiny," and with a pioneering frontier spirit, Americans spread from the Atlantic to the Pacific Ocean.

One of the most pressing problems facing Americans in the nineteenth century was the slavery question. It had long been abolished in the north but was vital to the Southern economy. The debate over this and the degree to which states were to control internal affairs led to the secession of the South and the establishment of the slave-holding Confederate States of America in 1861. The objective of a united American nation was finally achieved with the surrender of the southern states in 1865, and the government began a policy of reconstruction to reintegrate the South.

The years following the Civil War saw the arrival of millions of immigrants from Europe and Asia. European immigrants came through the northeastern states, particularly the port of entry at Ellis Island, New York, where Irish fleeing famine, Italians fleeing poverty and Jews fleeing pogroms came in their millions at the turn of the century. On the West Coast, Asian immigrants found employment, settling in San Francisco and Los Angeles. Filipinos, having served in the American Navy since 1901, settled in cities with naval traditions. These new immigrants were gradually absorbed into the new American society. At the same time, they contributed much to the evolving American culture and were vital to the emergence of the contemporary industrial and commercial economy.

America emerged from its relative isolation into a world power during the two World Wars. Prosperity saw the emergence of a new middle class culture, where suburbia and the automobile have become important elements. The 1960s witnessed a transformation in American social and political life, when the popular struggle for civil rights of African-Americans became widespread, embracing also the struggle for the rights of women, children, homosexuals, the disabled and Native Americans.

UNITED STATES OF AMERICA — CANADA see CANADA–UNITED STATES OF AMERICA.

UNITED STATES OF AMERICA — MEXICO see MEXICO–UNITED STATES OF AMERICA.

UNITED KINGDOM A country in Western Europe, the United Kingdom (area: 94,248 sq. miles [244,008 sq. km.]; estimated population: 58,000,000 [1994]) has land boundaries with Ireland (224 miles; 360 km.), on the Irish island, and, as sovereign bases, with Cyprus. The boundary of the Dhekelia Base is about 64 miles (103 km.) long, while the Akrotiri Base runs for approximately 30 miles (49 km.). The capital of the United Kingdom is London.

Until 900 years ago, the British Isles were periodically invaded from the European continent. The first to come, in prehistoric times, were the Celts, who were pushed farther inland by later arrivals. Today they preponderate only in Wales and the Scottish Highlands, but many cultural relics testify to their former preeminence. The same holds true for the Romans, whose range of influence subsequently determined the area inhabited by the English. The next wave consisted of Germanic colonists: Angles, Saxons and Jutes constitute the single most important substratum of the modern British. The last invasion was that of the Normans in 1066. The English soon became predominant among the British. They subjugated the Welsh and after a long process finally absorbed Wales in the sixteenth century. In 1707 the English united with the Scots to form Great Britain. Ireland, however, was treated as a colony until fully integrated by 1801. A struggle for independence resulted in 1920 in the partition of Ireland, with the Northern Irish remaining attached to Great Britain.

UNITED KINGDOM — CYPRUS see CYPRUS–UNITED KINGDOM.

UNITED KINGDOM — IRELAND   see IRE-
LAND–UNITED KINGDOM.

URUGUAY   A South American country (area: 68,500 sq. miles [177,415 sq. km.; estimated population: 3,200,000 [1994]), Uruguay is bounded in the north and northeast by Brazil (612 miles; 985 km.), in the east and south by the Atlantic Ocean and in the west by Argentina (360 miles; 579 km.). Uruguay's capital is Montevideo.

For nearly 200 years after the Spaniards first reached the Plata region, they established no fixed settlement in what is now Uruguay. The region was occupied chiefly by nomadic cattle herders (*gauchos*). There was no attempt to claim ownership of the land or even to establish ranch headquarters. The idea of landownership was slow to reach Uruguay, but once it did, the zone of *estancias* (ranches) moved northward from the Plata shore and the nomadic *gauchos* were pushed to more remote parts of the country. Landowners gradually replaced the *gauchos* with hired workers. As this type of occupation spread northward, Uruguay became a land of small scattered trading villages and of widely spaced ranches. By the 1830s, the country was already grazed by millions of cattle, but the only products exported were hides, tallow and salt beef.

In 1840 high grade merino sheep were introduced from Britain, and the grazing of wool sheep spread quite rapidly. In the 1870s two inventions reached Uruguay that initiated major changes in the pastoral economy. One was barbed wire, which made possible the fencing of pastures and control of animal breeding, the other was the refrigerator ship, which made possible the shipment of frozen meat across the tropics. It is estimated that by 1900 there were in Uruguay 18.5 million head of sheep and 7 million head of cattle.

This transformation was made possible by the initiative of European immigration during the nineteenth century. By 1852 more than a fifth of the Uruguayan population was foreign-born. Work was plentiful in the cattle industry and the *saladeros* (salted beef plants), due to the expansion of the British market for Uruguayan meat. The 1860 census revealed that the proportion of foreigners in Uruguay had grown to 35%, while 48% of the total population lived in Montevideo. Brazilians consti-

tuted the largest foreign colony, almost 20,000 people, or a fourth of the foreign total. Spaniards ran a close second with some 18,000. The Italians and French created communities which stabilized in number at around 10,000 each. Almost half the population of Montevideo itself was foreign-born. By 1908 foreigners constituted 42% of the labor force in the industrial sector of Montevideo and 28.4% at the national level. Between the middle of the nineteenth century and 1903, the population of Uruguay grew almost 13 times. By 1908 in Montevideo almost one-third of the inhabitants were foreigners. In the period 1881–1924, Italians made up 41% of the total immigrants, Spaniards, 30% and French, 6%. These immigrants made great contributions to the modernization of the country. The role of immigration in the rapid economic growth of Uruguay was crucial, especially in the secondary and tertiary sectors in the cities, as well as in the national urbanization process. Under the impact of immigration the old cultural patterns practically dissolved.

Uruguay's territory has served throughout much of its history as a buffer zone. The colonial empires of the Spaniards and Portuguese disputed the area, invading Uruguay repeatedly in the attempt to occupy and retain a strategic position at the mouth of the Rio de la Plata. Uruguay (Banda Oriental, or East Bank) was an integral part of the viceroyship of Rio de la Plata, and gained independence through the intervention of the British and an agreement between Argentina and Brazil to recognize its sovereignty.

The Uruguayan republic soon became the most stable and democratic state in Latin America. During the early twentieth century, it made rapid economic and social progress. Exports of meat, wool, leather and grain continued to expand the nation's prosperity until the 1950s. Uruguay attained distinction in Latin America through the sociopolitical model implemented by José Batle y Ordoñez, who organized the urban and working-class population under the banner of the Colorado party. He and his successors created a welfare state that provided social benefits seldom equaled elsewhere in the developed world. The welfare state collapsed by 1965, however, as the largely pastoral economy proved unable to support a system in which most people worked in nonproductive activities. Instead, an authoritarian political regime took power with military intervention in 1973 to fight armed insurgency (the Tupamaros guerrillas), and Uruguay became an oppressive state oriented by a neo-liberal economy policy that provoked a large wave of emigrants, including political exiles and refugees. Since 1984 redemocratization is gradually under way.

URUGUAY — ARGENTINA see ARGENTINA–URUGUAY.

URUGUAY — BRAZIL see BRAZIL–URUGUAY.

UZBEKISTAN A landlocked central Asian country, Uzbekistan (area: 172,742 sq. miles [447,400 sq. km.]; estimated population: 21,700,000 [1994]) is bounded in the north and west by Kazakhstan (1,369 miles; 2,203 km.), in the north by the Aral Sea, in the south by Turkmenistan (1,008 miles; 1,621 km.) and Afghanistan (85 miles; 137 km.) and in the east by Tajikistan (722 miles; 1,161 km.) and Kyrgyzstan (683 miles; 1,099 km.). The capital of Uzbekistan is Tashkent.

The ethnogenesis of the Uzbeks has been a long and steady process which is not yet complete. Its main component is the ancient central Asian Iranian ethnic groups which have been undergoing a centuries-long, almost latent, process of Turkification. The process has been artificially hastened by the authorities since the 1920s, which has caused strong resentment among the intellectual strata of Tajiks. Its second component was the older Turkic settlers of central Asia, whose first appearance in the present territory of the Uzbeks is traced back to the sixth century. The last component was the confederation of Turkic and Turkified nomad Mongols, known under the general name of Uzbeks, who began expanding into central Asia in the fifteenth century and finally conquered it in the sixteenth century. It was this Uzbek confederation to which all the rulers of the sixteenth- to nineteenth-century central Asian principalities belonged. (In the aftermath of the late 1860s' to early 1870s' Russian conquest of central

Asia one of them, the Khuqand (Kokand) principality, was abolished in 1876, and two others, the Bukharan and the Khivan, became, with very diminished territories, Russian protectorates.) It was this name that was chosen as a unifying ethnic designation for the population of a republic established in 1924 on most of the Russian territories in central Asia: the Uzbek Soviet Socialist Republic. In the longer run this engineering of a new ethnicity proved successful: the common Uzbek self-identification now strongly prevails over tribal identifications. Nevertheless, the latter still exist, albeit in a secondary and/or residual form. The following tribes deserve mentioning: the Qarluq, Qyphchaq, Jalair, Barlas, Qungrat, Manghit, Laqay and Yuz. Although not a tribe, the Kurama group that dwells near Tashkent also has a subethnic identity of its own (they are in all probability Uzbekified Qazaqs). In Afghanistan the Qarluq and Qypchaq regard themselves as distinct ethnic entities.

In 1991 Uzbekistan proclaimed its sovereignty but remained within the framework of the Commonwealth of Independent States (CIS). In Afghanistan Uzbeks were very active in the resistance to the 1979 Soviet intervention and played a leading role in the downfall of the Moscow-backed Afghanistani government in 1992.

UZBEKISTAN — AFGHANISTAN see AFGHANISTAN–UZBEKISTAN.

UZBEKISTAN — KAZAKHSTAN see KAZAKHSTAN–UZBEKISTAN.

UZBEKISTAN — KYRGYZSTAN see KYRGYZSTAN–UZBEKISTAN.

UZBEKISTAN — TAJIKISTAN see TAJIKISTAN–UZBEKISTAN.

UZBEKISTAN — TURKMENISTAN see TURKMENISTAN–UZBEKISTAN.

V-W

VANUATU A country consisting of a chain of islands, Vanuatu is situated in the South Pacific Ocean, east of Australia. Formerly known as New Hebrides, its total land area is 4,706 sq. miles (12,184 sq. km.) with an estimated population of 200,000 (1994). Its capital is Port-Vila and it has no land boundaries.

Until 1980 Vanuatu was jointly governed by an Anglo-French condominium established in 1906. The islanders achieved independence in 1980, and controversy over issues of land rights were settled by the new constitution, which ruled that the land belong to the indigenous owners and their descendants. In March 1988, Vanuatu signed an agreement with Papua New Guinea and the Solomon Islands to form the "Spearhead Group," which aimed to preserve Melanesian cultural traditions and to campaign for New Caledonian independence. The principal exports are cocoa, copra, beef and timber. In 1989 agriculture, forestry and fishing contributed about 18.9% of Vanuatu's national product, about half their proportional contribution in the early 1980s.

VATICAN CITY (Cittá del Vaticano) An independent country under the ruling of the Catholic pope, Vatican City is located within the Italian city of Rome. Italy's encompassing boundary with Vatican City measures 2 miles (3.2 km.). Its area is 0.17 sq. miles (0.44 sq. km.) with an estimated population (1994) of 1,000.

VATICAN CITY — ITALY see ITALY–VATICAN CITY.

VENEZUELA A South American country (area: 352,279 sq. miles [912,050 sq. km.]; estimated population: 20,700,000 [1994]), Venezuela is situated in the northern part of the continent. It is bounded in the north by the Caribbean Sea, in the east by Guyana (462 miles; 743 km.), in the south by Brazil (1,367 miles; 2,200 km.) and in the west by Colombia (1,274 miles; 2,050 km.). Venezuela's capital is Caracas. Venezuela was named "Little Venice" by Alonso de Ojeda, who sailed into the Gulf of Venezuela in 1499. The territory, Spanish control of which was fiercely resisted by Indians, was under the control of a German banking firm during much of the early 1500s. The indigenous people were decimated by smallpox in the late 1590s. From then until independence in 1811, Venezuela fared much the same as the rest of Hispanic America.

What established Venezuela most securely as a keystone in the modern history of Latin America, however, were the exploits of the Venezuelan Simon Bolívar, who entered Caracas as "the Liberator" in 1813 to establish the short-lived Second Republic. Bolívar, driven out of the country by royalists in 1814, regrouped his forces in Haiti and re-entered Venezuela, proclaiming the Third Republic of Gran Colombia, a union of Venezuela and Colombia, which subsequently collapsed, and Venezuela was declared an independent state in 1829.

The constitution of 1961 established a strong presidential form of government under a system of legislation which, through protection of private enterprises and a system of social welfare, effectively guarantees a mixed economy. Suffrage is both universal and compulsory.

VENEZUELA — BRAZIL see BRAZIL–VENEZUELA.

VENEZUELA — COLOMBIA see COLOMBIA–VENEZUELA.

Venezuela's boundaries with Brazil and Colombia

VENEZUELA — GUYANA see GUYANA–
VENEZUELA.

VIETNAM A Southeast Asian country (area:
128,115 sq. miles [331,689 sq. km.]; estimated population: 70,400,000 [1994]), Vietnam is bounded in
the north by China (796 miles; 1,281 km.), in the
east and south by the South China Sea and in the
west by Cambodia (763 miles; 1,228 km.) and Laos
(1,324 miles; 2,130 km.). The capital of Vietnam is
Hanoi.

The Vietnamese are descended from nomadic
groups from central China who migrated to the Red
River delta and intermingled with Indonesian immigrants in the pre-Christian era. They were subdued
by the Chinese in the second century B.C.E. and only
reasserted their independence during the mid-tenth
century. At the same time, they began migrating
southward to the Mekong River delta, dominating or
assimilating the local Cham and Khmer. For 900
years, Vietnam was an independent empire modeled
largely on the Chinese system. Cultural and religious activity centered on Chinese traditions and on

Buddhism, Taoism and Confucianism which coex-
isted alongside traditional beliefs in spirits and ancestor worship.

Vietnam reached its present territorial form only in
1780. Less than a century later, the French Conquered the country and divided it into three sections:
the colony of Annam in the south, and the protectorates of Cochin and Tonkin in the center and
north.

The French provided Western education, a Roman
alphabet to replace complicated Chinese ideographs
(almost 90% of the Vietnamese are literate) and
Catholicism. It was at this time that a native religion, Cao Dai, emerged, synthesizing Judeo-Chris-
tian traditions with Chinese religious values and Indian mysticism.

Led by Ho Chi Minh, Vietnamese students study-
ing in France were attracted to the Communist
teachings of Karl Marx and Vladimir Ilych Lenin
and sought to apply them in a future independent
Vietnam.

Following the Japanese occupation of the country
(1940–1944) a short-lived Communist regime was

established in Tonkin in the north but this was quashed by returning French colonial troops. In 1954, France promised to grant independence under emperor Bai Dai, but this was rejected by the Communists, now known as the Viet Minh, who were still influential in Tonkin. In the First Indochina War, French troops were severely beaten at Dien Bien Phu, and the partition of the country into North and South Vietnam was inevitable. The monarchy was deposed the following year.

The reunification of Vietnam was an important goal of the northern government and the two countries maintained a hostile relationship. By 1964 the two were at war, with the north being supported by China and the south by the United States. Until 1972 neither side had the advantage. Finally public pressure in the United States, sparked by American losses in such violent encounters as the 1968 Tet offensive, forced President Richard Nixon to reduce American troops in Vietnam. By 1975, the North Vietnamese and their Communist allies in the south, the Viet Cong, managed to break through South Vietnamese lines. By the end of April, the southern capital of Saigon (now Ho Chi Minh City) had fallen. Official reunification of Vietnam was proclaimed in 1976.

Scars of the Vietnamese War can still be felt among the Vietnamese. 2,000,000 civilians died in the conflict and many more were permanently injured. Moreover, Vietnam was soon involved in further conflicts with its former ally China and with neighboring Cambodia.

Many ethnic Chinese, once a flourishing middle class, fled the country, as did Vietnamese seeking security on foreign shores. Known as "boat people," they captured world attention for a short time, but many still remain in incarceration camps in neighboring countries, unable to return home and with no country willing to accept them. In Vietnam, however, Buddhist resolve and recent political and economic liberalization are enabling the slow reconstruction of the country.

VIETNAM — CAMBODIA   see CAMBODIA–VIETNAM.

VIETNAM — CHINA   see CHINA–VIETNAM.

VIETNAM — LAOS   see LAOS–VIETNAM.

VIRGIN ISLANDS, BRITISH   A British colony in the West Indies, the British Virgin Islands is an archipelago with a total land area of 59 sq. miles (153 sq. km.) and an estimated population (1994) of 13,000. Its capital is Road Town and it has no land boundaries.

VIRGIN ISLANDS, USA   A Caribbean archipelago that constitutes a US territory, the Virgin Islands of the United States has a total land area of 133 sq. miles (344 sq. km.) with no land boundaries. It has an estimated population (1994) of 118,000 and its capital is Charlotte Amalie.

WALLIS AND FUTUNA   A South Pacific archipelago, the Wallis and Futuna Islands form a French overseas territory. Its total land area is 98 sq. miles (255 sq. km.), with an estimated population (1994) of 18,000. Its capital is Mata-Utu (Uvéa) and it has no land boundaries.

The islanders hold French citizenship. The entire population is Roman Catholic. Many still engage in subsistence farming, supplemented by copra production. Most monetary income is derived from government employment and remittances sent home by relatives employed abroad.

WESTERN SAHARA   A west African country (area: 102,703 sq. miles [265,898 sq. km.]; estimated population: 200,000 [1994]), Western Sahara is bounded in the north by Morocco (275 miles; 443 km.), northeast by Algeria (26 miles; 42 km.), east and south by Mauritania (970 miles; 1,561 km.) and west by the Atlantic Ocean. Its capital is El Aaiún. Western Sahara's sovereignty is undetermined at present.

WESTERN SAHARA — ALGERIA   see ALGERIA–WESTERN SAHARA.

WESTERN SAHARA — MAURITANIA   see MAURITANIA–WESTERN SAHARA.

WESTERN SAHARA — MOROCCO   see MOROCCO–WESTERN SAHARA.

WESTERN SAMOA (Samoa i Sisifo)   A group of islands in the South Pacific Ocean, Western Samoa's total land area is 1,093 sq. miles (2,831 sq. km.). It has an estimated population (1994) of 200,000 and its capital is Apia. Western Samoa has no land boundaries.

Western Samoa was administered by Germany from 1899, and New Zealand from 1919. It became the independent State of Western Somoa in 1962.

The population of Western Samoa is on two main islands: Upolu, with the capital, Apia and Savi'i and about 20 small islands. It was a United Nations Trust Territory, under the administration of New Zealand, until achieving its independence in 1962.

X-Y-Z

YEMEN (Al-Yaman) A Middle Eastern country in the southernmost region of the Arabian Peninsula, Yemen (area: 205,356 sq. miles [531,667 sq. km.]; estimated population: 12,050,000 [1994]) is bounded by Saudi Arabia (906 miles; 1,458 km.) in the north and by Oman (179 miles; 288 km.) in the east. Its capital is San'a.

The Yemenis may descend from famous pre-Islamic kingdoms that thrived on long-distance trade. They were Islamicized by 650. In the nineteenth century the British occupied Aden and its hinterland in southern Yemen. After the collapse of the Ottoman Empire in 1918, northern Yemen became the independent kingdom of Yemen while southern Yemen was established as a British zone of influence in the Aden hinterland.

Northern Yemen was still a medieval kingdom when the last traditional ruler died in 1962. A bloody civil war broke out between republicans supported by Egypt, and royalists, aided by Saudi Arabia. This war reflected the tension between isolationism and openness to modernity. In 1970 a ceasefire established a republican regime; but many royalists kept key posts, and in fact Saudi, tribal and Islamic influences remained predominant.

The South Arabian Federation, which Britain had installed in 1959 in southern Yemen, was forced to give way to radical republican nationalists who eliminated the power of both the British and the sultans. In 1967 southern Yemen became independent as the Democratic People's Republic of Yemen, governed by a Marxist-Leninist regime which leaned increasingly toward the Soviet Union.

In North Yemen after 1974 a succession of violent government changes exacerbated tension between modernizers (supported by the South) and Islamic traditionalists (allied with Yemen's northern tribes and the pro-Saudi faction). Domestic strife soon expanded into war between the two Yemens. The "forgotten civil war" continued for years. In the mid-1980s, however, a more moderate trend became manifest in both North and South Yemen, leading to a rapprochement between them. The thaw thus ushered in has, over the past years, led to a liberalization of South Yemen's economic system, and to an expansion of political liberties in North Yemen. Finally reunited in 1991, Yemen is now experiencing the transition to a multiparty system with a free press. However, when it refused to abide by sanctions against Iraq, Saudi Arabia retaliated by suspending financial support and sent 800,000 Yemeni migrants back home, plunging the country into an acute financial crisis.

YEMEN — OMAN see OMAN–YEMEN.

YEMEN — SAUDI ARABIA see SAUDI ARABIA–YEMEN.

ZAIRE A landlocked central African country (area: 905,446 sq. miles [2,344,200 sq. km.]; estimated population: 40,250,000 [1994]), Zaire is bounded in the north by the Central African Republic (980 miles; 1,577 km.) and Sudan (390 miles; 628 km.), in the east by Uganda (475 miles; 765 km.), Rwanda (135 miles; 217 km.), Burundi (145 miles; 233 km.) and Tanzania (305 miles; 490 km.), southeast and south by Zambia (1,200 miles; 1,930 km.), southwest by Angola (1,560 miles; 2,511 km.) and west by Congo (1,010 miles; 1,625 km.). Its capital is Kinshasa.

The Congo formed a great kingdom that reached its zenith in the fifteenth and sixteenth centuries. The kingdom disintegrated during the seventeenth century but Congo linguistic and cultural dominance continued to be felt. Toward the end of the nineteenth century the kingdom was conquered and divided by the Portuguese, the French and Leopold II of Belgium (in the early twentieth century the part that was the king's private territory was taken by the Belgian parliament and became Belgian territory). Most Congo lived in the Belgian Congo (present-day Zaire).

During the period of colonial rule by the Belgians the Congo seized educational opportunities and, thanks to their close proximity to major cities, including Léopoldville (Kinshasa), were well represented in the colonial civil service. They were, however, among the first groups to demand greater liberties and eventually independence. Their anticolonial struggle was ethnic in character and included ideas of rebuilding the Congo kingdom. In 1950 they formed the Association des Congo to protect their culture from foreign influences in Léopoldville. Later this organization became a political party called the Alliance des Congo.

After independence the Congo party leader, Joseph Kasavubu, became president of Zaire and supported a Federation in which the Congo would have considerable autonomy. He was deposed by

The boundaries of Congo and Zaire

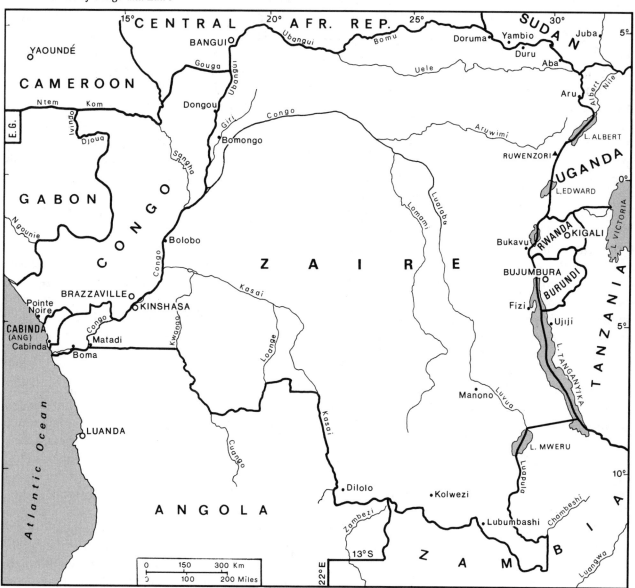

Joseph Mobutu (Mobutu Sese Seko) in 1965, however, before his program could be enacted.

Following the Katanga crisis of 1960–1963, Zaire was divided into 21 provinces. The Congo occupy the Congo Central province. They still dominate the government and civil service and are everywhere present in Zaire's capital.

The Congo of Angola were also active in the decolonization struggle against the Portuguese. In 1961 a revolt of Congo farmers that was brutally crushed by the Portuguese triggered the war of liberation that continued until independence in 1975.

Prior to independence from Belgium, granted in June 1960, Zaire was known as Belgian Congo. The Belgians left their colony without preparing it for self-rule and grave ethnic conflicts erupted almost immediately after independence. The foremost of these was the attempt of the Lunda and Yeke of the mineral-rich province of Katanga to secede. At first the Luba of Katanga regarded the struggle as a conflict between the impoverished locals and the rich foreigners from among the Kasai Luba and the Chokwe, who arrived in Katanga during the colonial period. Soon, however, the struggle became an ethnic one and the local Luba joined the Kasai Luba and the Chokwe in opposing secession. The Katanga crisis was resolved only in 1963. Since then Zaire has been ruled by Mobutu Sese Seko.

All groups in Katanga continued to feel disgruntled over the government's refusal to repay the money it appropriated from the region or to invest it in local development projects. In the 1970s two more crises shook the region, while the Lunda-Luba conflict simmered. In 1992 and 1993 many Luba fled Katanga (renamed Shaba by Mobutu) after violent Lunda attacks.

Since the early 1990s popular demands for democratization were heard, but Mobutu squashed all opposition harshly.

ZAIRE — ANGOLA see ANGOLA–ZAIRE.

ZAIRE — BURUNDI see BURUNDI–ZAIRE.

ZAIRE — CENTRAL AFRICAN REPUBLIC see CENTRAL AFRICAN REPUBLIC–ZAIRE.

ZAIRE — CONGO see CONGO–ZAIRE.

ZAIRE — RWANDA see RWANDA–ZAIRE.

ZAIRE — SUDAN see SUDAN–ZAIRE.

ZAIRE — TANZANIA see TANZANIA–ZAIRE.

ZAIRE — UGANDA see UGANDA–ZAIRE.

ZAIRE — ZAMBIA The boundary between Zaire and Zambia runs 1,200 miles (1,930 km.) through the heart of Africa, from the boundary junction with Tanzania in Lake Tanganyika to the border junction with Angola near the source of the Zambezi River. It marks the colonial Belgian–British boundary of that region.

Geographical Setting. This boundary line runs from the border junction with Tanzania, situated in the southern part of Lake Tanganyika, at about 8°13'S. It forms a straight line to the shore of that lake, directly to the right bank of the Luapula River, where this river issues from Lake Moero (Mweru). The line runs through the lake southward to the entrance of the river into the lake, where the boundary diverts south and west of the lake so as to include the island of Kilwa in Zambia. The line then follows the main channel of the Luapula River up to its issue from Lake Bangweulu, which is not a clear point since the river issues from the lake in a swampy area and only later forms permanent banks. However, boundary pillar no. 28 was erected at the assumed point, clearly defining the boundary there, south of Mkuku. Thence the line runs southward along the longitude meridian of the point where the river leaves the lake (Mpanta meridian) to join the watershed between the two great African rivers of the Congo and the Zambezi at boundary pillar no. 1. Then the boundary runs westward along the watershed between the Congo (north) and the Zambezi (south) rivers, which is lined with 46 demarcation pillars, to the border junction with Angola, where boundary pillar no. 46 is located, near the source of the Zambezi River.

Historical Background. The central area of Africa, known as the Zambezi, remained free of European occupation until the 1880s. The boundary of the Belgian Congo Free State extended as far as the Congo–Zambezi watershed and to the south lay the British protectorate of Bechuanaland. Portuguese possessions were still confined to the coastal areas, both west and east. The boundaries of the Congo with British possessions were established by the Anglo-Belgian Agreement of 12 May 1894 but this delimitation was imprecise and was based upon geographical misconceptions. By 1887 Portuguese claims upon territories dividing its possessions on the west and east coast prompted Britain to move north into the Zambezi and by 11 February 1888 had concluded an agreement which recognized Matabeleland as within the British sphere of interest. The British began to expand into the Zambezi after a Royal Charter of 29 October 1889 to the British South Africa Company. This was extended in 1891, to allow the company to pursue its operations north of the Zambezi, into most of what was to become Northern Rhodesia. The area was administered as Barotseland-Northwestern Rhodesia from 28 November 1899 and in 1900 the northeastern part was the subject of an order in council for its administration by the company. Between the Limpopo and Zambezi rivers lay the Matabele Kingdom and the Mashona people and to the west was the Barotse kingdom. From 1896 the high commissioner in Cape Town controlled company officials in Northern Rhodesia and by 1899 Northern Rhodesia was a colonial protectorate. It retained this status when the British South Africa Company's charter was cancelled in 1923. For 10 years, from 1953 to 1963, it was part of the Federation of Rhodesia and Nyasaland and became independent as Zambia on 24 October 1964. The Belgian Congo had also achieved independence, on 30 June 1960, and from 21 October 1971 it became the Republic of Zaire.

The Tanzanian tripoint is indefinite, having originally been described in the agreement of 1894 as "a line running direct from...Cape Akalunga on Lake Tanganyika, situated at the northernmost point of Cameron Bay at about 8°15'S, to the right bank of the River Luapula, where this river issues from Lake Moero." The location of Cape Akalunga is in doubt, and there is reason to believe that the name appears in the agreement by error. The latitude 8°15'S lies between Cape Kipimbi and Cape Pungu and International Boundary Survey No. 51 suggests that the tripoint should be at 8°13'S. The agreement continues to describe the boundary through Lake Moero, running directly to the entrance of the Luapula into the lake, but deflecting to leave Kilwa Island to Zambia. This rough description is uniformly interpreted as a median line that diverts around the west and south of the island, where local problems of delineation may be experienced. From Lake Moero the boundary is supposed, by the 1894 agreement, to follow the Luapula River *thalweg* to its issue from Lake Bangweolo. However, the river does not issue from the lake, but has its origins beyond the Bangweolo swamp, north of which it is known as the Chambezi River. The boundary is supposed to run south along the line of longitude at the point of its issue from the lake, until its intersection with the Congo–Zambezi watershed. Boundary pillar no. 1 on the watershed, erected by the Belgian section of a boundary commission of 1914, has been accepted and the line of longitude was to extend north from it to intersect the *thalweg* of the Luapula River where it issues from the swamp. This section, known as the Mpanta meridian, is demarcated by pillars that were placed during 1912–1914 and was recognized in an exchange of notes on 4 April and 3 May 1927. From here the boundary follows the Congo–Zambezi watershed, demarcated by pillars, to the Angolan tripoint at pillar no. 46. This section was demarcated by a mixed commission in 1911–1914, redemarcated in 1929–1930 and approved in an exchange of notes on 7 April 1933. The section from boundary pillar no. 11 to pillar no. 29 was redemarcated during 1927–1929.

Present Situation. Although some parts of this boundary are well defined, especially along the Congo–Zambezi watershed, which was redemarcated in 1929–1930, there are some indeterminate areas that still need to be defined. Since gaining independence no known disputes between Zaire and Zambia have been reported concerning the delimitation of the line as both adopted the colonial boundary as their common international boundary.

ZAMBIA A landlocked central African country (area: 290,586 sq. miles [752,327 sq. km.]; estimated population: 9,000,000 [1994]), Zambia is bounded in the north by Zaire (1,200 miles; 1,930 km.), in the northeast by Tanzania (210 miles; 338 km.), in the east by Malawi (520 miles; 837 km.) and Mozambique (260 miles; 419 km.), in the south by Zimbabwe (495 miles; 796 km.) and Namibia

(145 miles; 233 km.) and west by Angola (690 miles; 1,110 km.). Zambia's capital is Lusaka.

Zambian independence from Britain was officially declared in 1964. The new government was led by Kenneth Kaunda and his United National Independence Party (UNIP), of Bemba origin. Other parties were supported by other ethnic groups: the African National Congress was dominated by the Tonga and the United Party was the voice of the Lozi. At independence the Kaunda government was faced with the Lozi wish to maintain the separate status granted to them by the colonial government. Kaunda recognized these rights in the Barotse Agreement of 1964.

In time Kaunda consolidated his power by outlawing all opposition: a one-party state was instituted in 1972. Although minority rule has all but disintegrated in most of southern Africa, the economic situation in Zambia failed to improve and political disquiet increased. Most parliamentarians are Bemba but the diversity of other ethnic groups precluded political opposition movements based on ethnic divisions. Rather, opposition was led by trade-union leaders and politicians from different ethnic backgrounds. Discussions in 1990 over multiparty elections and constitutional amendments led to free elections in 1991, in which Kaunda was defeated by trade-union leader Frederick Chiluba.

ZAMBIA — ANGOLA see ANGOLA–ZAMBIA.

ZAMBIA — MALAWI see MALAWI–ZAMBIA.

ZAMBIA — MOZAMBIQUE see MOZAMBIQUE–ZAMBIA.

ZAMBIA — NAMIBIA see NAMIBIA–ZAMBIA.

ZAMBIA — TANZANIA see TANZANIA–ZAMBIA.

ZAMBIA — ZAIRE see ZAIRE–ZAMBIA.

Malawi and Zambia's boundaries

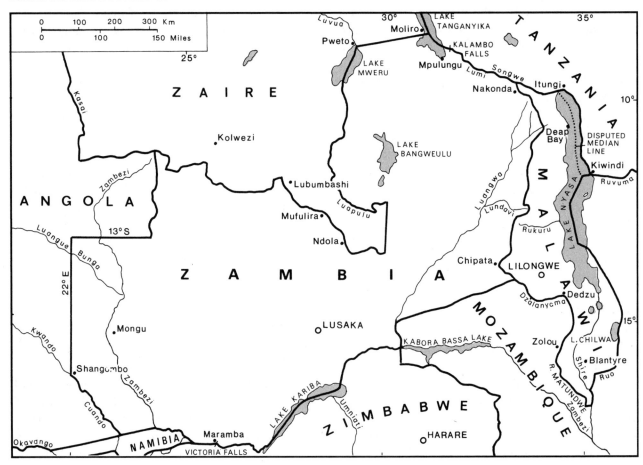

ZAMBIA — ZIMBABWE   From its boundary tri-point with Mozambique in the east this 495-mile (796-km.) boundary between Zambia and Zimbabwe runs along the Zambezi river and through the Kariba reservoir to the eastern edge of the Namibian Caprivi Strip in the west.

Geographical Setting. Setting out from the point where Mozambique's western border intersects the medium filum of the Zambezi River, the Zambia–Zimbabwe boundary keeps to this line and runs westward to the Katengathumbi group of islands and courses between these islands and the mainland of Zimbabwe and so to the Chikwenya group of islands. It divides this group and the mainland of Zambia, reaches Kanyemba island, runs between the island and Chipara island, continues to Umairi island and separates it from Zimbabwe. It then meets a point on the Kariba Dam wall, which is marked by a brass stud numbered NRT/T 153, at approximately 16°31'20"S and 28°45'40"E.

From there the boundary runs in a series of straight lines across the Kariba for the following approximate distances: on a bearing of 221°26' for a distance of 11,100 feet (3,384 m.) to 16°33'40"S and 28°44'30"E; on a true bearing of 259°06' for 37,200 feet (11,341 m.) to 16°33'50"S and 28°38'20"E; on a bearing of 247°11' for a distance of 143,330 feet (43,698 m.) to 16°43'20"S and 28°15'20"E; on a true bearing of 229°03' for 55,800 feet (17,012 m.) to 16°49'20"S and 28°08'10"E; on a true bearing of 245°44' for 117,600 feet (35,854 m.) to 16°57'30"S and 7°49'50"E; on a bearing of 214°39' for 125,300 feet (38,201 m.) to 17°14'40"S and 27°37'50"E; on a true bearing of 185°44' for 31,000 feet (9,451 m.) to 17°19'50"S and 27°37'20"E; on a true bearing of 221°06' for 39,500 feet (12,043 m.) to a point at 17°24'50"S and 27°33'E; on a true bearing of 232°10' for 102,100 feet (31,128 m.) to 17°35'20"S and 27°19'10"E; on a bearing of 218°16' for 10,000 feet (3,049 m.) to 17°48'20"S and 27°08'40"E; on a true bearing of 166°25' for 10,800 feet (3,293 m.) to 17°50'10"S and 27°09'10"E; on a true bearing of 226°51' for 34,400 feet (10,488 m.) to 17°54'S and 27°05'E; on a true bearing of 214°10' for a distance of 25,700 feet (7,835 m.) to 17°57'40"S and 27°02'30"E; and on a true bearing of 282°36' for 9,000 feet (2,744 m.) to 17°57'20"S and 27°01'E on the medium filum of the Zambezi River.

The boundary runs along the Zambezi River, between Mapeta island and the mainland of Zambia and on to the intersection of the median line of the river with the middle of the main gorge to the south of Rainbow Falls and Livingstone island. Then it follows the middle of this gorge to the west of Livingstone island, along the middle of the channel between Livingstone island and the island nearest to and west of Livingstone island and along the middle of the channel between Livingstone island and Princess Victoria island. It courses along the middle channel, placing Princess Victoria island, Princess Christian island, Princess Marie Louise island and Princess Elizabeth island on its west and Princess Helena Victoria island and Princess Margaret island on its east. It reaches King George VI island, continues along the middle of the channel to the south of this island and to a group of islands to the north of Princess Elizabeth island. The boundary divides King George VI island and the mainland of Zimbabwe, keeping to the median line between Queen Elizabeth island, King George VI island, Canary Island and the mainland of Zimbabwe. It reaches Kandahar island, runs between it and Palm island and continues along the medium filum to meet the boundary junction with Botswana and Namibia.

Historical Background. In 1886 Portugal concluded treaties with France and Germany which recognized its ambition to link its coastal possessions of Angola and Mozambique, on the west and east coasts of southern Africa respectively. Britain expanded into the Zambezi area of Africa in order to prevent Portugal from disconnecting its southern possessions from those in the north. A Royal Charter to the British South Africa Company in 1889 led to the seizure in 1893 of Matabeleland and an Anglo-German treaty on 1 July 1890 acknowledged Britain's interests in the Nyasa region. From 1896 the British South Africa Company officials in Northern Rhodesia (Zambia) were responsible to the high commissioner in Cape Town; those in Southern Rhodesia (Zimbabwe) had their own administrator and council.

The territory later known as Northern Rhodesia became a colonial protectorate by the orders in council of 28 November 1899, 29 January 1900 and 4 May 1911. In 1923 the British South Africa Company's charter was cancelled and Southern Rhodesia acquired self-government as a colony under Crown supervision. Northern Rhodesia remained a protectorate, as did Nyasaland (Malawi) with which the two Rhodesias formed a federation on 1 August 1953. This lasted until 31 December 1963 and Northern Rhodesia became independent as Zambia on 24 October 1964. On 11 November 1965 the Rhodesian prime minister unilaterally declared independence in Southern Rhodesia. Britain refused to recognize this and revoked Rhodesia's self-governing status, declaring it to be a colony. The Security Council of the United Nations supported Britain's attitude and prescribed economic sanctions. Britain resumed control at the end of 1979 and after 15 years of external pressure and internal strife Rhodesia became independent as Zimbabwe on 18 April 1980.

Present Situation. The alignment of the Zambia–Zimbabwe border is recognized by both countries, as both adopted the colonial boundary as their common international boundary.

ZIMBABWE A landlocked south African country (area: 150,873 sq. miles [390,610 sq. km.]; estimated population: 10,700,000 [1994]), Zimbabwe is bounded in the north by Zambia (495 miles; 796 km.), northeast and east by Mozambique (766 miles; 1,231 km.), south by South Africa (140 miles; 225 km.) and southwest by Botswana (505 miles; 813 km.). Its capital is Harare.

In 1923 Southern Rhodesia (as Zimbabwe was then called) became a white-dominated, self-governing colony with internal autonomy in all matters except foreign policy and legislation affecting the African population. In 1965 Ian Smith proclaimed his Unilateral Declaration of Independence and Rhodesia became independent of Britain under a white minority government. In response, African liberation movements, founded a few years earlier, launched a guerrilla war to end white rule. The Zimbabwe African Peoples Union (ZAPU), led by Joshua Nkomo, was supported by the Ndebele, and the Zimbabwe African National Union (ZANU), led by Robert Mugabe, was supported by the Shona. In 1980, after negotiations between ZANU, ZAPU,

Britain and the Smith regime, free elections were held: ZANU won the majority of seats in the new parliament. Mugabe aspired to establish a one-party state on the Marxist model after establishing a base of popular support throughout the country. Nkomo, who considered the election results to be invalid, rejected Mugabe's offer of the presidency and a merger between ZAPU and ZANU. In 1982 Nkomo and his colleagues were dismissed after arms were found on ZAPU property in Matabeleland. Despite some pro-Nkomo violence, the remaining ZAPU parliament members remained in the the government and Nkomo was not brought to trial. This was, however, only the beginning of the ethnic conflict. In 1982 the military wing of ZAPU initiated acts of violence in the poverty-stricken Ndebele region. In 1983 and 1984 a ZANU army unit was accused of committing atrocities against Ndebele civilians; despite objections from international organizations such as Amnesty International, the government denied the accusations. Mugabe's government then launched a military campaign against the dissidents in the Ndebele area. ZANU's representation in the government was increased, further alienating the two groups. In the midst of this deteriorating situation, talks between ZANU and ZAPU took place. In 1987 Mugabe withdrew from the talks, claiming that they had accomplished nothing. Only following a brutal massacre of Ndebele in November of that year were the talks resumed. They culminated in a merger of the two parties and the formation of a single-party Marxist state. This agreement, signed in December 1987, was ratified in 1988.

ZIMBABWE — BOTSWANA see BOTSWANA–ZIMBABWE.

ZIMBABWE — MOZAMBIQUE see MOZAMBIQUE–ZIMBABWE.

ZIMBABWE — SOUTH AFRICA see SOUTH AFRICA–ZIMBABWE.

ZIMBABWE — ZAMBIA see ZAMBIA–ZIMBABWE.

GLOSSARY

Irregular subjects, followed by the boundary items in which they appear.

ENCLAVE (EXCLAVE) A territory belonging to one country but which lies wholly within the territory of another country; it is an enclave with respect to the country in which it is located and an exclave with respect to the country to which it holds political affiliation.

ANGOLA–CONGO; ANGOLA–ZAIRE; ARMENIA–AZERBAIJAN; BANGLADESH–INDIA; BELARUS–LITHUANIA; BELGIUM–NETHERLANDS; BRUNEI–MALAYSIA; CAMBODIA–VIETNAM; CYPRUS–UNITED KINGDOM; EGYPT–SUDAN; FRANCE–SPAIN; FRANCE–SWITZERLAND; GERMANY–SWITZERLAND; GREECE–TURKEY; ITALY–SWITZERLAND; LESOTHO–SOUTH AFRICA; LITHUANIA–RUSSIA; MOROCCO–SPAIN; NAMIBIA–SOUTH AFRICA; OMAN–UNITED ARAB EMIRATES.

EQUIDISTANCE A line or point which is deemed to be at an equal distance from two other points or lines.

BENIN–TOGO; BRUNEI–MALAYSIA; COLOMBIA–PANAMA; ISRAEL–JORDAN; NIGER–NIGERIA.

LANDLOCKED STATE A state that does not possess an open sea coastline.

AFGHANISTAN; ARMENIA; AUSTRIA; AZERBAIJAN; BELARUS; BHUTAN; BOLIVIA; BOTSWANA; BURKINA FASO; BURUNDI; CENTRAL AFRICAN REPUBLIC; CHAD; CZECH REPUBLIC; ETHIOPIA; HUNGARY; KAZAKHSTAN; KYRGYZSTAN; LAOS; LESOTHO; LIECHTENSTEIN; LUXEMBOURG; MACEDONIA; MALAWI; MALI; MOLDAVA; MONGOLIA; NEPAL; NIGER; PARAGUAY; RWANDA; SAN MARINO; SLOVAKIA; SWAZILAND; SWITZERLAND; TURKMENISTAN; UGANDA; UZBEKISTAN; VATICAN CITY; ZAMBIA; ZIMBABWE.

LATITUDE The angular distance (measured in degrees [°], minutes ['] and seconds ["] of arcs) of a point on the earth's surface, north or south of the equator, as measured from the center of the earth.

ANGOLA–CONGO; ANGOLA–NAMIBIA; BELIZE–MEXICO; BOTSWANA–NAMIBIA; BOTSWANA–ZIMBABWE; BURKINA FASO–GHANA; BURKINA FASO–NIGER; CAMEROON–EQUATORIAL GUINEA; CANADA–UNITED STATES; CHINA–PAKISTAN; COLOMBIA–ECUADOR; COLOMBIA–

VENEZUELA; GHANA–LIBERIA; GUATEMALA–MEXICO; KENYA–SOMALIA; LIBYA–SUDAN; UGANDA–ZAIRE; ZAIRE–ZAMBIA.

LONGITUDE An angular distance (measured in degrees [°], minutes ['] and seconds ["]) of a point on the earth's surface from an adopted line, mainly the Greenwich Meridian (longitude 0°).

BOTSWANA–NAMIBIA; CANADA–UNITED STATES; CHAD–NIGER; KENYA–SOMALIA; ZAIRE–ZAMBIA.

MEDIAN LINE A line which at every point is equidistant from the lines (i.e., shores or banks) between which it is being drawn. A median line may delineate the shared boundary of two states.

AFGHANISTAN–UZBEKISTAN; ANGOLA–NAMIBIA; ARGENTINA–CHILE; BENIN–NIGERIA; BRAZIL–URUGUAY; BURUNDI–ZAIRE; CAMBODIA–LAOS; CAMEROON–CENTRAL AFRICAN REPUBLIC; CAMEROON–CHAD; CAMEROON–EQUATORIAL GUINEA; CHINA–HONG KONG; CHINA–RUSSIA; FRANCE–SWITZERLAND; GERMANY–POLAND; GREECE–TURKEY; GUATEMALA–HONDURAS; HUNGARY–SERBIA; INDIA–NEPAL; IRAQ–KUWAIT; IRELAND–UNITED KINGDOM; KENYA–UGANDA; MALAWI–MOZAMBIQUE; MALAWI–TANZANIA; MOZAMBIQUE–SWAZILAND; MOZAMBIQUE–TANZANIA; NIGER–NIGERIA; PORTUGAL–SPAIN; SYRIA–TURKEY; TANZANIA–ZIMBABWE; ZAMBIA–ZIMBABWE.

MERIDIAN A semicircle of longitude, e.g., the 75°W (West) meridian. All meridians extend from pole to pole.

ALBANIA–GREECE; ALGERIA–WESTERN SAHARA; ANGOLA–ZAMBIA; ARMENIA–AZERBAIJAN; AZERBAIJAN–GEORGIA; AZERBAIJAN–IRAN; BELIZE–MEXICO; BENIN–TOGO; BHUTAN–CHINA; BOTSWANA– NAMIBIA; BRAZIL–COLOMBIA; BRAZIL–PERU; BRAZIL–VENEZUELA; BURKINA FASO–GHANA; CHAD–LIBERIA; CHAD–NIGERIA; CHAD–SUDAN; CHINA–HONG KONG; CHINA–KAZAKHSTAN; COSTA RICA–PANAMA; EGYPT–LIBYA; GAMBIA–SENEGAL; GEORGIA–RUSSIA; GUATEMALA–MEXICO; GUYANA–VENEZUELA; INDIA–PAKISTAN; INDONESIA–PAPUA NEW GUINEA; LAOS–VIETNAM; LIBERIA–SIERRA LEONE; LIBYA–SUDAN; MALI–MAURITANIA; MALI–NIGER; MAURITANIA–WESTERN SAHARA;

MOZAMBIQUE–ZIMBABWE; NAMIBIA–SOUTH AFRICA; POLAND–RUSSIA; SOUTH AFRICA–ZIMBABWE.

PARALLEL   A line drawn around the earth parallel to the equator, and may be thus described as approximate circles with the two poles as centers.

ANGOLA–ZAMBIA; ARGENTINA–BOLIVIA; BELIZE–GUATEMALA; BENIN–NIGERIA; BOLIVIA–CHILE; BOTSWANA–NAMIBIA; BRAZIL–COLOMBIA; BRAZIL–PERU; BURKINA FASO–GHANA; BURKINA FASO–TOGO; CAMEROON–CHAD; CAMEROON–CONGO; COSTA RICA–PANAMA; EGYPT–SUDAN; ETHIOPIA–KENYA; ETHIOPIA–SOMALIA; GAMBIA–SENEGAL; GUINEA–SENEGAL; GUINEA–SIERRA LEONE; INDIA–PAKISTAN; INDONESIA–MALAYSIA; IRAQ–KUWAIT; KENYA–SUDAN; KOREA, NORTH–KOREA, SOUTH; LIBYA–SUDAN; MALI–MAURITANIA; MALI–NIGER; MAURITANIA–WESTERN SAHARA; MOROCCO–WESTERN SAHARA; MONGOLIA–RUSSIA; MOZAMBIQUE– SWAZILAND; NAMIBIA–SOUTH AFRICA; NAMIBIA–ZAMBIA; NIGER–NIGERIA; RWANDA–UGANDA; SUDAN–UGANDA; TANZANIA–ZAIRE; UGANDA–ZAIRE.

PLEBISCITE   A vote by which the people of an entire country or district express an opinion for or against a proposal; especially concerning a choice of government.

AUSTRIA–SLOVENIA—10 OCTOBER 1920; BENIN–TOGO—1956; CAMEROON–NIGERIA—1959, 1961; CZECH REPUBLIC–GERMANY; CZECH REPUBLIC–POLAND—OCTOBER 1921 (SILISIA); DENMARK– GERMANY—1919 (SCHLESWIG); EGYPT–SUDAN—1958; GERMANY–POLAND—11 JULY 1920 (EAST PRUSSIA)

THALWEG   A German term, literally "downstream," with reference to river navigation. Here referring to the deepest channel in a river, generally the most suitable channel for navigation at the normal lowest water level.

ANGOLA–NAMIBIA; ARGENTINA–URUGUAY; AUSTRIA–SLOVAKIA; AUSTRIA–SWITZERLAND; BANGLADESH–MYANMAR; BELIZE–GUATEMALA; BELIZE–MEXICO; BENIN–NIGERIA; BENIN–TOGO; BOLIVIA–PARAGUAY; BOTSWANA–NAMIBIA; BRUNEI–MALAYSIA; BURUNDI–RWANDA; CAMBODIA–VIETNAM; CENTRAL AFRICAN REPUBLIC–ZAIRE; DOMINICAN REPUBLIC–HAITI; ETHIOPIA–SOMALIA; ETHIOPIA–SUDAN; GUYANA–SURINAME; INDONESIA–PAPUA NEW GUINEA; IRAN–IRAQ; IRAN–TURKEY; KENYA–TANZANIA; IRAQ–KUWAIT; IRAQ–SYRIA; IRAQ–TURKEY; KENYA–SOMALIA; LAOS–MYANMAR; LAOS–THAILAND; LIBERIA–SIERRA LEONE; LIBYA–TUNISIA; MALAWI–MOZAMBIQUE; MOLDAVA–ROMANIA; MOZAMBIQUE– SWAZILAND; MOZAMBIQUE–TANZANIA; MOZAMBIQUE–ZIMBABWE; MYANMAR–THAILAND; NAMIBIA–ZAMBIA; NIGER–NIGERIA; NORWAY–RUSSIA; RWANDA–TANZANIA; RWANDA–UGANDA; RWANDA–ZAIRE; SUDAN–UGANDA; TANZANIA–UGANDA; TANZANIA–ZAMBIA; UGANDA–ZAIRE.

TRIPOINT   A point which is the junction of three boundary lines.

UTI POSSIDETIS   A Latin term, which states that rightful sovereignty should be based on occupation, utilization and effective control of territory—rather than on written or verbal claims. This served as a basis for many boundaries, especially in South America, whereby colonial boundaries were maintained as state boundaries as the European colonies achieved independence.

ARGENTINA–CHILE; BRAZIL–PARAGUAY; BRAZIL–PERU; BRAZIL–URUGUAY; BRAZIL–VENEZUELA; CHILE–PERU; COLOMBIA–ECUADOR; COLOMBIA– VENEZUELA.

WATERSHED   The elevated area separating headstreams that are tributaries to different river systems or basins.

AFGHANISTAN–CHINA; ALBANIA–MACEDONIA; ALGERIA–MALI; ANDORRA–FRANCE; ANDORRA–SPAIN; ANGOLA–ZAMBIA; ARGENTINA–CHILE; AUSTRIA–ITALY; AUSTRIA–SLOVENIA; BELGIUM–FRANCE; BELGIUM–GERMANY; BELGIUM–LUXEMBOURG; BELIZE–MEXICO; BHUTAN–CHINA; BOLIVIA–CHILE; BOLIVIA–PERU; BOTSWANA–ZIMBABWE; BRAZIL–COLOMBIA; BRAZIL– FRENCH GUIANA; BRAZIL– GUYANA; BRAZIL–PARAGUAY; BRAZIL–PERU; BRAZIL–SURINAME; BRAZIL–VENEZUELA; BRUNEI–MALAYSIA; BULGARIA–GREECE; BULGARIA–MACEDONIA; BULGARIA–SERBIA; BURKINA FASO–MALI; CAMBODIA–LAOS; CAMBODIA–THAILAND; CAMBODIA–VIETNAM; CAMEROON–CENTRAL AFRICAN REPUBLIC; CAMEROON–CONGO; CAMEROON–NIGER; CENTRAL AFRICAN REPUBLIC–CONGO; CENTRAL AFRICAN REPUBLIC–SUDAN; CENTRAL AFRICAN REPUBLIC–ZAIRE; CHINA–INDIA; CHINA–LAOS; CHINA–MYANMAR; CHINA–NEPAL; CHINA–TAJIKISTAN; COLOMBIA–PANAMA; CONGO–ZAIRE; COSTA RICA–PANAMA; CZECH REPUBLIC–GERMANY; CZECH REPUBLIC–POLAND; CZECH REPUBLIC–SLOVAKIA; ECUADOR–PERU; EL SALVADOR–HONDURAS; ERITREA–SOMALIA; ETHIOPIA–KENYA; ETHIOPIA–SUDAN; FINLAND–NORWAY; FRENCH GUIANA–SURINAME; FINLAND–SWEDEN; FRANCE–ITALY; FRANCE–SPAIN; FRANCE– SWITZERLAND; GEORGIA–RUSSIA; GHANA–TOGO; GREECE–MACEDONIA; GUATEMALA–HONDURAS; GUINEA–IVORY COAST; GUINEA– MALI; GUINEA–SIERRA LEONE; GUINEA-BISSAU–SENEGAL; GUYANA–SURINAME; GUYANA– VENEZUELA; HONDURAS– NICARAGUA; HUNGARY–SLOVAKIA; HUNGARY–SLOVENIA; INDIA–MYANMAR; INDONESIA–MALAYSIA; IRAN–PAKISTAN; IRAN–TURKEY; IRAN–TURKMENISTAN; ITALY–SLOVENIA; ITALY– SWITZERLAND; LAOS–THAILAND; LAOS–VIETNAM; LIBYA– TUNISIA; LIECHTENSTEIN–SWITZERLAND; MACEDONIA–SERBIA; MALAWI–ZAMBIA; MALAYSIA–THAILAND; MALI–MAURITANIA; MONGOLIA–RUSSIA; MOZAMBIQUE–ZAMBIA; MYANMAR–THAILAND; NAMIBIA–ZAMBIA; NORWAY–SWEDEN; OMAN–UNITED ARAB EMIRATES; POLAND–SLOVAKIA; POLAND– UKRAINE; PORTUGAL–SPAIN; RWANDA–UGANDA; SLOVAKIA–UKRAINE; SUDAN–UGANDA; SUDAN–ZAIRE; TANZANIA– ZAMBIA; UGANDA–ZAIRE; ZAIRE–ZAMBIA.

LIST OF BOUNDARIES

LIST OF MAPS

SELECT BIBLIOGRAPHY

General

Allcock, J. B. et al., editors. *Border and Territorial Disputes*. 3rd edition. London: Longman, 1992.

Anderson, E. *An Atlas of World Political Flashpoints: A Sourcebook of Geopolitical Crisis*. London: Pinter, 1993.

Bernstein, Itamar. *Delimitation of International Boundaries: A Study of Modern Practice and Devices from the Viewpoint of International Law*. Tel Aviv, 1974.

Blake, G. H., editor. *Maritime Boundaries and Ocean Resources*. London: Croom Helm, 1987.

British and Foreign State Papers.

Cukwurah, A. O. *The Settlement of Boundary Disputes in International Law*. Manchester, 1967.

Day, Alan J., editor. *Border and Territorial Disputes*. Detroit: Gale Research Company, 1982.

East, W. G. & Moodie, A. E., editors. *The Changing World: Studies in Political Geography*. London, 1975.

East, W. G. & Prescott, J. R. V. *Our Fragmented World: An Introduction to Political Geography*. London, 1975.

Encyclopaedia Britannica.

Gallusser, W., editor. *Political Boundaries and Coexistence*. Bern: Peter Lang, 1994.

Great Britain Treaty Series.

Gross, Feliks. *World Politics and Tension Areas*. New York, 1966.

Kurian, G. T., editor. *Encylopaedia of the First World*. Vol. 1. New York: Facts on File, 1990.

Luard, D. E. T., editor. *The International Regulation of Frontier Disputes*. London, 1970.

Prescott, J. R. V. *The Geography of Frontiers and Boundaries*. London, 1965.

Prescott, J. R. V. *Boundaries and Frontiers*. London, 1978.

Rumley, D. & Minghi, J., editors. *The Geography of Border Landscapes*. London: Routledge, 1991.

Sharma, Surya P. *International Boundary Disputes and International Law*. Bombay, 1976.

Stuyt, A. M. *Survey of International Arbitrations, 1794–1970*. Leiden, 1972.

Szajkowski, B. *Encyclopedia of Conflicts, Disputes and Flashpoints in Eastern Europe, Russia and the Successor States*. Harlow, Essex: Longman, 1993.

United States Department of State. *International Boundary Research Studies*. Department of State, Bureau of Intelligence and Research.

United States Department of State. *International Boundary Studies*. Department of State, Office of the Geographer.

Americas

Annual Reports of the International Boundary and Water Commission, United States and Mexico.

Annual Reports of the United States and Canada International Boundary Commission.

Braveboy-Wagner, Jacqueline. *The Venezuela–Guyana Boundary Dispute*. Westview, 1984.

Girot, Pascal O., editor. "The Americas." *World Boundaries*. Vol. 4. Routledge, 1994.

Grant, C. H. *The Making of Modern Belize*. Cambridge University Press, 1976.

Ireland, Gordon. *Boundaries, Possessions, and Conflicts in Central and North America and the Caribbean*. Harvard University Press, 1941.

Ireland, Gordon. *Boundaries, Possessions, and Conflicts in South America.* New York: Octagon Books, 1971.

Marchant, Alexander. *Boundaries of the Latin American Republics: An Annotated List of Documents, 1493–1943.* Washington: Department of State, 1944.

Nicholson, Norman L. *The Boundaries of Canada, Its Provinces and Territories.* Ottawa: 1954.

Van Zandt, Franklin K. *Boundaries of the United States and Several States.* Geological Survey Professional Paper 909. Washington, 1976.

Wood, Bryce. *Aggression and History; The Case of Ecuador and Peru.* University Microfilms International, 1978.

Zammit, J. A. *The Belize Issue.* The Latin American Bureau, 1978.

Middle East

Abdullah Omran Taryam. *The Establishment of the United Arab Emirates 1950–1985.* 1987.

Admiralty Handbook. Syria: British Admiralty, 1945.

Al-Baharna, Husain M. *The Arabian Gulf States: Their Legal and Political Status and Their International Problems.* 2nd revised edition. Beirut, 1975.

Blake, G. H., Dewdney, J. & Mitchell, J. *The Cambridge Atlas of the Middle East and North Africa.* Cambridge: Cambridge University Press, 1987.

Blake, G. H. & Drysdale, A. *The Middle East and North Africa: A Political Geography.* Oxford: Oxford University Press, 1985.

Blake, G. H. & Schofield, R. N., editors. *Boundaries and State Territory in the Middle East and North Africa.* Cambridgeshire: Middle East and North African Studies Press Limited, 1987.

Blum, Y. Z. *Secure Boundaries and Middle East Peace in the Light of International Law and Practice.* Jerusalem, 1971.

Burrel, R. M. *The Persian Gulf.* New York, 1972.

Dodd, C. H. & Sales, M. E. *Israel and the Arab World.* London, 1970.

Foreign Areas Studies. *Area Handbook for Saudi Arabia.* Washington, DC: American University, 1971.

Gilbert, M. *The Arab-Israeli Conflict: Its History in Maps.* London: Wiedenfeld & Nicholson, 1979.

Hitti, P. K. *Syria, A Short History: Including Lebanon and Palestine.* London: Macmillan & Co. Ltd., 1951.

The Israel-Jordan Peace Treaty. London Israeli Embassy, October 26, 1994.

Karsh, E., editor. *Peace in the Middle East: The Challenge for Israel.* Ilford: Frank Cass, 1994.

Kelly, J. B. *Eastern Arabian Frontiers.* New York, 1964.

Kelly, J. B. *Arabia, the Gulf and the West.* London: Wiedenfeld & Nicholson, 1980.

Lorimer, J. G. *Gazetteer of the Persian Gulf and Central Arabia.* Calcutta: Government Printing, 1915.

Risso, P. *Oman and Muscat: An Early Modern History.* 1986.

Roberts, J. *Visions and Mirages: Middle East in a New Era.* Edinburgh: Mainstream Publishing, 1995.

Schofield, C. & Schofield, R., editors. "The Middle East and North Africa." *World Boundaries Series.* Vol. 2. London: Routledge, 1994.

Schofield, R., editor. *Territorial Foundations of the Gulf States.* London: University College of London, 1994.

Schofield, R. N. & Blake, G. H., editors. *Arabian Boundaries. Primary Documents 1853–1960.* 30 vols. Farnham Common: Archive Research, 1988–1992.

United States Department of State. *Geographic and Global Issues.* Vol. 3, No. 2. Washington: Department of State, Bureau of Intelligence and Research, 1993.

United States Department of State. *Geographic and Global Issues.* Vol. 3, No. 4, Winter 1993/4. pp. 13–14. Washington: Department of State, Bureau of Intelligence and Research, 1993.

Vine, P. & Cassey, P. *United Arab Emirates.* London: Immel Publishing, 1992.

Wenmer, M. W. *The Yemen Arab Republic: Development and Change in an Ancient Land.* Boulder: Westview Press, 1991.

Wilkinson, J. C. *Arabia's Frontiers: The Story of Britain's Boundary Drawing in the Desert*. London: I. B. Tauris & Co. Ltd., 1991.

Africa

Bahru Zewde. *A History of Modern Ethiopia 1855–1974*. London, 1991.

Blake, G. H. & Drysdale, A. *The Middle East and North Africa: A Political Geography*. Oxford: Oxford University Press, 1985.

Brownlie, Ian. *African Boundaries: A Legal and Diplomatic Encyclopaedia*. London and Los Angeles: C. Hurst, 1979.

Cassel, C. Abayomi. *Liberia: History of the First African Republic*. New York: Fountainhead, 1970.

Faisal Abdul Rahman Ali. *The Sudan–Ethiopia Boundary Dispute*. Abu Dhabi, 1983.

Horell, Muriel. *The African Homelands of South Africa*. Johannesburg, 1973.

Hoskins, Catherine. *Case Studies in African Diplomacy 2: The Ethiopia-Somalia-Kenya Dispute, 1960–67*. Dar es Salaam, 1969.

Huberich, C. H. *The Political and Legislative History of Liberia*. Vol. 1. New York: Central Book Company, 1947.

Institute for Conflict Analysis and Resolution. *Chronology of Conflict Resolution Initiatives in Eritrea*. George Mason University, 1991.

McEwen, A. C. *International Boundaries of East Africa*. Oxford: Clarendon Press, 1971.

Morrison, G. *Eritrea and the Southern Sudan*. Report 5, New Edition Minority Rights Group, 1976.

Schofield, C. & Schofield, R., editors. "The Middle East and North Africa." *World Boundaries Series*. Vol. 2. London: Routledge, 1994.

Sherman, R. *Eritrea, the Unfinished Evolution*. New York: Praeger, 1980.

Touval, Saadia. *The Boundary Politics of Independent Africa*. Cambridge, Massachusetts: Harvard University Press, 1972.

Widstrand, Carl Gösta, editor. *African Boundary Problems*. Uppsala, 1969.

Asia-Pacific

Brown, D. E. *Brunei, the Structure and History*. Brunei Museum Publications. Star Press, 1970.

Chang, J. J. "Settlement of the Macao Issue 1887 Protocol and 1987 Declaration." *Occasional Papers Reprint Series*. Contemporary Asian Studies. No.4, p.188. 1987.

Patterson, George N. *The Unquiet Frontier—Border tensions in the Sino-Soviet Conflict*. Hong Kong: International Studies Group, 1966.

Watson, Francis. *The Frontiers of China*. London: Chatto and Windus, 1966.

Central and Southern Asia

Bremmer, I. & Taras, R., editors. *Nations and Politics in the Soviet Successor States*. Cambridge: Cambridge University Press, 1993.

Chew, A. F. *An Atlas of Russian History: Eleven Centuries of Changing Borders*. New Haven and London: Yale University Press, 1970.

Collier, H. J., Prescott, D. F. & Prescott, J. R. V. *Frontiers of Asia and South East Asia*. Melbourne: Melbourne University Press, 1977.

East, W. G., Spate, O. H. K. & Fisher, C. A., editors. *The Changing Map of Asia*. 5th edition. London, 1971.

Gondker Narayana Rao, *The India–China Border*, London: Asia Publishing House, 1968.

Lamb, Alistair. *The China–India Border*. Oxford University Press, 1964.

Lamb, Alistair. *Asian Frontiers*. London: Pall Mall Press, 1968.

Lewis, R. A., editor. *Geographic Perspectives on Soviet Central Asia*. London: Routledge, 1992.

Prescott, J. R. V. *Map of Mainland Asia by Treaty*. Melbourne, 1975.

Twining, D. T. *The New Eurasia: A Guide to the Republics of the Former Soviet Union*. Westport, Connecticut: Praeger, 1993.

Europe

Abbot, W. E. *An Introduction to the Documents Relating to the International Status of Gibraltar*. New York, 1934.

Baker, E. *Austria 1918–1972*. Macmillan, 1973.

Boban, Lj. *Croatian Borders 1918–1993*. Zagreb: Croatian Academy of Sciences and Arts, 1993.

Colonial Annual Reports 1947–53. *Gibraltar*. London: British Commonwealth Office.

Deak, F. *Hungary at the Paris Peace Conference: The Diplomatic History of the Treaty of Trianon*. New York, 1972.

Geographical Handbook. *Germany*. Vol. 1. British Admiralty, 1944.

Geographical Handbook. *Juyoslavia*. Vol. 2. British Admiralty, 1944.

Gibraltar, the Dispute with Spain. HMSO, 1969.

Hand, G. J. *Report of the Irish Boundary Commission 1925*. Shannon: Irish University Press, 1969.

Heller, R. P. & Long, E. *Free and Swiss*. London, 1970.

Kranz, W., editor. *The Principality of Liechtenstein: A Documentary Handbook*. Press & Information of the Government of the Principality of Liechtenstein, 1981.

Lucic, J. & Obad, S. *Konavoska Prevlaka, Dubrovnik:* Matica hrvatska Zbornik Slavonija, Sriejem, Baranja I Backa. *Zagreb: Matica hrvatska, 1994.*

Raton, P. The Principality of Liechtenstein. *Vaduz.*

Srkulj, S. Hrvatska povijest u devetnaest karata. *Zagreb, 1937.*

Treaty Series No. 4. Cyprus and Exchange of Notes. Nicosia, August 16, 1960 and maps, 1961.

International Boundaries Research Unit (IBRU) Publications

Englefield, G. "Yugoslavia, Croatia, Slovenia: Re-emerging Boundaries." *Territory Briefings*. No. 3. Durham: IBRU, 1992.

Kelly, I. S. "The Hong Kong–China Boundary." Boundary Briefings. No. 1. Durham: IBRU, 1990.

Klemencic, M. "Territorial Proposals for the Settlement of the War in Bosnia-Hercegovina." *Boundary and Territory Briefings*. Vol. 1, No. 3. Durham: IBRU, 1994.

Klemencic, M. & Schofield, C. "Croatia and Slovenia: The 'Four Hamlets' Case." *Boundary and Security Bulletin*. Vol. 2, No. 4, pp. 65–77. Durham: IBRU, 1995.

Kliot, N. "The Evolution of the Egypt–Israel Boundary, From Colonial Foundations to Peaceful Borders." *Boundary and Territory Briefings*. Vol. 1, No. 8. Durham: IBRU, 1995.

Kolossov, V. A., Glezer, O. & Petrov, N. *Ethno-Territorial Conflicts and Boundaries in the Former Soviet Union*. Durham: IBRU, 1992.

O'Reilly, G. "Ceuta and the Spanish Sovereign Territories: Spanish and Moroccan Claims." *Boundary and Territory Briefings*. Vol. 1, No. 2. Durham: IBRU, 1994.

Roberts, J. "Israel and Jordan: Bridges over the Borderlands." *Boundary and Security Bulletin*. Vol. 2, No. 4. Durham: IBRU, 1994.

Schofield, C. H. "The Northern Epirus Question." *Boundary Bulletin*. No. 4., May 1992. Durham: IBRU, 1992.

SUBJECT INDEX

BILATERAL TREATIES

Aachen Peace Treaty, 1748 → France–Germany

Aachen Treaty, 26 June 1816 → Germany–Netherlands

Adrianopol Treaty, 1829 → Armenia–Turkey; Romania–Serbia

Aigun Treaty, 16 May 1858 → China–Russia

Alcacovas Treaty, 1479 → Portugal–Spain

Aleksandropol Treaty, December 1920 → Armenia–Turkey

Algerian-Tunisian Agreement, 6 January 1970 → Algeria–Tunisia Convention

Amman Agreement, 9 August 1965 → Jordan–Saudi Arabia

Anglo-Belgian Agreement, 12 May 1894 → Zaire–Zambia

Anglo-Belgian Treaty, 1934 → Rwanda–Uganda

Anglo-Ethiopian Agreement, 29 September 1947 → Ethiopia–Kenya

Anglo-Ethiopian Agreement, 6 December 1907 → Ethiopia–Kenya

Anglo-French Agreement, 19 February 1910 → Chad–Nigeria

Anglo-Iranian Agreement, 27 December 1895 → Iran–Pakistan

Anglo-Italian Treaty, 24 March 1891 → Kenya–Somalia

Anglo-Russian Treaty, 1895 →

Afghanistan–China

Angora Frontier Convention, 9 April 1929 → Iran–Turkey

Ankara Treaty, 5 June 1926 → Iraq–Turkey

Argentina-Chile Agreement, 23 July 1881 → Argentina–Chile

Augsburg Peace, 1555 → Germany–Netherlands

Bamako Agreement, 26 April 1984 → Algeria–Mali

Bogotá Treaty, 15 July 1916 → Colombia–Ecuador

Britain-Mexico Agreement, 8 July 1893 → Belize–Mexico

British-French Agreement, 23 December 1920 → Israel–Lebanon

British-Russian Agreement, 1873 → Afghanistan–Tajikistan

British-Russian Protocol, September 1885 → Afghanistan–Turkmenistan

Brussels Treaty, 24 September 1956 → Belgium–Germany

Bur (Bura) Treaty, 20 August 1727 → China–Russia

Canas-Jerez Treaty, 15 April 1858 → Costa Rica–Nicaragua

Chuguchak Treaty, 1864 → China–Kazakhstan; China–Tajikistan

Dorpat Peace Treaty, 2 February 1920 → Estonia–Russia

Dorpat Treaty, 14 October 1920 → Finland–Russia

Erzurum Treaty, 1847 → Iran–Turkey; Iran–Iraq

Ethiopia-Kenya Agreement, 9 June 1970 → Ethiopia–Kenya

Franco-German Convention, 23 July 1897 → Burkina Faso–Togo

Franco-Italian Agreement, 12 September 1919 → Algeria–Libya

Franco-Ottoman Agreement, 19 May 1910 → Algeria–Libya; Algeria–Tunisia

Franco-Portuguese Agreement, January 1901 → Angola–Congo

Franco-Portuguese Convention, 28 August 1817 → Brazil–French Guiana

Franco-Spanish Convention, June 1900 → Algeria–Western Sahara

Franco-Spanish Convention, 1904 → Algeria–Western Sahara

Franco-Spanish Treaty, 3 October 1904 → Morocco–Western Sahara

Franco-Turkish Convention, 19 May 1910 → Libya–Tunisia

Franco-Turkish Convention, 30 May 1926 → Syria–Turkey

Franco-Turkish General Staff Agreement, 3 July 1938 → Syria–Turkey

French-Thailand Peace Treaty, October 1893 → Cambodia–Laos; Cambodia–Thailand

German-Portuguese Declaration, December 1886 → Angola–Namibia

Germany–Netherlands Boundary Treaty, 10 June 1963 → Germany–Netherlands

Ghent Treaty, 24 December 1814 →

MAJOR INTERNATIONAL TREATIES AND CONFERENCES

Ancón Treaty, 20 October 1883 ➤ Bolivia–Chile; Bolivia–Peru; Chile–Peru

Anglo-German Agreement, 1 July 1890 ➤ Botswana–Namibia; Malawi–Tanzania; Mozambique–Tanzania; Namibia–Zambia; Rwanda–Uganda; Tanzania–Uganda; Zambia–Zimbabwe

Anglo-German Agreement, 14 May 1910 ➤ Rwanda–Tanzania; Rwanda–Uganda; Tanzania–Uganda

Anglo-Portuguese Treaty, 11 June 1891 ➤ Angola–Namibia; Malawi–Mozambique; Mozambique–Zambia; Mozambique–Zimbabwe; Namibia–Zambia

Berlin Conference, November 1884–February 1885 ➤ Angola–Congo; Angola–Zaire; Congo–Zaire; Malawi–Mozambique; Mozambique–Swaziland; Mozambique–Zimbabwe

Berlin, Congress Of, 1878 ➤ Albania–Serbia; Armenia–Turkey; Bosnia–Serbia; Bulgaria–Macedonia; Bulgaria–Romania; Bulgaria–Serbia; Bulgaria–Turkey; Georgia–Turkey; Hungary–Romania; Iran–Turkey; Macedonia–Serbia; Moldava–Romania; Romania–Serbia; Romania–Ukraine

Franco-German Convention, 18 April 1908 ➤ Cameroon–Central African Republic; Cameroon–Chad; Cameroon–Congo; Cameroon–Gabon

Hanima Agreement, 17 September 1809 ➤ Finland–Russia; Finland–

Sweden

Kayes Treaty, 16 February 1963 ➤ Algeria–Mali; Mali–Mauritania

London Conference, May 1913 ➤ Albania–Serbia; Bulgaria–Turkey; Macedonia–Greece

London Treaty, 15 November 1831 ➤ Belgium–Luxembourg; Belgium–Netherlands

Niamey Convention, 20 June 1909 ➤ Algeria–Mali; Algeria–Mauritania; Algeria–Niger

Paris Convention, 14 June 1898 ➤ Central African Republic–Sudan; Chad–Libya; Chad–Nigeria; Chad–Sudan

Paris Peace Conference, 1919–1921 ➤ Albania–Greece; Albania–Macedonia; Albania–Serbia; Croatia–Hungary; Hungary–Ukraine; Italy–Slovenia

Paris Peace Treaty, 10 February 1947 ➤ Albania–Macedonia; Albania–Serbia; Austria–Italy; Bulgaria–Macedonia; Bulgaria–Romania; Bulgaria–Serbia; Croatia–Hungary; Djibouti–Eritrea; Finland–Norway; France–Italy; Hungary–Romania; Hungary–Slovakia; Hungary–Slovenia; Hungary–Ukraine; Libya–Tunisia; Moldava–Romania; Moldava–Ukraine; Romania–Ukraine

Paris Treaty, May 1814 Belgium–France; France–Switzerland

Petrópolis Treaty, 17 November 1903 ➤ Bolivia–Brazil; Brazil–Peru

Riga Peace Treaty, 18 March 1921 ➤ Belarus–Latvia; Belarus–Poland; Belarus–Russia; Belarus–Ukraine; Poland–Ukraine

Saint Germain, Treaty Of, 10 September 1919 ➤ Austria–Italy; Italy–Slovenia; Italy–Switzerland

San Ildefonso, Treaty Of, 1 October 1777 ➤ Bolivia–Brazil; Bolivia–Colombia; Brazil–Paraguay; Brazil–Peru; Brazil–Venezuela; Portugal–Spain

Sèvres, Treaty Of, 10 August 1920 ➤ Iraq–Turkey; Israel–Syria; Oman–Saudi Arabia; Syria–Turkey

Sykes-Picot Agreement, 16 May 1916 ➤ Iraq–Syria; Israel–Lebanon; Israel–Syria; Jordan–Syria

Trianon, Treaty Of, 4 June 1920 ➤ Austria–Hungary; Austria–Slovakia; Croatia–Hungary; Hungary–Romania; Hungary–Serbia; Hungary–Slovakia; Hungary–Slovenia; Hungary–Ukraine; Romania–Serbia

Utrecht, Treaty Of, 1713 ➤ Belgium–Luxembourg; Belgium–Netherlands; Gibraltar–Spain

Versailles, Treaty Of, 28 June 1919 ➤ Austria–Czech Republic; Austria–Germany; Austria–Liechtenstein; Austria–Slovakia; Belgium–Germany; Botswana–Namibia; Cameroon–Chad; Czech Republic–Germany; Denmark–Germany; Estonia–Latvia; France–Germany; Germany–Poland; Namibia–South Africa; Poland–Ukraine; Romania–Ukraine; Rwanda–Tanzania

Vienna, Congress Of, 1815 ➤ Austria–Switzerland; Belgium–France; Belgium–Luxembourg; Belgium–Netherlands; Brazil–Suriname; France–Germany; France–Luxembourg; Germany–Luxembourg; Germany–Netherlands; Germany–Poland; Germany–Switzerland; Italy–San Marino

Westphalia Peace Treaty, 1648 ➤ Belgium–Netherlands; France–Germany

INTERNATIONAL ARBITRATION

AFGHANISTAN–IRAN, 1872; 1889
➤ British Officer

AFGHANISTAN–IRAN, 1935 ➤
Turkish General

ANGOLA–ZAMBIA, 1903 ➤
King of Italy

Argentina–Brazil, 5 February 1895 ➤
President of the United States

Argentina–Chile, 20 November 1902; 1966 ➤ British Arbitration

Argentina–Chile, 21 October 1994 ➤
Arbitration Tribunal

Argentina–Paraguay, 12 November 1878 ➤ President of the United States

Bolivia–Peru, 15 May 1906 ➤
President of Argentina

Brazil–Guyana, 6 June 1904 ➤ Rome, Italian Arbitration

Burkina Faso–Mali, 22 December 1986 ➤ International Court of Justice

Cambodia–Thailand, 1962 ➤
International Court of Justice

Canada–United States, 1829 ➤ King of the Netherlands

Canada–United States, 1872 ➤
Emperor of Germany

Chad–Libya, 3 March 1994 ➤
International Court of Justice

Chile–Peru, 3 June 1929 ➤ President of the United States

Colombia–Venezuela, 16 March 1891 ➤ King/Queen Regent of Spain

Colombia–Venezuela, 24 March 1922 ➤ Swiss Federal Council

Costa Rica–Panama, November 1896 ➤ French Arbitration

Costa Rica–Panama, 1914 ➤ United States Chief Justice

Egypt–Israel, 1988 ➤ International
Tribunal

El Salvador–Honduras, 1970–1971 ➤ Uruguayen Moderator

El Salvador–Honduras, 11 September 1992 ➤ International Court of Justice

French Guiana–Suriname, May 1891 ➤ Czar Alexander III of Russia

Guyana–Venezuela, 1899 ➤
Arbitration Tribunal

Honduras–Nicaragua, 23 December 1906 ➤ King of Spain

Honduras–Nicaragua, 18 November 1960 ➤ International Court of Justice

India–Pakistan, 19 February 1968 ➤
International Tribunal

Iraq–Turkey, November 1925 ➤
International Court of Justice

Malawi–Mozambique, 1875 ➤
President of France

Mozambique–Swaziland, 1875 ➤
President of France

Mozambique–Zimbabwe, 1875 ➤
President of France

NAMES OF BOUNDARY LINES

Blue Line ➤ Kenya–Sudan

Blue Line ➤ Qatar–Saudi Arabia

Brussels Line ➤ Iraq–Turkey

Clifford Line ➤ Ethiopia–Kenya

Curzon Line ➤ Belarus–Poland; Lithuania–Poland; Poland–Ukraine

Durand Line ➤ Afghanistan–Pakistan

Green Line ➤ Israel–Jordan

Gwynn Line ➤ Ethiopia–Sudan

Hamza Line ➤ Saudi Arabia–Yemen

Line Of Control ➤ India–Pakistan

Mcmahon Line ➤ China–India

Oder (Odra)-Neisse Line ➤
Germany–Poland

Philby Line ➤ Saudi Arabia–United
Arab Emirates–Yemen

Red Line ➤ Kenya–Sudan

Red Line ➤ Saudi Arabia–United Arab
Emirates–Yemen

Riyadh (Ryan) Line ➤ Saudi
Arabia–United Arab Emirates

Schomburgk Line ➤
Guyana–Venezuela

Taif Line ➤ Saudi Arabia–Yemen

Violet Line ➤ Saudi Arabia–United
Arab Emirates–Yemen

BOUNDARY MOUNTAIN RANGES

Acaraí ➤ Brazil–Guyana

Adenburg ➤ Austria–Germany

Ala Tau ➤ China–Kazakhstan

Alantika ➤ Cameroon–Nigeria

Alasyskiy ➤ Kyrgyzstan–Tajikistan

Allgäu Alps ➤ Austria–Germany

Altai ➤ China–Kazakhstan;
China–Mongolia; Mongolia–Russia

Altai ➤ Kazakhstan–Russia;
Mongolia–Russia

Amambaí (Abambay) ➤
Brazil–Paraguay

Andes ➤ Argentina–Bolivia;
Argentina–Chile; Ecuador–Peru

Angland Shan ➤ China–Myanmar

Annam ➤ Cambodia–Laos

Annamatique ➤ Laos–Vietnam

Anti-Lebanon ➤ Lebanon–Syria

Arakan Yoma ➤ India–Myanmar

Ardennes ➤ Belgium–Germany

Atakora ➤ Benin–Burkina Faso

Bamba ➤ Angola–Congo

Bavarian Alps ➤ Austria–Germany

Belasica (Belashtiza) Planina ➤
Bulgaria–Greece; Bulgaria–Macedonia

Bernina Alps ➤ Italy–Switzerland

Bohemian Forest ➡ Czech Republic–Germany

Cardamoms ➡ Cambodia–Thailand

Carnic Alps ➡ Austria–Italy

Carpathian ➡ Hungary–Ukraine; Poland–Slovakia; Romania–Ukraine

Caucasus ➡ Azerbaijan–Russia

Cerra De Divisor ➡ Brazil–Peru

Chatkal'skiy ➡ Kyrgyzstan–Uzbekistan

Chimanimani ➡ Mozambique–Zimbabwe

Cóndor ➡ Ecuador–Peru

Cordillera ➡ Costa Rica–Panama

Cupy ➡ Brazil–Venezuela

Dangrek ➡ Cambodia–Thailand

Dinaric Alps (Dinara) ➡ Bosnia–Croatia

Dipilto ➡ Honduras–Nicaragua

Drakensberg ➡ Lesotho–South Africa

Dwarsberg ➡ Botswana–South Africa

Dzalanyama ➡ Malawi–Mozambique

Erzgebirge (Krusneberg) ➡ Czech Republic–Germany

Galendi ➡ Guinea–Senegal

Gata ➡ Portugal–Spain

Geres ➡ Portugal–Spain

Golija ➡ Bosnia–Serbia

Gory Bystrzyckie ➡ Czech Republic–Poland

Hazar Masjed ➡ Iran–Turkmenistan

Himalayas ➡ Bhutan–India; China–Nepal; India–Myanmar; India–Nepal

Hohe Tauern ➡ Austria–Italy

Imeri ➡ Brazil–Venezuela

Iran ➡ Indonesia–Malysia

Jablanica ➡ Albania–Macedonia

Jalapa ➡ Honduras–Nicaragua

Javorniky ➡ Czech Republic–Slovakia

Kacha ➡ Iran–Pakistan

Karakoram ➡ India–Pakistan

Karawanken Alps ➡ Austria–Slovenia

Kherbet Kopet ➡ Iran–Turkmenistan

Kom Balkan ➡ Bulgaria–Serbia

Konkoniouma ➡ Guinea–Senegal

Kozjak ➡ Macedonia–Serbia

La Botija ➡ Honduras–Nicaragua

Latome ➡ Kenya–Sudan

Lebombo ➡ Mozambique–South Africa; Mozambique–Swaziland; South Africa–Swaziland

Mabuara ➡ Cameroon–Nigeria

Macelj ➡ Croatia–Slovenia

Maglic ➡ Bosnia–Serbia

Makonjwa ➡ South Africa–Swaziland

Males ➡ Bulgaria–Macedonia

Maluti ➡ Lesotho–South Africa

Mangfallgebirge ➡ Austria–Germany

Maracaju ➡ Brazil–Paraguay

Matundwe ➡ Malawi–Mozambique

Medjerda ➡ Algeria–Tunisia

Mirjawa ➡ Iran–Pakistan

Mong Ling Shan ➡ China–Myanmar

Nemerchka ➡ Albania–Greece

Niari ➡ Angola–Congo

Nimba ➡ Guinea–Ivory Coast; Guinea–Liberia

Ödenburg ➡ Austria–Hungary

Oka ➡ Colombia–Venezuela

Pa Wan ➡ Myanmar–Thailand

Pakaraima ➡ Brazil–Guyana; Brazil–Venezuela

Pamirs ➡ Afghanistan–China

Parima ➡ Brazil–Venezuela

Patkai ➡ India–Myanmar

Peah ➡ Argentina–Bolivia

Perijá ➡ Colombia–Venezuela

Pindar ➡ Greece–Macedonia

Planina ➡ Bulgaria–Serbia

Pljesevica ➡ Bosnia–Croatia

Pou Den Dinh ➡ Laos–Vietnam

Pyrenees ➡ Andorra–France; Andorra–Spain; France–Spain

Rhaetian Alps ➡ Austria–Switzerland

Salinka ➡ Slovakia–Ukraine

Salzburg Alps ➡ Austria–Germany

Santa Ana ➡ Brazil–Uruguay

Sar ➡ Macedonia–Serbia

Satha ➡ Lebanon–Syria

Sayan ➡ Mongolia–Russia

Schellen Berg ➡ Austria–Liechtenstein

Siahan ➡ Iran–Pakistan

Silotwane ➡ South Africa–Swaziland

Silvreta ➡ Austria–Switzerland

Someswar ➡ India–Nepal

Stamnaungruppe ➡ Austria–Switzerland

Sudetic ➡ Czech Republic–Poland

Sumava ➡ Czech Republic–Germany

Tama ➡ Colombia–Venezuela

Tapirapecó ➡ Brazil–Venezuela

Tarbagatay ➡ China–Kazakhstan

Tatra ➡ Czech Republic–Poland; Poland–Slovakia

Tereteinia ➡ Sudan–Uganda

Tibesti ➡ Chad–Niger

Tien Shan ➡ China–Kyrgyzstan

Tumac-Humac ➡ Brazil–French Guiana; Brazil–Suriname

Valledupar ➡ Colombia–Venezuela

Volujaak ➡ Bosnia–Serbia

Wellerstein ➡ Austria–Germany

White Carpathian ➡ Czech Republic–Slovakia

Wugamba ➡ Rwanda–Uganda

Zaalayskiy ➡ Kyrgyzstan–Tajikistan

Zachodnie ➡ Poland–Slovakia

BOUNDARY JUNCTION MOUNTAIN PEAKS

'Anaiza ➡ Iraq–Jordan–Saudi Arabia

Dolent ➡ France–Italy–Swizerland

Forno (Ofen) ➡ Austria–Italy–Slovenia

Hermon ➡ Israel–Lebanon–Syria

Jongsong ➡ China–India–Nepal

Kremenec ➡
Poland–Slovakia–Ukraine

Kuh I Malik Siah ➡
Afghanistan–Iran–Pakistan

Kuytun ➡ China–Kazakhstan–Russia

Monte Cristo ➡
El Salvador–Guatemala–Honduras

Naafkopf ➡
Austria–Liechtenstein–Switzerland

Neun ➡ Guinea–Ivory Coast–Liberia

Orjien ➡ Bosnia–Croatia–Serbia

Petzen (Pec) Peak ➡
Austria–Italy–Slovenia

Piz Lad ➡ Austria–Italy–Switzerland

Plockenstein ➡ Austria–Czech
Republic–Germany

Povalo Shveykovski ➡
Afghanistan–China–Tajikistan

Roraima ➡ Brazil–Guyana–Venezuela

Sabinio ➡ Rwanda–Uganda–Zaire

Tumba (Bélès, Pole) ➡
Bulgaria–Greece–Macedonia

Uweinat ➡ Egypt–Libya–Sudan

Zapaleri ➡ Argentina–Bolivia–Chile

BOUNDARY LAKES

Abbe ➡ Djibouti–Ethiopia

Albert ➡ Uganda–Zaire

Aral ➡ Kazakhstan–Uzbekistan

Buenos Aires ➡ Argentina–Chile

Chad ➡ Chad–Cameroon–Niger–
Nigeria

Chala ➡ Kenya–Tanzania

Chiuta ➡ Malawi–Mozambique

Coboba (Tshoboba) ➡
Burundi–Rwanda

Cochrane ➡ Argentina–Chile

Constance (Bodensee) ➡
Austria–Germany–Switzerland

Dead Sea ➡ Israel–Jordan

Dojran ➡ Greece–Macedonia

Edward ➡ Uganda–Zaire

Erie ➡ Canada–United States

Erne ➡ Ireland–United Kingdom

Fagnano ➡ Argentina–Chile

Fianga ➡ Cameroon–Chad

Geneva ➡ France–Switzerland

Guaiba (Gaiba) ➡ Bolivia–Brazil

Guija ➡ El Salvador–Guatemala

Hazapin (Khozapini) ➡
Georgia–Turkey

Huron ➡ Canada–United States

Jipe (Yipe) ➡ Kenya–Tanzania

Khanka (Hanka) ➡ China–Russia

Kilpis ➡ Finland–Sweden

Kivu ➡ Rwanda–Zaire

Lake Of The Woods ➡
Canada–United States

Lugano ➡ Italy–Switzerland

Macnean ➡ Ireland–United Kingdom

Maggiore ➡ Italy–Switzerland

Melvin ➡ Ireland–United Kingdom

Mirim ➡ Brazil–Uruguay

Mweru ➡ Zaire–Zambia

Neusiedler ➡ Austria–Hungary

Nyasa (Malawi) ➡
Malawi–Mozambique–Tanzania

Ohrid ➡ Albania–Macedonia

Ontario ➡ Canada–United States

Orava ➡ Poland–Slovakia

Pangong ➡ China–India

Peipus (Chudskoye) ➡ Estonia–Russia

Prespa ➡ Albania–Greece–Macedonia

Rengen ➡ Norway–Sweden

Rudolf (Turkana) ➡ Ethiopia–Kenya

Rweru (Regwero) ➡ Burundi–Rwanda

Scutari ➡ Albania–Serbia

Spanggur ➡ China–India

Store ➡ Norway–Sweden

Superior ➡ Canada–United States

Tanganyika ➡
Burundi–Tanzania–Zaire–Zambia

Titicaca ➡ Bolivia–Peru

Uberaba ➡ Bolivia–Brazil

Uinamarca ➡ Bolivia–Peru

Untersee ➡ Germany–Switzerland

Victoria ➡ Kenya–Tanzania–Uganda

Vistytis ➡ Lithuania–Poland

White Lake (Laguna Blanca) ➡
Chile–Peru

BOUNDARY RIVERS

Ab-I-Pandj ➡ Afghanistan–Tajikistan

Abuná ➡ Bolivia–Brazil

Acre ➡ Bolivia–Brazil; Brazil–Peru

Afrine ➡ Syria–Turkey

Agatete ➡ Burundi–Rwanda

Agueda ➡ Portugal–Spain

Akobo ➡ Ethiopia–Sudan

Al Asi (Orontes) ➡ Syria–Turkey

Alazani ➡ Azerbaijan–Georgia

Al Khaiim ➡ Iran–Iraq

Al Tib ➡ Iran–Iraq

Alupe ➡ Kenya–Uganda

Amacuro ➡ Guyana–Venezuela

Amazon ➡ Brazil–Peru;
Colombia–Peru

Ammodar ➡ Uganda–Zaire

Amu Darya ➡ Afghanistan–Tajikistan;
Afghanistan–Turkmenistan;
Afghanistan–Uzbekistan

Amur ➡ China–Russia

Anar ➡ Finland–Norway

Anguiatu ➡ El Salvador–Guatemala

An-Ping ➡ China–North Korea

Aouk ➡ Central African
Republic–Chad

Apa ➡ Brazil–Paraguay

Apaporis ➡ Brazil–Colombia

Aras (Araks) ➡ Armenia–Azerbaijan;

Kolimbiné ➜ Mali–Mauritania

Kolok ➜ Malaysia–Thailand

Kom ➜ Cameroon–Gabon

Komadugu (Yobe) ➜ Niger–Nigeria

Konkama ➜ Finland–Sweden

Kouè ➜ Guinea–Ivory Coast

Kourou Kelle ➜ Guinea–Ivory Coast

Kunglong ➜ China–Myanmar

Kupa ➜ Croatia–Slovenia

Kura ➜ Georgia–Turkey

Kusiyara ➜ Bangladesh–India

Kutari (Cutari) ➜ Brazil–Suriname;
Guyana–Suriname

Kwando ➜ Angola–Zambia

Kwango ➜ Angola–Zaire

Kyè ➜ Cameroon–Gabon

La Brea ➜ Guatemala–Honduras

Lami ➜ Uganda–Zaire

Las petas ➜ Bolivia–Brazil

Lauter ➜ France–Germany

Lawa ➜ French Guiana–Suriname

Leaghany ➜ Ireland–United Kingdom

Lempa ➜ El Salvador–Honduras

Lendava ➜ Hungary–Slovenia

Lepenac ➜ Macedonia–Serbia

Leraba ➜ Burkina Faso–Ivory Coast

Limon ➜ Honduras–Nicaragua

Limpopo ➜ Botswana–South Africa;
South Africa–Zimbabwe

Little Scarcies ➜ Guinea–Sierra Leone

Logone ➜ Cameroon–Chad

Lorzot ➜ Libya–Tunisia

Losoyai ➜ Kenya–Tanzania

Loungou ➜ Congo–Zaire

Luangwa ➜ Mozambique–Zambia

Luapula ➜ Zaire–Zambia

Lubilia-Chako ➜ Uganda–Zaire

Lubirizi ➜ Rwanda–Uganda

Luia ➜ Malawi–Mozambique

Lukavica ➜ Bulgaria–Serbia

Lys ➜ Belgium–France

Macara ➜ Ecuador–Peru

Magowi ➜ Liberia–Sierra Leone

Mai Sai ➜ Myanmar–Thailand

Makhaleng ➜ Lesotho–South Africa

Makonda ➜ Guinea–Liberia

Malawa (Lwakhakha) ➜
Kenya–Uganda

Malosa ➜ Malawi–Mozambique

Mamoré ➜ Bolivia–Brazil

Managua ➜ Guatemala–Honduras

Mani (Mano/Saint John) ➜
Guinea–Liberia

Manne (Mano) ➜ Liberia–Sierra
Leone

Manunggul ➜ Brunei–Malaysia

Manyaga (Muniaga) ➜ Uganda–Zaire

Manzan ➜ Ghana–Ivory Coast

Maqta ➜ Libya–Tunisia

Marano ➜ Italy–San Marino

Mareb ➜ Eritrea–Ethiopia

Marico ➜ Botswana–South Africa

Maritsa ➜ Bulgaria–Greece;
Greece–Turkey

Mark ➜ Belgium–Netherlands

Maroni ➜ French Guiana–Suriname

Massiete ➜ Tanzania–Zambia

Mataje ➜ Colombia–Ecuador

Mathabhanga ➜ Bangladesh–India

Mauwa ➜ Liberia–Sierra Leone

Mazoe ➜ Mozambique–Zimbabwe

Mbéré ➜ Cameroon–Central
African Republic;
Cameroon–Chad;
Central African Republic–Chad

Mbomou ➜ Central African
Republic–Zaire

Mechi ➜ India–Nepal

Mekong ➜ Cambodia–Laos;
China–Myanmar; Laos–Myanmar;
Laos–Thailand

Mékrou ➜ Benin–Burkina Faso;
Benin–Niger

Meli ➜ Guinea–Sierra Leone

Meta ➜ Colombia–Venezuela

Meuse (Maas) ➜ Belgium–

Netherlands

Mina ➜ Brazil–Uruguay

Minha ➜ Portugal–Spain

Mininga ➜ Angola–Zambia

Mira ➜ Colombia–Ecuador

Mitji ➜ Guinea–Senegal

Mkumbaw ➜ Tanzania–Zambia

Mkumvura ➜ Mozambique–
Zimbabwe

Mo ➜ Ghana–Togo

Moa (Makona) ➜ Guinea–Sierra
Leone

Moei ➜ Myanmar–Thailand

Mohan ➜ India–Nepal

Molopo ➜ Botswana–South Africa

Mono ➜ Benin–Togo

Morava ➜ Austria–Slovakia;
Czech Republic–Slovakia

Morro ➜ Liberia–Sierra Leone

Moselle (Mosel) ➜ France–Germany;
France–Luxembourg;
Germany–Luxembourg

Motagua ➜ Guatemala–Honduras

Mounio ➜ Finland–Sweden

Mournebeg ➜ Ireland–United
Kingdom

Mpemba ➜ Tanzania–Zambia

Mukana ➜ Burundi–Tanzania

Muni ➜ Equatorial Guinea–Gabon

Mur (Mura) ➜ Austria–Slovenia;
Croatia–Hungary; Croatia–Slovenia

Muresul (Maros) ➜ Hungary–
Romania

Murghab ➜ Afghanistan–Turkmenistan

Murungu ➜ Uganda–Zaire

Mwibu ➜ Burundi–Tanzania

Naf ➜ Bangladesh–Myanmar

Nam Che ➜ China–Myanmar

Narayani ➜ India–Nepal

Nashiodo ➜ Uganda–Zaire

Natisone ➜ Italy–Slovenia

Ndhlozane ➜ South Africa–Swaziland

Negro ➡ Bolivia–Paraguay; Brazil–Uruguay

Negro ➡ Colombia–Venezuela

Negro ➡ Honduras–Nicaragua

Neisse ➡ Czech Republic–Germany; Germany–Poland

Neman ➡ Lithuania–Russia

Nera ➡ Romania–Serbia

Neun ➡ Ivory Coast–Liberia

Ngoko ➡ Cameroon–Congo

Ngou ➡ Cameroon–Central African Republic

N'gounie ➡ Congo–Gabon

Niabola ➡ Uganda–Zaire

Niagiaki ➡ Uganda–Zaire

Niamanka ➡ Guinea–Guinea-Bissau

Nianda ➡ Guinea–Liberia

Niger ➡ Benin–Niger

Nikoliç ➡ Greece–Macedonia

Nimoi ➡ Ivory Coast–Liberia

Nossob ➡ Botswana–South Africa

Notwani ➡ Botswana–South Africa

Ntem ➡ Cameroon–Gabon

Nyarugando ➡ Uganda–Zaire

Nyaura (Kigura) ➡ Sudan–Uganda

Nyemenek ➡ Latvia–Lithuania

Nyoue ➡ Cameroon–Central African Republic

Oder (Odra) ➡ Czech Republic–Poland; Germany–Poland

Oira ➡ Colombia–Venezuela

Okavango (Cubango) ➡ Angola–Namibia

Okpara ➡ Benin–Nigeria

Olopa ➡ Guatemala–Honduras

Opava ➡ Czech Republic–Poland

Orange ➡ Namibia–South Africa

Orinoco ➡ Colombia–Venezuela

Orlice ➡ Czech Republic–Poland

Oro ➡ Colombia–Venezuela

Orontes ➡ Syria–Turkey

Oti ➡ Ghana–Togo

Our ➡ Germany–Luxembourg

Oyapock ➡ Brazil–French Guiana

Pakchan ➡ Myanmar–Thailand

Pamir ➡ Afghanistan–Tajikistan

Pandaruan ➡ Brunei–Malaysia

Papurí ➡ Brazil–Colombia

Paraguay ➡ Argentina–Paraguay; Bolivia–Brazil; Brazil–Paraguay

Paraná ➡ Argentina–Paraguay; Brazil–Paraguay

Pasvikelv ➡ Norway–Russia

Paz ➡ El Salvador–Guatemala

Pedernales ➡ Dominican Republic–Haiti

Pena Blanca ➡ Honduras–Nicaragua

Penbi ➡ Mozambique–Zimbabwe

Pendjari ➡ Benin–Burkina Faso

Pepiri-Guacu ➡ Argentina–Brazil

Petit Ruzizi (Rusizi Rutoya) ➡ Burundi–Zaire

Pibor ➡ Ethiopia–Sudan

Pigeon ➡ Canada–United States

Pilcomayo ➡ Argentina–Bolivia; Argentina–Paraguay

Piva ➡ Bosnia–Serbia

Pocitos ➡ Argentina–Bolivia

Pomola ➡ El Salvador–Honduras

Poprad ➡ Poland–Slovakia

Poteca ➡ Honduras–Nicaragua

Pregel ➡ Poland–Russia

Prut ➡ Moldava–Romania; Romania–Ukraine

Purus ➡ Brazil–Peru

Putumayo ➡ Colombia–Ecuador; Colombia–Peru

Qabirri ➡ Azerbaijan–Georgia

Qanix ➡ Azerbaijan–Georgia

Qareh SU ➡ Syria–Turkey

Quaraí ➡ Brazil–Uruguay

Quebrada Grande ➡ Honduras–Nicaragua

Ramaquabane ➡ Botswana–Zimbabwe

Rapirra ➡ Bolivia–Brazil

Ravi ➡ India–Pakistan

Red (Yüan, Hong) ➡ China–Vietnam

Red Volta ➡ Burkina Faso–Ghana

Rezova ➡ Bulgaria–Turkey

Rhine ➡ Austria–Switzerland, France–Germany, Germany–Netherlands; Germany–Switzerland; Liechtenstein–Switzerland

Rio De La Plata ➡ Argentina–Uruguay

Rio Grande (Bravo Del Norte) ➡ Mexico–United States

Rumi (Lumi) ➡ Tanzania–Zambia

Ruo ➡ Malawi–Mozambique

Ruvu (Bangani) ➡ Kenya–Tanzania

Ruvuma ➡ Mozambique–Tanzania

Ruwa (Luhwa) ➡ Burundi–Rwanda

Ruzizi ➡ Burundi–Zaire; Rwanda–Zaire

Saar ➡ France–Germany

Sabor ➡ Portugal–Spain

Safu (Samfu) ➡ Tanzania–Zambia

Saint Croix ➡ Canada–United States

Saint Lawrence ➡ Canada–United States

Saint Paul ➡ Guinea–Liberia

Saissi ➡ Tanzania–Zambia

Sakarani ➡ Guinea–Mali

Salween ➡ Myanmar–Thailand

Salzach ➡ Austria–Germany

Samur ➡ Azerbaijan–Russia

San ➡ Poland–Ukraine

San Antonio ➡ Argentina–Brazil

San Gha ➡ Cameroon–Central African Republic; Cameroon–Congo

San Go ➡ Kenya–Uganda

San Juan ➡ Argentina–Bolivia

San Juan ➡ Colombia–Ecuador

San Juan ➡ Costa Rica–Nicaragua

San Luis ➡ Brazil–Uruguay

San Miguel ➡ Brazil–Uruguay

San Miguel ➡ Colombia–Ecuador

San On Kolè ➡ Mali–Senegal

San Pedro ➡ Gambia–Senegal

ACKNOWLEDGMENTS

The Publishers wish to express their appreciation to the following individuals and institutions for their help:

Illustrations:
p. 16 No'am Ron; p. 27 Dr. Peter Demant; p. 31 Dr. Zvi Ron; p. 38 Daniel Keren; pp. 41, 53 Dr. Avraham Arbel; p. 58 Anat Biger; p. 81 Dr. Avraham Arbel; p. 84 Daniel Keren; p. 90 Prof. Martin Glassner; p. 92 Gilad (Gili) Haskin; pp. 95, 97 (above) Dr. Avraham Arbel; p. 97 (below) Gilad (Gili) Haskin; p. 98 (above and below) Dr. Avraham Arbel; p. 99 (above and below) Prof. Martin Glassner; p. 100 Anat Biger; p. 101 (above) Dr. Avraham Arbel; p. 101 (below) Prof. Martin Glassner; p. 102 (above) Eyal Biger; pp. 102 (below), 103, 104, 105, 106, 107, 108 (above) Gilad (Gili) Haskin; p. 108 (below) Shlomo Gafni; p. 109 (above) Anat Biger; p. 109 (below) Shlomo Gafni; p. 110 (above and below) Prof. Martin Glassner; p. 111 (above) Gilad (Gili) Haskin; p. 111 (below) Eyal Biger; p. 112 Prof. Nili Liphschitz; p. 142 Dr. Avraham Arbel; p. 152 Prof. Martin Glassner; p. 154 Gilad (Gili) Haskin; p. 156 Shlomo Gafni; p. 157 Dr. Avraham Arbel; p. 168 Gilad (Gili) Haskin; p. 171 Daniel Keren; p. 181 Prof. Bracha Rager; pp. 187, 190 Eyal Biger; p. 195 Daniel Keren; p. 197 Efrath Biger; p. 201 David Harris; pp. 224, 226, 227, 228, 230, 233 Prof. Martin Glassner; p. 236 Anat Biger; p. 239 Prof. Martin Glassner; p. 242 Anat Biger; p. 245 Eyal Biger; p. 248 Prof. Martin Glassner; p. 265 Efrath Biger; p. 273 (above and below) Eyal Biger; p. 274 (above) Daniel Keren; p. 274 (below) Eyal Biger; p. 275 (above and below) Efrath Biger; pp. 276, 277 Anat Biger; p. 278 Prof. Nili Liphschitz; pp. 279, 280 (above) Gilad (Gili) Haskin; pp. 280 (below), 281 (above and below) Prof. Martin Glassner; p. 282 (above and below) Anat Biger; pp. 283, 284 Duby Tal and Moni Haramati, Albatross Aerial Photography; p. 285 (above) Gilad (Gili) Haskin; p. 285 (below) Prof. Martin Glassner; p. 286 (above) Daniel Keren; p. 286 (below) Dr. Gideon Biger; p. 287 (above) Prof. Martin Glassner; p. 287 (below) Dr. Gideon Biger; p. 288 Dr. Avraham Arbel; p. 290 Gilad (Gili) Haskin; p. 292 Prof. Martin Glassner; p. 294 Dr. Avraham Arbel; pp. 301, 308 Efrath Biger; p. 309 Anat Biger; p. 315 Duby Tal and Moni Haramati, Albatross Aerial Photography; p. 317 Efrath Biger; p. 320 Azaria Alon; pp. 323, 325 Prof. Martin Glassner; p. 330 Boaz Fletcher; p. 331 Efrath Biger; pp. 339, 340 Dr. Avraham Arbel; p. 350 Gilad (Gili) Haskin; p. 356 Prof. Martin Glassner; p. 363 Efrath Biger; pp. 366, 372, 382, 390 Prof. Martin Glassner; p. 397 Gilad (Gili) Haskin; p. 410 Prof. Martin Glassner; p. 416 Dr. Avraham Arbel; pp. 417 (above and below), 418 (above and below) Prof. Martin Glassner; p. 419 (below) Eyal Biger; p. 420 Daniel Keren; p. 421 Dr. Avraham Arbel; p. 422 Duby Tal and Moni Haramati, Albatross Aerial Photography; pp. 423, 424, 425 Gilad (Gili) Haskin; p. 426 (above) Efrath Biger; pp. 426 (below), 427 (above) Dr. Avraham Arbel; pp. 427 (below), 428, 429, 430 Gilad (Gili) Haskin; p. 431 Duby Tal and Moni Haramati, Albatross Aerial Photography; p. 432 (above and below) Gilad (Gili) Haskin; p. 435 Eyal Biger; p. 438 Prof. Nili Liphschitz; pp. 443, 459 Prof. Martin Glassner; p. 470 Prof. Bracha Rager; pp. 481, 483 Prof. Martin Glassner; p. 485 Eyal Biger; p. 495 Anat Biger; p. 499 Dr. Avraham Arbel; p. 506 Prof. Martin Glassner.

Typesetting and Pagination: Devorah Sowalsky Meyer—The Jerusalem Publishing House; *Secretary:* Shoshanna Lewis.

Films: Printone Ltd., Jerusalem.

Printing and Binding: Keter Enterprises Ltd., Jerusalem.